The yacht Australia II, representing Western Australia, defeated the New York Yacht Club's Liberty and became the first non-American vessel ever to capture the prized America's Cup.

1984 YI

EVI

FUNK & WAGNALLS NEW ENCYCLOPEDIA 1984 YEARBOOK

LEON L. BRAM
Vice-President and
Editorial Director

NORMA H. DICKEY
Editor in Chief
Special Projects

Funk & Wagnalls, Inc.

Publishers since 1876

Funk & Wagnalls offers a Standard Desk Dictionary.
For details on ordering, please write:

Funk & Wagnalls, Inc.
Dept. BPM
P.O. Box 391
Radio City Station
New York, NY 10101

ISBN 0-8343 0069-9

CONTENTS

MEMBERS OF THE STAFF

FOREWORD: THE EVENTS OF 1983

The year 1983 witnessed continued international conflict and tensions. In the Middle East, fighting flared up between rival Lebanese groups and factions of the Palestine Liberation Organization; in Beirut, U.S. and French peacekeeping troops suffered heavy casualties from terrorist attacks. In the Caribbean, U.S. and other troops invaded the island of Grenada, after a violent coup overthrew the existing Marxist government. Relations between Western nations and the Soviet Union were severely strained when the Soviets shot down a South Korean commercial airliner flying off course over Soviet territory; all 269 people aboard were killed. Finally, the deployment of U.S. intermediate-range missiles in Western Europe, to counter Soviet deployment of SS-20 missiles, aroused strong controversy and added to the issues that divided the Soviet Union and the West.

Voters in Great Britain and West Germany gave strong support to the existing governments; in other countries, such as Australia, Argentina, and Italy, elections during 1983 brought important changes of leadership. In the United States, the economy rebounded from a deep recession, enhancing President Ronald Reagan's reelection prospects.

Despite its many tragic headlines, the year had its share of records and triumphs, as physicist Sally Ride became the first American woman to travel in space, a U.S. federal holiday was declared in honor of the Reverend Martin Luther King, Jr., and Solidarity leader Lech Walesa won the Nobel Peace Prize. *Return of the Jedi* was a blockbuster at box offices, and *Australia II* became the first non-U.S. yacht to capture the coveted America's Cup.

As education became a focus of increased concern, the role of computers in the classrooms of today and tomorrow attracted greater attention; it is also the topic of the first feature article. Another feature article provides a look at selected art treasures from the Vatican collections, on display in the United States in one of the biggest traveling art exhibits ever mounted. A third article offers a tour of Florida's enchanting Everglades, focusing on renewed efforts to protect the region's distinctive plant and animal life.

THE EDITORS

COMPUTERS
in the Classroom

by ROBERT P. TAYLOR

Since the beginning of the 1980's, hundreds of thousands of microcomputers have been streaming into American schools, and the flood appears to be only starting. Dataquest Inc., a California market research firm, estimates that 140,000 computers were purchased by U.S. elementary and secondary schools in 1982— and that by 1987, schools will be buying 2 million units a year. At the college level as well, there is increasing demand for computer courses, both introductory and advanced, and computers are playing a greater role in all areas of the curriculum.

Children, teachers, school administrators, and parents today are deeply engrossed in learning how to use computers and in scheming to get more of them into the schools. They are aided and abetted by computer manufacturers, who have entered the educational market with machines suitable to the classroom and who sponsor programs to train teachers. The last few years have also witnessed the birth of hundreds of small producers of educational software (the programs that tell a computer what to do), the emergence of classroom computers as a topic in both educational journals and new computer magazines, and the entry of major educational publishers into software production and distribution.

The interest in computers stems partly from the fact that they are perceived as the wave of the future. Many parents and educators believe that, as we enter the computer age, familiarity with these machines and the ability to understand and use them—what is frequently called "computer literacy"—may be nearly as important in the job market and in life itself as the ability to read and write. Aside from the goal of computer literacy, computers can play an important role in helping students learn other things—in ways that

Robert P. Taylor, an associate professor at Teachers College, Columbia University, is director of its Graduate Program in Computing and Education. He is the author or editor of several books on computers in education, including The Computer in the School: Tutor, Tool, Tutee *(1980).*

Opposite page: Like typical youngsters everywhere, pupils at Atlanta's John F. Kennedy Middle School are curious about computers and eager for the chance to use them.

9

to some extent are still unexplored—and it's obvious that, to many youngsters, working with a computer is just plain fun.

For all of these reasons, computers have been introduced in a wide variety of settings and at every grade level from kindergarten to college. In kindergarten and even prekindergarten, children using a simple computer language called Logo can trace and manipulate shapes on a screen to learn basic geometric concepts, the difference between left and right, and at least something about how computers work. At a more advanced level, high school or college students might use computers to study Newton's Laws, or to plan a simulated city and work out the effects on it of different courses of action by city officials.

The many uses that a computer can have may seem overwhelming to parents and even to teachers and administrators seeking to plan curriculum and select the best hardware (physical equipment, including video screens, keyboards, and printers) and software

At the college level, students are vying to enroll in computer classes; some colleges have made basic computer courses mandatory. Here, undergraduates at Santa Ana City College in California look over their programs.

(programs) for their purposes. It is helpful to begin by considering four different basic ways, or modes, in which computers can be used in schools and colleges. The computer may be used (1) as a sort of private tutor, teaching a specific topic or subject; (2) as a tool to perform certain functions, like a calculator; (3) as a toy, in educational games; and (4) as a "tutee," when the student, by programming, in a sense instructs the computer, instead of the other way around.

In the first three uses, the pupil does not actually need to know how computers function and "think." For the "tutee" mode, though, the student must learn how to program, or create software, to give the computer instructions on how to perform a specified task. The "tutee" mode thus demands a deeper level of involvement with the computer itself.

Computer teachers come in all different sizes and ages. Above left: a whiz kid of 13 tutors an older-generation learner. Above: learning from peers in an elementary school class.

The Computer as Tutor

Using the computer as a tutor, to teach the learner a specific topic or subject, is perhaps the most traditional approach in schools; another term for this approach is "computer-assisted instruction," or "CAI" for short. The software used in CAI is designed to guide the learner through a sequence of material much as a human tutor might, by questioning and reacting to the learner's responses to the questions. For example, a geography lesson might show part of a map, leaving the learner to complete it or perhaps to correct mistakes in it. A music lesson might present a melody and ask the learner to write harmony for it. Depending on the particular program, pupils might compose a harmony completely on their own, indicating the notes by pressing buttons on the keyboard, or they might pick

Showing computer literacy at an early age are a studious nine-year-old in Lexington, Mass. (top), and two small scholars in a Glen Head, N.Y., school (bottom).

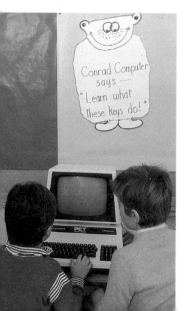

the notes from a "menu" (a list of possible choices) on the video screen—possibly using a "joystick," or control stick that can be tilted at different angles to move an arrow on the screen.

There are several possible advantages to this use of a computer. The material can be covered at a pace the student chooses, and feedback is immediate. Fast learners can move along without waiting for the rest of the class to catch up; at the same time, the machine, unlike a human teacher, never loses patience with the slower learner and can engage in seemingly endless drills to enable such students to master the subject without embarrassment. Testing is an integral part of the learning process, and complete records can be kept for the teacher's use in monitoring each student's progress.

There are disadvantages as well. Because the software must be very elaborate and complex to deal reasonably well with the wide range of responses learners can make, it is costly to create. Because it is designed only to tutor the learner on a specific topic, it cannot be used for anything else, despite its considerable cost. And since such software "controls" the learner rather than the other way around, the learner is usually effectively prevented from doing much exploration or discovery learning. Finally, our knowledge of what such software can or should do is still in its infancy, so even the experts aren't very good at creating it yet.

The Computer as Tool

The computer can also function as a tool, to help learners perform some specific task. One common example is the use of text-editing software to help students write stories or do research papers. Programs that do statistical analysis or financial projections can be utilized in mathematics, and the same software that helps composers write music can also be used by youngsters to create simple tunes.

The principal advantage of this kind of software is that much of it already exists. Businesses and specialists in various fields had a need for computer programs to perform such tasks as word processing and economic forecasting, and they were willing to pay for their development. Though created outside the school, many of these tools are reasonably suitable for use in educational settings. And because such tools have already been developed and are on the market, they tend to be relatively cheap and more readily available for tryout before purchase.

The principal disadvantage springs from the very fact that most of the existing software was designed for a specific use outside the classroom. The better such a tool suits members of the group for whom it was developed, the less fitted it may be to certain learners in schools, because of inappropriate vocabulary or format. In general, these tools were not designed to teach, and they do not usually allow for student discovery and exploration.

The Computer as Toy

The ubiquitous electronic game that eats up quarters in the local arcade is a not-too-distant cousin of the teaching computer when the latter is used as a toy to simulate or represent different situations. Students in the classroom can gain experience comparable to what they could get from the actual situation.

Older, well-known examples of educational computer games include Hammurabi and Oregon Trail, programs that let users find out what it is like, respectively, to rule a kingdom or to undertake a hazardous pioneer journey. Newer and more dramatic games include simulations of the operation of the Three Mile Island nuclear reactor and of flying a plane in specific regions of U.S. airspace. Both of these new games use color graphics and sound to heighten their realism, which adds to the overall interest and attraction.

By offering such games, schools can give students experiences that would otherwise simply not be accessible. These experiences may help students gain a

Computers can be used in the classroom as tools to perform some specific task. Here, two pupils at Field Elementary School in San Diego practice the art of composition by exchanging stories about themselves with Alaskan Eskimo pen pals, via computer.

broader understanding than reading and discussion alone could provide. But computers used as educational toys do have drawbacks. Good simulation software is complex and therefore expensive to develop and buy. And the experience each computer game provides is limited in scope.

The Computer as Tutee

Computers obviously teach students, but pupils can reverse the procedure, treating the machine as, in some sense, the pupil. To do so, the human learner must first learn an appropriate computer language—a formal grammar and vocabulary—such as Basic, Logo, or Pascal, and then use it to tell the computer how to do something or how to teach another person to do something.

The potential here is wide: students might write programs getting computers to conjugate French verbs, multiply fractions, keep and average grades, animate cartoons, or write harmony for songs. Working in the tutee mode, the learner might also create software for others to use in one of the other modes. By "teaching" the computer, the human student should learn something about how computers work and how to program; the student should also learn more about the specific subject matter, skill, or simulation that the computer is being taught.

Since computers come equipped with programming languages, which are the only software needed for this mode, no further expenditure is necessary. One of the

"SURE YOU CAN BECOME A SYSTEMS ANALYST IF YOU WANT TO— BUT TELL DADDY, WHAT IS A SYSTEMS ANALYST?"

disadvantages is that most computer languages are still rather hard to learn, particularly to the point where they can be used competently. Many students never get beyond the language to do much programming, and not all students seem able to master programming well enough to create software of any complexity.

In the high school classroom computers are usually introduced in separate programming or computer literacy courses, rather than as integral components of traditional courses. Above: students at a Wayne County, N.Y., high school learn programming.

Current Trends

While it is certain that computers are being used in many American elementary schools, recent surveys suggest that they are more commonly found in high school. Basic is still the dominant computer language, but Pascal is becoming more popular at upper levels, probably because high school students will soon be allowed to take Advanced Placement exams in Pascal for college credit.

The computer is also becoming more and more important in college itself; acquaintance with the machines is increasingly viewed as a prerequisite for success in future careers. As a result, enrollment in college computer courses has risen dramatically—by some estimates, registration was 30 to 40 percent higher in the 1982–1983 school year than in the previous year.

Some colleges are now requiring all students to enroll in computer literacy courses, and an increasing number are requiring each student to buy a personal computer. The Stevens Institute of Technology, Drexel University, Rensselaer Polytechnic Institute (RPI), Clarkson College of Technology, and Carnegie-Mellon University are among the institutions now experimenting with such requirements. Some, like Stevens and RPI, have tried different machines on different entering classes and have required them for

Students at Washington High School in Atlanta find that working with computers is fun. The computer terminal can have immense drawing power in the classroom.

only a select group in each class, trying to measure the impact by comparison. Others, like Carnegie-Mellon, have begun multimillion-dollar research projects with such industrial partners as the Digital Equipment Corporation and IBM to design and produce within five years personal computers many times more powerful than any now available for student and faculty use.

What Students Gain

In the last two or three years, many claims have been made about what students can and do gain from learning how to program. It has been said that besides acquiring "computer literacy," they will learn to think more logically, become better problem solvers, increase their proficiency in math, and so forth. Programming also continues to be emphasized in elementary school and high school because there has not till quite recently been much tutor, tool, or toy software available. Finally, it is easier to set up a separate computer programming course than to try to integrate the computer into a number of other courses. By adding a programming course at one or more grade levels, the school can prove that it is keeping up with the times with minimal disruption to the rest of the curriculum.

Unfortunately, what's being taught and learned in many of these classes may be only one small part of programming, the fairly mechanical task of learning a computer language. Mastering a computer language is very similar to a lot of other skills schools have long taught, but learning to program is a very complex activity, is not well understood, and is rather unlike what schools are accustomed to teach. Consequently, when youngsters are given courses in computer programming, the classes are usually heavy on Basic or Logo and short on actual guidance and practice in programming.

Even where appropriate emphasis is given to learning to program, by a teacher who understands what is involved and uses the most appropriate materials, there is as yet little commonly accepted evidence as to some of the benefits involved. Research in the field is only beginning, and it is simply too early to state unequivocally that children who have learned a significant amount of programming, compared to those who haven't, form hypotheses more easily, think more like mathematicians, or think more logically. Beyond "computer literacy," what children can definitely learn from programming is a good deal about the topic or topics the program is dealing with. A high school senior writing a program to drill freshmen in Spanish verbs must first study Spanish and needs to be aware of the errors those inexperienced in the language may make.

In high level college courses the graphic capabilities of computers are used to enhance mathematical and scientific concepts.

In the same way, students learn something about particular topics, or acquire certain skills in mathematics, language, or other areas, through computer-assisted instruction, where the computer serves as tutor. How much they learn depends largely on how well the programs are written and how well they lead students into the thick of the topic. The benefits are also more pronounced in the case of slower students, who can get the kind of patient, individual attention and drill that they may need.

More research is needed into what else students learn, or could learn, from using computers in the classroom.

A further question to ask is why so many youngsters of all ages, and adults as well, apparently enjoy working with computers, and especially programming them. People working with computers, particularly in programming, seem to undergo a certain self-renewal as a result of the creativity involved. Young people gain familiarity and ease from their early exposure to the machines, and they come to feel a heightened sense of control over their environment when a program is successfully written and a desired result achieved.

Problem Areas

As with all new developments, a number of problems remain to be solved in the educational use of computers. For one thing, the hardware now available is not particularly well-designed to fit the needs of

An extension of the computer classroom is the increasingly popular computer camp. Summer programs, whether offered on college campuses (above left) or in more typical camplike settings (above), generally provide extensive hands-on experience at various levels of expertise, for fees ranging around a few hundred dollars a week.

young users. Screens are too small and often hard to read. Keyboards remain the most common device to enter information, even though other instruments (like joysticks) are far easier for most people, especially youngsters, to use.

In addition, the software typically lacks imagination and often aims at what is easiest to produce (such as drills and practice exercises) rather than at challenging material designed to develop more sophisticated skills. This situation may change as more software is developed and sold. However, research is needed to learn more about how to design new software and, perhaps, structure learning differently in a dynamic medium with so many possibilities.

Beyond these drawbacks, a major problem is that few of today's teachers are computer literate. Most of them finished their schooling before the computer came to be regarded as significant to education, so they never had any formal training in computing. To overcome the problem, U.S. schools are instituting staff training programs, as are dozens of colleges and universities. Hardware and software vendors are also offering products and training programs for teachers. Finally, professional associations such as the Association for Computing Machinery and the Institute of Electrical and Electronics Engineers are drafting guidelines about what teachers should know and what courses they should take.

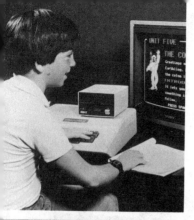

Whatever they do study, many teachers will find themselves rapidly outpaced by good students (some of whom have computers of their own at home) who are eager to learn as much as they can in every area of computer competence. In many cases, students will be teaching one another. Teachers may have to adapt themselves to a new role, that of the coach able to guide and encourage, rather than that of the authority figure and dispenser of knowledge.

Another concern that has recently come to the fore is the widening computer gap between wealthy and poor school districts. At present, according to one estimate, two-thirds of the public schools in wealthier districts have microcomputers available for use by students, while more than half of the schools in poorer districts do not. In the future, it is likely that the richer schools will get richer in computer hardware and software, while the poorer ones lag farther and farther behind.

A possible solution lies in a bill being sponsored in Congress by Representative Fortney (Pete) Stark (D, Calif.), providing tax incentives to computer manufacturers in return for donating computers to schools. The bill grew out of a conversation between Stark and Steven Jobs, the chairman of Apple Computer, who offered to give a computer to every school in the United States in exchange for such incentives; the so-called Apple bill passed in the U.S. House but failed in the Senate during 1982; it was reintroduced in both houses in 1983. A similar measure that also includes the donation of software and extends the proposal to colleges was introduced in 1983 by Senator John C. Danforth (R, Mo.). Other bills were introduced calling for the provision of federal funds for computer training in U.S. public schools.

In the classroom (above) computers are often used as "tutors," to teach and drill in particular subjects; in the library (below) they may be used as tools for research.

As yet we do not know the full potentialities of the computer and how it may change education and culture; whatever the future may hold, youngsters like the pupils shown here are getting in at the ground floor.

What the Future Holds

The future of the computer in education is difficult to predict, but we may pick up clues by examining what is different about computers. The main thing that makes computing different from educational television, books, and lectures is its interactivity—the ability to let the user engage in a give-and-take with the material embodied in the software. There is little such give-and-take between student and lecturer, and even less in the case of television or books.

A further difference between computers and printed matter is that there are more possibilities for graphic material. A program in physics might use an animated sequence of a ball rolling down a hill to demonstrate acceleration. In music, both visual and auditory information might be presented—for example, by displaying the notes of a tune in the form of a musical staff and then playing the tune and the sound of two alternative harmonies. By integrating graphic and sound information with material, computers can lead to richer learning experiences and raise graphics to a new level of importance in our culture.

Finally, students will be able to share information with other learners located miles away by using computers that are linked by cables or phone lines. There may well be a profound change in education as a result of the use of computers in increasingly imaginative and interconnected ways. In particular, schools may become places where children come to cooperate more with one another and realize more fully their interdependence. In short, the private learning now characteristic of the classroom may be broadened to include more shared learning.

Treasures From the Vatican

Over 230 objects from the Vatican's vast collection were sent abroad for display in New York, Chicago, and San Francisco during 1983 and early 1984, in one of the most elaborate traveling art exhibits of the century. The pieces ranged from ancient sculptures like the granite lion below (Egypt, circa 380–342 B.C.) to 20th-century paintings. Many, like the tapestry at right, *The Miraculous Draught of Fishes* (circa 1519, designed by Raphael), were restored specifically for the exhibit.

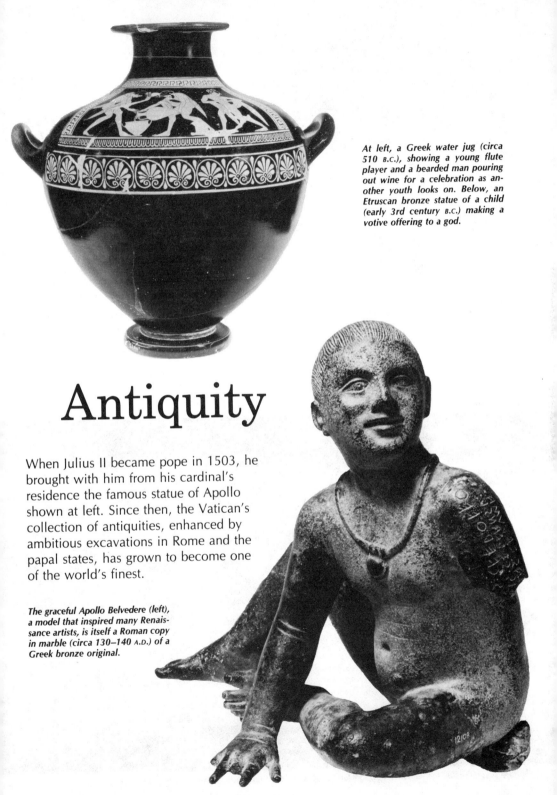

At left, a Greek water jug (circa 510 B.C.), showing a young flute player and a bearded man pouring out wine for a celebration as another youth looks on. Below, an Etruscan bronze statue of a child (early 3rd century B.C.) making a votive offering to a god.

Antiquity

When Julius II became pope in 1503, he brought with him from his cardinal's residence the famous statue of Apollo shown at left. Since then, the Vatican's collection of antiquities, enhanced by ambitious excavations in Rome and the papal states, has grown to become one of the world's finest.

The graceful Apollo Belvedere (left), a model that inspired many Renaissance artists, is itself a Roman copy in marble (circa 130–140 A.D.) of a Greek bronze original.

The prophet Jeremiah holding a scroll said to allude to Christ's coming; part of a fresco of the Baptism of Christ, in Roman style (circa 1120–1130).

Christian Themes

After the fall of Rome, religious art came increasingly into its own, and for many centuries themes from the Bible, as well as the lives of the Virgin Mary and the saints, inspired artists working in a variety of forms and styles.

Rare silk, depicting the Annunciation to Mary, probably from Constantinople (8th–early 9th century).

Madonna and Child (circa 1340), a fine treatment of a traditional subject, by Bernardo Daddi or his school.

27

Middle Ages and Early Renaissance

Vivid frescoes, altarpieces, and mosaics were in great demand during the Middle Ages and early Renaissance to adorn the splendid churches being built. By the 1400's, classical works were being widely studied for their humanistic values and mastery of balance and perspective. Rivalry among artists for honors and commissions was intense, and all of the decorative arts flourished.

At left, **The Music-Making Angel,** *from a famous fresco by Melozzo da Forlì (circa 1480); below,* **St. Nicholas Saves a Storm-Tossed Ship,** *from an altarpiece by Gentile da Fabriano (around 1425); above,* **St. Peter,** *depicted in a fresco fragment from the late 13th century by an unknown artist.*

High Renaissance and Baroque

Stimulated in part by Church patronage, the arts in Europe attained a new sophistication during the High Renaissance (1500's) and the Baroque period (1600's). Works from these times, by masters like Raphael, Bernini, and Caravaggio, were highlights of the Vatican exhibit.

At right, The Deposition (circa 1604), a dynamic, emotional masterpiece by the Baroque artist Caravaggio, depicting Christ's body being placed in the tomb; below, sharply contrasting in style, is a balanced, restrained Annunciation scene painted by Raphael around 1502 at the height of the Renaissance. Above, a Baroque altar cross (circa 1660), designed by Bernini.

Primitive Art

Although European art and classical antiquities form the bulk of the Vatican collections, popes since the 1700's have collected art objects from non-European countries around the world; a selection of these pieces, many originally acquired by missionaries, was included in the Vatican exhibit, in an effort to illustrate the universality of the religious impulse.

Above, a small statue in grayish stone, from Guinea or Sierra Leone, depicting a female with male headgear; it was probably venerated as a seat of spirits who guarded the land and ensured its fertility. Right, a wood and leather mask from the Congo, probably meant for use in religious ceremonies.

At right, a carved wooden hook from Papua New Guinea, representing a birdlike aquatic spirit, invoked for success in fishing. Above, a painted wooden mask from Nigeria, worn in ceremonial dances to appease spirits of the dead.

Modern Works

The Vatican's newest collection, installed in 1973, consists of some 500 paintings, sculptures, and other works from the 20th century, each donated by the artist or owner. A number of interesting pieces from this collection were included in the Vatican exhibit.

At right, **The Holy Face (Sainte Face),** *portrait of a suffering Christ, by Georges Rouault (circa 1946); below,* **The Church at Carrières-Saint-Denis,** *by André Derain (1909); at left,* **Adolescence (Portrait of Francesca Blanc),** *a bronze by Giacomo Manzù (circa 1940–1941).*

35

Saving the Everglades

Diminished and ecologically disturbed over the years, the Everglades nevertheless remains the finest subtropical wetland in the United States, known especially for its variety of bird life. Opposite page: a flock of egrets flies over the Glades. Above: the anhinga, or snakebird, a handsome resident of the area.

Juanita Greene writes on environmental subjects for the Miami Herald.

by JUANITA GREENE

Across the southern end of the Florida interior stretches a broad, flat expanse of green—the Everglades. The green is sharp-edged saw grass that can grow more than 12 feet high. For at least part of every year the grass stands in slow-moving water. Here and there small tree islands, called hammocks, punctuate the saw-grass plain.

The Everglades is the finest subtropical wetland in the United States, home to a wide variety of plant and animal life. It is a peaceful, enchanted place. A cool wind rustles through the broad river of grass. A warm sun reflects the clean, clear water. Small fish dart about.

Once the Glades covered 2½ million acres. The saw grass waved from the south rim of Lake Okeechobee, more than a hundred miles up the Florida peninsula, to the mangrove-fringed tip of Florida; in places the Glades stretched to a width of 40 miles or more. Today, braced by levees and bled by an elaborate system of drainage canals, the Everglades wetland has been shrunk to half the original size. A large part of what once was Everglades is now occupied by homes and farms; hundreds of thousands of acres have been planted with sugarcane and other crops. Much of what remains of the Glades is now included in Everglades National Park, at the southern tip of the state, and in Big Cypress National Preserve directly to the northwest.

Development of the Everglades region, over the

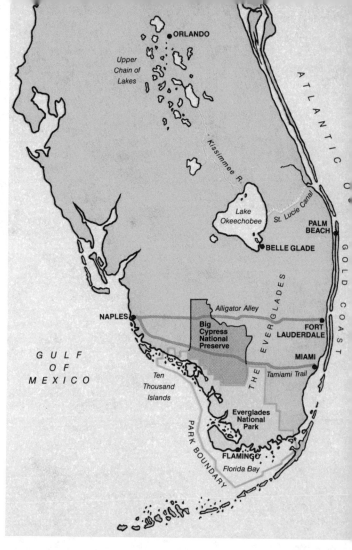

The map at right shows the Everglades drainage system from its beginning in central Florida to Big Cypress National Preserve and Everglades National Park, which include much of what remains of the Glades today.

years, has brought some economic benefits, but at a heavy price. The region's delicate and complex ecosystem, which depends on the flow of water from Lake Okeechobee southward to the tip of the peninsula, has been partially disrupted. Wildlife is struggling to survive. Where drainage has led to depletion of underground fresh water in coastal areas, salt water is seeping in, even threatening the giant aquifers (vast natural reservoirs of underground water) that underlie South Florida and guarantee the water supply of Miami and other cities along the Atlantic coast. At the same time, soil on the reclaimed farmland is drying up and blowing away.

Recently, however, the practical as well as the aesthetic value of the Everglades has become more fully appreciated, and a movement has grown up not only to preserve what remains of the Glades, but to restore as much as possible of the region to its original state.

The World of the Everglades

The broad sweep of the Everglades can be seen from the highways that cross it from west to east—Alligator Alley (Florida Route 84) from Naples to Fort Lauderdale and the Tamiami Trail (U.S. 41) from Naples to Miami. Along the Alley in winter, birds fill the occasional trees like large white blossoms. On the Trail they line the bordering canal. For a closer look, many visitors take the road that leads through Everglades National Park proper. It begins at the park's main entrance near Florida City, about 35 miles southwest of Miami, and runs through all the representative terrain of the lower Everglades, ending at Flamingo on Florida Bay, at the end of the peninsula. The park road traverses saw-grass plains, pinelands, forests of dwarf cypress, hardwood hammocks, freshwater sloughs (permanent water channels), and mangrove stands.

The vastness of the saw grass is relieved by the hammocks, where the ground rises 2 or 3 feet above the surrounding wetlands. On these hammocks grows the sabal palm, which appears all over Florida, as well as some trees found only in South Florida, the West Indies, and the Bahamas; they include the bronze-barked gumbo-limbo and the delicate paradise tree.

Saw-grass plains, dotted with tree-covered islands, or hammocks, stand in slow-moving water for at least part of every year.

A conservationist cradles one of many deer rescued from the Everglades, as hunters in another part of the Glades began a controversial "mercy hunt" to thin out the deer herd, starving because of flooding.

Fifth-graders from a Hialeah, Fla., school hike through Everglades National Park with a ranger, during a week-long camping trip aimed at initiating the youngsters into the wonders of the Glades.

There is native mahogany, too, found nowhere else in the United States.

Intruding into the southern Glades is the tail end of the ridge that runs along Florida's east coast; it is high enough to support a forest of Southern pine. In this forest are more hardwood hammocks, whose dark, damp interiors support a profusion of ferns. Liguus tree snails, whorled gems of moving color much sought after by collectors, have managed to survive in the more remote hammocks, feeding on the lichens that grow on the trunks of certain trees. Air plants growing in the hammocks include spiny bromeliads that bloom in passionate red and orchids in pale pastels.

On the fringe of the Everglades the water becomes brackish, then salty, from seawater pushed inland by wind and tide. Here the mangrove trees begin to grow, first as stubby bushes amid the short saw grass and finally in thick, tall forests along the coast. These mangroves sift runoff, collecting drifting soil and debris around their exposed roots to build land and thus protect coastlines. In addition, as fallen leaves decay, they provide important nutrients in the fish food chain.

Flamingo is a small settlement on Florida Bay at the end of the 38-mile road through Everglades National Park. It is a place of spectacular sunsets, with flocks of water birds casting silhouettes as they fly to their island roosts. Over the Flamingo campground the ibis and egrets fly so low that the fluttering of their wings can be

On the Anhinga Trail, in Everglades National Park, visitors get a close-up view of the watery flora and fauna but manage to keep their feet dry.

heard. Spoonbills streak the sky in pink. Flamingos also appear, but they are not a common sight. (Flamingos are not native to Florida; National Park Service biologists don't know if these specimens are immigrants from the Caribbean or escapees from the captive flock that parades at Hialeah Park racetrack near Miami.)

In the whole Everglades region, there are many endangered and threatened species. With luck, some can be seen by visitors, including the Southern bald eagle, the Everglade kite, the Florida sandhill crane, the great white heron, the wood stork, the manatee, and the alligator. More rarely seen are the short-tailed hawk, American peregrine falcon, Cape Sable seaside sparrow, American crocodile, and Florida panther. The crocodile, like the West Indian hardwood trees, is found in the United States only at the southern tip of Florida. The panther is the most endangered of all the Florida species. Only about 20 are believed to survive today, living a precarious existence in the park and in the adjoining Big Cypress Swamp.

The Water of Life

The making of the Everglades began more than 100,000 years ago, when Florida was still under water.

The alligator is perhaps the best known Everglades citizen. Once prized by poachers and threatened by habitat loss, it now enjoys a fairly comfortable home in the Glades.

The Florida peninsula was probably the last part of the United States to emerge from the sea. The land that today separates the Gulf of Mexico from the Atlantic Ocean is the high, dry part of a plateau that extends west about 100 miles under the Gulf and east a short distance under the ocean. Over the submerged portion of the plateau the water is no more than 500 feet deep. The Florida plateau was alternately exposed and submerged over the centuries as sea levels fluctuated with the forming or melting of glaciers far away. At times the dry area was twice the present size; at other times only a few spots escaped submersion. Florida as it appears today was uncovered about 20,000 years ago.

Of all the factors affecting the Everglades environment today, water is by far the most important. The average annual rainfall in South Florida is 60 inches, but there is great variation from one year to the next, as drought alternates with flood. By mid-1983, for example, the park was severely waterlogged after some 18 months of above average rainfall. Deer were endangered, alligator nests were virtually wiped out, and many wading birds were unable to nest.

Usually 75 percent of the rainfall occurs in the wet season, from May through October; when hurricanes rage, they can drop up to 2 feet of water within a few days. During the rainy season, a shallow, slow-moving flow of water (known as sheet flow) travels southward from Lake Okeechobee to the sea, creating large areas of aquatic habitat within the remaining Everglades region. The action of sunlight and plant life keeps the water clear and clean. When the dry season arrives and these areas shrink, fish, crustaceans, and other organisms become concentrated. This makes it easier for the wood stork and other nesting wading birds and for the alligator and other predators to find food.

Sheet flow also is important because it moderates the effects of the great yearly variations in rainfall. In the wet season, the peat soil of the Glades serves as a sponge, soaking up moisture to hold the water table high into the dry season and recharge the huge underground Biscayne Aquifer, sole source of water for most residents of Florida's southeast "Gold Coast." The high head of fresh water also holds back salt water from the sea.

The Everglades system does not work as effectively as it once did, since much of the water is drained off by the canals and carried to the eastern coast before it can reach the lower Everglades. Some scientists also believe that the shrinkage of the Everglades through drainage has diminished the rainfall over South Florida, because not enough moisture rises from the Glades to trigger rain in the same volume as before. With increasing water requirements for homes, agriculture, and other uses, the need to restore the full natural sheet flow wherever possible becomes ever more important.

The First Residents

People have lived in and around the Everglades for the last 4,000 years. The first inhabitants probably were the Glades Indians, who occupied both coasts, the Lake Okeechobee region, and part of the Everglades. In

Egrets are one of many species of birds that live and breed in and around Florida Bay. Above: two egret babies.

The panther is the most endangered of all animal species in Florida; about 20 are believed to survive today in Everglades National Park and the adjoining Big Cypress Swamp.

43

Much of the original Everglades has been lost to development. Here, on drained swampland south of Lake Okeechobee, migrant workers pick parsley; smoke in the background indicates the burning of harvested sugarcane to remove the leaves.

the early 1500's, when the first Europeans (the Spanish) arrived, the Glades people are believed to have numbered 5,000 or more. By the mid-1700's, only a few hundred survived. The tribes had been decimated by invading British-led Creek Indians from North Florida, who carried their captives off into slavery. Smallpox and other European diseases also took their toll. In 1763, when Florida became a British possession, what were believed to be the last 80 Indian families in South Florida left with the Spanish for Havana.

In the next century the Everglades began to shelter Indians of a different origin, the Seminoles. They were migrants from Georgia and Alabama who came to Florida to escape the land conflicts between Indians and settlers farther north. When the settlers followed and claimed land in Florida, the Seminoles resisted. In 1818, General Andrew Jackson led an expedition to subdue them. Fifteen years later, the U.S. government decided to remove the Seminoles to the West. The Indians rebelled, and in the course of the fighting, they were pushed ever southward until they reached the Everglades.

The Everglades became the last battleground, and the Seminoles soon adapted to this vast watery wilderness. Standing on platforms in the sterns of shallow cypress canoes, they pushed through the tall grass with long poles. They made camp on islands deep within the saw grass, where they planted crops and kept watch from tall trees. In all, the removal of the Seminoles required three wars extending over a period of 41 years, and it was never fully completed. Left to live out obscure lives in the Everglades were perhaps 100 to 300 Indians; their number has grown to an estimated 2,000 today.

Messing With Mother Nature

Beginning in the 1880's the Everglades region was invaded by new people—the dredgers and the drainers. White settlers began building canals and levees that made possible the cultivation of portions of the Everglades. The program was spurred on by the efforts of Napoleon Bonaparte Broward, a former riverboat captain who was elected governor of Florida in 1905 on a drain-and-development platform. By 1913, five main drainage canals were open in the Everglades. In all, about 225 miles of canals had been dug. People began to settle around the rim of Lake Okeechobee and near both ends of the canals leading from the lake to the Atlantic.

Real estate developers are in the fierce competition for land in southern Florida.

The making of the Everglades began over 100,000 years ago, when the Florida peninsula was still underwater; of all the factors affecting the Everglades environment today, water remains by far the most important. Above: an aerial view.

However, as the area developed, serious problems emerged. The rich black Everglades soil, created over the centuries from decayed vegetation, dries out when drained. It burns easily, it blows away, and it settles in a process that is called subsidence. Since farming began there, the layer of black soil near the lake has shrunk from 11 feet in thickness to 4 feet, and the process continues at the rate of about an inch a year. (On the steps of some old houses in the town of Belle Glade, near Lake Okeechobee, there is a gap of a foot or more between the bottom step and the ground.)

The Everglades region has also suffered from devastating hurricanes. In 1926 more than 400 people were killed during a tropical storm when a dike around Lake Okeechobee broke. Two years later, hurricane rains and winds caused the lake to overflow again, inundating the whole south shore. Estimates of the number of lives lost ran to more than 2,000.

Reclamation work came to a virtual standstill during the Great Depression and World War II. Then came the great hurricanes and flood of September and October 1947. Only the ridge along the east coast remained dry; most of the remainder of southeast Florida was under water. The disaster prompted a public outcry for flood protection. The federal government was called upon for help, and the U.S. Army Corps of Engineers responded with a massive flood-protection and drainage plan.

Today, most of the work envisaged in the Corps of Engineers plan has been completed. A great north-south levee about 100 miles long was built a few miles west of the Gold Coast to hold back the waters of the Everglades. West of the levee three water storage areas were created in the Glades. Existing canals were widened and deepened, and new ones were dug. The levee around Lake Okeechobee was raised and extended. The meandering 100-mile Kissimmee River was transformed into a straight 50-mile ditch. In all, the work has cost more than $500 million.

A state agency, the South Florida Water Management District, now controls water resources all the way from the Upper Chain of Lakes, in central Florida, to the tip of the peninsula. Reclamation has proceeded apace, and the fast-growing cities along the coast and around Orlando now have dry ground for expansion. South of Lake Okeechobee the farmland that once was Everglades has expanded to cover a total of 700,000 acres, most of them now planted with sugarcane. A protective dike surrounds the land.

Even while efforts to drain the Everglades were at their peak, however, a countermovement for preservation was at work. In 1947, not long before the adoption of the Corps of Engineers plan, conservationists succeeded in winning the establishment of Everglades National Park on the southwest tip of the peninsula. The park has since been expanded, and about one-fifth of the original river of grass lies within its confines.

In 1970 and 1971, while dredging was still in full swing, a parching drought began to crack the farm soil around Lake Okeechobee. It prompted a public reappraisal of the wisdom of the water-control and reclamation work. Evidence was mounting by the early 1970's, moreover, that the activities of the water management district were also apparently creating other problems. Lake Okeechobee, in a process called eutrophication, was suffocating from an oversupply of nutrients that no longer were given time to settle along the banks of the Kissimmee River. (When such substances build up, they feed a tremendous burst of algae and other plant growth; the plants then use up the oxygen in the water, which fish need to live.) Runoff water from the farms around the lake, laden

The Big Cypress Swamp covers more than 2,400 square miles in subtropical Florida. Its cypresses are mostly of the dwarf pond variety; the age-old giant cypress trees have nearly disappeared, victims of the lumber industry.

A Seminole girl, rowing her boat in the Everglades, serves as a reminder of the region's often stormy past, during a series of Indian wars.

with organic nutrients from fertilizers, and runoff from cattle lots along other streams feeding into the lake added to the problem.

In addition, Everglades National Park was threatened with too much water one year and too little the next. In years of heavy rainfall, the canals poured huge amounts of water into the park. When rainfall was light, on the other hand, more water was held back for residential, agricultural, and commercial needs.

In 1970, park supporters won legislation from Congress guaranteeing the park a certain amount of water each year, but in some years there was still not enough. Salt water began to creep inland along the coast, no longer held back by a constant high head of fresh water. Fishing fell off in Florida Bay, at the southern tip of the state; sports fishermen blamed the diversion of fresh water away from the bay. In the St. Lucie estuary up the east coast, on the other hand, too much fresh water was being dumped, damaging the marine breeding grounds there.

Restoring a Balance

Problems like these have led to recommendations for restoring the Everglades region to something approaching its natural state. Canals would be filled in and levees demolished; in certain places the historic sheet flow would again move through the Everglades along its natural course. The water management district itself is turning away from canal digging to more natural approaches. The district hopes to restore the Kissimmee River to some degree, so that some of its floodplains again will be wet for part of the year.

An ambitious, multimillion-dollar plan to acquire and restore major parts of the Everglades region was unveiled in 1983 by Florida Governor Bob Graham. The program also called for studies by state agencies to determine the best approach for restoring the Kissimmee River. Part of the plan would require federal aid and cooperation.

Conservationists hope that, in any event, not much more of the Everglades will be drained and that someday sizable dry parts will be reflooded. The most likely place for large-scale reflooding, eventually, would be the agricultural area south of Lake Okeechobee, where the vanishing soil is expected to be too shallow to plow by the end of the century.

No one believes it is possible for Florida to restore all of its former Everglades. The challenge is to save what's left, and there is hope for that.

1984 YEARBOOK
EVENTS OF 1983

CHRONOLOGY FOR 1983

January

21 ● The Labor Department reports that the U.S. inflation rate was 3.9 percent in 1982.

25 ● President Ronald Reagan, in his State of the Union message, asks for a broad freeze on domestic budget expenditures together with a continued military buildup.

31 ● President Reagan sends Congress a proposed $848.5 billion budget for fiscal 1984, with a projected deficit of $188.8 billion.

February

4 ● The Labor Department announces that U.S. civilian unemployment fell to 10.4 percent in January, the first drop in 17 months.

11 ● Ariel Sharon resigns as Israel's defense minister (but remains in the cabinet) after a commission of inquiry finds him "indirectly responsible" in the September 1982 massacre of Palestinian refugees by Lebanese Christian Phalangists near Beirut.

22 ● The Environmental Protection Agency announces a $33 million plan to buy out property owners in Times Beach, Mo., which had been contaminated by a highly toxic form of dioxin.

March

5 ● Australia's Labor Party, led by Robert Hawke, wins a solid majority in the lower house of Parliament, ending eight years of Liberal–National Party rule.

FEB. 22

6 • Christian Democrats capture nearly 50 percent of the vote in West German elections, ensuring the party continued control of the government in coalition with the Free Democratic Party.

9 • Anne Burford resigns as head of the EPA, amid continuing charges that the agency mishandled the toxic waste cleanup program.

14 • The Organization of Petroleum Exporting Countries cuts the benchmark price for its oil from $34 a barrel to $29 and assigns production quotas for member countries, in an effort to stop price slides.

23 • Sixteen weeks after receiving an artificial heart, Barney Clark dies in Salt Lake City.

April

12 • Chicago voters narrowly elect Democrat Harold Washington to be the city's first black mayor.

18 • A powerful bomb destroys much of the U.S. embassy in Beirut, killing at least 60 people, including 17 Americans.

20 • President Reagan signs a compromise social security reform bill designed to shore up the system for future years by increasing taxes and cutting back on the growth of benefits.

May

3 • The U.S. National Conference of Catholic Bishops approves a pastoral letter condemning nuclear war as immoral and calling for a negotiated halt to the production and deployment of nuclear weapons.

4 • The government of Iran dissolves the Tudeh (Communist) Party, charging it with espionage, and expels 18 Soviet diplomats.

6 • Israel and the United States sign an agreement, endorsed earlier by Lebanese leaders, providing for a withdrawal of Israeli troops

APRIL 18

from Lebanon, contingent on the simultaneous withdrawal of Syrian and Palestine Liberation Organization forces.

25 • Navy Lieutenant Commander Albert Schaufelberger is shot and killed in El Salvador, becoming the first U.S. military adviser to die there.

51

JUNE 9

June

9 • Prime Minister Margaret Thatcher's Conservative Party scores a resounding electoral victory, gaining a 144-seat majority in Britain's House of Commons.

11 • Canada's Progressive Conservative Party chooses Brian Mulroney as its new leader, succeeding Joe Clark.

17 • After meeting privately with former Solidarity leader Lech Walesa, John Paul II concludes an eight-day visit to his native Poland.

23 • The U.S. Supreme Court strikes down the so-called legislative veto, used by Congress to annul certain executive actions.

• Congress passes a compromise $849.6 billion budget resolution for fiscal 1984 calling for higher taxes, lower military spending, and higher domestic expenditures than President Reagan wanted.

24 • The space shuttle *Challenger* completes its second mission; its crew of five includes Sally Ride, the first U.S. woman in space.

• Syria expels Palestine Liberation Organization chief Yasir Arafat, who had accused Syrian officials of backing PLO factions in a rebellion against him.

July

1 • The third and last phase of President Reagan's income tax reduction program goes into effect, with a cut amounting to about 10 percent for most taxpayers.

18 • President Reagan announces the appointment of former Secretary of State Henry Kissinger to head a newly established bipartisan commission, charged with formulating recommendations for long-term U.S. policy in Central America.

21 • Poland announces the formal lifting of martial law and declares a partial amnesty for political detainees.

August

4 • Bettino Craxi becomes Italy's first Socialist premier, at the head of a coalition of five non-Communist parties.

52

8 • Guatemala's army leaders depose President Efraín Ríos Montt and replace him with General Oscar Mejía Victores.

10 • With Libyan aid, rebel forces in Chad oust government troops from the strategic oasis of Faya-Largeau.

21 • Philippines opposition leader Benigno Aquino is shot and killed at Manila airport as he returns home after three years; guards shoot to death the alleged assassin, later described as a professional killer.

• France dispatches combat aircraft to Chad in support of French troops setting up an east-west defense line to block further advances by Libyan-backed rebels.

27 • A rally to mark the 20th anniversary of the 1963 civil rights march draws an estimated 300,000 people to Washington, D.C.

September

1 • A Korean Air Lines jetliner straying into Soviet airspace is shot down near Sakhalin Island in the Soviet Far East; all 269 aboard are killed.

4 • Israeli forces in Lebanon complete a planned withdrawal southward to the line of the Awali River.

26 • After U.S. and Saudi mediation, a new cease-fire goes into effect in Lebanon, ending four weeks of heavy fighting near Beirut.

29 • Congress approves a compromise resolution under the War Powers Act, allowing U.S. peacekeeping troops to remain in Lebanon for 18 months.

October

2 • Britain's Labor Party chooses Neil Kinnock to succeed Michael Foot as party leader.

5 • Solidarity leader Lech Walesa is awarded the Nobel Peace Prize.

9 • Four South Korean cabinet ministers and 17 other people are killed by a bomb blast in Rangoon, during a state visit to Burma by South Korean President Chun Doo Hwan.

• James Watt, under fire for an off-the-cuff remark considered offensive to minorities and women, resigns as interior secretary.

10 • Israel's parliament approves Yitzhak Shamir as prime minister, succeeding Menachem Begin, who had announced his resignation.

13 • In a surprise move, President Reagan names National Security Adviser William Clark to be secretary of the interior.

23 • More than a million people demonstrate in West Germany, Britain, Italy, and other countries against deployment of U.S. medium-range missiles in Western Europe.

AUG. 21

53

DEC. 8

6 • In national elections in Turkey, the conservative Motherland Party wins a majority of seats in parliament, as a transition to civilian government begins.

15 • The leader of the Turkish sector in Cyprus declares the area an independent republic.

18 • On the last day of its 1983 session, Congress approves military spending of nearly $250 billion for fiscal 1984, including funds for 21 MX missiles.

23 • A day after the parliament reaffirms West Germany's decision to permit the stationing of U.S. intermediate-range missiles, the first Pershing II missiles arrive in the country, and the Soviet Union suspends talks with the United States on limiting medium-range missiles.

December

• A truck loaded with TNT is driven into a U.S. Marine headquarters at the Beirut airport, where it explodes, destroying the building and killing over 240 Americans; another blast nearby kills at least 58 members of the French peacekeeping force.

2 • The U.S. Labor Department reports a November unemployment rate of 8.4 percent, a two-year low.

4 • In response to Syrian attacks on U.S. reconnaissance aircraft, 28 U.S. carrier jets bomb Syrian targets in Lebanon; two U.S. aircraft are shot down.

25 • A few days after a coup by a radical Marxist faction, U.S. forces (and units from several Caribbean countries) invade Grenada and quickly seize control of key points despite some resistance, largely from armed Cuban personnel on the island.

8 • After a ten-day flight in which numerous scientific experiments are conducted, the space shuttle *Columbia* lands safely, despite a delay caused by extensive malfunctions.

30 • Raul Alfonsín of the Radical Civic Union is elected president of Argentina, ending eight years of military rule.

19 • Japan's ruling party sustains heavy losses in parliamentary elections.

November

20 • Yasir Arafat and 4,000 Arafat loyalists in the PLO are evacuated from Tripoli, Lebanon, in Greek ships, after a six-week siege by Syrian-backed PLO dissidents.

2 • President Reagan signs a bill making the third Monday in January a national holiday, beginning in 1986, to commemorate the birthday of Martin Luther King, Jr.

28 • A Pentagon commission publishes a report blaming Marine commanders and U.S. policy for failures that made possible the bombing of a Marine headquarters in Beirut.

• South African voters approve constitutional changes to create a tripartite parliament consisting of separate chambers for white, Indian, and mixed-race citizens.

31 • President Shehu Shagari of Nigeria is deposed in a military coup.

ACCIDENTS AND DISASTERS. The following were among the noteworthy accidents and disasters of 1983:

Jan.–Feb., California: Storms batter the California coast, causing flooding and mudslides; at least 28 deaths are reported, and damage is put at over $500 million.

Jan. 3, Turkey: A seven-story apartment building built on loose ground sinks and collapses in Diyarbakir, reportedly killing 80 people.

Feb. 11–12, United States: A powerful storm sweeps along the coast from North Carolina to Maine; at least 46 deaths are reported.

Feb. 12, Virginia: The coal carrier *Marine Electric* capsizes in a blizzard east of Chincoteague; 33 crew members perish.

Feb. 13, Italy: Fire breaks out in a Turin movie theater, killing 64 patrons, most of them young people.

Feb. 16–18, Australia: Brush fires in the south engulf bush, farms, and forests left bone dry by drought; at least 70 deaths are reported.

Feb. 19, Mexico: A freight train crashes into a stalled passenger train near Empalme; more than 70 people die.

Late February, Lebanon: Blizzards that rage for nearly ten days leave more than 70 people dead in mountainous north and central areas, many of them victims stranded in their cars.

March 1, China: An overnight ferry, traveling from Canton to Zhaoqing, turns over in a thunderstorm, leaving at least 166 people dead or missing.

March 7, China: Some 270 people are killed when a landslide engulfs a village in Gansu province.

March 7, Turkey: Two gas explosions rip through the Armutcuk coal mine near the

The Golden State was pounded by a series of storms in January and February that left at least 28 dead. Here, waves 15 to 20 feet high hit Pacifica, Calif., just south of San Francisco.

Black Sea town of Ereğli, leaving more than 100 miners dead, in the worst mining accident in Turkey's history.

March 31, Colombia: An earthquake devastates the historic Andean city of Popayán, as many pilgrims gather there for Holy Week ceremonies; over 260 people reportedly lose their lives.

Late March, Peru: Mudslides engulf two villages in northern Peru, causing more than 100 deaths.

April 18, South Korea: Fire sweeps through a crowded disco in Taegu, killing 25 people, many of them teenagers.

April 27, Ecuador: More than 100 people are killed when a landslide sweeps a convoy of trucks and buses over a cliff into a river.

May 7, Turkey: An explosion in a first-floor coffee shop starts a fire in an Istanbul hotel, leaving at least 40 people dead.

May 18–23, United States: Over 30 people are killed as flash floods, hailstorms, and tornadoes hit areas of eight southern states.

May 25, Egypt: A Nile River ferry explodes into flame and sinks in Lake Nasser; more than 300 people are drowned.

May 26, Japan: A powerful earthquake, centered off the northwest coast, triggers strong tremors and high waves; over 100 people perish, and property damage is estimated at nearly $600 million.

May 27, India: Sixty people are believed dead after a bus careens into a gorge in the central state of Madhya Pradesh.

Late April–May, China: The central province of Hunan is struck by hailstorms, tornadoes, and torrential rains that leave a death toll of more than 3,000.

June 2, Kentucky: Twenty-three people die as an Air Canada DC-9, engulfed in smoke and flames from a lavatory fire, makes an emergency landing at the Greater Cincinnati International Airport.

June 5, Soviet Union: The upper deck of the cruise ship *Alexander Suvorov* rams a railroad bridge on the Volga River near Ulyanovsk; well over 100 people are killed.

June 16, Turkey: Forty-seven people are killed when a Turkish jet crashes in sleet and high winds while landing at an airport near Ankara.

June 28, India: Nearly 1,000 people are reported dead or missing after four days of monsoon rains in the state of Gujarat.

June, Soviet Union: A nuclear-powered Soviet submarine sinks in the Pacific Ocean, off the Kamchatka Peninsula, according to U.S. intelligence reports; the whole crew, about 90, is believed lost.

July 11, Ecuador: A Boeing 737 slams into a mountain while trying to land at Cuenca; all 119 aboard lose their lives.

July 28, Colombia: Two avalanches about an hour apart pour down a mountainside in heavy rains, causing 160 deaths at a dam project east of Bogotá.

June–July, China: According to Chinese press reports, at least 273 people are killed and millions of acres of crops destroyed as heavy rains flood the Yangtze and Huang He Rivers.

Aug. 13, India: At least 60 people are killed at a shrine in the northern state of Himachal Pradesh, when a nearby market stall collapses and causes widespread panic.

Aug. 24, Taiwan: The roof of a high school auditorium in Fengyuan collapses during an assembly; at least 26 students die.

Aug. 30, Soviet Union: A Soviet Aeroflot airliner, with a capacity of 77 passengers and crew, crashes on its approach to the Alma-Ata airport, killing all aboard.

Sept. 1, Soviet Union: A South Korean commercial airliner on a routine flight strays into Soviet airspace and is shot down over the Sea of Japan by a Soviet jet fighter; all 269 persons aboard are killed.

Sept. 12, South Africa: Sixty-four miners lose their lives in an explosion at the Hlobane coal mine southeast of Johannesburg.

Sept. 23, Abu Dhabi: A Gulf Air Boeing 737 en route to Bahrain crashes in flames in the desert mountains, killing 112 people.

Sept. 28, Nicaragua: A passenger ferry, reportedly carrying 127 people, catches fire and sinks while crossing Lake Nicaragua; 90 people are reported dead or missing.

September, India: Monsoon floods inundate roads and villages, causing landslides and traffic accidents in five northern states; nearly 400 people are left dead.

Oct. 26, China: The U.S. oil-drilling ship *Glomar Java Sea* vanishes in a typhoon in the South China Sea, with the apparent loss of all 81 people aboard.

Oct. 30, Turkey: A major earthquake strikes eastern Turkey, reportedly devastating dozens of villages; the death toll is said to be at least 2,000.

Nov. 8, Angola: An Angolan Boeing 737 crashes shortly after takeoff from an airport at Lubango, killing all 126 aboard.

Late November, United States: Back-to-back snowstorms sweep through the Midwest, closing airports and highways in seven states and causing at least 56 deaths.

Nov. 21, Philippines: The *Dona Cassandra,* a 167-foot ferry, sinks in a typhoon off Mindanao Island; more than 200 people are reported missing.

Nov. 27, Spain: A Boeing 747 operated by Colombia's Avianca airlines crashes on its approach to Madrid's Barajas airport; at least 183 people are killed, in one of the ten worst aviation crashes in history.

Nov. 28, Nigeria: A Nigeria Airways airliner crashes 300 miles east of Lagos; at least 53 people are killed.

Dec. 7, Spain: In the second major accident in ten days, two Spanish jetliners collide on the ground at Madrid's Barajas airport, leaving 93 people dead.

Dec. 17, Spain: A fire sweeps through the Alcala 20, a Madrid discothèque; 81 people die and at least 21 are injured.

Dec. 22, Guinea: An earthquake reportedly destroys 16 villages in the northwest and kills over 200 people.   M.H.

ADVERTISING. In spite of the lingering effects of the recession, advertising prospered in the United States during 1983. Michael Drexler, executive vice-president of media and programming at Doyle Dane Bernbach, predicted a 10 percent growth in advertising over 1982, with volume reaching nearly $74 billion. Expenditure increases in the traditional media were expected to be about 10 percent, while cable advertising revenue was predicted to rise 48 percent because of the addition of new advertising-supported networks.

Regulation. While the advertising industry continued its effort to convince Congress to reduce the Federal Trade Commission's authority to regulate advertising, FTC Chairman James C.

Advertisers are keeping up with today's fashion for fitness. The Campbell's Soup kids, for instance, have lost the little paunches they sported back in the 1920's and are now into exercise.

Miller III expressed his firm belief that the commission should retain power over "unfair" advertising. In mid-July, the FTC ordered two major over-the-counter drugmakers to drop claims of superiority for their products. Both Bristol-Myers and Sterling Drug Inc. were informed that they could no longer claim their pain relievers were better or safer than others without scientific support in the form of well-controlled clinical tests.

Media. Advertising spending estimates for newspapers showed an increase of 10 percent over 1982, to a total of $20 billion, while newspaper advertising rates were expected to increase approximately 9 percent, less than the average 1982 increase, according to a Knight-Ridder Newspapers survey.

Magazine advertising page sales rose in 1983. Magazine advertising rates were expected to increase approximately 9 percent over 1982, according to the Magazine Publishers Association. Video and electronics magazines constituted the largest category of new magazines. Both in-home and arcade video game magazines proliferated, and numerous consumer and fitness magazines also started up. All of these allowed for more specifically targeted advertising.

An increase of 5 percent in both spot and network radio advertising rates was predicted for 1983. In May, the Federal Communications Commission voted to add stations to the FM radio spectrum, a decision expected to result in 600 to 800 new outlets.

Beginning in April, the three broadcast television networks allowed an additional two minutes of network and one minute of local advertising in prime time per week (these additions still fell under the current FCC ceiling on television commercials). Network commercial prices continued to skyrocket, with rates for the 1983–1984 season expected to increase 12 to 14 percent. The list asking price for one 30-second spot on the February 18 series-ending episode of M*A*S*H was $450,000, setting a new record for a prime-time series commercial. Sponsor commitments for the 2½-hour episode were greater than $11 million.

Advertising-supported cable television networks flourished. *Advertising Age* compilations indicated 1983 cable advertising revenues of about $383 million, a 58 percent increase over 1982.

In June, ten Public Broadcasting Service stations across the country completed an 18-month trial run of commercial messages intended to compensate for federal funding cut-backs. Progress reports indicated that some marketers were eager to pay a premium price to reach the PBS audiences, that participating stations were enthusiastic, and that audiences did not object to the introduction of advertising.

Advertisers. It was a year of rebuilding for Johnson & Johnson's Extra-Strength Tylenol capsules, which had been pulled off the market in the fall of 1982 after seven persons died from swallowing Tylenol capsules laced with cyanide. In January, the company reintroduced the pain reliever in tamper-proof packaging, stressing consumer confidence in the product, and it soon recaptured a large share of the analgesic market.

With the introduction of caffeine-free colas by Coca-Cola, Pepsi-Cola, Dr. Pepper, and Royal Crown Cola, advertising messages stressing the absence of caffeine in soft drinks flourished. Canada Dry ginger ale was touted as having "no caffeine since 1904," while Seven-Up stressed a "never had it" theme and also introduced Like caffeine-free cola.

The hamburger war between McDonald's, Wendy's, and Burger King continued. Burger King advertisements began emphasizing consumers' preference for its "flame-broiled" hamburgers over "fried" burgers, while veteran actor John Houseman extolled the quality and value of McDonald's product in television commercials.   B.G.V.

AFGHANISTAN. The war in Afghanistan between the rebel Mujahedeen (holy warriors) and forces of the Afghan government and the Soviet Union showed no signs of abating in 1983. Diplomatic efforts to achieve a cessation of hostilities as a prelude to a political settlement proved unavailing.

The war. The Mujahedeen, better armed and better trained than in the past, operated throughout the country, knocking out bridges, closing major roads, destroying convoys, and attacking Soviet military bases. The Mujahedeen made daring raids into the capital city of Kabul, attacking the airport and various Soviet installations, including the Soviet embassy, and temporarily knocking out electricity in the city.

The Soviets often relied on air power in striking back. In April and May, after a series of rebel offensives, Soviet helicopters and fighter-bombers attacked civilian settlements throughout Afghanistan, including Herāt, the country's third largest city. Reportedly, half the city was destroyed and 3,000 civilians were killed. In September and October, Soviet and Afghan troops waged new ground offensives with heavy air support, bombing villages in seven provinces; heavy bombardment of one small town near Kabul reportedly left several hundred people killed, including many women and children. In early December, Soviet forces reportedly withdrew from a valley north of Kabul, after suffering heavy casualties in an unsuccessful assault on rebel positions there.

Since the war began in 1978, casualties for the more than 100,000 Soviet troops in Afghanistan have been estimated as high as 5,000 killed and 10,000 wounded. Arrayed against the Soviets and the 30,000-man Afghan Army were 70,000–100,000 guerrillas. Morale was low in the Afghan Army, and conscription was being carried out by press gangs, who searched homes and rounded up young men on the streets.

Impact on the economy. The widening conflict had a profound effect on economic activity in Afghanistan. Disruption of farming caused severe food shortages in Kabul and other cities. As stocks of grain, meat, cooking oil, sugar, and other commodities became low, prices soared. The shortages were aggravated by the flight of the rural population to the relative safety of the cities, bringing about chaotic urbanization. Trade with the West, once an important source of income, dried up. Most of Afghanistan's exports, including some 90 percent of its natural gas, was going to the Soviet Union.

Political rivalries. In the ruling People's Democratic Party, the feud continued between the two major factions, the Parcham (flag) group, headed by President Babrak Karmal, and the Khalq (masses) group. In August, according to Western sources, members of the two factions clashed openly near Herāt. About a hundred pro-Parcham Afghan soldiers and pro-Khalq Interior Ministry police were killed or wounded in the gunfight.

In the guerrilla movement, the two most powerful groups, the Hizbe-Islami (Islamic Party) and the Jamiat-I-Islami (Islamic Association), both composed of fundamentalist Sunni Muslims, continued to fight separately against the common foe. In another example of the sometimes conflicting strategies of the Mujahedeen, Ahmad Shah Massoud, the young overlord of the vital Panjshir Valley north of Kabul, arranged a temporary separate truce in March with the Soviet military command in the capital. The truce allowed him to regroup his forces but also allowed the Soviets to transfer some of their troops to other areas.

Foreign affairs. International efforts failed again to bring an end to the conflict in Afghanistan. In March the summit conference of the nonaligned nations movement, held in New Delhi, India, called for a Soviet withdrawal. United Nations Undersecretary-General Diego Cordóvez continued negotiations in Geneva with the foreign ministers of Afghanistan and Pakistan in search of a political settlement. In addition to the removal of Soviet troops, the major issues included a secure return of Afghan refugees (said to number 4 million in Pakistan and Iran) and restoration of an independent, nonaligned government in Kabul.

None of the negotiations included the Mujahedeen, who had not formed a government in exile. In July, Afghanistan's exiled king, Zahir Shah, emerged from political retirement to offer his services to the resistance, but several guerrilla spokesmen said they would not recognize the former monarch as the symbol of the Afghan struggle.

Relations between Kabul and Washington deteriorated further. The Karmal government expelled several U.S. diplomats on charges of spying, which the United States denied. In July, U.S. Secretary of State George Shultz, meeting with Mujahedeen representatives while on a visit to Pakistan, reaffirmed U.S. support for Afghanistan's "fighters for freedom."

Dissent on Radio Moscow. Listeners to the English-language service of Radio Moscow pricked up their ears in May when they heard announcer Vladimir Danchev refer to the Afghan people's "struggle against the Soviet invaders." Danchev was apparently disaffected with his country's role in Afghanistan. For his "personal mistake," he was taken off the air and reportedly ordered to undergo a mental examination.

See STATISTICS OF THE WORLD.   N.P.N.

Africa

Much of Africa was beset in 1983 by serious drought, which put an added strain on economic resources. Conflict escalated in Chad and in the racially split southern African region, while tensions continued in Western Sahara and the Horn of Africa.

At least 22 African countries faced severe drought conditions in 1983. For many it was the second year of insufficient rain, and the United Nations Food and Agriculture Organization warned that conditions approaching the famine of 1973–1974 threatened an even wider area than at that time. Regions affected included the western and central African Sahel on the southern borders of the Sahara Desert, the Horn of Africa in the northeast, and most of the countries of southern Africa. The five countries identified as in the greatest need were Chad, Ethiopia, Ghana, São Tomé and Príncipe, and Mozambique. Some 3 million people in Ethiopia and 4 million in Mozambique were reported suffering from serious food shortages.

The drought accentuated the lingering effects of the world recession, which hit African countries especially hard. For developing countries in general, the International Monetary Fund (IMF) reported in September, the ratio of foreign exchange reserves to exports had dropped to about 17 percent at the end of 1982; for African countries the ratio had fallen to 6 percent, marking the virtually total depletion of reserves. Even industrialized South Africa suffered a drop in its gross domestic product, which declined at an annual rate of 6.5 percent for the first half of 1983. More than a third of African countries were forced to negotiate new special financing arrangements from the IMF during the year.

Organization of African Unity. The 20-year-old Organization of African Unity (OAU) succeeded in holding its long-delayed 19th summit, which had twice collapsed in 1982 over the divisive issues of Western Sahara and Chad. The meeting was held June 8–12 in Addis Ababa, Ethiopia, where the organization's headquarters is located, rather than in Libya as originally planned. Host country leader Mengistu Haile Mariam accordingly became the organization's chairman for the following year instead of the controversial Libyan leader, Muammar al-Qaddafi.

The delegation representing the Polisario front, the guerrilla movement that seeks recognition of an independent Western Sahara, agreed to absent itself voluntarily from the meeting, making it possible for a quorum to be convened. Morocco, which claims the territory of Western Sahara as its own, had mobilized a walkout of countries opposed to the seating of Polisario, blocking the necessary quorum of 34 members for an August 1982 meeting. The June summit adopted a resolution calling for direct negotiations between Morocco and the Polisario.

Chad conflict. The perennial civil war in Chad, which had blocked a second attempt to convene an OAU summit in 1982, continued to elude a solution. Fighting between Libyan-backed rebels headed by Goukouni Oueddei and Western-backed forces of Hissène Habré, who had overthrown Goukouni's government of national unity in 1982, escalated during the summer, as large-scale military action extended the rebels' control in the north. On August 10, Goukouni's forces, heavily reinforced by Libyan armored and artillery units, seized the important town of Faya-Largeau. In response to developments in Chad, the United States ordered two Awacs surveillance planes, eight F-15 fighter craft, and ground support forces to bases in neighboring Sudan. Zaire sent troops to aid especially in keeping order in the Chadian capital. France ultimately dispatched more than 2,000 troops to take up positions along an east-west line across the country, in effect blocking further major advances. Peace talks under OAU auspices, originally set for December 21, were postponed until early 1984.

Strife in the South. In South Africa, in a November referendum, white voters approved a new constitutional package that gave minority representation to Coloured and Indian South Africans in a three-chamber parliament and provided greater powers for an executive presidency. However, those of African descent remained excluded from participations in accordance with the apartheid, or "separate development," doctrine that assigns them to rural "homelands" on 13 percent of South Africa's land area.

During the year, guerrilla attacks by the banned African National Congress (ANC) in South Africa escalated. A major bombing, outside air force headquarters in Pretoria, killed 19 people and wounded more than 200. In South West Africa (Namibia) also, the guerrilla war continued, while Western-backed negotiations bogged down over U.S. and South African demands that any settlement providing for an independent Namibia be linked to the withdrawal of Cuban troops from Angola.

In Angola, military action by South Africa and by the South African–backed guerrilla group Unita (the National Union for the Total Independence of Angola) reached the highest point since 1976. Across the continent, Mozambique, which South Africa accused of harboring ANC guerrillas, suffered two South African attacks and stepped-up harassment from the Mozambique National Resistance, a guerrilla movement said to be South African–sponsored.

In Swaziland, a traditionalist faction ousted Prime Minister Mabandla Dlamini, as well as Queen Regent Dzeliwe, and stepped up cooperation with South Africa's counterinsurgency efforts. In Zimbabwe, domestic political strife continued between the ruling party of Prime Minister Robert Mugabe and two key opponents, Joshua Nkomo and Bishop Abel Muzorewa.

Leaders of the nine-nation Southern African Development Coordination Conference (SADCC), meeting at their annual summit in July in Maputo, Mozambique, denounced South African military actions in the region, which summit chairman President Quett Masire of Botswana said had created a "life and death" situation for SADCC members.

Other regions. In the north of Africa, there were no major shifts in political lineups, although a March visit by Algeria's President Chadli Benjedid to neighboring Tunisia was seen by some as the beginning of a rapprochement between the two neighboring countries. Morocco under King Hassan II and Egypt under President Hosni Mubarak continued to develop closer military ties with the United States, citing the threat of Arab radicals such as Libya's Qaddafi. Sporadic strife continued between

Supporters of Chad's Libyan-backed rebel leader Goukouni Oueddei were captured in August during the fight for Faya-Largeau, a strategic northern oasis. Here, rebel prisoners are put on display in N'Djamena, capital of Chad.

A young boy drinks water from a puddle in Lebowa, a black homeland in South Africa. Drought conditions in at least 22 African countries led to serious food shortages.

Moroccan troops and Polisario guerrillas seeking control of Western Sahara.

In the Horn, the conflicts pitting guerrillas of the Ethiopian provinces of Eritrea and Tigré, as well as ethnic Somalians, against the central government in Addis Ababa continued unabated. In the Sudan, insurgency threatened to escalate in opposition to President Jaafar al-Nimeiry's dissolution of a semiautonomous regional government in the south.

In West Africa, Nigerian elections in August returned President Shehu Shagari's ruling National Party of Nigeria to power with an increased majority, but the civilian government was overthrown December 31, in the nation's fifth military coup since it won independence from Britain. At the beginning of the year, Nigeria expelled as many as 2 million citizens of other West African countries. The largest number were from Ghana; others were from Togo, Benin, Cameroon, Chad, Mali, and Upper Volta. In French-speaking Senegal, President Abdou Diouf was reelected by a landslide in a February general election. In Upper Volta, Prime Minister Thomas Sankara overthrew the conservative government of Jean-Baptiste Ouédraogo, in an overnight palace coup on August 4–5 that left 13 dead. Sankara described the new government as nonaligned.

The Economic Community of West African States (ECOWAS) laid out plans for the gradual establishment of free trade and free movement of people among them. The target date for Ghana, Ivory Coast, Nigeria, and Senegal was set at 1986, with other, more economically vulnerable countries allowed a longer period to implement these reforms.

In October, a parallel organization for ten central African states was officially created by a treaty signed in Libreville, Gabon. The Economic Community of Central African States (CEEAC) is composed of Cameroon, Central African Republic, Chad, the Congo, Gabon, Burundi, Rwanda, Zaire, Equatorial Guinea, and São Tomé and Príncipe.

To the east, the Kenyan election in September confirmed President Daniel arap Moi in office by a comfortable margin. In the Indian Ocean nation of Mauritius, Paul Berenger, head of the Mauritian Militant Movement, was defeated by his former ally, Prime Minister Aneerood Jugnauth.

See also separate articles on many of the individual countries mentioned. W.M.

AGRICULTURE. Drought, floods, and agricultural policies of some producing nations brought a decline of about 3 percent in world agricultural output in 1983. Harvests were lower in most regions, including the United States, Europe, and Australia, and Africa was hard hit by drought.

World output. Total world grain production in 1983 was estimated by the U.S. Department of Agriculture (USDA) at less than 1.6 billion tons, well below the harvest of close to 1.7 billion tons in 1982. (All ton figures are metric tons.) The world wheat crop of 480 million tons was about the same as in 1982, but the coarse grain harvest of 685 million tons was down substantially. Rough rice production of 420 million tons was up slightly. Soybeans, cottonseed, and flaxseed declined.

Combined output of red meat and poultry meat was 103.5 million tons, about the same as in 1982. Output of eggs, milk, and other dairy products was up.

World production of centrifugal sugar (raw value) was 99.7 million tons, down slightly from 1982, but the world coffee crop was estimated at 95.0 million bags (of 60 kilograms each), a sharp increase. The world cotton crop yielded 66.5 million bales (of 480 pounds each, net weight), down from 1982. Tobacco production was forecast at 6.06 million tons (farm sales weight), down sharply from the 1982 record crop.

United States. Production of major U.S. crops dropped sharply from 1982 levels, reflecting government programs to reduce output and the effects of extremely hot, dry weather in important growing areas. In September, the USDA's "all crop" production index was a shocking 88 (1977 = 100)—the lowest since 1976 and 31 points below the revised record index of 119 in 1982.

Unusually hot, dry weather from the Rocky Mountains eastward during the summer damaged corn and sorghum grain and reduced yields of oats, barley, peanuts, and cotton. The corn harvest was forecast at 112 million tons (4.39 billion bushels), almost a 50 percent drop from the record 1982 figures. The 1983 cotton crop was 7.78 million bales, the smallest harvest since 1895.

Food grain production (wheat, rye, and rice) was forecast at 70.9 million tons. Rice, at 4.71 million tons (104 million hundredweight), was down 33 percent. These declines were due almost entirely to government acreage-reduction programs; the wheat yield, for example, was a record 39.5 bushels per acre. Soybeans totaled 1.53 billion bushels. Planted acreage was down, influenced by the government's reduction program. Tobacco production, at 1.36 billion pounds, was the smallest crop since 1941.

Livestock, poultry, and dairy products. The July 1 inventory of U.S. cattle and calves was 123,540,000, a moderate decline from the 1982 total. Conditions were not favorable for expanded cattle operations. For hog producers, expanded herds brought a sharp drop in national average prices from $57.80 per hundredweight in July 1982 to $43.50 in July 1983. Broiler producers responded to a cost-

Longhorn cattle graze on a Texas ranch. This hardy breed has become popular once again, because of their longevity and adaptability and because increasingly health-conscious consumers have come to prefer their lean meat.

price squeeze in the first half of 1983 by reducing the number of eggs allotted for hatching and chicks for third-quarter slaughter.

Combating surpluses. U.S. farmers in recent years have produced more of some commodities than domestic and foreign markets can absorb. In 1983, the USDA took several steps to bring commodity output more into line with demand, including a strengthening of acreage-reduction programs for planted crops and assessments on dairy farmers to help defray storage costs and encourage lower production. In November, Congress cleared and President Ronald Reagan signed a bill that for the first time paid dairy farmers for cutting back on milk production, at $10 per 100 pounds diverted from production.

Exports slump. A fundamental U.S. farm problem in 1983 was the continued slump in agricultural exports. Shipments in the first nine months of fiscal 1983 totaled $26.6 billion, down substantially from the year before. Factors behind the export drop included the low level of Soviet imports and the great strength of the U.S. dollar, as well as economic recession and increased farm production abroad. On August 25, Agriculture Secretary John R. Block signed a new five-year grain trade pact with the Soviet Union that, among other things, raised the minimum annual Soviet purchases of U.S. grain to 9 million tons.

Canada and Latin America. The wheat crop in Canada was forecast at 27.0 million tons, up slightly, but hot, dry weather lowered coarse grain production to 21.4 million tons. In June, Canada's Parliament passed a bill to establish Canagrex, a government-owned agricultural export corporation aimed at increasing exports.

Argentina harvested a large wheat crop in 1982–1983, 14.5 million tons; the 1983–1984 crop was expected to decline to 11.0 million tons. Beef production also fell. Brazil's coffee crop was estimated at 31.50 million bags, compared with only 17.75 million in 1982–1983; coffee trees affected by the 1981 freeze had almost entirely recovered. Brazilian sugar production was also up, to 9.3 million tons.

Some countries suffered disastrous losses. Bolivia was hit by its worst drought in more than a century, which affected almost 40 percent of the country's territory and left about 1 million people in near-famine conditions. Peru lost an estimated 11 percent of crop and livestock production because of floods and drought.

Western Europe. The 1983 projected Western Europe grain harvest of 153.8 million tons was down about 6 percent from the 1982 crop, largely because of reduced barley production. The European Economic Community continued to push wheat exports, with authorizations up 20 percent from 1982. Production of beef and veal was up 3 percent, and output of pork rose 1 percent. Poultry meat production declined 2 percent, to 3.9 million tons.

Soviet Union and Eastern Europe. After several successive years of poor harvests, Soviet grain production in 1983 was expected to exceed 200 million tons, as compared with 174.4 million in 1982 and only 154.4 million in 1981. Corn and oats crops were estimated at near record levels. Wheat production, however, at a projected 85.0 million tons, was virtually unchanged from the 1982 harvest. The Soviet Union was expected to require continuing grain imports in the period ahead. In Eastern Europe, grain production dropped sharply, to an estimated 96.3 million tons, as drought took its toll.

Africa. The 1982–1983 drought that afflicted Africa was one of the worst in its history, as crops failed or were greatly reduced in a vast

Swine Jewelry

A single earring that costs $500 may be an extravagance for most people, but when the bauble is designed for the pierced ear of a male pig, it can be well worth the price tag. The earring in question is used to give each porcine wearer exclusive access to its own feed bin, which opens on command of an electromagnetic signal from the earring. Farmers can then monitor how much each pig eats, and the pigs that grow fattest on the least amount of feed can be picked for breeding. Developed by American Calan Inc., the earrings are available in 12 decorator colors, including lilac and pink, and are said to appeal to the pigs themselves. One problem is that pigs like to nibble each other's ears.

The rains stopped around July 4 in much of the Middle West, and scorching weather set in, devastating crops. Here, an Illinois farmer examines his field of drought-stricken corn.

belt of countries stretching from the Atlantic to the Indian Ocean. For many rural people, the hot, dry weather brought hardship and even starvation. Ethiopia was hit very hard; in late July, United Nations officials estimated that 50 to 100 children were dying there every day as a result of the drought. The U.S. Agency for International Development announced a $3 million allotment for immediate food aid to Ethiopia. Grants of $5 million and $6.7 million for humanitarian assistance were also made for fiscal 1984.

Asia and Australia. Grain production in 1983 in China was estimated at 313 million tons, a good crop. Output of wheat and coarse grains was up; that of rice was down. China's cotton crop was up to an all-time record of 17 million bales. Tobacco production continued to increase; in May, a Chinese cigarette company signed a preliminary joint venture agreement with R. J. Reynolds Tobacco International to produce cigarettes in China. Accounting for China's improved agricultural situation were good weather and the government's new "responsibility system," stressing material incentives for greater output.

India's grain production was 159.9 million tons, above crops of the preceding two years. The cotton crop was on a par with the 1981 and 1982 crops. Tea production was 568,000 tons. In Sri Lanka the tea crop was 175,000 tons, down from 1982. Thailand's rice crop was 17.7 million tons, up somewhat. Australia's drought-damaged 1982–1983 wheat crop of 8.8 million tons was about half the 16.4 million harvested in 1981–1982. However, cattle numbers in Australia were not seriously affected, declining only about 7 percent, to 22.0 million head.   H.W.H.

ALABAMA. *See* STATISTICS OF THE WORLD.

ALASKA. *See* STATISTICS OF THE WORLD.

ALBANIA. Albanian party chief Enver Hoxha remained in charge, but having turned 75 in October 1983 and being in poor health, he seemed unlikely to hold office for very long. Meanwhile, he strove to ensure that the country would continue along the course he had set by eliminating opponents, especially adherents of the late Prime Minister Mehmet Shehu. According to foreign observers, at least 30 ministers and undersecretaries have been killed or imprisoned since Shehu's mysterious death in December 1981, and trials of officials associated with Shehu continued.

President Ramiz Alia, who succeeded the purged Haxhi Lleshi in late 1982, made highly publicized tours around the country, during which he lauded Hoxha, urged the continued supremacy of the Workers' (Communist) Party, and echoed Hoxha's denunciations of neighboring Yugoslavia, with which Albania continued to have troubled relations.

In April, a national conference on the state of the economy was held in Tirana. Almost the entire politburo attended except for Hoxha, who was rarely seen in public during the year. President Alia contrasted what he called Albania's healthy economic situation with that of capitalist countries and Yugoslavia. Albania, he declared, had no foreign debt; whatever economic problems it might have he blamed on former Prime Minister Shehu.

In foreign relations, there were signs of a reconciliation with China. Albanian officials signed a trade and payments protocol in Peking on October 4, and Chinese advisers returned to Albania to oversee industrial projects abandoned by the Chinese government in the mid-1970's after Albania denounced the Chinese for alleged ideological deviations. There also were indications that Albania was seeking improved relations with Greece.

See STATISTICS OF THE WORLD.   R.A.P.

ALBERTA. See STATISTICS OF THE WORLD.

ALGERIA. In foreign affairs, Algeria in 1983 continued to seek solutions to regional issues and conflicts. Domestically, attention focused on preparations for an early 1984 convention of Algeria's ruling National Liberation Front (FLN) party.

In February, President Chadli Benjedid of Algeria and King Hassan of Morocco met in Akid Lotfi, a village near the Moroccan border, to seek a way out of the costly war between Morocco and the Algerian-backed Polisario guerrillas over Western Sahara, the former Spanish colony Morocco has annexed.

The diplomatic atmosphere created by the summit encounter was promising but uncertain. Algeria stressed that it had no direct quarrel with Morocco, declaring its "total readiness to work in behalf of a rapprochement between our brothers of Western Sahara and

our brothers of Morocco." The absence of any representative of Polisario at Akid Lotfi testified to the desire of the two states to engineer a settlement, but the Algerian position nonetheless implied some future negotiation directly between the Western Saharans and the Moroccans.

There were other signs as well of a search for regional reconciliation. In March, Benjedid went to Tunisia to sign a treaty of friendship and an agreement that definitely demarcated the border between the two countries; earlier in the year, a similar treaty was concluded with Niger. In early April, the border between Algeria and Morocco was reopened.

The political setting appeared stable as the FLN congress approached, with Benjedid exercising firm control over party, military, and bureaucracy. Benjedid nonetheless continued to sanction progressive policies that angered fundamentalist Muslim circles. The government approved a new birth control program to encourage the "spacing of births," and the Central Committee endorsed a liberal family code that strengthened women's rights in marriage and the workplace.

The decline in oil prices and in the share of the global oil market controlled by the Organization of Petroleum Exporting Countries, of which Algeria is a member, was a setback to the national economy, but the growth in natural gas sales took up the slack. As an encouragement to the agricultural sector, the government raised the price that it paid to wheat producers and allowed the price of such basic foodstuffs as bread, cooking oil, and eggs to rise.

See STATISTICS OF THE WORLD. See also MOROCCO.   R.A.M.

AMERICAN SAMOA. See STATISTICS OF THE WORLD.

ANGOLA. In 1983, Angola experienced the most significant escalation since 1976 of attacks by the South African–backed Angolan guerrilla movement, the National Union for the Total Independence of Angola (Unita). The Lomaum dam, which supplies electricity to Lobito and Benguela, was seriously damaged during January. In March, 66 Czechoslovak citizens, who had been working at an industrial complex at Alto Catumbela, were abducted by Unita guerrillas; later, 45 of them, including

17 women and 21 children, were released to the Red Cross. In late July, Unita forces attacked a passenger train, killing some 50 people. The key southeastern town of Cangamba was captured during August. In September, Unita released 21 Portuguese citizens after having held them captive for several months; 17 other Europeans were seized in November.

The Angolan government charged that the latest offensive was the result of a decision made by South Africa and the United States. Unita's leaders themselves have admitted receiving support from South Africa but have denied involvement of South African commandos and aircraft in actual operations. The U.S. government, for its part, was barred by the congressional Clark Amendment from giving military aid to Angolan dissident groups. The Reagan administration, however, made plain its sympathies for Unita and its opposition to the presence of Cuban troops in Angola. In January, China established diplomatic relations with Angola, leaving the United States as the only major country besides South Africa that had not done so.

Negotiations to settle the conflict in South West Africa (Namibia) continued, with a meeting in February between representatives of Angola and of South Africa, which controls Namibia. No progress was reported. In April, Angolan Interior Minister Manuel Rodrigues met with U.S. Vice-President George Bush; Angola and other African countries continued to reject the linkage proposed by South Africa and the United States between a Namibian settlement and the withdrawal of Cuban troops from Angola. In December, South Africa launched a major action into Angola against bases of guerrillas fighting for independence in Namibia.

At its February meeting, the Central Committee of the ruling Popular Movement for the Liberation of Angola adopted a "General Emergency Plan" for dealing with the worsening domestic situation. It stressed improved access to consumer goods for skilled workers and greater attention to the peasant farming sector. Also in February, the People's Assembly postponed elections until 1986.

Angola's principal source of income continued to be oil exports. By the end of 1983 the average output was expected to reach 190,000 barrels per day, earning some $2 billion in revenue for the year. Almost every other sector of the economy continued to suffer from shortages of trained personnel and from inadequate infrastructure and planning.

See STATISTICS OF THE WORLD.   W.M.

ANTHROPOLOGY. The validity of pioneering research by the late Margaret Mead, a possible connection between Sir Arthur Conan Doyle and the Piltdown hoax, and the significance of a 3.5-million-year-old humanlike fossil were among topics of lively debate in 1983.

Mead under attack. The publication in early 1983 of anthropologist Derek Freeman's new study, *Margaret Mead and Samoa: The Making and Unmaking of an Anthropological Myth,* caused a mild storm in anthropology. Freeman, a professor emeritus of anthropology at Australian National University in Canberra, charged that Mead, one of the world's best-known anthropologists, had radically misrepresented Samoan culture in her best-selling, widely influential 1928 book, *Coming of Age in Samoa.* He contested Mead's conclusions—that Samoans were "one of the most amiable, least contentious, and most peaceful people in the world" and that premarital sex among them was free and easy—arguing that she had been misled by her teenaged informants in the field and misguided by the cultural determinism of her mentor, Franz Boas, a major figure in early 20th-century anthropology. According to Freeman, Samoans actually were a violent people who had strict rules on sexual behavior.

A common view among anthropologists was that Freeman and Mead were both guilty of oversimplifying Samoan culture. In any event, many anthropologists doubted that Freeman's study would do long-term harm to Mead's scholarly reputation, which was based on much more than her Samoan research. Ward Goodenough of the University of Pennsylvania said that the book did not create a revolution in anthropology; the real crisis it engendered was in "the public's image of a public idol."

Piltdown hoax revisited. After seven years of investigative work, American scientist John Hathaway Winslow, in an article in the September 1983 issue of *Science 83* Magazine, named Sir Arthur Conan Doyle—the creator of

The theories of the influential anthropologist Margaret Mead came under fire in a controversial study published in early 1983.

master detective Sherlock Holmes—as prime suspect in the infamous Piltdown Man hoax.

For four decades, many anthropologists and paleontologists had believed that a fossilized skull and jawbone "discovered" in the English village of Piltdown and unveiled to scientists in 1912 constituted the "missing link" in human evolution. Although the skull was clearly human, the associated jawbone was very ape-like. Their combination suggested the existence of a human predecessor even older than fossils previously found in France, Germany, and Java. Lacking modern means of dating, early 20th-century scientists seeking to estimate a fossil's age had to rely on more subjective clues, based on geological and anatomical interpretations. The geological site where the Piltdown fossils were reportedly found placed them in the early Ice Age—about 1 million years ago. Key pieces of the skull and jawbone were missing, making it impossible for anatomists to discern how the jaw and skull were joined or to prove whether they did, in fact, belong together. Nevertheless, Piltdown Man came to occupy a prominent place in the British Museum and in human history.

In 1953, when the Piltdown fossils were finally scrutinized with modern chemical and X-ray techniques, it became obvious that the skull dated back only 500 to 600 years, that the jawbone came from a modern female orangutan, and that the bones and teeth had been deliberately stained or altered so as to appear ancient. Several people have since been suspected of perpetrating the fraud, but Winslow thinks the evidence points to Doyle.

At the time of the Piltdown discoveries, Doyle resided near the fossil site, which he had visited. A retired physician, he knew anatomy and dabbled in geology and archaeology. He was an avid collector of fossils, and he had a taste for hoaxes, adventures, and complex fictional plots. Most importantly, Doyle had a motive: he nourished a grudge against the British scientific establishment, for he firmly believed in spiritualism and strongly resented scientists' out-of-hand rejection of his views. Winslow argued that Doyle masterminded the intricate hoax in order to gain revenge and that he left clues to the prank in his novel The Lost World, which he wrote and published before the Piltdown discoveries were made public.

Controversy over Lucy. During a 1983 meeting at the Institute of Human Origins in Berkeley, Calif., scientists advanced two opposing interpretations of the significance of Lucy, a 3'6" hominid (humanlike) fossil discovered in 1974. Lucy, who had a humanlike posture and a chimplike head, inhabited the Afar region of present-day Ethiopia about 3.5 million years ago.

Donald C. Johanson, the institute's director and principal discoverer of the fossil remains, reiterated his contention that Lucy was a fully upright biped who lived on the ground. His interpretation supports the theory that humanity's ancestors achieved upright stature and mobility on two legs long before they developed human-sized brains. Anatomists Randall Susman and Jack Stern of the State University of New York disagreed. In their view, Lucy's apelike anatomy suggests that humanity's early ancestors, some 3 to 4 million years ago, still lived in trees. Johanson and his supporters sought to counter this position by arguing that Lucy's apelike traits are only "evolutionary excess baggage."

Susman and Stern agreed with Johanson that Lucy was a member of an evolutionary line leading to early humans. Her descendants, they believe, eventually evolved into *Homo erectus*, who, 1.5 million years ago, was definitely a ground-dweller, with a larger brain and body and with tool-making ability. A still different interpretation of Lucy's place in history has been offered by two well-known paleoanthropologists, Mary Leakey and her son, Richard. They maintain that Lucy's line did not lead to *Homo erectus*, but met a dead end, fading away with the Australopithecines, about 1 million years ago.   P.J.M.

ANTIGUA AND BARBUDA. *See* Statistics of the World.

ARAB LEAGUE. In 1983 Arab differences over such issues as the conflict with Israel, civil strife in Lebanon, and the Iran-Iraq war prevented the Arab League from even meeting on any of these issues.

At the center of the league's diplomatic efforts in 1983 was a peace plan adopted at a league summit meeting held in Fez, Morocco, in September 1982. That plan had called for the withdrawal of Israel from all territory captured during the Six-Day War of 1967, the abandonment of Israeli settlements in occupied territory, UN guarantees of peace for "all states" in the Middle East, and the creation of a Palestinian state with East Jerusalem as its capital. A major dispute arose when an Arab League delegation sent to explain the Fez plan was not received by the British government because it included a member of the Palestine Liberation Organization (PLO). The Arab states retaliated in January by informing the British foreign secretary that his planned visit to Saudi Arabia, Qatar, and the United Arab Emirates would be unwelcome, and Saudi Arabia initiated an embargo on British goods. A compromise was reached in which a Palestinian professor and another member of the Palestine National Council (PNC) would participate in the delegation, neither being a member of the PLO "as such." The delegation subsequently received a full ceremonial welcome in London.

The Fez peace plan was endorsed at the 16th session of the PNC held in Algiers during February, despite opposition from radical factions of the PLO. The UN Conference on Palestinian Rights, held in Geneva during September, also approved it. Five radical Palestinian factions denounced the plan at a conference in Tripoli sponsored by Libya during January. The plan also widened the rift between radicals and moderates in the PLO, and it was one cause of the fierce fighting between the diverse PLO factions that erupted in Lebanon during 1983.   D.P.

ARCHAEOLOGY. Nautical archaeologists in 1983 recovered the anchor of the Civil War ironclad *Monitor* and discovered ships of Napoleon Bonaparte's fleet off the Egyptian coast. Also receiving attention were the excavations at the Roman city of Bath and well preserved cave art discovered in eastern Tennessee.

Long-lost ironclad. Ever since the wreck site of the U.S.S. *Monitor* was discovered in 1974, archaeologists and historians have been intent on salvaging the long-lost ironclad, which went down in a storm 16 miles off Cape Hatteras, N.C., on December 31, 1862, coming to rest at a depth of about 220 feet. The ship, which gave its name to the monitor class of warship, took part in the first battle between ironclad vessels when it engaged the Confederate ship

This figure of a bird, possibly a great horned owl, is one of the well-preserved drawings discovered on the walls of a cave in east Tennessee. They were probably made by Mississippian Period Indians, between the 12th and the 16th centuries.

Virginia (formerly the *Merrimack*) in Virginia's Hampton Roads harbor on March 9, 1862. The battle ushered in the age of the battleship and spelled the end of the wooden man-of-war.

In August, archaeologists used inflated fabric bags to raise the first piece of the *Monitor*: its distinctive four-fluked anchor, weighing about 1,200 pounds, along with 6 feet of anchor chain. The finds were declared to be in good condition. By comparing the anchor with the drawings made by the *Monitor*'s designer, John Ericsson, researchers hoped to learn more about the ship. Videotapes made of the *Monitor* were examined with a view to organizing a future expedition to raise the vessel's cylindrical gun turret.

Napoleonic fleet. In July, French and Egyptian researchers announced that they had found two ships belonging to the 13-vessel fleet that transported Napoleon and his troops to Egypt and was sunk in the Battle of the Nile in 1798. One was believed to be either *L'Orient,* flagship of the fleet, or *Le Guerrier,* its second largest ship. The vessels sit beneath Egypt's Abukir Bay, where the fleet, commanded by Admiral François Brueys, was destroyed on August 1, 1798, by a British fleet commanded by Horatio Nelson. The British victory played a major part in Napoleon's ultimate defeat.

Archaeologists located the sites by using a minesweeper equipped with electronic sensing devices and sonar, a sophisticated approach that also enabled them to roughly locate any metal aboard the ships before sending down the divers, who had to contend with extremely poor visibility. Jacques Dumas, the leader of the expedition, and his team of divers proceeded to salvage a variety of artifacts, including 5-foot metal nails, pottery, a rifle, cannon fragments, and, from the floor of the bay, an object identified as the remains of a Roman pottery urn. Plans for the future include an expedition to lift up major parts of the warships.

Bath excavations. Visitors to the ancient Roman city of Bath, England, were able to witness the excavation of one of its most important monuments. Dig members concentrated their efforts on the remains of the Temple of Sulis Minerva, the goddess who presided over the hot springs for which the city is named.

The exact location and details of the temple were not known until 1983, even though some dramatic discoveries had come to light beginning in the 18th century. For instance, a gilded bronze head of Minerva, belonging to a life-size statute, was found by workmen in 1727. Today, much of the temple's inner precinct and many of its monuments are visible deep beneath modern Bath. The temple precinct covers an area of some 4,000 square yards and lies beneath other archaeological relics, including a medieval cemetery and the famous 18th-century Pump Room. The temple area includes a reservoir spring, which was eventually placed inside a vaulted hall used as a place of worship. Thrown into the spring were countless offerings to Minerva—coins, pewter "curses" (thin sheets of copper with inscribed messages), vessels, and trinkets.

Parts of the temple itself are now on view to the public. The first phase of its construction consisted of a small building with Corinthian columns and a sculpture depicting a Gorgon's head. Later a new facade was added, and further additions were made when the reservoir spring was enclosed and roofed.

Tennessee cave art. Archaeologists have uncovered some unusually well preserved drawings etched on the mud-coated walls of a cave in eastern Tennessee. The etchings, called glyphs, which include anthropomorphic stick figures, depictions of woodpeckers and turtles, and symbolic motifs, were probably created by Indians of the Dallas culture, in the Mississippian Period (12th–16th centuries). The closest parallel to this type of cave art is the Ice Age art of France and Spain, where modeled clay and mud figures of animals survived for thousands of years alongside the famous cave paintings of bison and other wildlife. The Tennessee discovery, dubbed the Mud Glyph Cave, is unique to North America and provides archaeologists with a remarkably undisturbed view of prehistoric art on the continent.

Charles Faulkner, professor of anthropology at the University of Tennessee, directed the team that researched this find, whose exact location was not disclosed in order to protect it. The investigations indicate that the Indians who fashioned the glyphs probably used the cave only for ritual or artistic purposes, since there were no artifacts suggesting that it was used for mining or shelter. The only other items found were charcoal bits from torches, which were radiocarbon-dated to reveal the date of the art and ultimately the identity of the artists.

B.R.

ARCHITECTURE. Art museums dominated new American architecture in 1983, although Philip Johnson and I. M. Pei drew attention for their innovations in skyscraper and hotel design in the United States and abroad. Controversy continued to surround two recently completed American works, for opposite reasons: one because of its restraint, the other because of its boldness. Meanwhile, two famous older buildings were the focus of disputes between pragmatic and preservationist interests, with the latter winning out in both cases.

New buildings. Several of the new art museums were designed by leading architects, including one in Portland, Me., by Harry Cobb, chairman of the architecture department at Harvard Uni-

The new Portland (Me.) Museum of Art, designed by Harry Cobb and called the most intriguing recent work of architecture in New England, features a giant brick facade with a strongly decorative pattern of arches, squares, and circles on an otherwise featureless wall.

The Fragrant Hill Hotel near Peking, designed by I. M. Pei & Partners, is an unusual blend of traditional Chinese and contemporary Western styles of architecture. The Chinese-born Pei has expressed the hope that the hotel will stimulate China's architects to create a modern idiom for their work.

versity's Graduate School of Design and a member of I. M. Pei & Partners; one in Atlanta by Richard Meier; and one in a new cultural center in Dallas by Edward Larrabee Barnes. Meanwhile, Cesar Pelli's addition to the Museum of Modern Art in New York, which included a tall apartment tower, was being completed. The Whitney Museum of American Art in New York was also scheduled to get an addition with a tower, to be designed by Michael Graves.

The building at 333 Wacker Drive in Chicago, designed by the firm of Kohn Pedersen Fox Associates, was praised for its imaginative use of a difficult site. The tower of bluish-green glass on a granite, stainless-steel, and marble base forms a gentle arc that reflects the curves of the Chicago River beneath it.

The most prolific architectural firm of the year was John Burgee, Architect, with Philip Johnson, Consultant (formerly Johnson/Burgee). In major cities from coast to coast, skylines were being altered by the firm in

inventive ways. Johnson and Burgee's headquarters for the American Telephone and Telegraph Company was nearing completion in Manhattan; Johnson has claimed that the building, with its distinctive crest reminiscent of Chippendale furniture, signaled the demise of pure modernism. In Houston the firm designed the vaguely Renaissance-style RepublicBank Center; in Pittsburgh, the somewhat Gothic Pittsburgh Plate Glass Industries headquarters; and in San Francisco, 580 California Street, a shimmering cylinder of glass set in a concrete bunker.

The most didactic building of the year was the Fragrant Hill Hotel near Peking, China, by I. M. Pei & Partners. Pei, a Chinese-American, very deliberately set about designing the hotel in a way that might generate a new Chinese architectural vernacular. He rejected a tower as unsuitable and instead made the hotel a horizontal building, organized around a series of pools and courts in the traditional Chinese manner. He also drew upon the Chinese ornamental tradition, although in form the building is characteristically simple and modern. Overall, he successfully sought "Chineseness" without lapsing into quaintness or cliché, and he offered the design to the architects of China as a model to "accept and adapt."

Vietnam Veterans Memorial. In February, the U.S. Fine Arts Commission, which reviews the architectural design of federal buildings in Washington, D.C., gave final approval to a plan to place a flagpole and statute near the entrance to the Vietnam Veterans Memorial on the Mall in Washington. The memorial has generated controversy ever since its design, by Yale University architecture student Maya Lin, was first chosen in a 1981 competition. It consists of two dark granite walls recessed below ground level, on which the names of Americans killed in the Vietnam war are inscribed. Lin's stark design received nearly unanimous praise from professional architects, and it was also supported by major veterans' organizations. A dissident group of veterans and a number of conservative political figures, however, criticized the design for being too somber and devoid of patriotic symbolism, calling it, among other things, "a political statement of shame and dishonor."

These critics eventually persuaded the memorial's sponsor, the Vietnam Veterans Memorial Fund, to add, at the intersection of the walls, a large flagpole and a heroic statue of soldiers—additions opposed by Lin and various art and architecture organizations. Finally, after the Fine Arts Commission directed that the statue and flagpole be clustered near the entrance to the memorial, away from the walls themselves, the flagpole was installed on July 3, and sculptor Frederick Hart began work on the statue, a larger-than-life trio of young servicemen.

Portland Building. Another center of controversy was the Portland Building, a municipal office building in Portland, Ore., designed by Michael Graves, that is one of the most publicized examples of the postmodernist movement. This design called for a simple, somewhat squat box, punctured with small, widely spaced square windows but boldly decorated with bright colors, masonry garlands, and other ornamentation. The controversy reached a cli-

A tower of bluish-green glass atop a base of granite, stainless steel, and marble, this building by Kohn Pedersen Fox Associates at 333 Wacker Drive was highly praised for its creative use of its Chicago River site.

max in May, when the building won one of the 1983 American Institute of Architects honor awards. One honor awards juror called the building "ordinary" except for its "idiosyncratic exterior decor." Charles Gwathmey, the chairman of the jury, defended the award but conceded that the "meanings and interpretations of the building are more powerful than the reality."

Lever House. One of the acknowledged masterpieces of the long-dominant modernist style, the Lever House in Manhattan, was also a subject of dispute in 1983. Built in 1952, the metal-and-glass building by Skidmore, Owings & Merrill was designated a historic landmark by the New York City Landmarks Preservation

Commission just as it reached the minimum 30-year age required for such designation. The landmark designation was then challenged before the city's Board of Estimate, whose approval is required, by a real-estate developer who hoped to replace the Lever House with a bold, decoratively fluted 40-story glass tower. The architect for the new tower testified before the board that the Lever House was in disrepair and architecturally unworthy of landmark status. Other architects, however, testified to the historical importance of the building, and the board approved the designation in March.

U.S. Capitol. One of architecture's oldest controversies was resolved in 1983, when both the House and the Senate voted to preserve and restore the crumbling west front of the U.S. Capitol, the last remaining original wall of the building still exposed. For 20 years, a debate had raged between those who wanted to restore the wall and those who wanted to replace it in the process of expanding the Capitol.

Awards. Pei was the winner of the 1983 Pritzker prize, at $100,000 the most lucrative of architectural awards. The prize was given for the body of his work rather than a single building. Pei is a master craftsman among architects, and the Pritzker jury noted that he has "elevated the use of material to an art." Perhaps his best-known work is the East Building of the National Gallery of Art in Washington.

American architecture's premier individual honor, the gold medal of the AIA, was awarded in 1983 to Nathaniel Alexander Owings, a founding partner of Skidmore, Owings & Merrill, perhaps the best large firm in the world in terms of consistent design quality. The award also honored Owings' work as chairman of the Pennsylvania Avenue Development Corporation in Washington and his environmental activism, especially in the Big Sur area of California, where he now lives.

The increasingly prestigious AIA Firm Award went in 1983 to Holabird & Root of Chicago, which in 1982 had celebrated its 100th year of continuous practice. The firm achieved early renown as part of the pioneering Chicago School of architecture and had a second flowering in the Art Deco movement of the 1920's

and 1930's. After World War II, it employed a conventional and somewhat tired modernist style. In recent years, however, the firm has tried new approaches with considerable confidence and success.

In addition to Graves's Portland Building, winners of the 1983 AIA honor awards were the Best Products Company headquarters in Richmond, Va., by Hardy/Hardy/Holzman/Pfeiffer; the Masterson branch of the YWCA in Houston, by Taft Architects; the Mecklenburg County Courthouse in Charlotte, N.C., by Wolf Associates Architects; the Coxe/Hayden house and studio on Block Island, R.I., by Venturi, Rauch & Scott Brown; the Hartford (Conn.) Seminary, by Richard Meier and Partners; Immanuel Presbyterian Church in McLean, Va., by Hartman/Cox Architects; the restoration of the California State Capitol in Sacramento, by Welton/Becket and Associates; the Douglas County administration building in Castle Rock, Colo., by Hoover/Berg/Desmond; the Suntech Townhomes in Santa Monica, Calif., by Urban Forms; and the Haj Terminal at the King Abdul Aziz International Airport in Jidda, Saudi Arabia, by Skidmore, Owings & Merrill.

The AIA gave its Twenty-five Year Award for distinguished and enduring architectural design to Frank Lloyd Wright's engagingly exotic Price Tower in Bartlesville, Okla. The $25,000 R. S. Reynolds Memorial Award for 1983 went to Architektengruppe U-Bahn of Vienna for their work on that city's subway system. The project included the restoration of the Green Line stations designed by the eminent early modernist Otto Wagner and the design of stations for a new Red Line. D.J.C.

ARGENTINA. Seven years of military rule came to an end on December 10, when Raúl Alfonsín, elected two months before in a surprise upset, took office as president of Argentina. The new civilian government inherited persistent economic problems, including severe inflation and a crushing foreign debt.

Presidential campaign. The presidential campaign dominated the period leading up to the elections on October 30. The country's reactivated political parties flourished as 5.6 million people registered for party membership, the highest number ever recorded. Of these, more than 3 million registered as members of the

Argentina's New Civilian President
At his inauguration on December 10 as Argentina's first democratically elected president since the military takeover in 1976, Raúl Ricardo Alfonsín, 57, assured the nation that "we are going to be a decent government." Three days later, Alfonsín, long an outspoken advocate of human rights, issued a decree to prosecute former members of the military junta responsible for the torture and disappearance of more than 6,000 Argentines between 1976 and 1982. It was one of a series of bold steps which he took shortly after assuming office. A member of the Radical Civic Union, Alfonsín had formed an insurgent faction in 1972 and unsuccessfully challenged the party's leadership. Eleven years later, he captured the party's nomination for president and won the presidency, upsetting the Peronist front-runner.

Raúl Ricardo Alfonsín

Peronist Party, which remained the largest political grouping; about 1.5 million were affiliated with the moderately left-of-center, traditionally middle-class Radical Civic Union.

Within the Peronist Party, there was considerable factional feuding, but at a party convention in early September the Peronists were able to unite behind the candidacy of Italo Luder, who was regarded as front-runner in the presidential race. A former leader of the Senate (upper house of parliament), Luder had served as provisional president for one month in 1975 during the illness of President Isabel Martínez de Perón, widow of Juan Perón. In contrast to the charismatic tradition of Peronism, Luder in his campaign speeches projected an image of moderate pragmatism. He called for a nonaligned foreign policy and greater governmental control of the economy. (At the same convention, Isabel Perón, in exile in Spain, was named titular head of the party. She was also pardoned by Argentina's president, retired Major General Reynaldo Bignone, for her conviction on charges of having embezzled charity funds while in office. In early December, she returned to Argentina.)

The other main presidential contender, Raúl Alfonsín, was nominated in August as the presidential candidate of the Radicals. He described himself as a left-of-center social democrat. In his campaign speeches, he attacked the military and called for ending Argentina's draft and cutting back arms purchases to provide more money for education, health, and development.

Election of a new government. In a stunning upset, Alfonsín took 52 percent of the vote to win the presidency in the October election. The Radicals also won a small majority in the Chamber of Deputies (lower house of parliament), taking 131 of the 254 seats; 111 seats went to the Peronists. Alfonsín named an eight-member cabinet, which included close personal confidants in key posts.

Almost immediately after his inauguration, Alfonsín moved to fulfill key campaign pledges. Among other steps, he announced on December 13 that the government would prosecute former junta members, including three ex-presidents, responsible for the disappearance of more than 6,000 Argentines between 1976 and 1982, as well as seven leftist terrorist leaders. Three days later, he asked Congress to repeal an amnesty law promulgated by the junta in September, and he set up a commission of inquiry into the disappearances, in the meantime retiring about half of the army generals and two-thirds of the navy admirals in his efforts to bring the armed forces under strict civilian control. Alfonsín had excluded Big-

Protests erupted in Buenos Aires after President Reynaldo Bignone went on national television on April 28 to deliver what many considered an inadequate report on the "disappeared"—the more than 6,000 persons missing since government antiterrorist campaigns in the 1970's. Here, a young man kicks a policeman who had driven through a group of demonstrators.

none from those to be prosecuted, but a court subsequently indicted the former president for the 1976 disappearance of two Communist army draftees under his command. On December 17 the new government also introduced legislation to curb Argentina's powerful unions, most of them traditionally Peronist, by requiring periodic elections of union leaders and limiting the number of their terms. The Peronists vowed to oppose the legislation.

Two days before Alfonsín's inauguration, the United States announced that, in view of improvements in human rights and the imminent return of democratic rule to Argentina, it would remove its ban on arms sales to that country. No actual sales, however, were planned.

The Bignone government. Shortly before the restoration of civilian rule, the military decided to court-martial former President Leopoldo Galtieri and two associates for their conduct of the 1982 Falkland Islands war with Great Britain. Earlier, dealing with another issue embarrassing to the military, the junta issued an official statement on the "disappeared," the more than 6,000 Argentines believed to have been abducted and killed by security forces. The statement admitted that "mistakes were

made . . . as in all wars" but said no further details would be released. The report generated protests.

Economy. The country's foreign debt remained a serious impediment to economic development. Total indebtedness rose to almost $40 billion in 1983; the major components of repayment had to be rescheduled through the International Monetary Fund in January. In return, the Bignone government agreed to certain unpopular austerity measures; these included capping the monetary supply increase at 160 percent, holding the public sector deficit down, and raising charges for public services by 2.5 percent. In September the junta narrowly escaped default on the foreign debt when it won an extension from an international group of banks to meet some of Argentina's overdue payments. On coming to office, Alfonsín promised to pay his country's debt, the developing world's third largest, but sought more generous terms, such as lower interest rates and longer payback times. On December 15 his government requested a six-month delay, to June 30, 1984, in repaying nearly $9 billion in debt due and some $3.5 billion in interest either already accrued or expected to accrue by then. The new civilian government, as part of its efforts to come to grips with Argentina's economic problems, also ordered a 40-day price freeze and limited wage hikes, while planning drastic cuts in public spending for 1984.

Consumers and workers suffered under the cumulative effects of Argentina's runaway inflation, which by late 1983 had risen to an annual rate of more than 600 percent. A national strike protesting economic conditions had paralyzed the country on October 4.

Nuclear capacity. The National Atomic Energy Commission announced in mid-November that Argentina had achieved the capacity to make enriched uranium and thus fuel nuclear explosives. The Commission president, Rear Admiral Carlos Madero, said at that time that Argentina would use its nuclear capacity for peaceful ends but would not submit to international inspection of its nuclear facilities.

See STATISTICS OF THE WORLD.   J.F.

ARIZONA. See STATISTICS OF THE WORLD.

ARKANSAS. See STATISTICS OF THE WORLD.

ART. Several major exhibitions, highlighted by a superb showing of works by Edouard Manet mounted in Paris and New York, made 1983 a memorable year in art. Other noteworthy events included the unveiling of new works by Christo and George Segal, several high-level appointments in the museum world, and record prices paid for a number of works.

Christo and Segal. In 1983 the world of art showed a healthy diversity. Two individual works that attracted considerable attention in the United States, for example, could hardly have been more different. In May, the artist Christo encircled 11 islands in Florida's Biscayne Bay with pink plastic sheets. *Surrounded Islands,* as Christo called the work, received wide international press coverage and induced reactions that ranged from adulation to utter skepticism. In sharp contrast was George Segal's discrete, almost classical sculpture *The Holocaust.* Shown in the spring in a plaster version at the Jewish Museum in New York City, it was scheduled to be cast in bronze and

Day-glo pink plastic rings an island in Florida's Biscayne Bay near Miami—part of environmental artist Christo's $3.1 million creation titled Surrounded Islands.

A mammoth exhibition organized by the Louvre and New York City's Metropolitan Museum of Art presented to the public the great achievement of Edouard Manet, the 19th-century French artist. One of the nearly 200 works on view in New York was The Bar at the Folies-Bergère (1881–1882).

moved to its permanent home in San Francisco early in 1984. *The Holocaust,* composed of a group of figures representing inmates of the Nazi death camps—only one of whom is standing erect—has more in common with the centuries-old tradition of monumental sculpture than it does with the work of Christo.

Appointments. Several important curatorial and directorial appointments were made in 1983. One of the most significant was the appointment in May of John Walsh, Jr., as director of the J. Paul Getty Museum in Malibu, Calif., where he will preside over a huge $1.5 billion endowment. Walsh, a former curator at the Metropolitan Museum of Art in New York and the curator of paintings at Boston's Museum of Fine Arts since 1977, is a specialist in Dutch art of the 17th and 18th centuries and is widely respected as a solid scholar and administrator.

Another well-received appointment was that of Professor Sidney Freedberg as chief curator of paintings at the National Gallery of Art in Washington, D.C. At the as yet unopened Los Angeles Museum of Modern Art, Pontus Hulten resigned his directorship to head the projected Expo '89 in Paris (which shortly thereafter was canceled); he was succeeded by deputy director Richard Koshalek.

Multiartist exhibitions. Two large and much-touted major exhibitions opened with mixed results in London and New York. "The Essential Cubism," organized for London's Tate Gallery by Douglas Cooper and Gary Tinterow, was predictably beautiful but, in the view of many observers, contributed little to the understanding of that most important 20th-century artistic revolution. Presenting a narrow, traditional view of Cubism, the show focused on Pablo

Picasso and Georges Braque, with a nod to their colleagues Juan Gris and Fernand Léger. Although they did include some Cubist sculptures by Henri Laurens and a few works by lesser known artists, the organizers did not try to integrate these works into public understanding of the movement. More successful in concept was the Metropolitan Museum's blockbuster "Treasures From the Vatican," which contained some stunning works and presented a very interesting study of the history of aesthetic taste and art collecting (see the feature article Treasures From the Vatican).

Two other exhibitions were both successful, although totally different in intent, scope, and public. Baron Hans Heinrich Thyssen-Bornemisza, the famed collector of works by old masters, successfully negotiated a rare exchange show with the Soviet Union. In exchange for 40 of the most magnificent old master paintings from his collection, which were to be displayed in Moscow and Leningrad, the Soviet Government loaned 40 of its little-exhibited modern works from the Pushkin and Hermitage museums. Thus, from June through October a superb collection of rarely seen works by, among others, Matisse, Gauguin, Cézanne, Monet, Renoir, and Picasso was accessible to Western art lovers in the baron's villa near Lugano, Switzerland. Much larger in

scale and intent was a major collection of American paintings borrowed from many sources by Theodore Stebbins, Jr., for the Museum of Fine Arts in Boston. After stops at the MFA and the Corcoran Gallery in Washington, D.C., the exhibition was scheduled to travel to Paris.

One-man shows. The largest retrospective ever held of the works of Alexander Calder, one of the most beloved of American sculptors, was assembled in 1983 at the Palazzo a Vela in Turin, Italy. Comprising more than 400 works, borrowed from the Calder family as well as from various institutions, the show was elegantly installed by architect Renzo Piano. The Turin exhibition not only contained excellent examples of Calder's mobiles and stabiles, but also included earlier constructions and paper works that clearly showed the younger Calder's debt to the European Surrealist movement.

Equally fascinating, but a good deal smaller, was the retrospective of works by the Spanish-born sculptor Julio Gonzalez that was organized by Margit Rowell for the Guggenheim Museum. Gonzalez was the first sculptor to work directly with raw metal, using technological advances in welding to create increasingly abstract works. The Guggenheim exhibition, which went on display in March, contained 91 major pieces, plus drawings and

Abstract expressionist Willem de Kooning's Two Women *was sold for a record $1.2 million at Christie's in New York; it was the most money ever paid for the work of a living artist.*

early works that ranged from paintings to jewelry and decorative metalwork.

Manet centennial. The most spectacular and simultaneously satisfying exhibition of 1983 was a splendid Manet retrospective, organized jointly by the Louvre and the Metropolitan Museum of Art and shown successively at the Grand Palais and the Metropolitan Museum. The New York show, comprising 95 paintings and 95 drawings and other works, differed from its French counterpart only in the omission of a few major works (principally *Olympia* and *Déjeuner sur l'herbe*) that could not be moved from France. Metropolitan curator Charles Moffett and French curators Françoise Cachin and Michael Melot presented in the exhibition catalogue one of the clearest explanations of both the development of a brilliant transitional artist and the rise of Impressionism.

An exhibition largely devoted to the same artist—and also mounted in honor of the 100th anniversary of his death—was organized earlier in the year by Professor Theodore Reff of Columbia University for the National Gallery. Titled "Manet and Modern Paris," the Washington show also included some 100 works by Manet, as well as a sprinkling of paintings by such other Parisian artists as Jean-Louis Forain and Theodore Steinlen.

The market. As the world economy appeared to be coming out of its doldrums, so did the art market, although top dollar was paid mainly for top works. Among the big sales, Willem de Kooning's *Two Women* went for $1.2 million at auction, the highest amount paid for a work by a living artist. The Amon Carter Museum in Fort Worth, Texas, paid $1.5 million for a fine painting by William Merritt Chase—a record price for that artist's work. Mark Rothko's abstract *Black, Maroons and White* was sold for $1,815,000. Egon Schiele's excellent *Portrait of the Painter Zakovsek* went for $2.4 million, the record for any German Expressionist work. Finally, in early December, a beautifully illustrated medieval gospel manuscript, said to be the finest treasure of its kind ever put up for auction, was sold to a West German consortium for $11.7 million, by far the most ever paid for any book or work of art.

In other market news, an American takeover bid for the major London auction house of Sotheby Parke Bernet resulted in a debate in Parliament and a ruling by the Office of Fair Trading that the famed firm was a "national treasure." However, in September the British government approved the sale of Sotheby's to Alfred Taubman, a wealthy American businessman and art patron.

Contemporary art. The Whitney Museum's Biennial Exhibition, held during the spring of 1983, was as usual very mixed in style, but as in the commercial galleries throughout the year, Expressionism seemed predominant. Most artists were first-time exhibitors in a Whitney Biennial, but the show did include such stellar veterans as Louise Bourgeois, Jasper Johns, Joan Mitchell, and Frank Stella. The major innovation of the show, reflecting a change within the art world itself, was the size and diversity of the section devoted to film and video works.   E.S.R.

ASTRONOMY. In 1983, research was proceeding toward the possible discovery of intelligent life on other worlds. In addition, a meteorite was identified as having come from the moon, a new comet was sighted and analyzed, and astronomers found evidence of a solar system beyond our own.

Life on other worlds. The Search for Extraterrestrial Intelligence, or SETI, once again has the approval of the U.S. government. In 1981, Senator William Proxmire had won passage of a bill barring the National Aeronautics and Space Administration from spending money on such a program, which can involve the use of radio telescopes to hunt for radio wave patterns that might be evidence of intelligent life on other worlds. But a pro-SETI campaign conducted by many scientists eventually persuaded him to drop his opposition to such research, and NASA's budget allowed up to $1.5 million for the program during fiscal 1984.

In March a private SETI project began its own search, using a small radio telescope at Harvard, Mass. The effort was being funded by the Planetary Society, an organization founded by Cornell University astronomer and SETI proponent Carl Sagan.

Planets and their allies. Much has been learned recently about the solid bodies of the solar system. Among the smallest of these are the meteorites—meteors that pass through the earth's atmosphere and land on its surface. In 1983 a 1-ounce fragment discovered in Antarctica was identified from its chemical composition as having come from the moon. Thus, for the first time, a meteorite's place of origin was identified. This discovery also revealed that pieces can be knocked off bodies in the solar system and transported to earth.

The outermost planets of the solar system have also yielded important secrets. Three teams of scientists independently reported evidence that auroras occur in Uranus' hydrogen-rich atmosphere. These analogues to the earth's northern lights indicate that Uranus has a magnetosphere (a region surrounding a celestial body where the motions of electrically charged particles are dominated by a magnetic field). Thus, it joins a growing list of planets with such magnetospheres: Mercury, the earth, Jupiter, Saturn, and, perhaps, Mars.

Triton, the largest satellite of Neptune and the fifth biggest in the solar system, has long been a mystery world. If findings announced in 1983 are correct, it may also be the strangest. Near its south pole, Triton probably has a shallow sea of liquid nitrogen.

New comet. Astronomers were taken by surprise when the comet IRAS-Araki-Alcock sped past our planet only eight days after it was first identified as a comet, by two amateur astronomers—Genichi Araki of Japan and George Alcock of England. The unexpected visitor was first detected by the British-Dutch-American Infrared Astronomical Satellite (IRAS), which had been searching for asteroids. On May 11, when the comet was nearest the earth, its

The IRAS-Araki-Alcock comet, shown here in a nearly head-on view, passed within an astronomical stone's throw of earth—a mere 3.1 million miles—only eight days after it was first identified by two amateur astronomers. (The lines in the photograph are the paths of stars during the relatively long time the picture was being taken.)

distance was only about 3 million miles (12 times farther away than the moon). Observers with the advantage of clear, dark skies saw an amazing sight when IRAS-Araki-Alcock was at its closest—it appeared as a fuzzy glow six or more times larger than the full moon. Of particular interest to scientists was the fact that it was the first comet in which sulfur molecules were detected.

Another solar system? In August, IRAS scientists announced the discovery of what seemed to be a cloud of solid particles around the star Vega, about 26 light-years from the earth. While aimed at Vega, IRAS had detected an unexpected amount of infrared radiation emanating from the region around the star. Much of the observed radiation corresponded to material at very low temperature, indicating that Vega is surrounded by bits of solid debris. It was speculated that some of this solid material could take the form of bodies as large as asteroids. The Vega discovery was regarded by a number of scientists as providing the first direct evidence that the sun might not be the only star to have solid objects of considerable size revolving around it. Evidence of yet another solar system, around the star Fomalhaut, was reported in December by scientists analyzing IRAS data.

The Longest Day

In case you didn't notice, June 30 was longer than any other day in 1983—by exactly one second. The "leap second" was added on by observatories around the world at 11:59:59 Greenwich time, to keep pace with the gradually slowing rotation of the earth. Leap seconds are routinely decreed by international agreement every 12 to 18 months. Actually, days are getting imperceptibly longer all the time; 500 million years ago, each day was only about 20 hours long.

Fast pulsars. Pulsars are dying stars, thought to consist of closely packed neutrons, that emit radio waves or X rays in sharp bursts, or pulses. During 1983 the importance of our Milky Way galaxy's so-called millisecond pulsar, discovered in late 1982, became evident. This highly magnetized neutron star, spinning at a rate of 642 times a second, is likely to turn out to be the most accurate clock known in the universe. Already its period of rotation is known to an accuracy of one part in 10^{14} (1 followed by 14 zeros), which equals the accuracy of the atomic clocks used by scientists as time standards.

A new cosmic antenna receives a champagne baptism at Harvard, Mass. Part of a privately funded Search for Extraterrestrial Intelligence (SETI) program, the antenna will be used to listen simultaneously to 131,072 channels for possible messages from other worlds.

The physics of this millisecond pulsar is equally fascinating. It is a tiny body, only a mile or two in diameter, with a density more than 10^{14} times greater than that of water. If the millisecond pulsar were not so small and dense, its gravity couldn't hold it together against the centrifugal force created by its rapid rotation—the equator of the star is moving at a significant fraction of the speed of light. No one is sure how this object came to be, but a leading guess is that two neutron stars coalesced to form the millisecond pulsar.

Supernova. On July 3 an Australian amateur astronomer discovered a supernova in Messier 83, a relatively nearby galaxy in the constellation of Hydra. Supernovas are exploding stars of extreme brightness, and this one was one of the most brilliant—at its peak it shone with the light of 10 billion suns. For many months, astronomers examined this "new" star with detectors that scanned the radiation spectrum searching for clues to the origin of supernovas.

Black holes. It has yet to be proved that black holes—hypothetical bodies with gravitational fields so powerful that nothing, not even light, can escape from them—actually exist. But evidence continues to mount that these bizarre products of theoreticians' minds are real features of our universe. Since star-size black holes, if they exist, cannot be seen, they can only be detected by their gravitational effects on visible bodies. Perhaps the only way of hunting for a black hole is to look for a binary (double) star system in which a visible star has an unaccountably massive, unseen companion. (According to theory, any stellar object with a mass greater than about twice the sun's must either shed its excess mass in some way or eventually become a black hole.) In 1983 a scientific team found the best black-hole candidate yet, in the binary star LMC X-3 in the Large Magellanic Cloud. The scientists concluded that the unseen companion of LCM X-3's visible component has a mass of more than nine suns, and thus is very likely a black hole.   L.J.R.

AUSTRALIA. With the election of a Labor government in Australia on March 5, 1983, that party came to power for only the second time since 1949. The new Labor prime minister, Robert Hawke (see biography in PEOPLE IN THE

Powered entirely by solar cells, the tiny car dubbed the Quiet Achiever rolls into Sydney after completing a 2,500-mile trek across Australia. Despite discomfort in temperatures that reached as high as 116 degrees, the two drivers, who took turns at the wheel, maintained an average speed of 15 miles per hour.

News), presented a marked contrast to the remote manner of his Liberal predecessor, Malcolm Fraser. He had relatively little experience in Parliament, but he demonstrated a mastery of public relations that was novel in Australian politics.

General election. On February 3, Prime Minister Fraser called an election to take place on March 5. He hoped to catch Labor off guard and win a mandate for his Liberal–National Party coalition and its conservative policies. He expected to be running against the uncharismatic Bill Hayden, then leader of the Labor Party. However, on the very day Fraser announced the elections, Hayden agreed to resign, after receiving guarantees of fair treatment for his supporters and a promise of the foreign affairs portfolio in the prospective new Labor government for himself. Hawke was formally elected party leader by a Labor Party caucus on February 8.

Hawke's program, which promised tax cuts and stimulatory spending, undertook to achieve "national reconciliation, national reconstruction, and national recovery." For its part, the Liberal–National Party government late in 1982 had passed legislation freezing the incomes of federal employees for 12 months; the government had also induced the Conciliation and Arbitration Commission to impose a temporary wage freeze in the private sector. During the campaign a drought produced devastating brushfires in Victoria and South Australia and seriously damaged crops, adding to the country's already severe economic problems. High unemployment and double-digit inflation were issues in the campaign.

Despite poor showings in the opinion polls, Fraser maintained to the end that he would win. The results, however, showed an overall swing to Labor of more than 5 percent, far more than needed for victory. Labor came away with a solid 75–50 margin in the House of Representatives. Fraser tersely conceded defeat and promptly resigned as leader of the Liberal Party. On March 11, his former challenger for the party leadership, Andrew Peacock, was elected to succeed him. Soon after, Fraser announced his retirement from parliamentary politics, resigning a seat he had held since 1955.

New government. The new Labor government, assembled by Hawke and sworn in on March 11, was drawn basically from the right wing of the party. It included an inner cabinet of 13 members—among them, Bill Hayden, as foreign minister; Paul Keating as treasurer; and Lionel Bowen, as deputy prime minister and minister of trade.

The day after the election, Hawke was shown Treasury estimates that the federal deficit for 1983–1984 would reach $9.6 billion. He promptly stated that such a deficit was unac-

ceptable, and Labor policies for tax reductions and stimulatory spending became "inoperable." Hawke also ordered a 10 percent devaluation of the Australian dollar. On April 11, he convened a national "summit conference" of government, business, and labor leaders to seek a consensus on economic management. Employers agreed reluctantly to reintroduce "centralized" wage determination, which meant abandonment of the case-by-case approach adopted by the Conciliation and Arbitration Commission two years earlier. In October 1983 the commission granted a general 4.3 percent wage increase, ending the wage freeze.

The federal budget for 1983–1984, introduced on August 23, did not increase direct taxation and did not greatly increase benefits for the least advantaged. It was criticized from the Labor left, which also sought greater economic stimulus than was anticipated from the projected $8.4 billion deficit.

A schoolhouse in Cockatoo, 30 miles east of Melbourne, goes up in flames. Australia's southeast coast, parched by February's 100-degree heat, was devastated by fire storms propelled by gale-force winds.

Foreign affairs. In June, Hawke embarked on a 19,000-mile world tour, which took the new prime minister to London, Paris, and Washington, D.C., among other capitals. Despite some anti-Western positions taken by the Labor Party when it was in opposition, Hawke appeared anxious to establish cordial relations with the United States and other Western powers. He stressed that Australia, while it might criticize U.S. policy, "is not and cannot be a nonaligned nation"; he pledged to maintain joint military installations on Australian territory and to stand by the defensive alliance between Australia, New Zealand, and the United States.

State politics. A split in Queensland's long-dominant National-Liberal Party coalition led to the resignation of the Liberals from the government and to elections on October 22; the National Party succeeded in winning a majority by itself, capturing 43 out of 82 seats. Earlier, in February 19 elections, the Labor Party won control in Western Australia.

In New South Wales, Premier Neville Wran was cleared of improper involvement in the dismissal of theft charges against a rugby official. In Victoria, the minister of industrial affairs had to step down because of conflict of interest charges.

Bright spots. On March 20, the Prince and Princess of Wales, accompanied by nine-month-old Prince William, undertook a four-week tour of Australia. In September the yacht *Australia II* became the first challenger ever to win the America's Cup, ending the 132-year hold of the United States on that prized yachting trophy (*see also* SPORTS: Yachting).   B.J.

AUSTRIA. In general elections held on April 24, 1983, Chancellor Bruno Kreisky's Socialist Party (SPÖ) won only 90 seats in the 183-member Nationalrat (lower house of parliament), down from 95. The conservative People's Party (ÖVP), the leading opposition group, won 81 seats, up from 77. The right-wing Freedom Party (FPÖ) took 12 seats and thus held the balance of power. Regarding the Socialist setback as a rebuke to his leadership, Kreisky resigned the chancellorship after 13 years in office. He was replaced by Vice-Chancellor Fred Sinowatz, who on May 18 announced the formation of a coalition government of the SPÖ and the FPÖ. Sinowatz also became SPÖ party chairman.

To reduce unemployment, the Kreisky government early in the year had proposed a series of public spending programs intended to create jobs. It also proposed such compensatory revenue-raising measures as a 20 percent tax on interest earnings. The tax proposal drew immediate fire from the ÖVP and FPÖ. After the formation of the SPÖ–FPÖ coalition, the FPÖ's opposition to increased government spending compelled the Sinowatz government to moderate its socialist policies.

In January, Chancellor Kreisky made an official visit to the United States, with which relations had been strained because of Kreisky's support of Palestinian statehood in the Middle East and a political settlement involving the left in Central America. His trip reportedly left both sides satisfied.

The year 1983 marked the 300th anniversary of two momentous events in Austrian history. In 1683 the people of Vienna, besieged by about 300,000 Turks, held out for two months until a Polish-led international Christian army arrived to beat back the invaders. That same year the first coffeehouse appeared in Vienna; according to legend, the new beverage was brewed from a sack of beans left behind by the fleeing Turks.

The anniversary of the Turkish defeat served as the occasion for a four-day journey to Austria in September by Pope John Paul II. The pope received a warm welcome.

See STATISTICS OF THE WORLD.   R.S.

AUTOMOBILE INDUSTRY. Substantial increases in sales and profits marked the 1983 automotive scene in the United States.

Sales. U.S. automobile sales totaled 8,804,033 during the 1983 model year (ending September 30), up 14.6 percent from 1982. Domestic producers sold 6,475,222 units, up 16.8 percent from 1982, but still the second-worst year for U.S. manufacturers in 20 years. General Motors took the largest share (44 percent) of the market. Ford, with 16.8 percent, and Chrysler, with 9.3 percent, ranked second and third. The Ford Escort was the industry's top seller, with sales of 323,900 units; GM took second spot with the Oldsmobile Cutlass, and the Chevrolet Impala/Caprice ranked third.

An estimated 2,328,811 imported cars were sold in the United States in the 1983 model year, up 8.8 percent from 1982. Imports took 26.5 percent of the market, trailing a high of 28 percent in 1982. Toyota topped the imports, selling 536,982 cars.

In truck sales, Chevrolet was the industry leader, selling 917,240 units (up 20.9 percent over the 1982 model year). Ford was runner-up, on sales of 898,648 (up 19 percent).

Profits. Automakers posted their highest profits in four years. GM netted $2.4 billion in the first nine months of 1983, up from $818 million in the first nine months of the previous year. Ford reported profits of $1.09 billion for the first nine months, compared with a loss of $422 million in the period a year earlier. Chrysler made $482.4 million by the half-year mark, more than the $423 million it earned in all of 1976, previously its most profitable year. (For the first nine months of 1983, Chrysler earned $582.6 million.) The return to profitability helped Chrysler repay federally guaranteed loans of $813.5 million, plus interest, seven years early. American Motors Corporation, in contrast, lost $145 million during the first six months of 1983.

New models. American automakers introduced a variety of new cars for the 1984 model year. The most exotic was GM's Chevrolet Corvette, said to be able to stop, corner, and accelerate faster than any other mass-produced car ever made. A rolling high-tech showcase, the fiberglass two-seater carried a base list price of $23,360. Chevrolet also launched a Cavalier convertible, and Cadillac unveiled an Eldorado convertible. Ford introduced an all-new Continental Mark VII, with headlights mounted flush with the face of the car and with the model's traditional spare tire bulge on the trunk lid. AMC brought out a compact Jeep XJ, the first totally new Jeep in 20 years, in the form of smaller Cherokee and Wagoneer sports wagons. AMC also launched the Encore, a hatchback derivative of its popular Alliance, which in 1983 accounted for 91 percent of the firm's sales.

Prices and warranties. GM raised prices an average of $280 per car (2.4 percent) for the 1984 model year; Ford, $254 (2.3 percent); Chrysler, $191 (1.9 percent); and AMC, $232

(2.5 percent). Volkswagen of America, on the other hand, trimmed prices $45 (0.4 percent). On the average, a car made by the Big Three (GM, Ford, and Chrysler) during the 1984 model year will cost $10,933.

Ford introduced a lifetime service guarantee, obtainable at extra cost, that will protect owners from having to pay more than once for certain repairs for as long as they own their vehicles. Engines, transmissions, suspensions, and heating, cooling, and electrical systems are among items covered. The plan supplements Ford's standard 12-month, 12,000-mile warranty.

Fuel economy. During the 1983 model year, GM and Ford failed to meet government standards on Corporate Average Fuel Economy (CAFE), marking the first time any automakers had fallen short of the standards since they took effect in 1978. GM and Ford asked the government to ease its requirements—26, 27, and 27.5 miles per gallon (mpg) in 1983, 1984, and 1985, respectively. Chrysler and AMC, which met the standards because they were selling mostly small cars, argued that CAFE standards should be retained. GM's cars averaged 23.5 mpg in 1983 and Ford's 23.8; Chrysler's averaged 27, AMC's 31.6, and VW's 30.2.

Japan's Honda Civic CRX, a plastic-and-steel-bodied, two-passenger hatchback powered by a 1.3-liter, four-cylinder gasoline engine, captured the top spot in the government's annual fuel economy ratings, dislodging VW's diesel-powered Rabbit. The CRX was rated by the Environmental Protection Agency at 51 mpg.

Safety. The U.S. Supreme Court overturned a Reagan administration ruling that would have removed a requirement for air bags or automatic safety belts in passenger cars manufactured after September 1, 1983. However, the Court gave the Department of Transportation a year's time to impose the requirement or justify its failure to do so.

In August the U.S. Department of Justice, in a suit asking for more than $4 million in damages, charged General Motors with having knowingly built 1.1 million 1980 W-body cars with faulty brakes and then having issued "false and misleading" statements to federal investigators. GM said the suit was "unwarranted."

In October, GM offered to correct problems in nearly 500,000 cars and trucks; most of the recalls were to correct flaws in dual braking systems. Also in October, VW agreed to recall nearly 1 million cars to fix safety problems in their braking and electrical systems. According to the National Highway Traffic Safety Administration, the VW braking defects involved 650,000 Rabbit and Scirocco models produced in West Germany between 1975 and 1980 and more than 900,000 VW and Audi models with electrical problems. (The total number of cars came to less than a million since some cars had both problems.)

Labor. Chrysler and the United Automobile Workers in September approved a billion-dollar contract providing for an immediate $1-per-hour wage increase retroactive to August 15 and additional wage increases of $1.42 per hour, along with cost-of-living and productivity adjustments over the 25-month life of the agreement. The settlement gives Chrysler workers parity in wages and benefits with their counterparts at GM and Ford. VW's UAW-represented workers ratified a three-year contract calling for a basic wage freeze, plus retention of a scaled-back cost-of-living clause.

Around the world. General Motors and Toyota, which together manufacture about 25 percent of the world's automobiles, received Federal Trade Commission approval to start joint production of a front-wheel-drive subcompact car in late 1984 at GM's shuttered Fremont, Calif., assembly plant. Ford and Chrysler opposed the joint venture.

AMC became the first U.S. automaker to establish a joint venture in China, obtaining a 31.3 percent share in the newly established Peking Jeep Corporation Ltd. in exchange for $8 million in cash and another $8 million in technological assistance. Renault, the French government–backed automaker that owns nearly half of American Motors, boosted its stake in American-based Mack Trucks from 20 to 45 percent, paying $100 million for the additional ownership.   D.L.L.

The chairmen of Toyota and General Motors, Eiji Toyoda and Roger B. Smith, at the now idle GM plant in Fremont, Calif., where the two companies plan to cooperate in the production of 200,000 compact cars a year.

B

BAHAMAS. See STATISTICS OF THE WORLD.

BAHRAIN. See STATISTICS OF THE WORLD. *See also* PERSIAN GULF STATES.

BANGLADESH. Although Bangladesh remained under martial law in 1983, the nation's martial law administrator, Lieutenant General H. M. Ershad, announced in November that presidential elections would be held in May 1984. On December 11, he dissolved his cabinet, proclaimed himself president as a means of providing a "transition to democracy," and said that martial law would remain in effect until after the election. As president, Ershad replaced A.F.M. Ahsanuddin Choudhury, whom he had appointed after the bloodless coup by which he gained power in March 1982. On December 14, Ershad ordered the release of about 200 political prisoners who had been detained after a series of antigovernment riots in late November.

Violence had broken out sporadically during the year, most destructively in mid-February, when the army was called in to quell disturbances in various parts of the country. The February riots, in which several people lost their lives, were sparked by Ershad's proposal to require the study of Arabic and the Koran in the schools. The violence began when demonstrations spilled over the bounds of the Dhaka (formerly spelled "Dacca") University campus. In response, party leaders were arrested, and the university was closed for several months.

In April, a 15-party alliance of opposition parties put forward a series of demands, including an end to military rule, restoration of civil liberties, and a judicial inquiry into the February disorders. Ershad generally rejected the demands, but he made some concessions, easing press censorship and allowing indoor meetings of political parties.

Dhaka's military regime continued its cordial relations with Washington. Ershad visited the United States and conferred with President Ronald Reagan in October, and in late November, he requested the Soviet government to reduce its 36-person staff by half and to close

its cultural center in Dhaka. It was reported that the government suspected the Soviet representatives of inciting the November protests.

Earlier in the year, an Indian-Bangladeshi joint commission reached agreement on the amount of water to be released to Bangladesh from the Tista River in the Indian state of West Bengal.

The economic outlook improved somewhat. Significant increases in aid were arranged from Saudi Arabia, and there were substantial new Arab investments. Overall economic growth for fiscal 1982–1983 was 3.8 percent. Food production reached a record 15.1 million tons, and higher jute production contributed to a 20 percent rise in export earnings. Industrial growth, however, was less than 1 percent.

See STATISTICS OF THE WORLD.   S.-A.R.

BANKING AND FINANCE. The recovery of the U.S. economy in 1983 was reflected in a surging stock market and a strong dollar, but banks were still troubled by problem loans, both domestic and international.

Federal Reserve policies. During 1983, the Federal Reserve Board faced the delicate task of regulating the growth of the U.S. money supply and influencing interest rates in such a way as to fuel the economy's recovery from recession without reigniting inflation. For much of 1983, the money supply was growing faster than the Federal Reserve had desired. For example, M-1 (the money-supply measure that includes cash in circulation and checking-account deposits) increased at an annual rate of about 14 percent in the first half of the year, well above the Fed's target of 4–8 percent. In July, Federal Reserve Chairman Paul Volcker announced that for the second six months of 1983, M-1 would be permitted to grow in the range of 5–9 percent, and the Fed took steps to rein in what it considered an overgrown money supply.

By the time he announced the new money supply targets, Volcker had already been renominated by President Ronald Reagan for a second four-year term as chairman of the Federal Reserve Board. He was confirmed by the Senate and began his new term on August 6. Volcker had been criticized by some for keeping an overly restrictive grip on the money supply until late 1982. Detractors said this had prolonged and deepened the recession. Volcker supporters credited his policies with bringing down inflation from 13.3 percent in 1979 to about 4 percent in 1983.

Stocks and bonds. Investors, convinced that the economy was pulling out of the recession and encouraged by declining interest rates, sent the stock market into one of the strongest rallies of the last 50 years. On April 26, the Dow Jones Industrial Average, the major market barometer, closed above the 1,200 mark for the first time in history. The market advance stalled in the summer, because of concern over a resurgence in interest rates, but further records were set later in the year. The market absorbed billions of dollars in new stock offerings, allowing companies to build their recession-battered businesses. Economists also said the soaring stock market bolstered consumer confidence and thus boosted the economic recovery.

The somewhat lower interest rates sent corporations to the bond market for money to finance their growth and operations. During the first six months of 1983, corporations sold 358 issues of bonds totaling $30.7 billion, nearly three times as much as was sold during the first six months of 1982.

In late July, after months of well-publicized difficulties, the Washington Public Power Sup-

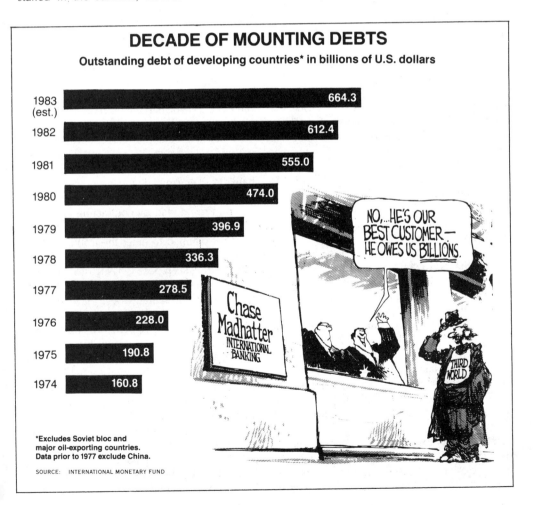

DECADE OF MOUNTING DEBTS
Outstanding debt of developing countries* in billions of U.S. dollars

1983 (est.)	664.3
1982	612.4
1981	555.0
1980	474.0
1979	396.9
1978	336.3
1977	278.5
1976	228.0
1975	190.8
1974	160.8

Chase Madhatter INTERNATIONAL BANKING

NO,...HE'S OUR BEST CUSTOMER— HE OWES US BILLIONS.

THIRD WORLD

*Excludes Soviet bloc and major oil-exporting countries. Data prior to 1977 exclude China.

SOURCE: INTERNATIONAL MONETARY FUND

ply System defaulted on $2.25 billion in bonds, the biggest default ever in the municipal bond market. The nation's largest issuer of tax-free municipal bonds, WPPSS had issued bonds for the construction of five nuclear power plants. The default came on the bonds for Projects 4 and 5, which had been canceled in 1982 because of huge cost overruns and lower-than-expected demand for electricity. The market for municipal bonds in general was nevertheless strong during the year.

Interest rates. A rise in interest rates during the summer was partly due to the Fed's tightening of the money supply. The prospects of huge federal budget deficits also contributed to higher interest rates. Economists warned that businesses and other private borrowers might be crowded out of the bond markets and interest rates forced up as the U.S. government soaked up too much of the available credit to finance its budget shortfall.

The prime lending rate, the base rate that banks charge business borrowers, remained at 10.5 percent from February through early August, but on August 8, the banks raised the prime to 11 percent. New three-month Treasury bills fetched around 8.5–9 percent in the autumn, compared with less than 8 percent at the beginning of 1983.

Banking industry. Even though recovery was well under way, banks still felt the effects of the recession. Problem loans continued to rise at many institutions, especially loans to borrowers in the energy industry. At the ten largest U.S. banks, nonperforming loans—loans on which the borrower is unable to make payments—reached 3.4 percent of total lending at the end of June, up from 2.25 percent a year earlier.

Although most banks still reported profits, a relatively large number of bank failures occurred. Ten of the failures were at banks controlled by Jake Butcher, a flamboyant Tennessee financier, and his brother, C. H. Butcher, Jr. The first and largest of the Butcher failures occurred at the United American Bank of Knoxville, with assets of $760 million. Experiencing heavy losses from bad loans, the bank was closed by state regulators in February. As other closings followed, questions mounted about the banks' lending practices. Many of

the institutions had made sizable "insider" loans, that is, loans to their own officers and directors or their families and friends.

Losses on energy loans were a key factor in the second largest commercial bank failure in U.S. history, which occurred at the First National Bank of Midland, Texas, in mid-October. After it was declared insolvent, the bank, with assets of $1.4 billion, was purchased by the Dallas-based RepublicBank Corporation and reopened as RepublicBank First National Midland.

Deregulation. The deregulation of the banking industry accelerated during the year. The money market deposit account, which was allowed to pay unlimited interest rates beginning December 14, 1982, proved very popular with consumers. Another major innovation was the deregulation of interest rates on consumer time deposits. New federal regulations that went into effect on October 1, 1983, removed federal interest rate ceilings and minimum balance requirements on certificates of deposit that are purchased after that date and mature in 32 days to 2½ years; penalties for early withdrawal were also eased.

Some states sought to attract new capital by easing banking regulations. South Dakota, for instance, relaxed laws designed to prevent banks from engaging in the insurance business, and New York's giant Citicorp banking corporation responded by contracting to buy the tiny American State Bank of Rapid City, through which it planned to enter the insurance business.

Withholding tax repeal. On August 5, President Reagan signed into law a measure repealing earlier legislation that would have required banks and other financial institutions to withhold for federal taxes 10 percent of most interest and dividend payments to depositors and shareholders. The repeal was due in great part to lobbying by the banking industry, which complained that withholding would be difficult and expensive. Banks rallied the support of depositors, who waged a massive letter writing campaign directed at members of Congress. The drive was deemed one of the largest grass-roots political efforts ever undertaken.

International debt crisis. Many of the world's financially strapped developing countries

The world's largest Scrabble game? No—only workers carting away no-longer-needed letters from the United American Bank of Knoxville, which changed both owner and name when auditors revealed an estimated $160 million loss in bad loans.

struggled to renegotiate their staggering debts to creditors in the industrialized nations. Doomsayers predicted defaults that would precipitate chaos in the financial markets and possibly the collapse of some of the world's biggest banks. But the bankers, with the help of their governments and world lending agencies, managed to patch together solutions for each crisis that arose.

The International Monetary Fund estimated that the non-oil-exporting developing countries owed foreign creditors $612.4 billion at the end of 1982, and the IMF predicted that the total would rise to $664 billion at the end of 1983. Most of this vast sum was owed to commercial banks, many of them in the United States. While dozens of developing countries sought to reschedule debt, seven debtor nations—Mexico, Brazil, Argentina, Venezuela, Chile, Yugoslavia, and Poland—were said to account for about 81 percent of the debt that was renegotiated. Of these, the most heavily in debt was Brazil, which owed $90 billion, including $22 billion to U.S. banks.

The seeds of the debt dilemma were planted a decade ago when the Organization of Petroleum Exporting Countries initiated a series of price increases that brought the benchmark price of a barrel of oil from less than $3 to a peak of $34. These oil-rich nations deposited billions of dollars of oil revenues in the world's major banks, which found the developing world an eager market for loans, to finance both oil imports and development projects. Then the world recession hit. Interest rates skyrocketed in the late 1970's and early 1980's, and in many countries the squeeze was exacerbated by slumping exports.

Varying agreements were struck in efforts to renegotiate each country's debt. The terms often included a grace period, in which no payments were required, a lengthening of the maturity of the loans, and the lending of further sums. Generally, only debt falling due in the near future was renegotiated.

Some banks, however, wanted no more of the risks of international finance. A report by the International Monetary Fund showed that in 1982 banks had cut back their foreign lending for the first time in five years, by about 40 percent. The IMF projected a further marginal decline in lending during 1983.

IMF quotas. The IMF decided in February that an increase of over $40 billion in its own funding was needed in order for it to serve its members and keep the developing countries afloat. Although most member countries readily agreed to specified increases in their contributions, the U.S. share of $8.4 billion was hotly debated in Congress, where the funds were ultimately approved in November.

To facilitate passage, the Reagan administration pressed for, and got, an IMF agreement to reduce each country's level of access to loans. Starting in 1984, each country will generally be allowed to borrow only 102 percent of its quota, or deposit in the fund, per year over a three-year period; in some cases, access could be raised to 125 percent. The limit had been 150 percent since 1981. The percentage reduction, combined with the increased contributions, meant that the actual

At a growing number of Sears, Roebuck & Company stores, customers can now buy securities or insurance or consult a real estate broker.

dollar limits on loans would be virtually unchanged.

Bankers' worries. The biggest U.S. banks have lent vast sums abroad, particularly in Latin America. To cover loan losses, most multinational banks have reserves equal to about 1 percent of loans; such reserves would be wiped out if any major debtor country defaulted. The banks' second line of defense, shareholders' equity, varies by the size of the bank. The top ten banks in the United States had lent, on average, amounts equal to over 150 percent of their shareholder's equity to just five Latin American countries by the end of 1982.

Many bankers grumbled that the debtor countries had complicated the problems by borrowing from banks around the world and not telling each lender where or how much they had borrowed elsewhere. In response, the banks created a private institute to gather and distribute information and to consider solutions to the world's debt dilemma. Founded in January, the body is called the Institute of International Finance and is based in Washington, D.C. By midyear, the institute counted more than 100 member banks from 29 countries.

World financial markets. The international currency markets were unsettled during 1983. On March 21, the eight European nations that make up the European Monetary System agreed to realign their currencies, the third such realignment in 13 months. The West German mark was revalued upward 5.5 percent and the French franc devalued 2.5 percent, in effect devaluing the franc by 8 percent against the mark.

Meanwhile, the dollar's value in relation to other currencies soared, partly because of high real interest rates (after allowing for inflation) in the United States. In early August it reached its highest point against the mark in nine years, and its highest against the French franc in more than 60 years. The United States central bank (the Federal Reserve) intervened in world currency markets, selling dollars in an attempt to bring down the currency's value. The Fed was joined in this effort by the central banks of West Germany, Japan, Switzerland, and France.

Stock markets all over the world showed impressive gains in 1983, as investors became convinced that the industrial nations, notably the United States, were shaking themselves out of the lingering recession. Gold, which often appeals to investors in times of crisis or when other investments are performing poorly, declined in value.   T.C.

BARBADOS. *See* STATISTICS OF THE WORLD.

BEHAVIORAL SCIENCES. Researchers in 1983 uncovered clues that may help in understanding two serious and troubling eating disorders, bulimia and anorexia nervosa. Other studies related depression to sleep cycle disturbances and questioned the desirability of expressing anger.

Bulimia and anorexia nervosa. Bulimics indulge in eating binges, especially of sweets; they often force themselves to vomit after eating to avoid putting on weight. This forced vomiting may lead to serious health problems involving, for example, tooth decay and acid-chemical imbalances from the loss of stomach acid. Anorexics restrict themselves to severe diets, losing so much weight that their lives may be endangered. Psychiatrist James Gibbs and co-workers at the New York Hospital—Cornell University Medical Center, on the basis of experiments with rats, suggested that bulimia may be linked to a disturbance in the integration of two competing signals in the central nervous system. One signal is triggered by the sweet taste of food. The other is provided by the digestive system, which releases two chemicals called bombesin and cholecystokinin. When these two chemicals circulate to the brain, they normally produce a feeling of satiety. In bulimics, however, the signals from these chemicals apparently fail to overcome the force of the sweet taste that drives the bulimics to continue eating. This finding also helps to explain why bulimics tend to prefer sweet foods.

Another group of researchers, headed by Jack L. Katz at the Montefiore Medical Center in New York, found links between depression and some cases of anorexia nervosa. In some of the 20 young female anorexics they studied, the researchers found a correlation between a sleep abnormality called short REM latency, and patients' complaints of feelings of sadness. REM (for rapid eye movement) is a stage of sleep during which the eyes move rapidly and dreams most frequently occur; in short REM

The pop singer Karen Carpenter, who died from heart failure in February at the age of 32, was a longtime victim of the eating disorder known as anorexia nervosa; researchers are now learning more about its possible causes.

latency, people enter this stage abnormally quickly. Katz and his group found that anorexics suffered from this abnormality of the stages of sleep, which researchers had already identified as occurring in patients suffering from major emotional depression. Each of these anorexics also appeared to have abnormally high levels of the hormone cortisol (which is produced by the adrenal glands), another commonplace finding among depressed patients in general.

Katz and his colleagues concluded that some forms of depression may be manifested in the appearance of anorexia. It was unclear, however, whether the eating disorder in these cases was actually caused by depression, or was independent in origin but became closely associated with depression.

Depression. Researchers have theorized that certain symptoms of depression—short REM latency, the tendency to wake up early in the morning, and abnormal cycles of rising and falling blood levels of the hormone cortisol—may all reflect a disorder in the patient's circadian (approximately 24-hour) rhythm of activity.

This theory was supported by recent findings at the University of California at San Diego, where researchers succeeded in treating seriously depressed patients by using bright light in an attempt to readjust their biological clocks, which presumably had fallen out of synchronization with the natural 24-hour cycles. Psychiatrist Daniel F. Kripke and his co-workers exposed 24 hospitalized depressed patients to a bright white light during a "critical photoperiodic interval." Bright light during this interval, around 5 A.M. to 6 A.M., led to significant improvement in the mood of the patients by afternoon. The light may exert its effect, the researchers theorize, through its effect on the secretion of a brain hormone called melatonin, which helps reestablish the appropriate rhythm. Symptoms of depression returned when researchers discontinued the treatment.

Expressing anger. When it comes to feelings of anger and frustration, the conventional wisdom has been to "let it all hang out." Otherwise, it is said, pent-up feelings may lead to depression, heart disease, ulcers, and other disorders.

Psychologist Carol Tavris, however, attacked the generally accepted view in her book *Anger: The Misunderstood Emotion*. According to Tavris, venting anger may create more problems than it solves, although she conceded the need to express anger on occasion. The expression of anger is most likely to be effective and healthy, she said, when it meets three conditions: it represents a legitimate cry for justice, it is directed against the person who provoked the anger, and it leads to a desirable change of the situation or, at least, does not bring retaliation.

Home computers and mental health. Mental health professionals reported seeing an increase in the incidence of marital stress and divorce caused by one spouse's preoccupation with a home computer. The computer-obsessed spouse may work at the computer for hours each day, becoming withdrawn and unresponsive in the process. According to Thomas McDonald, a psychologist with Transition Associates, a La Jolla, Calif., counseling service, the basic problem is the conflict between the supposedly perfect computer and imperfect people. McDonald leads group therapy sessions for "computerwidows" (or widowers) and their mates. M.K.

BELGIUM. In 1983 the center-right coaliation government of Premier Wilfried Martens, the first Belgian government in seven years to have lasted more than a year, continued the austerity program launched in early 1982. A major priority was reduction of the budget deficit, which proved difficult, partly because of lower-than-anticipated tax revenues. The Martens government proposed additional austerity measures during 1983, including postponement of annual bonuses to public sector workers, a tax on unemployment benefits going to high-income households, and increased social security contributions. In mid-September, government employees staged wildcat strikes to protest postponement of their bonuses and other proposals. Postal service and public transit facilities were sharply cut back. On September 26, however, after agreeing to a compromise proposal, the striking government workers returned to their jobs.

The national economy showed signs of modest recovery in 1983, after two years of declining output. Gross domestic product was expected to rise by 0.25 percent, with a further increase of 1.5 percent forecast for 1984. The unemployment rate fell gradually but remained the second highest in the European Community, at 12.3 percent in September. The government was seeking to alleviate unemployment through a voluntary program; where accepted by employers and unions, it provided for wage restraint and reduced working hours in return for the creation of additional jobs. The Martens government also proposed a $143 million rescue plan to bail out the ailing Cockerill-Sambre steel company, a major industry in southern Belgium. The plan, subject to worker approval, called for a reduction in production capacity, stringent pay cuts, and early retirement schemes.

The government made clear its plans to proceed with the deployment of medium-range U.S. nuclear missiles if U.S.–Soviet arms control negotiations in Geneva reached no satisfactory conclusion. Meanwhile, Belgium expelled six Soviet and Romanian diplomats in August, during an investigation of technological espionage. The expulsions followed the arrest of Eugene Michaels, an Eastern bloc specialist in the Foreign Ministry, who admitted having sold secret documents to the diplomats. In October, two other Soviet diplomats, said to have been seeking military information, also were expelled.

Two persons were killed when Belgium's worst earthquake in 45 years struck the city of Liège, also doing damage to many buildings. *See* STATISTICS OF THE WORLD. W.C.C.

BELIZE. *See* STATISTICS OF THE WORLD.

BENIN. *See* STATISTICS OF THE WORLD.

BHUTAN. *See* STATISTICS OF THE WORLD.

BOLIVIA. Bolivia's ruling coalition, Democratic and Popular Unity, which was dominated by President Hernán Siles Zuazo's Leftist National Revolutionary Movement (MNR–I), began to unravel in January 1983, when six cabinet members from the Leftist Revolutionary Movement (MIR) resigned. Efforts to revive the coalition failed, and the MIR ultimately joined the opposition in the legislature, leaving the government without a majority. The entire cabinet resigned August 5 to allow Siles Zuazo to restructure the government. The new cabinet was dominated by the MNR–I; it also did not have a legislative majority.

As part of its antinarcotics campaign, the Siles Zuazo government instituted a purge of high officers within the armed forces who had allegedly become involved in the drug traffic. In April, Bolivia signed an accord with the U.S. government for a $75 million aid program, to be used for coca leaf eradication and for producing substitute crops.

Interest on Bolivia's huge foreign debt threatened to exceed the country's export income. U.S. and European banks that had lent $1.3 billion to Bolivia tentatively agreed to renegotiate $450 million in payments due between 1983 and 1985. However, the renegotiation was contingent on Bolivia's reaching agreement on a financial program with the International Monetary Fund. In November, the government announced austerity measures that

The economic woes of Bolivia were reflected in the call for a general strike on November 21–22 protesting government policies.

included a 60 percent devaluation of the peso and food price increases of up to 79 percent. Worker protests and a 48-hour nationwide general strike were called. The cabinet again resigned on December 14, to make possible the formation of a cabinet of national unity.

Klaus Barbie, a former Nazi police officer called "the butcher of Lyon," was expelled from Bolivia on February 4 and turned over to France, which had long sought his extradition. He was held in France, awaiting trial.

See Statistics of the World.   L.L.P.

BOTSWANA. *See* Statistics of the World.

BRAZIL. In 1983, Brazil experienced its third straight year of severe recession, as inflation and unemployment soared and the country's foreign debt reached massive proportions. The worsening economy posed a grave problem for the government as it sought to maintain social order while meeting the stringent demands of foreign creditors.

Economic crisis. By 1983, Brazil had become the world's biggest debtor; it owed $90 billion to foreign creditors and was already in substantial arrears on its payments. In February, the International Monetary Fund agreed to grant Brazil a standby credit of more than $4 billion in return for government austerity policies, but credits were cut off after the budget deficit and rate of money supply expansion began to exceed agreed-upon targets in May. Protracted negotiations followed between the Brazilian government and the IMF. The IMF insisted, in particular, that Brazil modify its innovative wage indexing system, according to which wages were automatically raised every six months in accordance with the rate of inflation. However, there was considerable domestic resistance to these and other IMF demands, and militant labor activists mounted sporadic strikes and protests during the year.

In mid-October, the Brazilian Congress defeated an austerity package that would have cut state spending and limited wage increases to 80 percent of the rise in the cost-of-living index. In response, President João Baptista Figueiredo issued a decree providing for spending cuts and for reduced wage increases on a sliding scale that placed greater burdens on higher paid workers. The Congress ratified this decree on November 9. Later the same month an agreement was finalized with the IMF, resuming the flow of credits to Brazil and paving the way to rescheduling of $3.8 billion in debt to Western governments and $6.5 billion in commercial bank loans.

Although inflation had begun to decline in recent years, it actually soared upward again in 1983, reaching an estimated annual rate of close to 200 percent by November. In February, the government devalued the cruzeiro by 23 percent in the hope of attaining a trade surplus of $6 billion by year's end, another demand of the IMF. Further devaluations were ordered in August. These moves, however, contributed to the fueling of inflation during the year. Under terms agreed to in November, Brazil was committed to reducing inflation to 75 percent by the end of 1984—as opposed to an earlier commitment to 55 percent.

Political developments. Speculation persisted about the presidential succession in 1985, when President Figueiredo's term expires. Figueiredo himself reaffirmed his intention not to seek a new term, and in mid-July he temporarily relinquished office in order to undergo coronary bypass surgery in the United States. Vice-President Aureliano Chaves officially took over in his absence.

Foreign affairs. Brazil pursued an independent course in foreign affairs, sidestepping efforts by the Reagan administration to win its support for American policy in Central America. The major diplomatic flurry involved Libya, Brazil's second biggest arms client. It arose in April when four Libyan aircraft en route to Nicaragua and purported to be carrying medical supplies stopped for refueling in Brazil and were found to contain arms and ammunition. Libya apologized for the incident, and after extended negotiations, the planes were ultimately allowed to depart in June, on the condition that they would be flown directly back to Libyan soil.

Brazilian malaise. Burdened by its economic problems, Brazil seemed to be weighed down by a pervasive sense of malaise. Urban centers were thronged with refugees from the impoverished rural interior. Street demonstrations were attracting white-collar workers and government employees, as hardship increasingly affected Brazil's salaried middle class. Lootings of supermarkets by hungry Brazilians were not uncommon, and crimes such as muggings, armed robbery, and car theft increased dramatically, leading many wealthy families to hire armed guards.

See STATISTICS OF THE WORLD.   R.M.L.

Brazilian jungle troops patrol Manaus Airport as Libyan planes carrying arms to Nicaragua are impounded. Libya, which had claimed the planes were transporting medical supplies, later apologized to Brazil.

BRITISH COLUMBIA. See STATISTICS OF THE WORLD.

BULGARIA. Continued economic failures forced Bulgaria in 1983 to review its new economic program. In foreign affairs, the government faced lingering Western suspicions of Bulgarian involvement in the 1981 assassination attempt against Pope John Paul II.

Prime Minister Grisha Filipov announced in January that Bulgaria would introduce a revised economic reform plan to replace the initial so-called New Economic Mechanism (NEM), put into effect in 1982. Apparently, the NEM had failed to meet goals set for it by the government, including improved industrial production and more efficient industrial management and planning. At an economic conference in May, President Todor Zhivkov criticized the continued lack of labor discipline and the poor quality of Bulgaria's manufactured goods. Agriculture also was suffering, especially because of a major drought; in response, the government in May decreed price rises of about 20 percent for certain foods, including, pork, poultry, and ground meat.

Mehmet Ali Agca, the Turkish gunman convicted of the 1981 papal shooting, stirred wide attention in July when he asserted to reporters in Italy that he had been recruited and aided by the KGB and the Bulgarian secret service. Agca had made similar statements privately to Italian authorities. Both the Soviet Union and Bulgaria continued to deny involvement. In late 1982, acting on Agca's sworn statements, the Italians had arrested Sergei Ivanov Antonov, head of the Bulgarian Airlines office in Rome, on suspicion of "active complicity." In September 1983, however, while Antonov remained in custody, Italian authorities were reported preparing to indict Agca for "slandering" him. In December, Antonov was moved from jail for health reasons, but he remained under house arrest.

The arrest of Antonov led to deteriorating relations between Italy and Bulgaria, but there also was cooperation between the two countries. In July, Italian officials were permitted to visit Bulgaria to interview persons named by Agca, and in October two Bulgarian magistrates went to Rome to question Agca.

See STATISTICS OF THE WORLD.   R.A.P.

BURMA. During 1983 there was a political shakeup in Burma, the government stepped up action against insurgents, and in October, Rangoon was the scene of a bloody terrorist bombing.

Burma's ailing soldier-strongman, Ne Win, alarmed by the audacious political activities of his most likely successor, Brigadier General Tin Oo, removed him from power. Forty of his followers lost or changed positions as well. Tin Oo, former head of the Military Intelligence Service, third-ranking official of the ruling Burma Socialist Program Party, and longtime close adviser to Ne Win, was subsequently tried and convicted on charges of misusing state funds and property; he was sentenced in November to five life terms in prison.

In February and March, the government mounted major offensives against the Karen ethnic-minority insurgents, and in June, the army launched an unprecedented attack against the Karens deep in their own territory.

Real growth of the gross national product for the fiscal year that ended in March was 7.1 percent, significantly above the government's earlier projection of 5.9 percent, but the cost of Burma's exports rose in 1983, and prices for its exports declined. Burma's continued progress toward industrialization was demonstrated by the expanded production of electronic goods and automobiles in Japanese-franchised factories in Rangoon.

Burma's policy of neutrality was severely tested when a bomb explosion on October 9 killed 21 people, including four South Korean cabinet members, during a wreath-laying ceremony in Rangoon. South Korean President Chun Doo Hwan had been delayed from attending the ceremony and thus escaped injury. On October 17 the Burmese government announced the capture of two North Korean army officers in connection with the incident; they were tried and sentenced to death on December 9. Police had killed a third suspect, also said to be a North Korean commando, when he tried to escape arrest. The Burmese government broke off diplomatic relations with North Korea, which, for its part, denied any connection with the bombing.

See STATISTICS OF THE WORLD.   R.B.

BURUNDI. See STATISTICS OF THE WORLD.

C

CABINET, UNITED STATES. The resignation of Interior Secretary James G. Watt and the appointment of the first women to the Reagan cabinet made headlines in 1983.

Watt resigns. Watt, the most controversial member of the cabinet, resigned his post as secretary of the interior on October 9. The resignation followed intense criticism of the latest in a series of verbal gaffes made by Watt—a purportedly humorous comment that the Interior Department's Coal Advisory Committee was made up of "a black . . . a woman, two Jews, and a cripple." Watt later apologized for the remark, which came while he was addressing a group of lobbyists, but calls for his departure mounted from Republicans and Democrats alike, and a Senate resolution calling for his ouster had seemed likely to pass if he did not bow out before it came to a vote. President Ronald Reagan on October 13 named William P. Clark, the national security adviser, to succeed Watt.

Other cabinet changes. On January 5, Reagan nominated Elizabeth H. Dole to succeed Andrew L. Lewis, Jr., who had resigned the previous month, as secretary of the Transportation Department, making her the first woman to serve in his cabinet. Dole, who was approved by a 97–0 Senate vote and took office on February 7, had been serving as White House assistant for public liaison to special interest groups; previously she had served in federal consumer affairs posts and as a longtime member of the Federal Trade Commission. Later in January, Richard S. Schweiker announced his resignation as secretary of the Department of Health and Human Services, to take a post as head of the American Council of Life Insurance. On January 12, Reagan revealed his choice of former U.S. Representative Margaret M. Heckler (R, Mass.) to succeed Schweiker. After serving eight terms in Congress, Heckler had lost a bid for a ninth term in November 1982. Heckler, a founder and former cochairwoman of the Congressional Caucus for Women's Issues, was confirmed by an 82–3 Senate vote and was sworn in on March 9.

Cabinet structure. President Reagan vetoed a crime bill on January 14 largely because it would have allowed the creation of a cabinet-level director of federal efforts to combat drug trafficking. The president and the Justice Department concurred in the opinion that such an official, with authority over several agencies, could have disrupted the administration's antidrug campaign and caused friction among cabinet members.

After generating an uproar with a public remark considered offensive to women and minorities, Interior Secretary James Watt announced his resignation on October 9. Accompanied by his wife, Leilani, Watt made the announcement while on vacation at a California ranch.

Membership. Cabinet-level officers (officials who hold cabinet rank without holding cabinet posts) included Edwin Meese, counselor to the president; Jeane J. Kirkpatrick, U.S. representative to the United Nations; David A. Stockman, director of the Office of Management and Budget; William E. Brock III, U.S. trade representative; and William J. Casey, director of the Central Intelligence Agency.

The executive departments, the years of their establishment and their heads during 1983 follow:

Department of State, 1789: Secretary, George P. Shultz.

Department of the Treasury, 1789: Secretary, Donald T. Regan.

Department of the Interior, 1849: Secretary, James G. Watt, followed by William P. Clark.

Department of Agriculture, 1862: Secretary, John R. Block.

Department of Justice, 1870: Attorney General, William French Smith.

Department of Commerce, 1913: Secretary, Malcolm Baldrige.

Department of Labor, 1913: Secretary, Raymond J. Donovan.

Department of Defense, 1949: Secretary, Caspar W. Weinberger.

Department of Health and Human Services, 1953: Secretary, Richard S. Schweiker, followed by Margaret M. Heckler.

Department of Housing and Urban Development, 1965: Secretary, Samuel R. Pierce, Jr.

Department of Transportation, 1966: Secretary, Andrew L. Lewis, Jr., followed by Elizabeth H. Dole.

Department of Energy, 1977: Secretary, Donald P. Hodel.

Department of Education, 1979: Secretary, Terrel H. Bell. A.E.N.

CALIFORNIA. See STATISTICS OF THE WORLD.

CAMBODIA. In 1983, as Vietnamese troops stepped up action inside Cambodia (Kampuchea), the Heng Samrin regime, upheld by the Vietnamese occupation forces, tightened its grip over the country, actively repressing the Buddhist faith and curtailing both freedom of movement and contacts between Cambodians and foreigners. The three principal resistance groups—the Communist Khmer Rouge, the non-Communist Khmer People's National Liberation Front (KPNLF), and Prince Norodom Sihanouk's National United Front—continued to oppose the regime and seek the ouster of its Vietnamese protectors. In April reports that the Vietnamese government in Hanoi planned to install up to 400,000 Vietnamese settlers in eastern Cambodia provoked charges by the resistance groups and several foreign governments that the program would lead to colonization. Hanoi, confirming the program, claimed that it would bring economic gains to Cambodia.

Vietnamese forces launched the biggest action in Cambodia since their 1978 invasion of the country. Fighting began in January with small KPNLF probes against Vietnamese outposts. The Vietnamese responded with a massive attack against the KPNLF camp at Nong Chan, destroying the homes of over 40,000 refugees. In March, Vietnamese forces overran an important Khmer Rouge base at Phnom Chat. In April the Vietnamese pursued Cambodian resistance troops inside Thailand, where for the first time in the war the Vietnamese engaged in sustained combat with Thai forces. The Vietnamese also attacked the base camps of the National United Front, and by mid-April an estimated 50,000 Cambodian civilians had fled to Thailand. Refugee sources alleged that in an April assault on Sihanouk's military headquarters, hundreds of civilians were massacred by the attacking forces.

The Vietnamese withdrew from their forward positions in late April, and on May 3 the Heng Samrin regime held a ceremony marking the alleged removal of 10,000 Vietnamese troops from Cambodia. Thai intelligence sources claimed, however, that 2,000 fresh Vietnamese troops were sent to Cambodia the day after the ceremony.

In its first year of existence, the Coalition Government of Democratic Kampuchea, formed in mid-1982 by the Khmer Rouge, the KPNLF, and the National United Front, suffered from temporary rivalries within the leadership, but it gained valuable foreign recognition. In his role as president of the coalition, Sihanouk accepted the credentials of the ambassadors of Malaysia, China, North Korea, Bangladesh, and Mauritania at a ceremony held on the

Prime Minister Pierre Elliott Trudeau puffs on a symbolic peace pipe as government leaders and Indian representatives met to discuss Indian rights.

Thai-Cambodian border on April 30. A week earlier, French President François Mitterrand had welcomed Sihanouk to Paris, a gesture tending to counter the impression among some observers that France was leaning toward Vietnam on the Cambodian question.

At a summit meeting in February, Vietnam, Laos, and Cambodia formalized their relations as an emerging bloc dominated by Hanoi. The three governments reiterated their expectation that Cambodian resistance would eventually wear out and the Heng Samrin regime ultimately win broad recognition.

The Cambodian rice crop was up some 30 percent, to an estimated 2 million metric tons. Nevertheless, the United Nations Food and Agriculture Organization predicted a food deficit of 100,000 metric tons for 1983, and a Unicef report found that 60 percent of the nation's rural children suffered from malnutrition.

See STATISTICS OF THE WORLD.   E.H.B.

CAMEROON. *See* STATISTICS OF THE WORLD.

CANADA. The severe recession that had been throttling the Canadian economy came to an end in 1983, with an upsurge in economic activity. Nevertheless, unemployment remained high and the governing Liberal Party's popularity continued to drop.

Economic developments. By the beginning of the year, despite a reported unemployment rate of 12.8 percent for December 1982—a post-Depression record—Canada began to show signs of economic recovery. Housing starts climbed upward, reaching a five-year high in May, the final month of the federal government's Home Ownership Stimulation Plan, which provided $3,000 grants to buyers of new homes and first-time buyers of existing homes. (Canadian dollars used here and throughout.) Subsequently, the demand for single homes continued strong. Actual starts in urban areas alone were up by 84 percent in July over the same month of 1982. Other industries followed housing's trend. Bankruptcies dropped, and consumer confidence rose. Retail sales of major items increased; car sales, for example, were up 41 percent in the second quarter over the same period of 1982.

The relatively low inflation rate, about 6 percent, was also good news for Canadians. In January, the Bank of Canada cut its lending

101

rate to the lowest level since 1978. The rate declined further until midsummer; a small flutter produced a slight increase in July and August, but the rate dropped again in the fall.

Two serious problems, however, continued to haunt the Canadian economy and the governing Liberals: the high unemployment rate, still 11 percent in November, and the growing federal deficit. Unemployment insurance payments were at record levels; premiums paid by working Canadians were raised in January to cover the deficit. The federal deficit, which doubled in the first ten months of the 1982–1983 fiscal year, was blamed on unemployment insurance and welfare costs, rising debt charges, and decreased tax revenues as a result of the recession.

The Trudeau government. Rumors of Prime Minister Pierre Elliott Trudeau's pending retirement as leader of the Liberal Party grew stronger through much of the year as the party's ratings dropped in the polls (see biography in PEOPLE IN THE NEWS). A poll released at midyear showed 55 percent of committed voters ready to support the opposition Conservatives, while only 27 percent supported the Liberals.

Trudeau reshuffled his cabinet in August. It was the third shakeup of the year and by far the biggest, as five ministers were dismissed and others switched portfolios. Among the most notable changes, Minister of Defense Gilles Lamontagne, the cabinet's oldest member, was succeeded by Jean-Jacques Blais, who had been minister of supply and services. Jean-Luc Pepin ceded the transport portfolio to Lloyd Axworthy, who gave up his post as employment minister; the employment portfolio went to John Roberts, and Pepin was demoted to minister of state for external affairs. Judy Erola was named minister of consumer and corporate affairs, replacing André Ouellet, who took over from Charles Caccia as minister of labor. Caccia was given Roberts's former post as environment minister.

In early December, Trudeau outlined before Parliament a national agenda for 1984. It called for renewed efforts to bring about peace and disarmament abroad, and at home it committed

In a French immersion program in Ottawa, children from English-speaking homes spend six school hours a day speaking, reading, and writing French. The latest Canadian census showed that the number of people who could speak both official languages had increased by 27 percent over a ten-year period.

the Liberal government to a legislative program aimed at stimulating jobs and productivity while keeping public spending down. Later, the Liberals introduced legislation to withhold federal medical insurance funds from provinces that allowed overcharging of doctor and hospital fees. In a surprise move, the Progressive Conservatives on the federal level also endorsed the measure.

New Conservative leader. For Conservatives, as the year began, dissension within the party was a sore that would not heal. Party leader Joe Clark failed to win a clear mandate at the January leadership review, for the second time in two years. And so he called for a Tory leadership convention.

No one was surprised when Clark and Brian Mulroney, a veteran of the 1976 leadership race, Quebec-born and fully bilingual (see biography in PEOPLE IN THE NEWS), were quickly established as front-runners. Former Finance Minister John Crosbie of Newfoundland mounted a late but ineffective challenge. At the party convention in June, Mulroney won on the fourth ballot, to become the first Conservative leader from Quebec in nearly 100 years.

After capturing the leadership, Mulroney, who was not a member of Parliament, ran for a seat in the traditionally Conservative Nova Scotia riding of Central Nova. On August 29, Mulroney defeated his nearest rival, the Liberal candidate, winning 60 percent of the vote.

Cruise missile testing. After months of protests by marchers in cities across Canada, the cabinet announced in mid-July that it would permit testing of unarmed cruise missiles by the United States in Canada's north. Almost immediately, the decision came under heavy criticism from peace groups and federal politicians from all three major parties. A national peace march took place on October 22 to coincide with peace demonstrations in Europe.

Later in the year, as the U.S.-Soviet arms control talks in Geneva appeared doomed because of the scheduled U.S. missile deployments in Europe, Prime Minister Trudeau set out on a peace initiative of his own "to reintroduce dialogue in a very tense situation." He visited several major capitals, among them Peking, Moscow, and Washington, to persuade world leaders to return to negotiation in re-

solving disputes. His crusade drew plaudits from the Commonwealth of Nations meeting, held in India in November.

Airliner downing. In September, Canada revoked landing rights for the Soviet airline, Aeroflot, for 60 days in protest against the downing of a South Korean airliner by a Soviet fighter plane over Sakhalin Island early in the month. Several Canadians were among the 269 people killed.

Crowsnest Pass controversy. The federal government announced in February that the Crowsnest Pass rail freight rate, a special discount to western farmers, would be eliminated as part of a plan to raise funds to rehabilitate the western railroads. The federal government and the railroads pointed out that deteriorating conditions on the western lines impeded transportation, costing Canada millions of dollars in grain sales each year. Reaction to the proposal was stormy.

The "Holy Crow" was a vestige of the days when the Canadian Pacific Railway was being built through the rugged Crowsnest Pass in the Rockies. The special rate, for shipments of certain western grains, such as wheat, was part of the bargain struck by the federal government when it granted the land for the right-of-way to the rail line. As a result, farmers in recent years had to pay only about one-fifth of the actual transport costs to ship their grain. The government's proposal, which initially raised the rate from one half-cent to 2.53 cents per ton mile, was vigorously debated in the House of Commons; it finally won passage in November by a vote of 141–114.

Criminal justice. A bill amending the criminal code to redefine the law on sexual assault (rape) came into force early this year. The new law allows any married person to charge a spouse with sexual assault; it provides equal protection for men and women. The new law defines three degrees of gravity, carrying sentences ranging to a maximum of life imprisonment.

Energy. The federal government in 1983 continued to lock horns with the provinces over energy policies. In the east, Newfoundland lost its legal struggle for control of its offshore oil when the Supreme Court ruled against the province in February.

The Exchange on the move

Top hat and tails was the attire as members of the Toronto Stock Exchange moved to a new $25 million trading floor with the latest in electronic aids. The exchange hoped that high-tech trading facilities would keep it competitive with other markets.

As world oil prices fell, the federal government modified its 1981 energy agreement with Alberta, which was designed to keep the price of "old" Canadian oil (found before 1981) at no more than 75 percent of the world price. Under the new formula, which took effect July 1, oil found before 1974 is pegged at 79.3 percent of the world price, while "new" oil (found since 1974) is at full world price.

1981 census. Some highlights of the 1981 census were made public this spring. Average family income (all income figures in constant 1980 dollars) rose 28.5 percent between 1970 and 1980, to $26,748 per year. The rise was due partly to the increase in the number of people working per famiy. The average income of individual Canadians aged 15 years and over was $12,993, an increase of 18.6 percent. The number of Canadians able to speak both French and English rose 27 percent.

Academy awards. Canadians brought home three Oscars from the 55th annual Academy Awards presentation in Los Angeles in April. A controversial antinuclear film, *If You Love This Planet,* carried off the award for best documentary short subject. A Canadian Broadcast-

ing Corporation production, *Just Another Missing Kid,* won as the best documentary feature. *Quest for Fire* won for best makeup.

Royal visit. Royalty watchers in the Atlantic provinces, along with those in Ottawa and Edmonton, were excited at the opportunity to catch their first glimpse of Diana, Princess of Wales, as she joined Prince Charles on an 18-day tour of Canada. The June visit was Diana's first trip to Canada.

See STATISTICS OF THE WORLD. G.W.

CAPE VERDE. *See* STATISTICS OF THE WORLD.

CARIBBEAN COUNTRIES. The year 1983 was marked by increasing U.S. efforts to contain revolutionary movements in the Caribbean Basin, which, in the view of the Reagan administration, were instigated by the Soviet Union and Cuba. American involvement in the region reached a climax with the U.S.-led invasion of Grenada in October.

Grenada. On October 14, Grenada's Prime Minister Maurice Bishop was deposed in a power struggle within the ruling Marxist party. Bishop and others were killed a few days later. The Organization of Eastern Caribbean Nations, which includes Dominica, St. Vincent and the

Grenadines, Antigua and Barbuda, St. Lucia, and the newly independent Federation of St. Christopher and Nevis (St. Kitts–Nevis), requested and joined in an invasion of the island on October 25. Jamaica and Barbados also supported the invasion, and it was Jamaica that actually provided the largest share of the 300 Caribbean troops, which joined thousands of U.S. troops in the operation. The governor general, Sir Paul Scoon, had reportedly approved an invasion. The Caribbean Community (Caricom), a regional economic organization, at a special meeting on October 22–23, limited itself to supporting sanctions against Grenada. After the operation, rifts developed, as the Bahamas, Belize, Guyana, and Trinidad and Tobago were sharply critical of the action. (*See also* GRENADA.)

Regional economy. The centerpiece of U.S. policy in the region was the Caribbean Basin Initiative (CBI), which was approved by Congress in two segments. The initial legislation, in 1982, approved $350 million in emergency aid to the region, while legislation passed in July allowed a variety of Caribbean goods to be imported into the United States duty-free. Some Caribbean leaders strongly supported the program; others regarded the CBI as "too little, too late."

Caribbean countries experienced severe trade imbalances in 1983, with tourism, export commodity prices, and manufacturing all generally depressed in comparison with the late 1970's. Tourism was stagnating in much of the region as a result of the world recession, increased transportation costs, and overvalued local currencies, which were in many cases pegged to the U.S. dollar.

But it was commodity prices that declined the most. The "Spice Island," Grenada, suffered economic setbacks from the downturn in nutmeg prices. Sugar prices dropped sharply in the region, and sugar production in Caricom had fallen to a 30-year low in 1982. Declines in coffee prices and banana production also inflicted severe financial stress.

Dominican Republic. President Salvador Jorge Blanco's first full year in office was tarnished by the country's worst economic crisis in two decades. Exports and tax revenues were down. Jorge Blanco did succeed in stretching out payments on the Dominican Republic's $2 billion foreign debt over three years (1983–1985) and in securing $455 million in loans from the International Monetary Fund for that period. The prolonged austerity program to which the government committed itself in exchange, however, raised unemployment above 30 percent and caused hardship among workers and discontent among businessmen.

Jamaica. Jamaica's Prime Minister Edward Seaga began his fourth year in office in October amid increasing signs that his conservative policies were failing to have any great effect on the economy. Unemployment was high, and the trade deficit was increasing. In November the government devalued the dollar and increased some prices as part of an austerity program, adopted to win support from the International Monetary Fund for standby credits. In the swell of popularity arising from the successful invasion of Grenada, Seaga called for elections on December 15, two years ahead of schedule. Michael Manley, leader of the opposition People's National Party, declared a boycott of the elections, claiming that electoral reforms were needed. Seaga's Jamaica Labor Party captured six contested seats and won the remainder without opposition. Jamaica was thus left with a one-party Parliament.

Haiti. The year began with an abortive attempt on January 1 to assassinate President Jean-Claude ("Baby Doc") Duvalier. The Hector Riobé Brigade, named after a victim of the Haitian police, planted a bomb outside the presidential palace in Port-au-Prince, but Duvalier was away from the city when the explosion occurred. Led by the charismatic Jean-Claude Luis-Jean, the small Miami-based brigade had been carrying out a series of daring commando actions against the government since its founding in March 1982.

The Haitian government stepped up arms purchases and called for municipal elections, the nation's first in 26 years; the arrest of prominent opponents before the May balloting, however, called into question the Duvalier dictatorship's commitment to restoring democracy. Still, in Cap-Haïtien, the country's second largest city, the government-backed candidate lost to Wilson Borjella, a local hotel owner who promised to combat corruption.

The economy continued to decline in 1983. A drought in central and southern Haiti devastated the sugar crop and reduced the citrus, coffee, rice, and bean harvests as well. An epidemic of African swine fever necessitated the slaughter of the nation's entire population of pigs, the peasants' primary source of wealth and the country's major source of animal protein. The global recession hit hard at Haiti's 250 foreign-owned, export-oriented assembly plants and at its important tourist trade, which did only half the business it had done in 1979.

Suriname. In 1983, Suriname felt the aftereffects of the December 1982 liquidation of 15 prominent dissidents. The country's existing cabinet resigned and was replaced in February with a new 12-member cabinet, headed by sociologist Errol Alibux. The killings also caused the Netherlands and the United States to suspend aid; Brazil stepped in to provide a $300 million aid package in return for shipments of rice and alumina.

In late October the government expelled Cuba's ambassador and more than 100 other Cubans. President Desi Bouterse suggested that Cuba was involved in Bishop's mid-October overthrow in Grenada. In December, there was renewed labor unrest, posing a challenge to the Bouterse regime.

St. Kitts–Nevis. Following 360 years of colonial status, the two-island state of St. Kitts–Nevis received independence from Britain on September 19, as the Federation of St. Christopher and Nevis. Kennedy Simmonds, who was elected premier in 1980 on the People's Action Movement ticket, became prime minister.

See STATISTICS OF THE WORLD. *See also* CUBA; PUERTO RICO.   P.W. & W.M.W.

CENTRAL AFRICAN REPUBLIC. *See* STATISTICS OF THE WORLD.

CEYLON. *See* SRI LANKA.

CHAD. Fighting resumed in June 1983 between the forces of Chad's President Hissène Habré and those of former President Goukouni Oueddei. In mid-June, an estimated 2,500 to 3,000 rebels, led by Goukouni, seized the important north-central crossroads town of Faya-Largeau. By July 8, Goukouni's forces had also taken the oasis town of Oum Chalouba; and, continuing southward, they captured Abéché in east-central Chad. These initial rebel victories could

not have occurred without considerable support from Libya, whose leader, Muammar al-Qaddafi, still recognized Goukouni as the only legitimate leader of Chad.

Bolstered by the arrival of an estimated 2,000 Zairean troops to help guard N'Djamena, Habré's army began a counteroffensive on July 10 that routed the rebels from Oum Chalouba, Abéché, and Faya-Largeau. At this point, however, Libyan planes pounded Faya-Largeau for over a week, and on August 10, Goukouni's forces, now heavily reinforced by Libyan armored and artillery units, retook the town.

In early August, President Ronald Reagan dispatched three U.S. military advisers to Chad and ordered two Awacs surveillance planes, eight F-15 fighter craft, and ground support forces to bases in the Sudan. France initially refused to commit its ground forces to provide sorely needed air defenses. During the third week of August, however, more than 2,000 French troops poured into Chad and took up positions along an east-west line across the country, effectively conceding the northern half of Chad to Goukouni and his Libyan allies. With French forces committed, the United States was able to withdraw its Awacs and advisers. Fighting broke out again around Oum Chalouba early in September, but the government retained control of the town—its only major outpost north of the French defense line. Peace talks under the auspices of the Organization of African Unity were scheduled for January 1984.

Habré appeared to enjoy the support of a majority of African governments. One indication was the June meeting of the OAU, held in Addis Ababa, Ethiopia, with no representation for Goukouni's side. Libya had originally been slated to host the summit, in November 1982, with Goukouni seated as Chad's representative, but a number of OAU members boycotted that meeting as a result, making it impossible for a quorum to convene.

See STATISTICS OF THE WORLD.   G.L.

CHEMISTRY. During 1983 there were controversies over dioxin, acid rain, the contraceptive drug Depo-Provera, and the use of paraquat to spray marijuana plots on federal land.

Chemicals and the environment. In February, the EPA announced a plan for the federal and

A Drug Enforcement Agency helicopter flies over Cleveland, Ga., on its way to spray marijuana plots with paraquat, a potentially lethal chemical. Charging that paraquat spraying could contaminate nearby crops and livestock, opponents challenged the spraying program in the courts, leading the federal agency to suspend the program pending further research.

state governments to purchase the town of Times Beach, Mo. Government investigators had found high dioxin concentrations in the soil throughout the town, and it was feared that the chemical, among the most toxic known, had been stirred up by the devastating floods that inundated Times Beach in late 1982. The residents were asked to evacuate the town, and by June 1983 only a handful remained.

A direct link between sulfur dioxide emitted from industrial smokestacks and automobile exhausts and the acid rain that is damaging the environment in the northeastern United States and southeastern Canada was asserted in a report issued in June by the U.S. National Academy of Sciences. Contending that 90–95 percent of acid rain comes from artificial sources, the report concluded that a reduction in sulfur emissions would produce a proportionate decrease in acid rain. Two months after the report was published, the United States and Canada signed an agreement to monitor the flow of pollution from industrial sites in Ohio and Ontario.

See also ENVIRONMENT.

Contraceptives. One of the most controversial birth control products has been depot-medroxy-progesterone acetate, produced by the Upjohn Company as Depo-Provera. The drug, one injection of which can provide contraception for at least three months, was banned in the United States by the Food and Drug Administration in 1978 after studies linked it to cancers in dogs and monkeys. In the June 1983 issue of the *Journal of the American Medical Association,* two groups of scientists argued that the drug was probably safe and should be approved as studies of its possible side effects continued. Other scientists disagreed. The FDA scheduled a public board of inquiry to review its 1978 decision.

Also under development were rubber-like implants that release small amounts of progestins (synthetic female hormones) daily into the bloodstream, disrupting the menstrual cycle. The Population Council, a nonprofit organization active in contraceptive research, has developed two versions (one of which has received FDA approval for U.S. tests) that release different dosages of a certain progestin.

And Still Counting

Scientists are constantly synthesizing new chemicals, mostly for research purposes, and keeping track of them is no easy task. The American Chemical Society's Chemical Abstract Service, which has been identifying and registering chemical compounds since 1965, this February logged its 6 millionth entry: 2-cyclohexyl-3-methyl-4-(pentyl-amino)-2-cyclopentene-1-one. And the list continues to grow, as the registry identifies 6,000 more chemicals every day.

The implants can prevent pregnancies for at least five years, but they cause some menstrual irregularities.

Paraquat. The spraying of the herbicide paraquat on marijuana plants in Central and South America may present substantial health risks to people who later smoke the drug, according to the U.S. Centers for Disease Control. In July, CDC scientists contradicted State Department officials who had stated that there is no risk. The evidence, the CDC specialists argued, indicates that frequent exposure to paraquat could lead to scarring of the lung. They also said that dipyridyl, a paraquat residue, causes bleeding of the lungs in test animals.

The U.S. Drug Enforcement Administration began spraying paraquat in August on marijuana plots found on federal lands in the United States. As part of a Reagan administration antidrug campaign, the DEA said it had plans to spray in as many as 40 states. In September a federal district judge temporarily blocked the DEA from spraying paraquat because the agency had failed to obtain an environmental impact study, as required by law. The DEA subsequently agreed to halt further use of paraquat until such an impact study could be filed.

Rodenticides. Two new chemicals found to be highly effective in controlling rat populations were approved for use in 1983. One of them, alpha-chlorhydrin, was discovered by an Upjohn Company chemist to cause massive lesions in the male rat's reproductive tract, producing, in effect, a chemical vasectomy. The chemical's action is rat-specific, so that it will not harm children or pets. The second

chemical, discovered by chemists at Lilly Research Laboratories, is an odorless poison called bromethalin. It inhibits transmission of nerve impulses, producing paralysis and death. A third new compound of potential use as a rodenticide is 1-alpha-hydroxyvitamin D_3, often called simply 1-alpha. Investigators at the University of Wisconsin found that it causes calcium to be removed from rats' bones and deposited in the heart, liver, kidneys, and other soft tissues.

Combating viruses. Successful treatment of both type A (the most common) and type B influenza has been obtained with ribavirin, a new drug marketed as Virazole in several countries other than the United States. A team at Baylor College of Medicine reported that ribavirin sharply reduces both the duration of fever and the communicability of influenza. The drug was also found to alleviate the discomfort of common colds.

Another antiviral agent, ara-A (marketed as Vira-A by Parke-Davis), is used as an ointment to treat herpes infections of the eye. Ara-A has also recently been shown to speed healing and prevent complications of herpes zoster, or shingles, in some patients.

Einsteinium. The chemical and physical properties of the element einsteinium were measured for the first time by John Ward and his colleagues at Los Alamos National Laboratory. They found that the element is divalent, meaning that it can combine chemically with two atoms of another element, and that it evaporates more readily than barium or calcium, the most readily vaporizable divalent elements previously known.   T.H.M.

CHILE. President Augusto Pinochet Ugarte celebrated the tenth anniversary of his seizure of power on September 11, 1983, amid a rising chorus of demands for his resignation and a restoration of democratic government.

In May, opponents of the Pinochet regime had launched the first of a series of demonstrations calling for democratic elections. The protests were scheduled for around the 11th day of each month, to mark the overthrow of the elected government of President Salvador Allende Gossens by Pinochet and his military associates on September 11, 1973. Residents of shantytowns and well-to-do neighborhoods alike showed their support of the protesters by banging on pots and pans in a traditional Chilean show of disapproval. By mid-October, the so-called National Days of Protest had claimed over 60 lives in violent confrontations between protesters and police and army units. A particularly large demonstration occurred on October 11, when 40,000 gathered peacefully in Santiago under the leadership of the Socialist and Communist parties. Violent demonstrations followed.

Rumors of the president's impending resignation or assassination and of coup attempts were widespread. Speculation about a possible successor to Pinochet centered first on General Santiago Sinclair Oyender, the president's chief of staff, and later on conservative National Party leader Sergio Onofre Jarpa Reyes, who was named interior minister in August. The appointment of Jarpa to the interior ministry (to a cabinet with a majority of civilians) was seen by many as a sign of a coming transition to civilian rule. Jarpa began by cutting back on curfews, press curbs, and other emergency measures, but then reversed field in the face of continuing demonstrations.

In an apparent goodwill gesture, the government announced in June that several exiled political leaders would be allowed to return to Chile. They were the first prominent figures given permission to return since a limited amnesty was declared in December 1982. By midyear, the shape and size of the opposition was becoming clearer. A Democratic Alliance of five mainstream parties was formed early in August, as pressures for elections grew.

The government's political problems were aggravated by its inability to arrest Chile's economic decline. Foreign debt was near $18 billion late in the year, the highest in the world on a per capita basis. Unemployment was around 25 percent, and inflation was running at an annual rate of about 40 percent. An agreement was reached with the International Monetary Fund and international banks on credits and loans, but the economy continued

Students clash with police at the University of Santiago in Chile's capital during June. With high unemployment and inflation, Chile was convulsed by a series of violent protests against the ten-year-old military regime of General Augusto Pinochet.

to stagger, and more economists were calling for protectionism and greater government intervention in the economy.

See STATISTICS OF THE WORLD.   F.M.N.

CHINA, PEOPLE'S REPUBLIC OF. The aging Communist Party bureaucracy remained firmly in the saddle in 1983. In an effort to renew itself, the party retired many elderly officials, but few members of the top leadership stepped down. The economy was a prime concern. Relations with the United States, despite some agreements, were clouded by disputes over trade and Taiwan.

Politics and government. In March, Peking announced the formal retirement of the aged

A Tibetan woman is shown here paying homage to the Buddha in Jokang Monastery in Lhasa. The Chinese authorities have adopted a more tolerant attitude toward religions in border areas such as Tibet, hoping thereby to gain the support of local minorities for economic development projects.

ex-soldier Ye Jianying as chairman of the National People's Congress Standing Committee and titular head of state. His departure appeared to indicate a weakening of Maoist influence. It was paralleled lower down by the compulsory retirement of more than 2 million elderly party and state officials at both the national and local level.

The Sixth National People's Congress was held from June 6 to June 21. The major speech, delivered by Premier Zhao Ziyang, stressed the economy. The main innovation he announced, however, was the establishment of a ministry of state security, whose chief mission was stated to be counterespionage. The office of president was bestowed by the Congress on Li Xiannian, a senior official with a background in economic affairs and foreign relations. Deng Xiaoping, China's acknowledged strong man and key member of the Communist Party's Politburo, was named to lead the Central Military Commission.

Economy. To encourage economic development, official permission was given for state-owned economic enterprises to use a portion of their profits as they saw fit. However, Premier Zhao Ziyang declared that decentralization of economic authority from the national to the provincial level and to individual enterprises had led to overinvestment in heavy industry at the expense of light industry. As part of a campaign to shift the emphasis back to light industry, the government imposed higher taxes on the profits of most state enterprises.

In April, the State Statistical Bureau released figures on economic performance in 1982. For the first time, gross national product (GNP) was given: $524.3 billion, a surprisingly high figure. Grain output for 1982 was given as 353.4 million metric tons (a record), and the value of industrial output as $291.3 billion. The plan for 1983 called for a 4 percent growth rate for both industry and agriculture and for an increase in the output of consumer durables. In May, the Communist Party Central Committee decided to try to develop the island of Hainan as a competitor with Taiwan, and Shanghai as a rival to Hong Kong.

Agriculture has been doing better than other sectors largely because of partial decollectivization. Under the so-called production re-

Chinese leader Deng Xiaoping rides horseback with his granddaughter during a rural inspection tour.

sponsibility system, a household may contract with the local authorities to produce an agreed amount of some officially favored crop or crops, usually grain; the household may then sell anything it can raise over and above its quota on the open market and may keep the proceeds. Serious summer floods along the Yangtze River, however, served as a reminder that not all of China's agricultural problems can be solved through liberalizing policy changes.

Peking has been enlarging the scope and financial rewards for individual economic activity in the urban sector as well; it has also been doing something to make official prices approximate actual costs of production. In January, for example, the prices of cotton textiles were raised by 20 percent, whereas those of synthetic fabrics and some other consumer goods such as watches and television sets were lowered. Certain types of private individual and cooperative enterprises (in trucking, for example) were being allowed to coexist with comparable state enterprises. Private retail trading was flourishing as never before under Communist rule.

Foreign trade and investment. Chinese leaders reaffirmed their determination to keep China's economy open to the outside world. In 1982, total exports accounted for $22.15 billion and imports for $19.15 billion, leaving a favorable balance of $3 billion. According to official predictions, China's foreign trade situation in 1983 was to be markedly different as a result of a planned 40 percent increase in imports, while exports were expected to hold nearly level.

By mid-1983, China had attracted a total of $5.8 billion in foreign investment over the preceding four years. One of the biggest projects being built with foreign (in this case, Japanese) credits and technology was the Baoshan steel complex, located on muddy ground near Shanghai and without ready access to supplies of domestic iron ore. Work was resumed in 1983 on the second stage of this ambitious project, whose furnaces Peking hoped to feed at least partly with iron ore to be coproduced in Australia. In other innovations, offices of foreign banks operating in China were permitted to make loans to Chinese enterprises. For the first time also, Chinese firms were allowed to invest abroad, including in the United States, and not merely in Hong Kong as before. In an effort to attract greater foreign investment, China in September issued new economic regulations giving more preferential treatment to joint ventures.

Occidental Petroleum scored something of a coup by signing a contract in March to develop a coal mine, said to be potentially the world's largest, in the North China province of Shanxi. At midyear, Peking began to sign a new round of contracts with foreign oil companies for exploratory drilling in the South China Sea.

Although U.S.-Chinese trade was inevitably affected by the political disagreements between the parties, it continued at a respectable level. For 1982, trade in both directions came to $5.2 billion, down from $5.5 billion in 1981. Eager to improve its trade balance, Peking wanted to increase its sales of textiles, especially cotton textiles, in the U.S. market. Chinese negotiators demanded preferential treatment in the matter of U.S. import quotas, but the U.S. side offered equal treatment only and in the absence of agreement imposed its proposed quotas unilaterally in January. In retaliation, Peking promptly suspended purchases of U.S. grain, cotton, soybeans, and synthetic fibers. In July, however, a compromise was reached permitting an increase of around 3 percent each year, over the five-year life of the pact, in Chinese textile exports to the United States.

In late May, during a visit to China, Secretary of Commerce Malcolm Baldrige pledged to ease U.S. restrictions on the transfer to China of high technology with possible military application. A month later, Baldrige succeeded in getting White House permission to announce a favorable change in China's trade status to that of a friendly country, thus allowing U.S. manufacturers to export any civilian high-technology equipment to China unless the government specifically objects to certain items.

Foreign affairs. Chinese foreign policy was marked by a continuing aloofness toward the United States and a limited improvement in relations with the Soviet Union.

In February, Secretary of State George Shultz visited China. His talks with the Chinese were described as full and frank, but he brought no new concessions, and Peking's public comments on his visit were rather unenthusiastic. On April 4, the Reagan administration enraged Peking by granting political asylum to a Chinese tennis player, Hu Na, who had defected while in the United States. In retaliation, Peking canceled a number of scheduled cultural and athletic exchanges with the United States.

The most contentious single issue in U.S.-Chinese relations remained the continuation of U.S. arms transfers to Taiwan. The fact that the United States was transferring obsolescent weapons to Taiwan did not appease Peking, which objected to all such transfers on principle. By July, Washington was preparing to sell Taiwan a $530 million arms package.

On the other hand, there were some elements of improvement in relations between the two countries. A delegation of Chinese nuclear technicians visited the United States in July, marking a step forward in U.S.-Chinese cooperation in the nuclear field. In September, Secretary of Defense Caspar Weinberger made a trip to China, during which it was announced that Premier Zhao Ziyang and President Ronald Reagan would exchange official visits in 1984.

China's relations with the Soviet Union were seemingly on a slow upward curve. A second round in the ongoing series of Sino-Soviet talks at the vice foreign minister level was held in Moscow in March (the first round had taken place in 1982). The Soviet side reportedly agreed in principle to seek a reduction of tensions between Chinese and Soviet forces along their common border but refused to discuss the Soviet presence in Mongolia, Vietnam, or Afghanistan. The main positive development was an increase of trade. A third round of talks ended in October, with no agreement reported.

China and Great Britain continued to hold talks over the future status of the British colony of Hong Kong. On November 9, Peking affirmed that it would announce its plans for Hong Kong unilaterally, no later than September 1984, if it failed to reach agreement with Great Britain on transition of the colony to Chinese sovereignty after Britain's lease over most of the colony expires in 1997.

Relations with Japan were somewhat cool, because of mixed feelings toward Japan's "hawkish" and seemingly pro-American Premier Yasuhiro Nakasone. Relations toward other neighbors in Asia showed little change. In mid-January, Premier Zhao Ziyang concluded a tour of 11 African countries, in keeping with Peking's emphasis on its Third World status.

See STATISTICS OF THE WORLD.　　H.C.H.

CHINA, REPUBLIC OF. See TAIWAN.

"We Still Have a Dream" was the slogan for the 1983 March on Washington organized by civil rights leaders to commemorate the 1963 demonstration led by the Reverend Martin Luther King, Jr. Heading this year's march were Jesse Jackson (on right), president of Operation PUSH, the Chicago-based civil rights organization, and Coretta Scott King (center), King's widow.

CIVIL LIBERTIES AND CIVIL RIGHTS. The Reagan administration continued to attract opposition from civil libertarians in 1983 for its conservative positions on such issues as federal enforcement of civil rights laws, women's rights, and church-state relations. In what some said was a political response to such criticism, the administration in July filed its first desegregation suit, against state colleges and universities in Alabama.

Civil Rights Commission. A compromise worked out in November ended a long-drawn-out battle between Congress and the White House over the makeup of the Civil Rights Commission, which monitors the enforcement of federal civil rights policies. President Ronald Reagan had attempted to replace some CRC members with appointees sympathetic to his own policies, while the Senate fought back by refusing to confirm new appointees. Compromise legislation signed by Reagan in November provided that the CRC be expanded from six to eight members, that Congress and the president be allowed to appoint four members apiece, and that the CRC be removed from the executive branch and set up as an independent body. In December, however, some members of Congress and civil rights leaders charged Reagan with violating an informal agreement by refusing to reappoint two Republican commissioners who had supported civil rights initiatives opposed by the White House.

Equal education. In a major decision May 24, the Supreme Court upheld the authority of the Internal Revenue Service to withhold tax-exempt status from racially discriminatory private schools and colleges. The decision in *Bob Jones University* v. *United States* and *Goldsboro Christian Schools* v. *United States* involved two institutions that based their racial policies on religious belief; Goldsboro Christian Schools, in Goldsboro, N.C., denied admission to blacks, and Bob Jones University, in Greenville, S.C., restricted black enrollment and prohibited interracial dating and marriage among its students. The Reagan administration had

113

argued that the IRS had no legal authority to deny exemptions on such grounds, and, along with the institutions in question, had sought a ruling by the Supreme Court. The Court held that racial discrimination is contrary to public policy, that the IRS does have authority to deny tax exemptions on that basis, and that the national interest in ending racial discrimination substantially outweighs any limitation placed on religious belief in such cases.

Civil rights march. Commemorating the 1963 March on Washington led by Martin Luther King, Jr., 300,000 people gathered in Washington, D.C., on August 27 to call for a renewed national commitment to civil rights and social change. (Later in the year, Congress enacted legislation creating a federal holiday to honor the slain civil rights leader.) Unlike the 1963 march, which was dominated by black civil rights organizations, the 1983 march included labor, peace, environmental, feminist, and other social action groups.

Women's rights. Two Supreme Court decisions gave strong support to "economic equity." In *Arizona Governing Committee for Tax Deferred Annuity and Deferred Compensation Plans* v. *Norris,* the Court held that an employer-sponsored retirement plan may not provide smaller monthly benefits to women than to men. The Court held that the fact that women as a group live longer than men as a group does not justify different benefits, because workers must be treated as individuals. In a similar decision, the Court held, in *Newport News Shipbuilding and Dry Dock Co.* v. *Equal Employment Opportunity Commission,* that a company health insurance plan may not, under the Pregnancy Discrimination Act of 1978, provide less generous pregnancy coverage for wives of male employees than for female employees, because such a plan illegally discriminates against the male.

Abortion. On June 15, the Supreme Court, in *Akron* v. *Akron Center for Reproductive Health,* struck down an ordinance considered by many antiabortion groups a model for abortion regulation. The Court ruled that the city of Akron could not require that all abortions after three months of pregnancy be performed in a hospital; that physicians obtain parental consent for an abortion on a minor under 15 years old;

that physicians recite to women seeking abortions information about fetal development, possible complications, and alternatives to abortion; that the attending physician inform the patient of risks associated with abortion; that a 24-hour waiting period take place after a consent form for abortion is signed; and that fetal remains be given a "humane" disposal. However, in *Planned Parenthood* v. *Ashcroft,* the Court did uphold a Missouri law requiring that "unemancipated" or "immature" minors obtain parental or judicial consent for an abortion and that a second physician be present at abortions late in pregnancy.

On June 28, just two weeks after the *Akron* decision, the Senate defeated a constitutional amendment proposal that stated, "A right to abortion is not secured by this Constitution." The proposition fell short of obtaining a simple majority, in a major setback for antiabortion forces.

GM settlement. In what was described as the largest out-of-court settlement of an employment discrimination case, the General Motors Corporation agreed in October to pay $42.5 million to settle a ten-year-old complaint charging discrimination against blacks, Hispanics, and women. The agreement established numerical goals for the hiring, training, and promoting of minority-group members and women. It also provided $15 million for scholarships and other educational aid for General Motors employees and members of their families. The company, which did not admit practicing discrimination, agreed to provide $4 million in back pay and other relief to individuals who had filed complaints.

Church-state issues. In a 5–4 decision in *Mueller* v. *Allen,* the Supreme Court upheld a Minnesota law providing an income tax deduction of up to $700 for the cost of tuition, textbooks, and transportation for children in elementary and secondary schools, whether public or private. The Court majority found the law constitutional because the funds were available as a result of choice by individual parents and because the law met the three principles of constitutionality set in earlier cases—it had a secular purpose, it did not have the primary effect of advancing religion, and it did not entangle the state in religious affairs. The Court ruling heartened supporters of a federal tuition tax credit program, but a bill setting up such a program was voted down in the Senate on November 16.

An Alabama law permitting public school teachers to lead "willing" students in prayer was upheld by a federal district judge in January but was struck down in May by the federal appeals court in Atlanta. In October, a federal district judge struck down a New Jersey law requiring a minute of silence for "contemplation or introspection" in public schools.

National security. Attorney General William French Smith announced new guidelines March 7 for FBI investigations of groups advocating violence to achieve social or political change. The rules ease restrictions on infiltration, the use of informants, and the gathering of information. On March 11, President Reagan ordered that all government employees with access to classified information be required to sign pledges not to reveal any such information without permission.

Criminal law. In a case expected to be a test of the controversial "exclusionary rule," which bars the use in criminal trials of evidence obtained illegally by police, the Supreme Court sidestepped the issue; it merely ruled, in *Illinois* v. *Gates,* that police may use anonymous tips to obtain search warrants under somewhat less restrictive standards than previously imposed. In *Michigan* v. *Long* the Court held that police may conduct a "protective search" of the interior of a car they have stopped if the search is limited to areas where a suspect might seize a weapon.

For the first time, the Supreme Court ruled that the duration of a prison sentence must bear some relationship to the nature of the offense. In *Solem* v. *Helm,* the Court held that a life sentence without parole was cruel and unusual punishment in the case of a multiple offender who had never committed a violent crime and whose last offense was passing a bad check. In *Jones* v. *United States,* the Court ruled that a person found not guilty of a crime by reason of insanity may be confined in a mental institution for longer than he or she could be imprisoned if found guilty.

See also NEGROES IN THE UNITED STATES; WOMEN.   M.Gr.

COINS AND COIN COLLECTING

COINS AND COIN COLLECTING. In 1983, as the United States prepared to host the 1984 Summer Olympics, coin collectors helped underwrite the cost of the games. The United States Mint had been authorized by law to strike three special coins commemorating the XXIII Olympiad, scheduled for Los Angeles in July and August of 1984. The Olympic coin set includes one silver dollar dated 1983, a second dated 1984, and a $10 gold piece dated 1984. The law provided that surcharges of no less than $10 for each silver dollar and $50 for each gold coin be used to promote the Olympics. By mid-1983 more than 840,000 Olympic coins had been sold, with gross sales in excess of $62 million. The Los Angeles Olympic Organizing Committee and the United States Olympic Committee shared equally in surcharges amounting to $14.5 million.

The $10 gold piece, the first gold coin produced by the U.S. Mint in over 50 years, has a design featuring a male and a female runner. The 1983 silver dollar features a discus

Donna DeVarona, 1964 Olympic gold medalist, shows both sides of the 1984 Olympic gold coin. The first U.S. Olympic gold coin depicts a male and female runner on one side and an eagle on the other.

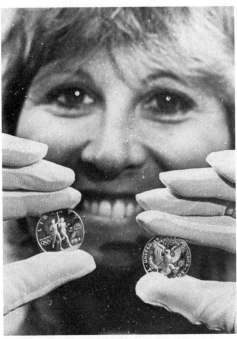

thrower, and the 1984 dollar shows the entrance to the Los Angeles Coliseum, where most of the 1984 Olympic competitions are scheduled. Both silver dollars are of the same fineness and weight as pre-1935 silver dollars.

The year 1983 marked the first full year of production of noncopper cents. Prior to 1982 the metallic content of all cents was a 95 percent copper–5 percent zinc alloy. In 1982, some cents were made of an alloy that is 97.5 percent zinc with a little copper and plated with a very thin layer of copper. When the public did not object to the change, a complete switchover was made for cents dated 1983.

The U.S. Treasury continued to issue 1-ounce and ½-ounce gold medallions to compete with the South African Krugerrand. The bullion coins were made more competitive in early 1983 when notification of the weight and fineness was included on the design and reeded edges were placed on the coins. The mint awarded a contract to J. Aron and Company to market the pieces under the American Arts Gold Medallion Act. The 1983 designs, released in August, featured poet Robert Frost on the 1-ounce and sculptor Alexander Calder on the ½-ounce medal.

While 1982 collector-item prices reflected the sluggish economy and showed a sharp drop in speculative values of silver dollars and gold pieces, prices realized in 1983 indicated an increasing interest in the hobby of coin collecting. This resurgence was marked by the record price paid for a 1927-D Saint-Gaudens double eagle. This U.S. gold coin, one of only ten or 12 known to exist, was sold for $290,000 in mid-1983; it had been purchased for $160,000 the previous October. Major auctions around the country brought generally higher prices, particularly for coins in finest condition.

Outside the United States, the National Bank of Poland, in an unprecedented move for a Communist country, issued five legal-tender coins in commemoration of the visit of Pope John Paul II to his native land in June. The three gold coins of the set (the other two are silver) show the pope holding up a crucifix—a remarkable image for the money of an officially atheistic state. An explanation for the coinage could be inferred from the fact that the bank hired an international firm to market

the coins for several times their face value, thus helping to alleviate Poland's severe foreign exchange shortage. E.C.R.

COLOMBIA. Colombia's President Belisario Betancur retained much of his personal popularity in 1983, but guerrilla violence continued, despite the conciliatory efforts of the Betancur government. That government had pushed a partial amnesty bill through Congress in November 1982. On March 7, 1983, American oil executive Kenneth S. Bishop was abducted by guerrillas, in the 83rd such crime since the beginning of the year. He was released five weeks later, after his family paid a ransom of several hundred thousand dollars to the leftist People's Revolutionary Organization. In mid-April the M-19 guerrilla group claimed responsibility for a bombing at the Honduran embassy in Bogotà and announced plans for intensified antigovernment activity; that group had previously declared a cease-fire. In late November, leftist guerrillas kipnapped the president's brother; 15 days later, he was freed unharmed, after pleas from world leaders.

Early in the year, the chief prosecutor's office submitted to Betancur an unpublished special report on a right-wing death squad, Death to Kidnappers (MAS); the report allegedly linked 60 military officers to the MAS, which it held responsible for the deaths of 300 peasants and guerrillas since its formation in 1981.

The Betancur government expected the gross domestic product to increase by 3 percent in 1983, although it was estimated that coffee export earnings would be only $1.5 billion, down slightly from 1982. Illegal earnings from Colombian cocaine sales in the United States were estimated to run into tens of billions of dollars annually, but the portion of the total being returned to the Colombian economy reportedly declined. A balance-of-payments deficit of more than $1 billion was forecast, up from the previous year. In an effort to protect domestic production, especially from cheaper goods made in Ecuador and Venezuela, the government sharply limited foreign exchange transactions, placed licensing controls on most imported products, and sharply curtailed imports of luxury products.

In January, Betancur's foreign minister, Rodrigo Lloreda Caicedo, met with the foreign ministers of Mexico, Panama, and Venezuela on the island of Contadora in Panama; there they drafted a proposal aimed at bringing about a negotiated settlement of current conflicts in Central America. Betancur personally pressed the Contadora proposals on government leaders in Nicaragua, Honduras, El Salvador, and Guatemala in July. Meanwhile, reaffirming its move toward nonalignment, Colombia attended, for the first time, a conference of the so-called nonaligned countries, held in New Delhi in March.

See STATISTICS OF THE WORLD.   L.L.P.

COLORADO. See STATISTICS OF THE WORLD.

COMMONWEALTH OF NATIONS. In 1983 the heads of government of the Commonwealth of Nations gathered in New Delhi and Goa, India, for their biennial meeting. A major preoccupation of the conference, which lasted from November 23 to November 29, was concern over tensions between the United States and the Soviet Union and over the failure to achieve progress in arms limitation negotiations.

Indian Prime Minister Indira Gandhi, who opened the conference, warned that "disaster looms on the horizon" because of this failure. Canada's prime minister, Pierre Elliott Trudeau, received support for his ongoing efforts to visit political leaders in major capitals and promote a lessening of tensions through political dialogue.

The conference was split over reaction to the U.S.-led invasion of Grenada on October 25. Several Caribbean members had themselves requested and joined in the invasion; other members, including Guyana and several African countries, strongly condemned it. The final conference document, while stating opposition to any infringement on a country's territorial integrity, did not condemn the United States, stressing instead a need for "reconstruction, not recrimination" in relation to Grenada. The leaders offered to support a peacekeeping force to be drawn from Commonwealth Caribbean countries.

The conference did criticize the United States for its policy with respect to South West Africa (Namibia). In particular, the final conference document condemned the U.S. view that any settlement leading to independence for South West Africa (Namibia) should be linked to the withdrawal of Cuban troops from neighboring Angola.

Another issue facing the Commonwealth was the situation in Cyprus, where on November 15 the Turkish Cypriot sector had declared itself an independent republic. The conference participants condemned the declaration and created a five-member action group to help promote renewed talks between the island's Turkish and Greek Cypriot communities.

On economic matters, Commonwealth leaders agreed to create a ten-member consultative group, drawn from both developed and developing nations, to promote improvements in world economic institutions, in part through the convening of an international conference similar to the 1944 Bretton Woods conference that had led to the creation of the International Monetary Fund.

On September 19, St. Christopher and Nevis (St. Kitts–Nevis) joined the Commonwealth of Nations as the 48th member.   T.G.S.

COMMUNISM. Communist parties throughout the world counted more than 78 million members in 1983. Despite its size and strength, the Communist movement continued to suffer from internal rivalries and from serious economic and political problems. The deployment of U.S. medium-range missiles in Western Europe was a major issue.

Soviet Union. Yuri Andropov, who became head of the Soviet Communist Party after Leonid Brezhnev's death in November 1982, attempted to consolidate his power in 1983 (see also biography in PEOPLE IN THE NEWS). In addition to filling numerous party and governmental positions with old associates from the KGB (the Soviet security police and foreign intelligence agency)—which he headed until 1981—Andropov sought to expand his power base outside the military and secret police factions that had provided much of his initial political support. Andropov also devoted serious attention to the economic problems facing the Soviet Union, calling for wide-ranging economic reforms to instill greater efficiency in the Soviet labor force. In late summer, however, Andropov dropped from public sight for the rest of the year, and it was rumored that he was seriously ill.

Рабочее место—не место попойки.
Пьянчугу, бездельника—
вон со стройки!

As part of Soviet leader Yuri Andropov's stern campaign against alcoholism and sloth at the workplace, a poster warns, "The job is no place for boozing. Get drunks and loafers off the site!"

Poland. Although the Polish military government officially lifted martial law in July, the underlying political and economic problems that had spawned the Solidarity labor movement in 1980 and challenged the position of the Polish United Workers Communist Party remained largely unresolved. There was no evidence that the government of General Wojciech Jaruzelski had established legitimacy among the population. Indeed, high points of the year for most Poles were two events that underlined the regime's lack of popular support: the long-awaited visit of Pope John Paul II (the former Karol Cardinal Wojtyla of Poland) in mid-June and the announcement in October that Lech Walesa, the leader of the now-outlawed Solidarity movement, had been awarded the Nobel Peace Prize.

Afghanistan. As civil war in Afghanistan continued unabated, the Afghan Communist regime and its Soviet ally seemed no closer to eliminating the armed resistance of the rebel Mujahedeen (holy warriors). Despite the presence of more than 100,000 Soviet combat troops, guerrilla groups controlled much of the countryside and were able to make periodic raids on Afghan government and Soviet military installations. Thousands of civilians reportedly were killed in Soviet air strikes launched in retaliation for guerrilla attacks on Soviet troops, and an estimated 4 million Afghan refugees remained in neighboring Pakistan and Iran.

Comecon. Economic conditions failed to improve for the ten member states of the Council for Mutual Economic Assistance (Comecon)—consisting of the Soviet Union, East Germany, Poland, Czechoslovakia, Hungary, Bulgaria, Romania, Cuba, Mongolia, and Vietnam. In the Soviet Union and in Eastern Europe, growth rates stagnated, shortages of consumer items were widespread, and political leaders seemed unwilling or unable to implement serious economic reforms. A particular danger was posed by the economic disaster in Poland and the resultant inability of the Poles to repay outstanding loans to Western banks. Because of the Polish situation, as well as similar problems facing Romania, Western banks and governments showed increasing reluctance to grant new loans to Communist countries; as a result, Comecon governments were finding it increasingly difficult to pay for imported Western goods needed to supplement domestic production.

At the annual Comecon meeting, held in East Berlin in October, national leaders called for more cooperation in energy conservation and food production. Beneath the surface unity, Western analysts said, was concern among many members over the relatively high price of oil and natural gas imports from the Soviet Union and low prices for farm exports, a major income source for smaller Comecon countries. Even countries such as Hungary and East Germany, which had enjoyed substantial economic growth during the 1970's, were encountering economic difficulties.

The Warsaw Pact. The major concern facing the Soviet Union and its European Communist allies in the Warsaw Pact was the NATO alliance's plan to begin deploying new U.S. intermediate-range cruise and Pershing missiles in Western Europe. Rejecting the NATO position that the new missiles were needed to counterbalance the intermediate-range SS-20 missiles introduced by the Soviet Union in recent years, the Warsaw Pact countries, at a conference in Moscow during the summer, issued a joint statement deploring the "unprecedented" U.S. buildup and vowed that they would not allow the West to achieve "military superiority." Similar observations, accompanied by threats of possible countermeasures, were made at other occasions and gatherings, including a meeting of Warsaw Pact defense ministers in late October in East Berlin. All of the Warsaw Pact countries adhered to Moscow's position, with the notable exception of Romania, which advocated that the Soviet Union begin dismantling SS-20 missiles. Reportedly because of this rift, Romania failed to send a representative to an important strategy meeting of Communist parties, held in Moscow in early December.

On November 23, a day after the West German Parliament reaffirmed West Germany's decision to allow deployment of Pershing II missiles on its soil, the Soviet Union withdrew from U.S.-Soviet medium-range missile talks in Geneva. Moscow also announced that new Soviet missiles would be deployed in East Germany and Czechoslovakia, as well as on submarines. Strategic arms reduction talks and talks on conventional armed forces in central Europe were recessed in December.

Far East. China and the Soviet Union continued to conduct negotiation sessions aimed at resolving mutual differences, but no major positive results emerged from these discussions. The Chinese strongly opposed both the Soviet role in Afghanistan and Soviet support for the Communist government of Vietnam in the latter's continuing occupation of Cambodia (Kampuchea). Vietnam maintained its domination of Communist Indochina in 1983, continuing a significant military presence in Laos and employing an estimated 150,000 or more Vietnamese troops to buttress the regime of Heng Samrin in Cambodia.

The Caribbean. In mid-October, a split within the Marxist leadership in Grenada led to the overthrow and assassination of Prime Minister Maurice Bishop at the hands of a radical faction led by General Hudson Austin. Soon thereafter, however, a military force consisting of troops from the United States, with a small number from several Caribbean nations, invaded Grenada and overthrew the new regime. In justifying the invasion, U.S. officials cited the threat posed by the regime to American residents on the island and requests made by other countries in the region to eliminate a radical government closely allied to Cuba that reportedly was planning to use Grenada as a base for military subversion. A few hundred Cubans and some Grenadians put up strong resistance.

Up, Up, and Away

They had no superpowers, but two East Berliners and a family of Czechs made headlines in 1983 by showing they had enough daring and ingenuity to more than make up for the lack. In early April, the two Germans successfully glided over the Berlin Wall under cover of darkness on pulleys attached to a high wire. (They had used a bow and arrow to string the cable from a rooftop to the far side of a building in the Western sector, where it was secured by a friend.) And in September, a Czechoslovak cyclist escaped to Austria with his wife, children, and bicycle, in a hot-air balloon sewn together out of raincoats and kept in the air by a cannister of lighted propane gas.

Nonruling parties. Electoral setbacks beset both the French and the Italian Communist parties, the largest such parties outside of Communist-run countries. The French Communist Party (PCF) suffered reverses in municipal council elections held in March. Subsequently, party leader Georges Marchais sharply criticized the PCF's coalition partner, the Socialist Party, for allegedly retreating from left-wing goals in economic and military matters. The Italian Communist Party (PCI) suffered slight losses in nationwide balloting on June 26–27; earlier in the year, at its first party congress since 1979, the PCI reaffirmed its opposition both to Soviet actions in Poland and Afghanistan and to NATO plans to base missiles in Sicily.

At a Spanish Communist Party congress in December, party leader Gerardo Iglesias, considered a moderate, defeated former party leader Santiago Carrillo, a pro-Moscow hardliner, to win reelection for a three-year term. In Portugal, where the party is solidly united behind Moscow, Alvaro Cunhal was reelected leader at a December congress.

See articles on individual countries mentioned. R.E.K.

COMOROS. See STATISTICS OF THE WORLD.

COMPUTERS AND ELECTRONICS. A price war in the home computer business in 1983 benefited consumers but brought financial troubles to manufacturers. In the consumer electronics sector, innovations involving videocassette recorders attracted attention.

Personal computers. People in the market for home computers—personal computers at the low end of the price scale—found a wide variety of models on sale at declining prices. However, while consumers benefited, able to buy popular models that once cost $200 to $300 for less than $100, some producers went into the red. Texas Instruments Inc. posted second-quarter losses of $119 million, and Warner Communications Inc., the parent company of Atari Inc., lost $283.4 million in the same period. By the summer, only Commodore International Ltd. had gained from the price war, reporting $28 million in earnings for the fiscal year ending June 30. Texas Instruments canceled production of its 99/4A and bowed out of the home computer field. Other companies announced price hikes to take effect in 1984. The biggest loser turned out to be the Osborne Computer Corporation—maker of the first portable computer—which filed for bankruptcy on September 13.

Coleco Industries Inc., one of Atari's chief video game competitors, entered the computer field with a home computer system called Adam. It includes a keyboard and microprocessor unit, 80K (kilobytes) of internal memory (roughly 80,000 units of information), a data storage device, a letter-quality printer, a built-in word processing program, and two joysticks. Atari, facing large losses, revamped its product line by discontinuing its 400 and 800 computers and introducing four new models, the 600XL, the 800XL, the 1400XL, and the 1450XL, which can all use existing Atari software. The 1400XL featured 64K of internal memory, a built-in modem (for communicating by telephone with other computers), and a speech synthesizer.

The long-awaited entry into the home computer market of the IBM PCjr ("PC junior") was scheduled for early 1984. It was to be sold in two versions: a basic model with 64K of internal memory for about $700 and a higher-priced model (around $1,200) with 128K of memory and a disc drive—both partially compatible with the more sophisticated IBM Personal Computer (PC).

The PC itself continued to dominate among more expensive microcomputers. Numerous companies rode IBM's coattails, producing computers that were compatible with the PC. Also, a host of firms specialized in either manufacturing peripheral equipment for the PC or writing programs for it and compatible models. To help maintain its place in the field, Apple Computer Inc. in January introduced Lisa, a $10,000 computer, designed for office use, that was said to be the first of a new generation of "user-friendly" machines. Lisa's sales were lower than anticipated, however, and in September, Apple cut its price to around $8,000.

The portable computer market continued to grow. Radio Shack, a division of the Tandy Corporation, introduced the battery-powered, notebook-sized TRS-80 Model 100, with up to 32K of internal memory, a full-sized keyboard, a built-in modem, and a liquid crystal display

The New York City police have introduced robots to handle bombs by remote control. Above, a bomb squad detective operates controls at a video monitor. Right, the robot moves a suspicious briefcase.

(LCD) screen. Another new model was the Sharp Electronics Corporation's PC-5000, which is somewhat larger and heavier but offers a host of interesting features, such as 128K of internal memory (expandable to 256K), a built-in, 80-column by eight-line LCD screen, and an optional modem and automatic dialer. There were also developments in transportable computers—portable computers that weigh about 25 pounds and are about the size of a sewing machine.

Manufacturers looked as well toward affordable large-capacity storage devices. One such device, called the Bank, was introduced in mid-1983 by Corvus Systems Inc. at an initial price of $2,195. It holds an amazing 200 megabytes of data in the form of a continuous loop of 100-track magnetic tape encased in a removable cartridge; 100-megabyte cartridges are also available.

Computer raiders. With more and more people buying personal computers, often capable of communicating with other computers via ordinary telephone lines, the risk of unauthorized individuals gaining access, through a personal computer, to important government, business, or academic computer systems has grown drastically. Breaking into computer systems in this way has become a sport for many young computer buffs, or hackers (as they style themselves). One case that attracted wide notice in mid-1983 was that of a group of hackers in Milwaukee who had gained access to the computer systems of a number of government and private organizations in the United States and Canada, including a U.S. government nuclear weapons laboratory at Los Alamos, N.M. In mid-October, FBI agents across the country raided the homes and seized the equipment of 15 other hackers suspected of intrusions into the systems of NASA, the Defense Department, and many companies.

Video. Stereo videocassette recorders, or VCR's, were previously capable of recording FM simulcasts and of playing back prerecorded stereo cassettes, but a new system called Beta Hi-Fi, from the Sony Corporation, uses an FM-modulated design to record high-fidelity sound, providing the next best thing to digital sound. Perhaps the most interesting innovation in video cameras was the built-in VCR. Sony's BetaMovie is a portable, self-contained VCR and camera combination that uses standard-sized videocassettes and weighs roughly 5 pounds. The RCA Corporation's CC030 is an innovative camera that includes a color electronic viewfinder, a new automatic focus system, a continuous white balance system that constantly sets the correct color, a character generator for on-screen titles, and an MOS (metal oxide semiconductor) image sensor in place of the normal imaging tube.

Liquid crystal display TV screens were placed on the market, and the Seiko Time Corporation used the technology to create a wristwatch TV. The tiny black-and-white screen measures 1.2 inches diagonally and features a receiver that fits in a shirt pocket. The Casio Computer Company also used an LCD screen in its compact pocket TV, which has a 2-inch screen.

Audio. The eagerly awaited compact digital audio discs and disc players finally became widely available. This new technology uses a laser beam to read digital information encoded beneath the surface of a plastic disc. The palm-sized records are not affected by scratches, dust, and fingerprints. Tuner technology also has been changing, and two new tuner designs seem to transcend all others. Found in the NAD 7150 tuner is the Schotz circuit, which greatly reduces multipath distortion from surrounding buildings and offers greater sensitivity overall. Similar in use but not in design is the Carver TX-11 tuner from the Carver Corporation, which uses a computerized logic system.

D.G.

CONGO. See STATISTICS OF THE WORLD.

CONGRESS OF THE UNITED STATES. As the first session of the 98th Congress convened on January 3, 1983, the Democrats, heartened by major gains in the House of Representatives in the November 1982 elections, seemed ready to take a more aggressive and partisan stance. The Republicans, grateful that they had preserved intact their slim majority in the Senate, were equally determined to defend the policies of President Ronald Reagan.

Along with the perennially difficult budget battle, foreign affairs dominated the congres-sional agenda, as the Democrats sought a stronger voice in foreign policy decisions. A more bipartisan spirit led to an agreement on funding for the MX missile, a jobs creation program, and a major overhaul of the social security system (see SOCIAL SECURITY). Congress found itself at odds with the Reagan administration over the makeup of the Civil Rights Commission (see CIVIL LIBERTIES AND CIVIL RIGHTS) and over such environmental issues as sales of coal-leasing rights and the activities of the Environmental Protection Agency (see ENVIRONMENT).

Foreign affairs. Congress generally divided along party lines in responding to the administration's widening involvement in El Salvador and Nicaragua. Both houses, however, slashed the presidential requests for supplementary military aid to the right-wing Salvadoran government. President Reagan in March requested $110 million more in military aid for El Salvador in fiscal year 1983. Both houses eventually approved only $55 million in supplemental aid, and only after extracting a promise from the administration to limit the number of U.S. military advisers in El Salvador to no more than 55 and persuading Reagan to appoint a special U.S. ambassador to Central America—a post that went to former Senator Richard Stone, a Florida Democrat.

For fiscal 1984 (beginning October 1, 1983), the president requested $86 million in military aid to El Salvador. In mid-November, both houses voted a stopgap spending measure providing a lower level of aid. Congress voted to extend for another year a condition that the administration certify every six months that the Salvadoran regime was respecting human rights, but Reagan vetoed that measure.

The congressional debate over El Salvador was complicated by growing anxiety over administration support of rebels fighting the left-wing Sandinista government of Nicaragua. On July 28, following a rare secret session to discuss U.S. covert activity in Central America, the House voted, 228–195, to ban any further covert aid to Nicaraguan rebels. On October 20, the House, voting on an intelligence authorization bill, again struck down such aid. In mid-November, however, Congress approved $24 million, enough to continue the aid at existing levels for a few months, pending further possible action.

Congressional attention also was fixed on Lebanon, particularly after U.S. Marines stationed there began suffering casualties. Resulting demands in Congress for a greater voice in controlling U.S. military action in Lebanon provoked a major congressional-executive confrontation that hinged on interpretation of the War Powers Act, passed by Congress in 1973 over President Richard Nixon's veto. That act requires the president to report to Congress whenever sending U.S. troops "into hostilities or into situations where imminent involvement in hostilities is clearly indicated by the circumstances." Once such a report "is submitted or required to be submitted," the troops must be withdrawn within 60 days, unless Congress declares war or specifically authorizes their continued deployment—a time limit that the president can unilaterally extend to 90 days. Arguing that these conditions applied to the Lebanon situation, numerous legislators urged President Reagan to invoke the act by submitting the required report. But the president,

insisting that the fighting in Lebanon was only sporadic and not directed at the Marines, declined to take such action.

In September, both Democrats and Republicans introduced resolutions requiring Reagan to abide by the provisions of the 1973 act. Behind the scenes, representatives from both branches worked to hammer out a compromise. Their labors bore fruit in a measure passed by Congress on September 29 and signed by the president on October 12, stating that the War Powers Act did apply to the Lebanon affair and that the president was authorized to keep U.S. forces there for another 18 months.

Defense. Congress once again missed the fiscal-year deadline for appropriating funds for the Defense Department. In June, the lawmakers adopted a $268.6 billion defense budget target, and in September they authorized the spending of $187.5 billion on weapons, research, and military operations. The latter figure represented a 5 percent after-inflation increase over fiscal 1983 spending levels, rather than the 10 percent rise sought by the Reagan administration; nevertheless, the pres-

At a meeting of the Senate Foreign Relations Committee, Senator Charles Percy (R, Ill.), the chairman (left), confers with Senators Paul Sarbanes (D, Md.) and Alan Cranston (D, Calif.), prior to voting on a resolution applying the War Powers Act to the U.S. military presence in Lebanon.

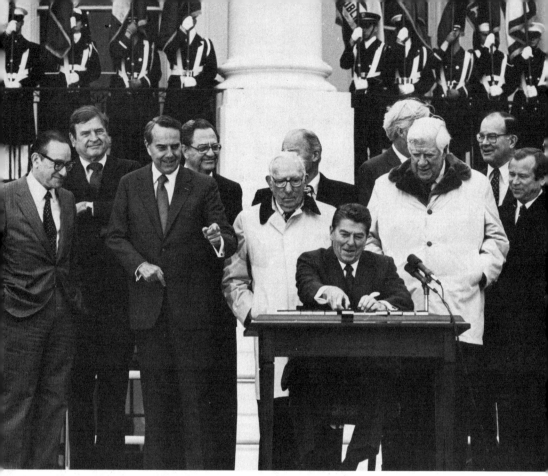

Congressional leaders look on as President Ronald Reagan signs a bill overhauling the U.S. social security system, thus ending a bitter two-year partisan fight. Among the changes were increased payroll taxes and raising of the retirement age from 65 to 67 early in the next century.

ident signed the measure on September 24. As for the appropriations bill, Congress in November voted in favor of a measure providing $249.6 billion for overall Department of Defense spending.

Included in the defense budget was funding for production of the MX missile—an item agreed upon only after a heated political battle over a method for basing and protecting the missile. A Reagan-appointed commission of defense experts recommended in April that work on the missile should continue, and in May, Congress approved $625 million for research and flight testing of the MX. In return, Reagan promised to undertake a comprehensive review of the administration's arms control policies and to attempt to carry out the com-

mission's suggestions for stabilizing the U.S.-Soviet nuclear balance. Finally, in September, Congress authorized production of 21 MX missiles.

In May, the House adopted a resolution calling on the president to negotiate an "immediate, mutual and verifiable" freeze on the production and deployment of all nuclear weapons. Opponents of the nonbinding resolution, however, succeeded in tacking on an amendment linking any freeze to negotiated arms reduction.

Budget. On January 31, President Reagan sent to Congress a proposed budget of $848.5 billion for fiscal 1984, including a projected $188.8 billion deficit. Besides a 10 percent increase in military spending, the proposal called for a freeze on most nonmilitary domestic spending and for funding cuts for transportation and energy development. In all, the president proposed $245.3 billion in military outlays, $603.2 billion in nonmilitary outlays, and $659.7 billion in budget receipts.

The compromise budget passed by both houses on June 23 set overall government spending at $849.5 billion, which would rise to $858 billion if the legislators subsequently approved various antirecession programs grouped together in a special reserve fund. Including the reserve fund, which was to be added to the budget if Congress approved the programs comprising it, Congress arrived at a deficit of $178.4 billion. These budget targets were predicated on accomplishing the politically difficult task of finding more than $12 billion in new revenues from additional taxes, as well as saving an equivalent amount through further domestic spending cuts. (No deficit reduction package was approved in 1983.) The congressional budget differed from that offered by the president principally by calling for approximately $5.3 billion less in military outlays and about $6.3 billion more in nonmilitary spending and by proposing tax increases that the president opposed.

With President Reagan warning that he would veto any tax or appropriations measures that did not reflect his budget targets, Congress in September resumed work on the specific appropriations measures needed to fulfill the budget resolution. By September 23, its self-imposed deadline for passage of all budget measures, Congress had passed only four of the 13 necessary appropriations bills. In an unusual display of bipartisanship and self-discipline, representatives and senators from both sides of the aisle collaborated to finish work on the necessary stopgap money bill without the all-night sessions and political wrangling that had accompanied such bills in past years.

Tax cut. Despite a concerted effort on the part of House Democrats, Congress refused to cancel or modify the third installment of the administration's three-year (1981–1983) tax cut. With the last stage scheduled to take effect July 1, the House on June 23 did vote to limit the tax benefit to a maximum of $720 per family; on the 229–191 vote, not a single

Republican sided with the Democrats. In the Republican-controlled Senate, an almost strict party-line vote resulted in a 55–45 rejection of a similar measure.

Recession relief. Democrats introduced a two-stage recession relief and jobs program in January. The first segment, which Reagan agreed to support, was enacted in March; it provided $4.6 billion for an estimated 40,000 new jobs, principally on public-works and construction projects, along with more than $5 billion for payment of jobless benefits. Phase two, a $5 billion jobs creation program, did not win passage.

Capitol bombing. At about 11 p.m. on November 7, a time bomb exploded outside the Capitol office of the Senate Democratic leader, causing no injuries but resulting in moderate damage. A group called the Armed Resistance Unit claimed responsibility for the bombing, which it said was in protest against the U.S. military "aggression" in Grenada and Lebanon.

Congressional affairs. A congressional scandal surfaced in July, when it was disclosed that two members of the House, Daniel B. Crane (R, Ill.) and Gerry E. Studds (D, Mass.), had had sexual relationships with teenage pages. Crane admitted to having had a relationship with a female page in 1980; Studds admitted having had a relationship with a male page in 1973. Although the House ethics committee recommended a reprimand—the least severe punishment the chamber could have meted out—the full House overturned that judgment and voted to censure both men.

See also ELECTIONS IN THE UNITED STATES; UNITED STATES OF AMERICA.

M.D.W.

Unlikely Détente

When they passed the Social Security rescue bill in March 1983, U.S. House members did not look too closely at the wording. It turned out that the text as originally adopted in the House referred to "Soviet Security" instead of "Social Security" in several places. Embarrassed lawmakers quietly voted for a second time, passing a corrected version of the bill.

MEMBERSHIP OF THE 98th CONGRESS IN 1983

Senators	Term Expires
ALABAMA	
Howell T. Heflin (D)	1985
Jeremiah A. Denton, Jr. (R)	1987
ALASKA	
Ted Stevens (R)	1985
Frank H. Murkowski (R)	1987
ARIZONA	
Barry M. Goldwater (R)	1987
Dennis DeConcini (D)	1989
ARKANSAS	
Dale Bumpers (D)	1987
David H. Pryor (D)	1985
CALIFORNIA	
Alan Cranston (D)	1987
Pete Wilson (R)	1989
COLORADO	
Gary Hart (D)	1987
William L. Armstrong (R)	1985
CONNECTICUT	
Lowell P. Weicker, Jr. (R)	1989
Christopher J. Dodd (D)	1987
DELAWARE	
William V. Roth, Jr. (R)	1989
Joseph R. Biden, Jr. (D)	1985
FLORIDA	
Lawton M. Chiles, Jr. (D)	1989
Paula Hawkins (R)	1987
GEORGIA	
Sam Nunn (D)	1985
Mack Mattingly (R)	1987
HAWAII	
Daniel K. Inouye (D)	1987
Spark M. Matsunaga (D)	1989
IDAHO	
James A. McClure (R)	1985
Steven D. Symms (R)	1987
ILLINOIS	
Charles H. Percy (R)	1985
Alan J. Dixon (D)	1987
INDIANA	
Richard G. Lugar (R)	1989
Dan Quayle (R)	1987
IOWA	
Roger W. Jepsen (R)	1985
Charles E. Grassley (R)	1987
KANSAS	
Robert Dole (R)	1987
Nancy Landon Kassebaum (R)	1985
KENTUCKY	
Walter D. Huddleston (D)	1985
Wendell H. Ford (D)	1987
LOUISIANA	
Russell B. Long (D)	1987
J. Bennett Johnston (D)	1985
MAINE	
William S. Cohen (R)	1985
George J. Mitchell (D)	1989
MARYLAND	
Charles McC. Mathias, Jr. (R)	1987
Paul S. Sarbanes (D)	1989
MASSACHUSETTS	
Edward M. Kennedy (D)	1989
Paul Tsongas (D)	1985
MICHIGAN	
Donald W. Riegle, Jr. (D)	1989
Carl Levin (D)	1985
MINNESOTA	
David F. Durenberger (R)	1989
Rudy Boschwitz (R)	1985
MISSISSIPPI	
John C. Stennis (D)	1989
Thad Cochran (R)	1985
MISSOURI	
Thomas F. Eagleton (D)	1987
John C. Danforth (R)	1989
MONTANA	
John Melcher (D)	1989
Max Baucus (D)	1985
NEBRASKA	
Edward Zorinsky (D)	1989
John James Exon, Jr. (D)	1985
NEVADA	
Paul Laxalt (R)	1987
Chic Hecht (R)	1989
NEW HAMPSHIRE	
Gordon J. Humphrey (R)	1985
Warren B. Rudman (R)	1987
NEW JERSEY	
Bill Bradley (D)	1985
Frank R. Lautenberg (D)	1989
NEW MEXICO	
Pete V. Domenici (R)	1985
Jeff Bingaman (D)	1989
NEW YORK	
Daniel P. Moynihan (D)	1989
Alfonse M. D'Amato (R)	1987
NORTH CAROLINA	
Jesse Helms (R)	1985
John P. East (R)	1987
NORTH DAKOTA	
Quentin N. Burdick (D)	1989
Mark Andrews (R)	1987
OHIO	
John H. Glenn, Jr. (D)	1987
Howard M. Metzenbaum (D)	1989
OKLAHOMA	
David L. Boren (D)	1985
Donald L. Nickles (R)	1987
OREGON	
Mark O. Hatfield (R)	1985
Robert W. Packwood (R)	1987
PENNSYLVANIA	
H. John Heinz 3rd (R)	1989
Arlen Specter (R)	1987
RHODE ISLAND	
Claiborne Pell (D)	1985
John H. Chafee (R)	1989
SOUTH CAROLINA	
Strom Thurmond (R)	1985
Ernest F. Hollings (D)	1987
SOUTH DAKOTA	
Larry Pressler (R)	1985
James Abdnor (R)	1987
TENNESSEE	
Howard H. Baker, Jr. (R)	1985
James R. Sasser (D)	1989
TEXAS	
John G. Tower (R)	1985
Lloyd Bentsen (D)	1989
UTAH	
Edwin J, "Jake" Garn (R)	1987
Orrin G. Hatch (R)	1989
VERMONT	
Robert T. Stafford (R)	1989
Patrick J. Leahy (D)	1987
VIRGINIA	
John W. Warner (R)	1985
Paul S. Trible, Jr. (R)	1989
WASHINGTON	
Slade Gorton (R)	1987
Daniel J. Evans (R)[1]	1989
WEST VIRGINIA	
Jennings Randolph (D)	1985
Robert C. Byrd (D)	1989
WISCONSIN	
William Proxmire (D)	1989
Robert W. Kasten, Jr. (R)	1987
WYOMING	
Malcolm Wallop (R)	1989
Alan K. Simpson (R)	1985

Representatives

ALABAMA
1. Jack Edwards (R)
2. William L. Dickinson (R)
3. William Nichols (D)
4. Tom Bevill (D)
5. Ronnie G. Flippo (D)
6. Ben Erdreich (D)
7. Richard C. Shelby (D)

ALASKA
At large: Donald E. Young (R)

ARIZONA
1. John McCain (R)
2. Morris K. Udall (D)
3. Bob Stump (D)
4. Eldon D. Rudd (R)
5. James F. McNulty, Jr. (D)

ARKANSAS
1. William V. "Bill" Alexander, Jr. (D)
2. Edwin R. Bethune, Jr. (R)
3. John P. Hammerschmidt (R)
4. Beryl F. Anthony, Jr. (D)

CALIFORNIA
1. Douglas H. Bosco (D)
2. Eugene A. Chappie (R)
3. Robert T. Matsui (D)
4. Vic Fazio (D)
5. Sala Burton (D)[2]
6. Barbara Boxer (D)
7. George Miller (D)
8. Ronald V. Dellums (D)
9. Fortney (Pete) Stark (D)
10. Don Edwards (D)
11. Tom Lantos (D)
12. Ed Zschau (R)
13. Norman Y. Mineta (D)
14. Norman D. Shumway (R)
15. Tony Coelho (D)
16. Leon E. Panetta (D)
17. Charles Pashayan, Jr. (R)
18. Richard H. Lehman (D)
19. Robert J. Lagomarsino (R)
20. William M. Thomas (R)
21. Bobbi Fiedler (R)
22. Carlos J. Moorhead (R)
23. Anthony C. Beilenson (D)
24. Henry A. Waxman (D)
25. Edward R. Roybal (D)
26. Howard L. Berman (D)
27. Mel Levine (D)
28. Julian C. Dixon (D)
29. Augustus F. Hawkins (D)
30. Matthew G. Martinez (D)
31. Mervyn M. Dymally (D)
32. Glenn M. Anderson (D)
33. David Dreier (R)

34. Esteban Edward Torres (D)
35. Jerry Lewis (R)
36. George E. Brown, Jr. (D)
37. Alfred A. McCandless (R)
38. Jerry M. Patterson (D)
39. William E. Dannemeyer (R)
40. Robert E. Badham (R)
41. Bill Lowery (R)
42. Dan Lundgren (R)
43. Ron Packard (R)
44. Jim Bates (D)
45. Duncan Hunter (R)

COLORADO
1. Patricia Schroeder (D)
2. Timothy E. Wirth (D)
3. Ray Kogovsek (D)
4. Hank Brown (R)
5. Ken Kramer (R)
6. Dan Schaefer (R)[3]

CONNECTICUT
1. Barbara B. Kennelly (D)
2. Samuel Gejdenson (D)
3. Bruce A. Morrison (D)
4. Stewart B. McKinney (R)
5. William R. Ratchford (D)
6. Nancy L. Johnson (R)

DELAWARE
At large: Thomas R. Carper (D)

FLORIDA
1. Earl Hutto (D)
2. Don Fuqua (D)
3. Charles E. Bennett (D)
4. Bill Chappell, Jr. (D)
5. Bill McCollum (R)
6. Buddy MacKay (D)
7. Sam Gibbons (D)
8. C. W. Bill Young (R)
9. Michael Bilirakis (R)
10. Andy Ireland (D)
11. Bill Nelson (D)
12. Tom Lewis (R)
13. Connie Mack (R)
14. Dan Mica (D)
15. E. Clay Shaw, Jr. (R)
16. Lawrence J. Smith (D)
17. William Lehman (D)
18. Claude Pepper (D)
19. Dante B. Fascell (D)

GEORGIA
1. Robert Lindsay Thomas (D)
2. Charles Hatcher (D)
3. Richard Ray (D)
4. Elliott H. Levitas (D)
5. Wyche Fowler, Jr. (D)
6. Newt Gingrich (R)
7. George Darden (D)[4]
8. J. Roy Rowland (D)
9. Ed Jenkins (D)
10. Doug Barnard, Jr. (D)

HAWAII
1. Cecil L. Heftel (D)
2. Daniel K. Akaka (D)

IDAHO
1. Larry E. Craig (R)
2. George Hansen (R)

ILLINOIS
1. Charles A. Hayes (D)[5]
2. Gus Savage (D)
3. Martin A. Russo (D)
4. George M. O'Brien (R)
5. William O. Lipinski (D)
6. Henry J. Hyde (R)
7. Cardiss Collins (D)
8. Daniel Rostenkowski (D)
9. Sidney R. Yates (D)

10. John Edward Porter (R)
11. Frank Annunzio (D)
12. Philip M. Crane (R)
13. John N. Erlenborn (R)
14. Tom Corcoran (R)
15. Edward R. Madigan (R)
16. Lynn Martin (R)
17. Lane Evans (D)
18. Robert H. Michel (R)
19. Daniel B. Crane (R)
20. Richard J. Durbin (D)
21. Melvin Price (D)
22. Paul Simon (D)

INDIANA
1. Katie Hall (D)
2. Philip R. Sharp (D)
3. John P. Hiler (R)
4. Dan Coats (R)
5. Elwood Hillis (R)
6. Dan Burton (R)
7. John T. Myers (R)
8. Frank McCloskey (D)
9. Lee H. Hamilton (D)
10. Andrew Jacobs, Jr. (D)

IOWA
1. James A. S. Leach (R)
2. Thomas J. Tauke (R)
3. Cooper Evans (R)
4. Neal Smith (D)
5. Tom Harkin (D)
6. Berkley Bedell (D)

KANSAS
1. Pat Roberts (R)
2. Jim Slattery (D)
3. Larry Winn, Jr. (R)
4. Dan Glickman (D)
5. Robert Whittaker (R)

KENTUCKY
1. Carroll Hubbard, Jr. (D)
2. William H. Natcher (D)
3. Romano L. Mazzoli (D)
4. Gene Snyder (R)
5. Harold Rogers (R)
6. Larry J. Hopkins (R)
7. Carl D. Perkins (D)

LOUISIANA
1. Bob Livingston (R)
2. Lindy Boggs (D)
3. W. J. Tauzin (D)
4. Charles Roemer III (D)
5. Jerry Huckaby (D)
6. W. Henson Moore (R)
7. John B. Breaux (D)
8. Gillis W. Long (D)

MAINE
1. John R. McKernan, Jr. (R)
2. Olympia J. Snowe (R)

MARYLAND
1. Royden Dyson (D)
2. Clarence D. Long (D)
3. Barbara A. Mikulski (D)
4. Marjorie S. Holt (R)
5. Steny H. Hoyer (D)
6. Beverly B. Byron (D)
7. Parren J. Mitchell (D)
8. Michael D. Barnes (D)

MASSACHUSETTS
1. Silvio O. Conte (R)
2. Edward P. Boland (D)
3. Joseph D. Early (D)
4. Barney Frank (D)
5. James M. Shannon (D)
6. Nicholas Mavroules (D)
7. Edward J. Markey (D)
8. Thomas P. O'Neill, Jr. (D)

9. Joe Moakley (D)
10. Gerry E. Studds (D)
11. Brian J. Donnelly (D)

MICHIGAN
1. John Conyers, Jr. (D)
2. Carl D. Pursell (R)
3. Howard Wolpe (D)
4. Mark D. Siljander (R)
5. Harold S. Sawyer (R)
6. Bob Carr (D)
7. Dale E. Kildee (D)
8. Bob Traxler (D)
9. Guy Vander Jagt (R)
10. Donald Joseph Albosta (D)
11. Robert W. Davis (R)
12. David E. Bonior (D)
13. George W. Crockett, Jr. (D)
14. Dennis M. Hertel (D)
15. William D. Ford (D)
16. John D. Dingell (D)
17. Sander M. Levin (D)
18. William S. Broomfield (R)

MINNESOTA
1. Timothy J. Penny (D)
2. Vin Weber (R)
3. Bill Frenzel (R)
4. Bruce F. Vento (D)
5. Martin Olav Sabo (D)
6. Gerry Sikorski (D)
7. Arlan Stangeland (R)
8. James L. Oberstar (D)

MISSISSIPPI
1. Jamie L. Whitten (D)
2. Webb Franklin (R)
3. G. V. Montgomery (D)
4. Wayne Dowdy (D)
5. Trent Lott (R)

MISSOURI
1. William Clay (D)
2. Robert A. Young (D)
3. Richard A. Gephardt (D)
4. Ike Skelton (D)
5. Alan Wheat (D)
6. E. Thomas Coleman (R)
7. Gene Taylor (R)
8. Bill Emerson (R)
9. Harold L. Volkmer (D)

MONTANA
1. Pat Williams (D)
2. Ron Marlenee (R)

NEBRASKA
1. Douglas K. Bereuter (R)
2. Hal Daub (R)
3. Virginia Smith (R)

NEVADA
1. Harry M. Reid (D)
2. Barbara F. Vucanovich (R)

NEW HAMPSHIRE
1. Norman E. D'Amours (D)
2. Judd Gregg (R)

NEW JERSEY
1. James J. Florio (D)
2. William J. Hughes (D)
3. James J. Howard (D)
4. Christopher H. Smith (R)
5. Marge Roukema (R)
6. Bernard J. Dwyer (D)
7. Matthew J. Rinaldo (R)
8. Robert A. Roe (D)
9. Robert G. Torricelli (D)
10. Peter W. Rodino, Jr. (D)
11. Joseph G. Minish (D)
12. Jim Courter (R)
13. Edwin B. Forsythe (R)
14. Frank J. Guarini (D)

NEW MEXICO
1. Manuel Lujan, Jr. (R)
2. Joe Skeen (R)
3. Bill Richardson (D)

NEW YORK
1. William Carney (R)
2. Thomas J. Downey (D)
3. Robert J. Mrazek (D)
4. Norman F. Lent (R)
5. Raymond J. McGrath (R)
6. Joseph P. Addabbo (D)
7. Gary L. Ackerman (D)[6]
8. James H. Scheuer (D)
9. Geraldine A. Ferraro (D)
10. Charles E. Schumer (D)
11. Edolphus Towns (D)
12. Major R. Owens (D)
13. Stephen J. Solarz (D)
14. Guy V. Molinari (R)
15. Bill Green (R)
16. Charles B. Rangel (D)
17. Ted Weiss (D)
18. Robert Garcia (D)
19. Mario Biaggi (D)
20. Richard L. Ottinger (D)
21. Hamilton Fish, Jr. (R)
22. Benjamin A. Gilman (R)
23. Samuel S. Stratton (D)
24. Gerald B. H. Solomon (R)
25. Sherwood L. Boehlert (R)
26. David O'B. Martin (R)
27. George C. Wortley (R)
28. Matthew F. McHugh (D)
29. Frank Horton (R)
30. Barber B. Conable, Jr. (R)
31. Jack F. Kemp (R)
32. John J. LaFalce (D)
33. Henry J. Nowak (D)
34. Stan Lundine (D)

NORTH CAROLINA
1. Walter B. Jones (D)
2. Tim Valentine (D)
3. Charles Whitley (D)
4. Ike F. Andrews (D)
5. Stephen L. Neal (D)
6. C. Robin Britt (D)
7. Charles Rose (D)
8. W. G. Hefner (D)
9. James G. Martin (R)
10. James T. Broyhill (R)
11. James McClure Clarke (D)

NORTH DAKOTA
At large: Byron L. Dorgan (D)

OHIO
1. Thomas A. Luken (D)
2. Willis D. Gradison, Jr. (R)
3. Tony P. Hall (D)
4. Michael G. Oxley (R)
5. Delbert L. Latta (R)
6. Bob McEwen (R)
7. Michael DeWine (R)
8. Thomas N. Kindness (R)
9. Marcy Kaptur (D)
10. Clarence E. Miller (R)
11. Dennis E. Eckart (D)
12. John R. Kasich (R)
13. Donald J. Pease (D)
14. John F. Seiberling (D)
15. Chalmers P. Wylie (R)
16. Ralph S. Regula (R)
17. Lyle Williams (R)
18. Douglas Applegate (D)
19. Edward F. Feighan (D)
20. Mary Rose Oakar (D)
21. Louis Stokes (D)

OKLAHOMA
1. James R. Jones (D)
2. Michael Lynn Synar (D)
3. Wes Watkins (D)
4. Dave McCurdy (D)
5. Mickey Edwards (R)
6. Glenn English (D)

OREGON
1. Les AuCoin (D)
2. Robert F. Smith (R)
3. Ron Wyden (D)
4. James Weaver (D)
5. Denny Smith (R)

PENNSYLVANIA
1. Thomas M. Foglietta (D)
2. William H. Gray III (D)
3. Robert A. Borski (D)
4. Joe Kolter (D)
5. Richard T. Schulze (R)
6. Gus Yatron (D)
7. Robert W. Edgar (D)
8. Peter H. Kostmayer (D)
9. Bud Shuster (R)
10. Joseph M. McDade (R)
11. Frank Harrison (D)
12. John P. Murtha (D)
13. Lawrence Coughlin (R)
14. William Coyne (D)
15. Don Ritter (R)
16. Robert S. Walker (R)
17. George W. Gekas (R)
18. Douglas Walgren (D)
19. William F. Goodling (R)
20. Joseph M. Gaydos (D)
21. Thomas J. Ridge (R)
22. Austin J. Murphy (D)
23. William F. Clinger, Jr. (R)

RHODE ISLAND
1. Fernand J. St Germain (D)
2. Claudine Schneider (R)

SOUTH CAROLINA
1. Thomas F. Hartnett (R)
2. Floyd Spence (R)
3. Butler Derrick (D)
4. Carroll A. Campbell (R)
5. John M. Spratt, Jr. (D)
6. Robin Tallon (D)

SOUTH DAKOTA
At large: Thomas A. Daschle (D)

TENNESSEE
1. James H. Quillen (R)
2. John J. Duncan (R)
3. Marilyn Lloyd (D)
4. Jim Cooper (D)
5. William Hill Boner (D)
6. Albert Gore, Jr. (D)
7. Don Sundquist (R)
8. Ed Jones (D)
9. Harold E. Ford (D)

TEXAS
1. Sam B. Hall, Jr. (D)
2. Charles Wilson (D)
3. Steve Bartlett (R)
4. Ralph Hall (D)
5. John Bryant (D)
6. Phil Gramm (R)
7. Bill Archer (R)
8. Jack Fields (R)
9. Jack Brooks (D)
10. J. J. Pickle (D)
11. Marvin Leath (D)
12. Jim Wright (D)
13. Jack Hightower (D)
14. William Patman (D)
15. E. de la Garza (D)
16. Ronald D. Coleman (D)
17. Charles W. Stenholm (D)
18. Mickey Leland (D)
19. Kent Hance (D)
20. Henry B. Gonzalez (D)
21. Tom Loeffler (R)
22. Ron Paul (R)
23. Abraham Kazen, Jr. (D)
24. Martin Frost (D)
25. Michael A. Andrews (D)
26. Tom Vandergriff (D)
27. Solomon P. Ortiz (D)

UTAH
1. James V. Hansen (R)
2. Dan Marriott (R)
3. Howard C. Nielson (R)

VERMONT
At large: James M. Jeffords (R)

VIRGINIA
1. Herbert H. Bateman (R)
2. G. William Whitehurst (R)
3. Thomas J. Bliley, Jr. (R)
4. Norman Sisisky (D)
5. Dan Daniel (D)
6. James R. Olin (D)
7. J. Kenneth Robinson (R)
8. Stanford Parris (R)
9. Frederick C. Boucher (D)
10. Frank R. Wolf (R)

WASHINGTON
1. Joel Pritchard (R)
2. Al Swift (D)
3. Don Bonker (D)
4. Sid Morrison (R)
5. Thomas S. Foley (D)
6. Norman D. Dicks (D)
7. Mike Lowry (D)
8. Rod Chandler (R)

WEST VIRGINIA
1. Alan B. Mollohan (D)
2. Harley O. Staggers, Jr. (D)
3. Robert E. Wise, Jr. (D)
4. Nick Joe Rahall II (D)

WISCONSIN
1. Les Aspin (D)
2. Robert W. Kastenmeier (D)
3. Steve Gunderson (R)
4. Clement J. Zablocki (D)[7]
5. Jim Moody (D)
6. Thomas E. Petri (R)
7. David R. Obey (D)
8. Toby Roth (R)
9. F. James Sensenbrenner, Jr. (R)

WYOMING
At large: Richard Bruce Cheney (R)

[1] Appointed and subsequently elected to fill the unexpired term of the late Henry M. Jackson.
[2] Elected June 21, 1983, to fill vacancy due to the death of Phillip Burton.
[3] Elected Mar. 29, 1983, to fill vacancy due to the death of John L. Swigert.
[4] Elected Nov. 8, 1983, to fill vacancy due to the death of Larry McDonald.
[5] Elected Aug. 23, 1983, to fill vacancy due to the resignation of Harold Washington.
[6] Elected Mar. 1, 1983, to fill vacancy due to the death of Benjamin S. Rosenthal.
[7] Served until his death, Dec. 3, 1983.

CONNECTICUT. *See* STATISTICS OF THE WORLD.

CONSTRUCTION. On the whole, the U.S. construction industry enjoyed a comeback year in 1983. In August, the value of new construction put in place, at an annual rate, came to $276.1 billion, a 2 percent increase compared to August 1982. The year-to-date actual value of new construction was $165.9 billion by August, a 12 percent increase over the 1982 January-to-August period. Residential building was responsible for most of the improvement in the construction industry, which also includes nonresidential building and nonbuilding construction.

Infrastructure. The urgency of rebuilding the nation's crumbling infrastructure (roads, bridges, and transportation terminals) led to some action by the federal government. On the average, two bridges collapse, sag, or bend daily somewhere in the United States. On January 6, President Ronald Reagan signed into law a federal tax increase on gasoline and diesel fuel, the first federal gas tax increase in 23 years;

the five-cents-a-gallon increase (to nine cents), which took effect April 1, was expected to raise $5.5 billion a year during the next ten years. Proceeds from the increased tax were to be used to resurface 4,000 miles of interstate highways, to repair or replace 23,000 bridges, and to aid mass transit systems. The law was also expected to create close to 200,000 jobs in surface transportation programs. Partly as a result of the law, highway construction, which had been declining, was expected to grow about 5 percent a year through 1986.

In October, a report commissioned by business and labor leaders urged federal, state, and local governments to spend up to $11 billion more each year to stem the "tragic deterioration" of highways, bridges, and water systems. The document was issued by the Labor Management Group, chaired by AFL-CIO President Lane Kirkland and Exxon Chairman Clifton Garvin, Jr.

Economic trends. Construction equipment sales were expected to increase by the end of the

A Connecticut Turnpike bridge in Greenwich collapsed into the Mianus River on June 28, causing the death of three persons. Investigators cited faulty bridge design; the firm that designed the bridge blamed the collapse on rust buildup in a crucial joint holding the structure together.

year to a level 10 percent above 1982; the export market, however, showed a decline. The office construction market was sagging, as many major cities reported a glut of unrented office space. Military construction was strong, getting a boost from increased government spending.

Productivity. Construction productivity received attention from the Business Roundtable, a group of 200 executives from large American corporations. The industry could save $10 billion a year, the Roundtable suggested, by taking such steps as developing standard training procedures to increase productivity, using more innovative contracting methods, and making safety a higher priority in selecting contractors.

Disasters. There were a number of construction tragedies in 1983, several of them related to the nation's aging infrastructure. Five people were killed and four injured when their cars plunged into a culvert that had collapsed under a county road near Antwerp, Ohio. Three people died and three others were injured when a section of the Connecticut Turnpike bridge spanning the Mianus River collapsed in June. Investigators blamed shortcomings in the bridge design for the collapse, but the engineering firm that designed the bridge said the collapse had been caused by rust buildup on the crucial pin-and-hanger assemblies that held the bridge together. In August, in Jersey City, N.J., a 50-ton concrete ceiling caved in over the main concourse of a commuter rail terminal, killing two and injuring nine. The ceiling collapsed as workers began to repair a sag in the structure found in April by an inspector, but transportation officials responsible for the station said that there had been no indication that a collapse was imminent, and they ordered an investigation.

Employment. The construction employment figure brightened somewhat in 1983, but the unemployment rate in the industry was still almost twice as high as the national rate. In August, 990,000 wage and salaried construction workers were out of jobs, compared with 1.05 million in August 1982. The August 1983 unemployment rate for construction workers was 18.1 percent, as against 20.4 percent a year earlier.

Brooklyn Bridge centennial. The world-famous Brooklyn Bridge turned 100 years old on May 24, and the event was celebrated with as much fanfare as was the bridge's opening to traffic in 1883. The bridge, which crosses the East River between the New York City boroughs of Manhattan and Brooklyn, has a central span of 1,595½ feet. The engineering marvel of its time, it was for several years the longest bridge in the world. During the centennial celebration, attended by 2 million people and marked by the biggest fireworks display in the city's history, much credit was given to civil engineers John and Washington Roebling, the father-and-son team that designed and built the bridge under the harshest conditions. The bridge continues to meet the demands of modern-day traffic loads, even though a full century has passed since its completion.   J.C.

COSTA RICA. Costa Rica in 1983 remained a haven of relative stability in Central America, but economic problems placed severe strains on the government. President Luis Albert Monge sought to implement austerity measures, while also trying to keep his pledges to maintain basic services and protect the poor, especially by holding down food prices. The effort proved increasingly difficult, however, because of a recessed economy, high inflation, widespread unemployment, and the necessity to make cutbacks mandated by a December 1982 agreement with the International Monetary Fund. The liberal wing of the president's National Liberation Party increasingly raised objections to austerity measures, and internal party pressures, backed by large public demonstrations, induced the administration to make some concessions.

Troubles with neighboring Nicaragua dominated Costa Rica's foreign relations. Costa Rica accused Nicaragua of interfering with shipping on the San Juan River between the two countries; there were also charges of armed Nicaraguan incursions and frequent overflights, and even reports of Nicaraguan links with nascent terrorist organizations. For its part, Nicaragua charged that anti-Sandinista guerrillas were using Costa Rican territory to launch air attacks on Nicaragua.

Relations between Costa Rica and the United States remained cordial. Presidential visits were exchanged, and U.S. economic and military assistance was increased. However, President Monge declined U.S. invitations to observe military exercises in Honduras and to send members of the Civil Guard (Costa Rica has no army) to a U.S.-run military training center there. In November, Monge officially declared a policy of "unarmed neutrality" for Costa Rica, while reaffirming Costa Rica's faith in Western democracy and its right to assistance in case of invasion, under existing collective security arrangements.

Pope John Paul II visited Costa Rica on March 2–4. In his speeches there he stressed a need for peaceful solutions to problems.

See STATISTICS OF THE WORLD.   R.L.M.

COUNCIL FOR MUTUAL ECONOMIC AS-SISTANCE. See COMMUNISM.

CRIME AND LAW ENFORCEMENT. Major U.S. crime stories in 1983 included the gangland-style slaying of an influential Teamsters Union figure, a new wave of airliner hijackings, several mass murder cases, and the two largest robberies in U.S. history. Also, the crime of drunk driving drew increased attention.

Teamster figure slain. Allen M. Dorfman, an insurance executive who earned millions in fees through his connections with the Teamsters Union's Central States Pension Fund, was shot to death in a suburban Chicago parking lot on January 20. Dorfman, Teamsters President Roy L. Williams, and three other men associated with the pension fund had been convicted in December 1982 of attempting to bribe then–U.S. Senator Howard Cannon (D, Nev.), whose cooperation they had sought in defeating a trucking deregulation bill. Law enforcement officials speculated that Dorfman was killed to keep him from supplying the government with information on mob figures.

Williams originally was sentenced to 55 years in prison, but under an agreement an-

New Jersey Governor Thomas Kean (center) and officers of the state's Automobile Dealers' Association stand in front of a billboard that is part of an association-sponsored campaign against drunken driving. Changing indulgent attitudes could play a major role in keeping intoxicated drivers off the roads.

"WELCOME TO CUBA.... HIJACKED FLIGHT #243, YOU ARE CLEARED FOR LANDING ON RUNWAY 12.... HIJACKED FLIGHT #57, HOLD YOUR PATTERN, PLEASE...I KNOW YOU'RE LOW ON FUEL.... HIJACKED FLIGHT #6, STILL THERE? THANK YOU FOR WAITING...."

nounced on April 15, the prison sentence was voided in return for his pledge to sever all ties to the union. He was the third Teamsters president in recent years to be convicted of federal crimes while in office.

Drug scandals. In the much publicized case of millionaire automobile entrepreneur John De Lorean, who was arrested in October 1982 and charged with conspiring to distribute 220 pounds of cocaine, two of De Lorean's co-defendants, William M. Hetrick and Stephen Lee Arrington, pleaded guilty to federal co-caine-smuggling charges. The trial of De Lorean, who pleaded not guilty, was postponed after CBS News broadcast a tape of his arrest provided by Larry Flynt, publisher of the por-nographic magazine *Hustler*. Flynt had ac-quired a copy of the tape from a clerk in the office of De Lorean's original defense lawyers.

The U.S. Justice Department and the House ethics committee conducted separate probes into allegations of drug use on Capitol Hill. Specific targets of the investigations included Representative Charles Wilson (D, Texas), for-mer Representative Barry Goldwater, Jr. (R, Calif.), and Representative Ronald V. Dellums (D, Calif.). All three vigorously denied the charges. On July 27, the Justice Department announced that its investigation would be dis-continued because of insufficient evidence for criminal indictments but added that all relevant evidence would be turned over to the House ethics committee.

Robert F. Kennedy, Jr., son of the late Senator Robert F. Kennedy, was arrested in September in South Dakota for possession of heroin. Kennedy, a former assistant district attorney in New York City, acknowledged having a drug problem and said he had admitted himself to a hospital for treatment.

The professional sports world was also shaken by drug scandals. Five football players were suspended after admitting to illegal activities involving cocaine, and three members of the Kansas City Royals baseball team pleaded guilty to cocaine possession, drew three-month jail sentences, and also were suspended. Later, former Royals pitcher Vida Blue also drew a prison sentence after pleading guilty to charges of possession of cocaine.

Skyjackings. There was a resurgence of hijackings of U.S. commercial airliners in 1983. Between May 1 and September 22, 12 U.S. airplanes were hijacked, several of them from Florida to Cuba by Cuban exiles. As the hijackings increased, the Federal Aviation Administration announced that it was reintroducing its sky marshal program, which had been credited with dramatically reducing the number of skyjackings in the late 1970's.

Ex-CIA agent sentenced. Former Central Intelligence Agency operative Edwin P. Wilson was sentenced in November to 25 years in prison for plotting to murder two prosecutors and six witnesses involved in earlier cases against him. In February he had been convicted of illegally exporting plastic explosives to Libya in 1977, and in 1982 he had been convicted of illegally transporting firearms to Libya; both of these convictions also carried prison sentences.

Brink's trials. Separate federal and state trials were conducted over the course of several months on charges stemming from the $1.6 million robbery of a Brink's armored car in Rockland County, N.Y., in 1981. Two Nyack, N.Y., police officers and a Brink's guard were killed in shootouts during the robbery and escape.

In the federal trial, which opened in April, five of the six defendants were accused of participating in a racketeering conspiracy that resulted in a series of robberies, murders, and other crimes, including the Brink's robbery. A sixth was charged with helping suspects avoid arrest. In a verdict handed down on September 3, the jury exonerated two of the defendants, convicted two others of conspiracy and racketeering, and found the remaining two guilty of having harbored a fugitive.

The state trial, which opened in August, focused specifically on the Brink's robbery and murders. Defendants Kuwasi Balagoon, David J. Gilbert, and Judith A. Clark refused legal representation and boycotted much of the trial. On September 14 they were found guilty of all charges against them—three counts of murder and four of armed robbery. They each received sentences of three consecutive terms of 25 years to life imprisonment. Two other suspects facing state charges, Kathy Boudin and Samuel Brown, were to go on trial in 1984.

Multiple murders. Two men who claimed to have committed, together or separately, a total of 300 murders were said to be prime suspects in 97 murder cases in 13 states. Authorities said that the two, Henry Lee Lucas and Ottis Elwood Toole, had described scores of murders in meticulous detail. Lucas pleaded guilty to killing an elderly woman in Texas, and in November a Texas jury found him guilty of the murder of his common-law wife; he was sentenced to life in prison. Lucas also had been formerly charged with several other murders in Texas. Toole was already charged with arson and murder in Florida and with murder in Texas. He was found guilty in another arson case in July.

After the longest criminal trial in U.S. history, lasting over two years, a Los Angeles jury found Angelo A. Buono guilty on nine of ten murder counts in the "Hillside Strangler" case, arising out of the murder of girls and young women in the Los Angeles area in 1977 and 1978. He was sentenced on November 18 to life in prison without parole.

In August, a 20-year-old immigrant from Hong Kong, Benjamin Ng, was convicted of the February 18 murder of 13 Chinese-Americans in a gambling den in Seattle's Chinatown section. Ng was sentenced to life imprisonment without possibility of parole. In October, another immigrant from Hong Kong, Kwan Fai ("Willie") Mak, was also convicted of participating in the murders and was sentenced to death.

Former prison guard George E. Banks received a death sentence on June 22 for each of 12 murder convictions stemming from a September 1982 shooting spree in Wilkes-Barre, Pa. The victims included three women Banks had lived with and five of his children. Another mass murderer, Douglas Daniel Clark, dubbed the Sunset Slayer, was sentenced March 16 to six death sentences for the sex-related murder and mutilation of persons who frequented night spots on Sunset Boulevard in Los Angeles.

Capital punishment. Five convicted murderers were executed in the United States in 1983, the highest number since 1965, when there were seven executions. In July, the U.S. Supreme Court directed the lower courts to restrict the ability of condemned inmates to impede the imposition of state court judgments by repeated petitioning; because the lower courts complied and because many of the nation's nearly 1,300 inmates on death row were running out of appeals, the rate of executions was expected to accelerate.

Biggest U.S. heists. Four defendants went on trial in October in connection with an $11 million robbery of the Sentry Armored Courier Corporation in the New York City borough of the Bronx on December 12, 1982—the largest cash theft in U.S. history. Among the suspects was Christos Potamitis, the lone guard on duty at the time of the robbery. From the start, police had suspected that the thieves, who neutralized the alarm system and cut a hole through the roof to gain entry to the building, had inside help. A fifth defendant remained at large, and only $1 million had been recovered.

Another armored-car company, the Wells Fargo Armored Service Corporation, was the

An Ohio deputy sheriff fingerprints an eight-month-old citizen as part of a voluntary program to help law enforcement authorities identify youngsters if missing or kidnapped.

target of both the second and third largest cash robberies in U.S. history. On the night of September 12, Victor Manuel Gerena, a Wells Fargo security guard, allegedly stole more than $7 million in cash from the company's West Hartford, Conn., garage. Wells Fargo offered a total of $350,000 in rewards for information leading to the conviction of the robber and the return of the money. On November 26, two men wearing Halloween masks forced their way into the Wells Fargo office in Memphis, Tenn., and stole $6.5 million in cash, negotiable securities, and checks.

Stolen computer secrets. Hitachi Ltd., one of Japan's largest computer companies, on February 8 pleaded guilty in a federal district court to charges that it had conspired to transport to Japan computer design information ostensibly stolen from the International Business Machines Corporation. Also entering guilty pleas were two Hitachi employees involved in the company's purchase of the information, Hitachi was fined $10,000, the maximum permitted under the law; the employees were fined $10,000 and $4,000, respectively, and placed on probation. Two other Hitachi employees were fined later in the year after having agreed to submit to U.S. jurisdiction. On May 13 the lone American in the case, Thomas Yoshida, pleaded no contest to one count of conspiracy; he was fined $7,500 and given two years' probation.

Drunk driving. Drunken driving may cause more than 20,000 deaths in the United States each year. By late 1983, 19 states had applied for grants under new federal legislation, rewarding states that have taken certain steps against the crime. Among the steps is a mandatory jail or community service sentence for repeat offenders and automatic suspension of the license of any driver who refuses to take a test for intoxication.

Prison population rises. U.S. prison populations continued to soar, reaching a record high of 431,829 inmates in mid–1983, according to figures released by the federal government in October. An increase of nearly 43,000 inmates (11.6 percent) during 1982 was the largest one-year rise in prison population's in the United States since such statistics first became available in 1925.   R.A.

CUBA. In 1983, Cuba's chief concerns were the troubled situation in the Caribbean Basin and its tense relations with the United States, which were further strained after U.S. troops and Cubans engaged in actual combat during the U.S.-led invasion of Grenada launched in October.

Earlier in the year, President Fidel Castro had expressed a willingness to discuss outstanding differences with Washington. Cuba supported the peace initiative of the Contadora group on Central America, offering to play a "constructive role" in any multilateral peace talks. Washington conditioned a U.S.-Cuban rapprochement on Havana's break with Moscow. U.S. officials indicated that Cuba would also have to withdraw advisers from Nicaragua and troops from Africa, end its support for Third World "wars of liberation," and agree to take back "undesirables" sent to the United States during the 1980 Mariel boatlift, more than 1,000 of whom remained in federal custody. The United States also was concerned over recent Cuban arms buildups and alleged Cuban involvement in drug trafficking, as well as an increase in hijackings of U.S. commercial planes to Havana by Cuban exiles.

Talk of rapproachement faded after the invasion of Grenada on October 25 by U.S. forces, accompanied by troops from several Caribbean nations. Cuban construction workers and military personnel—in Grenada to complete a 10,000-foot airport runway that the United States feared would be used by Soviet and Cuban military supply planes—put up some of the stiffest resistance encountered by the U.S. troops. By early November, as resistance essentially ceased, hundreds of captured Cubans were returned home to heroes' welcomes. Castro subsequently disputed U.S. charges that documents found on Grenada indicated the existence of secret military agreements between Grenada and the Soviet bloc aimed at turning the island into a Communist base.

Within Latin America, Cuba enjoyed improved relations with Argentina and Venezuela. It resumed diplomatic ties with Bolivia after a 19-year break.

In Cuba, there were reports that five people had been executed for trying to establish a

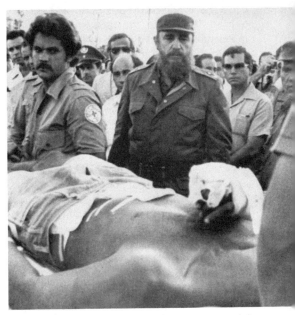

President Fidel Castro greets wounded Cubans being brought back from Grenada in November.

Solidarity-type union. A high Cuban official denied these reports but stated that 33 people had been jailed for acts of sabotage, such as burning canefields and work centers, and for allegedly planning the assassination of Cuban leaders.

The gravest internal problems facing the Castro government were, however, economic. The price of sugar, which accounted for more than three-quarters of all Cuban export revenues, fell to one-quarter of its 1980 level. Storms and floods in early 1983 destroyed much of the sugar and the high-quality tobacco crops. As a result, Cuba deepened its dependence on other Communist countries. According to Western sources, the Soviet Union was subsidizing the Cuban economy, through direct aid and concessionary trade, at a rate of $4 billion per year. At the same time, Moscow did not advance to Cuba the hard currency it needed to pay debts to Western banks and governments. The Castro government was obliged to renegotiate obligations, agreeing in return to slash public expenditures, increase consumer prices, and restrict imports.

See STATISTICS OF THE WORLD.   P.W.

CYPRUS. Events in Cyprus took a dramatic turn in 1983 with the proclamation of an independent Turkish Republic of Northern Cyprus in the Turkish-held northern part of the island on November 15. Turkey immediately recognized the new state, a move for which it was condemned by Greece and Great Britain, the other guarantors of Cyprus's 1960 constitution. The United States and other North Atlantic Treaty Organization members, fearing renewed tensions in the eastern Mediterranean, also strongly criticized the Turkish Cypriots' action and Ankara's support of it.

Turkish Cypriot leader Rauf Denktash asserted that the declaration, unanimously approved by the Turkish Cypriot Assembly, was intended to induce the Greek Cypriots, after nine years of fruitless intercommunal talks, to negotiate a "genuine federation" between the two communities. The UN Security Council, by a vote of 13–1, condemned the Turkish Cypriots' "legally invalid" move and demanded that it be reversed. Earlier, in May, the General Assembly had called for the withdrawal of occupying (Turkish) troops from the island as a way of facilitating efforts toward a settlement. (It was partly in response to that UN resolution, which he considered too one-sided, that Denktash decided to commit his government to a declaration of full independence.) On December 2 the Turkish Cypriots established a constituent assembly to draft a constitution for the newly proclaimed republic.

Greek Cypriot President Spyros Kyprianou declared that his government would not accept the Turkish Cypriot action as an accomplished fact but would seek, through "peaceful means," to have it reversed. Earlier, on February 13, Kyprianou had been elected to another five-year term as president. Heading an alliance between his centrist Democratic Party and the Progressive (Communist) Party of the Working People (AKEL), he gained 56.5 percent of the vote. Glafkos Clerides of the right-wing Democratic Rally, and Vassos Lyssarides, of the Socialist Party (EDEK), received 34 percent and 9.5 percent, respectively.

See STATISTICS OF THE WORLD.   P.J.M.

CZECHOSLOVAKIA. With one in every seven adults in Czechoslovakia a member or candidate member of the Communist Party—an unusually high proportion—there were recurrent complaints about the quality of party membership in 1983. It was said that many members were careerists and "people with low moral qualifications." Party units were criticized for having admitted newcomers indiscriminately. Corruption apparently remained a serious problem. Early in the year, the Crime Institute reported that private citizens were spending large amounts of money—a grand total of around $600 million a year—on illegal gratuities for all kinds of services. The Institute of Public Opinion in Bratislava found that almost half of those polled admitted having bribed a state employee to obtain better treatment.

In February the dissident playwright Václav Havel was transferred from jail to a civilian hospital in Prague because of serious illness. The following month, he was temporarily released from the hospital to recover at home. One of the founders of the Charter 77 human rights movement, Havel had been arrested in 1979 and sentenced to 4½ years' imprisonment for "subversion."

In June what was described as an international peace assembly was held in Prague. It was sponsored by the Czechoslovak government and attended by 3,625 people from 130 countries. After an inaugural address by Czechoslovak party leader Gustáv Husák, the assembly held a series of sessions dealing with "global problems." Delegates' speeches showed a strong bias in favor of the Soviet Union and against the United States.

Police were reported to have detained 120 members of the Franciscan religious order, after a series of raids at the beginning of Holy Week in March. Residences were searched, and religious literature and other materials were confiscated. The raids reportedly affected some 250 priests and lay Catholics from all parts of the country. Nine of those actually detained were released in 24 hours; the rest were held for a longer period. The Franciscan order, like other Roman Catholic orders and congregations in Czechoslovakia, was violently suppressed in 1950 and in 1983 remained sharply restricted by the government.

In January a contract for $1.5 billion worth of Soviet crude oil and oil products was signed in Moscow. Although Czechoslovakia paid a much higher sum for Soviet oil than it had in the past, the amount of oil to be provided was actually smaller; as a result, factories were again exhorted to meet their production targets while consuming less energy than planned. On the brighter side, Czechoslovakia in 1982 and 1983 managed to pay off $3.5 billion of its debt to the West.

See STATISTICS OF THE WORLD.   R.A.P.

DAHOMEY. *See* BENIN.

DANCE. The American dance world was saddened in 1983 by the death of choreographer George Balanchine. The New York City Ballet, which he helped found, flourished during the year, but American Ballet Theatre was beset by problems. The Joffrey Ballet was warmly received in a second home on the West Coast.

Balanchine and the NYCB. George Balanchine, arguably the most creative and influential figure in dance in the 20th century, died on April 30 at the age of 79. Balanchine was innovative and prolific. He utilized the classical academic dance tradition he had absorbed as a youth at the Russian Imperial Ballet School in his native St. Petersburg, transforming that tradition, through the impress of his distinctive mind and profound musicality, into a personal style. Between *La Nuit*, choreographed in 1920, and the revision of Stravinsky's *Variations*, done in July 1982, he produced a magnificent succession of ballets, among them *Apollo, Serenade, Concerto Barocco, The Four Temperaments, Divertimento No. 15, Agon, Liebeslieder Walzer, Jewels,* and *Mozartiana*. The Russian-born choreographer contributed greatly to the emergence of New York as the dance capital of the world, after moving to the United States in 1933 at the invitation of arts patron Lincoln Kirstein.

At the onset of Balanchine's illness, Peter Martins, one of the finest classical dancers of his generation, took charge of the day-to-day running of the New York City Ballet company, in collaboration with choreographer Jerome Robbins. In March the board of directors named them ballet masters in chief. Under their leadership, the company seemed determined to express its affection for Balanchine by dancing with a fresh dedication and zest.

Helgi Tomasson's choreographic essay *Ballet d'Isoline*, set to music by André Messager, was one of the two hits of City Ballet's spring season. The other big hit was Robbins's *Glass Pieces*, based on three short pieces by Philip Glass. Audiences also warmly applauded Robbins's other new work, *I'm Old Fashioned*, a set of variations on an excerpt from the 1942 film *You Were Never Lovelier*, in which Fred Astaire danced with Rita Hayworth.

In December, Martins retired as a dancer to concentrate on choreography and administration. Still, the company was generously stocked with talent: Along with elevating the remarkable Maria Calegari to the status of principal dancer, it welcomed to its ranks David McNaughton, a powerful virtuoso from the San Francisco Ballet, and Leonid Kozlov and Valentina Kozlova, who had defected from the Bolshoi Ballet in 1979.

American Ballet Theatre. American Ballet Theatre had less success. A lockout of dancers at the beginning of its 1982–1983 season, because of a labor dispute, entailed cancellation of a large part of the schedule, leaving a lavish *La Sylphide* as the company's only new evening-length production. Additions to the repertory included Twyla Tharp's *Once Upon a Time;* though brief, it gave better scope to the virtuosity of ABT's artistic director, Mikhail Baryshnikov, than did John McFall's *Follow the Feet,* pairing Baryshnikov with the promising Robert La Fosse. Two vehicles showcasing principal dancer Martine van Hamel—Lynne Taylor-Corbett's *Estuary* and Jiri Kylian's *Torso*—aroused little enthusiasm.

ABT had a disastrous drop in ticket sales during its New York season, with only 63 percent of the seats filled. By the end of the season, in July, ABT had an operating loss of nearly $1.8 million, and critical voices were being raised about the company's direction. In late September, the board of trustees announced that new donations, plus financial guarantees that could be used as collateral for a bank loan, would still enable the company to prepare for a full 1983–1984 season. In October the company announced that Herman Krawitz, apparently held responsible for some of ABT's problems, would no longer serve as executive director.

West Coast events. When the Joffrey Ballet opened its first season, on April 30, as the resident company of the Los Angeles Music Center, the first-night audience was studded with Hollywood luminaries and Southern California's business and social elite. The latter group had raised $2 million to bring the New York-based Joffrey Ballet to Los Angeles, making it the first major dance company to have homes and fund-raising sources in two cities. The opening night program featured the U.S. premiere of *Love Songs,* an Expressionist ballet originally created in Munich in 1979 by William Forsythe, to recordings by the pop singers Aretha Franklin and Dionne Warwick. Forsythe returned to the Joffrey to create a new work, *Square Deal,* in the fall.

Another major event on the West Coast was the week-long gala put on by the San Francisco Ballet, beginning January 29, to celebrate its 50th anniversary. The performance was conceived and directed by Michael Smuin, the company's codirector (with Lew Christensen), and gave an overview of the company's history, from its beginnings with Adolf Bolm's *Ballet Mécanique.*

Modern dance. Martha Graham gave the world premiere of her *Phaedra's Dream* in Athens in June. Paul Taylor offered three new works during his company's four week stay at City Center in April—among them, *Sunset,* a bittersweet idyll, set to Edward Elgar's *Elegy for Strings* and *Serenade for Strings.* Merce Cunningham offered *Quartet,* for four dancers and the aging choreographer himself, in March at City Center; in October, his company marked its 30th anniversary by launching a world tour.

Taking a New Step
Danish-born Peter Martins, long acknowledged as one of the world's best male dancers, assumed a major new role in March. He was placed in charge of day to day operations at the New York City Ballet (as co-ballet master in chief, with choreographer Jerome Robbins), after his mentor, George Balanchine, had become too ill to carry on at NYCB. (Balanchine died on April 30.) Late in the year, shortly after turning 37, Martins retired as a dancer in order to devote full time to his duties. Tall, blond, and classically good-looking, he personifies the title role in Balanchine's *Apollo,* which he performed in his first appearance with NYCB; he won wide acclaim as a dancer for his cool dignity and the near-perfection of his technique. As a choreographer, he has been noted for the precision and symmetry of his style, highly evident in such works as *Calcium Light Night* and his 1983 *Rossini Quartets.*

Peter Martins

The illustrious career of one of the world's greatest choreographers came to an end when George Balanchine, artistic director of the New York City Ballet, died at the age of 79. An innovator firmly grounded in tradition, he had the genius to visualize music as pure dance. Balanchine is shown here conducting a dance rehearsal.

Visiting companies. The Brooklyn Academy of Music in New York played host to a string of foreign companies, including the Basel Ballet from Switzerland, the Hamburg Ballet, and the London Contemporary Dance Theatre.

The Royal Ballet, touching down for a week in April at the Metropolitan Opera House, reunited the dancers Antoinette Sibley and Anthony Dowell in the world premiere of Sir Frederick Ashton's short but witty Varii Capricci, set off by David Hockney's brightly colored sets and Sir William Walton's breezy score. In May the Zurich Ballet, with Rudolf Nureyev as guest artist, visited the United States for the first time, dancing Nureyev's Manfred (its U.S. premiere), as well as his Don Quixote. (These were among Nureyev's last U.S. appearances before taking over as director of the Paris Opera Ballet.) In June, Roland Petit's Ballet National de Marseille visited Washington, D.C., Montreal, and New York, with guest artists Richard Cragun, Patrick Dupond, Natalia Makarova, and Rudolf Nureyev. Maurice Béjart's Ballet of the 20th Century visited the United States in the fall.

Black dance. The Dance Black America festival, held in April at the Brooklyn Academy of Music, celebrated more than 300 years of black dance. Katherine Dunham, the doyenne of black dance, was honored in a symposium on black style, held in June and sponsored by the Dance Critics Association. The Dance Theatre of Harlem put on company premieres of Bronislava Nijinska's Les Biches and Agnes de Mille's Fall River Legend. The spring season of the Alvin Ailey American Dance Company featured the first New York performance of Bill T. Jones's Fever Swamp.   K.F.R.

DELAWARE. See STATISTICS OF THE WORLD.

DEMOCRATIC PARTY. For the Democratic Party, 1983 was a year of preparation for the arduous 1984 campaign trail. By December 1983, eight Democrats were in the race to unseat President Ronald Reagan, whose own candidacy looked very much less vulnerable late in 1983 than it had earlier in the year. Party leaders, examining the off-year election returns, found comfort in the fact that the coalition of interest groups whose support the party would need in order to win in 1984—

139

Of the eight Democrats who hit the campaign trail in 1983, former Vice-President Walter Mondale (above) was the front-runner for the party's 1984 presidential nomination; Ohio Senator John Glenn (left) was another strong contender.

urban voters, organized labor, blacks, and women—appeared to be holding together.

Election results. Democratic candidates, especially women and blacks, fared well in the November balloting. For example, Kentucky Lieutenant Governor Martha Layne Collins won handily to become the state's first—and the nation's only—woman governor. San Francisco Mayor Dianne Feinstein easily beat back a recall attempt on April 26 and went on to win reelection in November; she was one of a few women frequently mentioned as potential vice-presidential nominees. Another prominent Democratic woman, Houston Mayor Kathy Whitmire, also won reelection. On April 12, U.S. Representative Harold Washington survived a bitter campaign, in which race was the leading issue, to become Chicago's first black mayor. Two other black Democrats, W. Wilson Goode and Harvey Gantt, won mayoralty races in Philadelphia and Charlotte, N.C., and another black Democratic mayor, Richard Hatcher of Gary, Ind., was reelected.

The party lost a U.S. Senate seat, however, after the death of Senator Henry M. ("Scoop") Jackson (D, Wash.) on September 1; Republican Daniel J. Evans, the temporary appointee, held onto the seat after a special election in November. The Democrats also lost a House seat when Representative Phil Gramm (D, Texas) resigned his seat and, after switching parties, regained it as a Republican in a special election.

See also ELECTIONS IN THE UNITED STATES.

Gearing up for 1984. By general consensus, the front-running Democratic presidential candidate was former Vice-President Walter F. ("Fritz") Mondale, with Senator John Glenn of Ohio, the ex-astronaut, in second place (see biographies in PEOPLE IN THE NEWS). Also in the race were former Florida Governor Reubin Askew; Senate Minority Whip Alan Cranston (D, Calif.); Senator Gary Hart (D, Colo.), Senator Ernest F. ("Fritz") Hollings (D, S.C.); civil rights leader Jesse Jackson (see biography in PEOPLE IN THE NEWS); and former South Dakota

Senator George McGovern, who was swamped as the party's standard-bearer in 1972. Mondale's strength lay with the party establishment and with big labor; a negative factor was his association with the Carter administration. Glenn began the race aided by public recognition as a national hero and a reputation as an expert on defense matters; on the other hand, his campaign was far less well-organized than Mondale's, and his conservative positions on arms control and "Reaganomics" seemed to put him to the right of the Democratic mainstream.

On January 6, Democratic National Chairman Charles T. Manatt announced a series of delegate-selection rules that would enhance the role of the Democratic officeholders and party officials at the 1984 convention. Of 3,923 delegate seats, 568 would be reserved for the party leaders, both elected and unelected, who would be unpledged to any presidential candidate. Other rules provided thresholds below which a candidate would not win a share of delegates proportionate to the candidate's share of the vote in primaries or caucuses. Jesse Jackson strongly criticized the new rules as discriminatory against minority groups and long-shot candidates and threatened a floor fight at the 1984 national convention; in a compromise, Manatt agreed to allow him to present his case at a January 1984 meeting of the Democratic Executive Committee.

See REPUBLICAN PARTY. G.M.H.

DENMARK. In 1983, Prime Minister Poul Schlüter survived his first full year in office with a mixed record. Austerity measures initiated in 1982 and new measures introduced in 1983 helped to reduce the budget deficit and the inflation rate, but unemployment remained high.

Schlüter, Denmark's first Conservative prime minister since 1901, presided over a coalition government consisting also of the Liberals, the Center Democrats, and the Christian People's Party. Lacking a majority in the Folketing (parliament), it depended on the support of most members of the maverick Progressive Party.

The chief goal of the Conservative-led coalition was to reverse the country's economic slump of recent years. The government had slashed planned public expenditures for 1983, primarily by reducing unemployment compensation and sick pay and by suspending cost-of-living pay increases. In August the coalition introduced further spending reductions for 1984, to be achieved by raising fees for various public services, including day-care centers; by increasing individual contributions to unemployment and medical insurance programs; and, for higher-income groups, by charging new fees for medical services. In October agreement was reached on an austerity package that included budget cuts and measures to help agriculture and construction.

The government's austerity program helped reduce the inflation rate from 9.8 percent in 1982 to an estimated 5.8 percent for 1983, and lower petroleum prices contributed to an estimated 25 percent reduction in Denmark's international payments deficit. However, projected industrial investments rose only 1 percent in 1983, while unemployment was expected to reach close to 11 percent.

Mogens Glistrup, the controversial leader of the Progressive Party, began serving a three-year prison term for tax evasion on September 1. Earlier, the Folketing had voted to strip Glistrup of his parliamentary immunity.

A four-year war of words over fishing rights ended in January when Denmark and the other members of the European Economic Community (EEC) agreed on a formula regulating access to waters off the west coast of Scotland and near the Shetland Islands. Under the agreement, Danish fishermen were allowed a total catch, after 1983, of 20,000 metric tons of mackerel in EEC (but not Scottish) waters.

The Folketing narrowly endorsed a resolution in May calling on the United States to postpone plans to install medium-range missiles in Europe, even if U.S.-Soviet negotiations failed to produce an arms agreement. However, the talks broke down and deployment was proceeding late in the year.

See STATISTICS OF THE WORLD. M.D.H.

DISTRICT OF COLUMBIA. *See* STATISTICS OF THE WORLD.

DJIBOUTI. *See* STATISTICS OF THE WORLD.

DOMINICA. *See* STATISTICS OF THE WORLD.

DOMINICAN REPUBLIC. *See* STATISTICS OF THE WORLD. *See also* CARIBBEAN COUNTRIES.

E

EARTH SCIENCES. The occurrence of an unusually strong El Niño, a current of warm ocean waters appearing off South America, attracted the attention of climatographers and oceanographers alike in 1983. Meanwhile, earthquakes and volcanic eruptions in many parts of the world were of interest to geologists.

CLIMATOLOGY

The winter of 1982–1983 was the northern hemisphere's warmest in 25 years, with temperatures about 5° Fahrenheit above average, and flooding and storms were unusually severe. Many meteorologists believed an important factor in producing the unusual weather was the massive oceanic disturbance known as El Niño (Spanish for "the Child," a reference to the Christ child). This name was originally applied to a warming of water near the west coast of South America that sometimes occurs around Christmas. Research by meteorologists and oceanographers has shown that this patch of warm water is really the reflection of an interrelated shift in winds, temperatures, and ocean currents that may cover huge areas of the Pacific Ocean. The unusually intense 1982–1983 El Niño was first observed in the mid-Pacific rather than near South America. By the time it began to taper off, it may have been instrumental in causing more than 2,000 deaths and $13 billion in damage worldwide.

Storms and floods. The state of California was pounded by storms through much of the winter. The storms, which sometimes carried winds of up to 90 miles an hour, killed at least 28 people, washed homes into the ocean, and triggered massive mud slides. Other western states, particularly Colorado, Wyoming, Utah, and Texas, were also extensively affected by storms. The same weather systems moved eastward to the Mississippi Valley, where torrential rains and snow killed close to 30 and drove thousands from their homes. At least 46 deaths were attributed to a February snowstorm that traveled from Virginia to Cape Cod.

A New York City resident pushes his child across a snowy Manhattan intersection, in the wake of a February blizzard that blanketed the Atlantic seaboard.

Record rains caused heavy flooding in some southern states during early April; here the swollen waters of the Pearl River inundate homes in southeastern Louisiana.

In early April a landslide brought on by heavy rain and snow buried U.S. 50, the main highway between Sacramento, Calif., and Lake Tahoe, under 30 feet of rocks and soil. Subsequently, melting snow caused flooding and mud slides in many areas of the West. The town of Bountiful, Utah, for example, was hit by a 30-foot-high wave of mud and water that roared through the community at a speed of 15 miles an hour; more than 1,000 residents had to be temporarily evacuated. In late June and early July the continuing snowmelt caused disruption along the Colorado River. Rain and flooding also caused problems farther east. In April a deluge of rain led to 13 deaths and forced the evacuation of nearly 30,000 people from their homes in Louisiana, Mississippi, and Tennessee. In mid-May another storm hit the south central states, with tornadoes and more flooding, causing another 24 fatalities.

Drought, heat, and hurricane. The exceptional weather continued into summertime, with a drought and abnormally high temperatures that persisted into mid-September in much of the United States east of the Rocky Mountains. The National Weather Service announced that August 1983 was the hottest month on record for the United States, as well as one of the driest. The first tropical storm of the season, Hurricane Alicia, struck the Texas coast on August 18 with winds of up to 130 miles an hour. At least 22 deaths were attributed to the hurricane, and property damage was estimated at more than $1 billion.   N.M.R.

GEOLOGY

On May 2, an earthquake measuring 6.5 on the Richter scale struck the small oil and farming community of Coalinga, Calif., 150 miles southeast of San Francisco. A large number of aftershocks later shook the area, including two with a magnitude of 5.5. About $30 million in damage was done, and more than 1,000 people were displaced from their homes. However, no one was killed, and only about 50 people were injured. The thrust fault that caused the Coalinga quake was tens of

Workers clear away rubble inside the cathedral in Popayán, Colombia; over 260 people were killed in an earthquake that devastated the city on March 31.

Volcanic eruptions. Kilauea volcano on the island of Hawaii erupted on January 3, its third and largest eruption within a year. U.S. Geological Survey scientists were able to predict the eruption a day in advance and alerted public agencies. The first eruptive phase, which lasted nine and a half hours, began in Hawaii Volcanoes National Park at Napau Crater and extended northeast with lava fountains for a distance of about 4 miles. Kilauea continued to erupt intermittently. Mount St. Helens also had further eruptions. In early February explosive activity began on the upper east flank, followed by extrusion of a new lobe of lava. Further ash and steam emissions and lava extrusions were reported later in the year. Veniaminof volcano on the Alaskan Peninsula began to erupt on June 7, with plumes containing ash rising to nearly 3 miles. Several days later, the crater began throwing out cinder-like lava and semimolten rocks.

Sicily's Mount Etna, Europe's tallest volcano, erupted in the spring, sending out lava flows that destroyed buildings. Efforts to divert the flow by erecting large earthen barriers achieved some success. Other volcanic eruptions were reported in May and June on the Soviet Union's Kamchatka Peninsula, beneath a large glacier in southern Iceland, and on Miyake Island in Japan.

Volcanic hazard alert. In 1982 the U.S. Geological Survey issued a notice of potential volcanic hazard for the Long Valley area of California, along the eastern front of the Sierra Nevada. As of late 1983, there had been no eruptions, but a swarm of more than 3,000 small earthquakes that began on January 6 caused some minor damage, as did a moderate earthquake in early July. Many scientists believe that the earthquakes were related to the movement of magma (molten rock material) beneath the Long Valley caldera, in which the Mammoth Lakes ski resort is located; they contend that the possibility of a volcanic eruption or a major earthquake did not diminish after the swarm ended. If the earthquake swarms are produced by tectonic forces (friction between crustal plates), the possibility of a major earthquake cannot be excluded.

In August, U.S. Geological Survey scientists reported that the earth was growing more

millions of years older than the better known San Andreas fault, which is of a different type and closer to the surface.

A stronger quake, of magnitude 6.9, struck a rural area of Idaho on October 28, with two deaths reported. In a more populated area it would have been more devastating.

Around the world there were other notable earthquakes, some of them devastating. On May 26, for example, an earthquake measuring 7.7 on the Richter scale occurred in the Sea of Japan. More than 100 people on the islands of Honshu and Hokkaido were killed by the quake or the tsunami (huge sea wave) that followed. On March 31, a quake devastated the Colombian city of Popayán, killing over 260 people. On October 30 a quake measuring 7.2 on the Richter scale killed about 2,000 people in eastern Turkey, and left tens of thousands homeless. Officials said it was the worst quake in the area since 1952.

restless beneath the Sierra Nevada and Cascade mountain ranges and pointed to several sites where serious eruptions were possible. Besides Mount St. Helens and the Mammoth Lakes area, they include Mount Lassen and Mount Shasta in California, Mount Rainier and Mount Baker in Washington, and Mount Hood in Oregon.   R.L.K.

OCEANOGRAPHY

The unusual weather conditions of 1983 were apparently caused in part by widespread changes in the equatorial oceans, including the century's strongest El Niño, the current that appears along the west coast of Ecuador and Peru. Since the disastrous El Niño of 1972, the current has been closely studied by U.S. and Peruvian oceanographers.

Southern oscillation. One atmospheric phenomenon related to El Niño is the southern oscillation, involving a large-scale exchange of air between the eastern Southern Pacific and the Indian Ocean around Indonesia. When the oscillation occurs, normally strong east-west trade winds along the equator weaken, and accumulated warm seawater off southeast Asia travels as a surge, or wavelike motion, across the Pacific. On hitting South America it causes similar wavelike movements of water along the coast to the north and south, with devastating effects on Peru and neighboring areas. Northward, the picture is complicated, owing to North America's irregular coastline. Unusual oceanic conditions, including altered sea-surface temperatures, were reported as far north as the Gulf of Alaska in 1983. The effect on North Pacific fisheries will probably not be known for years. One concern is that the changed ocean conditions may have upset the spawning of certain commercially valuable fish, such as salmon.

Walker circulation. The conditions that trigger an El Niño affect weather by changing wind patterns along the equator. One such pattern is the Walker circulation, named for Sir Gilbert Walker, who in the 1930's described it and pointed out its influence on weather.

The basic mechanism of the Walker circulation is related to water temperature. Where surface seawater temperatures are high, the overlying air is warmed and begins to rise. As the air rises, it cools, and the water vapor in

it condenses, resulting in local rains. In general, areas of warm sea-surface temperatures are areas of heavy rainfall. Conversely, when sea-surface temperatures are low, the overlying air is cooled, becomes more dense, and sinks. Areas of sinking air have clear skies and generally desert conditions.

During an El Niño, the distribution of warm and cool sea-surface temperatures shifts. For example, the normally cold areas off Peru are warm, causing the heavy rainfall and floods that plagued the South American coast during 1982–1983. By the same principle, land near ocean areas with unusually cold surface temperatures is likely to experience drought. Severe droughts were in fact particularly troublesome during 1982–1983. Australia saw its worst brush fires of the century, and crop failures occurred in India and parts of Africa.
                                                M.G.G.

ECONOMY AND BUSINESS. The U.S. economy led a worldwide recovery in 1983 from what was generally considered the worst recession since the Great Depression. The U.S. gross national product rose steadily, inflation remained low, and unemployment fell. These trends also were discernible in most other non-Communist industrial economies by midyear. Many economists, however, feared that large projected U.S. budget deficits and interest rates that remained relatively high could cut the recovery short.

U.S. recovery. The real, or inflation-adjusted, gross national product rose at an annual rate of 2.6 percent in the first quarter of 1983. In the second quarter, the recovery took off, with real GNP surging ahead at an annual rate of 9.7 percent. In the third quarter, the GNP rose at a 7.7 percent rate, with the government projecting fourth-quarter growth at a 4.5 percent rate. This cooling off was a welcome sign to economists who feared that too much strength over a sustained period of time would only lead to high interest rates as a result of the high federal deficits.

The recovery was led by the auto and housing industries, but it became more broadly based as the year progressed. Corporate profits after taxes rose 14.7 percent in the second quarter, the largest gain in nearly eight years, with manufacturing firms and financial institutions

Inspectors return from a mine due to be reopened in Johnstown, Pa., shortly before 1,100 Bethlehem Steel workers went back on the job there. With the turnaround in the U.S. economy, millions of workers were returned to the payroll.

accounting for most of the increase. Personal income was buoyed by expanding employment opportunities, lower inflation, and the third installment of President Ronald Reagan's tax cut, a 10 percent reduction which went into effect July 1. Investors found the stock market more alluring; the Dow Jones Industrial Average exceeded the 1,200 mark for the first time and set new record highs in 1983.

The increase in personal income led to a sharp rise in consumer spending. Consumer installment debt increased as much in the first six months of 1983 as in all of 1982. During the Christmas shopping season, retailers reported exceptionally high sales, and it was predicted that retailers' pretax earnings in the fourth quarter would be the highest since 1978.

Interest rates. The U.S. recovery was sparked by two factors: lower interest rates and lower inflation. The prime interest rate charged by banks began 1982 at 16.5 percent, then steadily declined as bank loan demand collapsed. At the end of 1982, the prime had fallen to 11.5 percent. In 1983 it dropped further, to 11 percent in January and 10.5 percent in February, before edging back up in August to 11 percent, where it remained late in the year. In the early part of the year, other market-sensitive interest rates followed the prime rate down, and consumers, finding the cost of borrowing more affordable, began to take on more debt to buy goods and services. Corporations, too, found the lower rates beneficial because they were able to decrease their own business costs and better repair their battered balance sheets.

Playing a key role in the interest rate decline was a decidedly more expansionary monetary policy by the Federal Reserve Board. In the early part of 1983, sharp increases in the money supply—well beyond the Fed's target range—raised fears that the Fed would tighten up again to bring monetary growth under control. Although it did tighten up somewhat in midyear, the central bank continued to be flexible.

Inflation. The record on inflation was the best news of all. The Consumer Price Index rose only 3.9 percent for all of 1982, and the increase in 1983 was only 3.8 percent, the lowest rate since 1972, a year of wage and price controls. Two particularly inflationary areas of the late 1970's and 1980—food and energy—showed dramatic improvement. Lower worldwide oil demand caused an oil glut that stabilized prices, and surpluses produced by American farmers moderated food prices.

Employment. In December 1982 the U.S. civilian unemployment rate had peaked at 10.8 percent, with over 12 million people out of work. The rate then began to decline, as the recovery took hold. In November, the civilian unemployment rate stood at 8.4 percent, and the overall rate (including military personnel) was 8.2 percent. Some 9.4 million people were unemployed.

The economy's shift away from manufacturing into services and information continued. In 1983 there were 2 million fewer manufacturing workers than there had been in 1979—but 5 million more workers in the services sector. This trend was especially troublesome for the heavily industrialized states around the Great Lakes. States dependent on such industries as steel, automobiles, coal mining, and textiles suffered the highest unemployment and found the way back to prosperity much more difficult. As a result of these labor force trends, wage increases were much more moderate than in the past. In a number of national wage contracts, employers won either freezes in wages or rollbacks of wage increases, as well as postponements of cost-of-living adjustments.

Deficits. The strong business recovery was threatened by the prospect of federal budget deficits in the range of $100 billion to $200 billion during each of the next five years. Economists feared that if left untouched, these deficits could create a scramble for available funds between an expanding private sector and a federal government hungry for money to cover its red ink. Such a scramble for funds, called "crowding out" by economists, could lead to another rise in interest rates and kill off the recovery sometime in 1984. In the view of these economists, the Federal Reserve Board could keep the recovery going by taking steps to print more money to feed the demands of the public and private sectors, but such a path would in the long run be inflationary.

Although the deficit situation frightened the financial markets and kept interest rates higher than they would otherwise have been, it was a stimulant to economic activity at the very time such a stimulus was needed. Heavy government borrowing may push up interest rates, but the government also uses its money to pay its employees and purchase goods and services, both of which spur the economy. Still, as Martin Feldstein, chairman of Reagan's Council of Economic Advisers, put it, the deficits looming over the next several years could cause a lopsided recovery, with industries that depend on credit for their success suffering the most.

Moreover, as high interest rates attract foreign investors to the U.S. financial markets, the value of the dollar in relation to other currencies becomes higher. In fact, the dollar was extremely overvalued in 1983—some suggested by as much as 20 percent. The high value of the dollar cost many U.S. workers involved in export industries their jobs because U.S. products became more expensive overseas. At the same time, imports became cheaper and poured into the country. The U.S. trade deficit for the year was projected at a record $70 billion.

U.S. trade did benefit when the United States and the Soviet Union signed a new grain pact, providing for Soviet purchases worth an estimated $7–8 billion over five years.

Bankruptcies, breakups, and mergers. In spite of the general recovery, the rate of business failures remained high. During the first 49 weeks of 1983, there were 29,550 business failures, according to a Dun & Bradstreet Corporation estimate, compared with 25,346

The breakup of American Telephone and Telegraph, effective January 1, 1984, produced a scramble for rate increases by phone companies unable to subsidize local services with the high profits from long-distance calls.

for all of 1982. Continental Air Lines, the eighth-largest U.S. carrier, filed for bankruptcy in September, citing "excessive labor costs." In the same month, Baldwin-United Corporation, a diversified financial services concern, also filed for bankruptcy, having announced in March that it was unable to meet its debts. Much of the debt had been incurred during an aggressive acquisitions campaign that had transformed the company from a piano manufacturer into a vast diversified concern. Other companies to declare bankruptcy included Wilson Foods Corporation, the largest U.S. fresh pork processor, and Bell & Beckwith, a Toledo, Ohio, brokerage firm.

There were a number of major corporate acquisitions. In January, Phillips Petroleum Company reached an agreement to purchase General American Oil Company of Texas in a complex acquisition costing an estimated $1.2 billion. In February, Goodyear Tire and Rubber Company announced the purchase of Celeron Corporation, an oil and gas concern based in Louisiana, for an estimated $825 million. Also in February, stockholders of the Kroger Company approved the acquisition of another food chain, Dillon Companies of Kansas, for $600 million in Kroger stock. The acquisition allowed Kroger to surpass Safeway as the largest supermarket operator in the U.S. market. In other retail business acquisitions, Associated Dry Goods purchased Loehmann's, one of the nation's best-known off-price apparel chains, and F. W. Woolworth bought the 102-store Holtzman's Little Folk Shop, Inc., a specialty store operator based in California.

In international mergers, the American Express Company acquired Trade Development Bank Holding S.A. in March, in a deal worth $550 million. The bank holding concern owned institutions in Geneva, London, Paris, Monte Carlo, and other cities. The acquisition would make American Express one of the five largest banks in Switzerland.

Under the terms of the court-ordered breakup of the American Telephone and Telegraph Company, scheduled to be implemented by January 1, 1984, the telecommunications giant was split into eight separate companies—seven regional companies, to handle local telephone service, and a greatly reduced AT&T, concentrating on long-distance telephone and electronic data-transmission services. The new arrangement was expected to result in considerably higher local telephone rates, since local service was no longer subsidized by long-distance

Huge quantities of grain are being shipped to the Soviet Union under a new trade agreement between Washington and Moscow, with total U.S. grain exports to the Soviet Union probably reaching $7–$8 billion over a five-year period.

revenues. Long distance rates, on the other hand, were expected to decline.

World outlook. Since the United States remains the strongest economic power in the world, accounting for some 20 percent of world production, U.S. recovery brought considerable cheer to leaders in other nations, who hoped that greater U.S. demand for imports would give their economies a boost. Most other industrial economies in the non-Communist world also were improving by summer, showing the first solid growth in three years. There were even some indications of an economic upturn in the developing nations.

Among the key indicators of economic improvement in 1983 was the fact that inflation was under better control. Prices in the non-Communist industrial world were up, on average, only about 5 percent in July 1983, compared with 12 months earlier. What made this significant was that the tendency during the last two decades for inflation to worsen with each business cycle (that is, with each bout of recession, recovery, growth, and decline) was stopped. During the 1974–1975 recession, the industrial world never saw aggregate inflation rates fall below 8 percent.

Most U.S. interest rates, another crucial factor in the global economy, were running in 1983 at about half their peak rates of late 1980 and early 1981. Nonetheless, with mortgage rates at about 13 to 14 percent during the summer, real interest rates—after subtracting the inflation rate—remained extraordinarily high. Interest rates in other countries had been dragged up by the high U.S. rates, and leaders of many Western European and other nations argued that American officials should do more to bring the U.S. rates down, believing that the high rates were retarding their own economic progress.

In the non-Communist industrial countries, the economic scene varied considerably in 1983. The British economy, revised statistics showed, was growing more rapidly than at first thought during the recovery that began in the spring of 1981. As a result of the Conservative government's earlier austerity program and the resulting high unemployment levels, productivity improved dramatically. In France, where the Socialist government of President François

The Cabbage Patch Kids—no-two-are-alike dolls that come with birth certificates and adoption papers— were snapped up by eager Christmas shoppers, as booming retail sales during the holiday season cheered merchants throughout the United States.

Mitterrand that came to power in 1981 had hoped to stimulate the economy through public spending, the government was forced by a severe balance-of-payments problem and a falling exchange rate for the franc to reverse directions in March 1983, with a severely deflationary budget. The French faced perhaps two years of slow growth, if not recession. West Germany made marginal economic progress, with growth running at an annual rate of 1 to 1½ percent.

The ninth annual economic summit meeting of the leaders of the seven major non-Communist industrial powers was held in Williamsburg, Va., in late May. It was, noted one economist, "long on rhetoric and short on substance." But the leaders did talk of trying for "convergent" national economic policies.

The debt crisis continued to overshadow the world economy. At a special meeting in February, the International Monetary Fund agreed to a 47.5 percent boost in quotas, or members' contributions, so as to extend new loans to debt-ridden countries.

By the end of 1982, the total external debt of non–oil-exporting developing countries exceeded $612 billion, and by the end of 1983, the total was expected to reach $664 billion. These countries were expected to pay some $93 billion on their loans in 1983. Reflecting lower interest rates and debt rescheduling, this sum is considerably less than the $107 billion they paid on debts in 1982.

One helpful factor for many debtor countries was a solid rise in the prices of commodities many of them export. An IMF index for 30 primary commodities—including such products as coffee, copper, cotton, rubber, jute, sisal, sugar, fats and oils, and rice—rose 11 percent between December 1982 and August 1983 and was expected to move up further. Because of a 25 percent drop in the same index between 1980 and 1982, combined with world recession, the average standard of living in the world's poor countries had been falling for three years. In 1983 the reversal in commodity prices, plus the decline in oil prices, meant a modest improvement in the situation.

See also BANKING AND FINANCE and articles on individual countries.   W.N. & D.R.F.

ECUADOR. Osvaldo Hurtado Larrea completed two years as Ecuador's chief executive on May 24, 1983. On that anniversary he said that his greatest achievement was the preservation of democracy during Ecuador's worst economic crisis.

As a condition for rescheduling a fourth of its $4.6 billion foreign public debt, Ecuador agreed to devalue the sucre for the second time in less than a year; it was projected to fall to 50 sucres to the dollar by year's end. Among other conditions imposed on Ecuador by the International Monetary Fund (IMF) and foreign lending banks was the removal of subsidies from milk, fuel oils, and other basic articles. As a result, the price of milk shot up by 40 percent in March, and that of fuel oils was expected to double within a year.

A massive general strike, called to protest government economic measures, halted nationwide production for 48 hours in March. The strike was called off when the government offered to negotiate wage increases in some cases. Later, government offices were paralyzed when employees went on strike, protesting a bill that would have reduced their wages. The bill was nullified when the IMF approved foreign debt rescheduling.

The inflation rate topped 50 percent in June. Hurtado blamed the high inflation mainly on food shortages resulting from heavy rains and flooding. Petroleum production, which came to earn more than 60 percent of Ecuador's export income, increased, and a rate of 250,000 barrels per day was anticipated by year's end. The price, however, declined to $27 per barrel on the spot market. In June, the government offered foreign companies 20-year oil exploration contracts on 11 tracts in the Amazon region and offshore.

See STATISTICS OF THE WORLD.   L.L.P.

EDUCATION. In 1983 national attention was focused on the state of public education in the United States. As a federally appointed commission released unfavorable findings, governors, presidential candidates, and a politically sensitive administration came forward with proposals to improve standards. Recommendations included adopting more stringent academic requirements, raising teachers' salaries on the basis of merit, and allocating more funds, on both the state and federal levels, for an expanded basic curriculum.

National report on quality of education. "We report to the American people that . . . the educational foundations of our society are presently being eroded by a rising tide of mediocrity that threatens our very future as a Nation." So began a hard-hitting report, *A Nation at Risk*, by the National Commission on Excellence in Education, an 18-member panel appointed by U.S. Secretary of Education Terrel H. Bell to study the state of American education and to prepare a report for President Ronald Reagan. The commission's recommendations, presented to President Reagan in April, included a required four-year high school course of study comprising four years of English, three years of math, three years of science, one-half year of computer science, three years of social studies, and for college-bound students, at least two years of a foreign language. The commission also urged school districts and state leg-

Carpenters at a Maryland school wall off traditional classrooms in a previously open teaching area; such efforts reflect nationwide concern for the quality of schools and a trend toward a more structured style of education.

islatures to consider lengthening their school day to seven hours and their school year to 200–220 days, to bring total schooling time in line with that in other modern industrialized nations. The report did not discuss how improvements were to be funded, but it called upon citizens to provide "the financial support necessary."

Merit pay. In a commencement address at Seton Hall University in South Orange, N.J., on May 21, President Reagan touched on the issue of merit pay for teachers, a concept strongly endorsed by the commission report. "Teachers should be paid and promoted on the basis of their merit and competence," he said. The next day, Mary Hatwood Futrell, the incoming president of the National Education Association, denounced Reagan's statement as a "disgraceful assault" on American schoolteachers. She also pointed out that the commission had also proposed increasing all teachers' salaries, a recommendation Reagan had ignored.

Meanwhile, the legislatures in California and Florida passed broad school reform bills that included key recommendations of the national commission. In Florida the development of a "master teacher" program was under way, in which highly rated teachers will be able to earn more for good work. A similar program,

the "mentor teacher" program, will be established in California, where certain qualified teachers can receive as much as $4,000 more a year for taking on added responsibilities, such as training novice teachers.

Decline of teaching profession. A study released in late August by the Carnegie Foundation for the Advancement of Teaching found that high school students planning to major in education score lower on the Scholastic Aptitude Test than any other group except those planning to major in "ethnic studies." The study cited low salaries as the major factor keeping better students from entering or staying in teaching. During the last decade, it found, teachers' salaries did not keep pace either with inflation or with the salaries of most other professions. Not only were starting salaries found to be low—an average of $12,769 in 1981–1982—but they failed to grow fast enough to be competitive.

Higher academic standards. The Carnegie Foundation study, while contending that schools and student performance had begun to improve in the late 1970's, asserted that there was a continuing need for major reforms, among them a central emphasis on writing and other English language skills and adoption of a "core curriculum" that would include mastery of a foreign language.

EDUCATION

Several states in 1983 raised graduation requirements, as well as salaries for teachers. The most notable example was Mississippi, which had had a firm lock on the 50th position among the states in support for its schools. Governor William F. Winter succeeded in persuading the Mississippi legislature to approve his Education Reform Act, which provided for, among other things, a 10 percent increase in teachers' salaries, the establishment of more rigorous certification requirements for new teachers, and the introduction of a testing program in the basic skills for grade school and high school students.

Florida became the first state to deny diplomas to high school seniors who had failed to pass a state functional literacy test. When the state announced that it might withhold diplomas from more than 3,000 seniors, suit was brought against it. In May, however, Federal District Judge George C. Carr declared that the state had the right to deny diplomas to those who had failed to pass the test in the five attempts allowed. The ruling was expected to spur other states to proceed with their plans to deny diplomas to students who failed to pass basic skills tests.

The actions of the state boards of education in Virginia and North Carolina, which increased the number of required high school courses from 18 to 20, were typical of the scurry to raise standards. California, which had abandoned all its state graduation requirements in 1969 and turned the responsibility over to local school boards, reinstated statewide standards. In July the New York Board of Regents (comparable to a state board of education), which had not followed the earlier trend toward lowering standards, nevertheless proposed additional required courses in math and the sciences.

Education as a political issue. These developments reflected two broader political trends that emerged in 1983: the adoption of education as a number one priority by state governors, particularly those in the South, and the emergence of education as a national political issue. Led by North Carolina Governor James B. Hunt, Jr., and Florida Governor Bob Graham, the Education Commission of the States concluded that high-quality education is cru-

"Master teacher" Quentin Merriman of Los Angeles handles extra duties and receives merit pay in addition to his regular salary; the fifth-grade instructor is taking part in a local program to reward good teachers and keep them in the classroom.

cial to economic growth. "Well-educated people are the raw material of high-tech corporations," said Governor Hunt in advocating more state support for public schools and colleges.

Meanwhile, leading Democratic presidential candidates voiced their support for increased federal funding of education. Former Vice-President Walter Mondale outlined a plan that would allocate $11 billion in additional federal funds for various programs, including teacher training, and a further $4.5 billion "fund for excellence" to be allocated to local governments. Ohio Senator John Glenn presented a $5 billion proposal stressing math and science education.

Education Secretary Bell contended that federal education support had risen during the Reagan administration, from about $14 billion to $15 billion. However, Reagan's budget proposals had actually called for cutbacks in education funding; these had been rejected by Congress, which had raised funding slightly. In March the House approved a bill authorizing more than $1 billion over the next five years to improve math, science, and foreign language programs. A similar bill was pending in the Senate.

Tuition tax credits. President Reagan's proposals to provide federal tuition tax credits of up to $300 per child for parents of children attending private schools got a boost during the summer. On June 29, the U.S. Supreme Court upheld the constitutionality of a Minnesota law that granted tax credits for parents of students in both public and private schools. This marked the first time the high court had upheld a state program of substantial aid to parents of private school students and appeared to signal that the court would not block a similar federal law. However, the Senate, on November 16, defeated an administration-supported tax-credit bill, in a 59–38 vote, leaving the issue dead in the view of many observers.

Computers. Pittsburgh's Carnegie-Mellon University announced this year that it will become the first "computer-wired" American university. Beginning in the fall of 1985, all students will have their own personal computers, linked to one another in a university-wide network. University President Richard Cyert predicted the school will have the most extensive computer network for everyday use anywhere in the world.

Nuclear-education movement. A new curriculum topic that has recently emerged in U.S. schools has stirred up considerable controversy among educators. "Nuclear war is *the* hot curriculum issue," said Herbert Wagner, executive director of Education for Social Responsibility, a teacher group founded in 1981 to promote classroom discussions of nuclear war. School boards all across the country, including those in Cambridge, Mass., Milwaukee, and New York City, have recently introduced or plan to introduce such topics as peace, nuclear war, and nuclear disarmament into their curricula.

Spending and enrollment. According to a report prepared by the National Center for Education Statistics, total education spending in the United States was expected to reach $230 billion in the 1983–1984 school year, up from an estimated $215 billion in 1982–1983. Elementary and secondary schools would account for $141 billion, while colleges and universities would account for $89 billion. The report also estimated that as of the fall of 1983, nationwide enrollment would decline by about 400,000, to 56.7 million, with most of the decline coming in the high schools. College and university enrollment would stay about the same, at 12.4 million.   D.G.S.

EGYPT. Egyptian President Hosni Mubarak continued to steer a middle course at home and abroad in 1983. In domestic policy he sought to eliminate corruption and to take a cautious but firm approach in dealing with the opposition. In foreign affairs he tried to enhance Egypt's position in the Arab world and the nonaligned movement while maintaining good relations with the West.

Domestic affairs. The government mounted a strong attack on corruption. Among the most prominent victims was Ismat as-Sadat, half brother of the late president. In February, Sadat and three of his sons, who had amassed a fortune estimated at $150 million, were found guilty on several counts of fraud; they were sentenced to a year in detention, and most of their illegally acquired assets were impounded. The Supreme Court of Ethics ordered their release in August but upheld the decision on impoundment. The trial led to action against other prominent figures, including the dismissal of two government ministers in March.

A major source of trouble to the regime was the desire of opposition parties to test the president's political colors and press for greater liberalization of the political system. There were repeated calls for an end to the emergency laws giving the president wide-ranging powers of detention. Mubarak largely ignored these calls, but in September two laws were repealed that involved the banning of demonstrations and the prohibition of harmful rumors.

In July the People's Assembly passed a law that would disqualify from representation any party failing to win at least 8 percent of the popular vote in a legislative election. (At the time the law was passed, Egypt's opposition parties together held only 3 percent of the seats.) The opposition won a victory in October, however, when judges of the Egyptian State Council declared the opposition New Wafd a legitimate political party.

The government carried on with its prolonged investigation of suspected religious dissidents arrested after Sadat's assassination. The trial of a group of 300 radical Muslims dragged on for months, its outcome still unknown by late 1983. In the meantime, internal security forces at the Ministry of the Interior, in August, arrested another group of alleged conspirators. Mubarak used the carrot as well as the stick in dealing with Islamic sentiment. During Ramadan, the holy month when Muslims fast from dawn to dusk, summer time was suspended so that the evening meal could come more quickly.

In economic policy, Mubarak reasserted his commitment to an "open door" policy, designed to attract foreign investment and establish productive enterprises in Egypt. Egypt's chronic problem of a high population growth rate (nearly 3 percent a year), combined with a failure to increase agricultural output dramatically, meant that it had to import half its food, at an estimated cost of $4 billion in 1983. To cover the heavy cost of food and other essential imports, Egypt relied on foreign exchange earnings from tourism, remittances from Egyptians working abroad, Suez Canal revenues, and oil exports. Tourism was finally rebounding from the shock waves of the Sadat assassination, and remittances by foreign workers were expected to remain high. Oil export revenues, however, were hit by the international economic recession and the related drop in world petroleum prices. Egypt anticipated a total current account deficit approaching $3 billion for the 1983–1984 fiscal year.

Egypt found some relief in its position as one of the world's largest recipients of foreign aid. It received more than $1 billion in economic aid from the United States in the 1983 U.S. fiscal year and $750 million in grants and credits from several Western European countries and Japan.

Foreign relations. In early March the Egyptian government resumed diplomatic contact with Israel, broken off after the massacre of the Palestinians in Lebanon in September 1982. However, Egypt stated that there would be no resumption of talks with Israel on Palestinian autonomy unless Israel withdrew its forces from Lebanon and stopped construction of new settlements in the West Bank and Gaza.

There were signs of improvement in relations with Arab nations. In February, Egyptian officials paid their first official visit to Iraq in four years. In March, Mubarak met informally with King Hassan II of Morocco and other Arab dignitaries. Relations with another neighbor, Libya, were at a low ebb. In February, when Libya appeared ready to support an abortive military coup in the Sudan, Egypt's close ally, Egypt made preparations to assist the Sudan, although no intervention proved necessary.

Mubarak traveled to New Delhi in March to deliver a speech at the nonaligned nations conference, and he also visited China, Indonesia, and North Korea. At the same time, he continued to foster close relations with the West, visiting the United States, Canada, Great Britain, and France. The Egyptian armed forces also participated in joint military exercises with the United States.

On December 22, Mubarak met with Palestine Liberation Organization leader Yasir Arafat in Cairo, after the latter had evacuated his forces from Lebanon. Despite an angry Israeli reaction, Israeli Prime Minister Yitzhak Shamir subsequently received a high-ranking Egyptian official in Jerusalem, for the first time in 18 months.

See STATISTICS OF THE WORLD.   K.J.B.

ELECTIONS IN THE UNITED STATES. Few distinct trends emerged in elections held across the nation in 1983. Perhaps the most significant aspect of the balloting was the electoral power exerted by black voters in key mayoral contests.

Congressional elections. Republicans gained one seat in the House and one in the Senate as a result of special elections held during the year. In a most unusual case, Representative Phil Gramm (D, Texas), after being stripped of his membership on the Budget Committee by the House Democratic leadership in January, resigned his congressional seat, switched parties, and regained his seat as a Republican in a February 12 special election. A more orthodox party changeover took place in the Senate, where the seat left vacant by the death of Democrat Henry M. Jackson on September 1 went to Republican Daniel J. Evans, the victor over Democrat Mike Lowry in an election held on November 8.

Another widely publicized congressional contest was that for the seat left vacant by the death of Representative Larry McDonald (D, Ga.), who was aboard Korean Air Lines Flight 007 when it was shot down by Soviet aircraft on September 1. George Darden (D) defeated Kathryn McDonald, the congressman's widow, in a runoff election on November 8. In other House elections, Gary L. Ackerman (D) was elected in March to fill the New York seat of the late Benjamin S. Rosenthal (D), who died in January; Daniel L. Schaefer (R) was elected in March to the Colorado seat left vacant by the death of Jack Swigert (R); Sala Burton (D) in June won the California seat that had been occupied by her husband, Phillip, who died in April; and Charles A. Hayes (D) in August gained the Illinois seat vacated by Harold Washington when the latter resigned to run for mayor of Chicago.

Gubernatorial elections. Of the three gubernatorial elections held in 1983, perhaps the most significant was the Kentucky contest won by Democrat Martha Layne Collins. In scoring a clear-cut victory over Republican opponent Jim Bunning (a former star baseball player) in balloting on November 8, Collins became the first woman governor of Kentucky and only the third woman ever to mount a successful campaign for governor without the advantage of a husband who had occupied the office. Also on November 8, Bill Allain (D) defeated Leon Bramlett (R) and three independent candidates for the Mississippi governorship. During the campaign, Bramlett had alleged that Allain was a homosexual who patronized male prostitutes; the accusation was categorically denied by Allain. On October 22, Edwin W. Edwards (D) was elected governor of Louisiana (a post he had held from 1972 to 1980) over incumbent David C. Treen (R) and several other candidates.

Municipal elections. Most prominent among the year's mayoral contests were the victories by black candidates in Chicago and Philadelphia, two of the nation's largest cities. Harold Washington's election as mayor of Chicago on April 12 capped a bitter and racially divisive campaign highlighted by an intense voter registration drive that added some 160,000 blacks to the voting lists, a narrow victory by Washington in the February Democratic primary over incumbent Mayor Jane Byrne and challenger Richard M. Daley (son of the late Mayor Richard J. Daley), and a large-scale defection

Upset Winner in Chicago

In winning the April 12 Chicago mayoral election, 61-year-old Harold Washington, a former U.S. representative from the city's South Side, pulled off the political upset of the year. As a black candidate bucking the fabled Democratic Party organization in a city polarized along racial lines, Washington initially seemed a rank outsider in the campaign. But, aided by a successful voter registration drive among the city's blacks, he upset the field in the February primary and then survived an often vicious, race-oriented campaign to triumph narrowly in April. In victory, he charged his supporters to seek ways to heal the divisions plaguing Chicago's political life. However, a bitter deadlock in the City Council between Washington's allies and foes all but paralyzed city government for much of the year. It may be that Washington's hardest battles lay ahead.

Harold Washington

of white Democratic voters to the camp of Republican candidate Bernard Epton. In the end, Washington barely managed to defeat Epton in a city that has not elected a Republican since 1927. Race was much less of an issue in the decisive victory of W. Wilson Goode over John J. Egan, Jr. (R) in the November 8 Philadelphia mayoral election.

Hispanic and women candidates also did well in municipal elections. In April, Henry G. Cisneros (D), the first Hispanic mayor of a major U.S. city, won an overwhelming 94 percent of the vote in his reelection to a second term as mayor of San Antonio. Two months later, Federico Peña (D) was narrowly elected as Denver's first Hispanic mayor; in the Democratic primary, Peña had defeated three-time incumbent William H. McNichol. Two women mayors of large cities won second terms in November: San Francisco's Dianne Feinstein,

Kentucky governor-elect Martha Layne Collins celebrates her victory over Republican Jim Bunning. Her election made her the state's first woman governor and the only current U.S. woman governor.

Federico Peña, shown (below right) working out with an aide, won a close election to become Denver's first Hispanic mayor. His victory was widely taken as a sign that Hispanics are wielding new political clout.

who had survived a recall vote in April, and Houston's Kathy Whitmire. Also in November, City Councilman Raymond L. Flynn defeated black candidate Melvin H. King to win the Boston mayoral race, 36-year-old Terry Goddard was elected the youngest mayor in the history of Phoenix, Maurice Ferre won a sixth term as mayor of Miami, and William Donald Schaefer was reelected to a fourth term as mayor of Baltimore. Earlier in the year, Republicans A. Starke Taylor, Jr., and Roger Hedgecock were elected mayors of Dallas and San Diego, respectively.

Referendums. Two local initiatives garnered significant national attention: a measure establishing strict limits on smoking in private offices, which was narrowly approved by San Francisco voters, and an attempt to ban nuclear arms research in the university town of Cambridge, Mass., which was handily defeated. Among statewide referendums, perhaps the most noteworthy were two Ohio proposals to slash the state income tax by almost 50 percent and to make any future increase in the tax subject to approval by a three-fifths majority in both houses of the legislature; both measures were soundly defeated.   D.J.F. & A.E.N.

EL SALVADOR. Fighting between Salvadoran government forces and leftist guerrillas continued intermittently in 1983, even as efforts were made to promote a political solution to the conflict. New elections, scheduled at one time for December 1983, were postponed until early 1984.

Civil war. The overall stalemate that had characterized the civil war since the March 1982 elections was punctuated from time to time by guerrilla or army offensives. Early in 1983, rebels captured and briefly held the city of Berlin and also laid siege briefly to Suchitoto, gateway to two hydroelectric dams. Moving out of the mountain areas, they roamed about in the lowlands, where they inflicted heavy damage on the nation's major export crops, coffee, cotton, and sugarcane. In June, the army launched a major new offensive; rebel forces withdrew ahead of them on all fronts, pulling back into their mountain strongholds. The army's success was attributed in part to leadership changes and to the effectiveness of the 55 U.S. military advisers then in El Salvador. Once the fighting had died down, a U.S.-financed aid program followed, resettling thousands of displaced peasants in time for the planting season. In the fall, however, the rebels

again seized the initiative, attacking more than 60 towns from central El Salvador to the Honduran border and opening up a corridor that allowed them to move freely across northern El Salvador. A government offensive in December scored no major gains; the guerrillas, on the other hand, overran a large army base north of the capital on December 30 and held it temporarily, reportedly inflicting heavy casualties on government troops.

Peace efforts and elections. A 21-point plan for peace in the region, proposed by members of the newly formed Contadora group of nations (Colombia, Mexico, Panama, and Venezuela), won acceptance from El Salvador and four other Central American countries outside the group. It called for future negotiations involving such issues as freezes on arms imports, reductions in foreign military advisers, human rights, and pledges to deny the use of territory to outside powers for aggression or destabilization efforts. In El Salvador itself, the government formed a peace commission to explore ways to bring leftist parties into presidential elections; commission members met with representatives of the rebels but reported no progress. The elections themselves were postponed until 1984, partly because of delays in approval of the final form for a constitution, submitted in draft form by a 16-member legislative commission in June. The two leading candidates were Roberto d'Au-

Two young Salvadoran rebels, armed with U.S.-made M-16 rifles, take part in an attack on the town of Tjutla, 45 miles from San Salvador.

buisson, the leader of the extreme right National Republican Alliance, and José Napoleón Duarte, the candidate of the Christian Democrats.

Human rights and terrorism. In May, the national legislature approved a limited amnesty for minor political prisoners; an offer of amnesty was also extended to guerrillas who agreed to lay down their arms. The case of the four American Roman Catholic churchwomen raped and killed in El Salvador in 1980 was reopened, after ballistics and fingerprint tests conducted by the FBI linked five Salvadoran national guardsmen to the crime. A judge ruled in March that the trial could not proceed until supporting evidence was collected locally. In late October, shortly after one of the guardsmen confessed to involvement, the five were ordered to stand trial, but the order was appealed. In the case of Michael Kline, an American murdered in 1982, three military suspects were turned over to the judiciary and were awaiting trial. In December the national police arrested a Salvadoran Army captain in connection with the 1981 killings of two American advisers; two national guardsmen were awaiting trial in the case.

Widespread killings of civilians, thought to be largely the work of right-wing "death squads," continued. In November there were reports that army troops had rounded up and killed more than 100 leftist sympathizers in three small towns. Some incidents also were attributed to leftist terrorists, including the murder of a U.S. military adviser on May 25.

In December the United States put pressure on the Salvadoran government to bring the death squads under control, indicating that U.S. aid might otherwise be lost.

Foreign relations. President Alvaro Magaña met in June with President Ronald Reagan and U.S. congressional leaders in Washington. Magaña said that his government could not accept the stipulation some legislators wished to attach to military assistance for El Salvador, calling for unconditional negotiations with the rebels. Earlier, Reagan appointed former U.S. Senator Richard Stone (D, Fla.) as special envoy to Central America. Stone met with Salvadoran leaders, including representatives of the rebels, but no progress in promoting negotiations was reported.

On July 18, Reagan named a bipartisan commission, headed by former Secretary of State Henry Kissinger, to make recommendations on long-range policy toward El Salvador and its neighbors. The commission visited Central America in October, and its members were reported to be "aghast" at the Salvadoran government's inability to control the armed forces or the judicial system. The commission's official report was expected in early 1984.

The U.S. Congress this summer approved an additional $55 million in military aid for El Salvador, over and above the sum previously allotted to the country for fiscal 1983. The Reagan administration had sought double that amount. In the fall, the administration sought stepped-up military aid for fiscal 1984, but Congress passed a stopgap spending measure that provided a lower level than the administration had sought. Congress also voted to extend for one year the condition that the administration periodically certify El Salvador's progress in respecting human rights and making political and economic reforms. Reagan vetoed that provision, however.

Economic affairs. The Magaña government met with considerable resistance from the private sector in May, when it announced a package of tax increases intended to reduce the large budget deficit estimated for fiscal 1983. The package included a 100 percent hike in the tax on imported vehicles, as well as increases in the value-added tax.

While protesting that El Salvador was not adhering to economic guidelines accepted earlier, the International Monetary Fund nevertheless agreed in May to lend the country $17 million. The U.S. economic aid program for the 1983 fiscal year came to $243.7 million. The central bank made credit available to agriculture and industry, in an effort to stem the decline in the gross domestic product, which had fallen by 25 percent since the insurgency began in 1980. Damage to the 1982–1983 coffee and cotton crops from guerrillas' economic-warfare tactics cut output of the two commodities. Unemployment reportedly surpassed 25 percent.

See STATISTICS OF THE WORLD. L.P.P.

ENERGY. Total U.S. energy consumption in 1983 fell for the fourth consecutive year, and the Reagan administration reduced federal support for energy programs. Production of coal was down from 1982 levels, while production of electricity increased slightly. Despite the abundant supplies of oil, solar energy was attracting interest as an economically viable energy source.

U.S. energy consumption. For the fourth consecutive year, energy consumption decreased in the United States. Energy conservation, high energy costs, high interest rates, and the weak state of the economy all contributed to the decline. According to government estimates, energy consumption in 1983 was expected to amount to 70.2 quadrillion British thermal units (Btu's), down from 70.9 quadrillion Btu's in 1972. Prior to the 1973–1974 Arab oil embargo against the United States, domestic consumption had been increasing at an average annual rate of 3.5 percent.

Federal budget. The Reagan administration backed off from its promise to dismantle the Department of Energy in 1983 and called for a DOE budget of $8.8 billion for fiscal 1984. Of this, only $3.3 billion was slotted for non-weapons energy programs—a 27 percent reduction from 1983—and funds for solar energy research, synthetic fuels, and fossil fuel research were to be cut by as much as 60 percent. Congress restored some of the cuts, authorizing a total allocation of $10 billion, of which $6.6 billion was earmarked for weapons.

Electrical energy. In 1982, for the first time in more than 30 years, electrical energy production by U.S. utilities declined from the preceding year, to 2,241 billion kilowatt-hours (kW-hrs.). Estimates for 1983 indicated a slight recovery, with an expected production of 2,260 billion kW-hrs.

Between 1950 and 1970, net electrical energy production by electrical utilities had increased at an average annual rate of 8.0 percent. In 1983 the utilities estimated that new electrical energy demand would increase at an average annual rate of only 3.2 percent between 1983 and 1991. Even this projected growth rate is considerably higher than the actual growth rate experienced since 1978.

Coal. The National Coal Association estimated that U.S. coal production for 1983 would total only about 780 million short tons. Coal production had increased 1.7 percent in 1982, to a record 838.1 million tons, and 27 percent of this coal came from the western states.

As oil prices dropped in response to the global oil surplus, the coal export market weakened. U.S. coal exports, which had reached a record 112.5 million tons in 1981, fell 5.6 percent in 1982. In early 1983 the export market for U.S. coal began to shrink more rapidly; not only were falling world oil prices continuing to reduce demand for coal, but South Africa and Poland made inroads into U.S. steam coal sales. Coal exports for 1983 were projected at 75 million tons, down sharply from the 105 million tons exported in 1982. Because of the faltering export market and the existence of large stockpiles of coal at electric utility plants, U.S. coal producers reduced output. While the majority of large coal producers sell most of their coal under long-term contracts, coal prices on the spot market in 1983 were as much as 20 percent below 1982 levels.

On April 28, 1982, the U.S. Department of the Interior had held the largest federal coal lease sale in the nation's history. It accepted bids totaling $43.5 million on ten tracts containing 1.1 billion tons of coal. In a follow-up sale in October 1982, two additional tracts containing 500 million tons of coal were leased for $23.7 million. The sales were severely

Mail Junkie

Unlike most folks, William Conklin, of Denver, doesn't mind junk mail. As a recent story in the *Wall Street Journal* recounted, Conklin has done everything possible to increase the daily deluge—signing up for numerous mailing lists and even using variations of his legal name to receive multiple copies of the same thing; he also accepts donations from overburdened friends. As the circulars, fliers, and catalogs pile up, Conklin just grins and feeds it all to his wood-burning stove, which he uses to supplement a conventional furnace. He can stay as warm as his neighbors without having to go out and chop firewood. The only drawback: Conklin occasionally misses a piece of valuable mail in all that junk—such as a $30 check he once burned by mistake.

New windmills line slopes at Altamont Pass, Calif., a result of tax breaks for alternate-energy investments and federal laws requiring utilities to buy power from small generating companies.

criticized; there were complaints that the coal had been sold too cheaply, and charges of unauthorized disclosure of proprietary coal data by Interior Department employees. After investigating the lease sales and the Interior Department's methods of determining the value of coal, the U.S. General Accounting Office, in a report released in May 1983, concluded that the coal had been sold for about $100 million less than fair market value.

Despite an oversupply of coal and falling coal prices, the Interior Department conducted another large coal lease sale on September 14. Eight tracts containing an estimated 543 million tons of lignite in the Fort Union formation along the Montana–North Dakota border were offered. Three tracts drew no bids, and the other five attracted one bid each totaling only $911,800, which amounts to about 1 cent a ton.

There was some question whether the leases would ever be issued. In a surprisingly strong rebuke to then Interior Secretary James Watt, the Republican-controlled Senate voted, 63–33, on September 20 for a temporary moratorium on coal lease sales in the West. (The House of Representatives had already approved a moratorium.) The leasing ban took effect on October 1. As a result of a lawsuit brought by environmental groups, the Interior Department was prevented from actually issuing the leases before the October 1 deadline.

Synthetic fuels. On June 30, the U.S. Synthetic Fuels Corporation, a semigovernmental agency, agreed to provide loan guarantees for a plant in California that would convert coal to gas. It was the first project the corporation had supported since Congress established it in 1980.

On August 18, Victor A. Schroeder, the corporation's president, resigned after several board members had demanded his ouster. He had been under investigation for misconduct by the Justice Department, which subsequently suspended the investigation. Late in the year,

Synfuels, under pressure from Congress and the Reagan administration, reversed a previous decision and agreed to consider price supports for the $2.1 billion Great Plains coal gasification project, which has already received about $1.5 billion in government-guaranteed loans. The consortium building the project had forecast significant operating losses without such aid.

Solar energy. The year 1983 offered some signs that solar energy could be economically viable. More than half of the 25 publicly held solar companies were showing profits, and many reported substantial sales. Late in the year, American Solar King Corporation, a major solar firm, admitted that it had drastically overestimated its revenues for the fiscal year. Its stock dropped rapidly, and dragged down the prices of other solar companies with it. Many analysts saw this setback as temporary, however, and anticipated long-term success for the industry. In addition to a largely untapped potential in solar heating, sales of photovoltaic systems—which convert sunlight directly into electricity—were projected to reach as much as $100 billion by the year 2000.

See also NUCLEAR POWER; PETROLEUM AND NATURAL GAS.   D.F.A.

ENVIRONMENT. Dominating environmental news in 1983 was a scandal that rocked the U.S. Environmental Protection Agency and led to the resignation or dismissal of the administrator and many key staff members. In addition, controversial Interior Secretary James Watt resigned his post in October.

EPA scandal. The EPA scandal arose out of an investigation begun by the U.S. House of Representatives in late 1982 into the agency's toxic waste cleanup program, specifically its enforcement of legal requirements to establish a $1.6 billion superfund to pay for cleaning up abandoned hazardous waste dumps. At an early stage of the investigation, House subcommittees subpoenaed thousands of EPA documents. In December 1982, when EPA Administrator Anne Burford withheld some of the documents, at the instructions of President Ronald Reagan, she was cited for contempt of Congress. (The documents were released to Congress many months later, and the contempt citation was then dropped.)

Meanwhile, investigators were focusing attention on the EPA's solid waste division and its chief, Assistant Administrator Rita M. Lavelle. She was accused of harassing and seeking the ouster of an EPA engineer who had criticized the handling of hazardous waste cleanup. Lavelle was also charged with having frequent meetings at expensive Washington, D.C., restaurants with representatives of the industries her office was supposed to regulate. It was alleged that one of the purposes of such meetings was the settling of "sweetheart" deals that eased cleanup costs for companies deemed of political value to the Reagan administration. The fact that Lavelle rarely met with environmentalists helped fuel charges of pro-industry bias. Accusations of general misuse of superfund money were also made.

One notable case of alleged EPA malfeasance concerned the Stringfellow Acid Pits, a toxic waste dump near Riverside, Calif. The EPA was accused of having delayed action on cleanup funding during the 1982 election campaign so that then California Governor Edmund G. Brown, Jr., a Democrat running for the Senate, could not take credit for the cleanup. (Brown lost the election.) One of the known Stringfellow dumpers was a former employer of Lavelle's, a California chemical firm, and several Reagan aides and associates reportedly had ties to other companies that used the site.

Reagan dismissed Lavelle on February 7 after she had refused Burford's request to leave voluntarily. Later that month, other high-level EPA officials resigned, reportedly at the urging of the White House. (More than 20 officials had resigned by the fall.) On March 9, Burford herself left office, stating that she hoped her action would end "the controversy and confusion that has crippled my agency." She was succeeded in May by the EPA's founding administrator, William D. Ruckelshaus, who faced the task of restoring stability and morale.

The same day Ruckelshaus was sworn in, the House voted to cite Lavelle for contempt, for failing to comply with a subpoena to testify before a subcommittee in March. Although she was acquitted of the contempt charge in July, Lavelle was subsequently tried and convicted on charges of perjury and obstructing a congressional investigation.

ENVIRONMENT

Hazardous wastes. With Ruckelshaus at the helm, the EPA made changes in its hazardous waste program. As part of stepped-up superfund efforts, the agency in August released $2.7 million of a total $10 million grant to begin cleanup at the controversial Stringfellow Acid Pits. In December, the EPA filed suit against the Occidental Petroleum Company to recover the nearly $45 million spent to clean up the Love Canal waste site in Niagara Falls, N.Y. At the same time, the Justice Department filed a $1.9 billion suit—the largest such suit ever brought by a federal agency—against the Shell Oil Company for damage to the environment allegedly caused by a Shell pesticide factory located within the U.S. Army's Rocky Mountain Arsenal, near Denver.

Under terms of a consent decree arising from a lawsuit filed by the Environmental Defense Fund, the U.S. Department of Health and Human Services agreed in May to establish an Agency for Toxic Substances and Disease Registry, as mandated by the superfund law. The duties of the new agency include studying and compiling data on the health effects of hazardous wastes, as well as maintaining a list of people exposed to toxic substances.

In August, the administration established a high-level working group under the auspices of the Interior Department to consider the use of federal lands for the disposal of hazardous wastes generated by private industry.

Watt resignation. On October 9, Interior Secretary James Watt resigned after he had come under fire for making a controversial public remark. Speaking before a group of lobbyists in Washington on September 21, Watt had jokingly described members of a newly named commission as "a black, a woman, two Jews, and a cripple." A furor immediately arose, and while President Reagan defended the secretary, congressional Republicans, as well as Democrats, called for his ouster. On October 13, Reagan named William P. Clark, the national security adviser, to take over the Interior Department.

Farmers listen as two agronomists, standing in front of a mobile experimental greenhouse, explain the effects of acid rain on crops.

Shortly before Watt's resignation, on September 28, a federal district judge blocked him from selling 140 million tons of federal coal reserves for mining by private industry. Congress had voted to place a six-month moratorium on the sale of coal leases, effective October 1; Watt had planned to issue the leases on September 30.

Dioxin. The toxic chemical dioxin—an inadvertent by-product of certain chemical processes—continued to make news. Although its exact health effects in humans have been a matter of controversy, the U.S. Centers for Disease Control has said that dioxin (more precisely, the form of dioxin known as TCDD) may be potentially dangerous even in concentrations as low as one part per billion. Concentrations substantially above this level have been detected in such states as Michigan, Missouri, and New Jersey.

At Times Beach, Mo., dioxin levels as high as 300 parts per billion were found. The dioxin was apparently contained in waste oils that were sprayed on the town's roads in the early 1970's to hold down dust. In February the EPA announced that the federal government would buy out the town for $33 million, with the state of Missouri appropriating several million dollars more. It was the first time that superfund money had been allocated for such a purpose. The buyout began in September.

Pesticides. Questions were raised in May about the safety of 212 pesticides and herbicides—15 percent of all such materials now on the U.S. market—when the EPA released a five-year study questioning the validity of laboratory tests done by a major private organization, Industrial Bio-Test Laboratories, Inc. In July the EPA told the manufacturers of 35 of the pesticides that they must submit new test data or the products would be suspended. The agency had determined that the other pesticides in question were safe.

Four former IBT officials were brought to trial in Chicago on charges of misrepresenting data used by chemical companies to obtain government approval for their products. One of the defendants was granted a mistrial in July, to undergo heart surgery; the other three were found guilty in October.

Action was taken against ethylene dibromide

The federal Environmental Protection Agency was attacked by critics for conflict of interest and mismanagement, particularly in its handling of toxic waste sites like the Stringfellow Acid Pits in California, shown here.

(EDB), a hazardous compound used in many pesticides and as a gasoline additive. On September 30, the EPA banned most agricultural uses of EDB. A week later, proposed regulations for protecting workers from EDB were published in the *Federal Register*. The standards, which substantially reduce the EDB levels to which workers could be exposed, were expected to take effect in 1984.

Marketing of new chemicals. The EPA issued final rules, effective in October, by which the maker of a new chemical must notify the agency at least 90 days before the substance is put on the market. If the manufacturer has any test results or other data on health and environmental effects of the new chemical,

163

these must be submitted with the notification. Many people, however, would like the submission of environmental, health, and testing data to be mandatory for all new chemicals before marketing. At present, the EPA can request a court-ordered ban on production of a chemical if the agency determines that it might pose an "unreasonable risk" or that the information submitted in the notification is insufficient.

Nuclear issues. In January, President Reagan signed the Nuclear Waste Policy Act, which had been passed by Congress late in 1982. The law instructs the U.S. Department of Energy to recommend three geologically stable sites as candidates for a permanent underground repository for radioactive waste by January 1, 1985. By 1987 the president must select one of the sites to be the first disposal repository, which would begin operation in 1998.

A series of decisions by the U.S. Supreme Court brought the nuclear power industry both good and bad news. On April 19 the Court unanimously ruled that the U.S. Nuclear Regulatory Commission need not take psycholog-ical stress on area residents into account in deciding whether to allow the restarting of a reactor at Three Mile Island, Pa., that had remained undamaged when a severe accident crippled a companion reactor in 1979. However, on April 20 the Supreme Court held that states could ban the construction of new nuclear power plants on economic grounds, such as the unpredictable future costs of waste disposal.

The NRC took action against a number of power plants during the year. For example, in May it imposed an $850,000 fine, for safety rule violations, on the company that operates the Salem nuclear power plant in New Jersey; the fine was the largest ever for safety violations. In the same month the commission unanimously ruled that it would shut down the two Indian Point nuclear power plants in Buchanan, N.Y., unless the facility's emergency evacuation plan was significantly improved; a plan was finally approved by the NRC in October. Also, a three-judge panel investigating Indian Point reported to the NRC that better safeguards were needed there.

Embattled Ex-EPA Head

When Anne Burford (Anne Gorsuch until her marriage on February 20) became head of the Environmental Protection Agency in 1981 after a career in Colorado politics, she quickly became unpopular with conservationists for her dedication to President Ronald Reagan's philosophy of loosening regulatory constraints on industry. Her troubles increased after House subcommittees began investigating the agency's $1.6 billion superfund for cleaning up hazardous wastes. When she refused, with White House backing, to supply certain records, the House cited her for contempt of Congress. Charges that the EPA had made "sweetheart deals" with toxic waste dumpers, revelations that paper shredders had been moved into the EPA building, and a spate of resignations in the agency followed during early 1983. On March 9, after the Justice Department declined to defend her in the contempt suit, the 40-year-old administrator also resigned, citing a need to restore agency morale.

Anne Burford

In September, NRC investigators charged that the companies involved in cleaning up the Three Mile Island site had followed improper procedures. A federal grand jury, in November, indicted the former operator of Three Mile Island for falsifying safety-test results before the 1979 accident at the plant.

The ultimate fate of the controversial Clinch River Breeder Reactor Project near Oak Ridge, Tenn., was in doubt through much of the year. In June, Congress had voted to end federal spending for the breeder reactor by September 30 unless the Energy Department developed a funding plan that would place some financial responsibility for the project on private industry. Such a plan was sent to Congress by the Reagan administration in early August, but Congress failed to vote on it by September 30. Site preparation work and equipment procurement continued temporarily, using budgeted funds that had been left over. On October 26, however, in a probably fatal action for the reactor project, the Senate voted not to provide additional funds.

Water and air issues. Considerable attention was focused on the need to protect underground water supplies. According to Representative Michael Synar (D, Okla.), chairman of a House subcommittee investigating groundwater, a survey showed that 2,830 wells in 20 states had become contaminated over a period of a few years as a result of poisons from hazardous wastes, pesticides, and various other pollutants. No specific federal program to address this problem existed, and there was increasing interest in developing appropriate legislation.

The U.S. government in 1983 seemed to be changing its position on the acid rain issue, which has been a source of major concern in U.S.-Canadian relations. The term "acid rain" is commonly used to refer to abnormally acidic precipitation—including rain, snow, and dry particles—that results when certain pollutants enter the atmosphere from various sources, both artificial and natural. Such precipitation has damaged forests and destroyed fish and plant life in lakes in a number of areas of the world, notably in southeastern Canada and the northeastern United States. For some time U.S. and Canadian officials had largely disagreed

Leave It to Beavers

Government and private sources have spent millions of dollars constructing concrete and wire-mesh dams on small streams, to reverse the process of erosion that muddies water and kills vegetation. Now the Federal Bureau of Land Management is studying projects on two Wyoming creeks, in which beavers released at the sites, aided by imported logs and strings of old tires, build the dams themselves. Results at both sites have been encouraging; the ecology is returning to normal, and, perhaps best of all, beavers work cheap. So far, the cost of both projects (including an electric fence to keep cattle away) has come to less than $3,000.

over the urgency of the problem and over the degree to which industry, especially U.S. industry, is the source of the pollutants affecting Canada. In June, however, a Reagan administration task force for the first time admitted the important contribution of man-made pollutants to the problem. And in the same month the U.S. National Academy of Sciences reported that there was a direct link between acid rain and the sulfur dioxide released into the atmosphere by industry. Two months later, the United States and Canada agreed to conduct a joint project to monitor the flow of pollutants from Ohio and Ontario, two areas suspected of contributing to acid rain.

Asbestos. In November, the U.S. Labor Department issued an emergency rule reducing by 75 percent the permissible level of asbestos to which workers may be exposed. Exposure to asbestos has been linked to cancer and other diseases. An asbestos industry group filed a suit challenging the government's action, which was temporarily suspended pending the outcome. J.J.

EQUATORIAL GUINEA. See STATISTICS OF THE WORLD.

ETHIOPIA. Political and military turbulence continued to plague Ethiopia in 1983. The Dergue, Ethiopia's ruling council, faced major military challenges from ethnic-based secession movements in the Ogaden, Tigré, and Eritrean areas of the country. In the Ogaden, bordering Somalia, the recently adopted policy of depopulating the area appeared substantially successful, but the continued movement of nomadic Somalis through the region permitted sporadic infiltration of Somali attackers. Ethiopian forces seized several small salients of Somali territory in the spring.

The war between the government and the separatists in Tigré province became the most serious threat to security. In April, guerrillas of the Tigré People's Liberation Front kidnapped ten foreign relief workers, and in August they abducted a group of Swiss nationals; all were eventually released unharmed. The TPLF increased its effectiveness by broadcasting in the Tigrinya language on the clandestine "Voice of the Broad Masses of Eritrea" radio station. Eritrean and Tigréan insurgencies tied down about half of the 250,000-member Ethiopian army.

The May Day speech by head of state Mengistu Haile Mariam focused on the devastating effect of drought on both domestic food supplies and the agricultural exports that normally help stabilize Ethiopia's precarious trade balance. Some of those hardest hit by the drought were in rebel-held areas, beyond reach of government assistance even if supplies had been available.

The Commission for Organizing the Party of the Working People of Ethiopia (COPWE), the Dergue's vehicle for the creation of a one-party socialist state, held a congress in January in Addis Ababa. During the congress, 34 commission members, including six members of the Central Committee, were expelled. In April, new ministers were named for foreign affairs, information, culture and sports, health, agriculture, and education. The government offered no explanation for the shifts.

In May, the Dergue issued a decree stating that all Ethiopians between the ages of 18 and 30 were liable for military service and that citizens up to the age of 50 could be called up if necessary. The conscription issue became a source of great controversy.

The diplomatic scene became busier during the year, as the Ethiopian government attempted to reach beyond its well-established links to the Soviets, Cubans, and Eastern Europeans. President Daniel arap Moi of Kenya

visited Addis Ababa in late April, as did UN Secretary-General Javier Pérez de Cuéllar. In June, when the Organization of African Unity met in Addis Ababa, Mengistu was elected chairman of the organization. Ethiopia's strong ties to the Communist states continued, and its arms debt to the Soviet Union reached $2 billion.

See STATISTICS OF THE WORLD.   R.B.

EUROPEAN COMMUNITIES, a supranational organization comprising the European Economic Community (EEC), the European Atomic Energy Community, and the European Coal and Steel Community. Because these communities share the same institutional framework, they are frequently referred to as the European Community (EC), or Common Market. In 1983 the ten member countries were Belgium, Denmark, France, Great Britain, Greece, Ireland, Italy, Luxembourg, the Netherlands, and West Germany.

In June the heads of government of the European Community held their semiannual meeting in Stuttgart. A major issue at stake was the allocation of funds from the Community's strained budget; central to the dispute was the British contention that the funneling of a majority of the funds to agriculture, largely in the form of subsidies, was unfair to Britain, whose agricultural sector was less important than most other members'. For several years, argued Prime Minister Margaret Thatcher, Britain had been contributing more to the organization than it was taking out. The dispute was not resolved, but the summit provisionally agreed to grant the British a rebate of $675 million from their 1983 contributions, contingent on overall resolution of the Community's financial problems. To make up partially for such a rebate, West Germany, the EC's largest contributor, offered to pay nearly $118 million more.

Each member promised to come up with comprehensive long-term proposals for the next summit meeting, held in Athens in December. Despite such plans, however, the Athens summit proved to be a fiasco, with no action taken to resolve financial problems. The ten members were far apart on a wide range of issues, including proposed reductions in farm subsidies and final resolution of the British demand for a rebate on its EEC budget

Common Market President Gaston Thorn lines up European leaders for a family picture during a summit in December. In the front row, from the left, are French President François Mitterrand, Italian Premier Bettino Craxi, Belgian Premier Wilfried Martens, Thorn, British Prime Minister Margaret Thatcher, Greek Prime Minister Andreas Papandreou, and West German Chancellor Helmut Kohl.

bution. As a result, for the first time, no communiqué was issued, and the organization was said to be facing the worst crisis in its 26-year history.

In March five of the eight members of the European Monetary System, a subdivision of the EEC, meeting in Brussels, agreed on a realignment of currency valuations. The move, taken because of heavy speculation against the French franc, resulted in the franc's devaluation by 2.5 percent. The German mark, the Community's strongest currency, was revalued upward by 5 percent; the other EMS currencies were also readjusted.

In June the EC called for cuts in finished steel making capacity by member countries, in accordance with a five-year plan aimed at streamlining Western Europe's steel industry in order to make it more competitive. By the end of January 1984, 30 million metric tons were to be cut from the 1980 level of 169 million. In late December, members also agreed to an emergency plan providing new minimum prices for steel products.

The June Stuttgart meeting also addressed foreign issues. The Community's leaders decided to unblock a small amount of aid to Israel (funds to Israel had been frozen after the 1982 invasion of Lebanon) and to reopen talks over Israel's request for association with the EC. The Community also called for a political rather than a military solution to the problems in Central America.

Jean Rey, a founder of the EC and president of the joint European Commission from 1967 to 1970, died in his native city of Liège, Belgium, on May 19. He was a staunch supporter of the concept of a federal Europe.

See also articles on individual countries mentioned.   J.O.S.

F

FASHION. American designers reinstated stylishness in the spring 1983 season. That pointedly feminine, sophisticated, slightly artificial quality that had been absent from clothing for many seasons was achieved by means of peplums, nipped-in waists, constricted hiplines, and such accessories as gloves, brimmed hats, handkerchiefs, and wide cinch belts. Fall clothes for women were more practical. Menswear was relaxed.

Spring and fall. Calvin Klein's collection proved to be controversial for its liberal use of bustiers (tightly fitted, brassiere-like tops without straps), fitted skirts, satin fabrics, and peplums lined with bright, contrasting colors. Better received were his double-breasted short wool jackets, cut with military precision. Ralph Lauren moved toward elegance with an emphasis on black and white linen in his dress and pant ensembles. Perry Ellis's carefully planned separates and sportswear also introduced a more dressed up, formal feeling than his designs of earlier seasons. His clothes were notable for their 5-inch-wide cinch belts, billowing blouse sleeves, and deeply plunging necklines.

A heavy military influence was typified by the use of crisp trim, brass buttons, nautical stripes, insignia-crested belts, white lapels against

In women's evening wear, Oscar de la Renta's provocatively ruffled design was typical of the tendency toward a sexier, glossier look.

Clothes by avant-garde Japanese designers received wide attention and challenged the fashion world with their aggressively different style. Favoring abundant use of rough fabrics, they produced a sense of strength and drama, as in this sweater-skirt combination by Kenzo.

sweater coat tapered from padded shoulders, while turtlenecks, crewnecks, or boat necks were layered with vests, cardigans, and shawls. An extension of the sweater was the knit dress, which also made a comeback. Classically cut, well-tailored pants were a mainstay for day and night. Almost every designer offered pants paired with jackets, pullovers, or cardigans for daytime suiting. There was a significant return to color in the fall: Sometimes two or three bright shades were used in the same garment or, more often, one explosive color set against black or gray.

Evening dress. Elaborate ball gowns gave way to sleeker, sexier shapes. Bill Blass offered a fuschia wool jacket featuring an outsize lapel embroidered with sequins to resemble a watermelon slice; it was teamed with trim black wool pants. Oscar de la Renta's evening collection was typically lavish. His collection included both sequined pullovers, in bright solid colors with white stars, and vampy black satin and velvet dresses. Geoffrey Beane showed a glitter-sparkled black evening suit. Klein maintained the high style for evening with strapless peplum bustiers of black satin, striped with sequins and worn with skintight ankle-length satin skirts.

Menswear. Men's clothes for spring were elegant but comfortable. Tailored clothes had a looser fit and softer construction, accomplished by removing most of the interlinings normally used for shaping. Still, suits were not baggy. They sported a fuller chest area, lower armholes, a slightly fitted waist, and lower button placement. Fabrics were generally draped, and pale plaids, fine stripes, two-toned herringbones, and fine checks were teamed with the traditional seersucker, poplin, tropical-weight worsteds, and gabardines. Alan Flusser styled his clothes after the 1930's draped look, which combined overall fullness, more room in the front and back of the shoulder, and slightly wider shoulders. Ralph Lauren emphasized details such as lapels on the vests of three-piece suits and elegant double-breasted jackets incorporating offbeat tones and patterns. Many designers paired patterned suits with patterned dress shirts and even added figured neck wear—for example, a herringbone sport coat over multicolor fair isle sweater-vest

navy blue, side stripes on skirts, and brilliant colors set off by white trimming or brass decoration.

At the opposite fashion pole were the new Japanese designers such as Issey Miyake and Rei Kawakubo, who received international attention for their shroudlike layered looks of somber rustic fabrics.

The more practical designs for fall hung from wide shoulders and fell into narrow yet loose and attractive lines. Form-flattering chemises appeared on runways from Paris and Milan to New York and Los Angeles. Hemlines hovered around the knee or dropped below it, but were no longer a fashion obsession. The focus had turned to the shoulders, where a wide yet rounded look prevailed.

Sweaters and slacks. Sweaters appeared dressed up and boldly proportioned as suit jackets. The

From Perry Ellis: A rugged tweed walking jacket with the casual comfort of a shirtfront closing, worn over a hand-knit Shetland sweater and tattersall wool trousers.

with striped shirt and foulard tie. Gray surfaced as a neutral alternative to pastel shades, and much emphasis was placed on gray and white linen.

A bigger, stronger sense of scale was evident in the fall, as the generous contours for outerwear gave rise to the layering of sweaters and jackets. The broad-shouldered topcoat; lighter, shorter jackets; fuller, more broadly draped and pleated trousers; and the season's big hit—the oversized cardigan—defined fall's sense of style.

Sport coats became the wardrobe's staple for day and evening. The prevailing silhouette, whether single-breasted or double-breasted, used generous proportions ruled by a well-defined shoulder line. Gianni Versace offered a boxy, double-breasted wool tweed sport coat mated with pleated wool trousers, Basile clustered stripes on a single-breasted sport coat, and Alexander Julian used pastel windowpane checks on gray tweed in his version. Scarves of rich textures and luxurious fabrics were the season's most dashing menswear accessory.

E.J.G.

FIJI. See STATISTICS OF THE WORLD.

FINLAND. National elections in Finland on March 20–21, 1983, resulted in the largest gains by the Social Democratic Party since the end of World War II. After extended negotiations, President Mauno Koivisto in May appointed Kalevi Sorsa, a Social Democrat who had headed the previous two governments, as head of a four-party coalition consisting of the Social Democrats, the Center Party, and the Swedish People's Party (as before), plus the Rural Party.

The Social Democrats advanced from 23.9 percent of the vote in 1979 to 26.7 percent in the March elections, increasing their numbers from 52 to 57 in the 200-seat Parliament. The other major winner was the Rural Party, which went from 4.6 percent to 9.7 percent and increased its seats from seven to 17. This gain was primarily at the expense of the Center-Liberal alliance, which declined from a total of 21 percent of the popular vote in 1979 to 17.6 percent and saw its strength in Parliament drop from 40 to 38 seats. The Conservative National Coalition Party advanced from 21.7 percent to 22.1 percent but lost three seats, for a total of 44 in the new Parliament.

The Communist-dominated Finnish People's Democratic League (SKDL) dropped from 17.9 percent to 13.5 percent, losing nine of its 35 seats in Parliament. The party's losses were attributed to its split into factions, whose quarrel over the defense budget in late 1982 had led to the resignation of one Sorsa coalition government and the installation of a new one that excluded the SKDL.

A decline in Finnish exports in 1982 had contributed to an increase in the rate of unemployment to 7 percent by the beginning of 1983. Ruralist leaders seized on unemployment as their central campaign issue, and Sorsa responded by assigning the Labor Ministry to a Ruralist.

During a visit to Moscow in June, President Koivisto renewed a long-standing treaty of friendship and cooperation between Finland and the Soviet Union. The Finns agreed to increase Soviet imports.

See STATISTICS OF THE WORLD.   M.D.H.

FISHERIES. Commercial landings (edible and industrial) by U.S. fishermen at ports in the 50 states amounted to 6.4 billion pounds in 1982, the latest year for which data were available. Although this total represented an increase of 7 percent over 1981, the value of the catch was about the same as in 1981 (about $2.4 billion). Record catches of menhaden and American lobster, along with increased landings of cod, flounder, jack mackerel, sablefish, and red hake, helped offset declines in other major species, such as crabs, tuna, shrimp, sea herring, and salmon. Prices of most edible species of fish and shellfish increased slightly.

Commercial landings by U.S. fishermen at ports outside the 50 states or transferred in the U.S. fishery conservation zone to foreign vessels (joint ventures) accounted for an additional 756.0 million pounds, valued at $175.8 million.

World production. World catches of fish and shellfish increased in 1981 (the latest year for which global data are available) for the fourth consecutive year, reaching a record 74.1 million metric tons. This represented an expansion of 2.5 percent over the revised figure for 1980 (72.3 million metric tons) and the largest increase since 1976. A significant role in the 1981 expansion was played by heavier catches of small pelagic, or open-sea, fish (such as pilchards, anchovies, and mackerels) in Japan, Chile, Mexico, Morocco, South West Africa, Norway, the Netherlands, and Ireland.

Aggregate landings in developed countries during 1981 reached 38.5 million metric tons, up only 172,000 tons from the revised figure of the previous year. Landings rose moderately in North America, with heavier catches in both Canada and the United States. In Canada heavier catches of Atlantic redfish (up 46 percent), salmon (31 percent), and crustaceans (20 percent) pushed up total landings by 28,000 tons.

Production in the European Economic Community rose by 85,000 tons in 1981, primarily because of heavier cod, herring, horse mackerel, and mussel catches in the Netherlands and a significant increase in mackerel landings in Ireland. These increases, and more moderate ones in West Germany and Italy, exceeded the decline in landings in Denmark, France, and the United Kingdom. The Soviet Union's total landings increased very slightly in 1981, reaching 9.5 million metric tons.

In Latin America production increased by over 952,000 metric tons in 1981, chiefly because of larger landings in Chile and Mexico. Developing countries in Asia registered an increase in aggregate landings of more than 570,000 metric tons in 1981. African developing countries recorded an aggregate increase in landings of over 100,000 metric tons in 1981. Landings in Near Eastern countries expanded in 1981, primarily because Turkey's catches increased by 32,000 metric tons.

Fishing treaties. A Common Fisheries Policy was signed by ten EEC nations in January. The accord, reached after several years of negotiations, set quotas on the amounts of seven species of fish member nations were allowed to catch. In March, Canada, retaliating for the violation of a 1982 fishing agreement, as well as for a European ban on the importation of seal pup skins, reduced by one-third (to 10,600 metric tons) the quotas of cod permitted to fishers from EEC countries.   D.R.W.

FLORIDA. See STATISTICS OF THE WORLD.

FORMOSA. See TAIWAN.

FRANCE. Municipal elections, a troubled economy, and French military involvement abroad dominated the news in France in 1983—a difficult year for President François Mitterrand (see biography in PEOPLE IN THE NEWS).

Municipal elections. On March 6 and again on March 13, French citizens went to the polls to elect municipal councils and mayors in the country's major towns and cities.

In the first round of the elections, in which only candidates who gained an absolute majority were elected, representatives of the various right-wing parties won 51 percent of the vote, while those of the left—led by the two ruling coalition partners, Mitterrand's Socialist Party and the Communist Party (PCF)—were left with only 49 percent. The chief beneficiary on the right was the neo-Gaullist party Rassemblement pour la République (RPR), headed by Paris Mayor Jacques Chirac. Chirac himself was reelected by a wide margin, as the RPR and its allies swept 18 of Paris's 20 districts.

In the second round the Socialist-Communist coalition made a partial recovery, but not without suffering some losses. Taking both rounds together, in 31 towns and cities with a population of more than 30,000 each, voters

FRANCE

replaced left-dominated municipal councils with those of the right.

Cabinet reshuffle. The election results reflected growing disaffection with the Mitterrand government's Socialist policies. Mitterrand responded in late March by reshuffling his cabinet, in the process reducing its size to 15 senior ministers from the previous 34. Three changes in particular indicated which way the wind was blowing. Two of the four Communist ministers were demoted to junior rank. Jean-Pierre Chevènement, on the left wing of the Socialist Party, was dropped as minister of technology and industry. Finally, Jacques Delors, a centrist respected by the banking community, was given expanded powers in his post as minister of finance and economy, to deal with all aspects of economic and fiscal policy.

Troubled economy. Economic troubles—signaled by stubbornly high rates of inflation and unemployment and by slow growth, or even decline, in the rate of industrial production—continued to plague the Mitterrand government. The franc was in difficulty, and the government was under continued pressure to hold down spending.

During the early part of the year, France's central bank, the Banque de France, borrowed heavily, depleting its foreign exchange reserves at an alarming rate, in order to reduce pressure on the franc, especially from the resurgent American dollar, and stave off another devaluation (the franc had gone through two devaluations in 1982). At the same time, it borrowed $1.2 billion of foreign currencies from other central banks and drew down foreign loans to about $2.2 million—all in defense of the franc. France remained under pressure from other members of the European Monetary System to accept a further, major devaluation of the franc, by up to 5 percent. On March 21 a compromise was worked out under which West Germany revalued the mark upward by 5.5 percent in relation to other Western European currencies, while France devalued the franc 2.5 percent. As part of the agreement, the Mitterrand government promised to adopt a conservative, anti-inflationary fiscal policy.

Three days later, on March 25, the government announced a major austerity program designed to reduce inflation, a growing foreign trade deficit, and consumer spending. It also was expected to slow the rate of decline in unemployment (nearly 10 percent at midyear). The most controversial element of the program was the limit of 2,000 francs on the amount of currency that French travelers could take out of the country, to prevent the conversion of large quantities of francs into foreign currencies at a time when the franc needed full support. (The limit was raised to 5,000 francs in December.) Also very unpopular was the program's call for a tax increase of up to 8 percent on alcohol and tobacco, for hikes in electricity and telephone rates, and for tighter controls on social security and welfare costs. The total austerity package was geared toward reducing the budget deficit by about $8.1 billion. These and other government measures sparked repeated public demonstrations.

The government's 1984 budget, unveiled in mid-September, provided for a series of tax increases, including a surcharge of as much as 8 percent on higher incomes, accompanied by a rise in public spending of only 6.8 percent, the smallest increase in 13 years. The proposed measures were intended to bring inflation down to 5 percent and to bridge the country's huge trade deficit by the end of 1984. The measures were widely attacked by business leaders.

Impeding Mitterrand's efforts to reduce public spending were the big corporations that the Socialists had nationalized after coming to power in 1981. Their steadily declining productivity forced the government to pour money into them in order to make them competitive. In 1983 the state provided $2.5 billion in new capital; another $1.8 billion was projected for 1984. On the brighter side, unprofitable subsidiaries were being sold or closed down, and several corporations were involved in major takeovers intended to strengthen their competitive position.

Chad and Lebanon. As the civil war in Chad, a former French colony, heated up, the Mitterrand government, abandoning its policy of noninvolvement, reluctantly intervened in support of President Hissène Habré. Prompting the French decision was an all-out attack, in June, by Libyan-backed rebel forces of former President Goukouni Oueddei on the strategic northern oasis town of Faya-Largeau. By the end of August, some 2,500 French troops, as well as French fighter-bombers and tons of armor, were in place in Chad or the neighboring Central African Republic, in effect halting further major rebel advances. Peace talks under the auspices of the Organization of African Unity were scheduled for early 1984.

In Lebanon, where a contingent of 2,000 French troops was serving as part of an international peacekeeping force set up in 1982, heavy fighting flared up in and around Beirut beginning in late August. French military personnel suffered several casualties when French positions were shelled, and in late September the French command ordered retaliatory air strikes against guerrilla gun batteries behind Syrian lines. On October 23 a terrorist bomb attack on the French headquarters in Beirut killed at least 58 French paratroopers. As in an even more devastating attack on U.S. military headquarters the same day, the bomb was

Klaus Barbie, the World War II Gestapo chief known as the Butcher of Lyon for his atrocities, was extradited from Bolivia in February to face charges of "crimes against humanity," under French law. Here, a top-security convoy delivers him to Lyon's Montluc Fort.

To celebrate the 200th anniversary of manned flight, two French balloonists recreated the 1783 flight over Paris by Joseph and Jacques Montgolfier in a replica of the original balloon.

carried aboard a truck that smashed into the military compound. The next day, Mitterrand made a personal visit to inspect the bombed site, pay tribute to the dead, and raise morale. Except for the Communist Party, which had called for withdrawal of French troops even before the bombing, French political parties supported Mitterrand's determination to continue maintaining the French troop presence in Lebanon. French aircraft launched a reprisal raid in mid-November against pro-Iranian Shiite Muslim militiamen in Lebanon; first reports by the French government indicated it had been highly successful, but later reports indicated that the damage had been limited.

Expulsions. In early April, the French government expelled 47 Soviet diplomats, journalists, and trade officials, accusing them of espionage. Among those ordered to leave within 48 hours were the chief of Soviet intelligence operations in France and his top aides. Later in the year, several Iranians suspected of terrorist activities were expelled.

Barbie case. Klaus Barbie, the Gestapo chief in Lyon during World War II, was extradited to France from Bolivia, where he had been living under an assumed name, in early February to stand trial on charges of "crimes against humanity." Already sentenced to death in absentia for the murder of French Resistance fighters, including Resistance leader Jean Moulin, Barbie was to be tried for the deportation of nearly 800 Jews to the death camps of Auschwitz and Ravensbruck, as well as for the torture and deaths of large numbers of civilians in Lyon.

Crackdown in Corsica. After a series of shootings and bombings in early January by the separatist Corsican National Liberation Front, the Mitterrand government took several stern measures, banning the Front, dismissing key police officials on Corsica, and assigning a tough and experienced cop as police commissioner on the island.

At the same time, the government announced plans to put into effect a partial autonomy program, providing for a regional assembly with limited powers over local expenditures, but many Corsicans remained dissatisfied. In late May, the Front unleashed another spate of bombings as a warning to Mitterrand before his two-day visit to Corsica, which took place as scheduled in the following month.

New Year's Eve bombings. Five people were killed and 50 wounded in two bombings on December 31. One bomb went off in the Marseilles railroad station; the other on a train 120 miles to the north. No immediate conclusion could be reached as to the group behind the bombings.

See STATISTICS OF THE WORLD. S.E.

G

GABON. *See* STATISTICS OF THE WORLD.
GAMBIA, THE. *See* STATISTICS OF THE WORLD.
GEORGIA. *See* STATISTICS OF THE WORLD.
GERMAN DEMOCRATIC REPUBLIC, or EAST GERMANY. Although trade with West Germany continued to expand, overall relations between East and West Germany remained tense. Meanwhile, the East German regime kept an eye on the domestic economy and celebrated the 500th anniversary of Martin Luther's birth.

Inter-German relations. In April, Erich Honecker, party chief of the German Democratic Republic (GDR), canceled a planned visit to West Germany. The visit was canceled at least in part because of public outrage in West Germany over the deaths of two West German citizens who had heart attacks during separate confrontations with East German authorities.

Trade relations between the two German states, on the other hand, flourished. In the first half of 1983, the value of inter-German trade rose 16 percent over that of the same period in 1982. In June the Bonn government guaranteed $400 million in loans to the GDR from private West German banks, hoping thereby to achieve a reduction in the amount of currency that Western visitors to East Germany were required to exchange on a daily basis. The East Germans had doubled the requirement to about $10 in 1980, cutting down the number of visits by 40 percent. In September the first sign of relaxation in the exchange policy came when the East Germans announced that children under 15 were exempted from the daily currency requirement. The $400 million West German credit enabled the GDR to meet interest and repayment obligations on its large debt to the West and to purchase oil and foodstuffs in hard currency markets. Soviet bloc countries could no longer provide these commodities to East Germany in sufficient quantities.

Economy. The centrally planned economy of East Germany continued to enjoy full employment, as the gross national product grew at a rate of 4.0 percent in the first half of the year.

Full employment, however, was secured only because labor productivity remained very low in the GDR—some 38 percent of West Germany's.

Martin Luther Year. East Germany, despite its official atheism, declared 1983 to be "Martin Luther Year," in celebration of the 500th anniversary of the birth of the Protestant religious reformer. In windows of stores throughout the GDR, one could see almost as many pictures of Luther as of Karl Marx, whose death in 1883 also was being commemorated. Luther's first home was restored with state funds, as was the Wartburg, a fortress near Eisenach where he translated the New Testament into German. Party chief Honecker personally led the cere-

The 500th anniversary of the birth of Martin Luther was celebrated in East Germany, despite its official atheism. Shown here is a religious ceremony at Wartburg Castle, where Luther went into hiding after being condemned for heresy.

monies officially opening the restored Wartburg in April.

Peace movement. Authorities appeared to be reducing pressure on the unofficial peace movement that came into being in East Germany in 1982. The movement, most of whose adherents are young people with close ties to the Protestant Church, actively opposed the militarism of the Eastern bloc states as well as that of the NATO countries. In April church leaders spoke out against the stationing of U.S. missiles in Western Europe and supported the regime's call for a nuclear-free zone in central Europe.

Foreign affairs. In the summer, Honecker became the first Eastern bloc leader to travel to Poland since martial law was lifted there. In May he had met with Soviet leader Yuri Andropov in Moscow.

See STATISTICS OF THE WORLD.   R.J.W.

GERMANY, FEDERAL REPUBLIC OF, *or* **WEST GERMANY.** In 1983, Chancellor Helmut Kohl of the Christian Democratic Union (CDU) led the parties of his coalition government to a decisive victory over the Social Democratic opposition (see biography in PEOPLE IN THE NEWS). Kohl continued to stand solidly behind the NATO plan to introduce new American intermediate-range missiles into Western Europe if U.S.-Soviet disarmament talks failed to produce results.

Christian Democratic victory. The Bundestag (lower house of parliament) was dissolved in January, almost two years ahead of time, so that federal elections could be held in March. In the campaign the Social Democratic Party (SPD), under Hans-Jochen Vogel, placed its major emphasis on job creation measures to combat unemployment, which was running at more than 10 percent. The SPD remained committed to NATO, but several party leaders spoke in terms that suggested a negative posture on the stationing of new American missiles in Western Europe. The Christian Democrats pointed to signs that the economy was beginning to mend and stressed the effective leadership of Chancellor Kohl since coming to office in late 1982.

In the federal elections, held on March 6, the CDU and its sister party, the Christian Social Union (CSU), led by Franz Josef Strauss,

minister president of the state of Bavaria, won their highest proportion of votes since Konrad Adenauer's 1957 landslide and close to a majority of seats in the 498-member Bundestag—48.8 percent of the vote, compared with 44.5 percent in 1980, and 244 seats. The third member of the ruling coalition, the liberal Free Democratic Party (FDP), under Foreign Minister and Vice-Chancellor Hans-Dietrich Genscher, won 7.0 percent of the vote, compared with 10.6 percent in 1980, for a total of 34 seats.

Among the opposition parties, the SPD dropped from 42.9 percent to 38.2 percent, winning 193 seats. The Greens, an environmental, pacifist, antiestablishment party, obtained 5.6 percent of the vote and 27 Bundestag seats. The Greens succeeded in hurdling the 5 percent barrier (mandated constitutionally for any party to gain representation in parliament) largely because some 1 million former SPD and FDP voters had switched.

State elections. Voting the same day as the federal election, citizens in Rhineland-Palatinate, where Kohl was formerly minister president, gave the Christian Democrats 51.9 percent of the vote. In Schleswig-Holstein one week later, the Christian Democrats, with 49 percent of the vote, again received an absolute majority of seats in the state legislature.

The pattern of Christian Democratic majorities was not repeated, however, in elections in Hesse and Bremen in September. In Hesse, where no party won a majority, the SPD, with 51 out of 110 seats, retained its minority government; and in Bremen the Social Democrats expanded their majority to 58 of 100 seats.

U.S. missiles. The issue that generated the most heat in West Germany was the deployment of U.S. intermediate-range missiles in Western Europe as a response to the Soviet SS-20 intermediate-range missiles aimed at Western Europe. Intense opposition to deployment arose mainly among church groups, left-wing Social Democrats, the Greens and other radical groups, and large numbers of young people. Late in the year, the SPD, at a special party congress, adopted a resolution opposing deployment, ignoring an appeal from former Chancellor Helmut Schmidt. Chancellor Kohl strongly

After scoring upset victories in West Germany's national elections, the 27 representatives of the antiestablishment group known as the Greens proceeded to discompose the staid Bundestag with their unorthodox dress and behavior. Here, Chancellor Helmut Kohl looks somewhat dubiously at a typical member of the Greens, Walter Schwenninger.

backed deployment, if significant progress were not made in the U.S.-Soviet arms limitation talks in Geneva. At the same time, during trips to Washington in April and May and to Moscow in July, Kohl urged that President Ronald Reagan and Soviet party chief Yuri Andropov hold a summit meeting. His efforts failed, and the Geneva negotiations produced no results.

Groups opposed to the missiles staged demonstrations in cities all over the Federal Republic. On October 22, in the largest series of protests to date, more than 600,000 people turned out for peaceful demonstrations in Bonn, Hamburg, Stuttgart, West Berlin, and elsewhere; perhaps 200,000 protesters formed a human chain over 60 miles long between U.S. military facilities in Stuttgart and Neu-Ulm. When U.S. Vice-President George Bush traveled to Krefeld in June to celebrate the 300th anniversary of German emigration to America, a crowd threw rocks and bottles at his entourage.

Despite the protests, the Bundestag on November 22, by a vote of 286 to 266, reaffirmed West Germany's 1979 decision to allow deployment. The first battery of Pershing II's began arriving the day after. Also on November 23, Moscow announced that it would withdraw

from the U.S.-Soviet medium-range missile talks in Geneva.

Brewing scandal. In late November a Bonn prosecutor announced that his office intended to indict Economics Minister Otto Lambsdorff, along with a leading West German banker and three others, on charges of accepting $50,000 in bribes from the Flick industrial conglomerate in exchange for tax favors. Lambsdorff, a leading member of the FDP, denied he had done anything illegal and declined to resign.

Economy. In July the rate of inflation was only 2.5 percent, compared with 5.8 percent at the same time in 1982. However, with 2.2 million West Germans out of work, the unemployment rate stood at 8.9 percent, compared with 6.8 percent the year before. Because investment capital was flowing to the United States to take advantage of high interest rates based on huge projected budget deficits, the Kohl government had to set West German interest rates at levels that discouraged borrowing for new investments. In September economists projected real growth of 1.0 percent for 1983.

Inter-German relations. The Bonn government announced in June that it would guarantee East Germany about $400 million in loans from private banks. The leading bank in the group, which obtained a very favorable rate of interest, was the official bank of the state of Bavaria. This helped explain the surprising role in the matter of CSU leader Strauss; although he and his party had always maintained a harder line against Eastern bloc states than other West German political groups, Strauss was highly active in securing the loan guarantee and later, in July, met with Communist leaders in Czechoslovakia, Poland, and East Germany on a private trip. His activities brought about the resignation from the CSU of a popular Bundestag deputy, Franz Handlos, who accused Strauss of failing to consult with the party over such a radical change in direction.

Hitler diaries hoax. The world was startled on April 22 when the West German weekly magazine *Stern* announced it had acquired 62 volumes of diaries and other works supposedly

Panic-stricken Ghanaians scramble for rides on their way home from Nigeria, after having been expelled as illegal aliens.

written by Adolf Hitler between 1932 and 1945. Press reports put the amount paid for the volumes as high as $3.8 million.

Initial skepticism about the authenticity of the works grew, until the West German Federal Archive, having examined selected volumes, declared them "primitive forgeries." *Stern* thereupon fired Gerd Heidemann, its star reporter who had acquired the supposed diaries, and accepted the resignation of two of its chief editors. Heidemann, who was subsequently held in custody, had purchased the volumes from Konrad Kujau, alias Konrad Fischer, an East German émigré living in Stuttgart.

See STATISTICS OF THE WORLD.   R.J.W.

GHANA. Ghana's economic and political stability were threatened in 1983 by Nigeria's repatriation of close to a million Ghanaians and by reported coup attempts against the government of Flight Lieutenant Jerry Rawlings.

Nigeria's January expulsion of between 700,000 (Nigeria's count) and 1 million (Ghana's figure) Ghanians generated tremendous hardship, both for those expelled and for the Ghanaian authorities. Ghana, already plagued with widespread unemployment, was confronted with the resettlement of hundreds of thousands of jobless citizens.

The first of the reported coup attempts occurred in late February, after the abrogation of the nation's 1979 constitution by the ruling Provisional National Defense Council (PNDC) and a cabinet reshuffle. In mid-April the government announced the thwarting of a second plot, involving "hundreds of mercenaries" said to have been recruited by the U.S. Central Intelligence Agency and the Israeli secret services. The third, and most serious, attempted coup followed another cabinet reshuffle; before this coup was put down, in late June, rebels managed to gain control of the Accra radio station and free 52 political prisoners.

Former PNDC member J. Amartey Kwei and two accomplices were executed in August, after having been implicated in the July 1982 murder of three High Court judges. In mid-December, Rawlings visited Ivory Coast to meet with President Felix Houphuët-Boigny; talks reportedly centered on Rawlings's concern that Ghanaian exiles in Ivory Coast were continuing to plot his overthrow.

An austerity budget introduced in April provided for a system of export bonuses and import surcharges which in effect devalued the national currency. Basic necessities such as rice and maize were exempt from the import surcharges, but a rise in the cost of petroleum products was immediately reflected in higher bus fares. These measures helped generate a series of protests, leading to closing of major universities.

See STATISTICS OF THE WORLD.   E.B.

GREAT BRITAIN. As Great Britain in 1983 emerged slowly from the deepest economic recession since the 1930's, the Conservative government of Prime Minister Margaret Thatcher (see biography in PEOPLE IN THE NEWS) won a strong vote of confidence in an early general election.

The elections. On May 9, Thatcher, yielding to arguments from her party that the time was ripe, announced a general election to be held one month later. One reason for setting an early election date (the current Parliament was not due to expire until May 1984) was the Conservatives' high standing in the polls. The public had responded favorably to what was seen as Thatcher's resoluteness during the 1982 Falklands conflict. That success also had the effect of imparting a favorable glow to her leadership at home, in areas where quick success had proved more elusive—the economy, for instance.

Another plus for the Conservatives was that the government appeared reasonably united. The Laborites, on the other hand, under the leadership of Michael Foot, were still beset by the ideological warfare that had consumed the party since it lost office in 1979. However, Labor had two exploitable issues that it might turn to its advantage: unemployment, which was then running at about 14 percent, and uneasiness at the nuclear arms buildup, as reflected in Britain's decision to allow U.S. deployment of cruise missiles at the end of 1983, failing progress in arms talks.

Challenging the Conservative government from the center was the Liberal Party, under the youthful David Steel, in alliance with the young Social Democratic Party (SDP), headed by Roy Jenkins.

The results of the June 9 elections amounted to a Conservative landslide in terms of seats won. In the 650-member House of Commons the Conservatives obtained 397 seats, which gave them an overall majority of 144, the largest since Labor's postwar victory in 1945. Labor won 209 seats, its smallest representation since 1935. The Liberal-SDP alliance captured a meager 23 seats.

Inspection of the votes cast gives a different picture. The Conservatives, with some 13 million popular votes, had 42 percent of the total vote. They had, in fact, fewer votes and a lower percentage than they had won in the general election of 1979. Labor had 28 percent of the vote and the alliance 25 percent, yet Labor won nine times as many seats. Thus, the Conservatives were less popular, and other major parties, especially the alliance parties, more popular than the numbers of seats won suggest.

The new government. After the election, Thatcher lost no time in reconstructing her government. She replaced moderates in her cabinet with hard-line Conservatives: for example, Francis Pym with Sir Geoffrey Howe as foreign secretary and William Whitelaw with Leon Brittan as home secretary. Howe was succeeded as chancellor of the exchequer by Nigel Lawson.

The new government listed the containment of inflation as its first domestic priority. It also promised to seek legislation compelling unions to poll their members for the election of senior officials, for declaring a strike, and for the maintenance of a political fund. In addition, it reaffirmed campaign commitments to the further sale of public property, such as British Telecom (the telephone part of the old Post Office's business) and British Airways.

By autumn, as Conservatives prepared for their annual party conference in mid-October, some storm clouds had begun to gather. The new trade and industry minister, Cecil Parkinson, disclosed that he had fathered a baby expected in January by his former secretary. Mounting criticism forced Parkinson to resign, a bitter blow to the party whose election victory he had managed as party chairman. Employment Secretary Norman Tebbit was named to replace him. The Thatcher government also suffered severe criticism for instituting sharp

A 14-mile human chain is formed by Britons protesting the planned installation of U.S. cruise missiles; the demonstration stretched from the Greenham Common Air Base, where the missiles were to be deployed, to the nuclear warhead factory at Burghfield.

cutbacks in financing for the National Health Service.

The opposition regroups. In the wake of Labor's rebuff by the voters, Foot resigned as party leader, and Denis Healey stepped down as deputy leader. At the annual party conference in early October, two principal contenders faced each other: Neil Kinnock, 41, a Welshman placed among the "soft left" of the party, and Roy Hattersley, a former cabinet minister ten years his senior and a right-winger in Labor terms. Kinnock took 71 percent of the vote to become the youngest Labor Party leader in British history. Hattersley won the deputy leadership.

In the SDP, Jenkins made way for the more forceful leadership of David Owen, a former Labor foreign secretary. An unresolved question for the alliance was whether the two parties forming it should emphasize their separate identities or move toward a merger. At its convention in Manchester in September, the SDP voted to reject any outright merger.

The nuclear debate. As part of the 1979 decision by the North Atlantic Treaty Organization to station 572 Pershing II and ground-launched cruise missiles in Europe, beginning in late 1983, if no progress were made at the U.S.-Soviet talks on medium-range missiles, Britain agreed to provide bases for 160 Tomahawk cruise missiles. Critics took the Thatcher government to task for not requiring joint U.S.-British control of the missiles. In response, Thatcher assured everyone that the use of American facilities in Britain in time of an emergency was "a matter for joint decision in the light of the circumstances at the time."

The Campaign for Nuclear Disarmament (CND) mounted strong protests against deployment. On April 2 at least 40,000 organizers descended on Greenham Common U.S. Air Base in Berkshire and, hand-in-hand, formed a 14-mile-long human chain linking the base with two other nuclear establishments in the vicinity. On October 22, a day of nuclear protests throughout Western Europe, hundreds of thousands jammed central London in the largest demonstration of its kind in British history. On November 15, soon after the first cruise missiles began arriving at Greenham Common, 141 members of a women's peace camp outside the base were arrested after tying themselves to the gates. That same day, protesters were arrested during a demonstration outside the House of Commons. Later in November, the U.S.-Soviet missile talks broke down when the Soviets walked out in protest over preparations for deployment.

The economy. The government introduced its budget on March 15. It offered a mild stimulus of some $2.2 billion, largely in the form of personal income tax cuts, while maintaining restraint in spending programs. The budget took a rosier view of the prospects for economic upturn, expecting, for example, a 2 percent rise in output in 1983, which could barely stabilize unemployment but would not significantly reduce it. By October the unemployment rate had fallen slightly, to 12.3 percent. Inflation, which had declined to 3.7 percent in June, was slowly climbing again (it reached 5 percent in October).

The government's worries about the future course of public spending were reflected in Chancellor of the Exchequer Lawson's announcement that the spending departments would have to save $745 million in 1983, including nearly $358 million on defense.

Northern Ireland. In the June 9 parliamentary elections, Unionist candidates won 15 of Northern Ireland's 17 seats (five more than before); the mainly Roman Catholic Social Democratic and Labor Party and Sinn Fein won one seat each.

In early August a Belfast judge convicted 34 members of the outlawed Irish Republican Army for terrorist offenses; 22 were given jail sentences, four for life. On September 25, 38 Irish nationalists broke out from maximum-security Maze Prison, near Belfast, after killing one guard and wounding five others in a gun battle. Most were recaptured.

Neil Kinnock and his wife Glenys acknowledge well-wishers' cheers after he became the youngest leader of the Labor Party in British history.

In the continuing sectarian violence, three Protestants were killed and seven wounded when gunmen opened fire in a Protestant church in Darkley on November 20. On December 7 a prominent Protestant leader, Edgar Graham, was gunned down in Belfast. In London itself, on December 17, a car bomb exploded outside Harrods department store, killing six people and wounding more than 90. The IRA admitted that some of its members had set the bomb but said they had acted without authorization. At the same time, the IRA claimed responsibility for a bombing a week earlier that killed several British soldiers in the Woolwich district of London. Another bomb exploded outside a London department store on Christmas day, injuring two pedestrians.

Falklands report. A six-member committee appointed to look into the background of the Falkland Islands war reported its findings in January. The committee found that it could not attach "any criticism or blame to the present Government for the Argentine Junta's decision to commit its act of unprovoked aggression in the invasion of the Falkland Islands" in 1982.

U.S.-British relations. Relations with the United States were strained in late October when U.S. troops led an invasion of the Caribbean island of Grenada, a former British colony, in the wake of a coup there. The invasion caused a furor over what was seen as inadequate U.S. consultation with the British government, which opposed military action. Disenchantment with the United States increased when the Reagan administration in December announced a lifting of its ban on arms sales to Argentina.

Royal trips. In mid-February, Queen Elizabeth II and Prince Philip embarked, aboard the royal yacht *Britannia,* on a month-long tour of the Caribbean, Mexico, and the western coast of the United States and Canada. In November they visited Kenya, Bangladesh, and India.

In March, Prince Charles and his wife, Diana, departed on a visit, of more than a month's duration, to Australia and New Zealand, accompanied by Prince William, their infant son. In June the Prince and Princess of Wales made another journey, to Canada.

Gold heist. On November 26 six gunmen pulled off the largest robbery in British history, stealing about $40 million worth of gold bullion from a security company warehouse near London's Heathrow Airport. On December 4 police arrested a guard for the company and charged him with the theft; other arrests followed as Scotland Yard continued its probe.

See STATISTICS OF THE WORLD. *See also* COMMONWEALTH OF NATIONS. T.J.O.H.

GREECE. In 1983, Greece's Socialist government renewed a major agreement with the United States, although it continued to take a highly independent position in most areas of foreign policy. In domestic affairs, the economy remained a central problem.

Foreign affairs. On July 15, after nine months of negotiations, the U.S. and Greek governments initialed an accord, ratified by the Greek Parliament in November, allowing the United States to maintain its military installations in Greece for another five years (1984–1988). These included four major bases, two near Athens and two on the island of Crete. The accord limited their use to an American defensive role; it allowed Greece to exercise titular command over them, obtain secret information secured through them, and suspend their operation in emergencies where Greek national interests might be jeopardized. In addition, the United States agreed to nearly double its military aid to Greece, to $500 million for fiscal 1984, thus preserving, at least temporarily, a seven-to-ten ratio in U.S. military assistance to Greece and to Turkey.

The Socialist government of Andreas Papandreou had been seeking to improve the terms of Greek membership in the European Economic Community, and in late March, the EEC Commission proposed, subject to approval by the Council of Ministers, that Greece be granted an additional $2.1 billion for agricultural, forest, and fishing development and be allowed temporarily to continue tariffs on ECC industrial imports. However, when Greece assumed the presidency of the council on July 1, the time was considered inopportune for Greece to press its claims.

Relations with Turkey were seriously strained late in the year after Ankara extended recognition to the newly proclaimed independent Turkish Cypriot republic in northern Cyprus. Greece, as a coguarantor, along with Britain

U.S. Marines check out a street in Greenville, Grenada, following the U.S.-led invasion of the Caribbean island in October.

and Turkey, of Cyprus's 1960 constitution, called for a reversal of the Turkish Cypriot move and for the resumption of intercommunal talks on the island. The new civilian government in Ankara appeared willing to discuss all outstanding issues with Athens.

In February, during a visit by Soviet Premier Nikolai Tikhonov, Greece and the Soviet Union signed a ten-year accord for economic cooperation. The two nations endorsed a nuclear-free zone in the Balkans and called for the withdrawal of foreign troops from Cyprus.

In May, the Greek government requested that Great Britain return the Elgin Marbles, famous classical sculptures removed from Greece by the British in the 19th century. The Greek request found little favor in Britain.

Economic developments. Greece faced serious economic problems, with inflation exceeding 20 percent, stagnant investment, and unemployment at 10 percent. Early in the year, the government imposed a wage freeze and a 15.5 percent devaluation of the drachma. A rash of protest strikes ensued, especially among state workers. In June, Parliament approved legislation curbing the right to strike in state-controlled industries.

Terrorist attack. On November 15 two gunmen killed a senior U.S. Navy officer in Greece, Captain George Tsantes, and his chauffeur as they waited for a traffic light to change on a highway outside Athens. A terrorist group, November 17, opposed to the presence of the Central Intelligence Agency in Greece claimed responsibility.

See STATISTICS OF THE WORLD.   J.A.P.

GRENADA. On October 25 a U.S.-led invasion force landed on the island of Grenada, overthrowing a hard-line Marxist regime that had come to power days before in a coup, and establishing an interim government that promised to restore democratic elections.

Relations between the United States and the previous (also Marxist) regime had reached a low in March when President Ronald Reagan pointed to the construction of the Point Salines Airport as evidence of Soviet-Cuban militarization; the Grenadian government maintained that the airport was needed to develop tourism. In June, Grenadian Prime Minister Maurice Bishop paid an unofficial visit to the United States and appealed for improved relations, reportedly winning a cool reception.

Bishop's New Jewel Movement (for Joint

Endeavor for the Welfare, Education, and Liberation of the People) had introduced a leftist program of social and economic change and had close links with Cuban President Fidel Castro. A split within the movement developed, as a faction reportedly led by Deputy Prime Minister Bernard Coard sought to curb Bishop's power. Bishop was put under house arrest and, a few days later, on October 19, was reportedly killed with at least 15 others, when soldiers fired on a crowd freeing him from custody. General Hudson Austin announced that a revolutionary military council had taken power.

On October 25, President Reagan announced that American troops, with a contingent representing other Caribbean nations, had landed in Grenada before dawn. He cited a threat to American citizens on the island, mostly medical students, and the need to prevent a Soviet-Cuban takeover. The approximately 6,000 Americans that eventually took part in the operation met stiffer resistance, particularly on the part of Cubans on the island, than had been expected, but by October 27 all the medical students had been airlifted out, and the major strongholds on the island had fallen. In all, 18 Americans, 25 Cubans, and more than 40 Grenadians died during the fighting, according to U.S. figures.

The invasion produced a flurry of protests, and the United States cast the sole negative vote (a veto) against a UN Security Council resolution condemning the invasion. On the other hand, polls and interviews on the island itself indicated widespread support for the U.S. action.

Austin and Coard were captured by the American forces and placed under guard by the Caribbean contingent. They were expected to be brought to trial. In November, Sir Paul Scoon, the governor general of the island (Grenada is a member of the British Commonwealth and therefore has a nominal representative of the crown in the country), appointed a nine-member advisory council, headed by Nicholas Braithwaite, to set the stage for elections.

The United States pledged more than $3 million in aid to help in reconstruction and to revive the economy, which had been brought to a halt by the invasion. All American combat troops were withdrawn by December 15, although about 300 soldiers were left behind to support a peacekeeping force from several Caribbean nations.

See STATISTICS OF THE WORLD. *See also* CARIBBEAN COUNTRIES; CUBA; UNITED STATES OF AMERICA.   R.D.

GUAM. *See* STATISTICS OF THE WORLD.

GUATEMALA. A military coup on August 8, 1983, installed Brigadier General Oscar Humberto Mejía Víctores, minister of defense, as Guatemalan chief of state, ousting Brigadier General Efraín Ríos Montt.

Ríos Montt had reduced administrative corruption and instituted some social reforms, but by mid-1983 his support had evaporated. In late June army hard-liners forced out reformist younger officers serving the administration. The Catholic church hierarchy feared the growing influence of Ríos Montt's evangelical Protestantism, conservative businessmen opposed his tax policies, hard pressed agricultural interests failed to persuade the government to defer loan payments, and civil rights advocates rejected his rural pacification program—charging that it had claimed thousands of lives.

President Mejía Víctores abolished the secret tribunals instituted by his predecessor that had taken the lives of at least 15 Guatemalan dissidents, and he promised balloting for a constituent assembly in mid-1984. Civil liberties were restored on the day after the coup, as Mejía Víctores ended the state of emergency; it had been declared by Ríos Montt in June, when a coup was threatened by a member of the former governing junta. In October and November, Mejía Víctores appointed a new chief of the armed forces and carried out a cabinet shakeup, replacing the labor and economy ministers. In December, the government issued a decree automatically retiring Ríos Montt and all other army officers who had served in the high command in previous governments.

By late 1983 observers noted an increase in political violence, with the murders of an influential Franciscan priest, three opposition politicians, and two U.S.-employed teachers. In September, Mejía Víctores's sister was kidnapped by four gunmen in an incident paralleling the June kidnapping of Ríos Montt's sister. Both women were released in late October

Soldiers escort Guatemalan ex-president Efraín Ríos Montt from his office in the National Palace in Guatemala City after his ouster in a military takeover on August 8.

after newspapers published a document from a group called the Rebel Armed Forces, condemning the Mejía Víctores government.

The United States reacted cautiously to the August coup; the U.S. embassy announced that it would not affect U.S. economic aid levels. In November, however, the U.S. Congress cut off $13 million in economic aid and refused to authorize military aid, which had largely been suspended since 1977 because of alleged human rights violations. Partly as a result, Guatemala was said to be losing interest in attempts to reactivate the Central American Defense Council, an anti-Communist military alliance involving Guatemala and four other Central American countries.

An agreement signed in August by the Mejía Víctores government and El Salvador provided that Guatemala would receive U.S.-supplied arms from El Salvador, in exchange for counterinsurgency training.

An unpopular value-added tax that raised the price of almost all consumer goods by 10 percent was introduced on August 1, after a massive budget deficit of $400 million in 1982. Expenditures in the 1983 budget were made 20 percent lower than in the 1982 budget, forcing the unemployment rate up to almost 30 percent.

See STATISTICS OF THE WORLD.   L.L.P.

GUINEA. See STATISTICS OF THE WORLD.

GUINEA-BISSAU. See STATISTICS OF THE WORLD.

GUYANA. See STATISTICS OF THE WORLD. See also VENEZUELA.

H

HAITI. See STATISTICS OF THE WORLD. See also CARIBBEAN COUNTRIES.

HAWAII. See STATISTICS OF THE WORLD. See also STATE GOVERNMENT REVIEW.

Health and Medicine

In 1983 the spread of the mysterious disease AIDS aroused often unfounded public fears, and the first person to receive an artificial heart succumbed to complications after surviving almost four months by means of the device.

MEDICINE

The most newsworthy medical stories of 1983 were the accelerating epidemic of AIDS (acquired immune deficiency syndrome) and the struggle of Dr. Barney Clark to survive sustained by an artificial heart.

Epidemic. By late 1983 over 3,000 cases of AIDS had been reported in the United States since the disease was first recognized in 1981, with an overall fatality rate of more than 40 percent. The disease had also been reported in more than 30 other countries, and its cause was still not understood.

Epidemiologists at the U.S. Centers for Disease Control (CDC) in Atlanta had first become aware of AIDS through outbreaks of certain previously rare diseases—a cancer called Kaposi's sarcoma and a form of pneumonia caused by the organism *Pneumocystis carinii*—in young homosexual men in New York and California. This pneumonia is classified as an "opportunistic" infection, one that seldom afflicts an individual with a healthy immune system. The CDC began requesting case reports of the pneumonia and Kaposi's sarcoma; as a result, AIDS became recognized as a new and serious disease syndrome.

AIDS involves a loss of the body's ability to fight certain kinds of infections and cancers. For instance, Kaposi's sarcoma, as found in the United States, was almost never fatal. In AIDS patients, though, it has shown itself to be quite malignant, and death usually results. Other symptoms seen in AIDS patients include a diffuse enlargement of the lymph glands and infections with various organisms, including the tuberculosis bacterium, the herpes simplex virus, and the cytomegalovirus (which is common in the homosexual community). Male homosexuals are not the only individuals in danger of contracting AIDS; intravenous drug users, Haitians, and hemophiliacs are also at risk. Most other people appear to have an exceedingly low risk; exceptions include infants of mothers in the high-risk groups (particularly intravenous drug users), female sexual partners of AIDS patients, and prison inmates with a prior history of drug use.

According to the classic definition of an epidemic as "an unusual occurrence of disease," AIDS should be considered a true epidemic. Reported cases by three-month periods increased from fewer than 25 in the first quarter that reporting was done (April to June 1981) to approximately 525 in the April–June quarter of 1983. Moreover, the rate of increase itself rose during this time. Some of the rise was undoubtedly the result of better diagnosis and reporting, but it is unlikely that these alone account for the whole increase. The underlying infection, suspected by most scientists to be the cause of AIDS, may occur months or even years before AIDS symptoms appear. Hence it is not known how many persons are now incubating the disease and could develop symptoms over the next two or three years. The current rates of disease may therefore be just a fraction of the rates that may be reported in the future.

In 1983, investigators found evidence of human T-cell leukemia virus in the lymphocytes of AIDS patients (lymphocytes are a type of white blood cells); it has not been determined whether the virus caused AIDS or is merely another opportunistic infection. If an infectious agent is responsible for AIDS, the infection could be transmitted in a number of ways. For male homosexuals, intimate sexual contact might be responsible, and the transmission of infected blood may provide the route for spread in intravenous drug users and some recipients of blood products. Research is planned in which apparently healthy persons in the high-risk groups, especially male homosexuals, will have their blood and immune functions studied periodically over a span of years; the expectation is that some will eventually develop AIDS, so that changes associated with its development can be scrutinized. In addition, the CDC is investigating AIDS cases that do not belong to the high-risk groups,. Much of the funding for ongoing AIDS research came from the federal government, which has put considerable effort and resources into AIDS research. No specific or very effective treatment has thus far been found, and the fatality rate has remained high.

One of the negative impacts of the AIDS epidemic for the general public resulted from a misunderstanding of the disease. People were apparently confused by reports linking AIDS with blood transfusions, and the rate of blood donations dropped significantly, especially in areas like New York City that have high AIDS rates. Public health officials assured prospective donors that there is *no* risk of acquiring AIDS from donating blood.

Artificial heart. The first recipient of a permanently implanted artificial heart, Dr. Barney Clark, died on March 23, after surviving a remarkable 112 days by means of it. The plastic-and-aluminum device, designed by Dr. Robert K. Jarvik of the University of Utah, had been implanted on December 2, 1982, just in time to save Clark's life. A retired dentist from the Seattle area, he had been suffering from cardiomyopathy, a progressive weakening of the heart muscle, which would no longer respond to drug treatment. At 61 years of age, he was more than ten years too old to be considered for a human heart transplant. But his stable personality and supportive family—as well as the gravity of his condition—made him a good candidate for the highly risky surgery.

The 7½-hour operation, performed by Dr. William C. DeVries at the University of Utah Medical Center, involved removing most of Clark's natural heart and replacing it with a

Expressing their concern about AIDS, 2,000 people carrying lighted candles marched down San Francisco's Market Street in May to join an estimated 8,000 other demonstrators near City Hall.

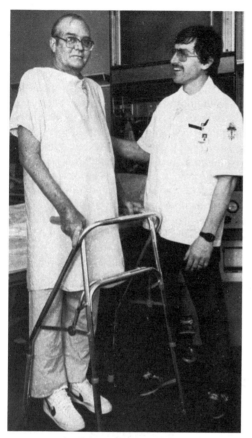

Dr. Barney Clark, recipient of the first permanent artificial heart, uses a walker to exercise in his hospital room at the University of Utah Medical Center. He died a few weeks after this photo was taken.

ethical questions, including those of cost and recipient selection, but it nevertheless was widely seen as an important step in the treatment of heart disease and the replacement of organs with artificial devices.

New hope for the infertile. Now that in vitro fertilization has become a relatively well-established technique, and "test-tube" babies are no longer as unusual as they once were, researchers in California have reported success with a new, still experimental method of fertilization that offers additional hope to couples with fertility problems. The technique, known as ovum (egg) transfer, involves taking sperm from the prospective father and then placing it in the uterus of a woman who has agreed to provide an egg. (With in vitro fertilization, on the other hand, the egg is obtained surgically from the mother's ovary and is then fertilized with the father's sperm, in the laboratory.) If fertilization occurs, the embryo is carefully flushed from the donor's womb through a narrow plastic tube. It is then transferred through a catheter to the uterus of the woman who will carry the fetus to term.

Ovum transfer offers at least one advantage over in vitro fertilization; no surgery is required for the recipient. However, the procedure, like artificial insemination, necessitates the participation of a third person in the process of conception, something that not everyone will find acceptable. Researchers suggest that ovum transfer will be most useful as an option in place of in vitro fertilization, when a woman has blocked fallopian tubes that cannot be opened surgically; in cases where the eggs cannot be removed surgically to allow in vitro fertilization; or where there is concern that the prospective mother might transmit a genetic disorder to her offspring.

Coffee and cholesterol. The debate over coffee's effects on health continued, as Norwegian researchers reported findings that could link coffee drinking to increased risk of heart disease. According to Dr. Dag S. Thelle and colleagues at the University of Tromsø, drinking large amounts of coffee may result in increased cholesterol in the blood, which has been linked in turn with the development of heart disease. The study examined the coffee-drinking habits of 14,581 Norwegian men and

device called the Jarvik-7, designed to mimic the action of the natural organ. The artificial heart was permanently connected by 6-foot-long hoses to a compressed-air pump that caused it to "beat"; the pump was housed in a wheeled cart. After the operation Clark suffered numerous complications, but he made more progress in recovering than many had anticipated. Two months after the procedure, he was able to take ten steps with the aid of a walker and pedal a stationary bicycle. His condition worsened a month later, however, and death eventually resulted. Clark's doctors stated that his death was caused not by any failure of the device, but by an overall failure of his own organ systems. The operation raised

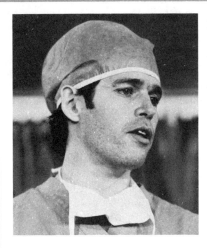

Artificial Heart Maker
When Dr. Barney Clark became the first person in history to receive an artificial heart, it was a proud day for 36-year-old Dr. Robert Jarvik. It was his plastic and metal device—the Jarvik-7—that was used in the pioneering operation. Originally a medical school dropout, Jarvik earned a master's degree in occupational biomechanics from New York University and, in 1971, went to work at the University of Utah's Division of Artificial Organs, developing mechanical hearts for test animals. He later found time to earn a degree from Utah's medical school, graduating in 1976. Jarvik continues to work at the Division of Artificial Organs; when not developing mechanical devices, he is an avid skier and sculptor.

Robert Jarvik

women. The results showed that people who drank between one and four cups of coffee daily had cholesterol levels about 5 percent higher than those who drank no coffee. Those who drank between five and eight cups daily had cholesterol levels that were 9 percent higher, and those who drank nine or more cups of coffee each day had levels about 12 percent higher than those of abstainers.

The researchers acknowledged that their findings by themselves did not settle the issue and that they left many questions unanswered, chief among them the question of why such an apparently strong relationship had not been well established by other research. The researchers suggested several distinctive characteristics of their study population that might have made the relationship more evident. One was the amount of coffee consumed by the subjects, 60 percent of whom reported drinking five or more cups of coffee daily; only about 20 percent of the subjects in similar American studies consumed that amount. Another factor might have been the strength of the coffee; in Norway, coffee is boiled rather than percolated or dripped through the grounds.

Huntington's disease. Huntington's disease, or Huntington's chorea, is a fatal hereditary disorder whose symptoms include jerky movements and mental deterioration. The child of an affected parent has a 50 percent chance of

also contracting it. Since symptoms do not usually appear until early middle age, victims may unknowingly pass the disease on to their children before a diagnosis can be made.

This situation may change as a result of the development of the first genetic test to detect the disease, announced in November by scientists at Massachusetts General Hospital in Boston. Using sophisticated gene-splicing techniques, the researchers discovered a "marker," or indicator, of the disease in human genetic material. Another year or two of study is required before the test can be widely applied, but it shows promise of making possible a diagnosis of the disease early in the life of those yet without symptoms, as well as prenatally.

High blood pressure. Despite years of advising people with hypertension (persistently high blood pressure) to eat less salt, physicians have lacked hard evidence that a low-salt diet does in fact result in lower blood pressure. In July, a study conducted by Dutch researchers offered the first evidence that lower salt intake may have a favorable effect on blood pressure. The study, conducted at Erasmus University Medical School in Rotterdam, compared 245 babies whose parents fed them a diet containing normal amounts of salt for the first six months of life with another group of infants who were fed diets containing two to three times less

189

salt. It was found that, after six months, the infants on the low-salt diets had blood pressure levels that were on average slightly lower than those who had taken in normal amounts of salt. The researchers contended that, though the difference was slight, the lower level, if maintained over a period of years, could "contribute considerably to the prevention of cardiovascular disease."

The issue, however, is far from settled. Another study, also described in July, found no link between high salt consumption, as reported by subjects, and high blood pressure, even among overweight people. A team of researchers in Connecticut questioned 1,655 men and 1,911 women as to the amount of salt they ate. Substantial differences in salt consumption were reported, but these did not correlate significantly with differences in blood pressure.

Alzheimer's disease. Alzheimer's disease, a neurological disorder that results in a progressive massive deterioration of mental functioning, is the underlying cause of perhaps 120,000 deaths in the United States each year. Although no way has yet been found to prevent the disease or halt its progress, certain drugs might possibly relieve symptoms.

One of the drugs, naloxone (sold as Narcan), is already used to treat narcotics overdoses. Because naturally occurring substances similar to naloxone may play a role in memory losses associated with Alzheimer's disease, Dr. Barry Reisberg of New York University Medical Center and colleagues tested the drug's effects on seven Alzheimer's patients. Tests of memory, perception, and other functions showed that all the patients improved somewhat after receiving the drug, with three improving so markedly that family members noted the change. Two of the patients experienced increased anxiety, but there were no other side effects.

Physostigmine (sold as Antilirium) is also being studied for use in treating Alzheimer's disease. In one preliminary study, Dr. Leon J. Thal and Paula Altman Fuld of New York's Albert Einstein College of Medicine found that eight of 12 patients tested with the drug improved their ability to carry out a recall task. When given higher doses, the patients did suffer significant side effects—nausea, vomit-

ing, sweatiness, or queasiness. In another study, Dr. Kenneth L. Davis and colleagues at the Bronx Veterans Administration Medical Center found that, in a small group of patients who received the drug, two became less disoriented and better able to relate to their environment.

In December researchers from the University of California reported that a substance known as prion, which is the smallest infectious substance known, might be the cause of Alzheimer's disease. Further tests were planned to confirm the initial test results. If they hold up, the discovery could ultimately lead to techniques for preventing and treating the disease.

Smoking. Smoking "light" cigarettes (those considered low in nicotine and other substances) apparently does not reduce the risk of cigarette-related heart attacks, researchers reported in 1983. Further confirming the notion that it's better to quit than switch, another study concluded that light cigarettes, in fact, have as much nicotine as regular cigarettes.

The first study, conducted by researchers from Boston and Harvard universities, compared the smoking habits of 502 men between the ages of 30 and 54 who were hospitalized after suffering first heart attacks with the habits of 835 men hospitalized for other reasons. It was found that the men who smoked faced almost three times the risk of heart attacks as those who did not smoke. Researchers also found that the level of risk did not change with the amount of nicotine and carbon monoxide apparently contained in the cigarettes.

The reason for the lack of difference may lie in part in the finding of the second study, conducted by Dr. Neal L. Benowitz of San Francisco General Hospital and Medical Center and colleagues. They found that despite the claims of cigarette manufacturers and contrary to the results of previous tests made by the Federal Trade Commission, the tobacco in low-yield cigarettes did not contain less nicotine than does that in most regular-strength cigarettes. The investigators reached this conclusion after extracting and measuring the nicotine content in different cigarettes,. To determine how much nicotine was consumed by smokers of low-yield cigarettes, the blood concentration of a nicotine by-product was measured after 272 subjects smoked various brands. The researchers suggested that their methods provided more accurate information than did the smoking machines used in the FTC tests.

In November, Surgeon General C. Everett Koop released still another report pointing out the dangerous health consequences of smoking. It suggested that in 1983, 170,000 Americans would die prematurely from heart disease because they smoked. The report also cited new research showing that the increased risk of death from heart disease begins to diminish as soon as the cigarette smoker quits.

Cancer and chromosomes. A study reported in July offered a new theory about why, when a large group of people are exposed to a cancer-causing agent, only some develop cancer. Dr. Jorge J. Yunis of the University of Minnesota suggests that chromosomal "fragile sites" caused by genetic weaknesses may make some people more susceptible to cancer than others.

Reporting his findings in *Science*, Yunis first explained how "characteristic defects," consisting of missing or rearranged genes, are now known to exist in most human tumor cells. In comparing tumor cell chromosomes to white blood cell chromosomes, he found that the latter had fragile sites, prone to breakage, in the same regions where the cancer cell chromosomes showed defects. Yunis was able to associate breakage points with fragile sites in a common type of lung cancer, two types of lymphoma, and two types of leukemia. If the finding holds up for other kinds of cancer, the sites could be used as a guide in identifying people who are most vulnerable to cancer.

Plague. In a two-month period from mid-April to mid-June, 16 cases of human plague were reported to the CDC by the health departments of four western states—New Mexico, Arizona, Utah, and Oregon. Four patients reportedly died of the disease, which is caused by a bacterium and is also known as bubonic plague. The cases were the result of exposure to wild-rodent plague. Fleas bite the rodents—including ground squirrels, chipmunks, and prairie dogs—and become infected with the plague bacteria. The fleas then transmit the disease by biting people.

Rabies in raccoons. Years ago in the United States, most rabies cases in raccoons were confined to Georgia and northern Florida.

However, over the last few years, raccoon rabies has moved up the Appalachian mountains, and in 1983 it struck hard in the Virginia and Washington, D.C., area. Raccoon rabies—which is potentially fatal if transmitted to humans—remained a problem in the Georgia and Florida area, and it also became a problem in sections of the Great Plains from Texas to Montana.

Prospective reimbursement. On April 20, President Ronald Reagan signed into law a statute altering the system by which U.S. hospitals are reimbursed by the government for care given to medicare patients. Under the new policy, known as prospective reimbursement or payment, hospitals will be reimbursed with fixed fees set in advance for each patient, based on

An Alzheimer's patient, with her program coordinator, at a rehabilitation center. Studies suggest certain drugs may alleviate some symptoms of the disease.

the problem diagnosed, rather than being reimbursed for the services and treatment the patient is actually given. The basis for deciding the amount of reimbursement is a list of 467 categories of illness called "diagnosis-related groups" (DRG's). The plan, which currently applies only to inpatient medicare services, will be phased in over a period of years, beginning October 1. The reimbursement rate is adjusted depending on which of nine U.S. regions the hospital is in and whether it is considered urban or rural. A number of states have been exempted from the system because they already have cost-containment programs that incorporate the DRG system in some way.

Under the new system, if a hospital can devise ways to provide care for a particular patient economically, spending less than the government has determined that that patient's condition requires, the hospital might well make a profit on that patient. On the other hand, if more care is given than the government estimates is needed, the hospital is likely to lose money. It is hoped that hospitals will be forced to provide more cost-efficient care.

MENTAL HEALTH

Among major mental health issues of 1983 was the role of stress in contemporary life. Psychi-atrists considered the plight of the increasing numbers of homeless, many of whom suffer from psychiatric disorders.

Stress. Some recent medical studies are lending support to the claim that the ability to cope with stress plays an important role in maintaining health.

One study unveiled in 1983 concluded that stress may contribute to the development of high blood pressure by causing the kidneys to retain salt. Previous investigations of rats indicated that stress causes their kidneys to excrete less salt and that rats that develop high blood pressure are more likely to retain salt than those that do not. To see whether the same pattern prevailed in humans, a team led by Dr. Kathleen C. Light of the University of North Carolina School of Medicine chose two groups of male college students; one was at high risk of hypertension, either because the students had family histories of high blood pressure or because they had borderline levels of hypertension themselves; the other was at low risk.

To place them under stress, the students were assigned competitive tasks. The researchers found that those in the high-risk group had increased heart rates and tended to excrete significantly less urinary sodium and fluid. The study concluded that "psychological stress appears to induce changes in [the kidney's] excretory functions that may play a critical role in long-term blood pressure regulation."

Blood pressure is not the only regulatory function that may be affected by stress; researchers also offered evidence for the theory that the body's ability to fight disease with antibodies varies with the amount of stress an individual experiences. In a one-year study, researchers from Harvard and Tufts universities and Beth Israel Hospital in Boston found that the levels of an antibody known as secretory immunoglobin A (s-IgA) dropped significantly when the subjects, 64 dental students, were in stressful situations, such as during examination periods. The researchers also discovered that the student's individual emotional reaction to a stressful situation affected the level of the antibody. Subjects found to be more competitive on the basis of standardized personality tests showed lower levels of s-IgA than less competitive peers subjected to the same type of pressure.

Mental health and the homeless. At the annual meeting of the American Psychiatric Association in May, psychiatrists focused on the growing number of the homeless living in the streets of American cities. Studies have indicated that as many as 80 percent are suffering from some kind of mental health problem. There was general agreement that the present system of care was inadequate and that new programs should be devised, concentrating on vocational rehabilitation and the re-establishment of family ties.

See also BEHAVIORAL SCIENCES. J.F.J. & S.W.

HONDURAS. Honduras was the subject of wide attention in 1983, as rebels based in that country continued an armed struggle against the Nicaraguan government and the United States strengthened its ties with Honduras, now considered its closest ally in Central America.

An estimated 7,000 to 10,000 Nicaraguan guerrillas operated from Honduras during the year. Nicaragua charged that the Honduran military, supported by the U.S. Central Intelligence Agency, was directly involved in training and equipping them. The Honduran government denied the charges and in turn accused

Nicaragua of violating Honduran territory and training left-wing Honduran exiles. Honduras specifically alleged that Nicaraguan forces had been responsible for the death in June of two U.S. journalists whose car was struck by a rocket-propelled grenade only yards from the two countries' frontier. The danger of war along the Honduran-Nicaraguan border was a major factor prompting the formation in January of the so-called Contadora group of nations (Colombia, Mexico, Panama, and Venezuela), which joined in efforts to promote a diplomatic settlement to the conflict in Central America.

During 1983 there were occasional bombings and other terrorist acts, but terrorist activity did not appear to be on the increase. There was an outbreak of guerrilla activity in the northern province of Olancho in the late summer, but by September the army seemed to have the situation there under control.

U.S.-supported contras—counterrevolutionaries opposed to Nicaragua's Sandinista government—conduct training exercises in Honduras, not far from the border.

HOUSING

Charges of official violations of human rights were frequent. Many of the alleged abuses appeared to be directed against foreign nationals, but increasing numbers of Hondurans complained of official harassment.

Ties between Honduras and the United States were growing increasingly close. The United States also increased its presence within the country. More than 300 U.S. engineers and technicians were stationed there. There were joint military maneuvers in Honduras in February. Another series of large-scale U.S.-Honduran military exercises, involving an average of 3,500 U.S. troops and several Honduran battalions, began in August; the exercises, known as Big Pine II, were expected to continue until March 1984. During 1983, Honduras received about $96 million in U.S. economic aid and $40 million in U.S. military aid. Government leaders were said to be seeking greatly increased levels of aid and guarantees of military security.

Honduras agreed in May to permit the United States to open a training base for Salvadoran soldiers on its territory. Honduran forces also continued to cooperate with the Salvadoran army in efforts to control the operations of Salvadoran antigovernment guerrillas along their common border. In October, Honduras joined with El Salvador and Guatemala in agreeing to reactivate a joint anti-Communist military pact, the Condeca agreement.

Economy. Despite increased international assistance the Honduran economy remained severely depressed. Unemployment was estimated at more than 25 percent and approached 50 percent in the major urban centers. Capital flight slowed in 1983, and the value of the currency was stabilized, but there were few signs of real recovery.

See STATISTICS OF THE WORLD.   R.L.M.

HOUSING. The strength of the housing industry's recovery in 1983 surprised many analysts. The annual rate of housing starts, month by month, ranged well above 1.5 million, a major improvement. Sales of existing homes improved as well, as mortgage rates remained moderately low in comparison to 1982.

Housing starts. The statistics on housing starts repeatedly surprised industry experts, beginning with a reported annual rate of 1.7 million

in January and 1.8 million in February. The Commerce Department reported an August figure of 1.9 million, the highest level in nearly five years, although rates before and after lagged slightly behind that figure. The number of housing starts for all of 1982, in comparison, was only 1.07 million.

Mortgages. The housing recovery was spurred by a decline in home mortgage interest rates. Lenders were charging approximately 13 percent for mortgage loans at the beginning of the year, down from close to 16 percent in mid-1982. Mortgage rates rose only slightly during 1983, creeping up close to 14 percent by August, then easing down slightly. The rate for Federal Housing Administration (FHA) insured loans and Veterans Administration guaranteed loans rose from a low of 11.5 percent to a high of 13.5 percent before leveling off at 12.5 percent by November.

With mortgage interest rates fairly low, monthly payments became affordable and more buyers came back into the housing market. Total mortgage borrowing reached record levels. Many lenders, flush with funds thanks to banking deregulation, gladly authorized the traditional 30-year fixed-rate loans favored by many home buyers. However, adjustable rate mortgages, in which monthly payments fluctuate, and various creative financing techniques were increasingly popular during the year. Adjustable rate mortgages grew from 23 percent of all mortgages issued, in the first quarter, to 44 percent in the third quarter.

In addition to lower interest rates, an emphasis on less expensive housing also helped pull the industry out of the recession. Builders found ways to construct and sell homes more cheaply, by decreasing square footage, building on smaller lots, and subsidizing interest rates. Many builders were designing housing specifically for first-time home buyers; traditionally, builders had left these buyers to the resale housing market, concentrating instead on selling to buyers of second and third homes. The industry found that the baby-boom generation of home buyers had money to spend and was a profitable market to tap.

Other signs of recovery. The sale of existing homes also fared well. In September, they were selling at an annual rate of 2.74 million, up

Carpenters in Agoura, Calif., raise a wall in the Oak View Ranch housing development. While construction unemployment remained comparatively high, the housing industry was reviving, and the situation was brighter than in 1982.

considerably from the 1.91 million of September 1982. The median sales price of a new home in September 1983 was $82,000 and for an existing home $70,400.

The subsidization of interest rates by builders was an important factor in the recovery of the housing market because in recent years a larger part of the cost of the home has consisted of financing (financing costs now account for about 15 percent of the price of the home, as compared with 7 percent in 1969).

Housing legislation. The U.S. House of Representatives in July passed an omnibus housing bill that would have authorized $76.8 billion for fiscal years 1984 to 1988 in a variety of federal housing programs, but the Senate did not go along. In November, Congress agreed upon legislation authorizing $63.4 billion in housing programs over the same period. The bill was expected to generate 100,000 newly subsidized housing units, including 30,000–40,000 newly constructed or rehabilitated units. It marked the first housing production program to be approved under the Reagan administra-

tion. The bill also created an experimental housing voucher program for low-income families, which would pay rent for low-income families up to a certain level and allow the family to find and select housing.

Mobile homes. The mobile home industry enjoyed a good year, with shipments expected to top 300,000 by year's end. Mobile homes, seen by many as a key component in efforts to keep housing costs down, were accepted into the same FHA program that insures loans for conventionally built housing. The nation's largest builder of for-sale housing, the Houston-based U.S. Home Corporation, acquired two manufactured-housing companies; these purchases were viewed as a sign that manufactured housing (scorned by some as being of lower quality) was winning acceptance by the traditional building industry.

Five acres and independence. U.S. Home also introduced a new housing concept in New Jersey, called Five Acres and Independence, based on a Depression-era book of the same name. The book's premise was that a home-

195

owner could support his family from crops grown on five acres and have enough surplus to sell and make money. The project attracted hundreds of interested home buyers.

Housing markets. Dallas/Fort Worth, Texas, was the nation's leading metropolitan housing market in 1983 in terms of new housing starts, outpacing the 1982 leader, Houston, which slipped to second place. Other top housing markets were Atlanta, Phoenix, Washington, D.C., Denver/Boulder, West Palm Beach/Boca Raton, Fla., Tampa/St. Petersburg, Fla., San Antonio, Texas, and Orlando, Fla.

Future outlook. A study by the U.S. League of Savings Institutions made a pessimistic assessment of the housing industry's ability to deliver affordably priced homes in the long-term future. Unless the United States increases its savings rate, especially among young people, there will be a growing shortage of capital available for loans to cover rising mortgage costs, the institute concluded.   J.C.

HUNGARY. In 1983 the Hungarian regime, under the leadership of Communist Party chief János Kádár, continued to deal with internal dissent and problems of heavy foreign debt. The regime has generally found it unnecessary to employ the repressive tactics of other Soviet bloc countries. However, Laszlo Rajk's "Samizdat Boutique," a Budapest apartment used as a publishing and distribution center for unofficial literature and a popular meeting place for dissidents, was closed down by the government in late January, 1983, after nearly two years in operation. Police emptied out the contents of the apartment, impounded the publications, and detained the tenants. The homes of a number of other dissidents were searched.

In May, officially declared as a month of "peace" in Hungary, there were more than 1,000 public events to mark the occasion, but all were held under the auspices of the officially approved National Peace Council. Adherents of several independent movements were blocked when they attempted to take part.

Crime continued to flourish in Hungary, as in other Communist societies, but statistics were published and discussion of the problem was not suppressed. Some 70,000 to 75,000 thefts a year were said to be reported by retail stores, and there were frequent cases of fraud, embezzlement, misappropriation of public property, and illegal handling of gold and foreign currency.

Hungary faced 1983 with a foreign debt of nearly $9 billion, the largest per capita debt in Eastern Europe, on which it was due to pay $3 billion to $5 billion in principal and interest. Since the government could not expect to obtain new loans for more than a fraction of this amount, it was necessary to repay as much as possible by domestic belt-tightening. The 1983 budget was therefore one of rigid austerity, with everything subordinated to fast and drastic reduction of the country's debt. Investment expenditures were slashed back to 1978 levels, per capita income was expected to fall to 1980 levels, real wages were sharply cut, and enterprises were given less financial independence.

See STATISTICS OF THE WORLD.   R.A.P.

I

ICELAND. Elections to Iceland's Parliament on April 23, 1983, produced a shift to the right, as the previous left-center coalition headed by Gunnar Thoroddsen was replaced by a right-center coalition, with Steingrímur Hermannsson the new prime minister. The Hermannsson government set about dealing with the nation's economic ills, the chief of which was severe inflation. Wage indexing (raising wages at a rate corresponding to the rate of inflation) was suspended for two years, and all wage agreements were extended to January 1984. The effects of this austerity program were to be alleviated by measures benefiting low-income groups. One of the first actions of the new government was to devalue the krona by 14.6 percent. Inflation declined later in the year, but remained relatively high, at close to 40 percent as of late October.

Figures for the fish catch for the first six months of 1983 were discouraging. The major cause was a 23.2 percent reduction in the take of codfish, the mainstay of Iceland's fish-export industry.

A new agreement covering the common Nordic labor market took effect on August 1, with Iceland a signatory for the first time. The agreement grants all citizens of Denmark, Finland, Iceland, Norway, and Sweden freedom of mobility throughout Scandinavia and equal rights regarding jobs.

See STATISTICS OF THE WORLD.   E.J.F.

IDAHO. See STATISTICS OF THE WORLD.

ILLINOIS. See STATISTICS OF THE WORLD

INDIA. India experienced natural disasters, political stress, and regional violence in 1983, but its democracy continued to function, The government of Prime Minister Indira Gandhi's Congress-I (for "Indira") party remained in firm control in New Delhi, despite growing clamor for political change in several states around the perimeter of the country.

Politics and regional conflict. In the northeastern state of Assam, state elections held in February triggered the worst violence in the strife-torn area's recent history. In one incident, at least 500 Muslims, mostly recent immigrants from neighboring Bangladesh, were reportedly massacred by Assamese tribespeople. Leaders of Assamese anti-Muslim groups had called for a boycott of the elections and the removal of illegal immigrants from the voting rolls. In some areas Assamese tried to forcibly prevent Muslims and others from voting.

The Congress-I easily won the Assam elections, but low voter turnout (under 20 percent in many districts) was evidence of the state government's unpopularity and tenuous authority. Assam had been placed under "president's rule," or emergency central government

Corpses wrapped in mats were piled up awaiting burial after anti-Muslim riots in the Indian state of Assam in February. Fears about the growing influence of immigrants from Bangladesh led to an outburst of violence that claimed thousands of lives.

administration, early in 1982; despite the expiration of president's rule in March 1983, central government troops and police remained in the state in large numbers.

Elections were held in Kashmir in June. In this instance, however, the Congress-I was easily defeated by the National Conference, the party of Chief Minister Farooq Abdullah. The election seemed to confirm that in Kashmir, where 75 percent of the people are Muslim, only a party that has special regard for Muslim interests could hope to gain an electoral victory.

In Punjab, New Delhi faced political opposition from the Sikh religious minority, whose most militant members wanted nothing less than independent nationhood. During April, 20 people were killed, at least 150 injured, and hundreds arrested as police clashed with Sikh demonstrators in the streets of Chandigarh, Amritsar, and other Punjab cities. The killing of eight people by terrorists on October 5–6 brought the total number of deaths connected with Sikh agitation to more than 175 since August 1982. Gandhi declared Punjab a "disturbed area," giving police the right to shoot to kill and to make arrests and search buildings without warrants. Violence continued, however; at least 16 people were killed, and more than 130 injured, in a train wreck reportedly caused by terrorists on October 21.

Developments in southern India also posed problems for the government in New Delhi. Early in January, the Congress-I went down to defeat in state elections in Karnataka and Andhra Pradesh, traditional Congress strongholds that the party had controlled since 1947. Even after these setbacks, Gandhi's party still held two-thirds of India's state governments and a solid two-thirds majority in Parliament; following the elections, nevertheless, Gandhi shook up her government, replacing several ministers. She also made changes in the leadership of the Congress-I, including the appointment of her surviving son and heir apparent, Rajiv, to be one of the party's five general secretaries.

Economic developments. India's economy continues to be markedly imbalanced, with a rapidly growing centralized urban elite enjoying great wealth and comfort while most of the population remains mired in the villages. The per capita gross national product was less than $300. Overall, the Indian economy grew at a rate of only 2 percent in fiscal 1982–1983, after two years of 5 percent growth; however, inflation also fell, to less than 2 percent.

Space satellites. On April 17, India's growing space program launched a 91-pound satellite; it was the third launch in a series aimed at perfecting a satellite launch vehicle. On September 1 the U.S. space shuttle *Challenger* launched for India the communications and weather satellite Insat 1-B, but the launch was not wholly successful, as the satellite's solar panels did not open fully.

Foreign affairs. Relations with the United States remained cordial despite continuing U.S. arms support for Pakistan. Gandhi visited the United States for the second time in two years in September, addressing the United Nations in her capacity as 1983 head of the nonaligned movement. (She had hosted the seventh summit conference of the nonaligned nations in March in New Delhi.) Gandhi met with President Ronald Reagan in the course of her visit.

India began reprocessing spent nuclear fuel into plutonium in 1983, enhancing the country's potential for developing nuclear weapons from its own materials, should it choose to do so. India still refuses to sign the treaty calling for nonproliferation of nuclear weapons, claiming that it must be ready to defend itself against any possible future danger. Indications that China has been helping Pakistan acquire sophisticated nuclear know-how (possibly enabling Pakistan to develop nuclear weapons without having to test them) added to India's anxiety.

At midyear, U.S. Secretary of State George Shultz went to New Delhi, where he promised to "forge an umbrella of understanding" over India; he also indicated that the United States was prepared to approve the sale of arms to India. In November, Queen Elizabeth II helped reaffirm ties between India and the United Kingdom with a ten-day state visit.

After undergoing a thaw, Indo-Pakistani relations chilled again somewhat. Violent mass protests raged for weeks in Pakistan's Sind Province, with students and others taking to the streets in opposition to the regime of

President Muhammad Zia ul-Haq. Zia accused "foreign elements" of fomenting the antigovernment demonstrations, looking toward New Delhi as he did so. India was uneasy about the presence of Soviet troop concentrations in Afghanistan, not far from its own frontiers; nevertheless, Indo-Soviet friendship remained firm.

Disasters. Floods racked the western states of Gujarat and Maharashtra; hundreds were drowned, thousands injured, and hundreds of thousands left homeless as floodwaters destroyed crops and ravaged villages and towns. In the extreme south, on the other hand, drought posed a serious threat to the states of Tamil Nadu and Andhra Pradesh, where millions faced another year without water for most of each day.

See STATISTICS OF THE WORLD.   S.A.W.

INDIANA. *See* STATISTICS OF THE WORLD.

INDIANS, AMERICAN. An Indian policy statement issued by President Ronald Reagan on January 24, 1983, drew sharp criticism from the Indian community. Many of the nation's 4.1 million Indians were also angered by earlier remarks by Interior Secretary James Watt, who had compared Indian reservations to the Soviet Union. In other developments, bingo became a major business enterprise on many reservations, oil and gas production from Indian lands reached a record high, and the tribes lost a series of water litigation battles.

Policy statement. In his policy statement on American Indians, Reagan outlined a program that would, he said, make Indian reservations more economically self-sufficient. The president said his administration intended to "enable tribal governments . . . to resume control over their own affairs," to create a "favorable environment for development of healthy reservation economies," and to begin the transfer of jurisdiction over Indian resources from the federal government to state and local governments. Acknowledging the governmental status of Indian tribes, Reagan promised to include a representative of the tribal governments on his Advisory Commission on Intergovernmental Relations. More concretely, the policy statement mandated the establishment of a Presidential Commission on Indian Reservation Economies. After some delay, members of the

commission were finally designated in August; they were sworn in on October 19 and were directed to submit a report to the president by November 30, 1984.

Indian reaction to the policy statement was generally cool because it did not provide new money or programs or, in the view of many Indian leaders, any real new direction. Some Indian representatives saw the statement as the administration's justification for budget cuts in existing Indian reservation programs.

Watt controversy. Just before the presidential Indian statement, James Watt, then secretary of the interior, made public comments that outraged many Indians. In a televised interview with *Conservative Digest* publisher Richard Viguerie, Watt, whose department included the Bureau of Indian Affairs, said: "If you want an example of the failures of socialism, don't go to Russia . . . come and see the Indian reservations." The reservations, he said, fostered the highest rates of divorce, drug addiction, alcoholism, unemployment, and social diseases in the country. Although Watt subsequently apologized for "causing hurt" to Indians, he did not retract his remarks, and several large Indian organizations called for his dismissal. (He resigned later in the year, after controversy involving other minority groups.)

Indian bingo. Federal budget cuts, which reduced funding of Indian programs by almost one-third, had devastating effects on many reservations, where unemployment ranged as high as 50–80 percent. About a dozen Indian tribes acted to alleviate their economic problems by initiating high-stakes bingo games on the reservations, which were exempt from state regulatory laws. In September the Kiowa, Comanche, and Apache tribes of Oklahoma announced plans for the construction of a $260 million, gambling-centered Indian development in Lawton, Okla., which would include a pari-mutuel horse racing track, a theme park, a hotel-conference center, multifamily residences, and a shopping and office center. The Oklahoma legislature had recently voted to permit horse racing as a county option, but tribal leaders indicated that they planned to seek neither state licensing nor a revenue-sharing arrangement with the state. In Minne-

The world's biggest bingo contest, with prizes totaling $1 million, was held by the Cherokee Indians on their reservation in North Carolina during July. These and other games on Indian reservations are exempt from state gambling laws.

sota the chairman of the Shakopee Sioux tribe, which had built a million-dollar bingo palace, said the operation "has created 100 percent employment, has improved the standard of living, and has made funds available for community improvement, health, and education."

The gambling operations also brought controversy. Some non-Indians complained that the games would attract organized crime, that they were unfair competition for regulated games, and that Indians should not have special privileges. Some federal officials expressed concern that professional managers hired by the tribes would be the main beneficiaries of the games, instead of the tribes and their people. In March the U.S. Justice Department proposed that the states be allowed to impose regulatory laws on the reservations, but the White House rejected the plan as contrary to its Indian self-determination policy.

Energy resources. While tribal revenues from energy resources soared (from $225 million in 1981 to $368 million in 1982), the Council of Energy Resource Tribes, organized in 1975 and publicized as an "Indian OPEC," had financial problems. The organization closed its Washington, D.C., offices, retaining only its technical assistance staff in Lakewood, Colo. Members of the executive committee acknowledged that the organization had accumulated a $1.2 million debt.

Court cases. Indian tribes suffered a number of court defeats on critical water rights issues. In March the U.S. Supreme Court voted, 5–3, against revising a 1964 Court-approved plan so as to increase the amount of Colorado River water allocated to five Indian tribes along the California-Arizona border. The Court, in so doing, rejected the findings of a special master it had appointed to study the case. In June, the Court unanimously ruled that the Justice Department could not seek modification of another previous plan, diverting the waters of Nevada's Truckee River from Pyramid Lake, owned by the Paiute Indian tribe. The Indians had sought to gain access to new water to fill the rapidly shrinking lake; farmers who relied on the existing allocation had contested reopening of the plan.

In another case, in May, water rights of the Wind River Reservation tribes were limited to agricultural use by a Wyoming district court, which asserted that the tribes' original claims had demonstrated "an avaricious appetite . . . for practically all the water in the Big Horn River system." Also, on July 1, the U.S. Supreme Court ruled, 6–3, that state courts, as well as federal courts, had jurisdiction in the adjudication of Indian water rights. The decision, directly affecting tribes in Montana and Arizona, was accompanied by a strong dissent from Justice John Paul Stevens, who noted that states and their citizens might well be "antagonistic toward Indian reserved rights."

On December 10, a federal appeals court affirmed a lower court decision rejecting the Oglala Sioux tribe's claim to the Homestead Mine in South Dakota, which is the largest gold mine in North America. The tribe claimed that the land where the mine was situated had been trespassed upon for more than 100 years and rightfully belonged to them.   V.L.

INDONESIA. In spite of economic difficulties, Indonesia remained politically stable in 1983. The Indonesian People's Consultative Assembly on March 10 named President Suharto to a fourth five-year term as president and, the following day, approved his choice for vice-president, General Umar Wirahadikusumah, to replace Adam Malik. At 58, Wirahadikusumah was only four years younger than Suharto and was not seen as a likely successor. A new cabinet, larger and including more civilians than the previous one, was also named and sworn in on March 19.

Executions of suspected criminals without trial became increasingly common during the first seven months of the year. The military was believed by many to be behind these summary actions. In August, a news blackout was imposed on information relating to the executions; by this time 553 individuals in Java and Sumatra with criminal ties or records had reportedly been killed.

Oil revenues, which account for about 70 percent of all state revenue, declined 18 percent in the 1982–1983 fiscal year; their continued low level, coupled with pressure from foreign lenders, compelled an austere budget. To curb deficits, construction of new public buildings was curtailed, civil service salaries were frozen, provision of cars for government workers was halted, food subsidies were ended, and motor and heating oil subsidies were reduced 25 percent. The national currency was devalued in March.

At a June meeting in The Hague, delegates from five international agencies and 12 industrialized countries, known collectively as the Inter-Governmental Group on Indonesia, agreed to increase aid and loans to Indonesia by 14 percent, to $2.2 billion. Major national assistance came from Japan ($279 million) and the United States ($106 million).

Japanese Premier Yasuhiro Nakasone visited Indonesia in May. He announced increased loans for development, a 50 percent increase in the import of industrial products manufactured by members of the Association of Southeast Asian Nations, and the intent to continue oil imports from Indonesia. Nakasone also brought a message from China's Deng Xiaoping, offering to resume relations with Indonesia. Suharto declined, citing Chinese support for insurgent Communist parties in the region.

In February, the United Nations Commission on Human Rights, voting 16–14, with ten abstentions, narrowly passed a resolution affirming the right of self-determination for the people of East Timor. Ever since it proclaimed the former Portuguese colony as the 27th province of Indonesia, in July 1976, the Suharto government has campaigned without success to have the UN drop the issue of East Timor. The government did confirm in July that recent talks had been held with the Front for the Liberation and Independence of East Timor (Fretilin) to end hostilities.

See STATISTICS OF THE WORLD.   K.M.

INTERNATIONAL CONFERENCES. Several major international conferences were held in 1983. For some not covered below, see AFRICA; ARAB LEAGUE; COMMONWEALTH OF NATIONS; NORTH ATLANTIC TREATY ORGANIZATION; ORGANIZATION OF AMERICAN STATES; ORGANIZATION OF PETROLEUM EXPORTING COUNTRIES; UNITED NATIONS.

Conference on Security and Cooperation in Europe. The 35-member East-West conference, convened in 1980 to review and expand provisions of the 1975 Helsinki accords on territorial security, human rights, and economic exchanges in Europe, reconvened in Madrid in February and reached agreement in July on a final document. The document, a 35-page addendum to the original accords, ended three years of intermittent, often deadlocked negotiations. It omitted or watered down many

Prime Minister Indira Gandhi convenes the seventh annual summit conference of nonaligned nations, in New Delhi; at her side is the host of the previous meeting, Cuba's Fidel Castro. Delegates from 101 countries approved a final communiqué critical of both the United States and the Soviet Union.

proposed human rights statements Western nations had sought to add, such as affirmations of the right to strike and to a free press, but it included some new human rights provisions. The agreement provided for convening of a conference on disarmament in January 1984, as the Soviet Union had wanted, although it broadened its agenda to include topics of particular concern to the West. A final meeting of foreign ministers, held in early September to mark reaching of the accord, was dominated by bitter exchanges over the Soviet downing of a South Korean airliner shortly before.

Nonaligned nations conference. The seventh summit of the nonaligned nations was held in March in New Delhi, under the chairmanship of Prime Minister Indira Gandhi. The group, expanded to a total of 101 members, called for economic reforms to aid developing nations, a ban on the production and deployment of nuclear weapons, and various political actions, including a halt to U.S. "imperialist interference" in Central America, establishment of a tribunal to try Israel for "crimes committed against the Palestinian people," and the withdrawal of unspecified "foreign troops" from Afghanistan.

Williamsburg summit. Leaders of seven major industrial nations—Canada, France, West Germany, Great Britain, Italy, Japan, and the United States—met in Williamsburg, Va., in May for their ninth annual conference. They jointly urged the Soviet Union to negotiate "constructively" on reducing medium-range nuclear weapons in Europe and warned against any attempt to divide the West on this issue. On economic matters, the conference declaration was mildly optimistic, pointing to "signs of recovery," but it urged action to reduce budget deficits and control money supply.

Asean conference. Foreign ministers of the Association of Southeast Asian Nations met in Bangkok, Thailand, in late June; the five member nations—Thailand, Indonesia, Malaysia, Singapore, and the Philippines—reiterated a call to Vietnam to withdraw its forces from Cambodia.   A.E.N.

IOWA. *See* STATISTICS OF THE WORLD.

IRAN. Iran's relations with the Soviet Union deteriorated sharply in 1983, and the Iranian government came down hard on the Communist, pro-Soviet Tudeh Party. In a bid to encourage trade and investment, Iran began settling its debts with a number of creditor nations. Meanwhile, the costs of the continuing deadlocked war with Iraq mounted steadily for both sides.

Conflict with the Soviet Union. A widening rift developed between Iran and the Soviet Union, to a large extent because of the Soviet Union's tilt toward Iraq in the Iran-Iraq war. Another factor was the Iranian government's continued opposition to the Soviet role in Afghanistan. Soviet troops in the Caucasus were placed on maneuvers early in 1983, inducing Iran to send its own troops from the war zone to protect its northern borders. It was also reported that Soviet arms were reaching Kurdish separatists locked in a losing battle with government forces in western Iran.

The regime in Tehran also accused Moscow of using the Tudeh Party to carry out espionage within Iran and began taking strong steps against the party, which had been the only non-Islamic party permitted to function openly. On May 4 the Tudeh Party was banned, and there were mass arrests of suspected party members. The same day, 18 Soviet diplomats were ordered out of the country within 48 hours; they left as anti-Soviet demonstrations were held throughout Iran.

U.S. relations. The Iranian government made regular payments on debts owed to U.S. banks and in late August paid nearly $420 million owed to the U.S. Export-Import Bank. Iran's exports to the United States (mostly oil) reached $932 million for the first ten months, triple the levels of a year earlier.

Political relations remained acrimonious. Tehran denounced as pro-Israeli the U.S.-mediated accord to end the occupation of Lebanon. Responsibility for the April 18 bombing of the U.S. embassy in Beirut was claimed by an organization of Shiite Muslims in Lebanon sympathetic to the Iranian government; the United States also accused Iranian terrorists of involvement in the October 23 bomb attack that killed more than 240 U.S. Marines in Lebanon, also stating that the Iranian embassy in Beirut may have been used as the staging place.

Economic developments. In addition to making good on U.S. debts, Iran settled a $350 million debt owed to two French oil companies and expressed interest in closer economic ties with West Germany. Japanese creditors in May rescheduled payments on $527 million owed by Iran on an unfinished petrochemical plant at Bandar-e Khomeini; in return, the Iranian government agreed to pay all remaining construction costs. Meanwhile, Iran's oil production began to return to prewar levels by early 1983, and Iran regained its position as the second largest producer in the Organization of Petroleum Exporting Countries (after Saudi Arabia).

Iran's economic outlook was generally improved. Official Central Bank figures for May showed inflation running at a relatively low 20 percent, although a thriving black market meant that effective inflation was significantly higher than the official rate. According to an official statement, the economy showed a growth rate

Bombed by Iraqi planes in March, Iran's Nowruz oil wells began gushing out thousands of barrels a day into Persian Gulf waters. As the two warring nations haggled over a cease-fire to allow workers to cap the out-of-control wells, the oil slick spread to the coastal areas of adjacent states.

of 7 percent in the fiscal year ended March 20, 1983.

War with Iraq. The war between Iran and Iraq, which was costing Iran an estimated $1 billion a month, entered its fourth year in late 1983, with the fighting basically stalemated. For much of 1983, Iran's "human-wave" invasions, in which large numbers of often ill-trained troops stormed Iraqi lines, had limited success, inhibited by Iraq's superior air power. Iran's own air force, according to some estimates, had fewer than 50 fighters and fighter-bombers available, a small fraction of its prewar strength. Iran refused to consider ending the war without a return to the prewar status quo along the Shatt al Arab waterway, with the two countries sharing sovereignty and shipping rights. Iran also held to its demand for $150 billion in reparations and for the resignation of Iraqi President Saddam Hussein.

The Gulf war heated up in October, as Iraq threatened to strike Iranian oil installations with its new Super Etendard aircraft from France. Iran said it would respond to an attack by blocking the Strait of Hormuz, thereby cutting off the supply of Gulf oil to most of the world. Late in the month, Iran announced it had begun an offensive into northeastern Iraq; subsequently, Iranians reportedly took the town of Penjwin, relying heavily on tanks and armored vehicles. Iraq for its part announced that it had mined the approaches to the port of Bandar-e Khomeini and later claimed to have destroyed several Iranian ships in that area.

Choice for the future. The Assembly of Experts, a body charged with the task of choosing Khomeini's successor, held its inaugural session in mid-July; the group was expected eventually to confirm Ayatollah Hussein Ali Montazeri—a man who shared Khomeini's strong dislike for Western-style democracy.

See STATISTICS OF THE WORLD.   A.T.S.

IRAQ. War with neighboring Iran dragged on inconclusively in 1983, draining Iraq of manpower and money. Iraqi President Saddam Hussein, still firmly in control of the government despite the growing unpopularity of the Gulf war, pursued an increasingly moderate course in foreign policy.

War with Iran. The war, which had begun in September 1980, appeared to have settled into

Iraqi POW's, blindfolded to prevent them from observing enemy positions, are evacuated from the front by Iranian soldiers. Iraq's losses in sporadic Iranian offensives were high, but Iraq prevented any decisive gains by Iran in the ongoing war.

a stalemate along the Iraqi-Iranian border, as Iran periodically mounted offensives with massed infantry only to be driven back in most cases by superior Iraqi firepower. Early in March, an Iraqi attack on Iran's Nowruz oil field heavily damaged offshore platforms, which began spewing crude oil into the Persian Gulf at the rate of several thousand barrels per day; it was one of the worst oil spills in history. Neighboring Gulf nations tried unsuccessfully to arrange a cease-fire so that the wells could be capped. Late in the year, Iran claimed to have capped them independently.

An Iranian offensive into northeastern Iraq, in the autumn, had some success; at the same time, Iraqis claimed to have sunk several Iranian ships in the Persian Gulf. In mid-December, Iraq fired surface-to-surface missiles at five Iranian towns, in retaliation for alleged bombings by Iranian terrorists of embassies and other sites in Kuwait, a country which had aligned itself with Iraq in the Iran-Iraq conflict.

Hussein was eager to negotiate an end to the damaging war but was not prepared to step down, as Iran demanded. Iraqi diplomacy was therefore directed largely toward securing supplies of advanced weapons. Deputy Prime Minister Tareq Aziz, who was given the additional post of foreign minister in January, made frequent visits to France, which was emerging as Iraq's largest Western arms supplier. A January visit brought Iraq an additional 29 Mirage F-1 fighter-bombers for delivery late in the year. In October, France went ahead with plans to loan Iraq five Super Etendard aircraft; when equipped with Exocet air-to-sea missiles, previously delivered to Iraq, the planes were expected to greatly enhance the Iraqis' ability to strike at Iranian oil ports and Persian Gulf shipping.

Foreign relations. Foreign Minister Aziz traveled to Cairo in early July, for the first such visit by an Iraqi official since Egypt signed a peace treaty with Israel in 1979. Iraq also showed signs of taking a more conciliatory stance toward Israel. In January the Iraqi government quoted Hussein as saying that Israel had the right to "a state of security." There was also some speculation that Iraq might be willing to cooperate with Jordan and Egypt to create a self-governing Palestinian "entity" on the West Bank, a solution favored by the United States. Hussein moved closer toward restoring official diplomatic relations with the United States, which were cut off after the 1967 war between Egypt and Israel. Important political differences remained, however.

Economic conditions. Damage to oil terminals and limited access to Mediterranean pipelines caused Iraq's oil exports to drop precipitously; 1983 production reached only 1 million barrels a day, still down from the prewar level of 3.5 million. Foreign exchange reserves plummeted from an estimated $35 billion, prior to the war, to a 1983 level of less than $6 billion, despite direct subsidies from the Persian Gulf states.

Foreign Minister Aziz flew to Paris in the spring to arrange a rescheduling of $1.8 billion in debts due to France, which agreed to accept 4 million tons of Iraqi crude oil over the next year to cover some of the weapons payments.

Iraq also owed West Germany $2.3 billion and Japan $1.5 billion. All foreign creditors agreed to reschedule payments.

Even with cutbacks, the government's budget for fiscal 1984, made public on June 1, reflected the regime's ambitious plans for the future more than it did the reality of Iraq's war-torn economy. In addition to $18 billion in annual investments, it called for $27 billion in current expenditures, up more than $3 billion from the previous year.

See STATISTICS OF THE WORLD.   A.T.S.

IRELAND, NORTHERN. *See* GREAT BRITAIN.

IRELAND, REPUBLIC OF. In 1983 the new Fine Gael–Labor coalition, under Prime Minister Garrett FitzGerald, attempted to grapple with Ireland's finances; headlines also told of a political scandal, a referendum on abortion, and the abduction of a prized horse.

As a result of elections in late 1982, FitzGerald's Fine Gael held 70 seats in the 166-member Dáil (parliament). In coalition with the Labor Party, it had a clear overall majority, but there were strains within the coalition. Labor, under its young new leader, Richard Spring, a former rugby star, advocated public spending for the purposes of job creation. Such a solution, however, conflicted with FitzGerald's priorities for tackling the combined problems of inflation, recession, and mounting foreign debt. In the end, the program agreed upon was almost but not quite so austere as the one advocated by FitzGerald. Seeking to raise more than $230 million in additional revenue, it imposed substantial tax increases. On the other side of the ledger, it called for expenditure cuts of over $400 million. The projected deficit of about $1 billion was over $170 million more than originally proposed—an effect of Labor's influence within the coalition.

Fianna Fáil, the major opposition party, contended with a growing movement in its ranks to replace Charles Haughey as party leader. Dissatisfaction asserted itself strongly early in the year, after the *Irish Times* reported that the justice minister in the Haughey government, Sean Doherty, had arranged with high police officials to wiretap politicians and journalists, apparently for political purposes. On January 20 the country's two top police officers resigned, and the following day Doherty quit his post in the party. Haughey, however, survived an attempt to oust him at a meeting of Fianna Fáil members a week later.

A referendum on a constitutional amendment confirming the ban on abortion was held September 7. Only half the electorate voted, but those who did approved the amendment by a two-to-one majority.

After a gap of more than two years, FitzGerald and British Prime Minister Margaret Thatcher met privately in early November to discuss the future of Northern Ireland and other issues of common interest.

In an unprecedented case of "horsenapping," armed men broke into the Aga Khan's stables in Ireland and made off with the racehorse Shergar (seen here winning the 1981 Irish Derby). Despite intense police work, Shergar remained missing.

Gulf Oil reported striking oil in offshore tests carried out in August. The news stimulated hopes, and financial speculation, that Ireland had at last struck oil in commercial quantities.

The racehorse Shergar, winner of the 1981 Epsom Derby and valued at over $10 million, was abducted by an armed gang from its stable at Ballymany Stud, Kildare, on February 8. Intense police activity and many false leads failed to find the hapless horse, alive or dead. *See* Statistics of the World.   T.J.O.H.

ISRAEL. The resignation of Prime Minister Menachem Begin and the continuing impact of Israel's June 1982 invasion of Lebanon dominated Israeli politics and public affairs in 1983.

Domestic affairs. Menachem Begin, who had served as prime minister since 1977, announced to the members of his cabinet on August 28 that he intended to resign. The announcement came as a shock to the ministers, who urged Begin to reconsider his decision. However, the prime minister remained firm in his determination to step down. Begin had appeared distracted, despondent, and far less vigorous during the year, which observers attributed partly to his ill health and to the death of his wife, Aliza, in November 1982.

Following Begin's announcement, a contest for leadership of his Herut Party arose between Deputy Prime Minister David Levy and Foreign Minister Yitzhak Shamir. The party's central committee voted 436–302 in favor of Shamir, who by mid-September had won the support of the other factions of the ruling Likud coalition. On September 21, Israeli President Chaim Herzog asked Shamir to form a new government, and on October 10, Shamir became prime minister when he won a parliamentary vote of confidence, 60–53.

The aftermath of Israel's invasion of Lebanon and the continued presence of Israeli soldiers there haunted every aspect of the country's politics. One of the most painful issues to be faced was that of responsibility for the September 1982 massacre of Palestinian civilians by Lebanese Christian militiamen, which occurred in refugee camps in an area near Beirut that was under the control of the Israeli army. On February 8, a commission—headed by the president of the Israeli Supreme Court—found that Israeli military and political leaders, including Defense Minister Ariel Sharon, were indirectly responsible for the killings because they had allowed the Christian Phalangists into the camps without seriously considering the possibility of a massacre, had improperly supervised the Phalange, and had not reacted quickly enough when reports of the atrocities began to arrive. Begin himself was criticized for indifference to Phalangist activities in the camps. Among other steps, the report recommended dismissal of the chief of military intelligence (carried out in March) and the resignation of Sharon.

Following release of the report, the Israeli cabinet met continuously, while violent clashes took place in the streets between demonstrators for and against Sharon. After three days the cabinet voted 16–1 to accept the report and its recommendations. Sharon, who cast the dissenting vote, was replaced as defense minister by Moshe Arens, the Israeli ambassador to the United States, but he remained in the cabinet as minister without portfolio.

Begin was able to persuade his coalition partners to vote along party lines to keep Sharon in the cabinet, but the prime minister proved unable to win the next major Knesset vote—the election of a new president in March. Begin sought the post for Supreme Court Justice Menachem Elon. The Knesset, however, voted 61 to 57 for the Labor Party's candidate, Chaim Herzog, who had served as Israel's ambassador to the United Nations and as head of Israeli military intelligence.

Despite a sharp rise in tourism, the Israeli economy stagnated overall in 1983. Exports dropped, and Israel's foreign debt rose to over $20 billion. Meanwhile, inflation by the summer had risen to an annual rate of 125 percent. The shekel was devalued by 7.5 percent in August. After a financial crisis in early October, the shekel was devalued by another 23 percent, food subsidies were slashed, and gasoline prices were raised.

Foreign affairs. On May 17, after U.S.-mediated negotiations, Israel signed a troop withdrawal agreement with the Lebanese government. Under its provisions, the state of war between Israel and Lebanon was formally ended, Lebanon agreed not to permit its territory to be used as a base for terrorists or foreign forces

After six years as prime minister, Menachem Begin resigned because of failing health; he was succeeded by his foreign minister, Yitzhak Shamir, who became prime minister in October.

hostile to Israel, and a security zone was to be established in southern Lebanon, with arrangements for joint Israeli-Lebanese supervision. The withdrawal of Israeli troops from Lebanon was, however, made contingent on the simultaneous withdrawal of Syrian and Palestine Liberation Organization forces, and Syria refused to go along. As a result of this development and increasing domestic pressures, Israel in September moved its forces southward out of the troubled Shouf region near Beirut to a more easily supplied and defended line along the Awali River.

In a terrorist attack similar to those on U.S. Marines and French troops in Beirut, a truck laden with explosives crashed into the Israeli military compound at Tyre in southern Lebanon on November 4, killing 60 people, 29 of them Israelis. Israel retaliated with air strikes behind Syrian lines. An Israeli Army report released in December concluded that adequate precautions had not been taken, despite ample warning from intelligence units that such an attack

Israeli soldiers carry away the body of one of the 60 people killed when terrorists crashed an explosives-laden truck into Israel's military compound at Tyre in southern Lebanon in November.

might occur. Terrorists also struck inside Israel. On December 6, a bomb planted on a crowded bus in Jerusalem killed six people; two competing factors of the PLO each claimed responsibility.

Early in the year, there was considerable friction between Israel and the United States, including tense confrontations in Beirut between Israeli troops and U.S. troops patroling the area as part of the multinational peace-keeping force. The Reagan administration pressured Israel to leave Lebanon by opposing increased military and economic aid and by withholding delivery of 75 F-16 fighter bombers. By the spring, however, U.S.-Israeli relations had begun to improve. Israel's standing in Washington was enhanced when Jordan refused to enter into peace talks with Israel, bolstering Israel's contention that Arab intransigence was holding up the peace process, and when Israel signed the troop withdrawal agreement with Lebanon. Following the signing, the Reagan administration lifted its ban on the sale of the F-16's and ended its opposition to increases in aid to Israel. The two countries also drew closer together after the terrorist attack on U.S. Marines in Beirut, when the United States came into direct conflict with Syrian and pro-Syrian forces in Lebanon. In November, Prime Minister Shamir visited Washington, and his meetings with President Ronald Reagan produced an agreement to coordinate U.S. and Israeli military planning in the Middle East.

Israel's relations with Egypt remained chilled. Egyptian President Hosni Mubarak frequently reiterated his commitment to the 1979 Egyptian-Israeli peace treaty but strongly condemned Israel's West Bank settlement policies and urged Israel to permit the Palestinians to exercise their "legitimate national rights." In late December, however, a high-ranking Egyptian official visited Israel and met with the prime minister—the first such event since the Israeli invasion of Lebanon in June 1982.

Tension remained high on the West Bank, as Arabs rioted in protest against the Israeli settlement policy and Israeli settlers retaliated. In February, a Jewish woman died after being struck by stones thrown by Arab youths in an Arab village. In July a Jewish seminary student was murdered in Hebron; Jewish settlers then burned down part of the old Arab market there. Subsequently three masked gunmen attacked the Islamic College in Hebron, killing three Arabs and wounding over 30 others; riots followed throughout the West Bank.

See STATISTICS OF THE WORLD.   R.O.F.

ITALY. National elections in Italy in 1983 led to the installation of the country's 44th government since the end of World War II and its first Socialist premier, Bettino Craxi.

Elections. Early in the year, internal disagreements over policy had prevented the recently installed coalition government of Christian Democratic Premier Amintore Fanfani from dealing effectively with economic problems.

On April 22, Craxi announced that his Socialist party would withdraw from the coalition and called for an early general election. A week later, Fanfani resigned; President Alessandro Pertini then dissolved Parliament and scheduled a general election for June 26–27, to coincide with planned local elections.

The election results showed a drop of more than five percentage points in the Christian Democrats' share of popular votes for the Chamber of Deputies (lower house of Parliament), from 38.3 percent in the 1979 elections to 32.9 percent. The Communist vote fell slightly, to 29.9 percent. The Socialists did less well than they had hoped, rising from 9.8 percent to only 11.4 percent.

New government. On July 21, after consulations with party leaders, President Pertini called on Craxi to form a government. Craxi, who had held no ministerial office before, secured support for a five-party coalition government and on August 4 announced his cabinet. It contained 16 Christian Democrats, six Socialists, three Social Democrats, three Republicans, and two Liberals.

On August 9, Craxi introduced his government's program. It proposed stern policies for economic recovery, modernization of the country's institutions, and continued support for the European Economic Community and NATO. The government secured a vote of confidence (361–243) in the Chamber on August 12. On October 22 hundreds of thousands marched in Rome to protest both the planned deployment of U. S. missiles in Sicily and the presence of Soviet missiles targeted on Western Europe. The Chamber, however, reaffirmed Italy's decision to allow deployment of U.S. missiles, and the arrival of the first missiles was announced November 27.

Internal violence. On January 24 the biggest antiterrorist trial in Italian history, that of 63 members of the left-wing Red Brigades, ended in Rome after nine months; 32 life sentences were administered for involvement in a total

Italy's First Socialist Premier

In the summer of 1983, when Bettino Craxi was called upon to form a government, few observers were surprised. Although the Socialists had won only 11 percent of the vote in the June parliamentary elections, the weakened Christian Democrats badly needed their support. Craxi himself was known as an astute, hard-working professional with more than a common touch of ambition. Italy's first Socialist premier had joined the party in his youth and risen through the ranks to become its head in 1976. A college dropout in a land where academic credentials are almost a political necessity, Craxi was also unusual among Socialists for his strong distrust of the Communists and his advocacy of close ties with NATO. His five-party coalition government, dominated by Christian Democrats, moved promptly to introduce austerity measures after its installation in early August.

Bettino Craxi

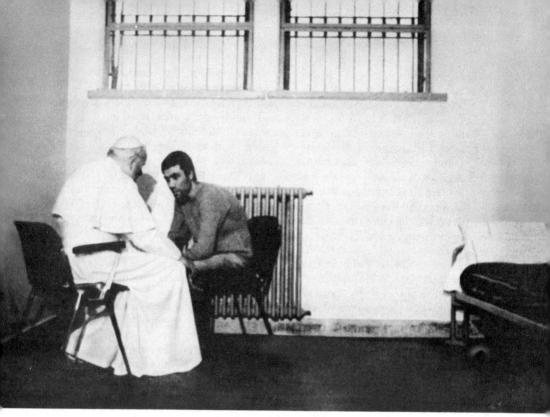

After conducting a Christmas service in Rome's Rebibbia Prison, Pope John Paul II met privately with Mehmet Ali Agca, the Turkish gunman who had severely wounded him two years before in an assassination attempt. John Paul had already publicly forgiven his assailant, who was serving a life sentence.

of 17 murders and four kidnappings committed during 1977–1980. Two Red Brigaders involved in the kidnapping of U.S. Brigadier General James Dozier in 1981 each received 16 years on other charges. On April 23, at the end of a six-month trial, a Florence court sentenced 83 members of an affiliated left-wing terrorist gang, Prima Linea, to prison terms of up to 30 years. On March 7, 71 persons arrested in 1979 on charges of involvement with an extremist group in Padua known as the Autonomists went on trial in Rome. The group's leading spirit, Antonio Negri, was released from jail in July after winning a seat in Parliament, but in September, when his parliamentary immunity was lifted, he fled Italy.

Organized crime was conspicuously active in Sicily, where an assistant public prosecutor was murdered on January 25. On March 5–6, in a large-scale sweep in south and central Italy, carabinieri (national police) arrested 834 suspects associated with the Mafia; its Neapolitan counterpart, the Camorra; and other criminal gangs. On June 17 arrest warrants were served on nearly 900 people, including well-known local Camorra personalities. In early April, in a fresh flare-up of Mafia violence, 12 people were killed in Palermo and Catania.

Economy. By August the budget deficit had reached nearly $57 billion, or around 17 percent of the gross domestic product. Craxi, in his program unveiled at that time, aimed to reduce this amount by a little more than $7 billion and to bring inflation down from the mid-1983 level of 16–17 percent by 1984. On September 30 he presented a stiff budget for 1984, seeking to cut the public sector deficit by close to $20 billion.

Foreign affairs. In September, Premier Craxi visited Paris, London, The Hague, and Bonn; the following month, he visited the United States, where he affirmed Italy's commitment to the installation of cruise missiles in Sicily. After terrorist violence escalated in Lebanon, Italy pledged to maintain its peacekeeping force there, although the government announced its intention to reduce the size.

Papal assassination investigation. In July, Mehmet Ali Agca, the Turkish gunman convicted of shooting Pope John Paul II in May 1981, told reporters he had been recruited and assisted by the KGB and the Bulgarian secret service. Both Bulgaria and the Soviet Union denied any connection with Agca. In September, Italian authorities were reported to be preparing an indictment against Agca for "slandering" Sergei Antonov Ivanov, a Bulgarian airline representative in Rome, whom Agca had accused of complicity in the papal assassination plot. In late December, Antonov, reportedly ill, was released from prison and placed under house arrest. Meanwhile, the Pope visited Agca in prison.

In a possibly related incident, Emanuela Orlandi, the daughter of a Vatican messenger, was abducted in Rome on June 22. On July 6 an anonymous caller to the Italian news agency Ansa demanded that the Italian government release Agca in exchange for her freedom. The pope appealed for her release.

Other developments. In March the High Court in London annulled a lower court verdict that the death of Roberto Calvi—the president of the collapsed Banco Ambrosiano found hanged under London's Blackfriars Bridge in 1982—had been a suicide. A subsequent inquest concluded that there was insufficient proof for a verdict of either suicide or murder.

On August 10, Licio Gelli, grand master of a banned secret Masonic lodge known as P-2 (Propaganda Two), slipped out of a Geneva prison where he had been awaiting extradition to Italy. A prison guard admitted having accepted a bribe to help Gelli escape. On December 24, Anna Bulgari Calissoni and her 16-year-old son, Giorgio, heirs to the Bulgari house of jewelers, were released by kidnappers after more than a month in captivity and payment of an undisclosed ransom. Kidnappers had severed Giorgio's right ear.

See STATISTICS OF THE WORLD.   M.G.

IVORY COAST. See STATISTICS OF THE WORLD.

J

JAMAICA. See STATISTICS OF THE WORLD. See also CARIBBEAN COUNTRIES.

JAPAN. After one year in office, Japan's Prime Minister Yasuhiro Nakasone called new elections for December 18, 1983, hoping to obtain an increased majority in the lower house of the Diet (Parliament). Nakasone and his Liberal Democratic Party (LDP), however, received a resounding setback, winning only 250 of the 511 seats, six short of a simple majority. The LDP was able to secure a working majority after nine independents joined its ranks. The small, conservative New Liberal Club joined the new government, putting another eight seats under government control, and Nakasone was formerly elected prime minister on December 26; his reshuffled 20-member cabinet was installed the next day.

The LDP had lost 36 seats in the elections, while the Socialists, the second-largest party, picked up 12. Another big winner was the centrist Clean Government Party, which won 24 new seats for a total of 58. The LDP's losses were not expected to lead to any major policy changes, but Nakasone stated in a press conference that the opposition's opinion on issues would have to be "humbly" requested.

Pre-election politics. Nakasone had sought a new mandate partly because of a boycott of the Diet by opposition members. They were pressing demands for the unseating of former prime minister and Nakasone supporter Kakuei Tanaka. Tanaka had been convicted in October on charges of accepting bribes from agents of the Lockheed Aircraft Corporation during his tenure in office (1972–1974). He was sen-

Former Prime Minister Kakuei Tanaka waves as he leaves court after his October conviction for accepting over $2 million in bribes from agents of the Lockheed Aircraft Corporation while he was in office.

tenced to four years in prison and fined more than $2 million, the amount of the bribes, but his lawyers then began an appeals process that could take as long as a decade. Tanaka, who remained free on bail, declined to give up his parliamentary seat despite massive rallies that called for his resignation. The opposition boycott ended in late November after Nakasone agreed to call new elections and establish a 20-member "political ethics council" to study means by which corruption could be thwarted. Tanaka himself easily won reelection on December 18.

Earlier in the year, Nakasone was under strong pressure from the right wing of the LDP to discard Japan's long-standing ceiling on defense expenditures (1 percent of the gross national product). The right wing also pressed for greater government control of education and the introduction of morality training in the schools. From big business came pressure to relax the antimonopoly laws. Nakasone sidestepped most of these rightist demands, which were opposed by many members of his own party as well as by opposition members. He did, however, strongly advocate increased spending on arms, among other conservative positions. Some analysts believed his rhetoric was partly responsible for the LDP's losses in December.

Economy. Slow growth continued to characterize the Japanese economy. The growth rate for fiscal year 1982 (ending March 31, 1983) was 3.3 percent, and the unemployment rate hit a 30-year high of 2.5 percent for the same time span—a figure that would be considerably higher if Japan used internationally accepted methods of measuring unemployment. Sluggish economic growth led to lower tax revenues, greater social welfare expenses, and weaker domestic demand for imports than had been expected. Government debt was expected to exceed $500 billion by the end of fiscal 1983. The fiscal 1983 budget of $214 billion represented a 1.4 percent increase over outlays in fiscal 1982—the lowest rate of increase in 28 years. The "second budget" (the fiscal loan and investment program) went up only 2 percent—the slowest growth rate in 25 years.

Foreign affairs. Nakasone received a warm welcome when he arrived in Seoul, South Korea, on January 11 with promises of $4 billion in low-interest loans over a seven-year period. Japan's concern for its ties to East Asian nations was reaffirmed on Nakasone's next major trip, to the five members of the Association of Southeast Asian States (Indonesia, Thailand, Singapore, Malaysia, and the Philippines) and Brunei between April 30 and May 10. Nakasone offered extensions of previous initiatives, including regular levels of aid and opening of the Japanese market to Asean products, but the real purpose of the trip was to assure these nations that Japan's defense buildup would remain limited. At the summit meeting of major industrialized nations, held in Williamsburg, Va., May 28–30, Nakasone took a strong stance linking Japan and East Asia to problems of arms control in Europe. At his initiative, Japan for the first time formally linked itself to the NATO countries and France in security matters, signing a joint pledge to "maintain sufficient military strength to deter any attack, to counter any threat, and to ensure the peace."

A severe blow to Japanese-Soviet relations came on September 1 when a Soviet fighter plane shot down a South Korean airliner over the Sea of Japan, killing all 269 people on board, including 28 Japanese passengers. The airliner, on a flight from New York City to Seoul, had strayed into Soviet airspace north of Japan.

Friction over trade again shadowed relations between Japan and the United States; the Japanese surplus in bilateral trade was expected to reach $20–25 billion in 1983. Despite earlier indications to the contrary, Japan announced in November that it would extend voluntary quotas on exports of cars to the U.S. market for another year, beginning April 1, 1984. Exports would be held to 1.85 million units for

the 12-month period; up from 1.68 million in each of the three preceding years. The Reagan administration, for its part, upheld a petition from Harley-Davidson, a U.S. maker of heavy motorcycles, for relief from Japanese competition. On April 1, in the face of stiff Japanese protests, it announced a tenfold rise in import duties on heavy motorcycles, almost all of which came from Japan. A further U.S. grievance was the theft of U.S. corporate trade secrets by Japanese companies. In October, Hitachi Ltd. reached an out-of-court settlement in a civil suit filed by the International Business Machines Corporation, in which Hitachi agreed to pay for the use of technology stolen from

The first Disneyland outside the United States opened in a Tokyo suburb in 1983. The Japanese owners (Disney Productions receives a percentage of the gross) insisted on American-as-apple-pie authenticity, counting on the enthusiasm of the Japanese for all things American and their passion for souvenirs to make a success of the enterprise.

A Great Leap Backward

While Japanese-made pocket and desk calculators proliferate in the United States, many business managers in Japan are reportedly urging a return to the ancient soroban, the counting board with movable beads known in the West as the abacus. Proponents claim that the soroban, when skillfully operated, comes up with the answer more rapidly, with less likelihood of error, and also provides insight into the mechanisms of calculation. Japan now has thousands of special schools for instruction on the soroban, and at least one electronics manufacturer is marketing a modern calculator mounted on a traditional abacus frame, allowing the user to switch back and forth between instruments.

IBM. Hitachi and the Mitsubishi Electric Corporation pleaded no contest in parallel criminal cases, and each was fined $10,000.

Easing these irritants were several positive developments in U.S.-Japanese relations during 1983. Primary among them was a growing appreciation in Washington of Tokyo's support for its foreign policies. In a mid-January visit to Washington, Nakasone and U.S. President Ronald Reagan discussed trade and defense issues; while the two leaders remained far apart on a number of points, Nakasone said he returned to Japan "with satisfaction and confidence." During a three-day visit to Tokyo in November, Reagan held a further series of cordial talks with Nakasone. While in Japan, Reagan addressed the Diet (the first time an American president had done so), attended a state banquet hosted by Emperor Hirohito, and visited the Meiji Shrine. Among developments associated with his trip were an agreement by the Japanese government, announced on the eve of his arrival, to export advanced military technology to the United States, and a U.S.-Japanese pact aimed at strengthening the yen's value relative to the dollar in order to help reduce the U.S. trade deficit.

See STATISTICS OF THE WORLD   M.S.B.

JORDAN. During early 1983, King Hussein unsuccessfully sought a formula that would enable Jordan to participate in negotiations on the creation of a Palestinian entity on the West Bank. Talks between Hussein and Palestine Liberation Organization leader Yasir Arafat in January produced an agreement that there would be a "special and distinctive relationship" between Jordan and a future Palestinian entity on the West Bank, a formulation that seemed compatible with the peace plan proposed by U.S. President Ronald Reagan in September 1982. The plan, however, cautiously approved by Hussein, was not accepted by other Arab states or by Israel. Further meetings between Hussein and Arafat in April resulted in an agreement that would have allowed the formation of a joint Jordanian-Palestinian negotiating team, the Palestinians being chosen by, but not belonging to, the PLO. Arafat, however, was unable to win the approval of radical PLO members for this plan.

Security remained an important concern for King Hussein. Jordan discussed the possibility of acquiring mobile Hawk missiles and F-16 fighter aircraft from the United States, but in view of congressional opposition made no formal request. The Reagan administration's $137 million aid request for fiscal 1984 represented a substantial increase over the $73 million in aid granted to Jordan for the previous year. Both Jordan and the United States were concerned over increasing deliveries of Soviet weapons to Syria.

In October it was reported that the Reagan administration was seeking $220 million in secret financing for a Jordanian strike force of 8,000 soldiers that the United States had been secretly training for 2½ years. The force was intended to move quickly to pro-Western Arab nations to quell uprisings or mutinies.

Meanwhile, two Jordanian ambassadors were attacked in separate incidents. Muhammad Ali Khourma, ambassador to India, was shot and wounded in New Delhi on October 25. A day later, the ambassador to Italy, Taysir Alaedin Toukan, was seriously hurt when assailants opened fire as his car left the embassy in Rome.

Aid to Jordan from other Arab nations was at low levels because of sagging oil revenues. As one means of giving a boost to the economy, the government allowed private companies to resume trade with Egypt, ending a boycott imposed in 1978.   C.H.A.

K

KAMPUCHEA. *See* CAMBODIA.

KANSAS. *See* STATISTICS OF THE WORLD.

KENTUCKY. *See* STATISTICS OF THE WORLD.

KENYA. In 1983, President Daniel arap Moi continued efforts to bolster his regime's security and consolidate his power within Kenya's sole party, the Kenya African National Union (KANU), in the aftermath of a 1982 coup attempt. By mid-1983, 900 members of the air force had been sent to jail and nine persons convicted of complicity in the coup attempt had been sentenced to death.

A persistent conflict between the two leading politicians of the historically dominant Kikuyu ethnic group, Vice-President Mwai Kibaki and Constitutional Affairs Minister Charles Njonjo, came to an unexpected climax in June, when Moi ousted Njonjo from the cabinet; Moi implied that Njonjo had been in the pay of an unnamed foreign power.

To further strengthen his political base, Moi had called for general elections to be held on September 26, over a year ahead of schedule. All candidates, as usual, had to be approved by KANU at the national level. Moi, Kibaki, and three other candidates were unopposed and were declared winners of their parliamentary seats by KANU at the conclusion of the nominating process in August. However, six cabinet ministers were defeated in the general elections, while other candidates whom Moi reportedly opposed won reelection. In the new cabinet appointed after the elections, Kikuyus were substantially reduced in both numbers and influence.

In foreign affairs, Moi continued as chairman of the Organization of African Unity for a second year, until early June, because the OAU was unable to convene a quorum to conduct an official session in 1982. During his two-year tenure, the Kenyan president spent considerable time mediating between African states in conflict over Libyan leader Muammar al-Qaddafi's bid to be the next OAU chairman and over the seating of a Chad delegation.

Shortages of foreign exchange severely constrained the domestic economy during 1983.

Prices for meat, milk, tea, and rice were raised in February. In April, expenditures for many government ministries were frozen to reduce the anticipated budget deficit. The shilling was devalued 4 percent in August.

See STATISTICS OF THE WORLD.   J.K.

KHMER REPUBLIC. *See* CAMBODIA.

KIRIBATI. *See* STATISTICS OF THE WORLD.

KOREA, DEMOCRATIC PEOPLE'S REPUBLIC OF, *or* **NORTH KOREA.** Internationally, the major development of 1983 for North Korea was its apparent implication in the bombing of South Korean leaders at a ceremony in Rangoon, Burma (see KOREA, REPUBLIC OF). North Koreans also complained that a South Korean-Japanese-U.S. offensive alliance had emerged against them.

Although Kim Il Sung continued to reign as unquestioned supreme leader of North Korea, his son and apparent successor, Kim Chong Il, was increasingly prominent: the son's writings were being quoted along with the father's as guides to action, and his portrait was carried in at least one public celebration.

The government adopted a balanced 1983 budget, with spending up 9.6 percent from the 1982 budget. Targeted for spending increases under the new budget were the rural sector, the mining industry, and the metal and chemical industries. Defense spending was scheduled to rise slightly, to 14.8 percent of the total budget. These increases in expenditures reflected the solid performance of the economy in 1982, as industrial production and grain output rose.

See STATISTICS OF THE WORLD.   D.S.M.

KOREA, REPUBLIC OF, *or* **SOUTH KOREA.** South Koreans were shocked and angered when a Korean Air Lines jet was shot down on September 1 by a Soviet fighter, killing all 269 persons on board, and were again stunned in October, when a bombing in Burma killed leading members of President Chun Doo Hwan's government.

KAL flight downed. In the early morning hours of September 1, Korean Air Lines flight 007, a Boeing 747 en route from New York to Seoul,

Family members grieve at an altar in Seoul's Kimpo International Airport after learning that relatives had been aboard Korean Air Lines flight 007, shot down by a Soviet jet fighter.

was shot down as it passed over the southern tip of Sakhalin Island, close to sensitive Soviet military installations. All 240 passengers (most of whom were South Koreans) and 29 crew members died when the plane was struck by a missile fired by a Soviet fighter and then crashed into the Sea of Japan. The plane, for unexplained reasons, was off course when it was shot down.

Formal demands by South Korea and the United States for a public apology and for compensation were rejected by the Soviets, who insisted (despite denials by Korean and U.S. intelligence agencies) that the plane was on a U.S. spy mission. In Seoul, six days of public demonstrations denouncing the Soviet action were climaxed by a huge memorial service at Seoul Stadium on September 7. Over 100,000 people jammed the stadium to share

the public grief of relatives of those killed. On the diplomatic front, South Korean representatives urged the United Nations to condemn the downing of flight 007. Eventually, 16 governments suspended access by Aeroflot (the Soviet airline) to their airports, as well as other flights to and from Moscow, for periods of two weeks to 60 days.

Rangoon assassinations. On October 9, 17 South Koreans, including four cabinet members and a number of other high government officials, were killed in a bombing at the Martyrs' Mausoleum in Rangoon, Burma, during the final minutes of preparation for a diplomatic wreath-laying ceremony. Four Burmese also died. President Chun, who was on a planned 18-day visit to several countries in Asia and the Pacific, escaped injury because his car had been delayed in traffic. Among those killed were Deputy Prime Minister Suh Suk Joon, Foreign Minister Lee Bum Suk, Chief of Staff Hahm Pyong Choon, and Senior Presidential Economic Adviser Kim Jae Ik.

Chun cut short his tour and returned to Seoul, where the new cabinet he appointed revealed no hint of major policy changes. Chin lee Jong was named prime minister, Shin Byong Hyon was named deputy prime minister and economic planning minister, Kim Mahn Je was chosen finance minister, and Sakong Il succeeded Kim Jae Ik as senior presidential economic adviser. Former Finance Minister Kang Kyong Shik was made chief of staff, and Lee Won Kyung was named foreign minister.

The ruins of the mausoleum yielded an explosive device from North Korea, and the Burmese government arrested two North Korean commandos in connection with the bombing. A third was killed trying to escape arrest. The two captured commandos were put on trial and sentenced to death.

Domestic affairs. The Chun government announced on February 25 that it was lifting the ban on political activity imposed in 1980 on 250 former politicians, leaving 305 still under proscription. In August, 1,944 convicts were released or otherwise amnestied; of these, 695 were political prisoners. Nevertheless, there were indications of continued opposition to government policies. Opposition leader Kim Young Sam, who was under house arrest, went on a hunger strike for three weeks in late May and early June. His bid to dramatize a demand for democratic reforms was joined by 15 other prominent dissidents. And throughout the spring, college students mounted demonstrations.

At the beginning of 1983, government officials predicted a real growth rate of 7.5 percent in the gross national product for the year. However, the goals of the fifth five-year plan (1982–1986) were revised to reflect both the decline in domestic inflation and the stagnant international economy.

U.S. relations. The continuing closeness of U.S.-Korean ties was underlined by the annual joint "Team Spirit" military exercise, conducted from February to April. In addition, President Ronald Reagan's two-day visit in November reaffirmed the American commitment to South Korea's security. Reagan became the first U.S. president to visit the demilitarized zone separating the two Koreas.

See STATISTICS OF THE WORLD.   D.S.M.

KUWAIT. Terrorism of the kind familiar in Lebanon also struck in Kuwait in 1983. On December 12, a truck loaded with explosives blew up at the U.S. Embassy compound, and remote control car bombs were detonated at the French Embassy and four other other places. Four people were reportedly killed and more than 60 injured by the bombings. Kuwaiti officials took 18 suspects into custody. According to the officials, most of the suspects were members of a fundamentalist Shiite Muslim group with close ties to Iran.

Kuwait, which is ruled by members of the Sunni branch of Islam, continued to support Sunni-ruled Iraq in its war against Shiite Iran, despite Kuwait's large Shiite population and Iraqi claims of sovereignty over most of Kuwait's oil fields. Kuwait's financial aid to Iraq in 1982 was estimated at well over $6 billion. The Iraqi government was angered by the Kuwait bombings, which it blamed on Iran; in retaliation, Iraq attacked targets in five Iranian towns with its air force and surface missiles.

Kuwait's relations with the United States were strained by a U.S. government ruling that U.S. corporations owned by Kuwaitis may not acquire any interests in U.S. federal mineral leases. Kuwait is the first and, so far, the only country to be denied this right. In August, the Kuwaiti government rejected the American choice for ambassador to Kuwait. The reason given was that the nominee had served as U.S. consul general in Jerusalem and reported from there directly to Washington—a disproof, according to Kuwait, of the U.S. claim that it does not recognize Israel's annexation of East Jerusalem.

Kuwait continued its aggressive overseas investment policies, purchasing nearly 10 percent of the Volkswagen corporation. The Kuwait Petroleum Corporation purchased Gulf Oil's refining and marketing operations in Belgium, the Netherlands, Luxembourg, Denmark, and Sweden. Kuwait thus became the first member of the Organization of Petroleum Exporting Countries to have its own fully integrated oil industry.

See STATISTICS OF THE WORLD.   L.A.K.

L

LABOR UNIONS. It was a difficult year for labor, as wage settlements registered record-low gains. During the first quarter, new wage settlements actually showed a 1.4 percent decline for the first contract year—the first such decline recorded in 15 years of collecting data on the subject. For the first nine months of the year, settlements showed a slight increase, but it was the slimmest on record for any nine-month period. The trend reflected a pattern of concessionary bargaining, in which many unions, in a period of slow economic growth, temporarily gave up gains as a way of protecting workers' jobs in ailing industries. Agreements between Dow Chemical Company and its steelworkers, between Kennecott Copper Corporation and its employees, and between the trucking industry and the International Brotherhood of Teamsters, among others, called for union sacrifices.

Steel and auto pacts. How the economic crosscurrents affected labor unions is illustrated in sharp relief by the two basic U.S. industries of steel and autos. In the steel industry, the United Steelworkers of America had bucked the trend to concessionary bargaining in 1982. In both July and November of that year, agreement on concessions had been reached between major steel companies and national union officials, only to be rejected by the presidents of the local unions, even though steel mills were operating at close to one-third of capacity and about one-half of the union members were jobless. Continued unemployment and plant shutdowns, however, finally brought for seven of the companies a new 41-month contract, ratified in March 1983, to take the place of the one scheduled to expire in July. The biggest concession by the workers was a $1.25-an-hour pay cut (plus elimination of a 6¢-an-hour increase based on cost-of-living adjustments), which would be restored in annual steps in February of 1984, 1985, and 1986. Other concessions included reduction in premium pay for regularly scheduled non-overtime Sunday work, loss of one week's vacation for everyone eligible for at least two

weeks' vacation, and elimination of one paid holiday, reducing paid time off to ten days.

The new contract also allowed companies to bargain with local unions for concessions beyond those granted in the national agreement. An example was a contract change approved in August at Bethlehem Steel's Lackawanna, N.Y., plant that called for the elimination of 59 of the existing 275 jobs and the early retirement of 70 employees. The seven-company steel settlement included an agreement by the companies that what they saved as a result of the union concessions would not be applied to any ventures outside the steel industry.

On the other hand, in the automotive industry, where the United Automobile Workers had consented to major givebacks in 1982, a dramatic turnaround occurred in 1983, as demand for cars increased and company profits grew. For example, Chrysler, which in 1979 had to borrow more than $1 billion from the federal government to stay afloat, recorded in

The Japanese style of management, stressing openness and cooperation, makes it difficult for unions, with their traditional adversary approach, to recruit workers. Shown here is a nonunion worker at the Honda automobile factory in Marysville, Ohio.

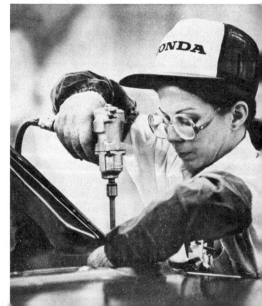

1983 its biggest second-quarter profits ever, so that it was able to pay back its entire debt before the due date, with a saving in interest payments of more than $300 million. Chrysler workers, who had made a series of concessions to aid the then ailing company, decided not only to try to win them back but also to bargain for new gains. The union already won some gains in late 1982. The next collective bargaining round was not scheduled to take place until January 1984, but in the last week of July 1983 the UAW reopened talks with Chrysler, asking for an immediate $1-an-hour raise. In early September, talks resulted in higher wages and an extension of the contract past its January 15, 1984, expiration date.

Winning back surrendered gains was not the only problem that concerned UAW leaders in 1983. Another problem was declining membership. Chiefly because of plant shutdowns, the UAW had lost nearly a third of its members since 1979. A task as difficult as keeping old members, union officials found, was attracting new ones, especially in areas not previously unionized. The UAW focused on three towns, where foreign firms, eager to penetrate the U.S. auto market, either had opened up or planned to open up new plants: Marysville, Ohio, where, since 1982, Honda has had an assembly plant; Smyrna, Tenn., where Nissan started manufacturing trucks in June 1983; and Fremont, Calif., where, beginning in late 1984, Toyota, in a joint venture with General Motors, planned to produce small cars at a plant closed down in 1982 by GM. In Fremont in September, union and management negotiators reached an accord under which the company recognized the UAW and agreed to pay its proposed 3,000 employees (mainly laid-off former GM workers) wages similar to those elsewhere in the U.S. auto industry.

Other settlements. On August 8 the Communications Workers of America, the International Brotherhood of Electrical Workers, and the Telecommunications International Union, representing a total of about 675,000 workers in the American Telephone & Telegraph system, went on strike. After 16 days, during which the company was able to continue operating because of the high degree of automation of its facilities, the unions and AT&T reached a three-year accord, providing for a maximum wage increase of 5.5 percent in the first year and additional increases of 1.5 percent, plus cost-of-living adjustments, in the subsequent two years. The settlement also provided for new retraining programs to help workers cope with technological change—a major issue in the strike. For its part, AT&T reserved the right to transfer and lay off workers.

A tentative three-year contract was negotiated by the International Longshoremen's Association on the Atlantic and Gulf coasts in April. It provided for a $1-an-hour pay increase (raising the hourly wage to $15) in the first year and a similar jump in each of the succeeding two years. The pact, which was supposed to take effect in September, was replaced in that month by another interim agreement; while keeping the wage gains contained in the first, it called for new contract negotiations by January 15, 1984.

A bitter 20-year battle between the J. P. Stevens Company and the Amalgamated Clothing and Textile Workers Union apparently ended in October when the National Labor Relations Board approved a $1.2 million settlement of all charges of unfair labor practices. Stevens had fought unionization by various means, including the dismissal of labor activists, and the union had responded with a boycott of Stevens products and intense organizing efforts at the company's plants.

Airline turbulence. As a result of deregulation, some of the older air passenger carriers continued to run into stiff competition from newer and smaller airlines promising lower fares. In late September, the nation's eighth-largest carrier, Continental Air Lines, which had been losing money steadily, filed for reorganization under Chapter 11 of the federal bankruptcy law. Thereupon, Eastern Air Lines, in a direct appeal from its president, implied to its 37,500 employees that unless they accepted a 15 percent pay cut, it might take the same action.

The unions, which had already signed agreements with several airlines for a series of wage and other reductions, were quick to charge that the airlines were using the bankruptcy laws as a means of doing away with existing labor contracts. Continental's pilots and flight attendants, whose salaries had been cut by up

Picketing Ma Bell workers wait to use a pay phone. For most consumers the strike by 675,000 telephone workers was barely noticeable, as automated equipment and supervisory personnel kept lines open.

to 50 percent, went on strike in early October to protest what they contended was the airline's union-breaking action; Continental continued operations using nonstriking employees. On the other hand, Eastern Air Lines employees reached an agreement with management in December, making major wage and work rule concessions in return for worker participation in management and holdings in common stock.

Political endorsements. The Executive Council of the American Federation of Labor and Congress of Industrial Organizations on October 1 voted to throw its support to former U.S. Vice President Walter Mondale in his quest for the Democratic Party's nomination for president in 1984. The decision was endorsed four days later by the delegates to the AFL-CIO convention. It was the first time the AFL-CIO had formally endorsed a presidential aspirant prior to a national party convention. Mondale had earlier won the backing of the National Education Association, the country's most important teachers' organization, with some 1.7 million members.

Legal decisions. The U.S. Supreme Court ruled, 5–4, that a union that fails to press a member's grievance for wrongful discharge may be held liable for part of any back pay due the member. The case arose from a complaint by an employee of the U.S. Postal Service whose dismissal, although judged unlawful by a lower court, had not been taken to arbitration by the union. In another 5–4 decision, the Court held that public employees are not protected by the constitutional guarantee of free speech when discussing internal office affairs; the case involved a New Orleans assistant district attorney who was fired for circulating among her fellow workers a questionnaire on office-related complaints. A federal circuit court ruled that disclosure of a union member's home address to a labor union—in the case at issue, the American Federation of Government Employees—was a "clearly unwarranted invasion of privacy."

Transition. A changing of the guard occurred at the International Brotherhood of Teamsters in April when Roy L. Williams resigned as president, in the wake of his December 1982 conviction in federal court for conspiring to bribe Senator Howard W. Cannon (D, Nev.). Williams was succeeded by Jackie Presser, president of Teamsters Local 507 of Ohio.

An era ended in the trade-union movement when Douglas Fraser retired as president of the UAW and was succeeded by 53-year-old Owen F. Bieber, who came from a younger generation of union leaders not directly associated with the legendary Walter Reuther, UAW head from 1946 to 1970.

Lloyd McBride, president of the United Steelworkers of America since 1977, died on November 6 at the age of 67. He had led the union through some of the industry's most troubled times. Lynn R. Williams was named temporary president, pending a March 1984 election.   S.L.W.

LAOS. In January 1983, a major reshuffling of the Laotian government was reported to have been completed—the first since the proclamation of the Lao People's Democratic Republic (LPDR) in December 1975. The government was enlarged and revamped, but there were no substantial changes in the roles of veteran leaders. Kaysone Phomvihan, head of the ruling Lao People's Revolutionary Party, retained the post of chairman of the Council of Ministers (prime minister). Nouhak Phoumsavan, first vice-chairman and second in party rank, surrendered the post of minister of finance but retained overall supervision of economic affairs.

On February 22–23, the top leadership of Vietnam, Laos, and Cambodia met in Vientiane for an Indochina summit conference, the first such gathering since the end of the Vietnam war. Laos subsequently put forth Vietnam's proposal for a direct dialogue between the Association of Southeast Asian Nations (Asean) and the three Indochina states. The proposal offered no compromise on Vietnam's military occupation of Cambodia, and Asean rejected it.

Laos remained closely linked to the Soviet Union and Vietnam, as opposed to China. China, for its part, announced support for a number of exiled political groups opposing the Laotian government.

There was a slight improvement in Laotian relations with the United States, marked by Laotian cooperation with the U.S. Department of Defense Joint Casualty Resolution Center. The latter's delegation was received in Vientiane in February for the first official discussions of specific cases of missing U.S. servicemen, and in December it was reported that Laos had given another delegation from the center the bodies of some missing servicemen. Earlier, the Reagan administration had disavowed the activities of James G. ("Bo") Gritz, a former U.S. Army Special Forces colonel, who led a band of American and Laotian guerrillas into Laos from Thailand in late 1982 and 1983 to look for missing American servicemen from the Vietnam war.

See STATISTICS OF THE WORLD.   J.J.Z.

LEBANON. The Lebanese civil war that began in 1975 flared up again in 1983. Muslim, Druze, Christian, and Palestinian factions fought each other and the Lebanese Army, and terrorist bombings exacted heavy death tolls. Syrian and Israeli troops continued to occupy most of the country, while the government of President Amin Gemayel controlled little more than Beirut and its immediate surroundings.

Lebanese-Israeli agreement. On May 17, after months of U.S.-mediated negotiations, Lebanon and Israel signed an agreement ending the state of war that had existed between them since Israel was founded in 1948. Under its provisions, Israel was to withdraw its forces from Lebanon, provided that Syria and the Palestine Liberation Organization did the same. The pact also provided for a continued Israeli presence in Lebanon after Israeli troops had pulled out. It designated the southern one-fourth of Lebanon as a security zone, with arrangements for joint Lebanese-Israeli patrols of the area. A side memorandum stipulated a role for Israeli ally Major Saad Haddad and his militia in the security zone. The agreement, however, was vehemently denounced by Syrian President Hafez al-Assad, and Syria refused to pull out its forces, in effect nullifying the agreement.

Civil war. The most bitter fighting in the renewed civil war took place in the Shouf Mountains east of Beirut, a region dotted with both Druze and Christian villages but regarded by the Druze as their territory. After Israeli forces drove Syrian troops from the region in 1982, Christian Phalangist militia forces were allowed to enter, setting off a struggle for control with the Druze. There were reports of massacres by both Druze and Christian forces.

Fighters in a Shiite Muslim group whose members are opposed to the Christian-dominated government of President Amin Gemayel conceal their faces while posing behind a picture of their leader.

In September 1983, Israeli troops, caught in the cross fire between Christians and Druze, withdrew from the Shouf region and took up more easily defended positions to the south, below the Awali River. The Druze, backed by Syria and reportedly joined by Palestinian guerrillas and Lebanese leftists, then made quick gains in the Shouf, taking several towns and besieging Suk al Gharb, held by the Lebanese Army, and Deir al Qamar, held by Christian militia troops. The Lebanese Army held on to Suk al Gharb, despite heavy fighting. In mid-December, the siege of Deir al Qamar was lifted, and the Christian militiamen and villagers who had fled there were evacuated.

The multinational peacekeeping forces in and around Beirut, made up of U.S., French, British, and Italian troops, were drawn into the conflict as Druze and other Syrian-backed forces fired on their positions from the nearby mountains. On September 19, the United States, which had 1,600 Marines stationed near Beirut, fired for the first time in support of the Lebanese Army rather than in direct reaction to attacks on its own positions. Two U.S. Navy ships off Beirut pounded Druze forces east of Beirut. Meanwhile, terrorists, operating from behind Syrian lines, attacked Western diplomatic and military headquarters. Early in the year, on April 18, a vehicle filled with explosives was driven up to the U.S. embassy in Beirut and blown up, causing the building's central section to collapse and leaving more than 63 dead and 100 wounded. Several months later, on October 23, a truck loaded with TNT crashed through barriers and blew up a U.S. Marine headquarters at the Beirut airport, killing over 240 people; minutes afterward, another suicide bombing destroyed a French paratroop barracks 2 miles away, causing at least 58 deaths. On November 4, a similar bombing of an Israeli military compound in Tyre in southern Lebanon killed 60 people. The terrorist attacks were believed to be the work of fundamentalist Lebanese Shiite Muslims with ties to the Iranian regime of Ayatollah Ruhollah Khomeini.

Both the French and the Israelis retaliated with air attacks on the bases of Shiite Muslim forces in eastern Lebanon. On December 4, U.S. carrier-based jets bombed Syrian antiaircraft batteries east of Beirut after U.S. reconnaissance planes were fired upon; two U.S. planes were downed, and one airman killed, while another was captured by Syria (he was released in early 1984). Also on December 4, eight Marines were killed near Beirut by Druze artillery fire. Terrorist bombings continued. On December 21, bombings of a French military post and a hotel bar in Beirut left at least 19 dead.

Reconciliation talks. The governments of Lebanon and Syria agreed to a cease-fire, effective September 26, which briefly halted the intense fighting in the Shouf Mountains, although heavy fighting there soon resumed. The agreement also called for a Lebanese conference of "national reconciliation," and President Gemayel accordingly issued invitations to the leaders of Lebanon's main religious and political groups; Syrian and Saudi Arabian observers also were invited. The conference opened in Geneva, on October 31, but was adjourned inconclusively on November 4. Participants agreed that they would neither ratify nor abrogate the Lebanese-Israeli accord but that the Gemayal government would open new discussions on a formula for the withdrawal of Israeli troops.

The chief aim of the reconciliation talks was to produce a new distribution of power to replace the governing arrangement established in 1943, which was opposed by Lebanese Muslims because it worked in favor of the Maronite Christians. Without a new governing arrangement, the country seemed likely to slide into partition. In July, Druze leader Walid Jumblatt and a group of Syrian-backed and leftist leaders formed an alliance called the National Salvation Front to administer areas of eastern and northern Lebanon occupied by Syria, and Israel's withdrawal to the Awali River was viewed by Gemayel as a consolidation of its position that could lead to permanent occupation. During a visit by Gemayel to Washington in late November and early December, U.S. officials urged him to move quickly to broaden the base of his government,

and he subsequently began consultations with all Lebanese factional leaders and with Syria in an effort to form a broadened cabinet.

Lebanese Army. Gemayel's hopes of unifying the country also depended on the Lebanese Army, which he planned to reconstitute and rebuild into a force that could replace the various militias. With new equipment supplied by the United States and intensive training, the army became a more formidable force during the year, acquitting itself well in the fighting at Suk al Gharb. The Lebanese Army also reported some successes in late December, in heavy fighting with Muslim militia forces just south of Beirut near the Shatila refugee camp, where the French had abandoned positions after heavy shelling and sniper fire. A new Lebanese cease-fire had gone into effect on December 16, but it did not hold.

See STATISTICS OF THE WORLD. See also ISRAEL; MIDDLE EAST; MILITARY AND NAVAL AFFAIRS; PALESTINE LIBERATION ORGANIZATION; SYRIA.

W.W.H.

LESOTHO. See STATISTICS OF THE WORLD.
LIBERIA. See STATISTICS OF THE WORLD.

U.S. Marine headquarters near Beirut lay devastated after a truck loaded with TNT blew up the structure, killing over 240 people. Here, rescuers search the rubble soon after the blast.

LIBRARIES. Circulation at public libraries in the United States has increased at more than twice the rate of population growth during the past four decades, according to a study by Herbert Goldhor, director of the Library Research Center at the University of Illinois. While the nation's population increased 70 percent from 1940 to 1980, public library circulation between 1941 and 1982 rose 160 percent. On the basis of data from a representative sample of public libraries serving communities of at least 25,000, Goldhor estimated that national circulation of all public library materials exceeded 1 billion for the first time in 1981 and reached nearly 1.1 billion in 1982. As a partial explanation for the increase, Goldhor noted that attractive new libraries had been built in many communities and that public libraries now circulate records, tapes, prints, video cassettes and movies as well as books and magazines.

Company libraries. The increasing use of data bases (computerized files on specific topics) by businesses has led to a rapid expansion of company libraries in the United States. Many corporations have created special libraries or have enlarged existing libraries to accommodate computer facilities, and trained librarians, often called information managers, have been increasingly relied on to cope with the growing mass of information accessible through data bases. Company libraries spend as much as $500 million a year, and their numbers are increasing; 600 company libraries were created between 1978 and 1983, bringing the total in the United States to over 5,600.

Library thefts. As libraries grow, the disappearance of valuable books and documents has caused increasing concern in recent years. Early in 1983 a work by the pioneer astronomer Nicolaus Copernicus, valued at $150,000, was among 370 rare books discovered missing from the John Crerar Library in Chicago. Drafts of a script for the film *Star Wars* recently vanished from the Theater Arts Library at the University of California at Los Angeles. At a two-day conference on library theft held in September at Oberlin, Ohio, speakers sought to make libraries more aware of the problem—which, it was estimated, costs public libraries a total of $50 million a year.

Kennedy tapes. The first sampling of President John F. Kennedy's secret White House tapes was made available to the public in June at the Kennedy Library in Boston. The tapes, the existence of which was first made known in 1973, contain 260 hours of conversation, recorded during the last 16 months of the Kennedy administration. The most interesting conversations on the portion of the tapes made available in June concerned the crisis surrounding the enrollment of James Meredith as the first black student at the University of Mississippi in 1962. Tapes related to the Cuban missile crisis and other developments were withheld because of national security regulations.

New libraries. Plans were announced for the construction of an 80,000-square-foot building to house the Richard M. Nixon Presidential Library, which will be built with private funds on a 13-acre site in San Clemente, Calif., the site of the Western White House during the Nixon administration. The library, which will include a museum, will be operated by the National Archives and Records Administration.

A 25,000-square-foot site for San Diego's new La Jolla branch library was donated by Florence Riford. The city has allocated $1 million for its construction, and matching fund donations were being sought from the community.

Library meetings. The International Federation of Library Associations' 49th general conference was held in Munich, West Germany, August 21–27. "Constant Change: Libraries Respond to the Challenge" was the theme of the 38th annual conference of the Canadian Library Association, convened in Winnipeg, Manitoba, June 16–21. More than 11,000 people attended the 102nd annual conference of the American Library Association, which was held in Los Angeles, June 25–30; its theme was "Connections." R.J.Sh.

LIBYA. In 1983, Libyan leader Muammar al-Qaddafi continued to seek influence abroad, through diplomacy and through military moves, including intervention in Chad.

Diplomacy. Qaddafi was rebuffed by the Organization of African Unity when the group held its 19th annual summit meeting in Addis Ababa, Ethiopia, on June 8–12. Because the meeting was held in Addis Ababa, instead of in Tripoli, Libya, as Qaddafi had wished, Ethiopian leader Mengistu Haile Mariam was automatically named chairman instead of Qaddafi. The OAU also resisted efforts to seat the Libyan-backed Polisario movement seeking control of Western Sahara. Shortly thereafter, Qaddafi embarked on a drive apparently designed to end his regional isolation, paying visits to Saudi Arabia, Jordan, Syria, and Morocco. Relations with the Palestinian Liberation Organization remained tense, and in November PLO leader Yasir Arafat accused Qaddafi of sending troops to back rebels seeking his overthrow.

Involvement in Chad. On June 23, Chadian President Hissène Habré announced that thousands of rebels, led by former President Goukouni Oueddei and with extensive Libyan assistance, had attacked Faya-Largeau in north-central Chad. On August 10, the town finally fell to some 3,000 rebels and 2,000 Libyans. Within days, French troops were deployed in a number of sites in Chad. Both Libya and France poured reinforcements into Chad; by late August, Libya was believed to have 3,500 troops there, while France may have had more than 2,500. By September, an uneasy stalemate had developed. (See CHAD.)

Gulf of Sidra incidents. Libya and the United States confronted one another on several occasions in the Gulf of Sidra. In February the United States moved the aircraft carrier *Nimitz* toward a position off the Libyan coast, after receiving reports of an alleged plot by Qaddafi to overthrow Sudanese President Jaafar al-Nimeiry. On February 18 the United States reported that F-14's based on the *Nimitz* had chased two Libyan fighters away. Large demonstrations in Libya's cities protested what were described as the "overt terroristic provocations of the U.S. Sixth Fleet." F-14's from the carrier *Eisenhower*, cruising off Libya during the Chad crisis, again intercepted Libyan MIG's off Libya's coastline on June 29 and on August 2.

Dispute with Brazil. On April 16, Brazil detained four Libyan transport planes after they set down to refuel at Manaus and Recife. The Libyans claimed they were carrying medical supplies to Nicaragua; however, U.S. intelligence informed Brazilian authorities that the planes were carrying arms. Brazilian military technicians boarded the planes and unloaded tons of weapons. Qaddafi insisted that the planes would not depart without the arms, while Brazil was equally adamant they would not leave with them. The impasse did not end until June, when Brazil dropped its demand, insisting, however, that the planes return directly to Libya.

See STATISTICS OF THE WORLD. A.D.

LIECHTENSTEIN. *See* STATISTICS OF THE WORLD.

LIFE SCIENCES. In 1983 developments in the life sciences included new techniques in genetic engineering and the evaluation of a new theory on the mechanisms of evolution. Botanists presented results suggesting that trees can communicate with each other, and zoologists considered some hard-to-digest facts about pandas' diets.

BIOLOGY

In 1983 genetically engineered organisms were released into the environment for the first time. Scientists were busy evaluating a new theory on evolutionary change, and new suggestions for conservation strategy were discussed.

Genetic engineering. Genetic engineering involves altering the genetic material within cells by manipulating the chemical substance DNA (deoxyribonucleic acid), which carries the cells'

Gardeners know every plant has a mind of its own; now studies show that plants send each other messages.

"*I don't mind the chirping of the birds or the buzzing of the bees, but the murmuring of those pines and hemlocks is driving me nuts!*"

genetic information, or genetic code. By transferring genes from the cells of one organism to those of another, scientists can give the second organism the specific traits governed, or coded for, by these genes. This technique is known as gene-splicing, and the altered genetic material is called recombinant DNA. Still a relatively new discipline, genetic engineering registered several "firsts" in 1983.

Bacteria. In September, Steven Lindow of the University of California at Berkeley became the first person to release genetically engineered organisms into the environment. The organisms were bacteria that Lindow sprayed on a potato plot near Tulelake, Calif., to see if they would protect the plants against freezing. Lindow had previously discovered that much frost damage to plants is caused by the presence of certain bacteria that have the ability to promote the formation of ice crystals. Plants bearing these "ice-nucleating" bacteria are damaged by frost at temperatures as much as 9° Fahrenheit higher than plants without them. Lindow and his colleagues isolated the genes that give the bacteria this ability and used genetic engineering techniques to remove the genes, in the hope that the bacteria altered in this way would thrive on the plants and displace the naturally occurring bacteria, thereby increasing the ability of the plants to tolerate low temperatures.

There was a great deal of discussion about Lindow's work before the Recombinant DNA Advisory Committee of the U.S. National Institutes of Health gave permission for the experiment. Some scientists think that winds may blow the natural ice-nucleating bacteria into the upper atmosphere, where they may play a role in regulating the climate. If these bacteria should be displaced by the engineered bacteria, changes in the weather could result. However, the committee decided that the risk of such an event is very small.

Plants. In January, teams working independently for the Monsanto Company and under Jozef Schell of the University of Ghent in Belgium announced they had transferred a bacterial gene into petunia-plant cells and achieved so-called expression—the first time this feat had been achieved in plant cells. Expression means that the trait coded for by the gene, in this case a resistance to antibiotics,

is actually exhibited by the cells. The petunia cells altered by the gene transfer were able to grow even when exposed to enough antibiotic to kill normal petunia cells. The Monsanto group later reported having grown whole petunia plants that were able to express the gene for antibiotic resistance, another first.

In another development, a team from Agrigenetics Inc. and the University of Wisconsin disclosed that they had taken from a bean cell a gene that codes for the production of a protein and transferred it into both sunflower and tobacco cells. In both cases, the gene was expressed and the bean protein was produced. This represented the first time that a gene from one plant had been transferred into cells from a second plant and expressed. Taken together, these results suggest that genetic engineering in plants may turn out to be somewhat easier than had been expected.

Human genetic defects. In August, scientists at the Salk Institute for Biological Studies in San Diego, the University of California at San Diego, and Baylor College of Medicine in Houston announced they had corrected a genetic defect in human cells by using a virus to insert a new gene into the cells. The defective cells were taken from patients suffering from Lesch-Nyhan syndrome, a severe brain disorder that causes mental retardation. The disease is due to a defect in a specific gene that controls the production of an enzyme needed for proper brain functioning. The scientists inserted a healthy gene into a mouse leukemia virus, altered the virus so that it would not cause cancer, and exposed the defective cells to the virus. The cells picked up the gene along with the virus and began producing the vital enzyme. The technique holds promise for use in treating a wide range of genetic diseases.

Evolution by molecular drive. The process of evolution involves change in the genetic makeup of isolated breeding populations or whole species of organisms, so that as time progresses they differ more and more from their ancestors. Two mechanisms for such change are currently recognized by most scientists: natural selection and genetic drift. Biologists may disagree about the relative merits of genetic drift and natural selection as explanations of the rich diversity of life, but for a long time few considered the possibility that a third mechanism might be operating. Such a third mechanism, a radically new concept termed molecular drive, was recently proposed. Throughout 1983 it kept evolutionary biologists busy at their computers testing the effects of this exciting new model on their simulations of rates and patterns of evolutionary change.

Natural selection, an idea dating back to Charles Darwin, is the most widely accepted mechanism today. In natural selection, those individuals best suited to their environment survive and breed more successfully, and consequently contribute more than their fair share of offspring to the next generation. In time, the whole population becomes composed of this sort of individual. Further genetic changes may be initiated by environmental change or may result from mutations (spontaneously arising errors in the genetic code), a small proportion of which may be advantageous.

The mechanism of genetic drift operates best in small populations, where purely random events are able to eliminate or bring to dominance certain gene combinations or mutations without environmental selection coming into play. The new gene balance is passed on to later generations.

The principle of molecular drive was originally set forth by geneticist Gabriel Dover of Cambridge University in late 1982 in a complex paper. As the name implies, molecular drive operates at the level of individual genes, or segments of the DNA molecules on the chromosomes of cells. It is now known that all higher organisms contain many important genes in multiple copies, or "families." Several hundred copies may be present, associated in one pair of chromosomes or distributed more generally over many. Such gene families govern the manufacture of many vital proteins, including the immunoglobulins of the immune system and the actin of muscles.

Dover noted that despite the large number of copies, the genes of a particular family in any one species are almost always identical, with little or no variation in an individual or between individuals; yet when the same gene family is found in a closely related species, it is dominated by a different gene variant. This pattern cannot be explained by genetic drift or natural selection, which generate far more variable genetic composition. Somehow, mechanisms must operate to create and maintain homogeneity within each gene family. Dover defined a series of complex but well documented ways whereby this can happen. He noted that DNA sections carrying genes are not rigidly fixed on chromosomes and can be exchanged, copied, and transferred by the cell's biochemical machinery. In addition, during some types of cell division one variant of a gene may replace, or "convert," a different variant to its own type. Since gene variants are likely to differ in their ability to undergo these alterations, some variants are able to spread more rapidly through their family than others and eventually come to replace all the alternative variants.

The most exciting implication of the molecular drive concept follows from the fact that the rate of gene conversion is slow compared to the rate of chromosome reshuffling in sexual reproduction. Because of this relatively rapid mixing of chromosomes there can be little variation in gene family composition between individuals in an interbreeding population. Consequently, with respect to the features of the organism determined by the gene families in question, the whole population evolves slowly and coherently. This is quite at odds with the way natural selection operates; natural selection favors a small proportion of the population, so that the population changes as a result of the increasing domination of a few bloodlines.

Isolated breeding populations evolving through molecular drive will tend to great internal uniformity in their gene families, but two such populations of a species may not become homogeneous with respect to the same gene variants. This greatly increases the genetic difference between the two populations and could prevent effective interbreeding. Molecular drive may even cause two large populations of a single species that exist in identical habitats to separate into distinct species, something that conventional evolutionary mechanics cannot easily undertake.

Dover remains cautious about the importance of his new evolutionary mechanism. He emphasizes that animals evolving in accordance with it remain subject to the influence of genetic drift and natural selection. Nonetheless, evolutionary biologists are hoping that the theory will provide new insights into the process of evolutionary change.

Conservation strategy. Successful conservation of endangered species and communities demands that the limited resources available be used as efficiently as possible in designing wildlife reserves. Reserves are akin to islands, and so the findings of island biogeography theory have often been used to assist in their planning. It is known that, regardless of climatic zone or degree of isolation, big islands can contain more animal and plant species than similar small islands. Correspondingly, a large wildlife reserve should contain more species and hence be a better reserve than a small one. But what happens if a reserve consists of several small isolated reserves with a total area equal to that of a single large reserve? Classic theory suggests that because of its larger size and, therefore, complexity the single big reserve should contain more species than the sum contained by the small reserves. This conclusion has influenced the design of wildlife refuges in urban and wilderness areas, although in many cases the presence of roads, settlements, and natural barriers has severely limited reserve size and made the notion of several small refuges more attractive to planners than a single large one.

Ecologists Daniel Simberloff and Lawrence G. Abele of Florida State University have suggested that conventional ideas of the superiority of a single large reserve may be incorrect. Attacking the SLOSS ("single large or several small") question through mathematical theory, the scientists showed that under most conditions, two small reserves equal in area to a large one should contain a *greater* number of species. These conclusions were also found to apply in real situations. Thus, a complex of small reserves, in addition to being possibly cheaper to purchase than a major plot of land and less subject to the effects of ecological disasters such as fire, disease, or freeways, may actually provide the better refuge.

But how small can a safe refuge be? Very small reserves may be able to house only a few individual animals or plants. If breeding numbers are too restricted, the likelihood of extinction caused by random environmental events increases. Biologists Thomas W. Schoener of the University of California at Davis and Amy Schoener of the University of Washington at Seattle carried out a careful five-year investigation of this effect on small islands in the Bahamas. Observing that islands smaller than about 2½ acres (all measurements refer not to actual island size but to total vegetated area) never contained lizards, the scientists artificially introduced small breeding groups to isolated, previously lizard-free islands varying in size from somewhat larger than a square yard to almost 10,000 square yards and then followed the fate of these introduced colonists. Populations on islands smaller than 12 square yards became extinct in less than a year. Above that size, survival duration rapidly increased, and on islands of more than 36 square yards, population levels remained high throughout the study period. The study demonstrated unequivocally that if islands or reserves are too small, species cannot maintain themselves. In addition it raised the further question of why there were no naturally occurring lizards on the larger experimental islands, which were able to maintain the introduced lizards for five years. The biologists suggested that hurricanes periodically reduced the vegetated area to below the critical 12-square-yard size, extinguishing species on islands normally able to support them. To maintain species safely, islands or reserves must be big enough not just to provide an adequate habitat under normal conditions, but to withstand the disasters that sometimes occur.

Acid rain. Biologists and other scientists cast new light on the problem of acid rain as two influential reports were released to the public. Acid rain—the term is used to cover all forms of acidic precipitation and airborne dust—has for several years been of prime concern to conservationists since it is responsible for killing all normal life forms in many lakes and streams and threatening plant life over wide areas. The source of the problem has been hotly debated, but reports in June by the U.S. National Academy of Sciences and the U.S. Interagency Task Force on Acid Precipitation both concluded that human-produced pollution was the main cause. The National Academy group reported unanimously that 90 to 95 percent of the northeastern United States's acid rain is the result of human activity, particularly industrial smoke and fumes and automobile exhaust. The Interagency study was somewhat more cautious but in basic agreement. Both studies suggested that the government can be assured that money spent in eliminating pollution will bear definite results in reducing acid rain.   S.M.H. & T.H.M.

BOTANY

Important contributions to botany in 1983 included a study that discovered a pattern in the many shapes, sizes, and colors of tropical fruit and a report suggesting that trees to an extent communicate with each other, releasing chemicals that serve as warnings of insect attacks. The Venus's-flytrap also was an object of interesting recent research.

Causes of tropical fruit diversity. Tropical-forest plants produce a bizarre range of fruits, diverse in color, size, shape, and smell. But Charles H. Janson of the University of Washington has discovered a remarkably simple unifying theme associated with the kind of animal that consumes them. Janson studied 258 plant species with fleshy fruits in the Manu National Park, Peru. For the fruit of each species he recorded the color, the size, and whether the fruit was protected by an inedible husk. The fruit colors could be grouped into two sets, which also reflected a difference in fruit protection. "Type A" fruits were red, white, black, blue, purple, or of mixed color and were unprotected. "Type B" fruits were protected by a husk and were colored orange, brown, yellow, or green. Although there was some overlap, over two-thirds of the fruits clearly fell into one or the other class.

Why should the fruits be so clearly grouped into two basic types? According to Janson, the governing factor is whether they are eaten by birds (type A) or mammals (type B). Birds and mammals differ in their color sense, that of birds being better developed. In addition, fruit-eating birds are generally smaller and have much weaker jaws than the equivalent mammals. Type B fruits were in fact notably bigger on the average than those eaten by birds. It would seem that the forest fruits have evolved

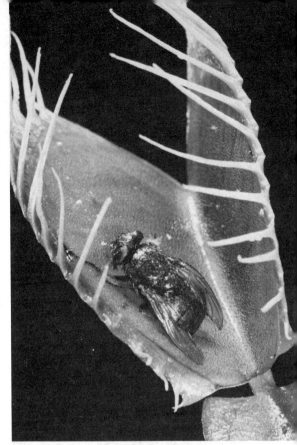

A Venus's-flytrap opens after consuming its insect prey. Botanists have found that the rapid closing of the trap—in only one to three seconds—is the result of sudden, irreversible cell growth on the plant's outside surface.

to suit the abilities of fruit eaters by offering the combination of color, size, and ease of access best suited to *either* birds *or* mammals. By ensuring palatability to one or the other group of fruit eaters, plants maximize their chances of dispersing the seeds associated with the edible fruit pulp. Plants with the wrong set of characteristics, intermediate between types A and B, might be ignored by both birds and animals, and so would tend to die out.

Communication in trees. Trees not only mount an active chemical defense against insects, but they also warn nearby trees to prepare for attack. Work by Ian T. Baldwin and Jack C. Schultz confirmed earlier reports that damage to leaves causes trees to change the chemical composition of the remaining leaves, making them less attractive, less palatable, and perhaps even lethal to insects. Similar chemical changes

229

were found in nearby unharmed trees, suggesting that airborne chemicals carried a message. This process may also explain other cases where trees seem to know what their neighbors are doing, such as the simultaneous flowering or fruiting of a grove.

Venus's-flytrap. Researchers at Cornell University and Lebanon Valley College in Annville, Pa., studied how the Venus's-flytrap rapidly closes to catch its prey and later reopens. Both actions were found to involve sudden, irreversible cell growth—on the outer surface in closing up, on the inner surface in reopening. Researchers found evidence that the growth results from changes in the acid-base balance of plant cell walls; a similar process is thought to play a partial role in other cases of plant growth.   S.M.H.

ZOOLOGY

Research by zoologists in 1983 included reports on pandas' eating habits, on how tapeworms survive the highly acid conditions of digestive systems, and on how and why some lizards lose their tails.

Panda diet. Although closely related to raccoons and other carnivores, the giant panda of China feeds almost exclusively on a vegetarian diet of bamboo. E. S. Dierenfeld and a team of scientists at Cornell University have recently shown that the skull, teeth, and paws of this rare animal are well adapted to eating bamboo, but, surprisingly, the digestive tract is not, since it lacks the important cellulose fermentation chambers found in most plant-eating animals. Consequently, the panda digests only about one-sixth of its food input and must eat huge amounts of bamboo to survive. Bamboo generally flowers once every 50–60 years over vast areas, then dies, with the result that the choosy pandas, reluctant to eat other food, may starve. This year, bamboo flowered in southwest China's Sichuan Province, where most panda reserves are located, and many of the animals were threatened with starvation. Under a program financed by China's Forestry Ministry, scientists spread food along forest trails to keep the pandas alive. Plans were also announced for placing some in captivity to

The giant panda of China, which feeds almost exclusively on bamboo, was threatened by a scarcity of its diet staple in 1983; under a government program, food was spread along forest trails in China's Sichuan Province, the site of most panda reserves, to keep the animals alive.

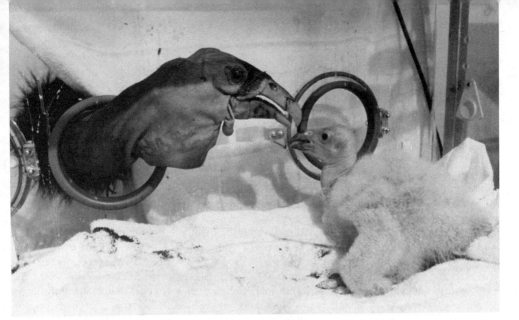

Sisquor, the first California condor born in captivity, takes its meal of minced-mouse pabulum from a hand puppet manipulated by its keeper at the San Diego Wild Animal Park. The puppet is needed to make the chicks of the endangered species think they are being cared for by a condor; otherwise, says the keeper, "they would want to live and mate with people and not be birds."

keep them properly fed and for relocating others to unaffected areas. The pandas would be returned to their original habitats when new bamboo seedlings are sufficiently grown to support them.

Defense against digestion. One of the least inviting habitats in which animals can be found is within the digestive system of vertebrates. The vertebrate gut secretes powerful enzymes that break up food into simple chemical components for use in the rest of the body. If chunks of meat and even bone can rapidly be digested by enzymes, how does an apparently unprotected animal like a tapeworm manage to survive in this hostile environment?

Two members of the Physiology Group at the School of Biological Sciences of the University of Kentucky investigated this problem using the common rat tapeworm *Hymenolepis diminuta*. Gary L. Uglem and John J. Just incubated tapeworms at blood temperature (37 degrees Celsius) in saline solution. The solution was maintained at pH 7.4, which is slightly alkaline and ideal for the action of the important protein-digesting enzyme trypsin. The pH scale runs from 0 (highly acidic) to 14 (highly alkaline), and pH 7 is neutral. After two hours

of incubation the worms were removed, and only a 16 percent inhibition of trypsin activity was found—not enough to give any protection from digestion. The researchers noticed, however, that when live worms were left in the saline solution, the pH tended to change. Placing worms in saline solutions ranging from pH 2.0 (very acid) to 8.0 (alkaline), they found that after incubation, the pH had changed toward 5.0. At this mildly acidic level, trypsin is almost completely inactivated, and the researchers found that only about 5 percent of its original activity remained. In the gut of the rat, the tapeworm manages to keep the environment much more acidic than normal, thereby protecting itself against attack by digestive enzymes, at the expense of the efficiency of its host's digestion.

A bizarre parallel to this behavior was reported some time later by a team of scientists headed by Michael J. Tyler and David J. C. Shearman of the Departments of Zoology and Medicine of the University of Adelaide in Australia. The female of the very rare Australian frog *Rheobatrachus silus* swallows her eggs and broods them in her stomach, eventually giving birth two months later through the mouth. How do the young avoid the unpleasant digestive effects of highly acidic stomach juices?

Only five female frogs were available for study in over eight years of research, but one expelled two dozen young larvae during handling, and these were carefully reared in clean water. The water was changed every day, and the old water containing the mucus and secretions from the tadpoles was concentrated for analysis. The researchers then used small sections of live stomach lining from a more abundant frog to assess the effect of *Rheobatrachus* larval secretions on acid release from the stomach. The extract proved to reduce acid secretion to less than a sixth of its normal level, and the active ingredient was found to be prostaglandin E_2. Prostaglandins are acids that have a multitude of functions within the body (for example, they help control blood pressure and smooth muscle contraction). However, this use by a larva to switch off its mother's stomach secretions is quite unique in the animal kingdom.

Tail shedding in lizards. When attacked by a predator, if other escape ploys fail, most lizards will shed their tails, leaving a distracting sacrifice for the predator while the truncated lizard escapes as best it can. Many tails thrash wildly for a number of seconds after shedding, and the function of this activity has never been clarified. Now Benjamin E. Dial of Texas A & M University's Department of Biology and Lloyd C. Fitzpatrick of the Department of Biological Sciences of North Texas State University have discovered the reason for this movement. They used two types of lizard, one with very active and one with very weak tail-thrashing, and they investigated how snake and cat predators could deal with them. Cats always ignored weakly thrashing or exhausted tails and attacked and ate the lizard body, but when the more active species was tried, the cats were attracted to the wildly thrashing tail, and the body made good its escape.

Snakes also attacked shed tails, but lacking paws to help them, they took much longer to subdue a thrashing tail, which they probably mistook for the whole animal. This gave the lizard body nearly forty seconds extra escape time. Thrashing tails accumulated very high levels of lactic acid in their muscles, suggesting that they are physiologically adapted to maximize the duration of activity, aiding the escape of the erstwhile owner by distracting and delaying the predator.   S.M.H.

LITERATURE. Among the major literary developments of 1983 were:

AMERICAN

Short story writers dominated the American literary scene in 1983. Several ambitious new novels were considered disappointments, and the more highly regarded new novels tended to be quieter and more modest efforts.

Fiction. Raymond Carver's third collection of short stories, *Cathedral,* was probably the most acclaimed work of fiction of the year. The stories depict in cool, deliberate, transparent prose the lives and sorrows of ordinary people; some of them were already being hailed as classics of the genre. Another highly praised collection was *The Stories of Breece D'J Pancake,* which convey a powerful vision of the impoverished coal-mining and farming country of West Virginia; they unfortunately constitute the only work of their author, who committed suicide in 1979 at the age of 26. *The Stories of Bernard Malamud* offered 25 stories from three decades, including such classics as "Idiots First" and "A Summer's Reading." The stories in Paul Theroux's new collection, *The London Embassy,* reminiscent of W. Somerset Maugham, were admired for their urbane prose style. M. F. K. Fisher, best known for her evocative books about food and France, brought out a collection of accomplished stories, *Sister Age,* which movingly depict the distress and small pleasures of old age.

Several writers, known for their short stories, chose to cultivate other fields. Cynthia Ozick published a collection of her reviews, *Art & Ardor,* and followed with a short novel, *The Cannibal Galaxy.* Mark Helprin, acclaimed for his 1982 collection *Ellis Island and Other Stories,* brought out a long novel blending realism and fantasy; called *Winter's Tale,* it won a less enthusiastic reception. Barry Hannah's novel *The Tennis Handsome* was derived in part from stories in his highly regarded collection *Airships* (1978). Laurie Colwin made a successful transition to novel-writing in *Family Happiness,* a perceptive study of upperclass urban life, as did James Wilcox in *Modern*

Baptists, a comedy with a complicated and flawless plot.

The most publicized and attacked novel of the year was Norman Mailer's long awaited *Ancient Evenings,* a vastly ambitious work that transmuted Mailer's contemporary concerns into ancient Egyptian history and myth. To some, the book seemed padded with undigested history and overly scatological. Another ambitious historical excursion, Russell Hoban's *Pilgermann,* the God-obsessed confession of a Jewish pilgrim during the Crusades, drew mixed reviews. Isaac Bashevis Singer's new novel, *The Penitent,* was widely criticized, as being more of a tirade against modern life than a novel. Critics were also hard on Gore Vidal's *Duluth,* a satire rumored to have been hastily written to pay off the author's debts for his abortive Senate campaign in California.

On the other hand, Gilbert Sorrentino's *Blue Pastoral,* which looked daunting, actually proved to be great fun; filled with parodies and word-plays, it was devoted to lampooning pop songs, academic prose, advertising, and other debased forms of English. William Kennedy, an author who had been quietly appreciated for years, won considerable acclaim for his third novel, set in Albany, N.Y., and entitled *Ironweed.* Joan Chase's first novel, *During the Reign of the Queen of Persia,* describing three generations of women on an Ohio farm, won glowing reviews and signaled the arrival of a new talent.

Among more established writers, Philip Roth, in *The Anatomy Lesson,* concluded his highly regarded comic trilogy about the vexations of a successful Jewish writer in America. Thomas Berger's *The Feud* hilariously recounted how two small towns waged a small war over a can of paint remover. Peter de Vries's *Slouching Toward Kalamazoo* took on the new morality; in the book, a schoolteacher who seduces her precocious student begins to sport not the scarlet letter A but the incandescent sexual grade of A-plus. In a more serious vein, Hortense Calisher published an ambitious, absorbing, densely plotted novel, *Mysteries of Motion,* centered on an imaginary future trip aboard a space shuttle.

Biography and history. A number of literary biographies appeared. Among them was Ian

Norman Mailer was both praised and castigated for his ambitious, long-awaited novel Ancient Evenings, set in ancient Egypt.

Hamilton's biography of Robert Lowell, which unsparingly described the tormented life of a major American poet. Joan Givner's *Katherine Anne Porter: A Life* presented the facts about Porter, but in a long, somewhat unwieldy chronicle. Andrew Field's *Djuna* was an informal life of Djuna Barnes, often neglected author of the avant-garde novel *Nightwood.* There were two accounts of the intense and extravagant life of a great detective novelist, William F. Nolan's unauthorized *Hammett: A Life at the Edge* and Diane Johnson's *Dashiell Hammett: A Life,* written with the cooperation of Lillian Hellman, Hammett's lover and literary executor. The most celebrated of the Beat writers was given a full and definitive treatment in Gerald Nicosia's *Memory Babe: A Critical Biography of Jack Kerouac.*

Major figures in 20th-century history were the subjects of new biographies. *Eisenhower: Soldier, General of the Army, President-elect,* by Stephen E. Ambrose, was the first volume of a comprehensive examination of Eisenhower's personal and professional life. *The Last Lion: Winston Spencer Churchill: Visions of*

Glory, 1874–1932, by William Manchester, told the story of Churchill's ambitious early years. There also appeared a posthumously published memoir by another crucial participant in World War II, *A General's Life: An Autobiography,* by Omar N. Bradley and Clay Blair.

Twenty years after the assassination of President John F. Kennedy, a number of books appeared on aspects of his life and career, including one full-length personal biography of the man behind the myth: *A Hero for Our Time: An Intimate Story of the Kennedy Years,* by Ralph G. Martin. Meanwhile, memoirs of Jimmy Carter's administration continued to appear. In *Hard Choices: Four Critical Years in American Foreign Policy,* by Cyrus Vance, and *Power and Principle: Memoirs of the National Security Adviser, 1977–1981,* by Zbigniew Brzezinski, the two chief foreign policy executives of the Carter administration assessed its successes and failures from different and often conflicting perspectives.

Two journalists who covered the Vietnam war returned to the subject as historians— Arnold R. Isaacs, with a critical account of U.S. policy in Southeast Asia in *Without Honor: Defeat in Vietnam and Cambodia;* and Stanley Karnow with *Vietnam: A History.* Vietnam policy also was a central theme of Seymour M. Hersh's harshly critical *The Price of Power: Kissinger in the Nixon White House.*

One of the most controversial historical works of the year was *The Rosenberg File: A Search for the Truth,* by Ronald Radosh and Joyce Milton. Drawing on trial records, interviews, and recently released FBI files, the authors conclude that Julius Rosenberg was guilty of spying for the Soviet Union and that his wife Ethel was an accomplice, but that government prosecution of the Rosenbergs was tainted by improper methods.

One of the most remarkable works of literary nonfiction was William Least Heat Moon's *Blue Highways,* an idiosyncratic travel book that describes the author's meandering journey on the backroads of America. Walker Percy's *Lost in the Cosmos: The Last Self-Help Book* was a rambling existentialist meditation that ranges from God and theology to television and popular culture. Among outstanding col-

lections of literary criticism were John Updike's *Hugging the Shore: Essays and Criticism* and Elizabeth Hardwick's *Bartleby in Manhattan and Other Essays.*

Poetry. One of the most exciting events of the year in poetry was the publication of Amy Clampitt's first collection, *The Kingfisher.* In the collection, which came relatively late in life for a poet, Clampitt espoused a new formalism, keeping her lines tight and her ear tuned. The poems evoked comparisons with the quiet and assured craft of Elizabeth Bishop, whose posthumous *Collected Poems* appeared during the year. A. R. Ammons, in *Lake Effect Country,* blended his observations of nature with philosophical and religious themes. Two other established poets brought out long, unified works. In *The Changing Light at Sandover,* James Merrill gathered three previous long poems into a single epic on the theme of the purpose and making of poetry. Hayden Carruth's *The Sleeping Beauty* was a sequence of 15-line rhymed lyrics using the framework of a Grimm fairy tale to explore the nature of love. M.D.

AUSTRALIAN

Australian literature in 1983 was marked by the publication of critically acclaimed novels by younger writers and by some fine writing from the ethnic community.

Fiction. Peter Kocan's *The Cure,* a semibiographical novel about the author's ten-year experience in a psychiatric institution following his attempted assassination of a public figure, received wide critical acclaim. It was a sequel to his first novel *The Treatment.* Both books were characterized by a bare and intense style and wry humor. Kocan has also published two award-winning volumes of poetry.

Brian Castro's first novel *Birds of Passage,* which won the Australian-Vogel literary award for an unpublished manuscript in 1982, traced a young Chinese Australian's search for ancestry and identity. It was a complex book marked by the young author's mastery of technique.

Australian aborigines produced some interesting work during 1983. Jack Davis's plays *Kullark* and *The Dreamers* celebrated the distinctiveness, humor, and resilience of the aboriginal character. Wherever they were per-

Rodney Hall won the Miles Franklin Award, Australia's most coveted literary prize, for his novel Just Relations.

formed on the stage they attracted warm acclaim. *Gularabulu* was an edited collection of aboriginal oral narratives, forming a bridge between aboriginal and European cultures. The stories are told by Paddy Roe, a well-known personality in the aboriginal community.

Ian Moffitt, who surprised readers with his first novel *The Retreat of Radiance*, a literate thriller, surprised again with *The Colour Man*, a psychological thriller full of insights and never dull.

Poetry. Notable poetry published during the year included Peter Porter's *Collected Poems;* a revised and updated edition of *Sometimes Gladness*, containing Bruce Dawe's collected poems from 1954 to 1982; *Welcome!,* the first major collection of Thomas Shapcott since his *Selected Poems* in 1976; and *Tide Country* by Vivian Smith, one of Australia's finest lyric poets.

Obituary. Christina Stead, probably Australia's most important woman novelist and, with Patrick White, the best known Australian writer internationally, died on March 31 at age 80. She had published 12 novels, among them *The House of All Nations* (1938), *The Man Who Loved Children* (1940), *For Love Alone* (1944), and *The Little Hotel* (1973).

Awards. Dimitris Tsaloumas, a Greek poet who settled in Australia in 1952 at age 30, won first prize in the National Book Council's Awards for *The Observatory*, a bilingual collection of poems. Olga Masters won second prize for

The Home Girls, a collection of tightly written, intuitive short stories.

Australia's most prestigious literary prize, the Miles Franklin Award, went to Rodney Hall's original novel of rural life *Just Relations*. The Australian Literature Society's Gold Medal was awarded to David Malouf for the novellas *Fly Away Peter* and *Child's Play*, the first dealing with Australians caught up in World War I, the second the story of a young Italian terrorist. Barry Oakley, Australian novelist and playwright, was named winner of the Canada-Australia Literary Prize, which is awarded annually in alternate years to an Australian or Canadian writer.   I.K.

CANADIAN

In spite of economic recession, which lowered book sales, Canadian literature displayed considerable vitality in 1983, and a wide variety of fiction and nonfiction was published. A number of short story collections in particular were well received by critics and the public.

Fiction. Among the noteworthy collections of short stories published in 1983 were Paul St. Pierre's *Smith and Other Events*, a sprightly collection of rural anecdotes; Veronica Ross's *Dark Secrets* and George Bowering's *A Place to Die*, both consisting of dour tales of alienation and death; and A. M. Klein's *Short Stories*, edited from manuscripts and Jewish periodicals of the 1930's and collected for the first time.

One of the most highly praised novels of the year was Clark Blaise's *Lusts*, set in the United

LITERATURE

States and India; in part it was a justification of a writer's life in the face of a fellow writer's suicide. The distinguished novelist Morley Callaghan, who turned 80 during the year, published *A Time for Judas,* an attempt to give the betrayer of Jesus a voice in his own defense. *Cold Heaven,* by Irish-born Brian Moore, is a quirky mystery about a man's disappearance and apparent death before his wife can divorce him.

Among the better novels in French were Madeleine Monette's lyrical *Petites Violences,* Yves Beauchemin's *Nuit battante,* and Jean Ethier-Blais's more realistic *Les Pays étrangers,* set in Montreal during the 1940's. Alice Parizeau's *La Charge des sangliers* continued the fiction sequence her earlier work began, and Claude Jasmin's *Masman-Paris, Maman-la-France* rendered the cultural shocks that await a Quebecker in France.

Poetry and drama. Margaret Atwood, best known for her novels, brought out a collection of prose poems called *Murder in the Dark;* they are sardonic fables about the reality of human cruelty and the need for vision, and also about how women may ironically lose their freedom as they struggle for liberation. Maria Jacobs's *Precautions Against Death* is a

The latest work by the Irish-born Canadian author Brian Moore was Cold Heaven, a mystery novel about the disappearance and presumed death of a man whose wife is about to divorce him.

In his novel A Time for Judas, *the distinguished Canadian author Morley Callaghan allowed Jesus's betrayer to speak in his own defense.*

highly personal work bringing together autobiographical poems and journals about the fate of Jews hiding in the Netherlands during the Nazi occupation.

A number of established poets brought out new volumes, including Dorothy Livesay, D. G. Jones, Daphne Marlatt, and Alan Safarik, and there were volumes of selected verse by Ralph Gustafson, Milton Acorn, Fred Cogswell, Raymond Souster, and Tom Wayman. Some very promising work by lesser known poets was also published, including Jacqueline Hogue's *Aube,* Sharon H. Nelson's *Mad Women & Crazy Ladies,* Barry Dempster's *Fables for Isolated Men,* Don McKay's *Birding, or Desire,* and John V. Hicks's *Silence Like the Sun.* Newly published plays included Louise Maheux-Forcier's *Un Parc en automne,* Leonard Angel's *The Unveiling,* and two plays by George Walker, *Science and Madness* and *The Art of War.*

Obituaries. The novelist Gabrielle Roy died on July 13 at the age of 74. Her first novel, *Bonheur d'occasion (The Tin Flute),* published in 1945, was a sympathetic portrait of working-class people in Montreal that became an international best-seller. On June 27, the poet and fiction writer Alden Nowlan died at the age of

50. A Nova Scotian, Nowlan portrayed the ordinary people of Atlantic Canada in his ironic and compassionate poems and plays.

W.H.N.

ENGLISH

Several of Britain's most eminent writers, including Anthony Powell and Iris Murdoch, made literary news in 1983. William Golding, however, captured the headlines by winning the Nobel Prize for literature (see PRIZES AND AWARDS). The theater was dominated by probing dramas, many of them with political themes.

Fiction. Veteran novelist Anthony Powell deflated various contemporary attitudes with wicked acuteness in *O, How the Wheel Becomes It!* The story explored one of his favorite themes: the apparent safety of maturity unexpectedly invaded by embarrassing reminders of youthful indiscretion. *The Philosopher's Pupil*, by Iris Murdoch, combined witty ironies of incident and relationship with the interplay of serious ideas. In portraying a crisis between the pupil, George, and his teacher, Rozanov, Murdoch probed with characteristic inventiveness and penetration her central question—the permissible limits of personal freedom.

Malcolm Bradbury's brilliant satire *Rates of Exchange* depicted the social, political, and economic confusions of an imaginary East European state, seen through the eyes of a mild English linguist bored by yet another cultural lecture tour. *The Little Drummer Girl*, by John le Carré, was a tensely gripping narrative that surveyed conflicts of loyalty in a young actress of radical sympathies, kidnapped by an Israeli intelligence unit and planted as an agent among Palestinian terrorists. The book was another major critical and popular success for le Carré.

In *The Handyman*, the seasoned feminist novelist Penelope Mortimer portrayed the problems of a timid widow in a rural retreat sadly different from what she had anticipated. Another accomplished woman novelist, Anita Brookner, again surveyed the plight of the woman alone in *Look at Me*. The sadness of solitude and pain of rejection were poignantly communicated through the experiences of a reclusive London librarian, initially dazzled and then disillusioned by her relationship with a charming but unprincipled couple.

There were two notable novels about the troubles of modern Ireland. William Trevor's *Fools of Fortune*, a chronicle of unfulfilled love, stemmed from the brutal destruction of a boy's home and family by British soldiers in 1918. *Cal*, a powerful second novel by Bernard Mac Laverty, depicted contemporary Ulster with vivid, sensuous immediacy.

Master Spy Novelist

Beginning in the early 1960's, John le Carré (real name: David John Cornwall) has produced some of the finest spy novels ever written, praised for their thoughtful exploration of moral dilemmas and for their skillfully plotted intrigue. The 51-year-old author's tenth novel, *The Little Drummer Girl*, soon reached the top of the best-seller charts in early 1983. Whereas most of le Carré's previous novels concentrated on the cold-war intrigues of British and Soviet spies, *The Little Drummer Girl* focused on an English actress called Charlie, enlisted by Israeli intelligence to penetrate a network of Palestinian terrorists attacking Israeli targets in Europe. Like its predecessors, however, le Carré's most recent work was notable for the intense scrutiny focused on the motives and behavior of its characters.

John le Carré

Biography. In *The Life of John Milton,* A. N. Wilson provided the most provocative literary biography of the year. It was attacked by some critics as a one-sided portrait that attempted to refurbish the image of Milton the man at the expense of historical accuracy. David Cecil's perceptive *A Portrait of Charles Lamb* appreciatively examined the life and work of this gentle, ironic man, while in *Robert Browning: A Life Within Life,* Donald Thomas offered an informative view of his subject's energetic personality, relations with his contemporaries, and poetic originality. The immense popularity of the contemporary poet John Betjeman was attributed by Patrick Taylor-Martin, in his comprehensive appraisal *John Betjeman: His Life and Work,* less to the poet's elements of "irony and subtle self-mockery" than to the sincerity of his expression of common emotions.

Drama. Two new plays by leading British dramatists contained striking similarities of theme and structure. The double setting of David Hare's *A Map of the World* was a Bombay conference on world poverty and a film studio where the event and its participants were re-created as a movie—with sharp shifts of emphasis. This thought-provoking play was pervaded by the author's awareness of issues clouded and principles flawed by human fallibility. Tom Stoppard's *The Real Thing* likewise presented the challenge of unresolved questions. Stoppard's ironic juxtaposition of the stage fictions of his playwright hero with the realities of the character's domestic life added a new dimension of emotional truth to the playwright's customary verbal brilliance.

There were two new plays by Caryl Churchill. *Top Girls* employed the device of an all-female dinner party (with guests taken from fiction and history) given by a tough, successful businesswoman who is sharply contrasted with her meek sister. The play questioned the worth of feminine freedom that sacrifices the weak or stupid to the clever and aggressive. Churchill's other play, *Fen,* set among farm workers, explored similar feminist dilemmas.

The threat of nuclear war was the subject of two arresting new plays. Raymond Briggs, in *When the Wind Blows,* starkly depicted the uncomprehending yet stoical response of an unimaginative English couple confronted by the reality of holocaust. Peter Whelan's subtly disturbing *Clay* dealt with the overshadowed future hopes and plans of four middle-aged childhood friends and their families.   M.W.

WORLD

One of the most surprising literary events of 1983 was the success of *The Name of the Rose,* an intellectually challenging first novel by an Italian literary critic, Umberto Eco, which became a best-seller in the United States and several European countries. Throughout the world, in both fiction and memoirs, authors

The British novelist William Golding, author of Lord of the Flies, and his wife, Ann, are shown in their garden shortly after the announcement that Golding had been awarded the 1983 Nobel Prize for Literature.

strove to find meaning amid political and social upheavals.

French. The ever-popular Colette received posthumous tribute in English in the form of a compendious biography by Joanna Richardson, publication of *The Collected Stories of Colette,* and publication, in a limited edition, of the midcareer autobiographical novel *Break of Day,* superbly illustrated by painter Françoise Gilot. Françoise Sagan's novel *The Painted Lady,* which subtly portrayed a group of blasé celebrities aboard a luxury liner, appeared in translation; French readers were attracted to her *Un Orage immobile* ("An Immobile Storm"), a historical novel set in 19th-century France. Cécile Wajsbrot's semi-occult novel *Une Vie à soi* ("A Life of Her Own") saw its heroine haunted by the ghost of the English writer Virginia Woolf and tempted by suicidal forces. A similar mood pervaded *Le Vent noir* ("The Black Wind"), a republished novel by the unjustly neglected Paul Gadenne, who died in 1956; the main figure is torn by a conflict between desire for a woman and a desire to be free from her.

The failure to reconcile narcissistic male fantasy and the needs of others was dramatized in Marguerite Duras's cinematographic novel *La Maladie de la morte* ("Fatal Illness"). Gothic horror stories and folktales of the demonic by Claude Seignolle, well-known in France for this genre, have now been translated into English as *The Nightcharmer. King Solomon* (part of *L'Angoisse du roi Salomon*) by the prolific Romain Gary was a complex semiautobiographical narrative that dealt with the visions and moral conflicts of a philanthropist.

The Paul Morand Prize of the Académie Française went to Henri Pollès for the novel *Sur le fleuve du sang vient parfois un beau navire* ("On a River of Blood Comes a Beautiful Boat Sometimes"), which portrayed the varied effects of World War I upon the inhabitants of a small town.

German. Thomas Bernhard, a severe critic of Austro-German society, turned from fiction to autobiography in *Wittgensteins Neffe: Eine Freundschaft* ("Wittgenstein's Nephew: A Friendship"). The title derived from a chance encounter with the nephew of Ludwig Wittgenstein, an Austrian who became one of the

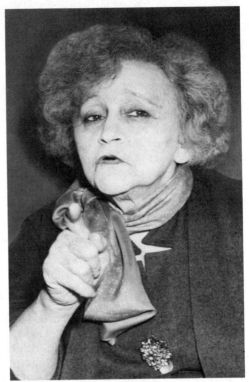

The French writer Colette, who died in 1954, won renewed attention with the publication in English of a major biography and a volume of collected short stories.

leading 20th-century philosophers. Wittgenstein saw language as useful nonsense, while his nephew regarded it as pernicious sense and found refuge in a madhouse; the contrast is central to Bernhard's view of himself as a writer. Bernhard is a stylistic successor to Heinrich von Kleist, who was the object of renewed interest in Germany and abroad in translation—as witnessed by the recent publication of *An Abyss Deep Enough* (letters) and a major biography of Kleist by Joachim Maass.

Gossipy details rather than substance marked the long-awaited memoir of Lion Feuchtwanger by his widow Marta, In *Nur eine Frau: Jahre, Tage, Stunden* ("One Woman Only: Years, Days, Hours").

Italian. Alberto Moravia's *1934,* which entangled his characters in a web of suicidal thoughts, cerebral sex, and politics, received a mixed critical response. Meanwhile, *The Name of* the *Rose,* a novel by a prominent Italian literary critic, Umberto Eco, caught readers' imaginations the world over. The book can be read on the level of a detective story, in which several Benedictine monks are mysteriously murdered in a wealthy monastery in the year 1372, or it can be interpreted as a parable of the return of the Dark Ages, with apocalyptic implications for the present.

Spanish and Portuguese. Familiar and new names continued to give vitality to Latin American literature. The stories *Chronicle of a Death Foretold* by Gabriel García Márquez and *We Love Glenda So Much* by Julio Cortázar enhanced established reputations. The brutal realities of South American life were described in novels by Argentina's Luisa Valenzuela (*The Lizard's Tail*), El Salvador's Manlio Argueta (*One Day of Life*), and Chile's Ariel Dorfman (*Widows*). In *Maíra* the Brazilian anthropologist Darcy Ribeiro mixed fact and fiction to depict the vanishing cultures of aborigines in outland villages. The renowned poetry of Antonio Machado (1875–1939) was translated into English in volumes by Alan S. Trueblood and Robert Bly.

Russian. Venedikt Erofeev's scathingly comic *Moscow Circles* exposed the dullness and desperation of regimentation. The Russian émigré Sergei Dovlatov chose Estonia for the setting of his novel *The Compromise,* which described a journalist's frustrations with censorship. Similar ironies about Russian life were pictured in Fazil Iskander's wickedly witty novel *Sandro of Chegem,* recounting the adventures of a Georgian dance troupe, and also in Vasily Aksyonov's *The Island of Crimea,* a fable about mad people who prefer Marxist authority to "decadent" freedom. Major memoirs came from the scholar Lev Kopelev (*Ease My Sorrows*) and the former army general Petro Grigorenko (*Memoirs*).

Other European. The 1983 Nordic Council Prize for Literature was awarded to the Danish novelist Peter Seeberg for *Om fjorten dage* ("In Fourteen Days"), a fictionalized survey of human history in which time and eternity have different meanings for humanity, animals, and God. The Pegasus Prize was awarded to Dutch writer Cees Nooteboom for his novel *Rituals,* in which a divorced man seeks distractions in Amsterdam's stock market, in women, and in Zen circles. The award may encourage translation of his other novels.

Japanese. Among recent translations were a number of notable novels. Fumiko Enchi's *Masks* was an exquisitely eerie tale about a modern female shaman. Michiko Ishimure's novel *Story of the Sea of Camellias* powerfully indicted the dumping of mercury wastes. Poetry was represented by *The Selected Poems of Shuntaro Tanikawa,* in Harold Wright's fine English versions.

Africa. Somalian Nuruddin Farah's novel *Sardines* captured with grim realism a range of sociopolitical, African feminist, and cultural problems. The Nigerian playwright Wole Soyinka's *The Forest of a Thousand Demons* was a translation of a classic Yoruba fantasy by D. O. Fagunwa, recounting exploits of fabled hunters, supernatural monsters, and tribal rites. *Expedition to the Baobab Tree,* by the Afrikaner novelist Wilma Stockenstrom, dramatized the harrowing experiences of a black slave in her life among bandits, assorted masters, and a pygmy tribe.   S.M.

BOOKS FOR CHILDREN

The children's book market appeared to be doing well in 1983. At midyear, *Book Industry Trends* projected that revenue from the sale of hardcover children's books would amount to close to $225 million in 1983, a 12 percent gain over 1982. Paperback sales were expected to exceed $65 million, gaining 13 percent.

Controversies. Questions about what books are unsuitable for children, and who has the right to decide, continued to stir controversy. In one notable instance, the public library systems of San Francisco and Milwaukee refused to circulate copies of *Jake and Honeybunch Go to Heaven* by Margot Zemach, a past Caldecott Medal winner, because librarians claimed the tale, based on black American folklore, perpetrated and reinforced negative racial stereotypes. On the other side of this controversy, the book's editor, Michael Di Capua of Farrar, Straus & Giroux, strongly denied the charges and noted that the book in question had been chosen by the New York *Times* as one of the 16 best children's books of 1982.

New and old. Picture, board, and tactile books for children six months to two years of age

It goes forth at night
to prowl around the fires.
It even likes to mingle
with the dancers.
Thus it is both prowler and dancer.

The 1983 Caldecott Medal, the American Library Association's award for best-illustrated children's book, went to Marcia Brown, who illustrated her own translation of an African-influenced French poem, Shadow.

proliferated in 1983. Publishers were discovering a sizable market for this so-called baby lit—parents anxious to expose their children to books as early as possible in order to make books a natural part of their world. One outstanding title for tinies was *Spot's First Christmas* by Eric Hill, a brightly colored, cheerful lift-the-flap book starring Spot, an irrepressible puppy. Hill also created a series of Baby Bear board books, illustrating very basic concepts without the use of words. *Me and My Kitty* by Nicole Rubel was a delightful look at a day a little girl spends with her cat, containing all the familiar daily activities youngsters do themselves and love to see in books. In *Who?, What?, Where?,* and *When?,* four wordless books by Leo Lionni, mice encounter situations that pose simple questions for toddlers to think about.

Novelty books of all kinds were rife (further evidence of the industry's effort to attract bookstore customers). Toy books, pop-ups, illustrated block books opening out to tell a story, books with moving pictures, and other innovations abounded. James Stevenson won raves for his *Barbara's Birthday,* a pop-up extravaganza in which sprightly pictures are set in motion when pages are turned and tabs are pulled. David A. Adler's *Bunny Rabbit Rebus,* a game in story form, with pictures by Madelaine Gill Linden, pleased tots and grown-ups alike. In it, a mother rabbit and her hungry bunny son go looking for carrots to eat; the narrative is advanced through a number of rebus puzzles. *Leonard Baskin's Miniature Natural History* was a four-volume set featuring superb watercolor portraits of animal life in miniature.

Retold fairy tales and newly illustrated versions of favorite stories were also abundant. A new edition of Daniel Defoe's *Robinson Crusoe,* with N. C. Wyeth's original illustrations that bring to life the tale of shipwreck and survival, was published, as was a 75th-anniversary edition of *The Wind in the Willows* by Kenneth Grahame, with pictures by Ernest H.

241

Shepard. *Beauty and the Beast,* retold by Deborah Apy, was adorned with new paintings by artist Michael Hague, and David Small added his illustrations to the classic *Gulliver's Travels* by Jonathan Swift. In addition, no fewer than four versions of the perennial Easter story, *The Velveteen Rabbit,* by Margery Williams found their way into print, as well as three editions of Charles Dickens's *A Christmas Carol.*

In a sequel to her award-winning *Marked by Fire,* Joyce Carol Thomas continued the story of Abyssinia Jackson in *Bright Shadow.* Julian F. Thompson, author of 1982's *The Grounding of Group 6* (his acclaimed debut), offered *Facing It,* the tale of a young man who finally learns to accept his past. *Slowly, Slowly I Raise the Gun* was another gripping mystery by Jay Bennett, who has twice won the Mystery Writers of America's Edgar award for juvenile fiction.

Prizes. The American Library Association's Newbery Medal was given to Cynthia Voigt for *Dicey's Song.* The Caldecott Medal, for the best American picture book, went to Marcia Brown, who illustrated and translated (from French) *Shadow,* an African-influenced dramatic poem by Blaise Cendrars. Maurice Sendak received the 1983 Laura Ingalls Wilder Award, presented every three years to an author or illustrator (published in the United States) whose books are found to have made a "substantial and lasting contribution to literature for children."

New Grimm fairy tale. A manuscript written by the German folklorist Wilhelm Grimm and containing an unpublished fairy tale was the first addition to be discovered to the collection of folktales published by Wilhelm and his brother Jacob in the early 19th century. The story, expected to be published in 1984 with illustrations by Maurice Sendak, tells of a virtuous little girl who is separated from her mother and faithfully serves a saint for 30 years. D.R.

LOUISIANA. *See* STATISTICS OF THE WORLD.

LUXEMBOURG. A major problem facing the center-right Social Christian–Democratic coalition government of Prime Minister Pierre Werner in 1983 was the required restructuring of Luxembourg's steel production, the country's largest industry. Steel production continued to be affected by weak foreign demand and growing international competitiveness. The restructuring measures, including modernization of capacity, further reduction of output, and the elimination of additional jobs, required an increase in government aid of about $200 million during 1983–1984. The government sought to finance the program mainly through added direct and indirect taxes, increased borrowing, and the sale of shares in subsidiaries of Arbed, Luxembourg's largest steel company.

The inflation rate was expected to hover around 9 percent through 1983. Unemployment was expected to be under 2 percent, the lowest level in the European Economic Community. Industrial output, however, was projected to decline by 2 percent.

In March, Parliament approved the creation of a Luxembourg Monetary Institute with authority to issue currency and to establish monetary policy. Formerly, both the issuance of Luxembourg currency and the setting of Luxembourg monetary policy had been regulated by the Belgium-Luxembourg Economic Union. *See* STATISTICS OF THE WORLD. W.C.C.

M

MADAGASCAR. *See* STATISTICS OF THE WORLD.
MAINE. *See* STATISTICS OF THE WORLD.
MALAWI. *See* STATISTICS OF THE WORLD.
MALAYSIA. During 1983 there was a constitutional struggle and a cabinet reshuffle in Malaysia. The government in August rushed through Parliament a series of proposed constitutional amendments, including two amendments intended to curb the power of the king. Under the two amendments, bills passed by Parliament would become law 15 days after being presented to the king, whether he signed

them or not, and the king would no longer have the power to declare a state of emergency. The amendments did, however, require the assent of the king, who appeared strongly opposed, as did the nine hereditary state rulers.

The ruling National Front government underwent a modest cabinet reorganization in early June. Anwar Ibrahim was named minister of culture, youth, and sports, replacing Mokhtar bin Haji Hashim, who had been convicted of murdering a political rival and sentenced to death in March. Chong Hon Nyan was switched from health minister to transportation minister, replacing Lee San Choon; named as the new health minister was Chin Hon Ngiam. Pengiran Othman bin Rauf, who had resigned as minister of federal territory, was replaced in that post by Shahrir Abdul Samad. James Ongkili, a deputy chief minister of Sabah, was named minister without portfolio in the prime minister's department, replacing Mohamed bin Nasir.

Parties within the National Front continued their internal struggles. In particular, there was strong rivalry between Deputy Prime Minister Musa Hitam and Finance Minister Tengku Razaleigh Hamzah for election in 1984 as deputy president of the United Malays National Organization (UMNO), the major party in the National Front. The Sarawak National Party, a National Front member, split over representation of Dayak interests within the party, which was headed by a Chinese, James Wong. Leo Moggie, the national minister of energy, telecommunications, and posts, was among a number of prominent Dayak members who withdrew to form a new National Front party, the Sarawak Dayak Party. Meanwhile, feuding within the Malay opposition Parti Islam (PAS) led to the suspension from the party of former party president Asri Haji Muda in January. Asri and other ousted members later formed a new opposition party, the Hisbul Muslimin (Islamic Front), to be known as Hamim.

In June the largely Chinese opposition Democratic Action Party won its second state by-election in eight months against the National Front. The PAS was less fortunate, as it lost a by-election to UMNO in March.

The economy showed signs of recovery, with growth in real gross domestic product for the year estimated at 5.5 to 6 percent. The growing foreign debt stirred concern; borrowing from international commercial sources exceeded $2 billion during the year, and public debt had doubled since 1980. The 1984 budget, announced in October, cut spending by almost 25 percent.

In foreign affairs, a British decision to give Malaysian students special preference for expanded scholarships provided an impetus for renewing close ties with Britain. After talks in London in March, Prime Minister Mahathir Mohamed announced in April the ending of the "buy British last" campaign that had been in effect for 18 months.

In September, Malaysia revealed that it had sent a commando force to occupy an atoll in the Spratly Islands in the South China Sea. Malaysia also claims another atoll in the Spratly Islands, most of which are occupied by Vietnam.

See STATISTICS OF THE WORLD.   K.M.

MALDIVES. See STATISTICS OF THE WORLD.

MALI. See STATISTICS OF THE WORLD.

MALTA. The Nationalist Party, headed by Edward Fenech Adami, ended its 15-month boycott of Malta's Parliament on March 29, 1983. As conditions for returning to Parliament, the Nationalists had demanded equal access to Malta's government-controlled broadcasting system; a redrawing of the constituency boundaries, which the Nationalists claimed had been gerrymandered prior to the last election; and a promise of early elections. Prime Minister Dom Mintoff reportedly promised his best efforts to fulfill these conditions.

Earlier in the year, the Labor government had taken measures in reaction to the boycott that strained diplomatic relations. For example, on January 10, the Maltese foreign minister sent notes to all diplomatic missions in Malta prohibiting them from making "contacts of any kind with members of the Nationalist Party." Most diplomatic missions objected; on March 11, the European Parliament passed a resolution sharply criticizing the government's action and recommended a cancellation of the European Community's aid to Malta.

Since his socialist Labor Party came to power in 1971, the strongly anticlerical Mintoff, who regards the Catholic Church as an ally of the Nationalist Party, has tried to reduce its influence in this predominantly Catholic country. On June 29 the Labor majority in Parliament unanimously approved a bill that could result in the state's seizure of an estimated 75 percent of church properties, with compensation to be well under current value. The 31 parliamentary members of the Nationalist Party left the chamber in protest without voting. On July 2, the Vatican warned that the seizure of its property would adversely affect "religious peace" on Malta.

See STATISTICS OF THE WORLD.

MANITOBA. *See* STATISTICS OF THE WORLD.

MANUFACTURING INDUSTRIES. In July 1983 the highly regarded National Bureau of Economic Research said that the recession that began in the United States two years earlier had come to an end by December 1982. The economic recovery continued during 1983; in November industrial production chalked up its 12th straight monthly gain; the increase pushed production by U.S. factories, utilities, and mines 16 percent above levels a year earlier. The recession had, however, left some U.S. manufacturing industries, notably steel, in a dangerously weakened state.

Steel. Although the nation's seven largest steel companies lost $3.2 billion in 1982, signs of health in the industry promised to lift some of them to a break-even level by the end of 1983. The long-term outlook for the U.S. steel industry, however, remained clouded. As the "steel intensity" of the U.S. economy, particularly in the huge automobile sector, continued to decline, total steel shipments were expected to drop from the 1982 level of 79.6 million tons to 67–68 million tons in 1983. According to many industry observers, moreover, the major steel producers would be hard pressed to retain their present share of the ever-diminishing steel market in the face of severe competition from low-cost, highly efficient overseas steel producers and domestic mini-mills.

Even with Japan and the European Economic Community agreeing to limit steel exports to the United States, imports accounted for more than 20 percent of the U.S. steel market through the first three quarters of 1983, and their share had been increasing steadily. Unfortunately for American steel producers, the void created by Japanese and European export restraints was quickly filled by low-cost steel from export-hungry Third World countries, especially Brazil and South Korea. Brazilian steel slab, for instance, was being sold in the U.S. market for $125 per ton delivered, or about $100 a ton below the price level at which U.S. producers could make a profit.

Subsidization by the governments involved played a key role in the skewed price patterns, but so too did lower labor costs and more modern facilities. The last two advantages also were enjoyed by U.S. mini-mills–small-scale specialty producers, whose share of the U.S. market rose to about 18 percent in 1983.

Squeezed by a shrinking market on the one hand and fierce competition on the other, the major producers were forced to streamline their operations, principally by shedding excess capacity and boosting the productivity of the operations they retained. Inland Steel, an industry leader in this type of effort, was following a ten-year program to boost return of equipment by cutting costs and raising operating efficiency. After cutting operating expenses by $126 million in 1982, Inland management forecast an additional $97 million in cost cuts in 1983. Eventually, the company hoped to realize a return on equity of 16–18 percent, a dramatic upswing from the 7 percent it had averaged over the previous five years. As for other companies, Bethlehem cut its steelmaking capacity 20 percent over the past few years, and National Steel, principally by selling its Weirton mill to the facility's employees in 1983, lopped off 39 percent of its capacity.

Another aspect of the streamlining process was an attempt by some steelmakers to divest themselves of their least efficient operations and put greater emphasis on more profitable elements. A typical example of this strategy was U.S. Steel's proposal to import steel slab from British Steel's Ravenscraig mill for finishing at the American company's Fairless Works, near Philadelphia. In December, however, U.S. Steel Chairman David M. Roderick announced that the proposed deal with British Steel was off; in addition, he revealed that the company intended to shut down three large plants and trim operations at several other facilities by April 1984, lopping more than 15,000 jobs off its payroll.

Machine tools. After suffering through what one industry spokesman characterized as an "abysmal" year in 1982, the machine tool industry rebounded slowly in 1983. A year-to-year rise of 80 percent in machine tool orders in September marked the eighth monthly increase in the first three-quarters of the year. Both orders and shipments, however, remained at relatively low levels by historical standards. The industry's cautious outlook was summed up in August by National Machine Tool Builders' Association (NMTBA) President John Gray. "It's nice to finally rise above rock bottom. But $170 million in monthly orders is still only half of what we need for a healthy industry."

The most serious long-range threat facing the industry was posed by imports, which in recent years claimed a growing share of the domestic machine tool market. In 1982, imports captured over 40 percent of the U.S. market, and foreign manufacturers appeared certain to match that level of penetration in 1983. Even these alarming industry-wide import figures, however, masked the full magnitude of the threat to domestic machine tool manufacturers. Much of the future of the industry lies in numerically controlled machine tools—the product of the marriage of computers to conventional machine tools. Although this technology was pioneered by U.S. industry, Japanese competitors subsequently took control of large segments of this market—principally, according to U.S. manufacturers, because of special assistance given to Japanese companies by their government. As a result, imports of numerically controlled machine tools came to account for more than 70 percent of the units sold in certain categories.

In response to this perceived threat from abroad, the NMTBA on March 10 petitioned President Ronald Reagan to limit imports of machine tools to 17.5 percent of the U.S. market through 1988. Describing the industry's products as "the tools of production," the petitioners cited the extra time required for retooling in the event of any rearmament program that might result from a threat to the national security. The Commerce Department was evaluating the petition and was slated to make a recommendation to the president by March 1984. A similar petition, submitted by

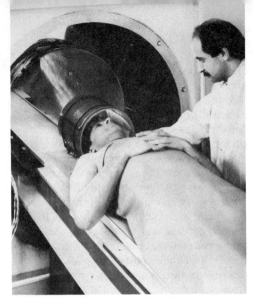

Orders for sophisticated medical diagnostic systems helped boost sales in the electrical machinery industry. Shown here, a nuclear magnetic resonance scanner, which picks up signals from body atoms exposed to a magnetic field.

Houdaille Industries, was denied by the Reagan administration in April 1983.

Paper industry. The U.S. paper industry responded well to the cyclical recovery of the economy in 1983. According to the American Paper Institute, paper and paperboard output was expected to reach an estimated 63.5 million tons in 1983, up from 59.5 million tons in 1982. A key factor in this rise was a growing demand for communication papers (those used in copy machines and computers and in magazines and other periodicals). Orders for packaging paper and paperboard also picked up, as industrial production in general, and the production of nondurable goods in particular, surged in the first nine months of the year. Yet another positive factor for the industry was the conclusion of restrained wage agreements with minimal strike disruptions. Overall, output per manhour at pulp, paper, and board mills was forecast to rise an extraordinary 10 percent in 1983.

Because of the lagging pace of the recovery outside the United States, as well as the strength of the U.S. dollar, U.S. exports of paper through September were down significantly from 1982 levels. Exports of market pulp, however, were expected to increase strongly over previous year levels, as were U.S. exports of paperboard.

Electrical machinery. According to the National Electric Manufacturers' Association (NEMA), electrical products sales in 1983 were expected to regain only about half of the 8.9 percent sales decline registered in 1982. Expected to outpace the industry average, however, were orders for diagnostic imaging and therapy systems (X-ray machines, computerized tomography scanners, and ultrasound and nuclear imaging equipment) and those products included in NEMA's Electronics Division (batteries, residential controls, electrical indicating instruments, semiconductor power converters, electronic power supplies, fire and security signaling systems, and traffic controls).

Textiles. The first half of 1983 presented a generally encouraging picture for the textile industry. Total fiber consumption over the period rose to 5.87 billion pounds, from the 5 billion pounds recorded during the first half of 1982. Similarly, cotton consumption experienced a sharp 17 percent increase (from 3.75 billion pounds to 4.4 billion pounds) on a year-to-year basis. Accompanying these encouraging increases in consumption were gains in textile mill employment, which rose to 750,000 workers by July, and in the length of the average workweek, which reached a comfortable 40 hours by midyear. By September, U.S. textile mills were operating at 84 percent of capacity—their highest level in nearly two years.

Despite these positive signs, however, U.S. textile manufacturers remained worried about imports. Heightening their concern was an agreement reached in July between the United States and China, under which Chinese textile exports will be permitted to grow an estimated 3 percent annually in the period 1983–1987. Although China is only the fourth largest exporter of textiles to the United States (after Taiwan, South Korea, and Hong Kong), industry spokesmen had opposed any increase in its export quota. Better news for U.S. manufacturers was President Reagan's decision, announced on December 16, to adopt new standards that will tighten controls on U.S. textile imports. The new standards could have the effect of keeping out imports from many countries, especially from low-wage countries in the Caribbean and Asia.   L.R.H.

MARYLAND. See STATISTICS OF THE WORLD.

MASSACHUSETTS. See STATISTICS OF THE WORLD.
MAURITANIA. See STATISTICS OF THE WORLD.
MAURITIUS. See STATISTICS OF THE WORLD.
MEXICO. In 1983, Mexican President Miguel de la Madrid Hurtado completed the first year of a six-year term, weighed down by the crushing economic burden he had inherited from former President José López Portillo. In foreign policy, the government participated in initiatives to achieve stability in Central America and maintained close, but at times tense, relations with the United States.

Economic developments. "We have spent beyond our means for a long time, borrowing to make up the difference," de la Madrid recently remarked, and the records backed up his contention. During the 1970's, Mexico had become the fourth-largest oil producer in the world. Taking advantage of record high petroleum prices, both the government and private industry had borrowed freely from foreign sources in a drive to modernize and expand the infrastructure. When oil prices fell in the early 1980's, Mexico had found itself all but unable to make payments on its debts. When de la Madrid took office on December 1, 1982, 40 percent of the population was unemployed or underemployed.

A sweeping austerity program formulated by the new president called for increased taxes on higher incomes, a hike in the value-added tax from 10 percent to 15 percent, a doubling of gas prices, and a 50 percent cut in the budget deficit. Public spending was to be reduced from 16.5 percent of the gross domestic product in 1982 to 8.5 percent of the GDP in 1983. Inflation, officially put at 98.8 percent for 1982, was to be brought down under control, with a target rate of 55 percent for 1983. In return for adopting austerity measures, the International Monetary Fund had agreed in late 1982 to provide $3.9 billion in credits.

A foreign debt of over $80 billion continued to plague the government throughout the year, but Mexico was able to negotiate major rescheduling agreements. In August international creditors agreed to reschedule $11.4 billion in principal payments falling due, and in September Mexico signed another accord with international banks, providing for a rescheduling of another $8.3 billion in public sector debt. Moreover, an agreement was reached in June with 16 international banks on rescheduling a portion of the private sector's $15 billion foreign debt.

By late 1983, Mexico appeared to be coming to grips with the economic crisis. International creditors were heartened during the year by figures showing substantial trade surplus. However, serious problems remained. The trade surplus primarily resulted from strict import controls, low factory output, and the weakened peso. The GDP was expected to decline by about 6.5 percent for 1983 as a whole. Unemployment had reportedly increased even further, and the high rate of joblessness made it possible to hold back large wage hikes demanded by organized labor. Inflation was far from under control—it was running at an annual rate of 80 percent according to official reports, and the government acted to increase prices of controlled items.

Politics and government. De la Madrid's Institutional Revolutionary Party (PRI), which has held a virtual monopoly on political power in Mexico since the 1930's, suffered a record number of reverses in local elections held in five Mexican states on July 3. The PRI's main opposition, the moderately conservative National Action Party, won ten of the 105 mayoralty elections, and another three mayoral

Mexican President Miguel de la Madrid Hurtado dealt with problems of inflation, unemployment, and foreign debt in his first full year in office.

seats went to small leftist parties. The PRI also lost five of the 61 state legislative seats being contested.

In previous years the PRI had not hesitated to resort to fraud in order to hold on to power. Yet in permitting opposition candidates to win some seats this year, the authorities undoubtedly eased political pressures that might otherwise have led to violence. In the same vein, the de la Madrid administration sought popular support by launching a campaign against corruption in government. The most notable case involved Jorge Díaz Serrano, powerful head of Petróleos Mexicanos, the state-owned oil monopoly commonly called Pemex, during the presidency of López Portillo. Díaz Serrano was charged by the government with having defrauded Pemex of $34 million.

Foreign affairs. The government continued to seek a settlement for the conflict in Central America. In January, the foreign ministers of Mexico, Venezuela, Panama, and Colombia met on the Panamanian island of Contadora to discuss holding negotiations to settle the conflict. Later in the year, the four nations—which became known as the Contadora group—issued a 21-point plan for future negotiations, to discuss such topics as the removal of foreign military bases and advisers in Central America, the establishment of international border patrols, and a freeze on the shipment of arms.

Central America dominated Mexican relations with the United States and was the main topic of conversation when de la Madrid met with U.S. President Ronald Reagan on August 14 in La Paz. The two leaders failed to reach any open agreement. U.S.-Mexican relations were further strained by the removal of some 50 items, including Mexican beer, from the U.S. duty-free list, by the issue of illegal immigration to the United States, and by the U.S.-led invasion of Grenada. Despite such sources of tension, relations between the two countries were better than they had been. There was a recognition that support from Washington, including advance payments for oil and credits to purchase U.S. grain, was helping to keep the Mexican economy afloat.

See STATISTICS OF THE WORLD.   J.H.B.

MICHIGAN. See STATISTICS OF THE WORLD.

MICRONESIA. See STATISTICS OF THE WORLD.

Middle East

Lebanon remained the most volatile spot in the Middle East in 1983; the country was the scene of a complex civil war, terrorist bombings, and continued foreign military intervention. The war between Iran and Iraq persisted despite international efforts to end it.

Most of the year's major events centered on Lebanon. The civil war that began there in 1975 erupted again, involving Maronite Christian, Druze, and Muslim factions, and the country was also the scene of fighting between opposing factions of the Palestine Liberation Organization. By year's end, PLO members loyal to Chairman Yasir Arafat had to evacuate their last positions in Lebanon. A U.S.-mediated peace accord failed to achieve a pullout of foreign forces, and Syria and Israel continued to occupy large sections of the country, with the Lebanese government in control only of the Beirut area. The four-nation peacekeeping force, especially U.S. and French troops, became more heavily involved in the action. Terrorist bombings, most of them apparently carried out by Shiite Muslims operating behind Syrian lines, increased the death toll; in the most serious incidents, on October 23, U.S. and French military compounds were devastated by suicide bomb attacks that killed a total of about 300 people.

Lebanese-Israeli agreement. In April, President Ronald Reagan gave Secretary of State George Shultz the task of expediting negotiations to bring about a withdrawal of Israeli, Syrian, and Palestinian forces from Lebanon. Shultz engaged in 12 days of shuttle diplomacy between Beirut, Jerusalem, Damascus, Cairo, and Riyadh, Saudi Arabia, attempting to obtain an agreement among the combatants and support for it from other Arab leaders. Eventually, a bilateral agreement was reached between Israel and Lebanon, which was signed on May 17. Under its provisions, Israel was to withdraw its forces from Lebanon within eight to 12 weeks, provided that Syria and the PLO also pulled out. Although Lebanon and Israel did not establish diplomatic relations, it was agreed that each could set up a liaison office on the other's territory. The pact also designated the southern one-fourth of Lebanon as a security zone, with arrangements for joint Lebanese-Israeli patrols of the area. A joint administrative committee of Lebanese, Israelis, and Americans would be established to take up future questions. Both the Lebanese and Israeli parliaments approved the pact, but Syria rejected it and refused to withdraw its troops. Damascus threatened to "take measures against the Lebanese state" for signing the agreement, arguing that it violated Lebanon's sovereignty and undermined Arab solidarity against Israel.

Lebanese civil war. As it became clear that there was no near prospect of troop withdrawal despite the pact with Lebanon, discontent with the occupation of Lebanon increased in Israel. There were numerous protest demonstrations, and in June the opposition Labor Party called for a unilateral phased withdrawal over the next three months. Continued Israeli casualties and clashes with diverse guerrilla factions finally led to a government decision to withdraw Israeli troops from the Beirut suburbs and the Shouf Mountains and to redeploy them in the south along the Awali River. The decision was taken against U.S. wishes; Washington feared that an Israeli withdrawal would lead to full-scale civil war in Lebanon.

Within hours after Israel's withdrawal from the Shouf, carried out in early September, intense fighting did in fact begin, involving Maronite Christians, Druze, Shiite Muslims, and other ethnic and religious factions as well as the Lebanese Army, which was trying to occupy the region. As the warfare escalated, American and French troops belonging to a

U.S. Secretary of State George Shultz meets with Lebanese President Amin Gemayel (far right) and U.S. special envoy Philip Habib (far left) during the spring in Beirut. Shultz's shuttle diplomacy helped bring about an Israeli-Lebanese agreement for the withdrawal of foreign forces from Lebanon, but the accord fell through because Syria refused to go along.

multinational peacekeeping force (which also included British and Italian troops) were attacked by antigovernment Lebanese. Initially, U.S. Marines in the multinational force withheld their fire, but as the intensity of the attacks mounted, U.S. warships stationed off Beirut shelled the hostile areas. As the Marines became more involved in support of the Lebanese government, and several were killed or wounded during late summmer and early fall, U.S. policy in Lebanon was sharply questioned in Congress. Congress finally approved a resolution involving the War Powers Act and authorizing the Marines' presence in Lebanon for 18 months; it was signed by the president on October 12. The criticism persisted, especially after a terrorist truck bomb attack on a Marine headquarters at the Beirut airport on October 23 resulted in over 240 deaths. A simultaneous attack on the French forces left at least 58 dead. (Earlier in the year, in April, the U.S. Embassy in Beirut was devastated by a similar suicide bombing that killed 63 people.) It was

believed that these attacks were staged by an Islamic extremist group sympathetic to and aided by the Iranian regime of Ayatollah Ruhollah Khomeini and had been undertaken from an area under Syrian control. The attacks were clearly aimed at driving out the multinational force by causing unacceptable losses. In late November the U.S. government said evidence indicated the attack on Marine headquarters had been carried out with the "sponsorship and knowledge and authority" of the Syrian government. All of the countries involved in the peacekeeping force indicated they would continue to maintain troops in Lebanon, although Italy announced it was reducing the number of troops there.

On November 4, a similar truck-bomb attack occurred at an Israeli military headquarters in Tyre, in southern Lebanon, leaving 60 dead. Israel retaliated with air strikes behind Syrian lines; it also sealed off the area it occupied from the rest of Lebanon. Fundamentalist Shiite Muslims also were blamed for terrorist bombings of the U.S. and French embassies and other sites in Kuwait on December 12 that left four dead. A previously unknown group called Black Hand claimed responsibility for later bombing attacks on a French military post and a hotel bar in Beirut, on December 21, that killed at least 19 people.

On November 17, French jets carried out a bombing and rocket attack on a pro-Iranian Muslim militia base near the eastern Lebanon city of Baalbek, in what French officials described as a reprisal for the terrorist attack on French forces.

On December 4, the United States launched an air strike against Syrian antiaircraft batteries that had fired on U.S. reconnaissance planes; two U.S. jets were downed, one airman killed, and another captured by Syria. (He was released on January 3, 1984, during a visit to Damascus by U.S. civil rights leader and presidential candidate Jesse Jackson, a visit aimed at negotiating the flier's freedom.)

Reconciliation talks. On October 31, leaders of Lebanon's main religious and political groups opened a national reconciliation conference in Geneva in an attempt to resolve the antagonisms behind the civil war. It was the first such meeting since fighting broke out in April 1975. Eight Shiite, Sunni Muslim, Druze, and Maronite leaders met under the auspices of President Amin Gemayel, with Syrian and Saudi Arabian representatives present as observers. The primary aim of the conference was to devise a new governing arrangement for the country to replace the constitutional system established in 1943, in which power was distributed proportionately among the country's various religious groups on the basis of the 1932 census. The system worked heavily in favor of the Maronite Christians, then the largest group, and continued to do so even after Muslims came to outnumber them. Lebanon's role in the Arab world and the May 17 peace agreement with Israel were also on the agenda. The talks, however, made little progress on any of these issues and were suspended on November 4. A series of truces arranged by Syria and the Lebanese government also failed to end the fighting.

PLO conflict. While civil war raged among the Lebanese, fighting also broke out between rival PLO factions in the country. A radical faction, based in areas controlled by Syria and supplied with Syrian weapons, rebelled against Yasir Arafat in May. The rebels opposed direct or indirect negotiation with Israel. They objected to Arafat's cautious interest in the Reagan peace plan, which called for the creation of a Pal-

Navy Lieutenant Robert O. Goodman, whose plane was shot down over Lebanon December 4 by Syrian antiaircraft batteries, is shown here in Syrian custody. He was freed on January 3, 1984, after Jesse Jackson, a candidate for the U.S. Democratic presidential nomination, traveled to Damascus and personally appealed to Syrian President Hafez al-Assad for his release.

estinian entity on the West Bank that would be associated with Jordan. They also rejected the Arab League peace plan, adopted at a league summit held in Fez, Morocco, in 1982; the Fez plan, while calling for a fully independent Palestinian state on the West Bank, also envisioned UN guarantees of peace for "all states" in the Middle East (apparently including Israel). The PLO radicals criticized the resolutions of the 16th Palestine National Council session in February, which endorsed the Arab League plan, and objected to Arafat's talks with King Hussein of Jordan on a possible combined Jordanian-Palestinian delegation for regional peace talks. In addition, they accused Arafat's associates of cowardice and poor military planning during the 1982 Israeli siege of Beirut and of corruption and misuse of the organization's funds.

When fighting among the Palestinians began, Arafat seemed to have the upper hand, but the dissidents, with Syrian assistance, had by November driven the pro-Arafat forces into the city of Tripoli in northern Lebanon. Besieged there and facing a humiliating defeat, Arafat arranged for the evacuation of his faction in Greek transport ships flying UN flags. The rebels halted their attack to allow him to leave. Israeli gunboats off the coast, which impeded the evacuation for several days by shelling the port area of Tripoli, also ceased fire, and the evacuation was carried out on December 20. The loss was clearly a major setback for Arafat, but he retained strong support among civilian Palestinians, especially those on the West Bank.

Israel. The effects of the June 1982 Israeli invasion of Lebanon continued to overshadow events within Israel. In February, a special Israeli commission, established to investigate the September 1982 massacre of Palestinians at refugee camps near Beirut, issued its report. While not holding Israeli officials directly accountable, it blamed Defense Minister Ariel Sharon, Army Chief of Staff Rafael Eitan, the chief of military intelligence, and other high-ranking officers for improper supervision of the Christian Phalangist militiamen sent into the camps to weed out terrorists. It called for the resignation of Sharon and the dismissal of other officials. The report also concluded that Prime Minister Menachem Begin and Foreign Minister

A Palestinian camp near Tripoli, Lebanon, is engulfed by the smoke of battle, as Syrian-backed dissidents in the Palestine Liberation Organization seek to dislodge Arafat's loyalists from one of their last strongholds in the region.

Yitzhak Shamir had made certain errors of judgment but did not recommend that they be penalized. The cabinet accepted the report, leading to Sharon's resignation as defense minister; he was, however, reinstated as minister without portfolio. Sharon was replaced as defense minister by Israel's ambassador in Washington, Moshe Arens. In August, Begin, Israel's prime minister since 1977, announced his intention to resign. He had been troubled by poor health and discouraged by the aftermath of the Lebanon war, and he was replaced as prime minister by Shamir. The Shamir government affirmed that it would continue Jewish

251

Israeli soldiers on a bus convoy in central Lebanon warily watch for signs of danger. In September, continuing Israeli casualties and attacks from diverse guerrilla factions helped induce Israel to move its troops southward to more secure positions in Lebanon.

settlement on the West Bank, maintain strict control of Arabs in the occupied territories, resist American pressure for concessions in peace negotiations, and remain in Lebanon until the Syrians and Palestinians withdrew.

The most immediate problem facing the new Israeli leadership was a severe economic crisis, which came to a head in October. After a run on the dollar and mass selling of bank shares, Finance Minister Yoram Aridor proposed replacing the shekel with the U.S. dollar as Israel's currency. His plan was quickly rejected, and Aridor resigned. The government, however, introduced a series of drastic austerity measures, including a substantial devaluation of the shekel and sharp reductions of food subsidies.

Iran-Iraq war. Elsewhere in the Middle East, the war between Iraq and Iran continued, with divisive effects on the Arab world. Syria, Libya, and Iran, at a meeting in Damascus in January, signed a pledge to overthrow Iraqi President Saddam Hussein. In February, Iran opened a major offensive, crossing into Iraq at a point 180 miles from Baghdad; Iran claimed to have recaptured 100 square miles of its own territory

that had been occupied by Iraq. By April, Iraq had become increasingly willing to compromise; it invited Iran's leader, Ayatollah Khomeini, to Baghdad for an Islamic conference on ending the war. Iran, however, had become increasingly belligerent; it threatened to close the Persian Gulf to outside shipping if other nations assisted Iraq, and it refused to agree to a local cease-fire to permit cleanup of a huge oil spill from Persian Gulf oil wells damaged in the fighting. An Iranian offensive into Iraq in the autumn reportedly had some success. Iran condemned the UN Security Council's call in October for a halt to hostilities as motivated by "a satanic spirit" that made the international organization incapable of resolving the conflict. Prospects that Iran might win a significant victory over Iraq aroused anxiety among conservative Arab regimes and in the U.S. government; many observers feared the possible further spread of Islamic militancy after a victory by the Khomeini regime.

See Arab League; Military and Naval Affairs; Palestine Liberation Organization; and articles on individual countries mentioned and other Middle Eastern countries.   D.P.

MILITARY AND NAVAL AFFAIRS. Military conflict in Lebanon heightened during the summer of 1983, and terrorist activity there climaxed in the October 23 bombing of U.S. and French military headquarters, leaving some 300 military personnel dead. It was the worst single day of casualties for U.S. personnel since the Vietnam war. Elsewhere, war between Iran and Iraq dragged on, and the civil war in Chad flared up again. Two days after the Lebanon bombings, the United States led an invasion of the Caribbean island of Grenada.

Within the United States, funds for the controversial MX missile and for preliminary laser weapons research were approved by Congress. Deployment of U.S. Pershing 2 and cruise missiles began late in the year in Western Europe; the Soviet Union meanwhile withdrew from talks with the United States on limiting medium-range missiles; U.S.-Soviet talks on strategic arms limitation (START) and East-West talks on reducing conventional armed forces in Central Europe also recessed indefinitely.

Lebanon. U.S. Marines and other members of the multinational peacekeeping force became increasingly involved in the hostilities in Lebanon. Terrorist attacks posed a very strong hazard. On October 23 a terrorist drove a truck loaded with explosives into a four-story Marine headquarters building adjacent to Beirut International Airport, where some 300 Marines in the U.S. peacekeeping force were asleep for the night. Entering an airport parking lot, the truck had gathered speed to penetrate a wire fence and a barbed wire perimeter, passed between two sentry posts without being fired on, evaded three sewer pipe barriers, and flattened a sandbagged guard booth at the building's entrance, before careening into the ground-floor atrium, where the explosion took place. More than 240 military personnel were killed and over 100 wounded. A similar attack minutes later against French barracks killed at least 58. About two weeks later, a suicide truck-bomb attack on an Israeli command post in southern Lebanon claimed the lives of 29 Israeli soldiers, plus 31 Arabs who had been detained there. The Israelis struck back with air attacks on Arab targets in Lebanon.

The truck-bomb attacks followed a usual pattern in war-ravaged Lebanon, where mass murder had come to serve as political statement. On April 18 a similar explosion at the American Embassy in Beirut had killed 63 people. A report by a special Pentagon commission, released in December, concluded that inadequate intelligence and security measures had played a role in the U.S. tragedy. The report stated that the Marines should not have been concentrated in one building; it also maintained that U.S. objectives, including the safety of the Marines, might have been better served by greater emphasis on diplomatic as opposed to military approaches. President Ronald Reagan announced that he himself accepted full blame for the lack of security and indicated that Marine commanders should not be subject to court-martial proceedings.

Following the October attack, the U.S. Navy assembled an unusually strong fleet in the eastern Mediterranean, including the aircraft carrier *Eisenhower* and the battleship *New Jersey*. On December 4, 28 carrier-based American fighter-bombers attacked Syrian antiaircraft batteries east of Beirut after the Syrians had fired on unarmed American reconnaissance planes. Two aircraft were reported downed, with one airman killed and another captured (later freed by the Syrians through the intervention of Democratic presidential contender Jesse Jackson). Later the same day, eight Marines were killed and two wounded during artillery attacks by Syrian-based militiamen. U.S. warships responded by firing on Syrian antiaircraft batteries east of the Lebanese capital. In mid-December, after reconnaissance planes were again fired upon, U.S. vessels again hit Syrian antiaircraft positions; this time, the *New Jersey* went into action with its heavy 16-inch guns.

Iran-Iraq conflict. The war between Iran and Iraq dragged on, with no decisive gains by either side. Early in the year, France agreed to supply Iraq with five Super Etendard fighter-bombers equipped with Exocet missiles. When the Iraqis said that the missiles might be used against Iranian petroleum installations and tankers, the Iranians threatened to attack Iraq's allies, Kuwait and Saudi Arabia, and to close the Strait of Hormuz, the crucial passageway for tankers carrying Persian Gulf oil to international ports. During November, owners of a

Greek freighter reported a possible hit from an Exocet missile as the ship approached an Iranian port in the Persian Gulf war zone. Meanwhile, communiqués from both Iraqi and Iranian sources during November confirmed strong Iranian thrusts into the northern sector of the war zone. Iran claimed to have wiped out three Iraqi battalions while occupying several villages and border posts. Iraq reported counterattacks that took a heavy toll among opposing forces and also claimed to have destroyed several Iranian vessels.

Chad. In August the intermittent civil war in Chad flared up anew when Libyan ground forces and warplanes intervened in support of the rebel troops of former Chadian President Goukouni Oueddei. The Libyan and dissident forces pushed southward from positions along Chad's northern border with Libya, prompting Chad's president, Hissène Habré, to request outside assistance. Zaire sent garrison troops to relieve Chadian soldiers for combat duty; France came to the aid of its former colony with troops and weapons. The United States, which had already planned the visit of two Awacs planes to Egypt, stepped up its timetable in order to monitor Libyan air strikes in Chad. It also dispatched Redeye antiaircraft missiles, along with American advisers to instruct Chadian troops in their use. The French intervention had the effect of checking the rebel advance; negotiation of the conflict was expected to begin in early 1984, under the auspices of the Organization of African Unity.

Grenada. Near dawn on October 25, some 700 U.S. Army Rangers made a low-level parachute drop at an airstrip under construction on the southwestern tip of Grenada. Thus began Operation Urgent Fury, a startling exercise of American muscle in the Caribbean.

The airstrip itself represented a focal point of American concern over events in Grenada since 1979, when Maurice Bishop, a leftist with a proclaimed admiration for Fidel Castro and the Cuban revolution, took power after a bloodless coup. Grenadian politics drifted sharply leftward, and Cuba began major financing of a new $71 million airport, featuring a 10,000-foot runway capable of handling planes as large as the Boeing 747. The Gren-

U.S. Marines seek cover after landing on Grenada in a Navy helicopter. Thousands of U.S. troops joined in an invasion of the tiny Caribbean island, launched October 25, after a coup overthrew the government.

adian government maintained that the airport was intended to serve what it hoped would become a growing tourist trade, but U.S. military experts, viewing the size of the runway and the extensive fuel storage facilities nearby, regarded the airport as a potential base for Cuban and Soviet military aircraft.

Events took a serious turn in Grenada in mid-October after the arrest of Bishop and the killing of Bishop and others by soldiers loyal to a new hard-line revolutionary military council. American students attending St. George's medical school on the island were restricted to their dormitories, and an American consular official from Barbados who had arrived in Grenada to assess the situation was not reassured, especially when the plane sent to fly him out was not allowed to land. Members of the Organization of Eastern Caribbean States became increasingly alarmed at the political turmoil on the island and asked for U.S. assistance in stabilizing the area. In announcing the U.S. intervention, President Reagan stressed the need to assure the safety of the U.S. students, as well as the need to neutralize the island's strategic location.

Following the Rangers into the airfield at Point Salines were aircraft carrying troops and equipment of the 82nd Airborne Division. Simultaneously, helicopters carried a contingent of about 600 Marines into Pearls airport, the old airfield on the island's north coast. Supported by planes from the aircraft carrier *Independence* and by choppers from the assault ship *Guam*, troops began to roll back rebel defenders, encountering many Cuban personnel. Although the Castro regime had steadfastly claimed that Cubans on the island were construction workers and advisers, American troops reported that they were heavily equipped and well-trained to engage in combat. The day after the landings, the medical students were evacuated by helicopters to the Point Salines airstrip, then flown to the U.S. aboard C-130 transports.

Thousands of American troops took part in the invasion, supported by air strikes. A few hundred additional personnel came from the Caribbean states whose governments were concerned about events on Grenada and about continued stability in the area: Antigua, St. Lucia, St. Vincent, St. Christopher and Nevis

U.S. Marines hit the beaches in Honduras during U.S.–Honduran joint maneuvers, part of the Reagan administration's show of force in Central America.

(St. Kitts–Nevis), Dominica, Jamaica, and Barbados. Some 300 troops from these seven nations were to remain on the island to maintain peace during an interim period and to guard hundreds of Cubans taken prisoner. According to U.S. sources, 59 Cubans were wounded and 25 were killed; prisoners and wounded were soon transferred back to Cuba. American casualties were reported as 18 dead and over 100 wounded. More than 40 Grenadians also reportedly lost their lives. Among the Grenadian casualties were 18 patients in a mental hospital hit in a U.S. air strike; U.S. officials said the hospital had been incorrectly identified as a military target. After the invasion, U.S. troops reportedly found extensive supplies of arms and copies of secret agreements between the Bishop government and the governments of Cuba, the Soviet Union, and North Korea, calling for the delivery of military equipment and the basing of Cuban military advisers. There

A Pershing 2 missile, scheduled for deployment in Western Europe, lifts off in a test launch from Cape Canaveral, Fla. Testing of the Pershing 2, which carries a single nuclear warhead and has a range of 1,000 miles, was successfully completed in September.

was no specific indication, however, that Cuba and the Soviet Union had actually been on the brink of taking over the island.

Central America. The events in Lebanon and Grenada overshadowed huge U.S. military exercises begun in the summer in Central America. The land and sea maneuvers, involving several thousand U.S. troops in Honduras and warships off the coasts of Nicaragua, were scheduled to last until early 1984. The administration announced the maneuvers—intended to demonstrate U.S. commitment to its allies in the area—in July after receiving intelligence reports of a massive influx of Cuban advisers and Soviet-built military gear in leftist Nicaragua. U.S. officials feared that a joint Cuban-Nicaraguan military strike might be launched against Honduras, a U.S. ally. Congressional critics of the Reagan administration argued that the president's aim was not protecting pro-U.S. governments in the region but overthrowing the Sandinista regime in Nic-

aragua. The United States did continue its covert support to anti-Sandinista guerrillas, known as the "contras." Meanwhile in El Salvador, a country allied with the United States, security precautions were tightened to protect U.S. military advisers, after the killing in San Salvador of one of their number, by terrorists on a San Salvador street in late May.

U.S.-Soviet balance. Assessing the balance between U.S. and Soviet forces in 1983, American defense officials noted comparatively higher expenditures by the Soviet Union and a narrower qualitative advantage for the West than in previous years. Soviet forces were enhanced by the new Typhoon-class nuclear submarine, larger than the Ohio-class American subs with Trident missiles. A new Soviet heavy bomber, Blackjack, currently in flight test, was approximately 20 percent larger than the American B-1. The Soviet ICBM force continued to expand. At the same time, the U.S. defense establishment received higher funding and experienced improvements in personnel and hardware.

Missiles and negotiations. After a prolonged congressional struggle, the controversial American MX intercontinental ballistic missile won $4.6 billion in funds for continued research and testing and for deployment of the first 21 missiles in underground silos located in Wyoming and Nebraska. The missile itself had made its first successful test flight in June. In exchange for political support for the MX, President Reagan agreed to be more flexible in arms control discussions with the Soviet Union.

The Reagan administration did soften its insistence in START negotiations that the Soviets gut their force of large, accurate land-based intercontinental missiles, and in early October, Reagan announced a proposal for a "build down" plan, under which two existing nuclear weapons would be destroyed by each side for every new weapon deployed. Despite proposals by both sides, however, START negotiations recessed in December with no progress reported.

There was considerable work on other advanced missile systems. The Navy continued to perfect its Trident 1, a sea-launched ballistic missile, carried by the new Trident nuclear-powered submarines like the U.S.S. *Ohio* and the U.S.S. *Michigan,* which in 1983 were joined by the U.S.S. *Florida.* In addition, the Navy proceeded with work on the advanced Trident 2 missile, scheduled for deployment in 1989.

International controversy continued to swirl around the Pershing 2 missile, built for the Army by Martin-Marietta. The Department of Defense had given production approval in 1982, even though the missile had not been flight-tested. After an abortive first flight during the summer of 1982, the Pershing made a successful launch in the winter of that year, and flight testing was completed in September 1983. Although a number of the trial flights experienced problems, the Pentagon stuck to its original plans for deployment of both Pershing and cruise missiles in Western Europe by the end of 1983. These plans had been subject to change if progress was made in U.S.-Soviet negotiations on medium-range missiles, but despite some proposals by both sides, no prog-

ress was reported. As the first Pershing missiles arrived in West Germany on November 23, the Soviet Union broke off negotiations with the United States on limitation of medium-range nuclear missiles.

The development of cruise missiles also moved rapidly forward. The Tomahawk cruise missile, developed by General Dynamics, was to be delivered in three versions: a ground-launched cruise missile (GLCM) for the Air Force; a sea-launched cruise missile for the Navy (SLCM); and a medium-range, air-to-surface missile (MRASM) for the Air Force. During August, British newspapers reported that nuclear warheads had already been delivered to the United Kingdom; the first GLCM's arrived at Greenham Common air base in mid-November.

The GLCM variant continued to make fully guided test flights in the United States at ranges of up to 800 miles; at the same time, the SLCM successfully began launches from submerged submarines, scoring hits at ranges of several hundred miles. The air-launched cruise missile (ALCM), built for the Air Force by Boeing, was in full production, with increasing numbers in

The U.S. Army introduced a new helmet, of a fiberglass-like material called Kevlar, which is said to offer better protection than the old "steel pot" type. First worn in combat during the Grenada invasion, the helmet drew some complaints because, as a result of its built-in webbing, it could not double as a cooking or washing pot.

operational status aboard B-52 bombers. The Air Force continued development of improved air-to-air and air-to-surface missiles, as well as new antiarmor weapons. The Army and Navy also pursued development of specialized antiaircraft missile systems.

"Star wars." Congress in November approved a final appropriation of $250 billion in defense funds for fiscal 1984, including money for preliminary studies involving various laser weapons, for defense against hostile satellites and ballistic missiles. Despite wide dismay at Reagan's initial endorsement of such a program, dubbed "star wars" research by critics, so-called space-based defensive systems had long been under analysis by U.S. defense agencies. Successful tests of an air-borne laser were conducted against a series of small air-launched missiles, although the Air Force prepared to scale down such efforts in order to acquire increased numbers of more conventional weapons and aircraft required in the next five years. A similar dilemma confronted

the Navy, which reported a shortage of combat planes. Critics continued to question the practicality of such costly items as the MX, which cut deeply into the budget for aircraft, tanks, and conventional arms.

U.S. aircraft. A variety of military aircraft were tested or put into accelerated production in 1983. With an advanced-technology "arrow wing," the F-16XL, manufactured by General Dynamics, began a series of flights to formulate data relative to increased range, payload, and combat speed. The Army's AH-64 helicopter gunship, produced by Hughes, entered volume production during the year, as did the B-1B bomber, produced by Rockwell International. First deliveries of the complex, swing-wing bomber were scheduled for the spring of 1985, with plans for 100 of the Mach 2 bombers to be in service by 1988. The Defense Department also cleared the way for production of the attack version of the F-18, marketed by McDonnell Douglas, whose foreign customers included Canada, Australia, and Spain.

The nuclear-powered Trident missile submarine USS Florida, shown here during commissioning ceremonies in June, was the third Trident-class submarine to join the U.S. Navy's fleet.

U.S. naval vessels. The Navy reported notable progress toward its goal of a 600-ship fleet by the end of the decade, listing 515 ships already in service and more than 100 in various stages of construction in 1983. The recommissioned battleship *New Jersey*, ultimately sent to Lebanon, had been refurbished with new Tomahawk surface-to-surface missiles and the Phalanx close-in weapons support system, in addition to its conventional 16-inch guns. The new Aegis missile cruiser, *Ticonderoga,* was also put to sea, where ocean trials raised the Navy's confidence that missile cruisers could serve as a defense against multiple threats from inbound missiles and aircraft. New contract-management procedures for two new nuclear-powered carriers, the U.S.S. *Abraham Lincoln* and the U.S.S. *George Washington*, were said to represent savings of $750 million. Against reports that contractors had charged thousands of dollars for simple items like wrenches, the Navy and all services instituted new cost-control programs.

U.S. Army weaponry. Production of the M1 Abrams heavy tank was stepped up, from 60 to 70 units per month, and improvements on the M1 and other existing equipment were continued. The Army also took delivery of several new combat weapons. The eight-wheeled Piranha light armored vehicle, equipped with a 25mm rapid-fire gun, began entering military service in late 1983. It provided both Army and Marine formations with a strategically deployable weapon with high tactical mobility and firepower. Additional firepower at the level of the infantry squad was expected to come from a new automatic weapon whose 800-meter range was 50 percent greater than that of the standard M16 automatic rifle. The Army also planned to step up purchases of recent equipment like the M198, a 155mm Howitzer that can be airlifted by helicopter and is capable of firing a variety of conventional explosives as well as nuclear rounds.

Bases and communications systems. The Air Force continued the low-key development of a contingency air base in a remote sector of Egypt. Formal negotiations for a large, permanent base had fallen through, although the Egyptian government agreed to a U.S. presence at a secret base. The base had already been used for deployment of Awacs planes to the Middle East, as well as for various training missions. Preparation of other foreign bases for use by U.S. aircraft and airborne forces was scheduled in Honduras, Liberia, Morocco, and Turkey.

The Navy prepared to enhance the capability of its missile-carrying submarines through a communications system known as Project ELF, for "extremely low frequency" radio waves. Construction was begun in Michigan's upper peninsula during the autumn. Much larger systems had been debated for two decades, but were suspended because of environmental concerns, including concern about low-level radiation effects. The ELF system was smaller and above ground, but it, too, found opponents, who charged that the system would give the United States a first-strike capability for a nuclear war.

See NORTH ATLANTIC TREATY ORGANIZATION, PALESTINE LIBERATION ORGANIZATION, and articles on individual countries mentioned.

R.E.B.

MINERAL AND METAL INDUSTRY. On January 4, 1983, President Ronald Reagan signed a bill reauthorizing the 1980 Deep Seabed Hard Mineral Resources Act for U.S. fiscal years 1983 and 1984. The act was intended to govern seabed mining up to 200 miles offshore until the U.S. government approved an international sea exploration treaty; the United States had declined to ratify the comprehensive Law of the Sea Treaty adopted by the United Nations in 1982.

Differences on an international level also led the United States to curb some of its mineral trade with the Soviet Union. On November 21 the Reagan administration announced that it would ban imports of Soviet nickel, contending that Soviet ingot shipments contained Cuban nickel. A U.S. trade embargo against Cuba has been in force since 1963.

A consortium of three mining companies, headed by CRA Ltd., an affiliate of the Rio Tinto-Zinc Corporation of Great Britain, opened a diamond mine near Lake Argyle, in the state of Western Australia. Experts indicated that the project could become the world's largest diamond-mining operation by 1984. Some 20–25 million carats of diamonds were expected to

Oil drilling rigs are left idle off the Texas coast. As recession and energy conservation caused the demand for oil to plummet, production fell off to the lowest levels since 1972.

be removed each year, for total revenues of more than $160 million at 1983 diamond prices. In a controversial decision, the state agreed to allow most of the mine's output to be marketed by the South African–owned De Beers Consolidated Mines, Ltd., through its Central Selling Organization, which already controlled 80 percent of the world diamond trade.

Drilling began in late 1983 at Noranda Mines Ltd.'s gold-mining operation at Hemlo, Ontario. Two deep holes were to be drilled simultaneously to depths of 6,000 and 8,000 feet. Early estimates were that the new find could yield more than $6 billion in ore, helping Canada retain its position as the world's third largest gold producer.

Also in late 1983, scientists of the U.S. Geological Survey discovered rich undersea deposits of cobalt—a metal widely used in alloys—in the Pacific Ocean between the Ha-

waiian Islands and Samoa. The earth specimens examined by geologists contained cobalt concentrations of 2.5 percent, or twice the amount found previously. The discovery was regarded as important for the United States, which has had to import all its cobalt supplies, mostly from African countries.

Total mineral output. On a worldwide basis, 1983 was a year of very modest recovery for a number of mineral and metal products. Output figures, based on preliminary data, approximated or slightly exceeded the low levels of 1982 for most commodities. However, petroleum, the most valuable single commodity, was a notable exception; a market glut continued in most of the market economy nations, and production was cut back from 1982 levels in an effort to reduce inventories. It was difficult to judge whether the final total value of world crude mineral production would exceed or fall short of the 1982 level of $562 billion, in constant 1978 dollars.

Data compiled by the U.S. Bureau of Mines indicated that, for 1982, the total value of U.S. crude nonfuel mineral production (in current dollars) was $19.8 billion, nearly 23 percent below the 1981 level. On the basis of 1982 figures, the most valuable commodity in terms of value of U.S. crude mineral output was cement; it was followed by stone (crushed and dimension), sand and gravel, copper, and iron ore.

Gold. World gold output in 1983 was estimated at 43.0 million ounces, slightly above the 42.7 million ounce 1982 level. South Africa again accounted for about half of the total, a much larger figure than the one-fifth estimated for the second-ranked Soviet Union. Canada, the United States, and Brazil were next in rank.

Aluminum. In the first half of 1983, world production of aluminum was slightly below that for the corresponding period in 1982. Output was up in Australia and the Eastern European countries but down in the United States, Canada, and Japan. In 1982 world bauxite output fell to 77.1 million tons, an 11 percent drop from 1981, and primary aluminum ingot production dropped 12 percent.

Copper. Preliminary data indicated that world copper output in 1983 slightly exceeded the 1982 level of 8.0 million tons. In 1982, Chile for the first time had become the world's leading copper producer, moving marginally ahead of the United States and accounting for 15.5 percent of the total. This was the result of a 15 percent growth in Chilean output in contrast to a 26 percent drop in U.S output. The decrease in U.S. production was reflected in the closing of the Anaconda Minerals Company's last operating copper mines in Butte, Mont., in 1983.

Iron and steel. World steel output rose by about 2.3 percent in 1983 over the 1982 level of 641 million tons, as most market economy nations slowly began recovering from the recession of the previous years. The Soviet Union remained the leading steel producer, with nearly one-quarter of the total. The upturn in steel production apparently occasioned a small rise in the world iron ore production level from the 795 million tons produced in 1982. In 1982 the Soviet Union led all other iron ore producers, with 30.7 percent of the world output.

Lead and zinc. Lead and zinc—traditionally related because they often occur together in ores—fared differently in 1983. Lead market conditions continued to be poor, but the zinc market seemed to be recovering. Mines in which lead was the predominant mineral received less attention than those primarily producing zinc.

World refined lead output had totaled 5.2 million tons in 1982, slightly below the 1981 level, with the United States the leading producer. Little improvement was expected for 1983. Canada was the leading mine zinc producer in 1982, accounting for 17 percent of the world total of about 6 million tons.

Nickel. World nickel production capacity remained considerably in excess of demand, and production was reduced in 1982. It was expected that final results for 1983 would reflect no significant increases. The Soviet Union ranked first in 1982 mine output, accounting for nearly 28 percent of 608,000 tons produced.

The Noranda Mines Ltd.'s gold-mining operation at Hemlo, Ontario, is shown during a blasting operation. Early estimates are that the new find may yield more than $6 billion in ore, helping Canada retain its position as the world's third leading gold producer (after South Africa and the Soviet Union.

Asbestos. The combination of economic downturn and the potential health hazard of asbestos products continued to cause decline in world output of asbestos in 1983. The Soviet Union accounted for about half of 1982 world production, followed by Canada with almost 20 percent of the total.

See also ENERGY. C.L.K.

MINNESOTA. See STATISTICS OF THE WORLD.

MISSISSIPPI. See STATISTICS OF THE WORLD.

MISSOURI. See STATISTICS OF THE WORLD.

MONACO. See STATISTICS OF THE WORLD.

MONGOLIAN PEOPLE'S REPUBLIC. See STATISTICS OF THE WORLD.

MONTANA. See STATISTICS OF THE WORLD.

MOROCCO. In 1983 there were several developments in the conflict over the Western Sahara, between Morocco, which had annexed the former Spanish colony in 1975, and the Polisario Front, which, backed by Libya and Algeria, was seeking the territory's independence. In August 1982, Morocco, opposing plans to seat a Polisario delegation at the scheduled Organization of African Unity summit, had led a boycott that left the organization unable to assemble a quorum. The OAU finally met in June 1983, after Polisario agreed "temporarily and provisionally" to suspend its OAU membership. The summit directed a seven-nation Implementation Committee, along with the parties to the conflict, to continue to work out plans for a referendum, in which the Western Saharans would decide whether they wanted to be integrated into Morocco.

A lull on the military front was shattered when Polisario launched four attacks in July against the town of Messeid in southern Morocco. In early August, Morocco employed air power to force Polisario to withdraw from the general area of battle. Action between Moroccan troops and Polisario was also reported in late December.

On the diplomatic front, Morocco achieved considerable success in improving relations with both Algeria and Libya. At a meeting in February between Morocco's King Hassan and Algerian President Chadli Benjedid—the first top-level talks between the two countries since the outbreak of the Western Sahara conflict—the leaders agreed on a series of steps toward a normalization of relations. The improvement

in relations with Libya came when Libyan leader Muammar al-Qaddafi suddenly declared that there was no dispute between the two nations and proceeded to visit Rabat from June 30 to July 3. On August 2 a Moroccan ambassador, withdrawn in 1982, was returned to Tripoli. Morocco also strengthened relations with France and Spain, during visits by French President François Mitterrand and Spanish Premier Felipe González.

In domestic politics, Prime Minister Maati Bouabid, presumably on instructions from the palace, in January formed the Constitutional Union Party, a "populist" group viewed widely as an attempt by the government to divide the leftist opposition during the upcoming elections. In June 10 balloting—the first in Morocco in six years—candidates without party affiliation took 22 percent of the contested seats on communal and municipal councils. No single party won more than 18 percent of the seats, and the CU made an unexpectedly strong showing.

The country's economic picture was clouded by a large balance-of-payments deficit, which the government sought to shrink in March by temporarily limiting imports. More drastic measures were taken by a special session of Parliament, which in July amended the national budget to reduce public spending and government subsidies on basic products and to eliminate 19,000 government jobs.

See STATISTICS OF THE WORLD. J.D.

MOTION PICTURES. Films like *Return of the Jedi, Flashdance,* and *Trading Places* were big hits at the box office in 1983; at the same time, with the growing popularity of cable television and videocassettes, more people were watching major movies at home than ever before.

Films of 1983. Movie theater business was booming in the United States and Canada, especially during the summer months. People flocked to see escapist fare all summer long, and the season's box office receipts reached a record $1.5 billion, of which *Return of the Jedi* alone accounted for $232.3 million. Although the popularity of *Superman III* ($62.5 million) and *Octopussy* ($62.9 million)—a new James Bond adventure starring Roger Moore—was expected, there were some surprises. Few would have predicted that *Flashdance* ($87.5

Return of the Jedi *provided more motion-picture magic, as George Lucas brought his* Star Wars *saga to an at-least-temporary halt. In the film, the Ewoks, two of whom are shown here, help the Rebels score a spectacular victory over the evil Empire.*

million) would become a hit, but it was the second most financially successful film of the summer, possibly as a result of extensive promotion over TV channels featuring pop music. Another sleeper was *Trading Places* ($80.6 million), the satirical comedy teaming Eddie Murphy and Dan Aykroyd. Although *Staying Alive* ($58.3 million), directed by Sylvester Stallone and starring John Travolta, was castigated by the critics, it also proved a winner at the box office.

WarGames ($68.2 million), starring Matthew Broderick, not only was a hit but also came to feature in the year's news stories. Some of the events described in this film about high school students who tap into a North American Air Defense computer and almost start World War III, were uncomfortably close to reality. In August the FBI revealed that a group of teenaged Wisconsin computer enthusiasts had electronically broken into and even tampered with a number of government and business computers in the United States and Canada, including one at a U.S. government nuclear weapons facility in Los Alamos, N.M. The break-ins had begun before the release of *WarGames,* but after seeing it, the tamperers began leaving the word "Joshua," the computer's password in the film, as their calling card, and even went so far as to reprogram one computer to respond with dialogue from the film.

A surprising number of this year's films confronted bold themes. *Silkwood,* starring Meryl Streep and directed by Mike Nichols, dramatized the case of Karen Silkwood, who was killed in an automobile accident under mysterious circumstances at a time when she was exposing alleged health hazards at a plutonium processing plant. One of the most daring films of the year was *Daniel,* directed by Sidney Lumet and scripted by E. L. Doctorow from his 1971 novel *The Book of Daniel,* suggested by the controversial Rosenberg spy case of the 1950's. Attitudes toward the film were inevitably related to how critics and viewers felt about the execution of Julius and

263

Ethel Rosenberg after their conviction for conspiracy to commit espionage.

Other topical films included *Under Fire,* starring Nick Nolte, which dealt with events in Nicaragua in the period just before the fall of the Somoza regime, and *The Final Option,* about antinuclear terrorists who infiltrate peaceful antinuclear groups and take over the American embassy in London. Costa-Gavras, long known for politically controversial films, such as *Missing,* cowrote and directed *Hanna K.,* which starred Jill Clayburgh as an American lawyer in Jerusalem who becomes involved in Israeli-Arab strife.

The Right Stuff, based on Tom Wolfe's book, indirectly bore upon the American political arena, since the dramatization recalling the heroism of the seven original U.S. astronauts included Ed Harris's portrayal of John Glenn, who was seeking the Democratic nomination for the presidency. The film walked a thin line between showing his stuffy side and reminding moviegoers of the courage it took to soar aloft during the pioneering days of the space age; the overall depiction of Glenn was generally considered favorable.

Bob Fosse's *Star 80* examined the frenzied search for success in the tinseled world of centerfold modeling; the film dealt with the murder of the model Dorothy Stratten by her estranged husband Paul Snider, who then committed suicide. The turbulent period of the late 1960's was recalled in Lawrence Kasdan's *The Big Chill,* about former college classmates who gather at a funeral and proceed to measure their current lives against their activist idealism while in school. Woody Allen was acclaimed for *Zelig,* his fanciful "documentary" about the life of a nonentity who, in Allen's screenplay, becomes a celebrity when he's discovered to be a human chameleon capable of turning into whatever type of person he's with. The film reflected the enormously detailed work required to insert Zelig (Allen) into 1920's and 1930's film clips and to match the visual and musical style of the period.

Mel Brooks was back with *To Be or Not to Be,* a remake of the 1942 Ernst Lubitsch comedy that starred Jack Benny. Other comedies included *The King of Comedy,* directed by Martin Scorsese, and Carl Reiner's *The Man With Two Brains,* starring Steve Martin. From Britain came *Monty Python's The Meaning of Life, Local Hero* by the Scottish director Bill Forsyth, and *Britannia Hospital,* Lindsay Anderson's spoof on contemporary British social conditions.

Britain's Ben Kingsley, who had scored a triumph in the title role of *Gandhi,* starred in *Betrayal,* based on Harold Pinter's play about a love triangle. Sean Penn, sometimes com-

Fast Eddie

Inventive, insouciant, and in a hurry, comic actor Eddie Murphy turned 22 in April and signed a $15 million, five-picture contract with Paramount Pictures in June. A star of TV's late-night comedy revue *Saturday Night Live* since 1980, Murphy has already appeared in two smash-hit films—*48 Hrs.* (1982) and *Trading Places* (1983)—and has created a gallery of instantly recognized characters, including militant film critic Raheem Abdul Muhammad and Mister Robinson, a ghetto-style version of TV's kindly Mister Rogers. In the fall, Murphy released his second album, cohosted the 1983 Emmy awards ceremony on television, and prepared to shoot his third movie, *Best Defense,* costarring Dudley Moore. The Brooklyn-born Murphy, who makes a point of stating that he does not smoke, drink, or use drugs, says his only vices are jewelry and fast cars.

Eddie Murphy

pared to Marlon Brando, appeared in *Bad Boys*. Vincent Spano was noticed for his work as a young working-class loser in *Baby, It's You*, John Sayles's first "commercial" film, and Kate Nelligan was praised for her acting in *Without a Trace*. Veteran character actor Robert Duvall starred in *Tender Mercies*, and also stepped forward as a director with *Angelo, My Love*, a film about a precocious gypsy boy whom Duvall had met. Another veteran actor, Sean Connery, once more put his stamp on the James Bond character by returning as agent 007 in *Never Say Never Again*, the second Bond film released this year. After a lifetime of character parts, Richard Farnsworth finally played a starring role and was lauded as the train robber in *The Grey Fox*. Barbra Streisand gained new prominence as the director and star of *Yentl*.

Late in the year, *Terms of Endearment*, with Shirley MacLaine, Jack Nicholson, and Debra Winger, won critical praise and also was doing well at the box office.

The most sophisticated film import to the United States was Ingmar Bergman's *Fanny and Alexander*, a three-hour drama about a theatrical family in Sweden in the early 20th century. Despite an earlier announcement that it was his farewell to cinema, Bergman continued making television films, and since these have been shown theatrically, there was every indication that the world would continue to see new works by the master. Another import was the late Rainer Werner Fassbinder's *Berlin Alexanderplatz*, a made-for-television series that ran 15½ hours and was shown theatrically in installments. Films from France included Andrzej Wajola's *Danton*, a political parable about the French Revolution starring Gérard Depardieu; Ettore Scola's *La Nuit de Varennes*, a dramatization of imagined events and relationships surrounding Louis XVI and Marie Antoinette's flight from Paris during the Revolution; Daniel Vigne's *The Return of Martin Guerre*, based on an actual 16th-century case in which a man who had disappeared returned many years later to his village and wife and had to face a trial to determine if he was who he claimed he was; and Eric Rohmer's *Pauline at the Beach*, a contemplative view of romantic love and misunderstandings. Michael Ver-

The seven original Mercury astronauts are portrayed in The Right Stuff; Ed Harris (back row, far right) plays the part of John Glenn, the earth-orbiting astronaut who later became an Ohio senator and a candidate for the Democratic presidential nomination.

hoeven's *The White Rose*, a docudrama about five university students and a professor who defied the Nazis and were executed, was a West German import. From Italy came a restored version of the late Luchino Visconti's 1963 film *The Leopard*, which had been cut for its original release. (This was a big year for restoration: *A Star Is Born* was also reconstituted in its longer version.) *La Traviata*, directed by Franco Zeffirelli, was a presentation of Verdi's opera with performances by Teresa Stratas and Placido Domingo.

Home movies. Although Americans were flocking to movie theaters, they were also seeing more films in their own homes, either

265

by subscribing to cable networks or by buying or renting prerecorded videocassettes. With more than 6 million homes owning videocassette recorders, the number of stores throughout the country where cassettes could be purchased or rented was approaching the 10,000 mark. Previously, X-rated movies had accounted for the major share of the market. But the proportion had changed considerably as the novelty of pornography wore off and current major movies became more readily available, often shortly after their release. Feature films came to dominate the videocassette market. During 1983, Hollywood film studios were projected to earn an estimated $240 million in cassette royalties, a figure representing about 7 percent of the total studio income.

The industry was growing so rapidly in 1983 that piracy became an increasing problem. In some cases, no sooner was a film released than it began turning up on illegal cassettes throughout the world. Studios took extra precautions to guard prints so that they were not "borrowed" from theaters overnight and copied. For example, *Return of the Jedi* was reportedly stolen six times within two weeks. Hollywood was also plagued by the common practice of recording films from television, which enables viewers to develop home libraries without paying royalties to studios or performers.

One of the giants of the television cable industry, Home Box Office, a division of Time, Inc., took the bold step of producing its own films specifically for cable. Its solid financial position offered the possibility of signing top stars, as was the case with *Mr. Halpern and Mr. Johnson,* starring Sir Laurence Olivier and Jackie Gleason, and *Between Friends,* teaming Elizabeth Taylor and Carol Burnett.

The studios themselves also were getting involved. A joint venture went into effect in August between Warner Brothers and the owners of two major cable services—Showtime, HBO's closest competitor, and The Movie Channel, the third largest cable movie service.

Academy Awards. The epic *Gandhi* won eight Oscars at the 55th annual Academy Awards ceremony, with *E.T., the Extra-Terrestrial* relegated to minor honors despite its starring performance at the box office. *Gandhi* won for best picture, best original screenplay (by John Briley), best director (Richard Attenborough), and best actor (Kingsley). It also took the awards

Woody Allen's Zelig, *the story of a human chameleon who could ingratiate himself with any group, won critical acclaim for its technical virtuosity and its wry, satirical treatment of American infatuation with oddities. Shown here, Allen in the title role, with costar Mia Farrow at his side.*

Shirley MacLaine and Debra Winger are shown in a touching scene from the film Terms of Endearment. *Playing mother and daughter roles, MacLaine and Winger were both lavishly praised by critics.*

for best cinematography, editing, art direction, and costume design. Meryl Streep was named best actress for her performance in *Sophie's Choice*. In the supporting categories, Louis Gossett, Jr., won for his portrayal of the tough drill instructor in *An Officer and a Gentleman,* and Jessica Lange for her role as Dustin Hoffman's girlfriend in *Tootsie*.

Tara still tops. With inflation, every blockbuster that comes along changes the lineup in the competition for all-time box office champion. But a ranking that treats movies from the 50-cent ticket era like those of today doesn't give a true picture of relative popularity through the years. The editors of the trade newspaper *Variety* and the management advisory firm Laventhol & Horwath devised a study that took inflation into account, figuring "constant millions" as adjusted by ticket price increases. On an unadjusted basis, *Gone With the Wind* had sunk to 13th place in the *Variety* listings. But fans of the 1939 epic were happy to learn that with inflation taken into account, it was still the number one film of all time in box office receipts.   W.W.

MOZAMBIQUE. The year 1983 witnessed continuing military pressure on the Mozambique government of President Samora Machel, from neighboring South Africa and from the Mozambique National Resistance (MNR), a guerilla movement said to be sponsored by South Africa. South Africa, in its conflict with the African National Congress (ANC)—an indigenous movement opposed to white majority rule in South Africa and operating in part out of Mozambique—carried out attacks in May and October against presumed ANC centers in Maputo, the Mozambican capital. The raids were made in reprisal for earlier ANC bomb explosions in South Africa. South Africa claimed that 64 people were killed in the May raid; Mozambique put the total at six. Meanwhile, the MNR extended its guerrilla activities to eight of Mozambique's ten provinces, inducing President Machel to personally assume the defense ministry and step up his military campaign against the rebels. A number of captured rebels were executed.

The fourth congress of the ruling Frelimo Party was held in late April. Decisions made by the 667 delegates reflected a new emphasis on decentralization. The Central Committee was doubled in size, to accommodate newcomers. The congress voted to put greater stress on small-scale projects, less dependent on capital and scarce technical skills.

267

Mozambican and South African officials met periodically in an effort to halt the deteriorating security situation in their countries. Mozambique also met several times with U.S. officials, asking them to urge restraint on South Africa. In July the United States named its first ambassador to Maputo since six U.S. diplomatic personnel were accused of spying and expelled from Mozambique in March 1981.

Mozambique's largely agricultural economy was devastated by what many believed to be the worst drought in the country's recorded history. One-third of the total population was estimated to be directly affected, and agricultural production in six of ten provinces was cut by as much as 80 percent.

See STATISTICS OF THE WORLD.   W.M.

MUSIC. Of the diverse events and trends in the music world during 1983, the following were among the most outstanding:

POPULAR MUSIC

If the year 1983 in popular music could be summed up in a single word, that word would be "electronic." Electronic sounds dominated both white and black pop music, and the electronic medium of television roared onto the scene, radically changing the marketplace in every type of pop music except jazz. Paradoxically, jazz musicians retreated from the electronic onslaught and found their most satisfying moments in reviving the acoustic jazz tradition.

Rock. In the world of rock 'n' roll, "videos" (that is, videotapes of live performances) dominated the scene. Leading the way was Warner/Amex's MTV (Music Television), a cable television station that offered rock video music 24 hours a day. By mid-1983, MTV had become the highest-rated 24-hour U.S. cable service ever, and a successful video was doing for an unknown act what a hit single used to do. Previously unknown heavy-metal bands such as Def Leppard, obscure British bands such as Duran Duran, and canny old-timers such as ZZ Top all turned MTV exposure into gold, and most of the year's top ten records probably would not have reached that exalted status without MTV exposure.

The one dark cloud over MTV was the allegedly racist nature of its programming. In midyear a rumor circulated that CBS Records President Walter Yetnikoff had threatened to withdraw all CBS videos from the channel unless it reconsidered its refusal to play videos

David Bowie's world-wide concert tour, his first in years, was a smash hit, and one of the few rock tours to make money in 1983.

An undaunted Diana Ross continued singing in the rain at a free concert in New York's Central Park that had drawn hundreds of thousands of her fans. When the storm increased, the vast audience was urged to leave slowly and return the next night.

from the year's best-selling album, *Thriller,* by black singer Michael Jackson. CBS denied the rumors, and MTV denied that it had refused Jackson's video on racial grounds. Immediately after the charges flew, MTV broadcast Jackson's "Billie Jean" video, as well as videos by Prince and Eddy Grant—black artists with heavy rock content in their music and considerable rock followings. "Billie Jean" and, later, Jackson's "Beat It" became two of the station's biggest hits. Jackson also teamed with Paul McCartney to create an elaborate ($300,000) video based on their hit single "Say, Say, Say."

MTV was not the only public outlet for rock videos. Most new-music clubs and discos had begun to feature video as part of their entertainment mix, along with records and/or live music, and there were numerous special video programs on cable television.

The Police, arguably the biggest-selling band in the world these days, mounted a very successful tour (copromoted by MTV), as did David Bowie, who had not toured in many years. Those were among the few tours to make money, however. Even such dependable stadium-fillers as Journey played to half-empty

houses. One concert that did make a splash— although not entirely in the way its promoters intended—was Diana Ross's performance before a vast throng in New York's Central Park. The July 21 show was cut short by a heavy thunderstorm. Also, at a rescheduled performance the next night, hundreds of youths rampaged through the park and the surrounding area, assaulting and robbing numerous concertgoers and passersby.

Record officials have noted that the United States is now the largest Spanish-language record market in the world, and Hispanic performers were increasingly seeking to appeal to non-Hispanic American audiences as well. Spanish crooner Julio Iglesias had a successful North American tour in 1983 and was cutting his first English-language record. In the field of rock music itself, RCA Records signed a long-term, multimillion-dollar contract with the Puerto Rican teen pop group Menudo, which was scheduled to release its first English-language album in early 1984.

The most notable death in the rock world was that of Dennis Wilson, drummer and singer of the Beach Boys; he drowned after diving

Fans of Menudo, a musical group of five Puerto Rican boys aged 13 to 15, turned out en masse for the group's U.S. tour. Menudomania came complete with Menudo T-shirts, jeans, and schoolbags.

from a boat in Marina del Rey, Calif., on December 28. Earlier in the year, Chris Wood, a founding member of the 1960's rock band Traffic, succumbed to severe liver problems caused by overdrinking, and Pete Farndon, bassist with the ill-fated British/American band the Pretenders, died of complications arising from drug abuse.

Soul. The black pop music scene was dominated by the runaway success of *Thriller,* which spawned an unprecedented five top-ten singles and sold over 5 million copies. That was only half of the story, however. Another large segment of the black record market was claimed by heavily electronic records featuring synthesized percussion, electronically altered vocals, and bizarre sound effects. This sound came principally from the New York dance club scene, where records by British electronic bands were combined with the latest "street sound" experiments.

Arthur Baker's Streetwise Records produced such remarkable electronic dance records as Afrika Bambaataa's "Searching for the Perfect Beat," a runaway-smash followup to last year's "Planet Rock," and even injected funk into the dark vision of England's New Order. Baker's other notable success was New Edition, a group of young blacks from Boston who sounded uncannily like the early Jackson Five.

Integral to the black music scene were break dancing and electro-boogie, two innovative dance styles that first got national exposure in a very brief scene in the movie hit *Flashdance.* In the film, a New York break-dance troupe called the Rock Steady Crew demonstrated the whirling, spinning, elastic dance style that youngsters perform on New York street corners for tips. Electro-boogie, in contrast, is performed by a line of dancers who move only isolated parts of their bodies to the music and pass the movement along the line.

Black pop music lost a great pioneer when Muddy Waters, born in Mississippi in 1915, died in his sleep on April 30 at his suburban Chicago home. Waters brought electricity to the Chicago blues scene, while retaining the Delta-blues guitar style he grew up with. He had been all but forgotten by the time the Rolling Stones took their name from one of his songs and recorded several other of his works, and he always thanked "those British cats" for reviving his career, which continued successfully until shortly before he died.

Country. Country got its own cable station, The Nashville Network, launched in March by Group W Satellite Communications and WSM, Inc. (owners of the Grand Ole Opry in Nashville). However, TNN was criticized for uninspired programming and failure to attract enough top-rate country performers. Another electronic highlight of the country year was country music's first sophisticated MTV-type video, a treatment of the Willie Nelson/Merle Haggard duet "Pancho and Lefty" that won awards and was one of country's top-selling records. (The video was ignored by MTV itself.) In fact, 1983 seemed to be the year of the duet, with Moe Bandy and Joe Stampley, Gary Stewart and Dean Dillon, Kenny Rogers and Sheena Easton, Dolly Parton and Lionel Ritchie, along with Nelson and Haggard, riding the charts with duets.

The new wave of country traditionalists gained ground on the airwaves, as the fad-oriented country stations founded around the time of the "urban cowboy" boom started to decline in number. John Anderson managed a pop crossover with "Swingin'," and George Strait's no-nonsense honky-tonk music continued to sell well. Ricky Skaggs not only had success with his own bluegrass-tinted music, but also was the producer of the Whites, a family (actually, his in-laws) bluegrass group that scored several hits. Finally, Delia Bell, a newcomer if not a youngster, made an album of songs that could have been released in 1960, and it was hailed as a masterpiece.

Jazz. Except for jazz-funk musician Herbie Hancock's hit record "Rockit," jazz was conspicuously nonelectronic in 1983. The newest jazz sensation was a 19-year-old trumpeter from New Orleans, Wynton Marsalis, who played a very conservative type of postbop that would not have been out of place in the 1950's and also released a highly regarded album of trumpet concertos by classical composers. Other young stars—guitarist Kevin Eubanks, flutist James Newton, saxophonists Chico Freeman, Hamiet Bluiett, and Paquito d'Rivera—also found both commercial and critical success in the same way. Newton and pianist Anthony Davis, among others, also turned out works that resembled European classical music

Romantic Crooner with a Worldwide Audience
One of the most successful recording artists of the century, Spanish singer Julio Iglesias was relatively unknown in North America until 1983, when he made a triumphant concert tour of the United States and Canada. He also recorded his first U.S. album, *Julio*, featuring ten of his biggest hits in six languages; a second album, sung entirely in English, was scheduled for early 1984 release. His skilled timing and casual, understated style bring a dramatic, emotional intensity to his performances; charm and movie-star good looks add to his appeal. Born in 1943, Julio Iglesias de la Cueva took up the guitar and started writing songs 20 years later, while recovering from an automobile accident. His career took off after he won a Spanish song contest in 1968. He is now said to have sold over 70 million albums worldwide, and his multilingual concert tours have taken him to as many as 46 countries in a single year.

Julio Iglesias

Gunnar Thygesen, librarian of the Odense Symphony in Denmark, proudly displays the earliest Mozart symphony. Composed when Mozart was about nine, it had been missing for 200 years; Thygesen discovered the manuscript tucked away in an old cellar.

as much as jazz—another trend of recent years that continued in 1983.

Not that electronic, funk-oriented jazz completely disappeared. It became apparent that Ornette Coleman's "harmolodic" language (a freely improvisational, atonal style) was best suited for electric instruments, both in Coleman's own Prime Time band and in ensembles by past and present Coleman sidemen such as Jamaaladeen Tacuma, Tonald Shannon Jackson, and James "Blood" Ulmer.

As always, jazz record labels operated on a shoestring, few radio stations played anything except the most blatantly commercial forms of jazz, and nightclubs and other performance spaces found it commercially difficult to present much jazz. Even the annual Kool Jazz Festival in New York, the successor to the Newport Jazz Festival, was poorly attended and aesthetically unsatisfying this year.

Jazz lost a pioneer with the death on April 22 of Earl "Fatha" Hines, a pianist whose "trumpet" style of playing (melodic improvisations in the treble range) influenced several generations of musicians. Another seminal figure, pianist-composer Eubie Blake, died on February 12 in New York City. Blake's ragtime compositions greatly influenced the development of early jazz.   E.W.

CLASSICAL MUSIC

The New York Philharmonic presented a special spring festival of modern music called "Horizons '83: Since 1968, a New Romanticism?" The Metropolitan Opera's centennial was launched with an afternoon and evening gala in October, featuring 100 artists in arias, duets, and ensembles. The New York City Opera faced a 54-day strike by musicians that forced cancellation of a major portion of the summer-fall season.

Operatic variety. Elsewhere in the operatic field a healthy variety and venturesomeness prevailed. The Los Angeles Opera Theater gave the first U.S. performance of Iain Hamilton's *Anna Karenina*. The Minnesota Opera presented the premiere of William Mayer's *A Death in the Family*, based on the novel by James Agee. The Waterloo Festival in New Jersey offered the first U.S. hearing of Wagner's second opera, *Das Liebesverbot* (The Edict Against Love) in a concert performance, an event of considerable historic interest. In San Diego, Saint-Saëns's little-known *Henry VIII*, in its U.S. premiere, provided a fine vehicle for baritone Sherrill Milnes. In Boston, Rimsky-Korsakov's *The Legend of the Invisible City of Kitezh and the Maiden Fevronia* was given its U.S. premiere by the Opera Company of Boston. Both praise and harsh criticism greeted Leonard Bernstein's new 110-minute *A Quiet Place*, given its world premiere in June by the Houston Grand Opera. Written as a sequel to *Trouble in Tahiti* (and presented with that work as a double bill), *A Quiet Place*, Bernstein's first opera in more than 30 years, encompassed contemporary themes of suicide, homosexuality, and mental illness.

Television made a serious contribution to opera by presenting the entire cycle of Wagner's *Der Ring des Nibelungen*, a videotape of the controversial Patrice Chereau-Pierre Boulez production at Bayreuth, West Germany.

The San Francisco Opera presented new productions of *Das Rheingold* and *Die Walküre,* with helmets, armor, and shields suggesting a kind of realism out of fashion in post–World War II Wagnerian presentations. A complete *Ring* cropped up in an unlikely place when conductor John Balme brought his Boston Lyric Opera Company into New York City's ramshackle Beacon Theater and amazed the public and critics with a convincing series of performances using minimal sets and mostly unknown singers. At the Spoleto Festival U.S.A. in Charleston, S.C., film director Ken Russell had his way with Puccini's *Madama Butterfly,* turning the heroine into a pre-Pearl Harbor prostitute and climaxing the opera with the atomic blast over Nagasaki. New York opera lovers responded warmly to the first U.S. visit of the Finnish Opera, which came to the Met with two impressive contemporary works, Joonas Kokkonen's *The Last Temptations* (1975) and Aulis Sallinen's *The Red Line* (1978).

Instrumental music. In the instrumental field, there was a generous array of premieres in 1983. Joseph Schwantner's *New Morning for the World,* written in celebration of Martin Luther King's 54th birthday, was performed at the Kennedy Center in Washington, D.C., by the Eastman Philharmonic. Dominick Argento's *The Andres Expedition,* a dramatic song cycle based on the journals of three Swedish explorers, was compellingly sung in a St. Paul, Minn., recital by Swedish baritone Hakan Haggegard. At the San Francisco Symphony, Vivian Fine's five-movement *Drama for Orchestra* (inspired by paintings by Edvard Munch) proved particularly evocative in the movement devoted to *The Scream.* Elliott Carter's characteristically complex new work, *Triple Duo,* was premiered in New York City by a visiting English group, The Fires of London.

Not all the premieres were of recent works. A remarkable 1948 violin concerto by the neglected American pioneer composer John J. Becker was finally heard in 1983, performed by Gregory Fulkerson with the Chattanooga Symphony. More of a curiosity was the unveiling in California, by Berkeley's Arch Ensemble for Experimental Music, of Ezra Pound's "opera" *Cavalcanti*—less a stage work than a song cycle based on poems by Dante's 13th-century predecessor Guido Cavalcanti. George Antheil's Violin Sonata No. 1, which caused a scandal at its 1923 premiere in Paris because of its barbarous rhythms and percussive effects, was successfully (and unscandalously) performed in Buffalo, N.Y., by violinist Thomas Halpin and pianist Yvar Mikhashoff. Perhaps the most unlikely premieres of all involved a piano trio by Debussy, played for what was believed to be the first time by the Western Arts Trio in Saratoga, Wyo., and the first

As the Metropolitan Opera in New York City celebrated its 100th birthday, it continued to serve as the showplace for great singers such as Placido Domingo, shown here in Berlioz's Les Troyens.

performance in the United States of a reconstruction of Schubert's Symphony No. 7 in E Major, presented by the Youth Symphony Orchestra of New York.

Mozart symphony found. The first symphony composed by Wolfgang Amadeus Mozart was discovered in manuscript form in Denmark early in 1983. The symphony, written in A minor, was believed to have been composed in London in 1764 or 1765.

Awards and appointments. Honors went to such music figures as composer Ellen Zwilich, who became the first woman to win the Pulitzer Prize for composition; pianist Jeffrey Kahane, who won the Arthur Rubinstein International Piano Competition; and composer Elliott Carter, who received the Edward MacDowell medal in recognition of a lifetime of achievement. Violinist Elmar Oliveira received the Avery Fisher Prize, and Van Cliburn was honored with the Albert Schweitzer Music Award for a life's dedication to music and humanity.

In September, the Metropolitan Opera announced the appointment of James Levine to the post of artistic director, with a five-year contract beginning with the 1986–1987 season. Levine will continue as the Met's music director and principal conductor until 1986. Boston opera director Sarah Caldwell was appointed artistic director of the New Opera Company of Israel; San Francisco Symphony conductor Edo de Waart accepted the position of music director and principal conductor of the Netherlands Opera beginning in 1985; and Stanislaw Skrowaczewski, conductor emeritus of the Minnesota Orchestra, was appointed principal conductor of the Hallé Orchestra. U.S. orchestras were also involved in musical chairs: Gerard Schwarz was named music adviser to the Seattle Symphony, Sergiu Comissiona was appointed music director of the Houston Symphony, and Swiss conductor Charles Dutoit was made principal guest conductor of the Minnesota Orchestra. Raymond Leppard assumed the same position with the St. Louis Symphony, and Joseph Silverstein was named artistic director of the Utah Symphony. In the opera field, Speight Jenkins, Metropolitan Opera television commentator, was appointed general director of the Seattle Opera, succeeding Glynn Ross.   S.F.

RECORDINGS

The compact disc (CD) hit the U.S. market in 1983. For several years, the "digital" LP— actually a hybrid since it was digitally recorded (that is, produced from a magnetic tape on which sound waves have been represented in numerical digits) but reproduced analogically, that is, on continuous tracks—had confused record buyers and aroused misgivings about the technique's vaunted potential. Once the average listener got to hear fully digital sound (reproduced on digital playback equipment), however, most of the doubts dissipated. Despite retail prices ($20–$25) double those of LP's, initial demand was enthusiastic, far outstripping supply. With only two CD manufacturing facilities functioning, in West Germany and Japan, the catalog seemed destined to remain sketchy for some time; other plants were under construction, including one by CBS in the United States.

Many early CD's have been hybrids of another sort—analog recordings digitally reproduced. Perhaps the intention was to reassure collectors that earlier recordings, too, stand to gain from the new technology's enhanced clarity and dynamic range (despite having the "faults" exposed in production techniques that were never intended to face such merciless scrutiny). This diversity and the burgeoning new series of cassette reissues, at both bargain and premium prices, together suggest the possibility of a brave new LP-less world—with new issues and major rereleases appearing on CD and with other catalog items recycled on cassette. One bellwether series, from In Sync Laboratories, applied "high-tech" cassette processing to historic recordings (by Karl Muck, Albert Coates, and others), to good effect.

Celebrations. As if to demonstrate its continuing sway in the classical recordings market, Deutsche Gramophon (DG) mounted yet another of its monumental celebrations. Just a year after its voluminous commemoration of the Berlin Philharmonic centennial, the German label did for Brahms's sesquicentennial what it had done for Beethoven's 1970 bicentennial, releasing the composer's complete works—62 discs in eight volumes. Some of the performances were reissues, such as Herbert von Karajan's symphonies with the Berlin Philharmonic (Leonard Bernstein's set with the Vienna Philharmonic was apparently not completed in time). Many others were new, including nine of the ten discs of songs, by Jessye Norman and Dietrich Fischer-Dieskau; the four discs of choral-orchestral works, with the Czechoslovakian Philharmonic Orchestra and the Prague Philharmonic Chorus conducted by Giuseppe Sinopoli; and another six discs of a cappella choruses led by Günter Jena. Among other important Brahms releases was a five-disc set of piano works and concertos by Claudio Arrau; this was itself part of another massive tribute—59 discs in all, reissued by Philips to mark the pianist's 80th birthday.

Ironically, given the time-honored animosity between the composers' camps, this Brahms year was also the 100th anniversary of Wagner's death. Much activity centered upon reissues, notably a seven-disc selection of historic material, "Wagner on Record, 1926–42" (Seraphim), and Wilhelm Furtwängler's 1950 La Scala Der Ring des Nibelungen, with Kirsten Flagstad (Fonit-Cetra). These were, however, significant new releases: Bernstein's Tristan und Isolde, with Hildegard Behrens and Peter Hofmann (Philips), recorded one act at a time at three widely spaced concerts, and Armin Jordan's Parsifal, with Yvonne Minton, Reiner Goldberg, and Robert Lloyd (Erato), recorded specifically to provide a sound track for Hans-Jürgen Syberberg's eccentric film interpretation.

Opera and song. A bold new German label, Orfeo, hit the American market in 1983 with a sizable catalog particularly rich in unhackneyed vocal literature. Its first three operas were Leoncavallo's La Bohème (Lucia Popp, Franco Bonisolli, Heinz Wallberg), Gluck's Alceste (Norman, Nicolai Gedda, Serge Baudo), and Egk's Peer Gynt (Norma Sharp, Roland Hermann, Wallberg). Noteworthy among its numerous song recitals was one devoted to Pfitzner (Fischer-Dieskau, Hartmut Höll). The French Erato label also continued its recent adventuring with first recordings of Dukas's Ariane et Barbe-Bleue (Katherine Ciesinski, Gabriel Bacquier, Jordan), Lully's Armide et Renaud (Rachel Yakar, Ulrik Cold, Philippe Herreweghe), and Rameau's Les Boréades (Jennifer Smith, John Aler, John Eliot Gardiner).

Despite some signs of an improved economy in 1983, traditional operatic fare remained at a trickle. Verdi was well represented, however, with new recordings of Falstaff (Katia Ricciarelli, Renato Bruson, Carlo Maria Giulini; DG), I masnadieri (Joan Sutherland, Bonisolli, Richard Bonynge; London), and Nabucco (Ghena Dimitrova, Placido Domingo, Sinopoli; DG).

Early music. The predictable seasonal Messiah's were of more than routine interest—major statements were offered by Nikolaus Harnoncourt (Telefunken) and Gardiner (Philips). Gardiner was also active on the Handel front with recordings of Hercules (Archiv) and Semele (Erato). Christopher Hogwood concluded his striking series of Mozart symphonies on original instruments (Oiseau-Lyre), while Trevor Pinnock did well by Bach's Brandenburg Concertos (DG). James Levine, after recording two Mozart symphonies for RCA, signed with DG to record, among other things, all the Mozart symphonies.

Moderns. Almost as unusual as the origin of Elliott Carter's Night Fantasies, a 1980 work jointly commissioned by four pianists, was its almost simultaneous release on recordings by two of those players, Paul Jacobs (Nonesuch) and Charles Rosen (Etcetera); the piece was coupled in each case with Carter's 1945–1946 Piano Sonata. Another 1980 work, David Del Tredici's In Memory of a Summer Day, was given its first recording by soprano Phyllis Bryn-Julson, with Leonard Slatkin and the St. Louis Symphony (Nonesuch). Sir Michael Tippett, blessed with beautiful recordings of his works in recent years, was given another in 1983: a stunning performance of his Triple Concerto, by György Pauk, Nobuko Imai and Ralph Kirschbaum, with Colin Davis leading the London Symphony (Philips).

New classical giant. Warner Communications Inc., the huge U.S. entertainment conglomerate, initiated steps to buy out the German Siemens group and take control of the powerful PolyGram group (a joint venture of the Dutch Philips corporation and Siemens). At a stroke, Warner, whose previous involvement in classical recording had been largely confined to the small U.S. Nonesuch label, became a major force worldwide.   J.R.O.

N

NAMIBIA. *See* SOUTH-WEST AFRICA.
NAURU. *See* STATISTICS OF THE WORLD.
NEBRASKA. *See* STATISTICS OF THE WORLD.
NEGROES IN THE UNITED STATES. During 1983, blacks won mayoral elections in two of the nation's largest cities, and black leader Jesse L. Jackson (see also biography in PEOPLE IN THE NEWS) entered the race for the Democratic presidential nomination. The late Martin Luther King, Jr., was honored by the establishment of a federal holiday in his name, and a successful reenactment of the 1963 March on Washington was mounted.

Political gains. Growing political gains by blacks were exemplified by the elections of Harold Washington and W. Wilson Goode as the first black mayors of Chicago and Philadelphia, respectively. Washington's victories in the Chicago Democratic primary in February and the mayoral election in April were particularly heartening to black political activists, because they came in a city long beset by racial tension and because they reflected the success of a massive voter registration drive. Goode's triumph, by a comfortable margin in November, was less surprising but equally welcomed; with his election, black mayors were in charge of four of the nation's six largest cities.

Galvanized by Washington's winning effort, black groups throughout the country had mounted intensive voter registration campaigns in the summer and fall. In Mississippi, for example, about 40,000 new black voters were enrolled prior to statewide primary elections on August 2, in which black turnout was the highest ever recorded. The NAACP announced in July that it was stepping up voter registration efforts nationwide, with a goal of signing up 4 million new black voters by the end of the year.

Jackson candidacy. A newfound sense of black political power, spawned by the voter registration drives, led to widespread speculation over the possibility of a black running for the 1984 Democratic presidential nomination. Many black leaders, judging that a black had little or no realistic chance of gaining the nomination, opposed a "token" campaign that might drain support from more viable candidates with liberal credentials; others argued that the time was right for blacks to make their mark in presidential politics. Thus, Jesse Jackson's declaration in November that he was entering the race for the Democratic nomination received mixed reactions from major civil rights spokesmen. Jackson, the head of Chicago-based Operation PUSH (People United to Serve Humanity, a human rights and minority self-improvement organization), has built a reputation as a brilliant orator and dynamic organizer. He greatly enhanced his reputation and visibility as a candidate when he went to Syria and, on January 3, 1984, won the release of a U.S. airman captured by Syrian forces in Lebanon a month before. But his provocative and flamboyant rhetoric (one slogan: "From outhouse to White House—our time has come") and his lack of political credentials were seen by some as serious drawbacks.

Commemorations. Fifteen years after his assassination, black leader Martin Luther King, Jr., was honored in two significant ways in 1983. In October, the Senate gave final approval to a bill designating the third Monday in January as a federal holiday commemorating King's birth, effective in 1986. President Ronald Reagan, who earlier had resisted the bill, signed it in a ceremony in the White House Rose Garden on November 2. At a press conference in October, Reagan had said that he did not "fault the sincerity" of certain opponents of a King holiday, such as Senator Jesse Helms (R, N.C.), who had sought access to sealed FBI files that, they claimed, would prove King had Communist beliefs and associations.

A second major event honoring King and seeking to promote his ideals, was a reenactment of the March on Washington that he had led in 1963. The August 27 March drew 300,000 people to Washington, D.C., where they heard speakers from civil rights, women's rights, environmental, disarmament, and other social action groups call for the forging of a new coalition for social change.

A federal holiday commemorating the birth of black leader Martin Luther King, Jr., was signed into law by President Ronald Reagan in November. At the ceremony were Vice-President George Bush; Coretta Scott King, Dr. King's widow; Senators Edward M. Kennedy and Bob Dole; and Representatives Jack Kemp and Katie Hall.

NAACP infighting. The NAACP, the country's oldest and largest civil rights group, was convulsed in midyear by an internal power struggle. The chief antagonists in the dispute were Chairman Margaret Bush Wilson and Executive Director Benjamin Hooks. In late May, Wilson announced that Hooks was being suspended from his post, which he had held since 1977, for alleged mismanagement and refusal to turn over internal records to the NAACP board of directors. Eight days later, however, Wilson bowed to widespread support of Hooks by reinstating him, and on June 11 the board stripped Wilson of all her powers. Finally, on July 11 a committee appointed by the board announced that it had found the charges against Hooks were "not substantiated by the facts."

Economic situation. According to a study conducted by the Center for the Study of Social Policy and released in July, the disparity between the average income of white and black families has remained approximately the same since 1960. The study did note some positive trends for black Americans: sweeping educational gains, to the point where the median level of schooling for whites and blacks has become virtually identical; large increases in the percentage of blacks holding various white-collar jobs; and a substantial increase in the number of blacks in the middle class. These gains were offset, however, by a substantial increase in the proportion of black households with children that are headed by females (from 21 percent in 1960 to 47 percent today). Because families headed by women are twice as likely as two-parent families to be poor, the average income of black families has suffered proportionately.

Newsmakers. Vanessa Williams of Millwood, N.Y., was crowned the first black Miss America in September in Atlantic City, N.J. Air Force Lieutenant Colonel Guion Stewart Bluford, Jr., became the first black American in space when he served as one of the four crew members on the flight of the space shuttle *Challenger* on August 30–September 5.

See also CIVIL LIBERTIES AND CIVIL RIGHTS.

M.Gr. & D.F.

NEPAL. See STATISTICS OF THE WORLD.

NETHERLANDS, THE. In 1983 the Netherlands' center-right government introduced new austerity measures and faced a growing protest movement against the deployment of U.S. missiles.

The coalition government of Christian Democratic Prime Minister Ruud Lubbers first announced public spending reductions of about $4.7 billion for 1983, with further annual cuts scheduled through 1986. Public sector wages and social security payments were frozen effective in January. The purpose of the austerity measures was to reduce the official budget

The Prince and Princess of Wales pose with their chubby Prince William during a quiet moment in their goodwill visit to New Zealand early in the year.

deficit from an expected record 11.9 percent of national income in 1983 to 7.4 percent by 1986.

However, a fall in revenue from natural gas sales required even more severe budget cuts to meet the deficit reduction goal. The interim budget published in April provided for a $5.4 billion decrease in spending for the year, including a 2 percent drop in social welfare benefits effective October 1 and a 2 percent pay cut for all civil servants and public service employees. Also, as a job-creating measure, the workweek of most private-sector workers was to be reduced from 40 to 36 hours in stages over the 1983–1986 period.

The economy remained in recession in 1983. Consumer prices rose only 2.4 percent in the 12 months ending in July 1983, and wages rose only 1.4 percent for the 12 months ending in June, both among the smallest increases in Western Europe. However, 17 percent of the work force was unemployed in mid-1983, the highest level in the European Community. A trade surplus of $3.8 billion for 1982 was due largely to gas exports; a surplus of about $3 billion was anticipated for 1983, one of the strongest performances in Western Europe.

During an official visit to Washington in March, Lubbers reaffirmed that preparations were under way for the installation of cruise missiles on Dutch territory. However, the government's position was that actual deployment

of the missiles would depend upon progress in arms control negotiations between the United States and the Soviet Union, and no final decision was made in 1983. The issue remained highly controversial throughout the Netherlands, where antinuclear sentiment was the strongest in Western Europe. A demonstration against deployment, on October 29 at The Hague, drew half a million people.

Alfred H. Heineken, the chairman of the Heineken brewery and thought to be the richest man in the country, was kidnapped at gunpoint, along with his chauffeur, on the night of November 9. After a ransom (reportedly over $10 million) was paid, Dutch police rescued the pair safely from an unguarded warehouse in Amsterdam; they also rounded up a large number of suspects.

See STATISTICS OF THE WORLD.   W.C.C.

NEVADA. See STATISTICS OF THE WORLD.

NEW BRUNSWICK. See STATISTICS OF THE WORLD.

NEWFOUNDLAND. See STATISTICS OF THE WORLD.

NEW HAMPSHIRE. See STATISTICS OF THE WORLD.

NEW JERSEY. See STATISTICS OF THE WORLD.

NEW MEXICO. See STATISTICS OF THE WORLD.

NEW YORK. See STATISTICS OF THE WORLD.

NEW ZEALAND. Prime Minister Robert Muldoon remained in office in 1983 as head of a National Party government with only a slender one-vote margin in New Zealand's one-chamber Parliament. Muldoon pressed efforts to develop large-scale industry in order to reduce unemployment; he also sought to make New Zealand less dependent on imported fuels. A major event of the year was the visit of the Prince and Princess of Wales to New Zealand in April. They were warmly received, but Muldoon himself attracted some controversy because of what critics alleged was an effort to use the occasion to thrust himself into the limelight. The slipping popularity of his government was evident in a public opinion poll, released the same month, in which the National Party received only 31.3 percent of the public's support, while the Labor Party received 52.4 percent.

Relations between New Zealand and China appeared to take a great step forward after a March economic mission to China headed by the minister for foreign affairs and leaders of the business community. After the visit, it was announced that business discussions with the Chinese had led to agreement on steps to settle a dispute keeping New Zealand livestock exports out of China.

New Zealand welcomed Japanese proposals for increasing investment in New Zealand, including a number of joint fishing ventures and manufacturing projects. It was hoped that the Japanese investments would herald a new phase of economic development by giving New Zealand access to new technologies, creating jobs, opening new markets, and providing an inflow of capital for further development.

In 1982, Muldoon had called for the convening of a conference to reform the collapsing international monetary system. In March 1983, on his first day back from a trip to Switzerland and Asia, he told reporters that he believed a groundswell of support for his reform proposals was developing.

On a visit to Great Britain in May, Prime Minister Muldoon strongly criticized the European Economic Community for placing stringent limits on butter and meat exports to Europe. Nevertheless, the EEC in October announced plans to further reduce New Zealand's butter export quotas, to a maximum of 75,000 tons by 1988.

In February, government statisticians reported that food prices had risen 7.2 percent in 1982 and that they had risen a total of 19.6 percent from 1980 through 1982. The annual inflation rate for 1983 was approximately 5 percent.

See STATISTICS OF THE WORLD.   F.D.S.

NICARAGUA. The Nicaraguan government continued to move to the left during much of 1983, but moderated some of its policies late in the year. The United States stepped up its covert support to antigovernment rebels, causing protests from Nicaraguan leaders.

Internal politics. Political power remained in the hands of the nine-member national directorate of the Sandinista National Liberation Front. The government adopted legislation recognizing the right of non-Sandinista political parties to compete for office, but the law also established strong government controls over their operations. Opposition parties, meanwhile, continued to be harrassed by roving gangs of Sandinistas, and many opposition leaders left the country or abandoned speaking out against the regime. A law providing for compulsory military service was enacted in late summer, despite strong protests.

Church and state remained in a state of conflict. The dispute peaked during Pope John Paul II's visit to Nicaragua in March. The Sandinistas were charged with having been disrespectful to the pope, after John Paul was beset by hecklers while trying to address a rally.

Late in the year the government moved to blunt criticism of its policies, easing censorship and granting amnesty to certain exiles and opponents of the regime. It also asked Salvadoran rebel leaders and a large number of Cuban military advisers to leave the country. Elections were to be held in 1985, with the date to be announced in early 1984.

Rebel activity. The Sandinistas faced a mounting military challenge from exile opposition groups, divided into two major factions: the Nicaraguan Democratic Force (FDN), operating out of Miami and Honduras, and the Revolutionary Democratic Alliance (ARDE), based in Costa Rica. Both groups were active sporadically during much of the year, and the level of activity picked up in September and October, with increased ground fighting and attacks on the international airport and on the

Celebrating the fourth anniversary of the Sandinista revolution with the slogan "All the people for defense!" the Nicaraguan government attempted to mobilize popular support for its fight against counterrevolutionary insurgents.

major ports of Benjamin Zeledón, Puerto Sandino, and Corinto. In December the government announced a new offensive against rebels, including many Miskito Indians, in the northeast.

Foreign relations. The issue of foreign support for armed exile attacks against Nicaragua dominated foreign relations in 1983. The United States was the main focus of Nicaraguan charges, although Honduras and Costa Rica also came in for growing criticism. Unofficially, Reagan administration spokesmen acknowledged that the CIA had been actively supporting rebel activities as a means of pressuring the Sandinistas to stop trying to "export revolution" and to introduce democratic reforms. In November, after a long deadlock over the issue, the U.S. Congress approved $24 million in continuing covert aid to anti-Sandinista rebels.

Earlier in the year, the Reagan administration cut by 90 percent the 1984 quota for Nicaragun sugar imports by the United States. In July and August, two U.S. carrier task forces were dispatched to Central American waters, amid rumors of possible plans to blockade Nicaragua.

Relations between Nicaragua and Honduras were very tense. Each side increased its military forces along the common border and charged the other with armed aggression. The threat of war was a major factor in the formation in January of the so-called Contadora group (Colombia, Mexico, Panama, and Venezuela), which sought a negotiated settlement to various Central American conflicts. In October, the group issued a 21-point peace program, which Nicaragua was said to have endorsed in principle.

Economy. A large part of Nicaragua's diplomatic efforts went toward securing external economic assistance. Trade credits were obtained from Spain, Sweden, the Soviet Union, and other nations. U.S. pressures resulted in a reduction of credits from such agencies as the World Bank and the Inter-American Development Bank, but some funding continued.

After two years of economic recovery following the civil war of 1978–1979, the economy dipped sharply in 1982 and continued to decline in 1983. Many Nicaraguans experienced growing hardship, as the economic slump generated high rates of unemployment and shortages of both food and manufactured goods.

See STATISTICS OF THE WORLD.   R.L.M.

NIGER. *See* STATISTICS OF THE WORLD.

NIGERIA. On December 31, 1983, elements of the Nigerian armed forces overthrew the civilian government of President Shehu Shagari, suspended the 1979 constitution, and announced the formation of a military regime. The new government was headed by Major General Muhammad Buhari, who declared that the coup had been necessary to rescue the country from "imminent collapse" brought about by "corrupt and inept leadership."

The deposed Shagari administration had been the first Nigerian government elected under civilian auspices since 1964. In the August 6 presidential election, the incumbent Shagari, of the National Party of Nigeria, won an unexpectedly massive victory, outpolling his nearest rival, Chief Obafemi Awolowo of the Unity Party of Nigeria, by more than 4 million votes. Opposition parties alleged that the electoral law had been flagrantly violated and that in some areas the ruling NPN had collaborated with local authorities to intimidate opposition polling agents and then rig the voting.

The controversy erupted into violence when the results of the August 13 gubernatorial elections showed the NPN increasing its governorships from seven to 13 in the 19 states. UPN partisans set fire to homes and businesses of NPN leaders, and more than 100 people were killed. Amid heavily reduced voter turnouts in subsequent legislative elections, the NPN won close to two-thirds of the National Assembly and gained legislative majorities in 12 states.

The Nigerian economy continued to stagnate in 1983. Oil revenue, which had declined from well over $20 billion in 1980 to $10 billion in 1982, was expected to reach only $8–10 billion. Export sales of crude oil stopped completely for a time, forcing Nigeria to announce a 15.5 percent price cut. Economic deterioration forced a painful refinancing of Nigeria's external debt. In mid-July, the government obtained from a consortium of international banks a high-interest loan of $1.6 billion to refinance short-term trade debts; later, preliminary agreement was reached with the International Monetary Fund on a loan of more than $26 billion. On January 17, 1983, the Shagari government announced that all unskilled foreigners residing in Nigeria illegally had to leave within two weeks. The sudden forced uprooting of some 2 million foreigners from other West African states (the official Nigerian estimate was 1,165,000) brought chaos and tragedy. Road and rail accidents caused at least 50 deaths; others died from cholera, hunger, and exhaustion while waiting in the crowded ports for evacuation.

A fierce border clash with Chad broke out in mid-April when a Chadian patrol attacked Nigerian troops on the disputed Kanisara Island in Lake Chad; the fighting escalated in May when Nigeria launched an offensive to recapture islands held by Chadian troops. An agreement that the two sides would return to the status prior to the clashes was formalized in early July.

See STATISTICS OF THE WORLD.   L.D.

NORTH ATLANTIC TREATY ORGANIZATION, abbreviated NATO. In 1983 the chief issue of concern to the nations of NATO was the deployment of Pershing II and cruise intermediate-range nuclear missiles, which began late in the year. Plans called for the eventual deployment of 572 missiles, in West Germany, Great Britain, Italy, Belgium, and the Netherlands. Growing numbers of Western Europeans joined in protests to demonstrate opposition to the missiles, but their governments had reaffirmed that they would accept deployment if no progress were made in the U.S.-Soviet disarmament talks in Geneva. In fact, governments in Britain and West Germany that were strongly committed to this policy won elections by comfortable margins.

Soviet efforts to discourage the deployment began in January when the Warsaw Pact allies released a series of disarmament proposals, with emphasis on an offer of a nonaggression accord with the members of NATO. The suggested accord would have included a joint pledge against first use of nuclear weapons, as well as an agreement to decrease military spending, and would have created a nuclear-free zone in Central Europe. NATO's response was cautious. Soviet Foreign Minister Andrei Gromyko visited Bonn, where he urged his hosts not to accept the 108 Pershings scheduled for deployment in West Germany. He repeated an earlier offer by the Soviet Union to dismantle some of its more than 350 intermediate-range SS-20 missiles if the United States did not deploy new medium-range missiles. Gromyko emphasized that the Soviet Union would never accept the so-called zero option proposal of the Reagan administration, which called for the dismantling of all SS-20's in return for the cancellation of Pershing and cruise deployment. In April, the Soviets also rejected a modified proposal put forward by President Ronald Reagan, which would allow some Soviet SS-20's to remain deployed on an interim basis, in return for a scaling back in U.S. deployment to equal the Soviet levels. The Soviets were willing to dismantle all but 162 SS-20's in return for cancellation of U.S. deployment plans—a number equal to the existing French and British missiles—but the United States, Britain, and France opposed inclusion of British and French national forces in the discussion.

Meanwhile, U.S. Vice-President George Bush made two trips to Western Europe to shore up U.S. relations with NATO allies. On the first, in February, he stressed the morality of the zero-option proposal, but insisted it was not a "take it or leave it" proposition. After a second trip in late June and early July, he said he was persuaded that the Western European governments would stand by their decisions to deploy U.S. missiles barring an agreement in Geneva. Bush's impression had been strengthened by a communiqué to the same effect issued early in June by NATO defense ministers. The statement, however, was not unanimous; Denmark urged postponement of the decision, and Greece and Spain did not sign.

Many Europeans saw the deployment of the U.S. missiles as increasing the likelihood that their countries could be the battleground for another major war. This fear led to massive popular demonstrations in the largest peace movement in Europe since the end of World War II. The demonstrations came to a head in late October, when on one weekend more than 600,000 West Germans in four cities, along with 200,000 Britons in London and numerous other marchers in Vienna, Rome, Paris, and elsewhere turned out in an attempt to persuade their governments to withdraw consent for the deployment. Former West German Chancellor Willy Brandt became the first mainstream politician to align himself with the peace movement, asserting that West Germans were "bitterly disappointed" at the lack of progress in the Geneva arms talks. Despite these signs of opposition to deployment, the governments of Margaret Thatcher and Helmut Kohl had won elections earlier in the year while strongly favoring deployment of the missiles, in the absence of an arms accord, to counter the Soviet deployment of SS-20's.

In October, President Reagan outlined new proposals to reduce nuclear weapons. His "build-down" plan allowed for the modernization of weapons arsenals and the destruction of old weapons as new ones were deployed. The plan included a guaranteed 5 percent reduction for each side in strategic nuclear weapons. The Soviet Union attacked the build-down proposal as a public relations ploy. Soviet leader Yuri Andropov reiterated that the appearance of new American missiles in Europe would make a continuation of the Geneva talks impossible.

Undeterred by Soviet threats or blandishments, the West German Bundestag on November 22 voted, 286–266, to allow deployment of the missiles if talks in Geneva to limit medium-range missiles failed to produce results. The next day, as the first Pershing missiles began arriving in West Germany, the Soviets withdrew from the talks. Also on November 23, Moscow warned that it would deploy new missiles targeted on the United States and its allies; such missiles, in the view of some analysts, would probably be both land based and submarine based. On December 8, in Geneva, the concurrent strategic arms limitation talks between the United States and the Soviet Union came to an abrupt halt; no date was set for their resumption. Later, on December 15, East-West talks in Vienna on reducing conventional armed forces in Central Europe were also indefinitely recessed.

In a related development, the Canadian government announced in July that the United States would be permitted to test cruise missiles over northern Canadian territory. Permission was granted in response to a U.S. request, and allowed for up to six annual tests over a five-year period beginning in January 1984. Thousands of Canadians demonstrated in protest, but the government saw the plan as a fulfillment of Canada's commitment to NATO. At the

U.S. Vice-President George Bush, flanked by the mayor of West Berlin (left) and West German Chancellor Helmut Kohl, looks across the Berlin wall during the first of two diplomatic visits made to U.S. NATO allies during the year.

same time, Prime Minister Pierre Elliott Trudeau set out on a peace initiative, visiting several major capitals, among them Peking and Washington, in an effort to promote a dialogue among the world's leaders and thus alleviate East-West tensions.

In September, after the Soviet downing of a Korean civilian jetliner, NATO leaders, meeting in Brussels, agreed to impose a two-week ban on all civilian flights to the Soviet Union from member countries. Twelve NATO members agreed to observe the ban, while France, Turkey, Greece, and Spain opposed it.

On December 8, NATO foreign ministers, in Brussels, nominated Lord Carrington, former British foreign secretary, to succeed NATO Secretary-General Joseph Luns, of the Netherlands, when his term expires in June 1984.

See also COMMUNISM; MILITARY AND NAVAL AFFAIRS; and articles on NATO member nations. J.O.S.

NORTH CAROLINA. *See* STATISTICS OF THE WORLD.

NORTH DAKOTA. *See* STATISTICS OF THE WORLD.
NORTHWEST TERRITORIES. *See* STATISTICS OF THE WORLD.

NORWAY. A faltering economy and controversy over the deployment of U.S. missiles in Europe dominated Norwegian political life in 1983, as the ruling conservative government sought to broaden its support by forming a coalition government. In June, Prime Minister Kaare Willoch invited two small parties to join his Conservative Party; together they commanded 79 of the 155 seats in the Storting (parliament). The Labor Party remained in opposition, with 66 seats.

The new government continued the economic policies of its predecessor, emphasizing fiscal restraint and the encouragement of private enterprise in exploiting North Sea oil. A growing budgetary deficit, however, had forced the first Willoch cabinet to limit itself to modest reductions in individual and corporate taxes. In October, Finance Minister Rolf Presthus submitted a 1984 budget proposal involving a deficit of $4.75 million—20 percent more than the budget originally approved for 1983.

Despite government efforts, economic performance continued to sag. The country's gross domestic product (GDP) was expected to fall for the first time in 25 years, by 0.6 percent.

At the same time, the unemployment rate rose from 1.7 percent at the end of 1981 to nearly 4 percent in 1983. As a first step toward reducing politically unacceptable unemployment levels, especially among younger people, the Willoch cabinet planned to spend the equivalent of $59 million in 1983 to create temporary jobs and 10,000 apprenticeships in private industry.

The economic doldrums caused relative constraint on the part of union leaders when they presented their wage demands for 1983–1984 to the national employers' confederation. In June, the two sides compromised on an average increase of slightly more than 7 percent.

The only exception to the spate of bad economic news was oil production. Oil exports were projected to rise to $7.6 billion in 1983, $700 million more than 1982 sales. The increase confirmed the growing importance of North Sea oil and gas for Norway.

At the Labor Party congress in April, delegates voted unanimously to oppose the deployment of U.S. Pershing II and cruise missiles in Western Europe. The party called instead for the continuation of bilateral talks in Geneva between the United States and the Soviet Union. The Storting, however, reiterated its support for eventual deployment if the Geneva talks failed.

Unidentified submarines were reportedly sighted in Norwegian coastal waters during the spring. The navy dropped depth charges along the western coast and conducted extensive searches, but no submarine was located.

See STATISTICS OF THE WORLD.   M.D.H.

NOVA SCOTIA. *See* STATISTICS OF THE WORLD.

NUCLEAR POWER. Falling demand for electrical energy and soaring construction costs due to delays and high interest rates continued to send shock waves through the U.S. nuclear power industry. New legislation provided both short-term and long-term procedures for the disposal of nuclear waste.

Nuclear power plants. On July 25 the Pacific Northwest's Washington Public Power Supply System (WPPSS) defaulted on $2.25 billion of tax-exempt bonds, which had been issued to finance construction of two nuclear power plants, known as units No. 4 and No. 5. It was the largest municipal bond default in U.S. history.

The WPPSS default spawned a rash of lawsuits. The bonds for units No. 4 and No. 5 are owned by about 75,000 investors, most of them individuals, according to estimates by the trustee for the bonds, Chemical Bank of New York. In June the Washington State Supreme Court had ruled that Washington utilities affiliated with WPPSS in the project were not obligated to pay off the bonds. Chemical Bank asked the court to reconsider its decision and said it would appeal to the U.S. Supreme Court if necessary.

WPPSS was only the most visible casualty in the nuclear power industry. In August the Puget Sound Power & Light Company, sponsor and 40 percent owner of the planned twin nuclear power plants at Hanford, Wash., announced its intention to abandon the project. Puget Power and its three partners (Portland General Electric Company, Pacific Power & Light Company, and Washington Water Power Company) had already invested $433 million in the project even though construction had not yet started.

In September owners of the financially troubled Seabrook nuclear power station in New Hampshire decided to halt almost all work on the second of two reactors planned for the site, until the completion of Unit No. 1, tentatively set for December 1984.

Among other developments, the Duke Power Company in April decided to cancel construction of Unit No. 1 at its Cherokee nuclear power plant near Gaffney, S.C. Unit No. 1 was about 17 percent complete; units No. 2 and No. 3 had already been canceled in November 1982. In late October 1983, the Senate voted not to spend $1.5 billion to complete the experimental Clinch River breeder reactor in Tennessee. The move was tantamount to cancellation of the project, which had already consumed $1.7 billion.

A U.S. Department of Energy study released in April showed that the nation's electric utility industry had substantially reduced its commitment to nuclear power: the industry had canceled almost half of the nuclear generating capacity it had ordered over the years. Three major reasons were cited by utilities for the cancellation of nuclear plants: (1) significant downward revision in the forecasted growth of peak electric power load, (2) constraints on construction financing, and (3) regulatory changes and uncertainty.

Reactor safety. On February 22 the Salem-1 reactor, owned by Public Service Gas and Electric of New Jersey, refused to halt the atomic reaction in its core when ordered to do so by a safety-control system. An operator had to shut the reactor down manually. The failure of the system, supposed to be an extremely rare occurrence, was repeated three days later, after the plant had been restarted without notification to the U.S. Nuclear Regulatory Commission. The NRC in November adopted regulations requiring most of the country's nuclear plants to install new mechanisms to ensure that the plants can be shut off if a major accident should occur. It was expected that the cost to each plant would be $3 million to $8.5 million, depending on the type of reactor used.

Pennsylvania's Three Mile Island plant continued to make news in 1983. In November, a federal grand jury indicted the nuclear subsidiary of Metropolitan Edison Company, which operated the reactors at Three Mile Island at the time of the 1979 accident, on charges of falsifying safety-related data.

Radioactive waste. On January 7, President Ronald Reagan signed the Nuclear Waste Policy Act, passed by Congress in December 1982. The legislation established a timetable and procedures for disposal of spent nuclear fuel from commercial power reactors in a permanent underground repository by the late 1990's. The act also authorized an interim federal away-from-reactor storage program, which would provide temporary federal storage for up to 1,900 metric tons of spent reactor fuel for those utilities that the Nuclear Regulatory Commission determines cannot reasonably provide sufficient storage at the reactor site.

The act mandated the Department of Energy to enter into contracts with all owners and generators of spent reactor fuel or high-level radioactive waste who need to have the department provide for its eventual disposal. The costs of disposal are to be paid from a special fund, the Nuclear Waste Fund, to be established from a special fee of 1 mill (one-tenth of a cent) per kilowatt-hour on all electricity generated by nuclear reactors after April 7, 1983.

Congressional passage of the act hinged on a compromise under which states received a stronger say in decisions. States targeted for storage will have the right to veto the chosen site, and the veto will stand unless overridden by Congress.   D.F.A.

The largest municipal bond collapse in U.S. history occurred when the Washington Public Power Supply System defaulted on $2.25 billion worth of bonds issued to finance nuclear power plants. Here, the cooling tower and reactor of a WPPSS unit only partly constructed.

O

OBITUARIES. Each entry below contains the name of a notable person who died in 1983. It also contains a brief description of the accomplishments and events that contributed to making each person notable.

Albright, Ivan, American painter. He won recognition for his meticulous images of human mortality and decay, as in the portraits he and his twin brother painted for the film of *The Picture of Dorian Gray.* Died Nov. 18, age 86.

Aldrich, Robert, American film director. Starting with *Big Leaguer* in 1953, he directed scores of films about society's misfits, including *Hush, Hush, Sweet Charlotte, The Dirty Dozen,* and *The Longest Yard.* Died Dec. 5, age 65.

Alemán Valdés, Miguel, Mexican politician. Elected president of Mexico in 1946, he served until 1952; his administration, although marked by charges of corruption, brought progress in agriculture, transportation, and industry. Died May 14, age 79.

Ameche, Jim, American radio performer. Widely known for his portrayal of Jack Armstrong, the All-American Boy, during the 1930's, he was also the announcer for the show *Amos 'n' Andy.* Died Feb. 4, age 68.

Anderson, Maxie Leroy, American balloonist. A participant in the first balloon crossing of the Atlantic in the *Double Eagle II,* in 1978, he financed his ballooning with a fortune made in mining. Died June 27 in a balloon crash, age 48.

Andrzejewski, Jerzy, Polish writer. A prominent political dissident and longtime opponent of censorship, he was best known for the novel *Ashes and Diamonds* (1948). Died April 19, age 73.

Aquino, Benigno Simeon, Jr., Philippine opposition leader. Imprisoned in 1972 after President Ferdinand Marcos declared martial law, he was allowed to leave for the United States in 1980, where he remained for three years. Intending to renew active opposition to the Marcos regime, he returned to Manila but was assassinated at the airport. Died Aug. 21, age 50.

Aron, Raymond Claude Ferdinand, French political thinker. Noted for his skepticism and moderate conservatism, he wrote *Peace and War Between Nations* (1962), among other works. Died Oct. 17, age 78.

Arran, Earl of (Arthur Kattendyke Strange David Archibald Gore), English peer. An eccentric columnist, he introduced in the House of Lords in 1966 the landmark Sexual Offenses Bill, which legalized homosexual acts between consenting adults. Died Feb. 23, age 72.

Aspinall, Wayne Norviel, American politician. A Colorado Democrat, he chaired the House Interior Committee a record 14 years. Died Oct. 9, age 87.

Auric, Georges, French composer. Youngest of the six French modernist composers called Les Six, he wrote for the stage and films as well as the concert hall; his best known work was the score for the film *Moulin Rouge* (1952). Died July 24, age 84.

A spirited ragtime pianist, Eubie Blake wrote Broadway's first black musical.

Averill, Earl Douglas, American baseball player. A Hall of Fame outfielder, he batted .318, with 238 home runs in 13 major league seasons, chiefly with the Cleveland Indians. Died Aug. 16, age 81.

Balanchine, George (Georgy Melitonovich Balanchivadze), Russian-American choreographer. Widely regarded as one of the most important figures in the history of dance, he helped establish the School of American Ballet in 1934 and the Ballet Society (later called the New York City Ballet) in 1946. His more than 200 major ballets included such classic works as *Serenade* (1934), *Concerto Barocco* (1941), and *Violin Concerto* (1972). Died April 30, age 79.

Baldwin, William, Jr. ("Billy"), American interior decorator. The most influential designer of his generation, he counted as clients such celebrities as Cole Porter, Jacqueline Kennedy Onassis, Mike Nichols, and Diana Vreeland. Died Nov. 25, age 80.

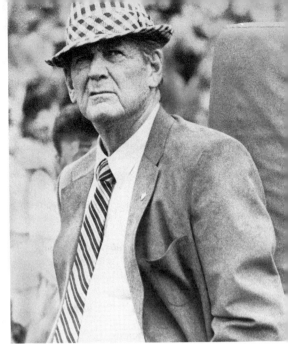

Paul "Bear" Bryant's 38-year career as a football coach included only one losing season.

Bee, Clair Francis, American basketball coach. His teams at Rider College and Long Island University had a combined 410–86 record from the late 1920's to the early 1950's, and he helped originate the 1–3–1 zone defense, the three-second rule, and the 24-second clock. He also wrote more than 40 books. Died May 20, age 87.

Bidault, Georges, French statesman. A leader of the French Resistance during World War II, he held such posts as premier and foreign minister in several postwar French governments. Died Jan. 27, age 83.

Bishop, Maurice, prime minister of Grenada. Leader of the Marxist New Jewel Movement, he had seized power in 1979 and was overthrown in a coup on Oct. 14. Killed with a group of associates, Oct. 19, age 39.

Black, William, American businessman and philanthropist. He built the multimillion-dollar Chock Full O'Nuts Corporation from a tiny shelled-nuts stand. Died March 7, age 80.

Blake, James Hubert ("Eubie"), American ragtime pianist. Composer of more than 1,000 songs and instrumental pieces, including "I'm Just Wild About Harry" and "Memories of You," he wrote the score for *Shuffle Along* (1921), the first black musical on Broadway. Died Feb. 12, age 100.

Bloch, Felix, Swiss-American physicist. He was cowinner of the 1952 Nobel Prize in physics for his work on nuclear magnetic resonance. Died Sept. 10, age 77.

Bluhdorn, Charles G., Austrian-American businessman. Starting with a small auto-parts company, he single-handedly built the giant conglomerate Gulf & Western Industries Inc. Died Feb. 19, age 56.

Blunt, Anthony Frederick, British art historian. The "fourth man" in the famous Guy Burgess–Donald Maclean–Kim Philby espionage ring, he was a longtime spy for the Soviet Union. Died March 26, age 75.

Boult, Sir Adrian (Cedric), British conductor. He was conductor of the BBC Symphony Orchestra from 1930 to 1950, then principal conductor of the London Philharmonic, and was known as a champion of 20th-century British music. Died Feb. 23, age 93.

Brandt, Bill, British photographer. His pictures, documenting all levels of English life, contained suggestive, often cryptic images. Died Dec. 20, age 79.

Bryant, Paul William ("Bear"), American football coach. In a 38-year career at four schools—Maryland, Kentucky, Texas A&M, and, from 1958, Alabama—he amassed a record 323 wins, along with only 85 defeats and 17 ties. His teams included such stars as George Blanda, John David Crow, Joe Namath, Ray Perkins, and Richard Todd. Died Jan. 26, age 69.

Buñuel, Luis, Spanish filmmaker. After his first film, the classic surrealist short *Un Chien andalou* (1928), made in collaboration with Salvador Dali, he went on to become one of the world's most prominent directors with such works as *Viridiana* (1961), *Belle de Jour* (1967), and *The Discreet Charm of the Bourgeoisie* (1972), which won an Academy Award for best foreign film. Died July 29, age 83.

Burton, Phillip, American politician. An influential liberal Democratic congressman from California, he helped pass important social security, welfare, and minimum wage legislation, as well as the largest national parks bill ever. Died April 10, age 56.

Canova, Juliette (Judy), American comedian. A hillbilly entertainer, she starred in films and in *The Judy Canova Show* on radio from 1945 to 1957. Died Aug. 5, age 66.

Carpenter, Karen (Anne), American pop singer. Her records of sentimental ballads, made with her brother Richard, sold more than 60 million copies in the early 1970's; their first and biggest hit was "Close to You." Died Feb. 4, age 32.

Carter, (Bessie) Lillian, mother of former President Jimmy Carter. An avid supporter of

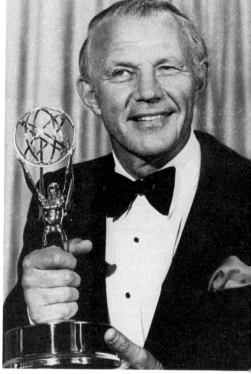

Michael Conrad won two Emmys for playing Sergeant Esterhaus in television's Hill Street Blues.

civil rights and women's causes, she joined the Peace Corps at age 68 and served as an unofficial ambassador during her son's presidency. Died Oct. 30, age 85.

Charles, Prince (Charles Theodore Henri Antoine Meinrad), Belgian ruler. Serving as regent of Belgium during the exile of King

Known as "Miss Lillian," President Jimmy Carter's mother, feisty Lillian Carter, went to India with the Peace Corps at age 68.

Leopold III from 1944 to 1950, he was credited with saving the monarchy. Died June 1, age 79.

Clark, Barney Bailey, the world's first artificial heart recipient. A retired dentist, he lived for 112 days after physicians at the University of Utah Medical Center implanted the device in his chest on December 2, 1982. Died March 25, age 62.

Clark, Kenneth Mackenzie, British art historian. Best known for his book and television series *Civilisation* (1969), he was director of London's National Gallery from 1934 to 1945 and chairman of the British Arts Council from 1953 to 1960. Died May 21, age 79.

Claude, Albert, Belgian-American scientist. A Nobel Prize–winner, he was a founder of modern cell biology and a pioneer in the use of the electron microscope and centrifuge in the study of cells. Died May 22, age 84.

Clayton, Jan, American actress. She was best known for her Broadway roles in *Carousel* and *Show Boat* and as the mother in the original *Lassie* television series. Died Aug. 28, age 66.

Cohen, Benjamin Victor, American lawyer. A key member of Franklin D. Roosevelt's "brain trust," he framed such New Deal legislation as the Securities and Exchange Act and the Fair Labor Standards Act. Died Aug. 15, age 88.

Conrad, Michael, American actor. A veteran film and television performer, he was best known for his award-winning portrayal of Sergeant Esterhaus in television's *Hill Street Blues.* Died Nov. 22, age 58.

Cooke, Terence Cardinal, American churchman. Spiritual leader of the Roman Catholic archdiocese of New York and of Catholics in the U.S. armed forces, he had been a cardinal since 1969. Died Oct. 6, age 62.

Corning, Erastus II, American politician. The longest-tenured big-city mayor in the United States, he had been mayor of Albany, N.Y., since 1942. Died May 28, age 73.

Cowles, John, Sr., American newspaper executive. A former newspaper publisher whose journalistic empire included the Minneapolis *Star* and *Tribune,* he was an advocate of internationalism. Died Feb. 25, age 84.

Crabbe, Buster (Clarence Linden Crabbe), American actor. An Olympic champion swimmer, he was best known for his film portrayals of Flash Gordon and Buck Rogers. Died April 23, age 75.

Cukor, George, American film director. Known for fostering the careers of such actresses as Katharine Hepburn, Ingrid Bergman, and Judy Garland, he made more than 50 movies, including *Little Women* (1933), *The Philadelphia Story* (1940), *Gaslight* (1944), and *A Star Is Born* (1954). Died Jan. 24, age 83.

Del Rio, Dolores (Lolita Dolores Martinez Asunsolo Lopez Negrette), Mexican-American film actress. After gaining fame in silent fiilms, including *What Price Glory?* (1926), she starred in such movies as *Flying Down to Rio* (1933) and the Mexican film *Maria Candelaria* (1946). Died April 11, age 77.

Spiritual head of the Roman Catholic archdiocese of New York, Cardinal Cooke was noted for his humility and patience.

Legendary former world heavyweight boxing champion Jack Dempsey was known as the Manassa Mauler.

Demarest, William, American actor. Best known as Uncle Charley in the television series *My Three Sons,* he appeared in dozens of comic character roles in films. Died Dec. 28, age 91.

Demaret, Jimmy, American golfer. The first golfer to win the Masters tournament three times (1940, 1947, and 1950), he was a member of the World Golf Hall of Fame. Died Dec. 28, age 73.

Dempsey, William Harrison (Jack), American boxer. Nicknamed the Manassa Mauler after the small Colorado town where he was born, he won the world heavyweight title in 1919 by demolishing Jess Willard in three rounds. His sixth title defense, in 1926, saw him lose the crown to Gene Tunney; a year later, he again lost to Tunney in the controversial "long count" rematch. Died May 31, age 87.

Dietz, Howard, American songwriter. He wrote lyrics for over 500 songs, including "Dancing in the Dark" and "That's Entertainment," and was Metro-Goldwyn-Mayer publicity director for many years. Died July 30, age 86.

Docking, Robert Blackwell, American politician. Democratic governor of Kansas for a record four terms (1967–1974), he was noted for fiscal conservatism. Died Oct. 8, age 57.

Dodson, Owen Vincent, American author and teacher. Professor of drama at Howard University for 20 years, he wrote fiction, plays, and poetry and was a major influence in black theater. Died June 21, age 68.

Dolin, Sir Anton (Sydney Francis Patrick Chippendall Healey-Kay), British ballet star. The first internationally acclaimed British male ballet dancer, he was a founding member of major ballet companies, including Ballet Theater (now American Ballet Theater), and later was a prominent choreographer, teacher, and lecturer. Died Nov. 25, age 79.

Dorticós Torrado, Osvaldo, Cuban politician. President of Cuba from 1959 to 1976 and the country's chief economic planner for many years, he had served as minister of justice since 1980. Committed suicide, June 23, age 64.

Drummond, Roscoe, American journalist. Author of the widely syndicated column "State of the Nation," he covered Washington politics for over 50 years. Died Sept. 30, age 81.

Ehrlich, Simcha, Israeli politician. Israel's deputy prime minister since 1979 and leader of the Liberal Party, he was a moderate ally of former Prime Minister Menachem Begin. Died June 19, age 67.

Emerson, Faye Margaret, American actress. She rose to prominence in the early years of television, and was the host of one of its first late-night talk shows, *Faye Emerson's Wonderful Town.* Died March 9, age 65.

Engle, Charles Albert ("Rip"), American coach. He was head football coach at Pennsylvania State University from 1950 to 1965, and his team never had a losing season. Died March 7, age 76.

Erickson, Eric, American-born Swedish oil executive. Posing as a Nazi sympathizer, he spied for U.S. intelligence in Germany during World War II; the film *The Counterfeit Traitor* (1962) was based on his life. Reported dead by his family in January, age 92.

Fielding, Temple Hornaday, American travel writer. He was the author and publisher of numerous best-selling travel books, including the annual *Fielding's Europe*. Died May 18, age 69.

Fitzgibbon, (Robert Louis) Constantine (Lee-Dillon), Irish-American author. He wrote fiction, biography, history, and translations, including *The Life of Dylan Thomas* (1965), and such novels as *When the Kissing Had to Stop* (1960). Died March 23, age 63.

Fontanne, Lynn (Lillie Louise Fontanne Lunt), British-American stage actress. With her husband, Alfred Lunt, she appeared in 27 plays, including *The Guardsman* (1924), *Design for Living* (1933), and *O Mistress Mine* (1946), setting a sparkling standard for sophisticated comedy. Died July 30, age 95.

Foy, Eddie, Jr., American actor. A clowning vaudevillian whose career began at the age of five in the family act "Eddie Foy and the Seven Little Foys," he later sang and danced on Broadway and in movies and television, gaining his widest fame for the stage and film versions of *The Pajama Game*. Died July 15, age 78.

Fuller, R(ichard) Buckminster, American inventor. His imaginative ideas in architecture,

An inventive genius, Buckminster Fuller was best known for his geodesic dome.

Arthur Godfrey's relaxed folksiness made him one of America's most popular entertainers.

engineering, cartography, and other fields ranged from the utterly practical to the stuff of futuristic dreams. Fuller's geodesic dome, patented in 1947, was widely used for its lightness and strength; in all, he held over 2,000 patents and wrote 25 books, including *Operating Manual for Spaceship Earth* (1969). Died July 1, age 87.

Gershwin, Ira, American songwriter. His clever, colloquial lyrics, set to melodies by his brother George and others, graced such shows as *Lady Be Good* (1924), *Strike Up the Band* (1929), and *Porgy and Bess* (1935); in 1932 the musical *Of Thee I Sing* made him the first lyricist to win a Pulitzer Prize for drama. Died Aug. 17, age 86.

Godfrey, Arthur, American entertainer. The brash, folksy, ukulele-playing radio personality became one of the pioneers of television; he had millions of fans from the 1940's until his retirement in 1959. Died March 16, age 79.

Gramm, Donald (Donald Grambsch), American opera singer. Noted for his rich bass-baritone and fine acting, he was particularly effective in such comic roles as Bartolo in *The Barber of Seville* and the title part in Verdi's *Falstaff*. Died June 2, age 56.

Gruenther, Alfred Maximilian, American military officer. The four-star army general was

OBITUARIES

European commander of NATO from 1953 to 1956; a brilliant military strategist, he helped plan the invasions of French North Africa and Italy during World War II. Died May 30, age 84.

Hackett, Joan, American film actress. She was best known for *The Group* (1966) and *Only When I Laugh* (1981). Died Oct. 8, age 49.

Halas, George, American football team owner. Cofounder of U.S. professional football and founder, president, and former player and coach of the Chicago Bears, he set the National Football League record for coaching wins. Died Oct. 31, age 88.

Hartline, Haldan Keffer, American biophysicist. He was cowinner of the 1967 Nobel Prize in physiology for his contributions to the study of the eye, specifically the electrophysiology of the retina. Died March 17, age 79.

Hines, Earl Kenneth ("Fatha"), American jazz pianist. His "trumpet style" playing influenced generations of musicians, and his Chicago big band of the 1930's and 1940's helped launch Sarah Vaughan, Charlie Parker, and Dizzy Gillespie. Died April 22, age 77.

Hoffer, Eric, American philosopher. A self-educated dockworker with a talent for perceptive aphorisms, he wrote on life, power, and

Dockworker-philosopher Eric Hoffer was awarded the Presidential Medal of Freedom in February.

society in such books as *The True Believer* (1951) and *The Ordeal of Change* (1963). Died May 21, age 80.

Hoffman, Julius Jennings, American judge. A U.S. district judge, he presided over the often tumultuous trial of the Chicago Seven on charges of inciting riots at the 1968 Democratic National Convention. Died July 1, age 87.

Holyoake, Sir Keith, New Zealand politician. First named prime minister for a brief period in 1957, he later served from 1960 to 1972 and also served as governor-general (1977–1980); he was knighted in 1970. Died Dec. 8, age 79.

Horner, Horace Mansfield (Jack), American aviation executive. Starting as a clerk in 1926, he worked his way up to the presidency of the United Aircraft Corporation (now United Technologies) in 1943 before serving as chairman from 1956 to 1968. Died May 9, age 79.

Humbert II (Umberto Nicola Tommaso Giovanni Maria), former king of Italy. He reigned briefly in 1946, losing his throne when Italy voted to become a republic. Died March 18, age 78.

Idris I (Muhammad Idris al Mahdi al Sanussi), former king of Libya. Deposed in 1969 by Muammar al-Qaddafi, he had led the Sanussi sect of Islam since 1917 and had, with British support, become king of the newly created state of Libya in 1951. Died May 25, age 93.

Jackson, Henry Martin ("Scoop"), American politician. Democratic senator from Washington since 1953, he was staunchly conservative on defense but liberal on civil rights and labor issues; he was a contender for his party's presidential nomination in 1972 and 1976. Died Sept. 1, age 71.

Jacobs, Paul, American musician. He played piano and harpsichord with the New York Philharmonic and was widely acclaimed for his performances of 20th-century music. Died Sept. 25, age 53.

James, Harry Haag, American band leader. A swing trumpeter and big band leader who was known for such romantic hits as "You Made Me Love You," he played with Benny Goodman's orchestra in the late 1930's, then started his own, which briefly featured the young Frank Sinatra. Died July 5, age 67.

An influential Democratic senator from Washington, "Scoop" Jackson was first elected to Congress as a U.S. representative in 1940.

Jones, Carolyn, American actress. A stage, screen, and television performer, she played the macabre Morticia in the television series *The Addams Family.* Died Aug. 3, age 50.

Kahn, Herman, American political philosopher. A leading thinker on nuclear strategy and the future, he was the author of such books as *Thinking About the Unthinkable* (1962) and *The Coming Boom* (1982). Died July 7, age 61.

Keats, Ezra Jack, American illustrator. An award-winning artist and author of children's books, his *The Snowy Day* won a Caldecott Medal in 1963. Died May 6, age 67.

Kline, Nathan Schellenberg, American psychiatrist. He pioneered the use of tranquilizers and antidepressants in the treatment of the mentally ill. Died Feb. 11, age 66.

Koestler, Arthur, Hungarian-British author. An essayist, journalist, novelist, dramatist, and cultural and scientific historian, he wrote the classic anti-Communist novel *Darkness at Noon* (1940). In turn a Zionist, Communist, and antitotalitarian, he also supported voluntary euthanasia; suffering from Parkinson's disease and leukemia, he took his own life in a double suicide with his wife. Found dead March 3, age 77.

Lansky, Meyer (Maier Suchowljansky), Russian-American underworld financier. The financial genius of organized crime, he rose from poverty by applying his talents to bootlegging, gambling, loansharking, stock manipulation, and the penetration of legitimate businesses. Died Jan. 15, age about 80.

One of the great political authors of the 20th century, Arthur Koestler wrote the classic novel Darkness at Noon *(1941). A supporter of voluntary euthanasia and suffering from serious illness, he committed suicide with his wife, also shown here.*

Leopold III, former king of Belgium. After 17 years on the throne, he abdicated in 1951 because of public furor over his surrender to invading German troops in World War II. Died Sept. 25, age 81.

Lewis, Robert Alvin, American pilot. He was copilot of the *Enola Gay,* the B-29 that dropped the atomic bomb on Hiroshima in 1945. Died June 18, age 65.

Liao Chengzhi, Chinese politician. A specialist in relations with Taiwan and Hong Kong, he had been expected to be elected vice-president of China. Died June 10, age 75.

Livingstone, Mary (Sadye Marks), American actress. A wisecracking comedian, she appeared with her husband Jack Benny on decades of radio and television shows. Died June 30, age 77.

Llewellyn, Richard (Richard Dafydd Vivian Llewellyn Lloyd), Welsh author. A playwright and novelist, he was best known for his first novel, *How Green Was My Valley* (1939),

Raymond Massey was best known for playing Abraham Lincoln on stage and Dr. Gillespie on TV.

which was made into an Academy Award–winning film in 1941. Died Nov. 30, age 76.

Lutyens, Agnes Elisabeth, British composer. Her many atonal works ranged from chamber concerti to opera to scores for radio plays and included the lyric drama *Isis and Osiris* (1969). Died April 14, age 76.

Macdonald, Ross (Kenneth Millar), American novelist. His carefully crafted mysteries featuring detective Lew Archer included *The Moving Target* (1949) and *The Blue Hammer* (1976). Died July 11, age 67.

Maclean, Donald Duart, British diplomat and spy for the Soviet Union. He fled the West in 1951 just before being exposed as a traitor; while serving in the British embassy in Washington, D.C., from 1944 to 1948 and as head of the British Foreign Office's American department in 1950 and 1951 he had access to vital secrets. Died March 6, age 69.

Markevitch, Igor, Russian-born musician. His early fame as a composer was overshadowed by his success as a conductor; he was especially noted for his precise control on the podium. Died March 7, age 70.

Marshall, Catherine (Catherine Marshall LeSourd), American author. She wrote such inspirational best-sellers as *A Man Called Peter* (1951)—a biography of her late husband, U.S. Senate Chaplain Peter Marshall—and the novel *Christy* (1967). Died March 18, age 68.

Massey, Raymond Hart, Canadian-American actor. Featured in more than 60 films, he won lasting fame for his Broadway portrayal of Abraham Lincoln in *Abe Lincoln in Illinois* (1938); he also played Dr. Gillespie in the 1960's television series *Dr. Kildare.* Died July 29, age 86.

McBride, Lloyd, American labor leader. A steelworker since the age of 14, the longtime union organizer had been president of the United Steelworkers of America since 1977. Died Nov. 6, age 67.

McCall, Thomas Lawson (Tom), American politician. A progressive Republican and ardent conservationist, he was governor of Oregon from 1967 to 1975 and fought for curbs on land development and on pollution. Died Jan. 8, age 69.

McDonald, Lawrence Patton, American politician. An ultraconservative Democratic congressman from Georgia since 1975, he was chairman of the John Birch Society. Died Sept. 1 when a Korean Air Lines jet was shot down in the Sea of Japan; age 48.

Medeiros, Humberto Cardinal, Portuguese-American churchman. Spiritual leader of Boston's Roman Catholics and a cardinal since 1973, he was a theological conservative and a champion of immigrant workers, the poor, and minorities. Died Sept. 17, age 67.

Mennin, Peter (Peter Mennini), American composer. President of the Juilliard School of Music since 1962, he wrote sonorous, often dissonant choral and instrumental works, including nine symphonies. Died June 17, age 60.

Micombero, Michel, former president of Burundi. Taking power in a 1966 coup that deposed the country's last king, he was himself overthrown in a 1976 coup. Died July 16, age 43.

Miller, William Edward, American politician. Republican candidate for U.S. vice-president on the 1964 ticket with Barry Goldwater, he served seven terms as a congressman from New York State. Died June 24, age 69.

Miró, Joan, Spanish artist. A profound influence on 20th-century art, he was a leader of the Surrealist movement and a painter, sculptor, muralist, and maker of constructions and assemblages; he was best known for his mosaic murals and brightly colored paintings. Died Dec. 25, age 90.

Model, Lisette (Lisette Seyberg), Austrian-American photographer. A longtime teacher at the New School for Social Research, she was best known for her fat and often grotesque subjects. Died March 30, age 76.

Monroe, Marion, American child psychologist. She was coauthor of the *Dick and Jane* reading books, read by millions of U.S. schoolchildren from the 1940's until the early 1970's. Died June 25, age 85.

Moorehead, Alan, Australian-born author. A World War II correspondent, he wrote many popular historical works, including *Gallipoli* (1956) and *The White Nile* (1960). Died Sept. 29, age 73.

Nearing, Scott, American environmentalist. Popular proponent of a self-sufficient, vegetarian life-style, he was an outspoken pacifist,

Debonair David Niven's Hollywood career spanned 48 years and included nearly 100 films.

socialist, and back-to-the-land movement leader; he and his wife Helen wrote *Living the Good Life* (1954). Died Aug. 24, age 100.

Niven, David (James David Graham Niven), Scottish-born American actor. He appeared in nearly 100 films, including *The Moon Is Blue* (1953) and *Separate Tables* (1958), for which he won an Academy Award as best actor; his two volumes of reminiscences, *The Moon's a Balloon* (1971) and *Bring on the Empty Horses* (1975) sold more than 10 million copies. Died July 29, age 73.

O'Brien, Pat (William Joseph O'Brien), American actor. Hollywood's archetypal Irishman, he acted in more than 100 movies, most notably *Knute Rockne—All American* (1940). Died Oct. 15, age 83.

Payne (Pierre Stephen) Robert, British-American author. A novelist, poet, translator, and journalist who produced more than 100 books, he was well known for his numerous biographies, whose subjects included Lenin and Hitler. Died Feb. 18, age 71.

Pelkey, Edward ("Fast Eddie"), American pool player. A high-stakes pool shark, he was portrayed by Paul Newman in the movie *The Hustler* (1961). Died Feb. 21, age about 85.

Pelshe, Arvid Yanovich, Latvian-born Soviet politician. A member of the Politburo since 1966, he was the last of the top Soviet leaders to have taken part in the 1917 Bolshevik revolution. Died May 29, age 84.

Pevsner, Nikolaus Bernhard Leon, German-British architectural critic and historian. He wrote such classic works as *An Outline of European Architecture* (1942) and the 46-volume *The Buildings of England* (1951–1974). Died Aug. 18, age 81.

Pickens, Slim (Louis Bert Lindley, Jr.), American actor. A rodeo performer turned cowboy movie star, he appeared in dozens of "B" pictures but was best known for his role as the B-52 commander in the film *Dr. Strangelove.* Died Dec. 8, age 64.

Pinheiro de Azevedo, José Baptista, Portuguese political leader. An officer in the Portuguese navy, he played a major role in the 1974 coup and served as prime minister in 1975 and 1976. Died Aug. 10, age 66.

Podgorny, Nikolai Viktorovich, Soviet politician. He served as chairman of the Presidium of the Supreme Soviet (titular chief of state) from 1965 to 1977. Died Jan. 11, age 79.

Qiao Guanhua, Chinese politician. As China's foreign minister from 1972 to 1974, he helped normalize Chinese-U.S. relations; he was dismissed after the arrest of the Gang of Four faction. Died Sept. 22, age 70.

Raphaelson, Samson, American playwright and screenwriter. His first play, *The Jazz Singer,* was a Broadway hit in 1925 and was made into the first sound movie; he also wrote the screenplays for such films as *Suspicion* (1941) and *Heaven Can Wait* (1943). Died July 16, age 87.

Renault, Mary (Mary Challans), British novelist. Her popular and highly praised historical novels of the ancient world included *The King Must Die* (1958), *The Bull From the Sea* (1962), and *The Last of the Wine* (1975). Died Dec. 13, age 78.

Reynolds, Frank, American television journalist. Beginning his career as a local broadcaster in Chicago, he was a widely respected

Sir Ralph Richardson had a long, distinguished theatrical career in England and the United States.

anchorman of ABC's *World News Tonight* from 1978 to 1983. Died July 20, age 59.

Richardson, Sir Ralph, British actor. Best known for such stage roles as Falstaff in *Henry IV* (1945) and a deranged old man in David Storey's *Home* (1970), he also appeared in such movies as *The Heiress* (1949) and *Doctor Zhivago* (1965). Died Oct. 10, age 80.

Robinson, Joan Violet, British economist. A collaborator with John Maynard Keynes on his major theories, she was an influential member of the so-called Cambridge School of economics. Died Aug. 5, age 79.

Robinson, John Arthur Thomas, British theologian. Ordained an Anglican bishop in 1959, he stirred controversy with his unorthodox interpretations of traditional doctrine in such books as *Honest to God* (1963). Died Dec. 5, age 64.

Rosenberg, Anna Marie (Anna Rosenberg Hoffman), Hungarian-born U.S. government official. The first woman to be awarded the

Medal of Freedom (1945), she was, as assistant secretary of defense from 1950 to 1953, the highest-ranking woman then to serve in the Pentagon. Died May 9, age 80.

Rosenthal, Benjamin Stanley, American politician. Democratic congressman from New York City since 1962, he was an outspoken supporter of liberal causes. Died Jan. 4, age 59.

Roy, Gabrielle, French-Canadian author. She was best known for her first novel, *Bonheur d'occasion* (1945; translated in 1947 as *The Tin Flute*). Died July 13, age 74.

Samples, Junior (Alvin Samples), American comedian. A regular performer on the television show *Hee Haw*, he was known for his deadpan delivery. Died Nov. 13, age 56.

Sartawi, Issam Ali, Palestinian diplomat. A moderate Palestine Liberation Organization official, he supported recognition of Israel. Assassinated April 10, age 47.

Savitch, Jessica, American television reporter. She was one of the first women to anchor an evening network newscast. Died Oct. 23 in a car accident, age 35.

Jessica Savitch was one of the first women to anchor an evening network television newscast.

Sert, José Luis, Spanish-American architect and city planner. A follower of Le Corbusier, he designed numerous buildings for Harvard and Boston University as well as Barcelona's Miró Museum. Died March 15, age 80.

Shearer, Norma, Canadian-American film actress. A star during the 1920's and 1930's, she made more than 60 movies including such films as *The Student Prince* (1927), *The Divorcee* (1930), for which she won an Academy Award, and *The Barretts of Wimpole Street* (1934). Died June 12, age about 80.

Slezak, Walter, Austrian-American actor. A stage and screen performer who specialized in character roles, he won a Tony award for his performance in *Fanny* (1955). Died April 22 of a self-inflicted gunshot wound, age 80.

Stankiewicz, Richard Peter, American sculptor. A pioneer of "junk art," he transformed such scrap material as pipes and boilers into pointedly witty constructions. Died March 27, age 60.

Stapleton, Ruth Carter, American evangelist. The sister of former President Jimmy Carter, she was a "born-again" faith healer and author of inspirational works. Died Sept. 26, age 54.

Stead, Christina Ellen, Australian novelist. She was best known for her novel *The Man Who Loved Children* (1940), which was hailed as a masterpiece on its 1965 reissue. Died March 31, age 80.

Stevens, Robert Ten Broeck, American government official. As secretary of the army (1953–1955), he debated Senator Joseph McCarthy in televised hearings that marked the beginning of the collapse of McCarthy's anti-Communist campaign. Died Jan. 30, age 83.

Struble, Arthur Dewey, American naval admiral. He directed naval operations in the 1944 Normandy invasion in World War II and commanded the fleet that carried out the 1950 landing at Inchon in the Korean war. Died May 1, age 88.

Swanson, Gloria (Gloria May Josephine Swenson), American film actress. Glamorous star of such silent movies as *Male and Female* (1919) and *Sadie Thompson* (1928), she made a stunning comeback in *Sunset Boulevard* (1950). Died April 4, age about 84.

Terayama, Shuji, Japanese playwright and film director. His movies, noted for their shock

Glamorous goddess of the silent screen, Gloria Swanson was a symbol of Hollywood's golden age.

than 60 years, he most recently did portraits of such celebrities as Eubie Blake and Muhammad Ali. Died May 15, age 96.

Vinogradov, Ivan Matveyevich, Soviet mathematician. As director of the Institute of Mathematics from 1932, he reportedly used his influence to bar the advancement of Jewish mathematicians. Died March 20, age 91.

Von Euler, Ulf Svante, Swedish scientist. A cowinner of the 1970 Nobel Prize in physiology or medicine, he discovered that the chemical noradrenaline is the key transmitter of nerve impulses in the sympathetic nervous system. Died March 10, age 78.

Vorster, Balthazar Johannes (John), South African politician. As longtime prime minister, from 1966 to 1978, he staunchly enforced apartheid policies. Died Sept. 10, age 67.

Wallenstein, Alfred (Franz), American conductor. A cellist, he was music director of the Los Angeles Philharmonic from 1943 to 1956; during the 1920's and 1930's, he helped introduce classical music to radio. Died Feb. 8, age 84.

effect, made him a leader in avant-garde circles. Died May 4, age 47.

Traynor, Roger John, American judge. In 30 years on the California Supreme Court (1940–1970), the last six as chief justice, he wrote over 900 opinions, establishing key precedents in such areas as discrimination, defendants' rights, and tax law. Died May 14, age 83.

Troisgros, Jean Georges, French chef. A leading practitioner of nouvelle cuisine, he ran, with his brother, one of the few restaurants to win three stars in the Michelin guide. Died Aug. 8, age 56.

Tunner, William Henry, American military officer. As a U.S. Air Force general, he directed the Berlin airlift of 1948–1949, which brought supplies to West Berlin during an 11-month Soviet blockade. Died April 6, age 76.

Tupper, Earl Silas, American businessman. He created the Tupperware plastic food containers and devised the popular neighborhood party method for selling them. Died Oct. 3, age 76.

Van Brocklin, Norman (Norm), American football player and coach. A National Football League Hall of Fame quarterback for 12 seasons (1949–1960), he later coached the Minnesota Vikings and the Atlanta Falcons. Died May 2, age 57.

Van Der Zee, James, American photographer. A portrayer of black middle-class experience in New York City's Harlem for more

Dame Rebecca West's literary output was characterized by intelligence, wit, and compassion.

Walton, William Turner, British composer. Among his best known works were the irreverent *Façade* (1923), the oratorio *Belshazzar's Feast* (1931), and coronation marches for George VI (1937) and Elizabeth II (1953). Died March 8, age 80.

Ward, Theodore, American playwright. His most acclaimed works, *Big White Fog* (1940) and *Our Lan'* (1947), depicted racial oppression and the spirit of American blacks fighting to overcome it. Died May 8, age 80.

Waterfield, Robert (Bob), American football player. A National Football League Hall of Fame quarterback, he led the Cleveland Rams to a world championship in 1945. Died March 25, age 62.

Waters, Muddy (McKinley Morganfield), American blues singer, songwriter, and guitarist. The developer of a hard-driving style that inspired British and American rock bands, he performed such hits as "Rollin' Stone" and "Hoochie Coochie Man." Died April 30, age 68.

Blues singer Muddy Waters was known for such hits as "Rollin' Stone" and "Hoochie Coochie Man."

Wechsler, James Arthur, American journalist. A former editor of the New York *Post,* he was an outspoken liberal columnist. Died Sept. 11, age 67.

Weiss, Louise, French author, A feminist who was the oldest member of the European Parliament, she received the Europa Prize in 1980 for her six-volume autobiography. Died May 26, age 90.

West, Dame Rebecca (Cicily Isabel Fairfield Andrews), British author. Her wide-ranging output included history, biography, criticism, novels, and political commentary; among her most notable books were *Black Lamb and Grey Falcon* (1941) and *The Meaning of Treason* (1947). Died March 15, age 90.

Wibberley, Leonard Patrick O'Connor, British-American journalist and author; he was best known for his 1955 best-seller *The Mouse That Roared,* later made into a movie starring Peter Sellers. Died Nov. 22, age 68.

Williams, Tennessee (Thomas Lanier Williams), American playwright. His best plays included *The Glass Menagerie* (1945) and, subsequently, *A Streetcar Named Desire* (1947) and *Cat on a Hot Tin Roof* (1955), both of which won Pulitzer Prizes; his lyrically passionate, richly symbolic works, which also included novels, short stories, and poems, typically portrayed the lonely, the odd, or the outcast and often reflected his Southern roots. Died Feb. 25, age 71.

Wilson, Dennis, American rock musician. Drummer, keyboardist, and singer for the popular group known as the Beach Boys, he specialized in songs about surfing. Died Dec. 28 in a drowning accident, age 39.

Winding, Kai Chresten, Danish-American jazz musician. One of the first to apply modern jazz principles to the trombone, he collaborated with Benny Goodman, Stan Kenton, and Miles Davis in recordings and appearances. Died May 6, age 60.

Young, Milton Ruben, American politician. A North Dakotan known as "Mr. Wheat," he served 36 years (1945–1981) in the U.S. Senate, the longest continuous Senate service by a Republican. Died May 31, age 85.

Zablocki, Clement John, American politician. A Wisconsin Democrat, he had served as a U.S. representative since 1949 and as chairman of the House Foreign Affairs Committee sine 1977; he was a staunch conservative and a skilled conciliator. Died Dec. 3, age 71.   M.H.

OHIO. See STATISTICS OF THE WORLD.

OKLAHOMA. See STATISTICS OF THE WORLD.

OMAN. See STATISTICS OF THE WORLD. See also PERSIAN GULF STATES.

ONTARIO. See STATISTICS OF THE WORLD.

OREGON. See STATISTICS OF THE WORLD.

ORGANIZATION OF AMERICAN STATES, abbreviated OAS. In September the Organization of American States sponsored an extraordinary conference in Caracas to discuss the massive foreign debt of the Latin American countries, estimated by the OAS at $330 billion. The four-day meeting concluded with a resolution directing the OAS's economic and social council to present to the United States, by March 30, 1984, a number of requests, including one for increased availability of export finance for Latin American and Caribbean nations.

The annual OAS General Assembly convened in Washington, D.C., in November. Defending the recent U.S.-led invasion of Grenada, U.S. Deputy Secretary of State Kenneth Dam asserted that "the overwhelming and positive reaction of Grenadians. . .confirmed the correctness" of the move. Supporting Dam, Salvadoran Foreign Minister Fidel Chávez Mena, following his election as president of the General Assembly, called Grenada's short-lived revolutionary government "a real threat to all its neighbors." The invasion, however, was criticized by many of the 30 nations represented. Mexico's Foreign Minister Bernardo Sepulveda Amor, leading the opposition, said there could be "no motive that would legitimize" it.

Mexico, Panama, Venezuela, and Colombia, which had established themselves as mediators in the Central American conflict, proposed to the General Assembly that the five Central American nations—Nicaragua, Costa Rica, Honduras, Guatemala, and El Salvador—sign peace treaties immediately. Assembly delegates quickly and unanimously endorsed the resolution and the activities of its sponsors, known as the Contadora group. The assembly had opened with a surprising announcement from OAS Secretary-General Alejandro Orfila of Argentina, who, after criticizing the United States for neglecting Latin America and blaming the OAS itself for a "lack of relevance and effectiveness," resigned as its leader, effective in early 1984. A new secretary-general was scheduled to be chosen at a special General Assembly of the organization, called for March 1984.   A.E.J.

ORGANIZATION OF PETROLEUM EXPORTING COUNTRIES, abbreviated OPEC. Internal differences among OPEC members over levels of production and price continued to threaten the unity of the organization during 1983, and its influence was threatened by the weakened world demand for oil. OPEC's dominant position was also undermined by growing competition in world markets from Egyptian oil and from North Sea oil produced by Great Britain and Norway.

The growing importance and cumulative price reductions of non-OPEC producers was one factor that by early 1983 had forced the organization to consider lowering its own prices. Crude oil exports of the 13 OPEC members had fallen 23 percent during 1982, and OPEC's share of world oil sales fell to 64 percent in 1982, from 72 percent in 1981. Production in 1982 fell from half to just over a third of the world's supply. In mid-February 1983, Great Britain and Norway announced oil price reductions of $3 a barrel, to $30.50. Within OPEC, Nigeria, faced with severe economic problems, attempted to increase its share of the market by producing more than its allocated quota and by lowering prices below the agreed $34 a barrel minimum, to $30. To prevent an internal price war among OPEC members, oil ministers from Arab Gulf states held urgent consultations during late February. Saudi Arabia and five other Arab states decided to lower their prices at that time by $4 a barrel and threatened further cuts if other OPEC members broke discipline.

On behalf of its Gulf allies, Saudi Arabia also warned dissident OPEC members to agree on a price minimum and a strict division of world markets or to be prepared for an all-out price war. The Gulf producers' share, still nearly 40 percent of all OPEC production, gave them a powerful position, although their share of production was on the decline.

At an emergency meeting of the organization in Geneva during January, OPEC nations had already agreed to reduce total production from 18.5 million to 17.5 million barrels a day, but a serious dispute remained over price adjustments reflecting differences in quality. Another major problem was allocation of production quotas among member states. Iran continued to dispute Saudi domination of OPEC policies, and threatened to raise its production levels to those of Saudi Arabia.

Some stability was achieved at OPEC's London meeting in March with an agreement to cut prices for the first time in the group's 23-year history. The basic reduction was 15 percent, to $29 a barrel, in Saudi light crude, the organization's benchmark for other oil prices. Agreement was also reached on national quotas, with Saudi Arabia, which was to act as the balancer of supplies on the world market, exempted from a quota. Members also agreed to avoid discounts.

At the organization's second biannual meeting in December, an Iranian call for the use of the "oil weapon" against the United States did not find support. Members agreed to maintain the 17.5-million-barrel-a-day production ceiling and the $29-a-barrel benchmark price. Member nations could not agree on a secretary-general to fill the position formerly held by Marc Saturnin Nan Nguema of Gabon; Kamal Hassan Maghur, Libya's oil minister, was named acting secretary-general, as well as being elected president of OPEC. D.P.

Qatar's oil minister, Sheikh Abdul Aziz bin Khalifa al-Thani (center), talked to reporters in London before the March OPEC meeting at which members agreed on the first price cut in the organization's 23-year history.

P

PACIFIC ISLANDS. In plebiscites during 1983, voters approved compacts of "free association" for three of the four units of the U.S. Trust Territory of the Pacific Islands—the Federated States of Micronesia (Yap, Truk, Kosrae, and Ponape), the republic of Palau (Belau), and the Marshall Islands. The compacts, providing for independence from the United States except in defense matters and for long-term U.S. aid, were ratified by local bodies in Micronesia in August and in the Marshall Islands in September; in Palau, however, the plebiscite was overturned by its Supreme Court, and a new compact was being drafted.

A cyclone called the worst in 50 years devastated Fiji on March 1, killing several people and causing extensive damage. A series of devastating cyclones also struck French Polynesia.

France announced a status of autonomy for New Caledonia in March. Discussions of arrangements for possible independence created an increasingly tense situation through the year.

Vanuatu's first general election since independence in 1980 was held in November. Prime Minister Walter Lini and his Vanuaaku Party were returned to power, but with a reduced majority of nine seats—down from 13—in the 39-seat Parliament. Vanuatu saw a marked decline in economic activity, compounded by the collapse in the price of copra. Western Samoa's economy was distressed as well; its poor state was reflected in a 16 percent devaluation in the Western Samoa dollar in March. After March general elections in the Cook Islands, the Parliament had 13 members from the Cook Islands Party and 11 from the Democratic Party. In a complicated series of events, the number of sitting members fell to 22, which left the two parties evenly represented and the islands without a prime minister until a second election, held in November, returned the Democratic Party's Sir Thomas Davis to the prime ministership.

See STATISTICS OF THE WORLD.   R.J.S.

PACIFIC ISLANDS, TRUST TERRITORY OF THE. See PACIFIC ISLANDS.

PAKISTAN. The military junta led by President Muhammad Zia ul-Haq gave particular attention in 1983 to the reconstruction of Pakistan's political life and to the country's diplomatic and security requirements. Protests and rioting taxed the stability imposed by martial law, but the country's economy improved, and the government spoke optimistically about its new five-year plan.

Politics and government. On August 12, President Zia announced the formation of a "new" political system, to go into effect in March 1985. Under the new system, the prime minister would be appointed by the president and made responsible to him. The Parliament could be dissolved by the president and new elections called by executive order. Political parties (banned since 1979) would not be permitted to run candidates for the Parliament or the provincial legislatures, and the president would be indirectly elected through the votes of the Parliament and the legislatures. Zia continued to maintain that factional politics are not in harmony with Islam. He indicated that martial law would remain in force until parliamentary and provincial elections in March 1985.

Two days after Zia's announcement, the Movement for the Restoration of Democracy, an alliance of eight political parties, began a campaign of civil disobedience to protest military rule. The campaign developed into large-scale antigovernment protests and rioting, centered in the southern state of Sind; the riots and police action against them had resulted, by the end of October, in the deaths of more than 60 people and the arrests of thousands. As the riots continued, Zia began discussions with opposition leaders about a return to civilian rule.

Foreign affairs. In January, a consignment of U.S.-made F-16's arrived in Pakistan, part of a $3.2 billion economic and military aid package agreed to in 1981. Despite such military

An estimated 3 million Afghans have fled to refugee camps in Pakistan to escape the fighting between Soviet forces and guerrillas.

assistance, Zia insisted his government was not interested in a new alliance with the United States, nor would it provide the Americans with bases in Pakistan.

On March 10, following an earlier meeting between Zia and India's Prime Minister Indira Ghandi, an Indo-Pakistani commission was established to promote a détente between the two old adversaries. Pakistani and Afghan foreign ministers met in Geneva, Switzerland, in April and June, but no agreement was reached about the withdrawal of Soviet troops from Afghanistan; Islamabad reiterated its refusal to recognize Afghanistan's Soviet-backed regime.

Economy and society. Pakistan's gross national product during 1982–1983 increased by 6.5 percent, compared with 5.4 percent for the preceding fiscal year. Self-sufficiency was achieved in wheat and sugar, and a surplus was projected for export purposes. A major wheat sale was negotiated with Iran.

The Zia government reported a $241 million surplus in the balance of payments for 1982–1983, and the country's rate of inflation in fiscal 1983 fell to 6.7 percent from 10.7 percent the year before. Nonetheless, the projected

1983–1984 budget envisaged a substantial deficit. Pakistan's sixth five-year plan, approved in May, gave special emphasis to literacy programs, seeking to raise the number of literates from 3.9 million to 33 million.

See STATISTICS OF THE WORLD.   L.Z.

PALESTINE LIBERATION ORGANIZATION, abbreviated PLO. The PLO, already weakened by its military defeat by Israel in the 1982 war in Lebanon, suffered another major setback in 1983. A Syrian-backed rebellion split the organization, and those loyal to Chairman Yasir Arafat had to evacuate their last base in Lebanon to avoid complete defeat by the rebels.

Although Arafat was unanimously reelected chairman of the PLO by the Palestine National Council in its February meeting in Algiers, discontent with his leadership had been building up since the 1982 defeat in Lebanon. The discontent was aggravated by Arafat's cautious interest in a peace plan set forth by U.S. President Ronald Reagan calling for a self-governing Palestinian entity linked to Jordan. Although the council endorsed the alternate Arab League plan, which reaffirmed the Palestinian goal of a completely independent state,

Arafat persuaded it not to explicitly reject the Reagan plan. Arafat's unsuccessful talks with Jordan's King Hussein in April, in which an attempt was made to create a joint Jordanian-Palestinian negotiating team for Palestinian autonomy talks, further angered elements in the PLO.

Open mutiny erupted in May within al-Fatah, the PLO's largest guerrilla group, headed by Arafat himself. The military leader of the rebellion was Said Musa, who had been displaced as military commander in Lebanon's Bekaa Valley when Arafat appointed two close associates to command al-Fatah forces there. (He later dismissed them as a concession to PLO rebels.) The dissidents, who included members of the other PLO groups, demanded that Arafat convene a general congress of al-Fatah to reject both the Reagan plan and the Arab League plan (which implied recognition of the state of Israel), to purge corrupt PLO bureaucrats, and to restore collective leadership. Arafat accused Syria of orchestrating the rebellion, a charge he repeated during a visit to Damascus, which resulted in his expulsion from Syria on June 24.

With Syrian support, the rebels managed to overwhelm pro-Arafat forces in the Bekaa Valley and the Shouf Mountains and take over al-Fatah offices in Syria. Arafat's followers were trapped in the Tripoli area of Lebanon and by early November were under siege in the city of Tripoli, where the fierce fighting caused many civilian casualties. Arafat ultimately arranged for the evacuation of himself and 4,000 armed followers on Greek transport ships flying United Nations flags. This operation, delayed several days when Israeli gunboats off the coast shelled Tripoli's port area, was finally carried out on December 20. About a month earlier, close to 6,000 other Palestinians and Lebanese were released from custody by Israel, in exchange for Arafat's release of six Israeli prisoners.

On December 22, Arafat, in a surprise move, went to Cairo and met with Egyptian President Hosni Mubarak. The meeting, suggesting a new shift toward moderation, was welcomed by U.S. officials but denounced by previously neutral members of the PLO as well as by the pro-Syrian dissidents. Afterward, Arafat met

PLO leader Yasir Arafat visits his troops in the Lebanese city of Tripoli, a few weeks before the evacuation of Arafat and 4,000 loyalists from their besieged stronghold.

with PLO associates in the Yemen Arab Republic and, late in the year, convened a policy meeting of the al-Fatah Central Committee in Tunisia.   W.W.H.

PANAMA. In spite of slow economic growth and high unemployment, Panama in 1983 managed to avoid the worst effects of the world recession and to maintain domestic stability. In April the Panamanian electorate approved a series of constitutional amendments proposed by a Constitutional Reform Commission. Most important was an attempt to reduce the public role of the National Guard, Panama's combined army and police force, by forbidding its members to enter politics. The amended constitution also provides for the direct election of a president, two vice-presidents, and a unicameral legislature no later than October

11, 1984, when President Ricardo de la Espriella's term of office ends.

The National Guard nevertheless remained a potent force in Panamanian politics. Its commander, General Rubén Darío Paredes, was initially regarded as a clear favorite for the presidency in 1984, and in August he resigned his post in what was assumed to be a prelude to his candidacy. However, Paredes proved unable to rally political support and the support of the National Guard, now commanded by General Manuel Antonio Noriega. In September, Paredes announced that he would not be a candidate and entered into an acrimonious public dispute with Noriega.

Relations with the United States were sometimes touchy. Early in the year, General Paredes charged that the U.S. ambassador was interfering in internal National Guard affairs and threatened to expel him from the country. Panama also objected to U.S. use of its Panamanian bases to support operations in Central America. Panama forged closer links with Costa Rica and became more critical of the Sandinista regime in Nicaragua. It opposed, however, putting military pressure on Nicaragua and helped found the so-called Contadora group (Panama, Colombia, Venezuela, and Mexico), which sought a negotiated political solution for the region's conflicts.

See STATISTICS OF THE WORLD.   R.L.M.

PAPUA NEW GUINEA. See STATISTICS OF THE WORLD.

PARAGUAY. On February 6, 1983, General Alfredo Stroessner was reelected president of Paraguay; he began his seventh term in August, still adhering to the system of close personal control he had followed since seizing power in 1954. Official returns showed him winning with 90 percent of the vote, but it was widely believed that the results had been manipulated by the government. In accordance with the election results, the government party received two-thirds of the legislative seats; the rest were split between opposition parties. Following the elections, the regime launched a vigorous campaign against "subversion," and in May leading members of independent student and worker organizations were arrested.

There was increasing evidence of tensions and wavering support within the pillars of the

Campaign posters in Asunción summon Paraguayans to vote for President Alfredo Stroessner. Stroessner won reelection to his seventh consecutive five-year term by garnering 90 percent of the vote according to an official, but disputed, tally.

Stroessner regime—the party, the army, and the business community. The party, for example, saw the revival of its old anti-Stroessner current, the Mopoco (Popular Colorado Movement), and the leading business associations—Feprinco and the Industrial Union—cautiously signaled their displeasure with government economic policies.

The major investment areas of the 1970's, hydroelectric projects and agribusiness, had begun to slow down, causing a 2.5 percent drop in gross domestic product in 1982—the worst performance in 30 years. Average real wages (after inflation was taken into account) fell 20 percent in 1982, and by early 1983 unemployment was around 15 percent. Foreign debt was increasing substantially, while export prices were depressed, and extensive portions of crops were wiped out by heavy floods. The result was a substantial trade deficit. The government made efforts to achieve closer ties with the United States and Western Europe, a reflection of its need for help from abroad for the shaky economy.

See STATISTICS OF THE WORLD.   J.F.Jr.

PENNSYLVANIA. See STATISTICS OF THE WORLD.

305

People in the News

Royal and presidential families claimed their usual share of public attention in 1983, as did the making and breaking of show business marriages. Feats and felonies catapulted others into the headlines, as people's fascination with the public and private lives of celebrities showed no signs of letting up.

The famous and the near-famous continued to surprise, disappoint, and inspire people-watchers in 1983. Actors and actresses, singers and comics, the socially prominent and the merely notorious shared the spotlight. Dominating the attention, however, were the occupants of the White House and those around them—as well as royalty from other lands.

Ex-president Jimmy Carter and wife Rosalynn remained in the public eye in 1983. Two chairs he made by hand were auctioned off for $41,000, the proceeds going to the Carter Presidential Library and the Carter Center at Emory University in Atlanta.

In his third year as president, **Ronald Reagan** did not officially announce that he would seek a second term, but observers believed it was only a matter of time. He did authorize a reelection committee to be formed, and he showed no signs of longing for a quiet retirement. Reagan faced serious crises abroad, ranging from the shooting down of a South Korean airliner to the bombing of U.S. Marine headquarters in Beirut; closer to home, while taking time off at the Augusta National Golf Course, the president was involved in a small but unnerving crisis when a Georgia man named **Charles Harris** crashed his pick-up truck through the club's fence, and held seven hostages at gunpoint while speaking to the president by phone. (The hostages were eventually released unharmed.)

The strains of life in the White House took their toll on **Nancy Reagan.** The first lady was looking unusually thin, and her office confirmed that she had lost a few pounds. Still vigorous, she kept up a hectic schedule, devoting special attention to her antidrug campaign. As part of that effort, she appeared on the television show *Diff'rent Strokes,* giving her first on-screen performance in 27 years; in the episode she congratulated the diminutive Arnold Jackson (played by **Gary Coleman**) for his exposé of drug dealing at P.S. 406.

Others in the Reagan family also attracted headlines. Son **Ron Reagan,** 24, caused the biggest stir, after making his debut with the first-string Joffrey Ballet Company, by announcing that he was quitting the ballet to become a writer. In an article published later in the year, Ron said he had quit partly because ballet dancers are "among the most grossly underpaid professionals in America." Son **Michael Reagan,** 38, and his wife **Colleen** had their second

President Ronald Reagan, Queen Elizabeth II, Nancy Reagan, and Prince Philip chat during the British queen's visit to California. Braving the elements, the queen was chauffeured over mountainous and flooded roads, and past an impromptu sign reading "WELCOME LIZ AND PHIL." She found the trip "delightful and terribly exciting."

child, **Ashley Marie,** on April 2. **Maureen Reagan,** 42 (who, like Michael, is the offspring of Reagan's first marriage, to actress **Jane Wyman**), made several television appearances as a commentator on *Entertainment Tonight,* and contributed some of her own Hollywood recollections. She also was hired by the Republican National Committee as a consultant on women's issues.

The Democrats were not to be outdone. House Speaker **Tip O'Neill** made a cameo appearance of his own on the television comedy *Cheers,* set in a Boston tavern. Looking quite at ease, O'Neill swapped repartee with the regulars. Former President **Jimmy Carter** spent most of the year quietly at home in Plains, Ga., but he remained in the public eye. Two pairs of chairs handmade by Carter fetched a total of $41,000 at a special Sotheby Parke Bernet auction; the proceeds from the auction went to the Carter Presidential Library and the Carter Center at Atlanta's Emory University. Carter also made political appearances, jetting,

for instance, to Ann Arbor, Mich., at the invitation of another former president, **Gerald Ford,** for a public policy conference. The year was not a happy one for Carter, however. His mother, **Lillian Carter,** who became an outspoken public figure during his administration and was universally known as "Miss Lillian," died of cancer October 30 at the age of 85. Just a month earlier his sister, evangelist and faith healer **Ruth Carter Stapleton,** 54, had also died of cancer.

Another former president, **Richard Nixon,** spent most of 1983 in his Saddle River, N.J., home, writing a new book on foreign policy, *Real Peace,* scheduled to be published in early 1984. He made his views public beforehand by traveling to Washington in October to testify before his former secretary of state, **Henry Kissinger,** head of a new bipartisan commission on Central America. Kissinger also made the requisite television appearance in a cameo role on the nighttime soap opera *Dynasty.* The filming took place at a gala celebrity fundraiser

Prince Hiro of Japan flanked by fellow students at Oxford University, where he matriculated in October. The 23-year-old prince is second in line to succeed Emperor Hirohito.

in Denver sponsored by oil tycoon **Marvin Davis.**

The Reagan administration bade farewell to the controversial **James Watt.** As secretary of the interior, Watt had continued alienating environmentalists and offending many other groups of Americans with his unorthodox decisions and intemperate remarks. On one occasion, he decided to ban the **Beach Boys,** a popular singing group, from Washington's Fourth of July celebration because they would attract "the wrong element." When the Reagans revealed that they themselves were Beach Boys fans, Watt apologized, eventually accepting the symbolic award of a plaster cast of a foot with a hole in it. Before long, however, he had slipped up again by describing his department's coal-leasing commission as including "a black . . . a woman, two Jews, and a cripple." It was the furor following this remark that led him to resign in October.

The Reagans welcomed Britain's **Queen Elizabeth** and **Prince Philip** to California in March, but the carefully planned royal tour of the state was nearly washed out by the worst weather in years. The visitors kept a stiff upper lip through the downpours—the queen even held her own umbrella—and the disrupted sched-

ules. They were able to enjoy a "Tex-Mex" meal at the Reagans' California ranch and entertain the president and first lady on their 31st wedding anniversary at a dinner aboard the royal yacht *Britannia.* But storms forced the royal couple to abandon plans for a voyage from Los Angeles to San Francisco. Toward the end of the week-long visit, the queen remarked that although many British traditions had crossed the Atlantic, "I had not realized before that weather was one of them."

The royal trip also included visits to the Cayman Islands and Mexico and to British Columbia. Later in the year, the couple made a state visit to Kenya; the visit included a tour of the game-viewing preserve in central Kenya where, in 1952, the queen, then Princess Elizabeth, had heard the news that her father, King George, was dead. The queen and Prince Philip went from Kenya to India, where they paid their respects to the memory of Indian leader Mohandas K. Gandhi at his cremation site.

Charles and **Diana,** the Prince and Princess of Wales, toured the Commonwealth, making a six-week trip to Australia and New Zealand in April and May and then heading on to Canada. Lady Diana caused a sensation in Australia by wearing a daring, off-the-shoulder gown. Little **Prince William** was along for the trip down under but did not go on with his parents to Canada, spending his first birthday, June 21, with his nanny in England. The Prince of Wales promised disappointed Canadians that he would bring his son along next time and perhaps a sibling or two. "Perhaps several by then, you never know," he joked.

Prince Charles's brother **Prince Andrew,** 23, made his own visit to Canada, in August for a two-week canoeing trip, but **Koo Stark** was nowhere in the vicinity. The American actress, who had appeared in a soft-core pornographic film and had scandalized the British in 1982 by taking a trip with the prince, did appear on the cover of *Tatler,* a British magazine, decked in jewels. Younger brother **Prince Edward,** 19, entered Jesus College at Cambridge in the fall, despite a petition by some students protesting that his grades were not high enough to be admitted. College officials promised the prince would meet the same standards and obey the same rules as any other student. Lady Diana's younger brother broke some rules, however. When **Viscount Althorp,** 19, allegedly became a bit raucous in an Oxford nightclub called Boodles, he was unceremoniously bounced. The unsympathetic British press promptly dubbed him "Diana's brat brother."

Despite such British peccadillos, Japan's royal family still believed that England was just the place for a young prince to be. They enrolled 23-year-old **Prince Hiro** at Oxford University in the fall. The family reportedly felt that the prince would be able to mingle more easily there and broaden his experience without the unblinking supervision of the Japanese press. The prince, who is second in line to the throne, had to share his rooms with a police inspector and an imperial household chamberlain.

Meanwhile, princesses were not only meeting, but marrying, young men. In Monte Carlo, **Princess Caroline of Monaco,** 26, daughter of **Prince Rainier III** and the late Princess Grace, married **Stefano Casiraghi,** 23, the Italian heir to an oil and real-estate fortune, at a private civil ceremony on December 29. Caroline's earlier marriage to French businessman-playboy **Philippe Junot** ended in a 1980 divorce.

Americans paid close attention to their own version of royalty—the Kennedys. **Jacqueline Onassis,** along with daughter **Caroline Kennedy,** 26, watched her son, **John Kennedy, Jr.,** 22, graduate from Brown University. Senator **Edward Kennedy** and **Joan Kennedy,** whose divorce became final in December, amicably attended the graduation of their daughter **Kara,** 23, from Tufts University, where the senator spoke; **Patrick,** 15, also got his father to speak at his graduation from the Fessenden school. More unexpectedly, Senator Kennedy appeared with the Reverend **Jerry Falwell,** of Moral Majority, to address an audience at Liberty Baptist College in Lynchburg, Va. The engagement came about after a membership

To mark the 20th anniversary of the death of John F. Kennedy, family members gathered for a graveside memorial service. From the left, JFK's brother-in-law Stephen Smith, his wife Jean, Senator Edward Kennedy, JFK's daughter Caroline, and sisters Eunice Shriver and Patricia Lawford.

Elizabeth Taylor and Richard Burton costarred in a Broadway revival of Noel Coward's play Private Lives, sparking rumors that the two would get back together in their own not-so-private lives. But Burton married his companion Sally Hay, and Taylor announced her engagement to lawyer Victor Gonzalez Luna, putting an end to the public's fantasies of a continued storybook romance.

card for Moral Majority was accidentally mailed to the senator. When the incident was made public, Kennedy was invited to Lynchburg.

Robert Kennedy, Jr., was the subject of unpleasant headlines. In September, while on a flight to South Dakota, he became ill; drugs were found in his flight bag, and he was arrested. He later announced he had admitted himself to a hospital "for treatment of a drug problem." Earlier in the year, the 29-year-old son of the late Senator Robert F. Kennedy walked out of the New York State Bar exam, which he had previously failed in 1982.

On November 22, many members of the Kennedy family gathered at the grave of President John F. Kennedy on the 20th anniversary of his assassination and later in the day attended a memorial mass in Washington, D.C. In Hyannisport, Mass., Jacqueline Onassis and **Rose Kennedy,** the 93-year-old matriarch of the Kennedy clan, attended a private memorial service.

Hollywood also commanded attention in 1983. Two leading lights, **Elizabeth Taylor** and **Richard Burton,** went to Broadway, where they starred in a revival of Noel Coward's play Private Lives. The critics gave the production mixed reviews, but the public was fascinated by the private lives behind the scenes. Offstage, Burton married companion **Sally Hay,** a production secretary, in a Las Vegas ceremony on July 3. Six weeks later, Taylor announced her engagement to Mexican lawyer **Victor Gonzalez Luna.**

Rolling Stones star **Mick Jagger,** who turned 40 in August, seemed ready to settle down. When his long-time girlfriend, model **Jerry Hall,** 27, who was expecting a baby, said they planned to marry, Jagger at first denied it but eventually agreed to set a date. He was beaten to the punch, however, by partner **Keith Richards,** who married actress-model **Patti Hansen,** 27, on his own 40th birthday in late December.

Many celebrities tied the knot during the year. Academy-Award-winning actor **Richard Dreyfus,** 35, married **Jeramie Rain,** a free-lance writer, on March 20. Supreme Court Justice **William Brennan,** 76, married **Mary Fowler,** 68, his secretary of 25 years, on March 9. The marriage was revealed in a brief memo left by the justice, saying the couple had gone to Bermuda. Comic actor **Dan Aykroyd,** 30, married television actress **Donna Dixon,** 25, on April 29 in Massachusetts. Flamboyant rock star **Jerry Lee Lewis,** 47, married **Shawn Michelle Stephens,** 25, on June 7 in Mississippi. It was his fifth marriage. Happiness turned to tragedy, however, when the bride was found dead of a suspected drug overdose on August 24. In New York, singer **Paul Simon,** 40, wed actress **Carrie Fisher,** 26, in August. The actress's parents, **Debbie Reynolds** and **Eddie Fisher,** were among the small audience. In November, actress **Mary Tyler Moore,** 45, wed

S. Robert Levine, 29, a cardiologist, at a ceremony in Manhattan's Hotel Pierre.

Other couples were separated or divorced. Playwright **Neil Simon** and actress **Marsha Mason** parted after nine years of marriage, during which time she had appeared in many of his films. *Star Wars* director **George Lucas** and his wife, **Marcia,** a film editor, announced their breakup before their movie company staff while holding hands; the couple divided an estate said to be worth $35 million. Perhaps the most widely publicized split was between *Tonight Show* host **Johnny Carson,** 58, and his wife of ten years, **Joanna,** 42, a former model. She demanded support payments of $2.6 million yearly, pending division of Carson's estimated $15 million net worth. On the air, the entertainer was unflappable. "I heard from my cat's lawyer today," he quipped on one show. "My cat wants $12,000 a week for Tender Vittles."

Several rising stars greeted people watchers in 1983. **Vanessa Williams,** 20, became the first black Miss America in the 62-year-history of the pageant. The Syracuse University theater major won the talent competition by belting out "Happy Days Are Here Again." Comic actor **Eddie Murphy,** 22, became a hot com-

A smiling Vanessa Williams clasps her scepter after being selected Miss America 1984 at the annual pageant in Atlantic City, N.J. She was the first black woman to win the title during the contest's 63-year history.

modity by appearing in two hit movies and signing a $15 million contract with Paramount Pictures—all this in addition to his regular appearances on television's *Saturday Night Live.* Actress **Brooke Shields,** 18, enrolled at Princeton in the fall, where she planned to

The cast of M*A*S*H *during the show's last days. After 10½ years on the air, the program finished up a winner: it ranked third in the ratings (behind 60 Minutes and Dallas), and its two-hour final show was the most watched entertainment special of the season.*

Counting her millions on her fingers, Marvein Jorich and her husband Nicholas, a retired steelworker, stand in front of their new Cadillac after they won $8.8 million in the Pennsylvania lottery.

concentrate on the humanities. She was in the news earlier in the year when an appeals court refused to block the sale of nude pictures of her taken when she was ten.

Television lost a platoon of veteran stars when the farewell episode of M*A*S*H was broadcast on February 28, concluding its ten and a half years as the medium's most successful series. Across the United States, many of the program's 125 million viewers held "M*A*S*H bashes" to mark the occasion. It wasn't ratings that ended the series but the decision of members of the cast and the producers. "I had too much respect for the show to let it become an imitation of itself," explained actor **Alan Alda,** who co-wrote and directed the final show.

Another show might have become an imitation of itself, but its audiences hardly seemed to care. Once again, **Bob Hope,** 80, was off to the front at Christmas with gags, girls, and golf clubs; this time, the stage was Beirut, where Hope performed seven shows aboard six ships, with a cast that included actresses Brooke Shields and **Cathy Lee Crosby.** "If this is peacekeeping," Hope cracked to an appreciative audience, "ain't you glad you're not in a war?"

Meanwhile, the irrepressible **Monty Python** group continued their outrageous ways in their latest movie, *Monty Python's The Meaning of Life.* A typically zany film, it included a scene in which **Graham Chapman,** as a condemned man, demands that his method of execution be pursuit by nearly naked women until he collapses.

John De Lorean reappeared in the headlines. The auto magnate was arrested in 1982 for allegedly conspiring to purchase and distribute $24 million worth of cocaine in an apparent attempt to salvage his failing motor company. During the fall a videotape of his arrest by the FBI was aired by CBS News just nine days before jury selection for De Lorean's trial was to begin. The presiding judge denounced the network and postponed the trial. CBS had obtained the tape from *Hustler* magazine publisher **Larry Flynt.** In a bizarre twist, Flynt later claimed that he had an audio tape proving that De Lorean was coerced into purchasing the drugs. Flynt refused, however, to produce the tape and later said it was a fake.

Among lesser known names, **Julie Ridge,** 26, became the first person to swim twice around the island of Manhattan without leaving the water. Previously claiming recognition only for her small part in the nude Broadway show *Oh! Calcutta,* the actress splashed into the record books by completing the 56 miles in 21 hours, 2 minutes, and 49 seconds. "It was an easy swim," Ridge maintained—but perhaps only by comparison with getting an acting job.

The best candidate for happiest person of the year was **Nicholas Jorich** of Harrisburg, Pa. The 59-year-old retired steelworker became the biggest lottery winner in U.S. history, receiving an $8.8 million grand prize in the state drawing. Jorich vowed the money would go toward taking care of his family, especially his 18-month-old granddaughter, Michelle. Life for the Jorichs promptly improved. Jorich's wife Marvein gladly retired after 30 years as a night-shift waitress, and Jorich himself immediately bought a Cadillac Eldorado.   P.L.W.

ANDROPOV, YURI V(LADIMIROVICH)

General secretary of the Soviet Communist Party, born June 15, 1914, at Nagutskaya in the Caucasus. A former KGB head, Yuri Andropov was little known in the West when he became party leader in November 1982 succeeding Leonid Brezhnev; and he remained somewhat of a mystery. Andropov shored up his power by appointing allies to top posts, and he himself was named chairman of the Presidium of the Soviet Union, or in effect head of state, in June. Throughout the year he appeared to retain authority and prestige, but he withdrew from public view beginning in late August, presumably because of illness.

During the year, he placed emphasis on the need to tackle problems of low productivity and excessive bureaucracy in the Soviet Union, and the Soviet economy did, in fact, show modest improvements in performance. One of his main foreign policy goals was to prevent the planned deployment of U.S. medium-range missiles in Western Europe, but in this he was unsuccessful. As talks on this subject continued in Geneva, Andropov, like President Ronald Reagan, periodically proclaimed compromise positions, but his proposals, seemingly aimed at influencing European public opinion as much as U.S. negotiators, did not gain acceptance. In late November, after U.S. missiles began arriving in Britain and West Germany, the Soviet Union broke off the talks.

Relations with the United States had worsened after a Soviet jet shot down a South Korean civilian airliner on September 1, killing 269 people. On September 28, after some delay, Andropov issued a personal statement repeating earlier Soviet charges that the airliner had been on a U.S. spy mission.

Andropov was apparently in poor health. The last time he was seen in public was at a meeting with U.S. senators on August 18. He did not appear even at the obligatory Revolutionary Day parade on November 7 or at the party Central Committee meeting in late December, although a speech of his, vigorously assailing economic failures in the Soviet system, was read at that time, and he was lavishly praised in the press. Andropov was officially said to be suffering from a cold; unofficial reports had him suffering from kidney trouble or a respiratory or circulatory ailment, among other possibilities. His whereabouts were not known.

ASSAD, HAFEZ AL-

President of Syria, born in 1928 or 1930 (sources vary) in Qardaha in northern Syria. In 1983, Hafez al-Assad, Syria's absolute ruler, played an increasingly important role in Middle East affairs. Assad repeatedly declared his vehement opposition to an Israeli-Lebanese agreement for the simultaneous withdrawal of all foreign troops from Lebanon. He particularly opposed provisions for Israeli reconnaissance flights and joint Israeli-Lebanese patrols in a 28-mile "security zone" to be established in southern Lebanon, and he refused to remove any of the tens of thousands of Syrian troops from Lebanon, thus preventing implementation of the accord.

The Syrian president later stepped up his support for factions fighting the Lebanese government's forces. He agreed to a cease-fire in late September (which held for a time) only on the understanding that Syria would have ob-

Despite apparent health problems—he was not seen in public from August 18 through the end of the year—Soviet leader Yuri Andropov managed to push through limited economic reforms and buttress his power with key appointments to the Communist Party's Politburo.

313

William Clark, President Ronald Reagan's longtime confidant, moved from his post as national security adviser to secretary of the interior after James Watt resigned under pressure. Often called upon to play the role of troubleshooter, Clark set to work making the department less of a political liability.

server status, and some influence, at "national reconciliation" talks among Lebanese factions on the future of Lebanon. (One session of the talks was held in late 1983, with no major progress reported.)

Assad got tough with Yasir Arafat, challenging his leadership of the Palestine Liberation Organization by supporting a mutiny of radical PLO guerrillas that broke out in Lebanon in the spring. The faction loyal to Arafat was ultimately trapped in the city of Tripoli, Lebanon, by Syrian-backed rebels and was forced to evacuate the country in December. The Syrian leader also made the news in early January 1984, when he met with the Reverend Jesse Jackson and apparently gave the nod for the release of a U.S. Navy flier who had been captured on December 4 during a U.S. bombing raid on Syrian positions in Lebanon.

The Syrian leader first rose to power when he led a secret Baathist clique of air force officers that in 1963 overthrew the existing regime and brought the Baath Party into office. He became commander of the air force and

later defense minister, and in 1970 he won the presidency in a bloodless coup.

Assad was out of the public eye for a period in late 1983 because of illness. He was originally said to have had appendicitis, but later was said to have been suffering from a heart problem that was brought under control.

CLARK, WILLIAM P(ATRICK)

U.S. secretary of the interior, born October 23, 1931, in Oxnard, Cal. In a move that surprised virtually everyone, President Ronald Reagan announced on October 13 that he had selected his national security adviser, William P. Clark, to become secretary of the interior. Clark was appointed to succeed James Watt, who had resigned a few days earlier amid a storm of controversy. Clark's selection was seen as reflecting both his uneasiness in the national security position—he had expressed a desire to leave—and Reagan's high regard for him as a troubleshooter. The president described him as a "God-fearing Westerner, fourth-generation rancher, and a person I trust." Environmentalists opposed the appointment because of his conservative views and lack of related experience.

It was not the first time Clark had been tapped for a key position for which he had little apparent background. He had come to the job of White House national security adviser, in January 1982, with less experience in foreign or military affairs than any of his predecessors. Yet he clearly had the confidence of his old friend President Reagan, and he soon became one of Reagan's most influential advisers. As national security adviser, Clark reportedly urged Reagan to follow his own hardline instincts in foreign affairs—a position at odds with the more moderate views of Secretary of State George P. Shultz, whose influence had seemingly waned as Clark's grew.

Clark gained Reagan's trust when he served as his chief of staff for more than two years after Reagan was elected governor of California in 1966. Reagan later appointed him to a county judgeship, eventually promoting him to the state appeals court and then, in 1973, to the California Supreme Court. After winning the presidency, Reagan summoned Clark to Washington to be deputy secretary of state under Alexander M. Haig, Jr. He proved his value, serving as a damage control officer in the feuds that constantly erupted between the volatile Haig and the suspicious White House staff. Then, when National Security Adviser Richard V. Allen resigned, Clark was asked by Reagan to take that key post.

GLENN, JOHN H(ERSCHEL), JR.

U.S. senator, born July 18, 1921, in Cambridge, Ohio. On April 21, after many months of testing the waters, Senator John Glenn, Jr. (D, Ohio), plunged in and formally announced his candidacy for the 1984 Democratic presidential nomination.

An authentic war hero, Glenn earned four Distinguished Flying Crosses as a combat pilot in World War II and the Korean war. He earned a fifth DFC when, as a military test pilot, he made the first transcontinental supersonic flight, on July 16, 1957. In April 1959, Glenn entered NASA's Project Mercury, the first U.S. attempt to put a human being in space. The highlight

Senator John Glenn (D, Ohio), the former astronaut who was the first American to orbit the earth, campaigned hard for the Democratic presidential nomination. Appealing to traditional values and presenting himself as a political moderate, Glenn sought to counter former Vice-President Walter Mondale's early lead by building grass-roots support.

of his career as an astronaut came on February 20, 1962, when he became the first American to orbit the earth, covering a distance of more than 80,000 miles in his space capsule, *Friendship 7.*

When President John Kennedy was assassinated in November 1963, Glenn was deeply affected, and he soon quit the space program to run for the U.S. Senate from Ohio. However, an accident that caused damage to his inner ear forced him to withdraw. In 1970, he lost the Democratic senatorial primary to Howard Metzenbaum, but he returned four years later to defeat Metzenbaum in a primary fight and win election to the Senate. He was reelected in 1980 by a margin of 1.6 million votes (an Ohio record).

Glenn appeals to traditional values and regards himself as a political moderate. Although he endorsed the principle of a nuclear freeze, he has taken a relatively conservative stand on foreign policy and defense. He initially supported President Ronald Reagan's three-year tax cut and his first budget cutbacks, but by 1982 he had joined in the Democratic attack on "Reaganomics." Glenn's early campaign efforts were hampered by a somewhat lackluster speaking style and poor organization on the part of his staff. Gallup polls in the fall of 1983 showed him running ahead in "trial heats" against Reagan, and he was expected to benefit from the flattering characterization of him in *The Right Stuff*, a movie based on Tom Wolfe's book about the first astronauts, released in September. Nevertheless, his chances of catching up with front-runner Walter Mondale were considered highly uncertain.

HAWKE, ROBERT J(AMES) LEE

Prime minister of Australia, born December 9, 1929, in Bordertown, South Australia. Australia's March 5 national elections, called hastily only a month earlier by Prime Minister Malcolm Fraser, were a resounding victory for the opposition Labor Party. The ruling Liberal–National Party coalition was unable to build up steam in the campaign, and when the ballots were counted, Labor's recently elected chief, Robert Hawke, had helped his party pick up 23 seats, engineering its most spectacular electoral triumph since World War II.

Never before had anyone with so little par-

On March 5, Robert Hawke led the Australian Labor Party to its biggest electoral triumph since World War II; he was installed a week later as prime minister.

liamentary experience won the country's highest office. Hawke was, however, a well-known and popular figure in Australia. The son of a country parson, he studied economics at the University of Western Australia and went to Oxford on a Rhodes scholarship. (While in England, he set an unusual record by downing 2½ pints of beer in 12 seconds, a feat inscribed in the *Guinness Book of World Records*.) In 1959, he became an economist and wage negotiator for the Australian Council of Trade Unions, and within ten years, he had worked his way to the council presidency, where he became known as an effective negotiator.

Hawke made an unsuccessful run for Parliament in 1963. He did not try again until 1980, when he ran from a safe Labor district and won. In February 1983, Labor's parliamentary representatives accepted the resignation of party leader Bill Hayden and chose Hawke to replace him. Hawke showed himself to be a charismatic, hard-hitting campaigner.

As prime minister, Hawke faced challenges both at home and abroad. His government's first budget drew mixed reviews; while providing for an ambitious job creation program, it also called for budget-trimming cutbacks in government benefits and tax concessions. Relatively inexperienced in foreign policy, Hawke set off in June on a 25,000-mile, 19-day world

tour, which included stopovers in Jakarta, London, Paris, and Washington, D.C. He reportedly impressed his hosts, but he caused turmoil within his own party, especially by his assertion to the president of Indonesia that Australia accepted Indonesia's annexation of the former Portuguese colony of East Timor.

JACKSON, JESSE L(OUIS)

Baptist minister and civil rights leader, born October 8, 1941, in Greenville, S.C. On November 3, Jesse Jackson formally announced his candidacy for the 1984 Democratic presidential nomination. Jackson had already captured considerable media attention with his would-be presidential candidacy and his ambitious series of black voter registration drives. The rallies inspired thousands of unregistered voters to sign up on the spot. They also served to prove, once again, that Jesse Jackson could move a crowd in a way not seen since his late mentor, the Reverend Martin Luther King, Jr.

Jackson's ties to King stretch back to the heyday of the black civil-rights movement, in

Jesse Jackson, the head of Operation PUSH, a Chicago-based civil-rights organization, announced his candidacy for the Democratic presidential nomination on November 3. Jackson received the enthusiastic support of many black voters, but left some black leaders with a hard choice: many felt they should support a white liberal with a better chance of being elected.

the mid-1960's. After earning a sociology degree in 1964 and doing graduate work at the Chicago Theological Seminary, Jackson joined King's staff at the Southern Christian Leadership Conference. He was with King when the civil rights leader was slain in 1968.

In 1971 he quit SCLC and formed the Chicago-based Operation PUSH (People United to Save—later changed to Serve—Humanity). For many years PUSH has used the threat of a black boycott to negotiate "covenants" with major corporations, committing them to hire more blacks, buy from black-owned suppliers, and the like. More recently, Jackson has headed PUSH-Excel, a controversial self-help program designed to encourage black parents and children to commit themselves to academic achievement.

A few weeks after formally declaring his candidacy, Jackson made a bold move when he traveled to Syria, at the invitation of Syrian government leaders, to discuss his interest in the possible release of a U.S. Navy flier, Lieutenant Robert Goodman, shot down December 4 in a bombing raid on Syrian positions in Lebanon. After some waiting, Jackson was able to meet with Syrian President Hafez al-Assad, and on January 3, 1984, he secured Goodman's release.

Some black leaders criticized the Jackson candidacy, believing that blacks should throw their weight behind a more viable contender; Jackson himself described his candidacy as a catalyst for black political activism at all levels. "My running will stimulate thousands to run; it will make millions register," he said. He hoped to win support from a "rainbow coalition" of the "poor and rejected of all races."

JOHN PAUL II

Pope of the Roman Catholic Church, born Karol Wojtyła on May 18, 1920, in Wadowice, Poland. In the fifth year of his pontificate, Pope John Paul II continued to display a conservatism in matters theological and a liberal concern for social and political issues. Both elements were in evidence as the pope journeyed to Central America in March and to his Polish homeland three months later. He also showed his commitment to ecumenism by taking part in a Lutheran church service in Rome on December 11.

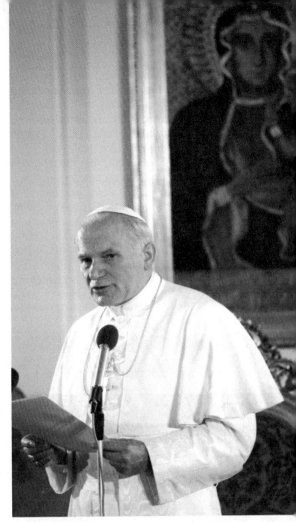

In 1983, Pope John Paul II paid dramatic visits to Central America and to Poland. Despite his frequent criticisms of governments and his appeals for social justice, he stressed that it was not the clergy's function to seek political change.

The pope's conservatism was demonstrated in January when he approved a new code of canon law evolving from the deliberations of the Second Vatican Council. The far-reaching new code, replacing one in force since 1917, decentralizes church power by granting more authority to local bishops. It also broadens the role of the laity. Unchanged, however, are traditional fiats on such issues as birth control and a married priesthood.

When the pope flew to Poland in June, he pitted his immense popularity among Poles against the Communist regime that had imposed martial law 18 months earlier. John Paul was greeted by massive crowds; many displayed the V-for-victory hand sign and banners with the name of Solidarity, the independent labor movement that was organized after his 1979 visit to Poland and later outlawed. John Paul and General Wojciech Jaruzelski, head of the military government, met twice, and it was reported that the two came to some sort of an agreement. Lech Walesa, who had been leader of Solidarity, also saw the pope privately.

When John Paul made his eight-day visit to seven Central American countries and Haiti, he confronted even more volatile situations. At times, he faced outright antagonism, especially in Nicaragua, where he was challenged with cries of "Power to the people!" while

Helmut Kohl, the Christian Democratic chancellor of West Germany, balanced firm support for deployment of U.S. medium-range nuclear missiles against development of economic relations with the Soviet Union.

celebrating mass. Throughout the trip, he delivered strong pleas for social justice.

In late December, John Paul met privately with Mehmet Ali Agca, the man who shot him in 1981 in St. Peter's Square; the two conversed quietly in a Rome prison cell for about 20 minutes. The pope said they had spoken as one brother to another.

KOHL, HELMUT

Chancellor of the Federal Republic of Germany, born April 3, 1930, in Ludwigshafen. In 1983, Kohl, a conservative, undramatic politician, found himself at the center of a dramatic controversy. The issue was NATO's planned deployment of U.S. medium-range nuclear missiles in West Germany and other European countries if U.S.-Soviet disarmament talks in Geneva failed to produce substantial progress. Kohl favored that course, but West Germany's Social Democrats and a strong antinuclear movement staunchly opposed it.

The missiles became a key issue in West Germany's national elections, held on March 6. (Unemployment and a stagnant economy were other major issues.) Kohl's opponent, Social Democrat Hans-Jochen Vogel, stressed NATO's expressed commitment to the U.S.-Soviet Geneva talks and charged that the United States was not willing to compromise with the Soviet Union. In the end, Kohl's policies and reassuring presence carried the day. His Christian Democratic Union and its coalition partners won a clear majority of seats in the Bundestag (lower house of parliament).

In July, Kohl visited the Soviet Union, where Communist Party chief Yuri Andropov warned him that deployment would have serious consequences for West Germany. Kohl stood his ground but assured Andropov of Bonn's interest in maintaining cordial relations with Moscow. Massive protest rallies were held in West Germany in October and November, but on November 22 the Bundestag, by a vote of 286–226, reaffirmed West Germany's decision to deploy the missiles; the next day, as the first missiles arrived, the Soviets suspended participation in the Geneva talks.

MITTERRAND, FRANÇOIS M(AURICE) M(ARIE)

President of France, born October 26, 1916, in Jarnac. During 1983 virtually nothing seemed

French President François Mitterrand faced problems both at home and abroad. His austerity programs were greeted with protests, and French troops were playing controversial roles in Lebanon and Chad.

Former Vice-President Walter Mondale, the Minnesota liberal who was Hubert Humphrey's protégé, jumped to an early lead in the race for the 1984 Democratic presidential nomination.

to go right for Mitterrand. On New Year's Day he was scheduled to give a live television interview from his country home in southwestern France. When the time came, however, a mobile crane needed for the television hookup was still in Nancy, at the opposite end of France, being used to trim trees. The affair of the bungled interview contributed to a growing feeling that the president did not have a firm hand on the tiller. As sweeping austerity measures went into effect, his approval rating sank—to 28 percent in July, a historic low for a French president. During the first half of the year, a series of demonstrations—by farmers, shopkeepers, students, and even disgruntled policemen—added to Mitterrand's worries.

Foreign affairs offered the beleaguered chief executive little relief. French troops were in Chad, intervening (against traditional French leftist policy) in a civil war on the side of the government, and in Lebanon as part of a multinational peacekeeping force. French and U.S. military installations in Beirut were devastated on October 23 when trucks laden with explosives penetrated the sites. At least 58 French troops were killed. Mitterrand flew to the scene the next day to bolster morale; he

later affirmed that France would not withdraw its forces.

Mitterrand's biggest headache, however, was France's ailing economy. The Socialist government had started out with a policy aimed at stimulating the economy, but high inflation and large foreign trade deficits had prompted initial austerity measures in 1982. In March 1983 the cabinet was reshuffled, producing what Mitterrand described as a "ministry of combat" to attack economic problems, and a new austerity program followed, featuring higher taxes, stringent currency restrictions, and steeper utility and mass transit rates.

There was some heartening economic news in the fall, with reports of a drop in the inflation rate and the trade deficit. But in September further austerity measures were announced for 1984, including steep tax hikes, cuts in government services, and limits on salary increases.

MONDALE, WALTER F(REDERICK)

Former U.S. vice-president, born January 5, 1928, in Ceylon, Minn. On February 21, 1983, Walter "Fritz" Mondale officially launched his campaign for the 1984 Democratic presidential nomination. "I am ready to be president," he declared before enthusiastic supporters in St.

Paul, Minn. Running as the candidate who could pull the party together after its disastrous defeat in 1980, Mondale leaped to an early lead as the field of candidates began to widen. A Gallup poll in December showed that Democrats preferred him to his nearest challenger, Ohio Senator John Glenn, by a wide margin of 47 percent to 19 percent. Mondale also won endorsements from the AFL-CIO, the National Education Association, and the National Organization for Women.

The son of a Methodist minister of Norwegian descent, Mondale studied law at the University of Minnesota. In 1948 he helped run the Senate campaign of Hubert H. Humphrey, who became his friend and political mentor.

Appointed and then twice elected state attorney general, Mondale was named in 1964 to fill the Senate seat vacated by Humphrey after he was elected vice-president. Mondale won election in 1966 and reelection in 1972 by comfortable margins.

In 1976, after having tested the waters as a presidential candidate himself, he was chosen by Jimmy Carter to be his running mate. Analysts credit Mondale, who had strong ties to traditional Democratic groups, such as labor unions and minorities, with bringing in the vote for Carter in the key northern states. After the Carter-Mondale ticket was defeated for reelection in 1980, Mondale joined a Washington, D.C., law firm.

Mondale's considerable experience in national politics was both a strength and a weakness for 1984. As a senator, he compiled a liberal voting record that reflected his state's progressivist political tradition. But now he had to prove that his record did not make him a "big-spending" Democrat whose answer for every problem was a new government program. His tenure as vice-president also was a liability as well as an asset, because it closely identified him with Carter, a somewhat unpopular president.

Mondale and his wife, Joan (Adams), whom he married in 1955, have three grown children: Theodore, Eleanor, and William.

MULRONEY, BRIAN M(ARTIN)

Leader of Canada's Progressive Conservative Party, born March 20, 1939, in Baie-Comeau, Quebec. At the Conservatives' convention at

Brian Mulroney replaced Joe Clark as the leader of Canada's Progressive Conservative Party. After 20 years of Liberal Party dominance, the Conservatives hoped that the media-friendly Mulroney could help revitalize the party.

Ottawa in June, Mulroney, campaigning vigorously, defeated Joe Clark on the fourth ballot to become the new party leader. Clark, whose nine months as prime minister in 1979–1980 constituted the only interruption in 20 years of Liberal rule, had decided to call the convention after failing to receive a clear mandate from the party to continue as leader.

There were sound political reasons for Mulroney's emergence as the party's choice. In contrast to Clark, he had the looks, the presence, and the smooth style to make full use of the power of television. Like most Tories, Mulroney favored a freer environment for business, the raising of Canadian oil prices to world levels, and less restriction on foreign investments.

Evincing an early interest in politics, Mulroney, after college, worked for the Conservative Party as a fund-raiser and speech writer before studying law. Bilingual, he practiced labor law in French-speaking Montreal, while remaining active in party politics. He came to prominence in the mid-1970's, when he served on a commission investigating corruption in Quebec's construction industry. In 1976, after failing in his first bid to be elected party head, he joined the Iron Ore Company of Canada, becoming its president a year later. Under his guidance, the once-troubled company reported increased productivity and profits.

In early 1983, Mulroney resigned his position at Iron Ore to try again for Conservative Party leader. His aggressiveness and success as lawyer and businessman made him the Tories' brightest hope in years—the sort of leader who party members believed might finally break the Liberals' long-standing grip on Canadian politics at the national level.

On August 29, Mulroney ran in a by-election in Nova Scotia for a seat in the House of Commons after the incumbent MP obligingly resigned. He won with a decisive 61 percent of the vote.

Mulroney was married to the former Mila Pivnicki. The couple had three small children: Caroline, Benedict, and Mark.

SHAMIR, YITZHAK

Prime minister of Israel, born October 15, 1915, in Ruzinoy in eastern Poland. When Menachem Begin unexpectedly announced his resignation as prime minister at the end of August, the Herut Party quickly turned to Begin's foreign minister and old comrade-in-arms, Yitzhak Shamir. Shamir then gained the support of the government's slender majority coalition in the Knesset (parliament), which voted October 10 to make him Israel's seventh prime minister.

Shamir quickly introduced measures to combat Israel's mounting economic problems, including a 23 percent devaluation of the shekel and a sharp cutback in food subsidies. He retained Begin's cabinet almost intact and continued Begin's tough foreign policy. In late November he made a three-day visit to Washington, where his talks with President Ronald Reagan produced an agreement on steps toward increased military cooperation between the two countries.

Shamir had migrated to Palestine in 1935 and, like Begin, joined the illegal Irgun organization, which advocated creating a Jewish state in Palestine through military action. When the Irgun split over wartime policy in 1940, Shamir joined its militant splinter, the Stern Group, which continued to attack the British in Palestine. Arrested by the British in 1946, Shamir was sent to a prison camp in Eritrea (now part of Ethiopia) but quickly escaped, and he spent two years in Paris before returning home after Israel achieved independence. He worked for Mossad, the Israeli intelligence agency, from 1955 to 1965 and was elected to the Knesset in 1973, eventually becoming

Yitzhak Shamir became Israel's seventh minister, after Menachem Begin's resignation in late August.

U.S. Secretary of State George Shultz gradually extended his influence over foreign policy, while maintaining his reputation as a conciliator.

speaker. He became foreign minister in 1980 and retained the foreign affairs portfolio after becoming prime minister.

Shamir's reputation as a hardliner was reinforced by reports that he had misgivings about the Camp David accords and by his abstention in the 1979 vote on the Egyptian-Israeli peace treaty. Foreign diplomats, however, have found him low-keyed and personable in negotiations. He lives quietly in Jerusalem with his wife, Shulamit. They have two children, a son, Yair, who is in the army, and a daughter, Gilada, a government employee.

SHULTZ, GEORGE P(RATT)

U.S. secretary of state, born December 13, 1920, in New York City. It was a frustrating year for Shultz, although his position within the Reagan administration, apparently being undermined early in the year, seemed improved by the end. The Middle East continued to be a major priority for the secretary of state. In May, after a wearying stint of shuttle diplomacy by Shultz, Israel and Lebanon reached a formal agreement on the withdrawal of Israeli troops from Lebanon. The agreement, however, proved impossible to implement, because Israel's withdrawal was conditional on the pullout of Syrian and PLO forces, and Shultz failed

to persuade Syrian President Hafez al-Assad to go along with the plan in private meetings in Damascus in May and July.

For much of the year, the influence of White House national security adviser William Clark seemed paramount in the making of U.S. foreign policy. In May, Clark successfully pressed for the firing of Thomas Enders, assistant secretary of state for inter-American affairs, and Deane Hinton, U.S. ambassador to El Salvador; Shultz reportedly went along with reluctance. In July, Clark's deputy, Robert McFarlane, replaced Philip Habib as special envoy to the Middle East. It was on Clark's advice that Henry Kissinger was chosen to head a special committee on Central American policy. In October, however, Shultz's position was apparently strengthened by Clark's departure from the foreign affairs arena to become secretary of the interior.

Shultz, who initially favored a conciliatory approach to U.S.-Soviet relations, met frequently during the early part of the year with Soviet Ambassador Anatoly Dobrynin. After the Soviet downing of Korean Air Lines flight 007 on September 1, however, Shultz harshly condemned the Soviet action and efforts to "cover up the facts." On September 8 he confronted Soviet Foreign Minister Andrei Gromyko in a stormy private meeting in Madrid and afterward called Gromyko's attitude "totally unacceptable." He nevertheless opposed any major unilateral sanctions against the Soviet Union, believing them to be counterproductive, and reportedly won over the president to his point of view. Shultz was also a major spokesman for the administration in defending the U.S.-led invasion of Grenada in October.

Shultz made two major trips to Asia—a 12-day visit early in the year to Japan, South Korea, Hong Kong, and China and a later tour of the Philippines, Thailand, Pakistan, and India.

THATCHER, MARGARET (HILDA ROBERTS)

Prime minister of Great Britain, born October 13, 1925, in Grantham, England. Slipping out of London secretly in January, accompanied only by her husband, Denis, and a few aides, Thatcher boarded a Royal Air Force VC-10 on the first leg of an 8,000-mile journey across the Atlantic Ocean. Twenty-three hours later, after her plans had been revealed, she began a highly publicized "personal pilgrimage" to the Falkland Islands—invaded by Argentina and recaptured by Britain in 1982. She visited British troops guarding the islands, paused tearfully at the graves of their dead, and talked with residents. Labor Party politicians charged that the trip was politically motivated, intended to remind voters of the popular Falklands campaign, which had reinforced an image of Thatcher as a resolute, vigorous, and victorious leader.

Thatcher therefore surprised no one when she announced on May 9 that general elections would be held exactly one month later. She clearly hoped to take advantage of a divided Labor Party and an improving economy as well as lingering memories of the Falklands triumph. The strategy paid off handsomely, as Thatcher, at age 57, won the most impressive electoral victory in Britain since 1945. Her Tories took 397 of the 650 seats in the newly enlarged House of Commons, giving her a stunning majority of 144 seats over the Labor and Social Democratic–Liberal opposition (compared with 34 in the previous Parliament). "It was a larger victory than I had dared hope for," she observed. Thatcher subsequently reshuffled her cabinet, but one of her new appointments—Cecil Parkinson, as minister of trade and industry—proved an embarrassment when he had to resign in October because of an adultery scandal.

During the summer, Thatcher took time off for a minor operation on her right eye. In September, after a visit to West Germany and the Netherlands, she traveled to Canada, where she addressed a joint session of Parliament (in the first Canadian visit by a British prime minister in more than 25 years), and to the United States, where she expressed concern about high U.S. budget deficits but reiterated her support for the deployment of U.S. nuclear missiles in Western Europe. She broke sharply with the Reagan administration, however, when she advised against the U.S.-led invasion of Grenada, in late October and afterward criticized the move.

TRUDEAU, PIERRE ELLIOTT

Prime minister of Canada, born October 18, 1919, in Montreal. During the year criticism seemed to be directed at Trudeau from all sides, prompting speculation by some that his long and often flamboyant political career was nearing an end. In January, a panel of Roman Catholic bishops issued a report that obliquely criticized Trudeau's economic policies and called for stronger government measures to create jobs for the 1.5 million unemployed. Bickering continued between the prime minister and the premiers of the ten provinces over distribution of energy resources and over Trudeau's notions of federalism, which, the provincial leaders maintained, increased Ottawa's powers at their expense. Peace groups attacked Trudeau for approving the planned testing of unarmed U.S. cruise missiles in the Canadian north. Even Canadian Indians and Eskimos were provoked into joining the chorus of criticism. In March, a delegation came to Ottawa to discuss the native peoples' status under the new constitution; when they declared that the land of Canada had been given them by God, Trudeau replied that God had also been responsible for sending Christopher Columbus and those who followed him to the New World.

Furthermore, public support of Trudeau's Liberal Party was declining. An August Gallup poll gave the Liberals only 27 percent of voter support, against 55 percent for the Conservatives. Some Liberals called on the prime minister to set a retirement date and convene a leadership conference to select a successor. At a party caucus in September, Trudeau soothed the dissidents, and the Liberals, despite the loss of several by-elections, clung to a slim majority in the House of Commons. Trudeau does not need to call a national election until February 1985, and, with the economy improving, many believed he would wait out the current wave of criticism.

In the meantime, Trudeau kept a high profile in international affairs. In May he attended the ninth annual economic summit of leading industrial democracies in Williamsburg, Va., and in November he traveled to capitals in Europe and Asia to promote an arms control initiative. His proposals included expanding arms limitation talks to all five countries known to have nuclear weapons and tightening controls on nuclear weapons development.

W.E. & S.L.D.

PERSIAN GULF STATES. The small Persian Gulf states faced lower world petroleum prices and decreasing reliance by the West on the region's oil supplies. With some analysts predicting that world oil demand would remain flat through the end of the century, the Organization of Petroleum Exporting Countries cut its benchmark price for oil to $29 a barrel in March. In an attempt to arrest the decline in oil prices, Arabian Peninsula states agreed to limit their overall production. The sale of less oil at lower prices led to drastic budget cuts by most governments in the area. Rather than deplete their diminishing foreign exchange funds, many states borrowed money to finance internal development.

Oil spilling from an Iranian oil field in the northern end of the Persian Gulf caused considerable damage to the gulf's ecology. The spill began early in the year and increased in magnitude after Iraq, at war with Iran, bombed the oil field in March. Until it was apparently brought under control, thousands of barrels of crude oil poured into the Persian Gulf daily. In addition to killing large numbers of marine animals and flora, the spill threatened the gulf's fishing industries and the desalination plants (which produce fresh water), causing people to hoard bottled water and fish.

Except for Oman and to a lesser degree Bahrain, the states of the gulf resisted U.S. overtures to establish a military presence there. The United States held two military operations in late 1982 and 1983 in Oman.

A Gulf Air jetliner en route from Karachi, Pakistan, to Bahrain crashed and burned near Abu Dhabi on September 23, killing all 112 persons aboard. It was the first crash in the 35-year history of Gulf Air, jointly owned by Bahrain, Oman, Qatar, and the United Arab Emirates.

See STATISTICS OF THE WORLD. *See also* KUWAIT; ORGANIZATION OF PETROLEUM EXPORTING COUNTRIES; SAUDI ARABIA; YEMEN, PEOPLE'S DEMOCRATIC REPUBLIC OF; YEMEN ARAB REPUBLIC.

L.A.K.

PERU. The government of Peruvian President Fernando Belaúnde Terry was besieged by a rising wave of terrorist violence in 1983. On May 30, after months of bloody conflict between the leftist insurgent movement Sendero Luminoso (Shining Path) and villagers and antiguerrilla forces, Belaúnde declared a state of emergency, suspending civil liberties. On July 11, Sendero Luminoso, which had previously dynamited power lines in Lima, blacking out much of the city, attacked Belaúnde's own party headquarters, killing two people. By August more than 800 Peruvians had died because of terrorist activities.

Despite continuing sporadic attacks within Lima itself, the government, on September 10, announced the lifting of the state of emergency except in three provinces in the Andes. Terrorist incidents continued. On October 22, Sendero Luminoso members set off more than 20 bombs in Lima, killing five people. Leftist guerrillas also vowed to disrupt the November 13 municipal elections; at least 26 people were reportedly killed after the balloting in one village, and numerous atrocities were reported. In the election itself, the government party suffered serious setbacks, losing most city halls to left and center-left parties.

The most optimistic observers predicted a deficit in the country's trade balance, as oil revenues tumbled (although the price of silver rose). The gross national product was expected to fall by roughly 8 percent from the 1982 figure, and inflation was approaching an annual rate of 100 percent late in the year. The government announced suspension of its ordinary cost-of-living wage increases, exacerbating tensions among workers.

Peru's indebtedness to foreign governments and commercial banks, which had reached about $7 billion, was under negotiation during the year; some creditors agreed to stretch out debt repayments and extend further loans to Peruvian government agencies. A loan request to the International Monetary Fund was also pending.

See STATISTICS OF THE WORLD.   F.M.N.

PETROLEUM AND NATURAL GAS. Declining demand for petroleum and natural gas combined with an abundant supply to produce a tumultuous marketplace in 1983. The Reagan administration's offshore oil leasing met legal challenges by environmentalists, and prices for natural gas continued to rise.

Oil. A slump in world oil demand that began in 1980 brought the international oil markets

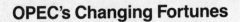

OPEC's Changing Fortunes

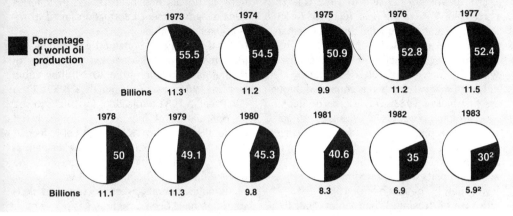

Percentage of world oil production

1973	1974	1975	1976	1977
55.5	54.5	50.9	52.8	52.4

Billions 11.3[1] 11.2 9.9 11.2 11.5

1978	1979	1980	1981	1982	1983
50	49.1	45.3	40.6	35	30[2]

Billions 11.1 11.3 9.8 8.3 6.9 5.9[2]

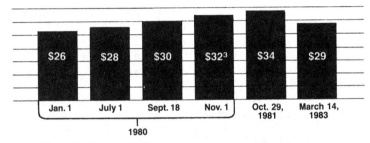

Official price per barrel

$26	$28	$30	$32[3]	$34	$29
Jan. 1	July 1	Sept. 18	Nov. 1	Oct. 29, 1981	March 14, 1983

1980

[1]Figures for all years are for total OPEC production, in barrels
[2]Projected
[3]From December 16, 1980, to October 29, 1981, Saudi Arabia's price remained at $32, while the rest of OPEC charged $36

SOURCE: U.S. DEPARTMENT OF ENERGY

perilously close to chaos by early 1983. The decline in demand was due to a worldwide economic recession and to a sharp increase in the crude oil prices of the Organization of Petroleum Exporting Countries in 1979 and 1980 that caused consuming nations to conserve energy.

As world oil demand continued to slide, some producers, notably Nigeria, Norway, and Great Britain (the last two are not OPEC members), began cutting prices early in 1983. An all-out price war was narrowly averted when the OPEC members agreed in March to trim $5 a barrel from the $34 benchmark price for Saudi Arabian light crude. It was OPEC's first official price cut since the organization was founded in 1960. At the same time, the OPEC ministers agreed to a production ceiling of 17.5 million barrels per day, with individual quotas for each producer (except Saudi Arabia), in an attempt to reduce the surplus of oil on the world market. The ceilings and prices were maintained at an OPEC meeting in December.

World oil production in the first half of 1983 averaged only 51.22 million b/d, 2.8 percent below the average in the same period of 1982 and almost 18 percent below the peak figure for a year, recorded in 1979. OPEC's share of the market was declining, and between the first half of 1982 and the first half of 1983, OPEC's production dropped 14.3 percent, to 15.91 million b/d. Thus, the world market could not absorb even the 17.5 million b/d production ceiling that OPEC had set. In the first half of 1983, OPEC production was only about half of its 1977 level. As the year progressed, however, the decline in world oil production began to level off, as the world economic recovery took hold. It was estimated that the final world average for 1983 would reach 53.26 million b/d, on the basis of increased production in the second half.

PETROLEUM AND NATURAL GAS

U.S. petroleum demand in 1982 was 18.8 percent lower than the peak recorded in 1978 and was essentially equal to the 1971 demand. Net imports accounted for only 28.1 percent of domestic consumption in 1982, compared with 33.6 percent in 1981. Preliminary data indicated that existing trends continued through the first half of 1983. Total domestic demand for petroleum products in 1983 was estimated to be 5.548 billion barrels, down just slightly from 1982. Domestic crude oil production rose about 0.5 percent in the first half of 1983, and net imports were approximately 14 percent lower than in the first half of 1982.

Offshore oil leasing. When James Watt (U.S. secretary of the interior from 1981 until his resignation in October 1983) approved an aggressive five-year offshore oil leasing program for the U.S. outer continental shelf in July 1982, environmentalists and Watt himself expected the schedule to spawn litigation everywhere. It has.

The schedule called for the Interior Department to lease about 1 billion acres of the shelf over a five-year period, with 41 separate lease sales being made by June 1987. On June 9, 1983, the U.S. Court of Appeals for the District of Columbia upheld the Interior Department's five-year lease sale schedule. In rejecting the arguments of the petitioners—in 13 suits brought by states and environmental groups and consolidated by the court—the court held that Watt's reliance on the competitive bidding process provided reasonable assurance that the government would receive fair market value for the resources. The court victory did not give the Interior Department any relief from litigation, however. Every lease sale Watt proposed outside the Gulf of Mexico has been the target of separate lawsuits.

In October, the Interior Department temporarily suspended its lotteries of onshore gas and oil drilling leases. The lotteries, held every two months, offer entrants noncompetitive ten-year leases on government tracts for $1 an acre; winners are chosen at random by computer. The halt was called to give officials time to correct abuses in the system. The tracts made available are supposed to be of unknown worth, but an internal investigation revealed that tracts in Wyoming potentially worth millions of dollars had been leased in lotteries because government information failed to reveal their true value.

Natural gas. The U.S. natural gas market was in turmoil in 1983. Marketed production of natural gas had fallen from 20.2 trillion cubic feet in 1981 to approximately 18.5 trillion cubic feet in 1982. Projections for 1983 showed a continuation of the trend, with marketed production down to 16.3 trillion cubic feet. A small rise in gas consumption in the residential sector was offset by large declines in the industrial and electric utility sectors.

Although natural gas production and consumption have been dropping, gas prices have been rising because of anomalies in the pricing system established by Congress. Since oil prices have been falling, industrial customers have switched to oil. Confronted with declining sales volumes, the pipeline companies sought rate hikes from residential customers to cover their fixed costs. In November the House Energy and Commerce Committee defeated a bill that would have rolled back natural gas prices by 5 to 10 percent, and it was estimated that residential gas rates for the winter of 1983–1984 would be an average 7 percent higher than the previous winter.

See also ENERGY; ORGANIZATION OF PETROLEUM EXPORTING COUNTRIES.   D.F.A.

PETS. American Kennel Club figures released early in 1983 showed only one change in relative rankings among the ten most popular breeds of dogs: The Labrador retriever replaced the German shepherd as fourth most popular breed. The poodle once again had the highest number of registrations, followed closely by the cocker spaniel. The Doberman pinscher remained in third place.

In May the AKC granted recognition to three additional breeds, which thereby became eligible for showing in the AKC's regular show classes as of January 1984. Each of the newly recognized breeds was placed in a different group among the AKC's seven group classifications. The Portuguese water dog was to be in the working group, the Tibetan spaniel in the nonsporting group, and the pharaoh hound in the hound group. The addition of the three new breeds brings to 128 the number of breeds in the AKC's regular classes.

Bone of Contention

In what may or may not have been a landmark decision, a judge in California recently granted a divorcing couple joint custody of the family dog. Both parties had pleaded for full custody of two-year-old Runaway, a cross between a poodle and a cocker spaniel, who owned an enviable collection of rubber toys and was said to enjoy such delicacies as lobster, scallops, and steaks. The judge ruled that the dog was a child substitute and was to be shared on a monthly basis.

Winner of the best in show award at the Westminster Kennel Club show in February was Ch. Kabik's The Challenger, an Afghan hound; this was the first time since 1957 that an Afghan hound had gone best in show at Westminster. More than 2,600 dogs were entered in competition at the 1983 show.

Dogfighting gained in notoriety because of its increasing popularity as both a spectator sport and betting activity. In Texas, a lobby called THIN (Texas Humane Information Network) persuaded the state legislature to pass a law making dogfighting a felony; by late 1983, some 20 states in all had similar legislation, and prosecutions were increasing. In Georgia, the state Bureau of Investigation raided a dogfight in October; 45 spectators drew varying fines, and the fight's three promoters drew prison sentences of up to seven years and fines as high as $16,000.

Nonvenomous snakes, particularly boa constrictors and pythons, continued to be the most popular reptilian pets. Possession of venomous snakes was being increasingly restricted by local laws, and these snakes became less sought after.

The price of canaries remained high, but common finches, such as zebra finches and society finches, were in good supply and relatively inexpensive. Budgerigars and cockatiels remained by far the most popular parrots, followed by the various lovebird species. Because of the uncertain future availability of imported birds and the increased demand for hand-tamed as opposed to wild-caught birds,

commercial dealers began to rely more on domestically bred stock than on imported birds.

Colorful rainbowfishes from Papua New Guinea and northern Australia captured the spotlight in the tropical fish field. Several new species, some of them unknown to ichthyologists until recently, were introduced, but they were very scarce; living specimens had been seen by only a handful of hobbyists.

The Persian cat remained the most popular of long-haired purebred cats and the Siamese the most popular short-haired cat, but several other breeds, among them the Abyssinian and the Maine coon cat, showed greater proportional gains.   N.P.

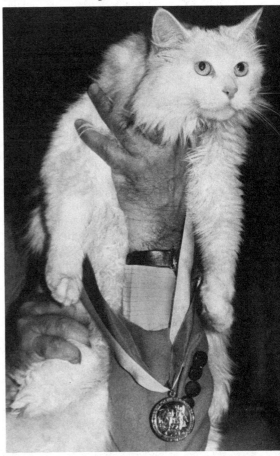

Chosen the ASPCA's animal of the year, the six-year-old cat named Pussycat was honored with a gold medal for saving the lives of its owners by awakening them when their Long Island home caught fire.

Sympathizers with Philippines opposition leader Benigno Aquino, Jr., surround the funeral hearse carrying him to Manila's Santo Domingo Church. The popular ''Ninoy'' was gunned down by an assassin just minutes after his return from three years' self-imposed exile in the United States.

PHILIPPINES. Philippines President Ferdinand E. Marcos came under increasing criticism after the assassination of opposition leader Benigno Aquino, Jr., at Manila International Airport on August 21, 1983, minutes after his arrival from the United States. Aquino was reportedly shot in the back of the head by a man dressed as an airline maintenance worker; the alleged assailant, said to be a hired killer, was shot dead by guards escorting Aquino.

A former senator, Aquino had long been an outspoken foe of the Marcos government. He was imprisoned after the imposition of martial law in 1972 but was permitted to travel to the United States for heart surgery in 1980. When he made known his plans to return to the Philippines, the government refused to renew his passport and warned he would be subject to arrest. Although Aquino's return had been expected, his exact flight had supposedly been kept secret; critics of the regime asked how the assassin had located Aquino and succeeded in getting so close to him. Marcos suggested that ''subversive elements'' were responsible for the assassination, but many citizens blamed the government. At least 1 million people watched Aquino's funeral procession along its 19-mile route, despite pouring rain. On September 21, violence broke out in Manila following a peaceful protest rally attended by an estimated 500,000 people, leaving 11 dead.

Shortly afterward, all the members of a commission appointed by Marcos to investigate the assassination resigned when opposition leaders questioned its impartiality; on October 22, Marcos appointed a new commission.

The ruling party attempted at its November caucus to allay uneasiness as to Marcos's possible successor. The president's wife, Imelda, publicly renounced any intention to succeed him, and the party supported restoration of the vice-presidency effective in 1987; in the interim, the speaker of the National Assembly would have the right of succession.

The New People's Army (NPA), a Communist guerrilla group, continued to be active, as did the Moro National Liberation Front, a Muslim separatist group. In April, the government reported that over 400 Communist and 160 Muslim rebels had been killed in a major sweep.

The United States and the Philippines signed a new five-year accord on June 1, providing for continued American use of Subic Bay Naval Base and Clark Air Base. On October 3 the United States announced that a visit by President Ronald Reagan to Manila, along with some other stops on a planned Asian tour in November, would be postponed because of a demanding legislative calendar. In a personal letter, however, Reagan sought to assure Marcos of his friendship.

See STATISTICS OF THE WORLD.   C.D.N.

PHOTOGRAPHY. Photography made a vigorous recovery in 1983 from the recession that afflicted most of the art market in 1982. Photography galleries experienced a renaissance, and auction prices reached record levels. In November, Charles Sheeler's 1939 photograph "Wheels" was sold at Sotheby Parke Bernet for $67,100, almost twice the previous auction record for a photograph.

Major shows. Several museums across the country sponsored important historical shows during the year, including two devoted to the calotype—a soft-focus paper-negative process invented in 1839, the same year as the better known sharp-focus daguerreotype. From December 1982 to February 1983, the Art Institute of Chicago offered "Paper and Light: The Calotype in France and Great Britain, 1839–1870," and in February and March, the Art Museum at Princeton University showed "Masterpieces of the French Calotype." The shows impressed on a large public the fact that photography was never a monolithic medium and that the possibilities of both soft-focus expression and sharp-focus explication were inherent from its birth.

Works of the Armenian-born Canadian portrait photographer Yousuf Karsh were displayed in the book Karsh: A Fifty-Year Retrospective. *Below, his 1941 portrait of a stubbornly determined Winston Churchill; above, the American artist Georgia O'Keeffe, posed with artifacts of the Southwest she herself liked to paint, and in a mood suggesting her own semi-abstract style.*

The first retrospective of America's preeminent 19th-century Western photographer, "Carleton E. Watkins: Photographer of the American West," opened in April at the Amon Carter Museum in Fort Worth, Texas, and traveled to Boston, St. Louis, and Oakland, Cal. The 102 images, made with his mammoth camera that produced 18×22-inch glass-plate negatives, covered not only his famous landscapes from Yosemite National Park but also urban panoramas, architectural studies, and industrial subjects.

The Museum of Modern Art in New York in late 1982 launched the second installment of its four-part survey of the work of Eugène Atget, this segment entitled "The Art of Old Paris." The show, which traveled during 1983 to Dallas, Cincinnati, Minneapolis, and St. Louis, presented 117 prints drawn from MOMA's own unmatched collection of the French photographer's documentation of his country in the early years of this century.

The most complete survey to date of the photographic work of Alfred Stieglitz was presented by the National Gallery of Art in Wash-

ington, D.C. Shown were 171 images spanning Stieglitz's career from 1894 to 1937. The show later traveled to New York's Metropolitan Museum of Art and to the Art Institute of Chicago. A related exhibit was "The Photo-Secession: The Golden Years of Pictorial Photography in America," originating at the Currier Gallery of Art in Manchester, N.H. The show provided a needed overview of the works created by Stieglitz's turn-of-the-century band of art photographers, including Gertrude Käsebier, Clarence White, and Edward Steichen.

Although vintage 19th-century material seems largely absorbed into museum and other collections, material by master artists from the 1920's and 1930's was also exhibited in commercial galleries and available at auction. Collectors bid heavily for the work of artists like Man Ray, Paul Outerbridge, and Florence Henri. The Prakapas Gallery in New York, which specializes in works from this period, reported great interest in three of its shows: "The Surrealist Spirit in Belgian Photography," "Constructivism and Photography," and "Die Neue Sachlichkeit in Photography," which featured German works of the 1920's.

Contemporary art photography flourished in 1983. David Haxton's huge color works, shown at the Sonnabend Gallery, attracted much attention for their romantic effects of abstract light and color. Eight photographers—Ellen Brooks, Eileen Cowin, John Coplans, Nic Nicosia, Cindy Sherman, John Baldessari, Barbara Kruger, and Kenneth Shorr—were included in the Whitney Museum of American Art's Biennial Exhibition of contemporary works.

Technology. Kodak introduced two major innovations in 35-millimeter color negative film. The first was the DX coding system, which will digitally code all 35mm film to instruct both the camera and the photofinisher on the film's identity, processing type, exposure latitude, and frame count. To encourage the system's adoption by all film and camera companies, Kodak is making its technology freely available to all. The second Kodak breakthrough was announced as "the most important advance in film emulsions in 50 years." A complex chemical technology, permitting the creation of a high-quality combination of high speed, fine grain, and accurate color balance,

was used in Kodacolor VR 1000, the fastest color print film ever made, which was put on the market in April.

The 3M Company's Color Slide 1000 Daylight became the world's fastest color-transparency film, and because it could be pushed to EI 4000, it was effectively the fastest 35mm film of any sort to date. Polaroid marketed Polachrome CS Color Transparency film, the first instant slide film and the first Polaroid film that could be used in any 35mm camera. The entire film can be processed in a separate unit called the Autoprocessor.   B.B.S.

PHYSICS. Major developments in physics in 1983 included the discovery of two new particles that confirmed recent work by theoreticians. The latest techniques in laser technology may ultimately lead to radically new applications, and an important stage in the search for energy from nuclear fusion was reached.

Particle physics. Heading the list of recent physics achievements is the discovery of the long-sought W and Z particles by two groups of experimenters using an extremely powerful particle accelerator, at the European Laboratory for Particle Physics, or CERN, near Geneva, Switzerland. The two groups, headed by Carlo Rubbia and Pierre Darriulat, during experiments in the fall of 1982 and the spring of 1983, found a total of 90 W's and ten Z's. This was enough to confirm the existence of the particles and verify their masses, which had been predicted to be 83 and 94 times larger than that of the proton, respectively.

The importance of the findings at CERN to elementary-particle physics is hard to overstate. Scientists use mathematically similar theories, known as gauge theories, to describe each of the three fundamental forces—the electromagnetic, strong nuclear, and weak—that influence the behavior of elementary particles. The forces are thought to be transmitted between the particles by means of intermediary particles called vector bosons. Photons, for example, are the vector bosons that carry the electromagnetic force. The so-called gluons do the same for the strong nuclear force. The W (which exists in electrically positive W^+ and negative W^- forms) and the Z (which is electrically neutral) had been theorized to be the intermediary particles of the weak force but had never been detected until the CERN experiments, because only CERN's powerful new accelerator could produce them. Their discovery thus completes this chapter of particle theory.

The focus of particle physics is now shifting to what is beginning to be called the new physics, where even more powerful accelerators will be required to detect additional particles. U.S. researchers are anxious to be the first to explore this new territory. In July a powerful new accelerator was successfully tested at the Fermi National Laboratory in Batavia, Ill. Meanwhile, the U.S. Department of Energy terminated another accelerator under construction at Brookhaven National Laboratory and urged a massive research and development effort leading to the completion in the mid-1990's of a super accelerator. The Department of Energy was reportedly preparing to spend $150–200 million just for planning such a machine, which would be huge in size. Its total cost would probably exceed $2 billion.

Lasers. In 1983 a joint French-American group working at the Laboratory for the Utilization of Electromagnetic Radiation (LURE is its French acronym) of the University of Paris-South in Orsay demonstrated the first free-electron laser to emit visible light. A group led by John Madey of Stanford University had demonstrated the first free-electron laser in 1976, using an electron linear accelerator to generate infrared light. The Stanford accelerator was not powerful enough to produce visible light. So Madey and his co-workers joined with the LURE researchers led by Yves Petroff to do an experiment on an accelerator in Orsay that had the requisite properties.

The name "laser" is itself an acronym standing for light amplification by stimulated emission of radiation. In conventional lasers, atoms (or molecules) in solids, liquids, or gases are boosted to a so-called excited state by injecting energy into them. As the excited atoms relax back to their low-energy "ground" state, they release the excess energy as light. This light

The Fermilab atom smasher, extending in a 4-mile ring beneath the Illinois prairie, was successfully tested in July. Using superconducting magnets to accelerate particles, the new device is expected to provide a major breakthrough in high-energy physics. Construction of a less successful atom smasher, at Brookhaven, N.Y., was halted.

can stimulate atoms still in their excited states to also relax. A kind of optical chain reaction ensues, in which each photon of light given off stimulates the emission of more light.

Two factors limit the usefulness of laser light generated in this way. The first is that the energy levels of atoms are quantized, or fixed at certain definite values. Owing to this quantization, the light emitted can have only certain distinct, or discrete, wavelengths. Although some lasers, dye lasers in particular, are tunable—that is, can emit light over a range of wavelengths—most lasers are not. The second factor is that the efficiency of most lasers, measured by the energy in the laser beam as compared to the energy originally injected to excite the atoms, is low.

Free-electron lasers provide one way to solve both problems. Their name comes from the use of "free" electrons in an accelerated beam, instead of electrons bound to atoms. The energies of electrons in a beam are not quantized, so any laser based on these particles is tunable. Theoretically, improved efficiency is also possible, although this has yet to be demonstrated in practice. Their tunability makes free-electron lasers an ideal tool for spectroscopic and structural studies of many kinds of materials, of interest to experimenters ranging from biologists to physicists. High efficiency would make free-electron lasers candidates for use in commercial chemical processes and for high-energy beam weapons, possibly for defense against missiles. The possibility that a free-electron laser could be tuned to ultraviolet or even X-ray frequencies is especially enticing to prospective users among scientists and in the commercial and military communities. The LURE experiments are an important step toward achieving these goals.

Fusion. Rounding out 1983 in physics was the initial testing of two fusion reactors, one in the United States and one in the United Kingdom, that are expected to attain a major milestone, called scientific breakeven, toward the development of nuclear fusion into an economically viable source of power.

In fusion, light atoms are made to form a dense gas heated to enormous temperatures, called plasma. The atoms then combine to form heavier elements, releasing energy.

Breakeven represents the point at which the energy received as product equals the energy used to start the fusion process and is a kind of proof that fusion may someday be economically viable.

Most research indicates that the ability to achieve fusion conditions in a plasma increases with the physical size of the reactor in which the fusion process takes place. Accordingly, the two new machines, costing over $300 million each, are the largest ever built. The U.S. machine, the Tokamak Fusion Test Reactor, or TFTR, at the Princeton Plasma Physics Laboratory, began operating on Christmas Eve 1982 and passed several important tests in 1983. The British facility, the Joint European Torus, or JET, stored its first plasma in June. A collaborative project of the European Economic Community, it is located at the Culham Laboratory. Actual demonstration of breakeven is expected by about 1986 at Princeton and somewhat later at Culham.

Researchers hope that commercial use of fusion power will become possible sometime in the next century. First, however, several other milestones will have to be passed. One of these is ignition, in which the fusion reactions generate enough energy to keep the plasma hot, so that it will not be necessary to continuously supply energy from outside the reactor. JET, which is a larger machine than the TFTR, may be able to achieve ignition toward the end of the decade.   A.L.R.

POLAND. Martial law, imposed in Poland in December 1981, was officially lifted in July 1983, but restrictive measures remained in force, and the government of General Wojciech Jaruzelski appeared to have made little progress in solving the country's political and economic problems. To the regime's embarrassment, Lech Walesa, leader of the banned trade union movement Solidarity, was awarded the 1983 Nobel Peace Prize.

Lifting the "state of war." Major confrontations between Solidarity supporters and police occurred on April 17 during demonstrations marking the 40th anniversary of the anti-Nazi uprising in the Warsaw ghetto; on May 1, the date of the traditional workers' holiday; and on May 3, the anniversary of the signing of the Polish reform constitution of 1791. Nevertheless, the government went ahead with its plans to bring martial law to a formal end. As of July 22, the 39th anniversary of the establishment of Communist rule in Poland, the "state of war" was officially lifted. However, the Jaruzelski regime pushed through a constitutional amendment giving the government the power to declare a state of emergency at any time, along with a whole new series of restrictive laws. They included "temporary" legislation (effective until 1985) empowering the authorities to dissolve organizations, to ban meetings, and to take over universities.

Just prior to the lifting of martial law, Parliament authorized the freeing of large numbers of political prisoners. In the fall, however, seven detained Solidarity leaders and four Solidarity advisers were formally charged with conspiracy to overthrow the system, which carries a penalty of one to ten years in jail. Meanwhile, nearly 700 Solidarity activists reportedly turned themselves in to authorities under a temporary amnesty that expired October 31 (later extended to December 31).

In November, without debate, Parliament approved legislation setting up a military National Defense Committee, with authority to determine when a "state of emergency" exists and assume sweeping powers at such a time. Jaruzelski, who resigned his post as defense minister, was named to head the National Defense Committee, in effect recovering the full authority he had held under martial law.

The opposition. Despite occasional arrests and communications problems, an underground Solidarity committee continued to function in 1983. Important moral support came from abroad. On October 5 the Norwegian Nobel Committee announced the award of the Nobel Peace Prize for 1983 to Lech Walesa for his efforts to solve Poland's labor problems "without resorting to violence." The leader of Solidarity said he intended to donate the prize money to the Catholic Church in support of a foundation to aid Polish farmers.

Walesa, who had returned to work at the Lenin Shipyard in Gdańsk in April, was the object of a growing government campaign to discredit him. Shortly before the award announcement, for example, the government broadcast a special television program, based

on an alleged secret tape of a conversation between Walesa and his brother in which Walesa supposedly talked about having a large sum of money abroad and complained that the pope was ruining his chances to win a Nobel Prize.

In other action against the opposition, the Communist regime in August abruptly dissolved the Polish Union of Writers, which had continued to express open sympathy for the goals of Solidarity.

Church and state. The spiritual and emotional high point of 1983 for most Poles was the

Solidarity leader Lech Walesa, shown here triumphantly waving the paper granting him leave from his job to visit Pope John Paul II in June, was awarded the Nobel Peace Prize for his "contribution, made with considerable sacrifice, to ensure the workers' right to establish their own organizations."

During Pope John Paul II's historic June visit to his homeland, an enormous crowd attending a mass he celebrated in Wroclaw heard him declare, "I bring you my solidarity and that of the Church," in a not-so-veiled allusion to the outlawed labor organization.

eight-day visit to Poland, in June, of Pope John Paul II. The visit had originally been scheduled for August 1982 to mark the 600th anniversary of the shrine of the Black Madonna of Częstochowa, but it was postponed because of political turmoil. Crowds of up to 1 million people, many with Solidarity banners, greeted the pontiff at his stops. John Paul criticized the repressiveness of the military regime and called for restoration of the Gdańsk accords of 1980, which had led to the creation of Solidarity. He conferred twice in private with General Jaruzelski. On the last day of his visit, after overcoming considerable official resistance, he was able to meet privately with Walesa at a remote mountain retreat. No details of the discussion were disclosed.

There were reports in mid-November that Polish authorities had sent a letter to the Roman Catholic primate, Jozef Cardinal Glemp, telling him to silence about 70 "antisocialist" priests. In a message delivered just before Christmas, Cardinal Glemp called for reconciliation between the government and its opponents; he also said he would ask priests "not to deal in politics." The government subsequently released 30 political prisoners, in what Glemp said was a gesture toward the Church.

Economy. The economy continued to suffer from serious problems. In March the government announced a three-year economic plan under which industrial production was projected to rise 14–16 percent. Its targets were still below actual 1980 production levels. In August, Warsaw reached agreement with Western banks on rescheduling $2.6 billion in debts due in 1983. In November, Jaruzelski dismissed the head of the state Planning Committee and instituted other cabinet changes, just as Parliament was approving the economic recovery plan he had put forward. The regime also announced controversial plans to raise food prices, effective in 1984.

See STATISTICS OF THE WORLD.   R.E.K.

PORTUGAL. In a general election on April 25, 1983—Portugal's fourth since the restoration of democracy in 1974—the Socialists, under Mário Soares, gained the largest share of the vote, with 36 percent of the ballots cast. The Socialist gains came at the expense of the ruling center-right coalition, the Democratic Alliance, which had been beset with internal dissension. After resigning in late 1982, Prime Minister Francisco Pinto Balsemão of the Social Democratic Party (PSD) had nominated Vítor Pereira Crespo, of the PSD, to succeed him. But President António Ramalho Eanes, exercising his constitutional prerogative, rejected Crespo's nomination and in February 1983 dissolved the Assembly of the Republic (parliament) and called for parliamentary elections. The Socialist electoral victory that followed gave Soares's party 99 seats in the 250-member Assembly, compared with its previous 71. The PSD gathered 27 percent of the popular vote, falling from 74 to 72 seats. The Communist Party, which captured about 18 percent of the vote, increased its total by three, to 44 seats.

Soares formed a coalition government with the centrist Social Democrats. Their leader, Carlos Mota Pinto, was named deputy premier and defense minister, and the new, 17-member cabinet contained nine Socialists, seven Social Democrats, and one independent. The combined parliamentary strength of the Socialist Party and the PSD gave the Soares government control of the Assembly. Soares, previously premier from 1976 to 1978, announced, upon taking office in June, that his government would be "austere, uncompromising and unpopular, if that is what it takes to secure recovery," and promised a "national emergency program" to deal with the economic problems besetting Portugal.

Soares kept his pledge of rapid economic action. On June 24, the Assembly, in granting the new government a vote of confidence, approved a set of austerity measures calling for tighter credit, new taxes, and sharp reductions in state spending. The government's program also included higher prices on several basic items, including bread, milk, and sugar. These measures, complemented by others, were designed to hold down Portugal's huge deficit and make a dent in the country's foreign debt, necessary if the government were to acquire new loans. Soares's austerity measures were rewarded in August, when it was announced that the International Monetary Fund had granted Portugal a $480 million standby loan, conditional upon a further pledge of governmental belt-tightening. Specifically, Portugal's national debt, then at $13.6 billion, was to be held to no more than $16 billion through 1984.

In December, Portugal and the United States signed an accord extending U.S. rights to an air base in the Azores for seven years, in exchange for increased U.S. economic and military aid. The agreement had been in negotiation for much of the year.

See STATISTICS OF THE WORLD.   J.O.S.

PRESIDENT OF THE UNITED STATES. Ronald Wilson Reagan, 40th president of the United States, was born February 6, 1911, in Tampico, Ill. In his third year as president, Reagan benefited from increasing public support, as the economy rebounded and a U.S.-led invasion of Grenada won public backing. A Gallup poll released in November gave the president an overall approval rating of 53 percent—up from 43 percent in August. Fifty-nine percent approved of the Grenada invasion, while 32 percent disapproved. Reagan's relations with Congress were strained by strong disagreements over defense spending, projected budget deficits, and other issues in both foreign and domestic policy; however, some important compromises were reached. (See also CONGRESS OF THE UNITED STATES.)

While all of his top advisers said they expected the president to seek a second term in 1984, Reagan resisted their pressure for an early official announcement. However, he began a series of campaign-style appearances in the summer, and a campaign committee was established in October.

Economic policy. In his State of the Union message to Congress on January 25, Reagan

335

declared that America was "on the mend." The economy, after 18 months of recession, was in fact beginning to recover. In the following months, the gross national product rose, and unemployment declined, though remaining high by historic standards. Inflation was low—in large part because of the policies of the Federal Reserve Board under Paul Volcker. (Reagan reappointed him in 1983 to a second four-year term.) The chief clouds on the horizon were persistently high interest rates and large projected budget deficits; the U.S. failure to solve these problems was criticized by representatives of the major industrial nations at the economic summit hosted by Reagan in Williamsburg, Va., in late May.

In his budget proposal for the 1984 fiscal year, submitted to Congress on January 31, Reagan called for an increase in military spending of 10 percent (after inflation) and a freeze on outlays for many domestic programs. The budget proposal was attacked by both Democrats and Republicans in Congress, and the budget as passed by Congress provided for higher domestic expenditures and a lower level of defense spending.

Foreign policy. The president was challenged by a series of foreign crises late in the year. On September 5, Reagan went on national television to discuss the recent downing by the Soviet Union of a South Korean civilian airliner flying off course over Soviet territory. He denounced the Soviet action, which cost the lives of all 269 people aboard the aircraft, as "an act of barbarism," and he announced sanctions against the Soviets. However, in what was generally considered a restrained response to the incident, Reagan did not cancel arms talks with Moscow or grain sales to the Soviets.

On October 23, a bomb-laden truck driven by a lone terrorist smashed through security lines and into a Marine headquarters at the Beirut airport, killing over 240. U.S. policies in Lebanon and the adequacy of security for American forces there were called into question in a Pentagon report, and Reagan said he himself took responsibility for the tragedy.

On October 25, U.S. troops invaded the Caribbean island of Grenada, where a power struggle in the Marxist ruling party had resulted in a coup. Reagan said that the invasion was intended to protect the 1,000 American citizens in Grenada and to restore democracy there. In a televised address on October 27, he described the island as "a Soviet-Cuban colony being readied as a major military bastion to export terrorism." Most members of a congressional delegation sent to the island concluded that the invasion had been necessary, although there was still questioning in Congress and in the press of the administration's stated reasons for the action and of its restrictions on press coverage during the first stage of the invasion.

Prior to these developments, Central America had dominated much of the president's time. Reagan blamed the Soviet Union and Cuba for fomenting revolution in Central America, particularly in El Salvador, and the United States became more deeply committed to helping the Salvadoran government combat leftist guerrillas. In addition, the Reagan administration channeled covert aid to rebels opposing the leftist Sandinista government of Nicaragua. In a controversial move that even caught some administration officials by surprise, the president approved large-scale military maneuvers in Honduras, Nicaragua's northern neighbor, and he dispatched a small fleet of warships for several months of patrolling off Nicaragua's coast. Partly in response to criticism of his policies from congressional Democrats, Reagan appointed a bipartisan commission, headed by former Secretary of State Henry Kissinger, to investigate long-term solutions to the region's problems.

Arms issues. Reagan managed to win support in Congress for the controversial MX missile, after a long lobbying campaign in which he repeatedly assured members of Congress that he would seek to be flexible in arms control negotiations with the Soviet Union. Two sets of U.S.-Soviet talks were held in Geneva—one centering on plans to base U.S. medium-range missiles in Western Europe, the other devoted to negotiations on strategic arms reduction. Reagan originally had proposed the so-called zero option—no deployment of U.S. medium-range missiles there; in 1983 he advanced "interim" proposals under which the United States would deploy fewer missiles in return for a Soviet decision to dismantle some of the

The invasion of Grenada by U.S. troops and a contingent from the eastern Caribbean is announced by President Ronald Reagan (with Prime Minister Eugenia Charles of Dominica) on October 25. Secretary of State George Shultz (far left), Secretary of Defense Caspar Weinberger, and White House Communications Director David Gergen (behind Weinberger) stand by in the wings.

existing ones. No agreement was reached, and missile deployment was begun late in the year. In early October, prior to the opening of a new session of the strategic arms talks (START), Reagan outlined what he termed a version of the build-down proposal supported by some members of Congress as an alternative to a nuclear freeze; it would allow each side to modernize its strategic weapons arsenal but require old weapons to be destroyed as new ones were added. The START negotiations recessed in December with no agreement. Earlier in the year, Reagan came under fire when he dismissed Eugene Rostow as director of the Arms Control and Disarmament Agency. His choice for a replacement, Kenneth Adelman, was confirmed only after a tough battle in the Senate, where many Democrats questioned Adelman's qualifications and his commitment to arms reduction.

Domestic affairs. On the domestic front, a series of controversies plagued the president. The Environmental Protection Agency came under congressional attack, for reputedly not vigorously enforcing a toxic waste cleanup law and allowing political considerations to influence decision-making. Reagan defended Anne Burford, the head of EPA, but accusations against the agency mounted, and in March, he accepted her resignation. Many others resigned or were dismissed, in a major shakeup of the EPA. The president named William Ruckelshaus, a Republican who in the early 1970's was the first EPA chief, to come back to head the embattled agency.

In another flap, administration officials acknowledged that Reagan's advisers had obtained, before Reagan's debate with Jimmy Carter in the 1980 presidential campaign, a copy of the briefing book being used by Carter to prepare for the debate. Reagan said he had never realized that his campaign staff had had the document before the debate. He insisted the controversy over "Debategate," as it was known in press reports, was "much ado about nothing." Later, however, he ordered his staff to cooperate with an FBI inquiry into the affair. A House subcommittee was investigating the matter as well.

On October 9, Reagan's most controversial cabinet member, Interior Secretary James Watt, resigned his position. Already under attack for his environmental policies and his frequently provocative remarks, Watt brought on a new storm of indignation with a joke, widely considered insulting to women and minorities, about the members of a newly appointed commission. Even prominent Reagan supporters called on him to step down. National Security Adviser William P. Clark was named the new head of Interior.

See also CABINET, UNITED STATES.   W.E.

PRINCE EDWARD ISLAND. See STATISTICS OF THE WORLD.

PRIZES AND AWARDS. The following is a selected listing of prizes awarded during 1983 and the names of the persons who received them. For some awards given in specific fields, see the appropriate subject entry, such as MOTION PICTURES.

NOBEL PRIZES

Americans gathered most of the Nobel Prizes in 1983, but probably the best known of the Nobel laureates were a Polish electrician and a bearded English novelist. The prizes, presented on December 10, carried a cash value of $190,000 each.

Chemistry. For his "work in the mechanisms of electron transfer reactions, especially in metal complexes":

Henry Taube (1915–), Stanford University chemistry professor. Born in Neudorf, Saskatchewan, Canada, Taube received his doctorate in chemistry from the University of California at Berkeley in 1940 and became a U.S. citizen in 1942. He taught at Berkeley, Cornell University, and the University of Chicago before going to Stanford in 1961. Taube found in experiments with chemical reactions in metallic solutions that electrically charged atoms, or ions, reacted through wholesale

William A. Fowler of the California Institute of Technology smiles as he poses with telescope at the Yerkes Observatory. Fowler shared the 1983 Nobel Prize in physics with Subrahmanyan Chandrasekhar, of the University of Chicago, for their research on the birth, composition, and death of stars.

migration of atoms or groups of atoms acting as a "chemical bridge"; it had previously been thought that the reactions involved simply a transfer of electrons. The Nobel committee said Taube had made 18 major discoveries in his field.

Economics. For his theoretical model of how in a free-market economy the forces of supply and demand can be balanced, through the agency of changing prices, at the point of maximum efficiency and, in general, for providing a mathematical foundation for supply-and-demand theory:

Gerard Debreu (1921–), professor of mathematics and economics at the University of California at Berkeley. Born in Calais, France, Debreu graduated from the École Normale Supérieure and received his doctorate in mathematics from the University of Paris. From

1950 to 1955 he was a research associate with the Cowles Commission for Research in Economics at the University of Chicago, and from 1955 to 1960 he was an associate professor of economics with that organization's successor, the Cowles Foundation, at Yale University.

He went to Berkeley in 1962 and became a U.S. citizen in 1975.

Literature. For his novels, which, "with the perspicuity of realistic narrative art, and the diversity and universality of myth, illuminate the human condition in the world today":

William Golding (1911–), British novelist and the first Briton to receive the Nobel Prize for literature since Winston Churchill's 1953 award. Golding is best known for his harrowing novel *Lord of the Flies*, in which a group of shipwrecked British schoolboys succumb to primordial savagery as their veneer of civilization is eroded. He was compared to Herman Melville and Jonathan Swift by the Swedish Academy, which awards the literature prize. Golding, who was born in Cornwall, England, pursued a teaching career after completing a degree in English literature at Oxford. He also served in the Royal Navy during World War II. *Lord of the Flies* (published in 1954) was instantly acclaimed in England. At first it met with an indifferent U.S. response, but the paperback edition, first published in 1959, quickly won an enthusiastic audience on American college campuses. Golding's other major novels include *The Inheritors* (1955), *Pincher Martin* (1956), *The Spire* (1964), and *Rites of Passage* (1980).

Peace. For his "contribution, made with considerable personal sacrifice, to ensure the workers' right to establish their own organizations":

Lech Walesa (1943–), leader of the 1980 shipyard workers' strike in Gdańsk, Poland, that led to the formation of the Solidarity trade union, of which he became president. Walesa served in the Polish army before he began his job as an electrician at the Lenin Shipyard in Gdańsk, where he participated in a 1970 strike that led to confrontation with security forces and to more than 100 deaths. When widespread strikes began in the summer of 1980, Walesa organized the Lenin Shipyard workers; he and other strike leaders made demands unheard of in a Communist country, including the right to strike and the right to establish independent trade unions. Most of the demands were agreed to in August 1980. Jubilant Poles ultimately swelled Solidarity's ranks to 10 million, but its fall was swift, when the government, claiming the union was plotting its overthrow, imposed martial law in December 1981 and interned Walesa. Solidarity was officially banned in October 1982, and Walesa was released a month later, although he remained the target of an intense government propaganda campaign.

Physics. The Nobel Prize in physics went to two U.S. astrophysicists for their work on the birth, composition, and death of stars.

Subrahmanyan Chandrasekhar (1910–), born in Lahore, India (now Pakistan), studied at the Presidency College in Madras and at Cambridge University in England, where he earned

Barbara McClintock, winner of the 1983 Nobel Prize in physiology or medicine for her research—revolutionary when published more than a quarter of a century ago—on the genetics of corn.

a Ph.D. in physics and a Sc.D. in astrophysics. From 1936 on, he worked at the University of Chicago and the Yerkes Observatory in Williams Bay, Wis., and he became a U.S. citizen in 1953. His theory about the density of collapsed stars led to the recognition of neutron stars and black holes.

William Alfred Fowler (1911–), born in Pittsburgh, graduated from Ohio State University in 1933. He earned his Ph.D. in physics from the California Institute of Technology, where he remained as professor and researcher.

Physiology or medicine. For research conducted during the 1940's and 1950's on Indian corn, which showed that genes could move from one place to another on chromosomes, influencing the genetic inheritance of future generations:

Barbara McClintock (1902–), a resident investigator at the Carnegie Institution's genetics laboratory at Cold Spring Harbor, N.Y. In the days when McClintock was investigating her theories of movable genes, the prevailing assumption was that genes were locked firmly in place on chromosomes and could only be transferred from parents to offspring; her work was for the most part ignored until relatively recent developments in molecular biology confirmed her theories. McClintock, born in Hartford, Conn., enrolled in 1919 at Cornell University, where she majored in botany. As a graduate student she turned to plant breeding and received her doctorate from Cornell in 1927. She eventually earned a research position at Cold Spring Harbor, where she remained.

PULITZER PRIZES

The 1983 Pulitzer Prizes were announced on April 18. The fiction award went to Alice Walker for her third novel, *The Color Purple*. Ellen T. Zwilich won the music award for *Three Movements for Orchestra*. Winner in the drama category was Marsha Norman for *'night, Mother*, a two-woman play about suicide. In journalism, the Jackson (Mississippi) *Clarion-Ledger* was given the public service award for a series of stories and editorials on public education in Mississippi. Galway Kinnell won the poetry award for *Selected Poems*.

Other Pulitzer Prizes in letters and journalism were as follows:

Biography. Russell Baker, for the autobiography *Growing Up*.

Commentary. Claude Sitton, editorial writer for the Raleigh (North Carolina) *News & Observer*.

Criticism. Manuela Hoelterhoff, arts editor of the *Wall Street Journal*.

Editorial Cartooning. Richard Locher, Chicago *Tribune*.

Growing Up to Win a Pulitzer
"It's only daily journalism," says 58-year-old columnist Russell Baker. "The readers throw it away and forget it." Characteristically modest, Baker's remark about his widely syndicated "Observer" column is also uncharacteristically inaccurate. Baker's humorous, incisively observant commentaries on the human scene won him his first Pulitzer Prize, in 1979, and have been published in five collected volumes over the years. In 1983, *Growing Up*, a wry, clear-eyed recollection of his rural Virginia boyhood and his coming of age during the Great Depression, was a best-seller and won its author a Pulitzer for biography. Baker's next stop was Broadway; he wrote the book for a musical tentatively scheduled to open in New York in the spring of 1984.

Russell Baker

Dallas Times Herald *photographer James B. Dickman (right) gets a champagne shower as he celebrates his winning the Pulitzer Prize for feature photography. Sharing the glory was the paper's director of photography Ray Adler (center) and fellow Pulitzer winner, from 1980, Erwin H. (Skeeter) Hagler.*

Editorial Writing. Miami *Herald*.

Feature Writing. Nan Robertson, New York *Times*.

General Nonfiction. Susan Sheehan, *Is There No Place on Earth for Me?*

History. Rhys L. Isaac, *The Transformation of Virginia, 1740–1790*.

Photography, Feature. James B. Dickman, Dallas *Times Herald*.

Photography, Spot News. Bill Foley, Associated Press.

Reporting, General Local. Fort Wayne (Indiana) *News-Sentinel*, for coverage of local flood.

Reporting, International. Thomas L. Friedman, New York *Times*, and Loren Jenkins, Washington *Post*, for dispatches from Lebanon.

Reporting, National. Boston *Globe*, for the special supplement "War and Peace in the Nuclear Age."

Reporting, Special Local. Loretta Tofani, Washington *Post*, for a three-part series on homosexual rape in a local jail, "Rape in the County Jail: Prince George's Hidden Horror."

OTHER PRIZES AND AWARDS

Among other awards were the following:

Academy of American Poets. $10,000 fellowships to Philip Booth and James Schuyler.

Albert and Mary Lasker Foundation. $15,000 divided by Eric R. Kandel of Columbia University and Vernon B. Mountcastle, Jr., of Johns Hopkins University for brain research. $15,000 divided by Saul Krugman of New York University and Maurice R. Hilleman of Merck Sharp & Dohme Research Laboratories for research on hepatitis B virus. $15,000 to F. Mason Stone, Jr., of Cleveland Clinic Foundation for heart disease diagnosis research.

American Academy and Institute of Arts and Letters. $5,000 each to Carl Andre, Jennifer Bartlett, Susan Rothenberg, Angelo Savilli, and Michael C. Spafford (art); Alfred Corn Stephen Dixon, Robert Mezey, Mary Oliver, David Plante, George Starbuck, Leo Steinberg, and Edmund White (literature); William Thomas McKinley, Bernard Rands, Bruce Saylor, and Joan Tower (music). Award for Distinguished

Service to the Arts: Congressman Sidney R. Yates of Illinois. Gold Medals: Bernard Malamud (fiction) and Louise Nevelson (sculpture).

American Business Cancer Research Foundation. $600,000 grants to Leland H. Hartwell and Robert A. Weinberg.

American Film Institute. Life Achievement Award to John Huston.

American Institute for Public Service. Jefferson Awards of $5,000 each and gold-and-silver medallions to Kirk Douglas, Paul A. Volcker, Jan Scruggs, and Helen Hayes.

Armand Hammer Foundation. $100,000 cancer research grant (shared) to J. Michael Bishop and Harold Varmus of the University of California–San Francisco, Raymond L. Erikson of Harvard, and Robert A. Weinberg of MIT and the Whitehead Institute.

Association of American Publishers, American Book Awards. Hardcover awards: fiction, Alice Walker; general nonfiction, Fox Butterfield; biography, Judith Thurman; children's books, Jean Fritz (fiction), James Cross (nonfiction); history, Alan Brinkley; science, Abraham Pais. Paperback: fiction, Eudora Welty; general nonfiction, James Fallows; biography, James R. Mellow; children's books, Paula Fox and Joyce Carol Thomas (co-winners, fiction); history, Frank E. Manuel and Fritzie P. Manuel; science, Philip J. Davis and Reuben Hersh. First novel, Gloria Naylor. Poetry, Galway Kinnell and Charles Wright (co-winners). Translation, Richard Howard.

Bristol-Myers Award. $50,000 prize for cancer research to Leo Sachs of Israel.

Martin Luther King, Jr., Nonviolent Peace Prize. Awarded to Martin Luther King, Sr., and Richard Attenborough.

Medal of Freedom. Highest U.S. civilian award to George Balanchine, Paul W. ("Bear") Bryant, James Burnham, James Cheek, R. Buckminster Fuller, Billy Graham, Eric Hoffer, Jacob K. Javits, Clare Boothe Luce, Dumas Malone, Mabel Mercer, Simon Ramo.

National Conference of Christians and Jews. Charles Evans Hughes Gold Medal to former New York Senator Jacob K. Javits.

Onassis Foundation. $100,000 to Polish film director Andrzei Wajda. $100,000 to Prince Sadruddin Aga Khan and the environmental organization Europa Nostra (co-winners).

Samuel H. Scripps–American Dance Festival Award. Prize of $25,000 to choreographer Paul Taylor.

Templeton Foundation. $200,000 Templeton Prize for Progress in Religion to writer Aleksandr I. Solzhenitsyn.

Wolf Foundation. $100,000 to physicists Leon M. Lederman and Martin L. Perl (co-winners).   A.E.N. & M.H.

PUBLISHING. Book publishing seemed to be emerging from the recession in 1983, as sales went up and companies showed greater stability. The entry of many publishers into potentially lucrative software computer ventures was another good sign. Newspapers and magazines made modest gains, as a number of ownership changes were announced.

Books. Estimates by the Association of American Publishers of sales in the first six months of 1983 showed strong upturns in several categories of books. Adult hardcover sales were 29.1 percent ahead of sales during the same period in 1982, and juvenile hardcover sales rose 30.4 percent. Statistics for other book categories also showed significant, if less dramatic, increases. Sales of mass-market paperbacks, for instance, were up 19.9 percent.

Books about business trends and management did well. Other best-sellers, besides the usual assortment of thrillers, histories, diet plans, and humor books, included fantasies of outer space (culminating in *Return of the Jedi: The Storybook Based on the Movie*) and grooming and fitness books by celebrities and ordinary people alike. Paperback romances continued their extraordinary showing, accounting, according to some analysts, for one in every five mass-market paperbacks sold.

The most exciting developments in the book industry had to do not with books but with computers. A dozen major publishers launched or announced plans for new lines of software disks and tapes. Random House and E. P. Dutton took aim at the mass market with informational and recreational disks, and Harper & Row began software publishing with programs for school use. Prentice-Hall entered the field with business-management software, and Macmillan's initial offerings were aimed at school, college, and professional markets. Books in the computer field were also creating excitement. Doubleday, for instance, paid a $1.3 million advance for the *Whole Earth Software Catalog,* possibly the highest price ever for a trade paperback.

One of the year's most lucrative deals for an author came when Norman Mailer left Little, Brown to sign a four-novel contract with Random House for a reported $4 million. Other million-dollar deals were made by John Irving, William Peter Blatty, and Jackie Collins.

The year had its share of bad news for publishers. A & W Publishers and Hastings House Publishers both filed for reorganization under Chapter 11 of the federal bankruptcy code. Dell Publishing and its hardcover imprint, Delacorte, had their ranks decimated by across-the-board firings, and the Dial Press, a Doubleday subsidiary, was absorbed into its parent company. Among booksellers, Crown Books, a young and aggressive discount chain, made its first public offering of stock, but long-ailing Brentano's prepared to sell its stock and the last of its bookstores, after trying to reorganize its debts under federal bankruptcy law.

In a case that attracted wide attention, a federal appeals court ruled in November that *The Nation* magazine had not violated copyright law by publishing excerpts from former President Gerald R. Ford's memoirs prior to their publication by Harper & Row. The court, overturning a district court decision earlier in the year, decided that the use of the excerpts, as part of an article in *The Nation,* was protected by the First Amendment and constituted news reporting, which is protected under the fair use statute of the copyright law. In another legal dispute of interest, Random House, threatened with a lawsuit, announced in December that it was recalling and would destroy some 58,000 copies of *Poor Little Rich Girl,* a biography of Barbara Hutton. The book was found to contain false statements about a physician who had treated the Woolworth heiress.

Magazines. With rates rising, magazine ad revenues for the year were expected to be at least 8 percent higher than in 1982, reaching a total of more than $4.2 billion. There was little improvement in overall circulation, but the magazines that reported gains outnumbered those suffering losses. Computer and video magazines were among the fastest growing

Condé Nast's original Vanity Fair *(above), which had a loyal readership for 22 years, was reincarnated (below) after more than four decades. The 732,000-copy first issue was dispatched to newsstands and some 600,000 charter subscribers.*

Books on business were big business. Megatrends, by John Naisbitt (above), was one of several books analyzing business trends to hit the top of the nonfiction best-seller lists during the year.

publications. Single copy sales remained soft, but circulation revenues, increasingly important as a source of income, continued to grow, largely as a result of further increases in cover prices and subscription rates. The Magazine Publishers Association said the average cover price would reach $1.90 during 1983.

There were several notable changes in ownership. The Washington-based American Psychological Association purchased *Psychology Today,* a 15-year-old monthly with a circulation of 850,000, from the Ziff-Davis Publishing Company for an undisclosed price. A group of investors headed by Mark J. Meagher, former president of the Washington Post Company, agreed to buy *Financial World,* an 82,000-circulation semimonthly, from Macro Communications for $7,250,000. Also, Century Publishing Company, publisher of seven sports-related magazines, announced it would acquire and revive *Inside Sports,* the monthly that Active Markets Inc. had bought from *Newsweek* in January 1982. The magazine had folded in November 1982; Century Publishing relaunched it in August, with an October cover date, and projected an initial circulation of 200,000. In September, Condé Nast Publications acquired *Gourmet* magazine from the estate of its founder, Earle R. MacAusland, for an undisclosed price.

TV-Cable Week, an ambitious venture by Time Inc. aimed at the more than 30 million U.S. households equipped with cable television, made its debut in April and bowed out in September. The 96-page weekly contained 40 color pages of national news and features covering both broadcast and cable television, plus cable television listings for the local market. It never gained sufficient readership, perhaps because of its $2.95-per-month price and because it was not enthusiastically accepted by the cable operators, who were responsible for its distribution.

Another new venture that aroused less enthusiasm than the publisher anticipated was the revival in February of Vanity Fair, the elite cultural monthly that won a devoted following between 1914 and its death in 1936. Believing that a resurrected Vanity Fair would appeal to today's cultural sophisticates, the Condé Nast company, publisher of the original magazine, invested a reported $15 million to revive it. The 732,000-copy first issue, sent to newsstands and 600,000 charter subscribers in late February, was a lavish production, with 290 slick pages (more than 160 devoted to advertising). Many critics found it to be uneven in quality and generally superficial. In May, after just three issues, S. I. Newhouse, Jr., board chairman at Condé Nast, fired Editor-in-Chief Richard Locke, replaced him with Leo Lerman, feature editor of Vogue magazine, and said Vanity Fair would try a "new approach."

Newspapers. The U.S. newspaper industry remained strong financially. More newspapers added special interest sections and individual editions for geographic zones, and many also switched from afternoon to morning publication. Although afternoon dailies still outnumbered morning dailies by nearly three to one, the American Newspaper Publishers Association reported in April that morning papers had taken the lead in total circulation during 1982 and were adding to their margin in 1983. The ANPA also noted that offset had replaced letterpress as the prevailing printing technology in U.S. and Canadian newspapers.

Two prospering metropolitan newspapers were sold by members of the owning families. In mid-April, Marshall Field V announced that he and his half brother, Frederick, planned to liquidate the Chicago Sun-Times Company and the related Field Enterprises. The dissolution was to include sale of the 651,000-circulation Chicago Sun-Times, the nation's ninth-largest daily. In early November, Rupert K. Murdoch, an Australian publisher who also owns such papers as the Times of London, the New York Post, and the Boston Herald, announced that he had agreed to buy the Sun-Times and the Field Newspaper Syndicate for $90 million in cash. In July, the 438,000-circulation Houston Post, the U.S. South's largest morning newspaper, also was put on the market by its owners, members of the Hobby and Catto families. Canada's Toronto Sun Publishing Corporation said in October it would purchase the Post for $100 million in cash plus the value of the paper's working capital.

In April, the Gannett Company sold the 109-year-old, 175,000-circulation Oakland Tribune to Robert C. Maynard, the paper's editor and publisher. Maynard thus became the first black owner of a general circulation metropolitan U.S. newspaper. Before taking over the Tribune, which had slipped into the red after earning a $2 million profit in 1979, Maynard obtained labor union concessions that were expected to save the paper $10 million over the next five years.

The St. Louis Globe-Democrat, scheduled by the Newhouse newspaper chain to cease publication December 31, got a new lease on life when Debra and Jeffrey Gluck, the publishers who had bought The Saturday Review in 1982, announced on December 23 that they had purchased the 131-year-old morning paper (for an undisclosed sum) and would continue its publication.

A notable new venture in 1983 was the Wall Street Journal's European edition, edited in Brussels and printed in the Netherlands. The Journal also reported that its Asian edition, started in 1976, had made a profit for the first time in 1982.

The Gannett Company's new national newspaper, USA Today, which had begun publication in September 1982, added new printing locations and spread into new markets during 1983. By mid-September it had become the third largest U.S. daily, with an average paid circulation of more than 1.1 million. Already sold in 2,500 communities, it was available to approximately two-thirds of the U.S. population.

In May a federal judge reversed a $2.05 million libel verdict against the Washington *Post*. The suit centered on a 1979 *Post* article that asserted that the president of Mobil Oil Corporation, William P. Tavoulareas, had used corporate funds to set up his son in the shipping business. The judge ruled that although the article fell "far short of being a model of fair, unbiased investigative journalism," it did not constitute libel according to the standards set by the U.S. Supreme Court.   G.B. & J.L.

PUERTO RICO. Despite some improvements, Puerto Rico's economy was still plagued by instability and uncertainty in 1983. Chronic high unemployment persisted, with the overall official figure reaching 24.7 percent in July, the highest rate ever. In some depressed urban and rural areas, unemployment exceeded the official figure by far, approaching or even surpassing 50 percent. In manufacturing, the most important sector of Puerto Rico's economy, newly opened plants were still fewer in fiscal 1983 than in the previous fiscal year. A major reopening, scheduled for 1984, will be that of the Commonwealth Oil Refining Company; closed in 1982, the company was acquired by a U.S. concern in September 1983.

Tourism, which accounted for approximately 5.5 percent of the gross domestic product in 1981–1982, declined 9.5 percent in 1982–1983. On the other hand, agricultural production increased by 5 percent during the ten-month period ending in May 1983.

A splinter movement within the governing New Progressive Party (NNP) culminated in the registration, this August, of the new Puerto Rican Renewal Party, under Hernán Padilla, mayor of San Juan. The new party did not specifically advocate any one of the three status formulas—statehood, independence, or commonwealth—proposed for the island's future.

In November, Puerto Rico Governor Carlos Romero Barceló admitted that two young independentista activists trapped by police in July 1978 had apparently been shot dead after surrendering. Two official investigations had cleared police of wrongdoing, but lingering suspicions led in 1983 to Watergate-style televised hearings and closed door testimony before the Puerto Rican Senate; ultimately, two police eyewitnesses, granted immunity from perjury prosecution for earlier testimony, testified that the activists, members of the small Armed Revolutionary Movement, had their hands up and may even have been pleading for their lives. The governor tentatively agreed to support appointment of a special prosecutor but backed away from giving such a prosecutor the strong powers sought by some.

See STATISTICS OF THE WORLD.   A.C–C.

Q

QATAR. See STATISTICS OF THE WORLD. *See also* PERSIAN GULF STATES.

QUEBEC. See STATISTICS OF THE WORLD. *See also* CANADA.

R

RADIO. See TELEVISION AND RADIO BROADCASTING.

RAILROADS. See TRANSPORTATION.
RECORDINGS. *See* MUSIC.

Religion

In 1983, political controversies often overshadowed theological concerns in the world of religion. The question of disarmament sparked intense debates within the Protestant and Catholic communities, echoes of the Holocaust drew the attention of the Jewish community, and the role of religion in secular government was a focus of concern in the Islamic world.

During 1983, Pope John Paul II made important trips to Poland and Central America, Protestants celebrated the 500th anniversary of the birth of Martin Luther, and strife between Hindus and Muslims afflicted parts of India.

ROMAN CATHOLIC CHURCH

For Roman Catholicism, 1983 was a year of frequent disputes over such issues as human rights and nuclear weapons, some involving Pope John Paul II directly and some involving national hierarchies of bishops.

Papal travels. The second visit by John Paul II to his native Poland since he became pontiff produced numerous sparks of controversy (see biography in PEOPLE IN THE NEWS). At every stop in the eight-day trip in June, the pope invoked powerful images identifying the Catholic Church with Polish nationalism and by extension with anti-Soviet and anti-Communist sentiment. The allusions were so blunt as to bring a warning at one point from the Polish government that politics was replacing what was to have been the essentially religious nature of the visit. The pope met twice with General Wojciech Jaruzelski, head of the Polish government. The talks were presumed to have covered such topics as political prisoners, the end of martial law, and the future of trade unionism, including that of the outlawed Solidarity union and its leader, Lech Walesa.

The pope was only hours back in Rome when *L'Osservatore Romano,* the Vatican City daily, published an editorial that appeared to ally the Vatican with Polish government efforts to undercut the leadership role of Walesa. The paper said that Walesa had "lost his battle" and indicated that he was no longer in a position to play a public role. The writer of the editorial, deputy editor Father Virgilio Levi, was forced to resign, but the editorial itself was not officially repudiated by the Vatican.

A tense eight-day trip in March to Costa Rica, Nicaragua, Panama, El Salvador, Guatemala, Honduras, Belize, and Haiti brought John Paul into contact with major concerns of his pontificate, including widespread social injustice and belligerent ideological rivalries. The pope, under constant guard because of military strife and civil unrest in much of the region, publicly scolded heads of state for violations of human rights, deplored violence by both right and left, admonished priests for involvement in politics, and demanded that Catholics be faithful to church doctrine.

A papal trip to Austria in September was largely pastoral in character, as John Paul dwelled on religious topics and emphasized the common heritage of Europe. The pope also made a pastoral visit in August to the shrine at Lourdes, France.

Peace messages. The American bishops' much-anticipated pastoral letter on nuclear arms was ratified by a 238–9 vote at a meeting in Chicago in May. The 45,000-word document, "The Challenge of Peace: God's Promise and Our Response," condemned nuclear weapons and cast grave doubt on the possibility of their ever being used morally, even in a limited conflict. The bishops called for a halt to the production and deployment of new nuclear weapons and gave only "strictly conditioned" acceptance to existing nuclear deterrents.

Calling out to men with a calling: Facing a severe shortage of priests, the Roman Catholic archdiocese of Toronto launched a recruitment drive using dramatic billboard advertisements.

The urgency of the nuclear arms issue for Catholics was pointed up as other national hierarchies issued peace statements of their own, some of which departed significantly from the American pastoral. The West German bishops, for instance, supported the NATO policy of "flexible response," which holds that nuclear weapons might be needed to halt an overwhelming enemy attack employing conventional weapons. The French bishops, in a statement issued in November, defended the moral legitimacy of nuclear deterrence in the face of the "aggressive and dominating character of Marxist-Leninist ideology." The Dutch bishops, on the other hand, stopped just short of urging unilateral disarmament as a means of controlling and reducing nuclear arsenals.

In a related development, the pope on November 12 called on the world's scientists to refuse involvement in "certain fields of research, inevitably destined . . . for deadly purposes." Instead of engaging in military research, the pope said, scientists should "work for justice, love, and peace."

World developments. The pope named 18 new cardinals on January 5, among them Archbishops Jozef Glemp of Poland and Julijans Vaivods of Latvia. The latter became the first publicly proclaimed cardinal in the Soviet Union. Three others from countries with Marxist governments received red hats: Archbishop Franjo Kuharic of Yugoslavia, Bishop Joachim Meisner of East Germany, and Archbishop Alexandre do Nascimento of Angola.

The pope also promulgated a new code of canon law. The new code—1,752 canons spelled out in seven books—removes many vestiges of authoritarian church law, broadens the role of the laity, decentralizes the church by extending more authority to bishops, stresses human needs and the church's responsiblity to serve them, and reaffirms traditional church law in a number of controversial areas, including abortion, contraception, divorce, and a male-only priesthood. In guidelines for sexual education issued on December 1, the Vatican reaffirmed the church's opposition to artificial birth control and labeled homosexual activity and extramarital sex as morally indefensible.

On September 13 the Society of Jesus (Jesuits) elected a new leader, Father Peter-Hans Kolvenbach, 54, a Dutch educator. The election was expected to reduce tension between the pope and the Jesuits, born of a disagreement over liberal tendencies within the order.

Europe. Voters in the Republic of Ireland approved a constitutional amendment September 7 acknowledging "the right to life of the unborn." The measure is intended to bar any possibility of legal abortion in the predominantly Catholic country, where abortion was already prohibited by statute. In March, Sweden and the Vatican resumed diplomatic relations after a break of more than 450 years, dating from the Reformation.

Investigations into the May 1981 shooting of the pope in St. Peter's Square by Turkish terrorist Mehmet Ali Agca continued, as authorities probed the possibility that Bulgarian secret services abetted Agca in the act. In July, in a surprise encounter with reporters outside police headquarters in Rome, Agca alleged that he had been part of a plot involving not only "Bulgarian services" but also the KGB. The following month, Emanuela Orlandi, 15, a citizen of Vatican City, was kidnapped by a group calling itself the Turkish Anti-Christian Liberation Front and demanding the release of Agca. The pope pleaded for the release of the girl but rejected as "unfeasible" the demand for Agca's release. The girl's whereabouts remained a mystery.

United States. Two prominent U.S. cardinals died in 1983: Cardinal Humberto Medeiros, archbishop of Boston, on September 17, and Cardinal Terence Cook, archbishop of New York, on October 6. Cardinal Joseph Bernardin, archbishop of Chicago, was awarded the 1983 Albert Einstein Peace Prize for his work on the U.S. bishops' pastoral letter on the morality of nuclear weapons.

A 52-year-old Sister of Mercy, Agnes Mary Mansour, resigned as a nun on May 11 rather than accede to demands by Detroit Archbishop Edmund Szoka and the Vatican that she quit as director of Michigan's Department of Social Services. At issue was the department's administration of a state-funded abortion program. Mansour declared that she was personally opposed to abortion but could tolerate government funding of abortion out of consideration for American religious pluralism.

Elsewhere. China jailed four elderly priests for up to 15 years in May for offenses that included

Prominent Catholic Leader
In 1983, Joseph Bernardin, recently named head of the Roman Catholic archdiocese of Chicago, emerged as an outspoken and energetic religious leader. The 65-year-old prelate spoke out against racism during the Chicago mayoral election and announced plans to establish a diocesan council composed of both clerical and lay members (an action that would have been unthinkable under his predecessor, Cardinal John Cody). He also headed a five-member committee of the National Conference of Catholic Bishops that drafted a widely publicized pastoral letter challenging the morality of U.S. nuclear arms policy. Bernardin was named a cardinal in January. For his work on the pastoral letter he was awarded the Albert Einstein Peace Prize in November.

Joseph Cardinal Bernardin

maintaining ties with the Vatican and sending abroad information about Catholics in China. In July, 12 Vietnamese priests were sentenced to jail terms of five years to life for "antistate activities and antirevolutionary propaganda," according to Vatican Radio. In April, the Vatican excommunicated Ngo Dinh Thuc, the former archbishop of Hue, Vietnam, now living in France, for ordaining several bishops without papal authorization.

In the Philippines a continuing tension between the country's Catholic bishops and the government of President Ferdinand E. Marcos reached a critical point in August, when a pastoral letter sharply critical of Marcos and condemning as immoral the president's power to have people imprisoned without trial was to be read at Sunday services. However, two days before the planned reading, the letter was withdrawn after Marcos decreed the repeal or modification of his powers to arrest suspected subversives.   J.G.D.

PROTESTANT AND ORTHODOX CHURCHES

Church-state issues, "political" involvement by interchurch organizations, and significant steps toward Christian unity were dominant themes in the Protestant churches.

Church, state, and politics. In January, a 30-minute segment on the CBS television program *60 Minutes* alleged that the National Council of the Churches of Christ in the United States of America (NCC) and the Geneva-based World Council of Churches (WCC) were funding violent revolution by giving money to Marxist organizations, including leftist guerrilla movements in various parts of the world. The two ecumenical groups, whose member churches include both Protestant and Orthodox bodies, were also criticized in a similar vein in an article published in the January issue of *Read-*

Nuns from the Russian Orthodox Church of the Soviet Union are shown here at the Sixth Assembly of the World Council of Churches, in Vancouver, British Columbia. The 930 representatives of roughly 440 million Christians passed a strong antinuclear statement.

er's *Digest.* In reply, NCC and WCC spokesmen charged that the media treatments of their organizations' programs ignored the fact that most of their money goes to fund relief work.

In May the U.S. Supreme Court upheld the Internal Revenue Service's revocation of the tax-exempt status of Bob Jones University in Greenville, S.C., and of Goldsboro Christian Schools in Goldsboro, N.C. Both schools had argued that any racial discrimination they practiced (the former restricted black enrollment, and the latter denied admission to blacks) was based on religious convictions and that the IRS decision to deny them a tax exemption was a violation of the religious freedom guaranteed in the Constitution. The Court ruled that the government has a clear secular interest in preventing racial discrimination, since it "contravenes public policy."

The 10,000-member Garden Grove Community Church in Garden Grove, Calif., whose pastor is the television personality Robert Schuller, was slapped with a heavy tax bill by the state Board of Equalization. The church, a highly atypical congregation of the Reformed Church in America, had its state property tax exemption withdrawn in 1982 when tax investigators declared it did not fulfill state requirements for a tax exemption, since its facilities were not being used for "exclusively religious" purposes. The church agreed under protest to pay $473,000 in back taxes, while accusing state officials of engaging in religious harassment.

WCC and NCC meetings. In July and August, the Sixth Assembly of the World Council of Churches convened in Vancouver, British Columbia—the first WCC Assembly in North America since the 1954 Assembly in Evanston, Ill. The secular as well as the religious press paid considerable attention to a highly important document relating to Christian unity called *Baptism, Eucharist and Ministry,* embodying statements brought to final form by the WCC's Faith and Order Commission at Lima, Peru. The Lima document figured in the Assembly's central eucharistic celebration, when 3,500 Christians from around the world participated in a service using the "Lima Liturgy." The rite is based on agreements, or "convergences," reached by Protestant, Orthodox, and Roman

Catholic scholars after 55 years of theological discussions. The Assembly also criticized U.S. policies in Central America and approved a statement on the Middle East interpreted as unsympathetic to Israel. Another key document supported nuclear disarmament.

The National Council of Churches continued to be faced with the question of whether to admit to council membership the Universal Fellowship of Metropolitan Community Churches, a predominately homosexual denomination founded in 1968. Delegates from several denominations threatened to pull out of the NCC if the Metropolitan group were admitted. At an NCC meeting in November, discussion of the Metropolitan's eligibility for membership was indefinitely postponed.

Unity and rapprochement. A split in American Presbyterianism over the slavery issue was mended after 122 years, when the 2.35 million-member United Presbyterian Church in the U.S.A. and the 815,000-member Presbyterian Church in the United States formally reunited. The merger was assured in February when a sufficient number of presbyteries (regional governing units) of the two churches approved the reunion plan previously passed by the churches' General Assemblies. The merged body, known as the Presbyterian Church (U.S.A.), officially came into being in June.

A group of 20 Roman Catholic and Lutheran theologians in the United States announced in September that dialogues between representatives of the two faiths, in progress since 1965, had resulted in a fundamental agreement on the doctrine of justification, which explains how humans who have sinned can be reconciled with God and achieve salvation. The new accord emphasizes a mutual belief that only God's grace can bring salvation.

Peace and disarmament. The issue of peace continued to dominate agendas at denominational assemblies. The Presbyterian Church (U.S.A.), the United Church of Christ, and the Christian Church (Disciples of Christ) issued individual statements favoring some form of nuclear disarmament.

Evangelical Protestant groups were also struggling with the disarmament question. A conference discussing "biblical perspectives" on peace and disarmament drew 1,500 evangelicals to Pasadena, Calif., in May. Organized by Fuller Theological Seminary and other sponsoring groups, it marked the first major gathering of evangelical Christians for the express purpose of examining issues of peace and nuclear war.

Seminaries. Amid controversy, a Southern Baptist scholar, Dale Moody, left Southern Baptist Theological Seminary in Louisville, Ky., after a 40-year teaching career. Moody accepted a paid leave of absence for the 1983–1984 academic year after ultraconservatives in the denomination threatened a heresy trial. His teaching contract would not be renewed, the seminary said. Moody said he disagreed with those Southern Baptists who believe that the mere acceptance of Christ guarantees salvation.

Christ Seminary–Seminex, the theological school formed by professors and students who walked out of the Lutheran Church–Missouri Synod's Concordia Seminary in St. Louis in 1974, graduated its last class in 1983 and shut down its St. Louis–based operations. Seminex, an abbreviation of "Seminary in Exile," came into being under the leadership of President John Teitjen, a key figure in the breakoff from the Missouri Synod of a "moderate" faction.

New translation. In October the NCC released a new translation of key Bible readings that studiously avoids characterizations of God, Jesus, and humankind as exclusively male. Intended for use in public worship on a voluntary and experimental basis, this Inclusive Language Lectionary is based on the Revised Standard Version of the Bible. Typical of its approach is the phrase "God, Father and Mother." Some American Christians welcomed the lectionary, but others attacked it for such failings as inaccuracy and stylistic inadequacy.

Other controversies. In June, 64 prominent leaders of various churches, including liberal and conservative Catholics and Protestants, delivered to Congress a signed resolution calling for a ban on genetic engineering experiments aimed at altering human cells in ways that could affect genetic inheritance.

A religious publisher prevailed upon its secular subsidiary to cancel publication of two novels containing what it deemed to be offensive language (distribution of a third book, already released, was curtailed). Thomas Nelson Inc. of Nashville, the world's largest publisher of Bibles, pressured Dodd, Mead & Co. (which it had purchased in 1982) to withdraw the books in August.

Fifty-nine of the United Methodist Church's 73 annual conferences in the United States passed resolutions or other legislation expressing their convictions on the ordination of homosexuals, a controversial question in the UMC as in other Protestant bodies. A majority of the conferences addressing the issue went on record against ordination of "avowed" homosexuals.

Luther anniversary. Lutherans and other Protestants around the world, joined in some instances by Roman Catholics, observed the 500th anniversary of Martin Luther's birth with special worship services, lecture series, scholarly dialogues, and publications that took note of the German monk and Protestant reformer's contributions. The event enjoyed official state support in East Germany, where 1983 was declared "Martin Luther Year." In November, East German leader Erich Honecker publicly referred to Luther as one of German history's "most meaningful personalities."   J.C.L.

JUDAISM

During 1983 the situation of Soviet Jews deteriorated seriously. Emigration was reduced to a trickle: in the first ten months of the year, fewer than 1,200 Jews were permitted to leave the Soviet Union. Officially sanctioned anti-Semitism was on the rise, and the government launched an intensive campaign against Zionism, apparently designed to discourage Jews from seeking to emigrate.

In Poland, in April, ceremonies and controversy marked the 40th anniversary of the Warsaw Ghetto uprising against the Nazis during World War II. Marek Edelman, the only known survivor of the uprising still in Poland, charged the Polish government with manipulation of the anniversary for its own political ends and urged a boycott of the ceremonies.

Years of effort by France and West Germany to have the Nazi war criminal Klaus Barbie, known as the "butcher of Lyon," extradited from Bolivia met with success. The Bolivian government arrested Barbie in January and

Survivors of the Holocaust point out their own faces in a photograph taken at the Auschwitz death camp in 1945. They were among the thousands of victims of Nazi persecution who gathered in April in Washington, D.C., many seeking friends and relatives lost since the war.

extradited him to France in February. French authorities said Barbie, who had twice been sentenced to death in absentia, would be put on trial under a new statute specifically enacted to deal with genocide and war crimes.

The American Jewish Commission on the Holocaust, established in September 1981 to study what the organized American Jewish community did or failed to do to save European Jewry during the Nazi period, released an interim report in February 1983. Prepared by the commission's chairman, former U.S. Supreme Court Justice Arthur J. Goldberg, the report found that American Jews were "so benumbed by the magnitude of the catastrophe" that they did not do all they could "to mount an all-out unified sustained mobilization for rescue." The report also noted, however, that in any event American Jews had "little power or influence" in the 1930's and 1940's to prevent the slaughter of Jews in Europe.

In April, 15,000 Holocaust survivors and their relatives gathered in Washington, D.C., for a three-day reunion of European Jews who survived the Nazi persecutions. President Ronald Reagan spoke at the opening ceremony. Vice-President George Bush and Speaker of the House Thomas P. O'Neill, Jr., presented to Elie Wiesel, chairman of the U.S. Holocaust Memorial Council, a symbolic key for a Holocaust memorial and museum, to be built with private funds near the Washington Monument.

The Central Conference of American Rabbis, a group of Reform rabbis, adopted at its March

Indonesia's famed Borobudur temple has been rededicated as a national monument. Covered with exquisite bas-reliefs depicting the life of Buddha, the structure's many levels symbolize the stages of enlightenment.

convention in Los Angeles a resolution recognizing the child of a Jewish man and a non-Jewish woman as Jewish. Orthodox groups announced that, as a result, they would review their association with Reform and Conservative rabbis in umbrella organizations.

The question of the ordination of women rabbis by the Conservative movement once again aroused heated debate. The movement's Rabbinical Assembly, at its annual convention, held in April in Dallas, voted by a narrow margin to reject the membership application of a Reform-ordained woman rabbi, Beverly Magidson. L.G.

ISLAM

Several Asian states grappled with the question of Islam's role in national government. General Muhammad Zia ul-Haq, the president of Pakistan, continued to work toward what he referred to as the Islamization of the Pakistani state, despite the objections of domestic critics that he was using Islamization chiefly to tighten the grip of his military government. In particular, Zia's Majlis-i-Shura (consultative council)

approved the creation of local shariat and qazi courts (theological courts) in an attempt to expedite the administration of justice according to religious law. Bangladesh, too, was attempting to extend Islamic traditions into secular areas, but with less immediate success. A government proposal to introduce the study of Arabic and of the Koran as compulsory subjects, beginning with the first grade, helped spark rioting by university students in February, and the proposal later was withdrawn. The opposite tack was taken by Indonesia, however. By reaffirming the primacy of Pancasila (the five principles of belief in God, sovereignty, unity, social justice, and humanity) as the official state ideology, the Indonesian government sought to counter the efforts of Islamic parties and groups to provide an Islamic foundation to the state.

In Iran, the Islamic government continued its attacks on the Bahai minority, numbering 300,000–400,000 in a total population of more than 40 million. Between 1979 and mid-1983, more than 150 Bahais were executed by the government. Later in 1983, 140 Bahais, mostly elected members of Bahai assemblies (later dissolved), were reportedly arrested.

In March, the Al-Azhar Mosque and University in Cairo celebrated its 1,000th year of existence as a center for Islamic learning and Muslim devotion. Staffed by a faculty of approximately 3,600, who provide instruction to a student body of about 90,000, this oldest of Islam's continuing educational institutions has offered a broad curriculum in secular fields while maintaining its widely acknowledged position as the outstanding Muslim theological university.

At a meeting of Islamic scholars held in Mecca in June, King Fahd of Saudi Arabia suggested that the practice of *ijtihad* be revived. *Ijtihad* (literally, "exertion") denotes a believer's conscientious striving for truth in the light of the Koran and other religious writings, tradition, reason, and one's situation in life; as a method of religious interpretation, it differs substantially from the literal reading of Islamic texts that has dominated theological inquiries since the suspension of *ijtihad* in the ninth century. In advocating revival of this approach, King Fahd argued that it could be useful in reconciling Islamic law with the complexities of modern life.

BUDDHISM

There were indications that the Chinese government was allowing greater religious expression to Tibetan Buddhists. Work was proceeding on the restoration of significant religious sites, and European journalists and film crews were allowed to photograph pictures, prominently hung in Tibetan buildings, of the Dalai Lama (high priest of Tibetan Buddhism). Also, construction was begun on a new Tibetan university, which, it was said, would include a center for Buddhist studies.

In northern China, restoration work began on the ancient Buddhist monastery in Shaolin; a few elderly monks still live in this monastic complex, which reportedly was an early center for Ch'an (Zen) and the martial arts. Meanwhile, restoration of a celebrated Buddhist shrine, the Borobudur in Java, Indonesia, was completed. The eight-year international effort to salvage and restore this priceless Buddhist monument, dating from the eighth century, was carried out under the aegis of the United Nations Educational, Scientific, and Cultural Organization. On February 23, Indonesian President Suharto unveiled a memorial plaque at Borobudur celebrating the accomplishment.

RELIGIONS OF INDIA AND SRI LANKA

Early in the year, violent clashes between Hindus and Muslims led to hundreds of deaths in the northern Indian state of Assam. Long-standing religious antagonism contributed significantly to the bloody conflict there. The immediate occasion of the violence was the holding of state elections in February, which brought to the surface resentments among many Assamese Hindus over the presence of millions of legal and illegal Muslim immigrants from densely populated Bangladesh and over increasing Muslim power at the ballot box. In Punjab, meanwhile, members of the Sikh religious minority continued to press religious and political demands on the national government. Shortly after the violent demonstrations erupted in Punjab in February, Prime Minister Indira Gandhi accepted several religious demands made by Sikh nationalists; among other things, her government agreed that Sikh religious sermons would be relayed and broadcast over All India Radio, that Sikhs would be allowed to carry ceremonial knives on domestic airline flights, and that the sale of meat, cigarettes, and wine in the vicinity of the Golden Temple in Amritsar would be prohibited. Violence on the part of Sikh extremists nevertheless continued (see INDIA).

In Sri Lanka tensions between the Buddhist Sinhalese majority and the Hindu Tamil minority similarly erupted in violence, looting, and arson. The disruptions were ignited in late July after an ambush apparently staged by extremist Tamils near the northern town of Jaffna killed 13 government soldiers. By the beginning of August, more than 200 persons had reportedly been killed, as mobs attacked Tamil homes, stores, and property. A national curfew eventually helped to curb the disorders. The Tamils, who constitute 20 percent of the population, have long been pressing for a separate Tamil political entity or state in the north; the Sinhalese majority have rejected the idea.

Another Indian religious minority, the Jains,

displayed more interest in unity than in strife. Jainism, whose followers in India number only a few million in a population of more than 700 million, is an offshoot of Hinduism stressing that all life is sacred, even the lowest forms, and that happiness in the next life can best be assured by strict asceticism in this life. Since the first century A.D., the Jains have been divided into two major sects, which disagreed initially over whether public nudity was permissible and whether women could attain salvation. In 1983, Jain leaders announced the beginning of a campaign aimed at reunification of the sects, the initial step of which would be cooperation in social welfare projects.

At India's 34th Republic Day celebration, held on January 26, the country's highest civilian award, the Bharat Ratna (the jewel of India), was conferred posthumously on Acharya Vinoba Bhave, who provided structure and guidance for the Sarvodaya and Bhoodan movements of material and spiritual uplift. Later in 1983, all Indians—not merely Hindus—mourned the passing of the industrialist-philanthropist Ghanshyamdas Birla, greatly admired for his contributions to the building of Hindu temples, who died in London on June 11 at the age of 89. J.R.C.

REPUBLICAN PARTY. Republican leaders had little to cheer about after the November 1983 elections, but their prospects in the upcoming presidential race were a good deal brighter in the fall of the year than they had been in the spring. Early in the year, with the recession barely over and the administration making little headway on its major domestic and foreign policy initiatives, there were doubts that President Ronald Reagan would run again. By the end of the year, however, the president's fortunes had risen with the economy, and a Reagan candidacy in 1984 seemed all but certain.

State and local elections. The off-year elections predictably resulted in numerous Democratic wins in the big-city mayoralty races. More disappointing to the Republicans were losses in the Kentucky and Mississippi gubernatorial elections, as well as the failure of a generously funded bid to gain control of the New Jersey legislature. Among the few Republican victors in important mayoral races were Richard Hud-

nut in Indianapolis and Donna Owens in Toledo, Ohio.

Congress. One bright spot for the party was the ability of former Washington State Governor Daniel J. Evans to hold onto the U.S. Senate seat to which he was appointed after the death in September of Henry M. ("Scoop") Jackson, a Democrat. Evans's victory left the Republicans with a 55–45 edge in the Senate—a little more breathing room for the 1984 Senate elections.

Among the most endangered GOP seats for 1984 were those held by two powerful senators who announced that they would not seek reelection: Majority Leader Howard H. Baker, Jr., (Tenn.) and Reagan loyalist John Tower (Texas), chairman of the Senate Armed Services Committee. In the running for the Republican nomination to succeed Tower was Representative Phil Gramm, formerly a pro-Reagan Democrat, or "Boll Weevil." Gramm, stripped of his Democratic seat on the House Budget Committee because of his support of the president's programs during the key budget battles of 1981 and 1982, resigned his congressional seat in January and then regained it as a Republican in a special election on February 12.

Reagan candidacy. Polls released in January gave President Reagan a national approval rating of only 41 percent—lower than the standing of any of his four elected predecessors at comparable stages of their presidential terms. Over the next few months, with legislative successes scarce and the administration beset by a series of minor but damaging scandals, there was speculation that Reagan might not run for a second term. Continuing economic recovery in the ensuing months brought a rapid rise in Reagan's popularity, however, and in mid-October, with the economic omens still favorable, Senator Paul Laxalt of Nevada, the Republican national chairman, announced that Reagan had authorized the formation of a reelection committee on his behalf.

Throughout 1983, Reagan moved to shore up what the pollsters perceived as his political weaknesses. For instance, partly to assuage women's rights critics, Reagan named two women to top cabinet posts. Also, in an apparent gesture to black voters, he signed into law a measure establishing a federal holiday to honor slain civil rights leader Martin Luther King, Jr. (an idea he had previously opposed).

Meanwhile, certain events overseas seemed to be working in Reagan's favor. The shooting down of a Korean jetliner by Soviet fighter planes on September 1 appeared to undercut Reagan's critics on defense policy by implying—as the president had said all along—that the Soviets could not be trusted. The U.S.-led military intervention in Grenada in late October, which apparently was supported by a majority of Americans, clearly left the Democrats groping for an adequate response and boosted the president's standing among the electorate, at least in the short run.

See DEMOCRATIC PARTY.   G.M.H.

RHODE ISLAND. See STATISTICS OF THE WORLD.

RHODESIA. See ZIMBABWE.

ROMANIA. Romania informed its major Western creditors in January 1983 that it would withhold repayment of $1.4 billion in debt principal due during the year until rescheduling agreements could be worked out. These agreements were hindered by Romania's recently enacted "education tax," which, designed to cut off emigration, levied a $10,000 to $20,000 hard-currency fee on would-be emigrants. Romanian citizens are not allowed to possess hard currency, and few would-be emigrants had relatives or friends in the West who could put up the required sums.

The United States, bound by U.S. law to deny most-favored-nation (MFN) trading status to any Communist-bloc nation restricting emigration, threatened revocation of Romania's MFN status in March. The loss would have cost Romania $200 million a year needed for repayment of its foreign debt. Finally, it was agreed unofficially that although the education tax would remain in effect, it would not be enforced, and on June 3, President Ronald Reagan informed Congress of his administration's intention to renew Romania's MFN status. In late June, Romania and the major commercial banks from which it had borrowed concluded an agreement to reschedule $600 million of the country's debt, with 30 percent of the money payable in 1983.

Drastic austerity and conservation measures were imposed during the year because of an

Writers Cramped

Plagued by a spate of antigovernment leaflets, President Nicolae Ceaușescu of Romania recently signed a decree prohibiting the possession or use of a typewriter by anyone posing "a danger to public order or state security." Current owners of typewriters had to register their machines with the police and supply a sample of the type; anyone wanting to buy a new typewriter was required to obtain state permission in advance. The decree also restricted ownership of copying machines to "socialist units and organizations."

energy shortfall, a cereal crop shortage, and Romania's desire to retire its whole $10 billion debt to the West by 1988. Party and state leader Nicolae Ceaușescu ordered citizens to reduce their consumption of electricity by 50 percent and submit to stringent food rationing. Beef, vegetables, and agricultural produce were being exported to raise cash, instead of being put on local markets.

The National Council for Environmental Protection, established in 1974, was proving unable to check the country's extensive air and water pollution. Major air pollutants include sulfur dioxide (from the lignite used in power plants) and lead concentrate (from nonferrous metallurgical plants). Effluents from chemical plants have tainted more than a thousand miles of rivers and continue to contaminate underground water supplies. Excessive lumbering has denuded large areas, causing soil erosion and flooding.

The observance of Ceaușescu's 65th birthday, on January 26, included a plethora of speeches, awards, and banquets, as well as a lavish output of commemorative books, articles, poems, sculptures, tapestries, and songs. Separate personality cults have also developed around Ceaușescu's wife Elena and his son Nicu, who was perhaps being groomed for the succession.

See STATISTICS OF THE WORLD.   R.A.P.

RUSSIA. See UNION OF SOVIET SOCIALIST REPUBLICS.

RWANDA. See STATISTICS OF THE WORLD.

S

SAHARA, WESTERN. *See* AFRICA; MOROCCO.

ST. CHRISTOPHER AND NEVIS (ST. KITTS-NEVIS). *See* STATISTICS OF THE WORLD.

ST. LUCIA. *See* STATISTICS OF THE WORLD.

ST. VINCENT AND THE GRENADINES. *See* STATISTICS OF THE WORLD.

SAMOA, AMERICAN. *See* STATISTICS OF THE WORLD.

SAMOA, WESTERN. *See* STATISTICS OF THE WORLD; WESTERN SAMOA.

SAN MARINO. *See* STATISTICS OF THE WORLD.

SÃO TOMÉ & PRÍNCIPE. *See* STATISTICS OF THE WORLD.

SASKATCHEWAN. *See* STATISTICS OF THE WORLD.

SAUDI ARABIA. Saudi Arabia, the world's largest oil exporter, was forced to cut back sharply on its output when world demand for oil produced by the Organization of Petroleum Exporting Countries slumped dramatically in 1983.

Oil. At the March quarterly meeting of the oil cartel, held in London, OPEC's benchmark price for a barrel of oil was reduced by $5, to $29. An overall production quota of 17.5 million barrels per day (mbd) was adopted, with individual quotas for countries other than Saudi Arabia. Saudi Arabia, in a concession to the less developed OPEC nations, agreed to adjust its production level to keep OPEC under the 17.5 mbd ceiling. That ceiling would allow the Saudis, if all other members kept within their individual quotas, to produce about 5 mbd. In March, Saudi production actually dropped to a low of 3.5 mbd, and in the third quarter it averaged under 5 mbd.

The drastic production cuts, representing about 60 percent of Saudi capacity, resulted in the major decision by Aramco, the now state-owned Arabian American Oil Company, to lay off 600 of its employees, mostly Americans. Final 1982–1983 production figures for Aramco, which produces 98 percent of Saudi Arabia's oil, showed output at a ten-year low of 2.3 billion barrels, down from 3.5 billion in 1981–1982.

Budget cuts. The budget for 1983–1984, released on April 13, showed total allocations of $75.6 billion. Defense and security, at $22 billion, remained the single largest category of spending, representing 29 percent of the budget. Other major areas of spending included education ($9.6 billion), transportation and communication ($8.6 billion), and internal loans and subsidies ($6.9 billion). Major cuts occurred in funds for the development of economic resources (at $4.5 billion, down 40

Lettuce is grown in an experimental field in the Saudi Arabian desert. The Saudis are pumping petrodollars into massive development projects, both agricultural and industrial, in order to diversify their economy before oil reserves dry up.

percent) and for municipal facilities (at $6.5 billion, down 27 percent).

In order to cut the 50 percent of the budget that goes to salaries and benefits for the 200,000 Saudis employed by the state, the government announced a public-sector salary and recruiting freeze. In another economic move, the Saudi currency, the riyal, was devalued slightly.

Figures for the first quarter of calendar year 1983 led many analysts to believe that the deficit for 1983–1984, officially forecast at $10.2 billion, might actually reach $30 billion. But second quarter figures were much more favorable, with oil production up and spending in line with budget projections.

Economic development projects. Not all the economic news was bad. For example, in Al Jubayl, an industrial city under construction on the Persian Gulf north of Dhahran, three major plants were opened—the Saudi Iron and Steel Company and two petrochemical plants. In April, King Fahd ibn Abdul-Aziz opened the Mahd al-Dhahab mine, northeast of Jiddah. The mine, first exploited in ancient times, had estimated reserves of 1.2 million tons of high-grade gold, silver, copper, and zinc ores. October saw the dedication of King Khaled International Airport, a $3.2 billion project near Riyadh. Saudi agriculture continued to be developed, at great expense.

Domestic politics. Despite rumors of an Iranian-sponsored coup attempt and opposition to King Fahd within the royal family, the king was able to consolidate his position (he had succeeded to the throne in mid-1982). In April and May, he presided over the first changes in the Saudi government since 1975. First came the resignation of the longtime head of the Saudi Arabian Monetary Agency, the country's central bank. Abd al-Aziz al-Quraishi reportedly quit over differences with Finance Minister Muhammad Aba al-Khail, who opposed his plan to dip into government reserves to pay for the anticipated budget deficit. Next, Fahd dismissed the information minister, Muhammad Abdu Yamani, and named General Ali Hassan al-Shaer in his place. Finally, the king filled a number of cabinet posts that had been vacant.

U.S.-Saudi relations. Despite some tensions in relations with the United States, Saudi Arabia remained important to U.S. strategic interests in the Middle East. In 1983, Washington approved the sale to Riyadh of $265 million worth of matériel, primarily spare parts for the Saudi navy and air tracking equipment. In August the U.S. government announced that it would also sell 100 M60A3 tanks to Saudi Arabia for $176 million.

In July, Prince Bandar bin Sultan, a nephew of King Fahd, was named ambassador to the United States. Prince Bandar gained international prominence in September, when he joined with U.S. Middle East envoy Robert McFarlane to help work out a cease-fire agreement in Lebanon.

See STATISTICS OF THE WORLD.   C.H.A.

SENEGAL. SEE STATISTICS OF THE WORLD.

SEYCHELLES. SEE STATISTICS OF THE WORLD.

SIERRA LEONE. SEE STATISTICS OF THE WORLD.

SINGAPORE. Prime Minister Lee Kuan Yew and his party continued to dominate politics in Singapore. In July rumors that the prime minister was critically ill or dead caused the volatile stock market to plummet. The market, however, more than recovered when the rumors were disproven, and the reclusive Lee pointedly made several public appearances. Earlier, Ong Teng Cheong, minister of labor and communications and a potential successor to high leadership within the ruling People's Action Party, was named as general secretary of the National Trades Union Congress, replacing Lim Chee Onn, who had been dismissed by Lee.

In August the prime minister sparked a furor by criticizing the performance of the national Family Planning and Population Board in promoting smaller families. Lee complained that the better educated were reducing family size, while the least educated continued to have large families. The nation's level of competence, he asserted, could decline as the uneducated increasingly came to outnumber the well educated.

During the first half of 1983, Singapore's real domestic product grew 5.6 percent (compared to 6.9 percent during the same period in 1982). Declines were noted in manufacturing (7.8 percent) and tourism (1.7 percent). There was a 1.5 percent drop in total foreign trade, with exports down 0.5 percent and imports down 2.2 percent.

The Monetary Authority of Singapore actively sought to attract Hong Kong financial institutions concerned about that colony's future when the British lease on most of the territory expires in 1997.

See STATISTICS OF THE WORLD.   K.M.

SOCIAL SECURITY. In January 1983 the bipartisan National Commission on Social Security Reform, appointed in 1981, released a compromise package of proposals aimed at restoring the solvency of the social security system. Congress approved the commission's recommendations without major changes in March, and President Ronald Reagan signed them into law on April 20.

The cornerstone of the changes adopted was an increase of $166.2 billion in the social security trust funds during the period 1983–1989. Additional funding was to come from a variety of sources, including increases in social security taxes ($57.9 billion), imposition of federal income tax on 50 percent of the social security benefits received by higher-income persons ($26.6 billion), the extension of social security coverage to government employees ($21.8 billion), transfers from general funds ($17.7 billion), benefit changes ($39.4 billion), and some smaller items. To help ensure the long-term solvency of the system, the new legislation also mandated that the age at which a person can retire with full benefits will rise from 65 to 66 by the year 2009 and to 67 by the year 2027.

The increase in social security taxes had two major components. First of all, the dates for two previously scheduled tax increases were moved forward—the scheduled 1985 increase up to January 1984, and part of the increase scheduled for 1990 up to 1988. Under the new, accelerated schedules, an individual wage earner's social security tax will rise to 7 percent in 1984 (up from 6.7 percent in 1983) and to 7.51 percent by 1988. The second major tax change involved the social security tax paid by self-employed persons. Since self-employed persons first became subject to social security taxes in 1950, their tax rate has been significantly lower than the combined employer-employee rate for other workers. (It was 9.35 percent in 1983.) To alter this situation and also raise revenue, the new law mandated that, as of January 1, 1984, self-employed workers were to be taxed at a rate of 14 percent—equal to the employer-employee rate. However, the law provided for temporary income tax credits which, for 1984, reduced the effective rate for

Senior Citizens' Senior Advocate

In 1983, Democratic Congressman Claude Pepper of Florida helped guide through the U.S. House of Representatives a bipartisan bill to rescue the nation's faltering social security system. As a member of the National Commission on Social Security Reform, he had played a key role in shaping the legislation, which essentially forestalled reductions in benefits by increasing the system's revenues. Pepper's contribution was the latest milestone in a congressional career that has focused on social benefit programs in general and the responsibilities of government toward the elderly in particular. Pepper has served 14 years in the Senate, where he vigorously supported Franklin D. Roosevelt's New Deal, and 21 in the House. In 1983 he became chairman of the powerful House Rules Committee and, at 83, was as fervent as ever in his zeal for causes.

Claude Pepper

wage earners to the previous 6.7 percent and made the actual rate for the self-employed only 11.3 percent.

The 1983 cost-of-living adjustment in social security benefits, scheduled for July, was delayed until January 1984, and in the future, all annual benefit increases will be given in January. Among other changes, as of 1984, up to 50 percent of social security benefits received by taxpayers with relatively high incomes (above $25,000 for single taxpayers and $32,000 for married taxpayers filing jointly) will be included in taxable income. All new federal civilian employees, along with all elected federal officials and presidential appointees in the executive branch, will be required to participate in the social security system.

Meanwhile, U.S. officials predicted that the medicare insurance fund would also go bankrupt if no action were taken. A federal advisory committee headed by former Indiana Governor Otis R. Bowen recommended, among other proposals, that the eligibility age for medicare be raised from 65 to 67 by 1991, that premiums be increased, and that increased excise taxes be levied on alcohol and tobacco, with the added revenue earmarked for the medicare trust fund.   J.A.R.

SOLOMON ISLANDS. See STATISTICS OF THE WORLD.

SOMALIA. Somalia's problems remained severe in 1983. The country was assailed by invasion, political disorder, economic hardship, and refugee inflows. A serious threat to internal order arose in March, when President Muhammad Siad Barre issued a decree banning the cultivation, import, and sale of qat, a narcotic leaf chewed by large numbers of Somalis. The ban resulted in sporadic rioting, but overall compliance with the decree appeared remarkably high.

The 20-year border war with Ethiopia continued at a relatively low level, with a number of minor skirmishes reported by both sides. Ethiopian forces won control of several small salients of Somalian territory. Meanwhile, the Kenyan foreign minister visited Mogadishu in May, and Djibouti's foreign minister visited in July. These consultations demonstrated Somalia's desire to improve its relations with formerly hostile neighbors. Romanian Com-

munist Party Secretary-General Nicolae Ceaușescu visited Mogadishu in July, and Romania agreed to provide Somalia with technical aid in a number of areas.

In mid-August, Somali and U.S. forces held large-scale joint military exercises, dubbed "Eastern Wind-83," in the Berbera region of northern Somalia; this indication of Somali–U.S. military cooperation met with protests from the Ethiopian and Soviet governments.

Economic conditions were miserable for the Somali people. Drought in East Africa continued to take its toll on crops, national income, and food supplies. The United Nations High Commissioner for Refugees, however, increased financial support for the 700,000 displaced Ethiopians living in Somali refugee camps. In April, Finance Minister Abdullahi Ahmed Addou visited Great Britain and Saudi Arabia to press for higher levels of assistance. He also conferred with U.S. and World Bank officials in Washington. The World Bank pledged continued support for the Juba Valley development projects, such as the Bardera Dam. In late October a group of foreign governments and institutions pledged $1.2 billion in aid to Somalia for its three-year economic development program, to begin in 1984.

See STATISTICS OF THE WORLD.   R.E.B.

SOUTH AFRICA. A new constitution, giving a limited role in governing South Africa to the nation's Coloured (mixed race) and Indian minorities, was approved by the white electorate on November 2, 1983. Continuing drought and internal security were major problems faced by Prime Minister Pieter W. Botha.

Constitutional reforms. The new charter provided for a tricameral Parliament consisting of separate chambers for whites (178 members), Coloureds (85 members), and Indians (45 members). The constitution also reserved substantial powers for an executive president, to be chosen for a maximum five-year term by an electoral college. The electoral college, in turn, was to be made up of 50 white, 25 Coloured, and 13 Indian members, selected by majority vote in each chamber. The president would appoint the cabinet, which could include Coloureds and Indians, as well as whites. The president would also appoint 25 members to a 60-member advisory body known as the President's

Council; the other members would be elected by each chamber of Parliament.

The constitutional reforms, approved earlier by Parliament, had encountered opposition from critics on both left and right. The former objected to the exclusion of black Africans, who make up more than 70 percent of the population; the latter charged that the reforms were a step toward "total integration."

Internal security. The most devastating act of political sabotage in the country's history occurred on May 20, when a car bomb exploded outside Air Force headquarters in the capital city of Pretoria at the peak rush hour; 19 people were killed and more than 200 wounded. The African National Congress, the black nationalist organization seeking to overthrow the government in South Africa, claimed responsibility for the attack.

In reprisal, South Africa launched an air raid three days later into neighboring Mozambique, whose government gives sanctuary and support to ANC guerrillas. South Africa claimed that 64 people were killed, including 41 ANC members and 17 Mozambican soldiers. International journalists reported that the visible damage had been surprisingly light. On June 9 three ANC guerrillas who had been convicted of murder and treason were hanged in Pretoria. The guerrillas had admitted taking part in attacks that killed four black policemen.

A lengthy inquest into the suicide in detention of trade unionist Neil Aggett, the first white to die in police custody in South Africa, ended in December 1982, when a Johannesburg magistrate ruled that Aggett's death, in February 1982, had not been induced by mistreatment on the part of the security police.

In November 1983, a young Afrikaner couple were found guilty of high treason for having aided the ANC; they were sentenced to prison terms. In December a high-ranking South African naval officer, Commodore Dieter F. Gerhardt, and his Swiss-born wife were convicted of high treason for having spied for the Soviet Union. Gerhardt was sentenced to life imprisonment; his wife was given a 10-year prison term.

Two members of the militant right-wing Afrikaner Resistance Movement were sentenced to 15 years in prison for terrorism in June, in

Prime Minister Pieter Botha of South Africa won a major victory in November, when a new constitution was approved overwhelmingly by the country's white voters.

a rare application of the country's tough security legislation against right-wing whites.

Saul Mhkize, a leader of African landowners and peasants in the southeastern Transvaal, was killed in April during an altercation with police; he had been leading a protest against government orders to remove the 5,000 residents of the tiny town of Driefontein and resettle them in camps in the government-created homelands. Meanwhile, violence flared for several months at a squatter camp in the Western Cape; government officials and police repeatedly raided the camp, tore down more than 600 plastic shelters, and arrested hundreds of black people.

Economy and labor. South Africa faced its worst drought of the century. The national economy was damaged, with food prices and the unemployment rate up. A preliminary survey showed that the drought cost the country at least $1 billion in lost export earnings.

See STATISTICS OF THE WORLD.   J.F.

SOUTH CAROLINA. *See* STATISTICS OF THE WORLD.

SOUTH DAKOTA. *See* STATISTICS OF THE WORLD.

SOUTH WEST AFRICA, also known as NAMIBIA. In late January 1983, the South African government dissolved the four-year-old National Assembly in South West Africa and announced that it was resuming direct rule in the territory it has administered since World War I. The move followed the resignation of the Council of Ministers, which had been controlled by the Democratic Turnhalle Alliance (DTA), a multiracial political group. On February 1, Willie van Niekerk replaced Danie Hough as administrator-general for Namibia.

Guerrillas of the South West Africa People's Organization (Swapo), which was fighting for the independence of Namibia, mounted a major offensive from their bases inside Angola into Namibia in February. The South African military responded in an action that reportedly left more than 100 Swapo guerrillas dead. During December, in what it said was a move to preempt an incipient guerrilla drive from Angola into Namibia, South Africa launched an offensive into Angola, involving motorized brigades, artillery groups, and aircraft. In early December, South Africa offered Angola and Swapo a 30-day disengagement of forces in Angola, to begin January 31, but they both rejected it. A separate effort to negotiate independence for Namibia—by the so-called contact group of Western nations, consisting of the United States, Great Britain, West Germany, Canada, and France—remained stalled over the joint South African–American insistence that Cuban troops in Angola must be withdrawn before a settlement could be achieved. Angola, backed by other black Africa states, continued to insist that the presence of Cuban troops in Angola was a separate issue. American and Angolan officials met in Paris in March, and in April a top Angolan government official went to the United States for further talks, the eleventh round of U.S.-Angolan talks in two years.

A special commission appointed by the Pretoria government released a report to the administrator-general of South West Africa in August criticizing the complex bureaucracy of separate racial and ethnic authorities within the territory. The commission concluded that this system, which, for example, provides 14 separate ethnic departments governing building regulations, allows corruption and inefficiency to flourish.

From a buoyant financial position in the 1970's, Namibia's economy had been sliding into decline since 1980. Production of one of the territory's key mineral resources, diamonds, fell by a third, and mining in general fell by 7.5 percent in 1982. The number of white South Africans in the technical, managerial, and business community has continued to shrink.

See STATISTICS OF THE WORLD.   J.F.

SOVIET UNION. *See* UNION OF SOVIET SOCIALIST REPUBLICS.

SPACE SCIENCE AND EXPLORATION. The United States launched some 30 spacecraft in 1983, including the *Challenger* space shuttle orbiter, which completed three manned flights, and the *Columbia* shuttle, carrying a European-built space laboratory and the biggest shuttle crew ever. The Soviet Union's approximately 100 launchings included two manned Soyuz spacecraft and two space probes.

U.S. space shuttles. On April 4–9, the space shuttle *Challenger* made its maiden flight,

Guion S. Bluford, the first black astronaut, checks an experiment on board the space shuttle Challenger *during its third flight.*

High Flier

With the words "Ride, Sally Ride" echoing across the nation, America celebrated its newest hero on June 18: Sally K. Ride, a 32-year-old Los Angeles native, had become the first U.S. woman in space. One of five crew members on the space shuttle *Challenger*'s second flight, Ride acted as flight engineer and, along with fellow astronaut John Fabian, successfully launched two communications satellites and made use of the *Challenger*'s mechanical arm. A scientist who received a doctorate in physics from Stanford University in 1978, Ride insisted that she was not a feminist symbol, but her flight was widely reported as a breakthrough for women, and she drew the lion's share of public attention for it.

Sally K. Ride

manned by Paul J. Weitz, commander, Karol J. Bobko, pilot, and Donald H. Peterson and F. Story Musgrave, mission specialists. The first in a series of tracking and data relay satellites (TDRS-A) was launched from the shuttle but, as a result of a malfunction, did not achieve its planned orbit; after subsequent adjustments by ground controllers, it was successfully fixed in the desired orbit on June 29. Three Getaway Special payloads (small cannisters carrying low-cost experiments) traveled in the cargo bay. On one occasion, two of the astronauts donned space suits and moved about in the cargo bay, 150 miles above the earth's surface.

Aboard the *Challenger*'s second flight, June 18–24, were Robert L. Crippen, commander, Frederick H. Hauck, pilot, and John M. Fabian, Sally K. Ride, and Norman E. Thagard, mission specialists. Ride, an astrophysicist, attracted wide media attention as the first American woman astronaut. A Canadian and an Indonesian communications satellite were launched from the shuttle, and the West German shuttle pallet satellite (SPAS), a platform designed to hold various instruments, was deployed and retrieved, using the shuttle's 50-foot-long, Canadian-built mechanical arm. The success of the arm was significant because future astronauts were expected to use it to retrieve orbiting satellites. Seven Getaway Special payloads, as

well as other payloads carried on the SPAS, were taken on this mission.

The *Challenger*'s third flight, August 30–September 5, featured the first night launch and night reentry of a shuttle; the crew consisted of Richard H. Truly, commander, Daniel C. Brandenstein, pilot, and Guion S. Bluford, Jr., William E. Thornton, and Dale A. Gardner, mission specialists. Bluford was the first black U.S. astronaut. An Indian communications and meteorological satellite was placed in orbit from the shuttle, which carried 24 Getaway Special payloads with a wide variety of experiments.

The space shuttle *Columbia*, which had been in "dry dock" for a year, carried the European-built Spacelab into orbit on November 28. The 17-ton, 23-foot-long, $1 billion Spacelab, built in West Germany for the 11-nation European Space Agency, contained instruments designed to conduct more than 70 experiments in astronomy, atmospheric physics, materials processing, earth observations, and physiology. *Columbia* carried a crew of six, the largest ever flown on a single spacecraft. Aboard were John W. Young, commander, Brewster H. Shaw, pilot, Robert A. Parker and Owen K. Garriott, mission specialists, and scientists Byron K. Lichtenberg and Ulf Merbold. Merbold, a West German physicist, was the first non-American to fly aboard a U.S. space vehicle;

he and Lichtenberg also were the first nonastronauts. The shuttle's orbit was higher than those of previous flights because of Spacelab's scientific requirements. Experiments conducted aboard *Columbia* included studies of the effects of prolonged weightlessness, ultraviolet and X-ray observations of the heavens, and measurement of the energy output of the sun. *Columbia*'s launch and ten-day flight were smooth, but its return on December 8, although safe, was marred by an eight-hour delay caused by a series of failures in its computer and navigation systems; the computer problems were later attributed to tiny pieces of gold and solder that apparently triggered short circuits.

Other U.S. missions. Pioneer 10, still relaying data on the solar wind, left the solar system on June 13, when it passed across the orbit of Neptune more than 11 years after its launch on March 2, 1972. Scientific instruments on Voyager 2 continued to monitor the interplanetary environments; that craft was on a trajectory expected to carry it past Uranus in 1986 and Neptune in 1989. The Infrared Astronomical Satellite (IRAS) was launched into a near polar orbit on January 25 from Vandenberg Air Force Base in California. The satellite was a joint project of NASA and agencies in the Netherlands and Great Britain. Designed to collect comprehensive data on sources of infrared radiation in space, it surprised the scientific community by discovering apparent evidence of other planetary systems in the universe. Its liquid helium supply exhausted, IRAS ceased to transmit data in November.

Soviet space activity. On March 10 the Soviets nearly doubled the size of the Salyut 7 space station by docking the module Cosmos 1443 with it. The unmanned Cosmos 1443, a space station tug and electric power module with a bell-shaped reentry vehicle, was said to be capable of returning 1,100 pounds of cargo to earth.

Soyuz T-8, with cosmonauts Vladimir G. Titov, commander, and Gennady M. Strekalov and Alexander Serebrov, was launched on April 20. As a result of a malfunction the rendezvous radar, to be used in docking with Salyut 7, did not fully deploy and docking was not accomplished. Soyuz T-8 reentered the earth's atmosphere and made a normal landing on April

A multiexposure photograph of the takeoff of the space shuttle Challenger *from Cape Canaveral on August 30, the shuttle's first nighttime launching.*

365

22. The Soyuz T-9 spacecraft, with cosmonauts Vladimir Lyakhov, commander, and Aleksandr Aleksandrov, flight engineer, was launched on June 27 and successfully docked with the Salyut 7 space station the next day. The Soyuz T-9 cosmonauts loaded 700 pounds of materials, including exposed film and spent hardware, onto the Cosmos 1443's reentry vehicle, which returned to earth on August 23. After 150 days in space, the Soyuz T-9 landed safely in Soviet Kazakhstan on November 23.

On September 27 a rocket carrying another Soyuz T transport craft exploded on its launch pad in Asia. The two cosmonauts on board reportedly survived. The Soviet Union subsequently launched the unmanned space freighter Progress 18 to carry supplies to Salyut 7.

Two space probes—Venera 15 and 16—were launched by the Soviets in June on a trajectory toward the planet Venus, which they reached and began orbiting in October. The Venera craft began returning the first high-resolution images of Venus's surface ever obtained through the planet's cloud cover. Astron, a Venera-class spacecraft modified for use in earth orbital missions, was launched by the Soviets on March 23 and placed into a highly eccentric orbit. It carried a nonimaging ultraviolet telescope with a spectral range of 1,100–3,600 angstroms.

Launches of other nations. On June 16, the European Space Agency, using the Ariane launch vehicle, successfully launched the European communications satellite ECS-1. In May,

The six-man crew of the Columbia *demonstrates the delights of weightlessness during their mission launching Spacelab, a joint project of NASA and the European Space Agency, into orbit.*

the ESA X-ray observatory satellite Exosat was launched by NASA and placed in polar orbit. A Japanese X-ray satellite called Tenma was placed in orbit on February 20. It carried three X-ray detectors, a gamma-ray burst sensor, and a radiation-belt monitor.   R.Y.D.

SPAIN. Under the moderate program adopted by Prime Minister Filipe González Márquez, Spain's Socialist government concentrated most of its efforts in 1983 on reviving the nation's troubled economy.

González's inauguration in December 1982 had raised hopes for new initiatives in the violence-ridden Basque province of northern Spain, where several million members of the country's Basque minority live. With the help of the Socialist Party, talks were set up between local leaders, but they were abandoned after a new wave of terrorist killings and a bank bombing in February. The terrorist wing of the Basque separatist organization ETA claimed responsibility for the violence, which continued sporadically during the year.

The cabinet in February approved changes in the penal code that would allow abortions to be performed under certain conditions. Legislation designed to make birth control information more easily available was also submitted to the Cortes, or parliament. The abortion measure was easily passed by the large Socialist majority in the Cortes in October, but the opposition, led by the conservative Popular Alliance Party and supported by the country's Roman Catholic bishops, declared its intention to challenge the measure before Spain's constitutional court.

Late in April, Spain's supreme court handed down new, more severe sentences on the military men involved in the February 1981 attempt to overthrow the government, and a number of lesser figures who had been acquitted in 1982 were found guilty and received prison terms. It was the first time since the Civil War of the 1930's that a civilian court had asserted its jurisdiction over military crimes. This blow to the status of the military came just a few weeks after Defense Minister Narcís Serra i Serra announced plans to reduce the size of the army by more than one-third. In addition, plans were approved by the cabinet in October for restructuring the military chain of command to strengthen government control of the armed forces.

Economy. In February, González moved to take over the 20 banks and several hundred other companies belonging to Spain's largest holding company, Ruíz Mateos S.A., commonly known as Rumasa. González stressed that the action would not lead to wholesale nationalization but instead was being taken to protect investors from mismanagement; he promised that eventually the companies would be returned to the private sector.

Despite González's earlier promise to provide jobs, the government was compelled to seek ways of reducing the work force in government-owned industry. Meanwhile, unemployment in Spain reached 17 percent by the end of September. In other economic developments, measures were taken to restrict the money supply in an attempt to curb inflation. In May, the government announced plans to borrow $600 million in international money markets. The loan, from a consortium of banks, was approved in July; it was to be used to help cover Spain's large budget deficit.

Foreign affairs. In March, Spain ratified a 1982 agreement permitting the United States to retain access to military bases. U.S.–Spanish relations were somewhat strained in June when Spain refused to sign a NATO communiqué affirming a 1979 commitment to begin the basing of U.S. intermediate-range missiles in Western Europe if no progress was made in U.S.–Soviet arms control talks. The Spanish government was still reviewing the question of Spain's membership in NATO and gave that as the reason for refusing to sign.

Also in June, González toured the nations of the Contadora group (Mexico, Colombia, Panama, and Venezuela), which seek a peaceful solution to the conflicts in Central America. The Spanish leader expressed support for their efforts and criticized U.S. policies in the area. He went on to Washington, where he met with President Ronald Reagan. The two leaders issued a communiqué stating that "no fundamental disagreement" existed between Spain and the United States on Central America; it was clear, however, that serious differences between the two countries remained.

See STATISTICS OF THE WORLD.   J.O.S.

Sports

The big winners in team sports in 1983 included the Baltimore Orioles in baseball, the Philadelphia 76ers in basketball, and the New York Islanders in hockey. Among the individuals who sparkled were Moses Malone, Wayne Gretzky, Mike Rozier, Martina Navratilova, Larry Holmes, Tamara McKinney, and Carl Lewis.

In 1983, upsets and surprises proved the rule rather than the exception in many sports. Leading the parade was the Australian yacht *Australia II,* victor in the America's Cup. Other surprising winners were the University of Miami in collegiate football, North Carolina State in collegiate basketball, and China in men's gymnastics.

Off the field, headlines were made by the innovative labor pact hammered out by pro basketball players and owners, drug-related scandals in several sports, and political wrangling over the choice of a host country for soccer's 1986 World Cup competition.

AUTO RACING

Grand prix racing, the most sophisticated competition in the sport and the most dangerous, became safer in 1983. With new rules reducing the speed of these sleek open-wheel, open-cockpit roadsters, there were no fatal accidents in the year's 15 Grand Prix Races. The most successful drivers were the Frenchmen Alain Prost in a turbocharged Renault and Rene Arnoux in a turbocharged Ferrari and the Brazilian Nelson Piquet in a turbocharged Brabham-BMW. Piquet took the Grand Prix of Brazil, Italy, South Africa, and Europe on his way to winning the overall championship.

The world's most important endurance race, the 24 Hours of Le Mans, France, was run June 18–19; the winning car was a factory Porsche 956 with three alternating drivers: Hurley Haywood and Al Holbert of the United States and Vern Schuppan of Australia. In the United States, a Porsche 935 driven by Bob Wollek of France and three others won the 24 Hours of Daytona race February 5–6 in Daytona Beach, Fla. A Porsche also emerged victorious in the 12 Hours of Sebring, March 20 in Florida.

Tom Sneva of Spokane, Wash., won the $2,411,450 Indianapolis 500, the richest race in the history of the sport. The greatest problem Sneva's March-Cosworth faced was passing Al Unser, Jr., to overtake his father, Al Unser, Sr.,

Tom Sneva takes the checkered flag as he wins the 67th Indianapolis 500, after placing second three of the last six years. He took the lead on lap 191 of the 200-lap race and held on to win.

who was leading. Sneva finally passed the Unsers on the 191st lap of the 200-lap race. Indianapolis-type cars also took part in the 12-race series run by Championship Auto Racing Teams; Al Unser, Sr., took the overall series.

In the National Association for Stock Car Auto Racing's Grand National series, Darrell Waltrip, Bobby Allison, and Cale Yarborough were the major winners. The series' richest race, the $1,015,577 Daytona 500, went to Yarborough.   F.L.

BASEBALL

The Baltimore Orioles proved once again that the accumulation of highly paid free agents is not the only way to build a world championship team. With a mostly home-grown team, the Orioles won the World Series over the Philadelphia Phillies. Baltimore was the sixth different team to win the Series in the past six years, and the first American League team to do so since 1978.

Off the field, Bowie Kuhn's second seven-year term as commissioner of baseball expired in August. The baseball owners appointed a search committee to find a replacement for Kuhn, who agreed to stay on the job temporarily.

The season. In the American League, the Orioles broke open a close race in early September in the Eastern Division and, with a classic display of pitching and power, won the division, perhaps the strongest in baseball, by six games. The Chicago White Sox were the entire story in the American League West, winning by 20 games over second-place Kansas City.

The White Sox, appearing in postseason play for the first time since 1959, hit only .211 in the best-of-five American League Championship Series, and that pretty much told the tale. Baltimore's winning effort was highlighted by rookie pitcher Mike Boddicker's ALCS-record 14 strikeouts in his second-game 4–0 win.

The National League's Eastern Division went to the Philadelphia Phillies, who showed that, at least in this case, older was better. With a lineup that sometimes averaged over 35 years of age, the Phillies won 21 out of 25 games in one stretch in August and September to take command for good in the East. In the West, the Los Angeles Dodgers floundered in the first half of the season, deprived of Steve Garvey

Foul Play

New York Yankee centerfielder Dave Winfield caused a big flap during a game with the Blue Jays in Toronto, when a ball he winged toward the dugout, after an outfield warmup, struck and killed a sea gull on the turf. As a ball boy covered the corpse with a towel and delicately removed it, Winfield held his cap over his heart in mock sorrow, inflaming the already angered Canadian fans, some of whom cursed him and threw debris in his direction. Afterward, he was arrested on charges of "causing unnecessary suffering" to an animal, a crime punishable by a fine of up to $500 or six months in jail. "It is quite unfortunate that a fowl of Canada is no longer with us," Winfield observed at the station house, where he had to post $500 bond. Toronto police, after thinking it over, later dropped the charges.

(lost to free agency) and Ron Cey (traded). However, their young players later held up well, and the team came on strong to claim the divisional crown.

The National League Championship Series thus featured age versus youth. Age won out, as the Phillies disposed of the Dodgers, who scored only eight runs in the entire series, in four games.

World Series. After the Phillies won the opening game, 2–1, behind John Denny's stellar pitching, the Orioles dominated the National League champs. In reeling off four straight victories, Baltimore relied mainly on the outstanding pitching of starters Mike Boddicker and Scott McGregor and reliever Tippy Martinez and on the timely hitting of Rick Dempsey and Eddie Murray. Dempsey, the Orioles' catcher, was named the Series' Most Valuable Player.

Landmarks. Philadelphia's Steve Carlton became the 16th pitcher ever to win 300 games and also took the major league lead in career strikeouts, with 3,709, passing Nolan Ryan of the Houston Astros; earlier in the season, Ryan had broken Walter Johnson's long-standing record of 3,508 career strikeouts. Another notable feat was turned in by Rickey Henderson of the Oakland A's, who stole 108 bases to become the first player ever to steal at least

Catcher Rick Dempsey of the Baltimore Orioles was named MVP of the 1983 World Series, going five for 13 with four doubles and one home run.

NATIONAL LEAGUE

Eastern Division	W	L	Pct.	GB
Philadelphia Phillies	90	72	.556	—
Pittsburgh Pirates	84	78	.519	6
Montreal Expos	82	80	.506	8
St. Louis Cardinals	79	83	.488	11
Chicago Cubs	71	91	.438	19
New York Mets	68	94	.420	22

Western Division				
Los Angeles Dodgers	91	71	.562	—
Atlanta Braves	88	74	.543	3
Houston Astros	85	77	.525	6
San Diego Padres	81	81	.500	10
San Francisco Giants	79	83	.488	12
Cincinnati Reds	74	88	.457	17

AMERICAN LEAGUE

Eastern Division	W	L	Pct.	GB
Baltimore Orioles	98	64	.605	—
Detroit Tigers	92	70	.568	6
New York Yankees	91	71	.562	7
Toronto Blue Jays	89	73	.549	9
Milwaukee Brewers	87	75	.537	11
Boston Red Sox	78	84	.481	20
Cleveland Indians	70	92	.432	28

Western Division				
Chicago White Sox	99	63	.611	—
Kansas City Royals	79	83	.488	20
Texas Rangers	77	85	.475	22
Oakland Athletics	74	88	.457	25
Minnesota Twins	70	92	.432	29
California Angels	70	92	.432	29
Seattle Mariners	60	102	.370	39

PENNANT PLAYOFFS

National League—Philadelphia defeated Los Angeles, 3 games to 1

American League—Baltimore defeated Chicago, 3 games to 1

WORLD SERIES—Baltimore defeated Philadelphia, 4 games to 1

100 bases in three seasons; no one else has done it more than once. Kansas City Royals' relief pitcher Dan Quisenberry had a major league record of 45 saves.

There were three no-hitters, including a 3–0 win over the White Sox by Oakland's Mike Warren, the first no-hitter by a rookie in ten years. The Montreal Expos' Bob Forsch threw his second career no-hitter, a 3–0 win over the St. Louis Cardinals, and Dave Righetti of the New York Yankees no-hit the Boston Red Sox, 4–0.

Two of baseball's all-time greats retired at the close of the 1983 season, after warm farewells in ball parks throughout the majors. Carl Yastrzemski left the scene after 23 seasons with the Boston Red Sox, during which he compiled over 3,000 hits and played in more major league games than any other player in baseball history. Johnny Bench, whom some consider to be the greatest catcher ever, quit after 17 years with the Cincinnati Reds.

Outstanding players. Baltimore's drive to the world championship was led by shortstop Cal Ripken, Jr., (.318, 27 homers, 102 runs batted in), first baseman Eddie Murray (.306, 33 homers, 111 RBI's), and starting pitcher Scott McGregor (18–7). Wade Boggs of the Boston Red Sox led the league with a .361 batting average; teammate Jim Rice led in homers with

39 and tied with Milwaukee's Cecil Cooper for the lead in RBI's, with 126. Among the American League pitchers, Chicago's LaMarr Hoyt (24–10) compiled the most victories, and Rick Honeycutt of the Texas Rangers (who was traded to the Dodgers in late August) led the league in earned run average (.242).

In the National League, the best all-around performer was Atlanta's Dale Murphy, who not only hit .302 with 36 homers and a league-leading 121 RBI's but also became only the fifth player in major league history to steal at least 30 bases and hit 30 homers in the same season. Mike Schmidt of the Phillies led the league with 40 home runs, and Pittsburgh's Bill Madlock hit .323 to win his fourth batting title. Individual pitching titles were won by Philadelphia's John Denny (most wins, 19) and San Francisco's Atlee Hammaker (lowest ERA, 2.25).

Ripken and Murphy were named the Most Vaulable Players in their respective leagues. The Cy Young awards for best pitcher went to Hoyt and Denny, and Rookie of the Year honors were bestowed on the White Sox' Ron Kittle and the New York Mets' Darryl Strawberry.

M.L.

BASKETBALL

North Carolina State, with a mediocre 26–10 regular-season record, surprised the collegiate basketball world by winning the 1983 National Collegiate Athletic Association championship. The Philadelphia 76ers, on the other hand, surprised no one in steamrolling their way to the 1983 National Basketball Association crown.

College. No team with ten losses during the regular season had ever won the NCAA national title. On April 4, 1983, before a crowd of 17,327 at the University of New Mexico in Albuquerque, the North Carolina State Wolfpack became the first. In the final seconds of the championship game against the favored Houston Cougars, the Wolfpack's Lorenzo Charles plucked teammate Dereck Whittenburg's wayward 35-foot desperation shot out of the air and dunked it to give his team a 54–52 victory. Charles's heroics were viewed by the largest television audience ever to watch a college or pro basketball game. Houston's Akeem Abdul Olajuwon, a 7-foot center who came to the

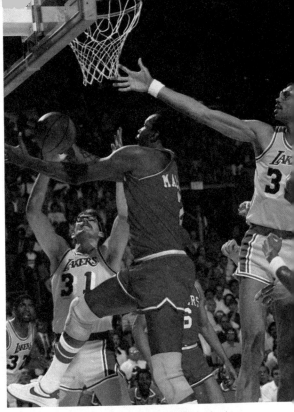

Philadelphia 76er Moses Malone attacks the basketball while seizing a rebound during the NBA championship series; Los Angeles Lakers Kurt Rambis (left) and Kareem Abdul-Jabbar (right) come down empty-handed. Malone's total dominance at center was the key factor in the 76ers' wipeout of the Lakers in four straight.

United States from Nigeria only four years ago, was voted the tournament's outstanding player.

For the third successive year, University of Virginia center Ralph Sampson was named college player of the year. In women's basketball, Southern California, led by Cheryl Miller, the nation's outstanding freshman, rallied from an 11-point halftime deficit to dethrone defending champion Louisiana Tech, 69–67, for the NCAA Division I title.

Professional. In professional basketball, Philadelphia dominated the NBA regular season, compiling a league-leading 58–24 mark. Past failures in the NBA playoffs, however, haunted the team's followers. After losing the 1977 NBA championship, the 76ers had tried to appease their fans with the slogan "We owe you one." Other slogans and promises followed in succeeding years. On May 31, 1983, at the

371

NATIONAL BASKETBALL ASSOCIATION
1982–1983 Regular Season

EASTERN CONFERENCE

Atlantic Division	W	L	Pct.	GB
Philadelphia 76ers	65	17	.793	—
Boston Celtics	56	26	.683	9
New Jersey Nets	49	33	.598	16
New York Knicks	44	38	.537	21
Washington Bullets	42	40	.512	23

Central Division	W	L	Pct.	GB
Milwaukee Bucks	51	31	.622	—
Atlanta Hawks	43	39	.524	8
Detroit Pistons	37	45	.451	14
Chicago Bulls	28	54	.341	23
Cleveland Cavaliers	23	59	.280	28
Indiana Pacers	20	62	.244	31

WESTERN CONFERENCE

Midwest Division	W	L	Pct.	GB
San Antonio Spurs	53	29	.646	—
Denver Nuggets	45	37	.549	8
Kansas City Kings	45	37	.549	8
Dallas Mavericks	38	44	.463	15
Utah Jazz	30	52	.366	23
Houston Rockets	14	68	.171	39

Pacific Division	W	L	Pct.	GB
Los Angeles Lakers	58	24	.707	—
Phoenix Suns	53	29	.646	5
Seattle SuperSonics	48	34	.585	10
Portland Trail Blazers	46	36	.561	12
Golden State Warriors	30	52	.366	28
San Diego Clippers	25	57	.305	33

PLAYOFFS

First Round
New York defeated New Jersey, 2 games to 0
Boston defeated Atlanta, 2 games to 1
Portland defeated Seattle, 2 games to 0
Denver defeated Phoenix, 2 games to 1

Second Round
Philadelphia defeated New York, 4 games to 0
Milwaukee defeated Boston, 4 games to 0
San Antonio defeated Denver, 4 games to 1
Los Angeles defeated Portland, 4 games to 1

Conference Finals
Los Angeles defeated San Antonio, 4 games to 0
Philadelphia defeated Milwaukee, 4 games to 1

Championship Finals
Philadelphia defeated Los Angeles, 4 games to 0

Philadelphia's drive to the NBA crown was led by center Moses Malone, who had been acquired from the Houston Rockets in September 1982 and signed to a lucrative six-year contract. Malone immediatley proved his worth by averaging 24.5 points a game in the regular season, winning his third straight rebounding title, and being named the league's Most Valuable Player. He was also unanimously voted the championship-series Most Valuable Player. Top scoring honors for the NBA regular season went to Denver Nuggets forward Alex English, who averaged 28.4 points per game.

The off-court turmoil that has been associated with the NBA in recent years again threatened to overshadow play on the court in 1983. In the spring and summer, a record number of coaching and franchise-ownership changes took place. Eight NBA teams changed head coaches, including the Boston Celtics, who fired Bill Fitch and hired K. C. Jones. Boston also was one of five teams to undergo a change in ownership; in August, the Celtics were sold to three businessmen headed by Don Gaston, formerly a high-ranking executive with Gulf & Western Industries.

The ownership changes reflected mounting financial losses that the NBA owners blamed principally on escalating salaries; by 1983, the average NBA salary had risen to approximately $250,000. With the owners insisting on relief from skyrocketing salaries and the players pressing for a share of the league's revenue, negotiations for a new contract between the NBA and the National Basketball Players Association seemed hopelessly deadlocked in late March. But on March 31, only two days before a strike deadline set by the players' union, the two parties announced that they had agreed upon a highly creative five-year labor pact. It set overall payroll ceilings for NBA teams, guaranteed the players 53 percent of the NBA's gross revenue, and established a profit-sharing arrangement whereby the league's richer teams would subsidize those in financial difficulty. In an addendum to the original pact, the two sides agreed in September to set up an innovative drug control program that allows for chemical testing of players for cocaine and heroin use and banishment from the NBA of any player found to be using drugs, after a

Forum in Inglewood, Calif., the 76ers repaid their debt to their fans by defeating the Lakers, 115–108, to complete a four-game sweep of the championship series. The final-game victory gave the 76ers their first NBA championship since 1967. The 76ers raced to the final round by eliminating the New York Knicks in four straight games and the Milwaukee Bucks in five. The startling sweep over the injury-plagued Lakers gave Philadelphia a 12–1 postseason record, the best in NBA history.

hearing of the player's case by an impartial arbitrator. Until December 31, 1983, however, a player could voluntarily turn himself in for drug treatment, with no penalty. S.G.

BOWLING

Earl Anthony, the PBA's all-time leader in tournament victories and earnings, won the PBA national championship for the third straight year and for the sixth time since 1973. In October he announced his retirement from the tour. A three-time PBA Player of the Year, Anthony departed the scene with 41 career titles. Meanwhile, Tom Milton took tournaments in January in Las Vegas, in April in Windsor Locks, Conn., and in May in Denver. Don Genalo also had notable successes.

On the Ladies Professional Bowling Tour, Aleta Rzepecki Sill won the 1983 earnings title. Also, in August in Dearborn Heights, Mich., newcomer Anne Marie Pike set world records for women. Pike started match play with eight-game scores of 166, 269, 196, 204, 299, 300, 243, and 300. The total of 1,977 pins was a women's all-time record. The total of 1,142 for the last four games was also a women's record. F.L.

BOXING

Rules changes instituted by the World Boxing Council after the ring death of lightweight Duk Koo Kim in November 1982 failed to prevent another such death in 1983. In a September 1 bout in Los Angeles for the WBC's vacant bantamweight title, Alberto Davila of Pomona, Calif., knocked out Francisco ("Kiko") Bejines of Mexico in the 12th round. The 20-year-old Bejines suffered massive cerebral contusions and died three days later.

Aaron Pryor, the World Boxing Association (WBA) fighter of the year in 1982, successfully defended his WBA junior welterweight title against Alexis Arguello of Nicaragua, whom Pryor had knocked out in a 1982 title bout. In their return match, held on September 9, 1983, in Las Vegas, Pryor knocked out Arguello in the 10th round. After the fight, Arguello announced his retirement. On October 26, Pryor declared that he, too, was retiring.

Among the heavyweights, WBC champ Larry Holmes successfully defended his title four times. On March 27, he outpointed Lucien Rodriguez of France. On May 20, he won a split decision over Tim Witherspoon of Philadelphia. Exactly four months later, Holmes stopped Scott Frank of Oakland, N.J., in five rounds, and on November 25, he knocked out Marvis Frazier, son of former heavyweight champion Joe Frazier, in the first round. On December 11, Holmes resigned his WBC crown

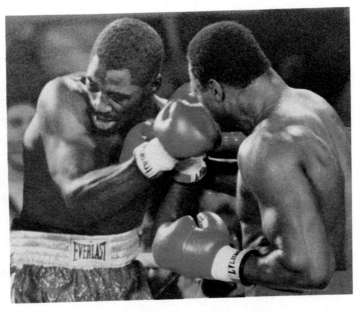

Larry Holmes (right) pounds Marvis Frazier during their brief November heavyweight championship bout. Holmes knocked out the son of former heavyweight champion Joe Frazier in the first round.

in favor of fighting as the heavyweight titlist of the newly formed International Boxing Federation. WBA heavyweight champion Michael Dokes, meanwhile, lost his crown to Gerrie Coetzee of South Africa, who dispatched Dokes in the 10th round on September 23.

The most impressive comeback of the year was mounted by Roberto Duran, the former lightweight and welterweight titlist who entered the middleweight ranks to knock out Davey Moore of New York City on June 16. However, Duran lost a decision to champion Marvelous Marvin Hagler—his legal name—on November 10.

F.L.

FOOTBALL

The University of Miami (Fla.) won the unofficial national college championship in the last minute of the last game of the season. Among professional teams, the Washington Redskins beat the Los Angeles Raiders to take their second straight National Football League (NFL) title, and the Michigan Panthers won the inaugural championship of the United States Football League (USFL), which played its first season in the spring and summer of 1983.

USFL. The new 12-team USFL was financed largely by two two-year television contracts— a contract for $9 million a year from ABC and one for $6 million a year from the Entertainment and Sports Programming Network (ESPN), a sports cable network. Though initial television ratings were much higher than expected, the ratings fell as the season went on and viewer curiosity diminished. The quality of play was uneven, and critics pointed to the large number of NFL castoffs on USFL rosters. The league did establish a measure of credibility, however, by signing several outstanding collegians, including at least half a dozen who were projected as first-round choices in the NFL draft.

In a controversial move in February, the USFL angered college officials by allowing the New Jersey Generals to sign Herschel Walker, the University of Georgia running back who had won the 1982 Heisman Trophy as outstanding college player, in the middle of his junior year. Although the USFL, like the NFL, had announced a policy against the signing of undergraduates, the league sanctioned the acquisiton of Walker, saying it represented a one-time exception.

The signing was an exception in another way, too. The Generals agreed to pay Walker an estimated $5 million over three years, the highest salary package in professional football history.

Money Player

In February 1983, 20-year-old Herschel Walker, the Heisman-winning University of Georgia running back, put an end to weeks of speculation by admitting that he had signed a three-year contract worth an estimated $5 million with the New Jersey Generals of the United States Football League. By signing Walker in the middle of his junior year, the Generals broke the announced USFL policy of not signing players before their college class graduates—a policy also adhered to by the rival National Football League. However, New Jersey felt it could not forego acquiring a gate attraction like Walker, whose college football records left star running backs of the past somewhere in the dust. Walker had denied he would turn pro right up until the signing was announced. As the highest-paid player in football, he generally lived up to his press clippings in his first pro season, leading the league in rushing with 1,812 yards— more than any other rookie in pro football history.

Herschel Walker

The league's credibility rose when it signed several talented NFL players to future contracts. Among its acquisitions were Gary Barbaro, Doug Williams, Joe Cribbs, Brian Sipe, Cris Collinsworth, and Dan Ross. Billy Sims, the Detroit Lion's star running back, signed one contract with the Houston Gamblers of the USFL and another with the Lions, and the matter was headed for resolution in the courts. The formation of the USFL also increased competition among non-USFL clubs for the best talent. Two players signed for salaries in the vicinity of $1 million or more a year: quarterback John Elway, in a five-year contract with Denver of the NFL, and quarterback Dan Fouts, who was pursued by the USFL but signed again with the San Diego Chargers, in a six-year contract.

In the USFL's 18-game season, the Philadelphia Stars (15–3) achieved the best record. The Michigan Panthers, however, defeated the Stars, 24–22, in the playoff final, on July 17 in Denver.

NFL. The 28 NFL teams averaged 59,000 spectators a game, as compared with 25,000 for the USFL. NFL television ratings dropped slightly overall, although they still were far ahead of the USFL's ratings. The NFL's decline in the ratings was attributed partly to poor matchups on games shown nationally. Also, the teams in such large population centers as New York, Chicago, and Philadelphia had losing seasons, and fans showed only moderate interest in winning teams in Los Angeles.

At the conclusion of regular-season play, the divisional champions were the Washington Redskins (14–2), the Detroit Lions (9–7), and the San Francisco 49ers (10–6) in the National Football Conference and the Miami Dolphins (12–4), the Pittsburgh Steelers (10–6), and the Los Angeles Raiders (12–4) in the American Football Conference. Wild-card berths in the playoffs went to the NFC's Dallas Cowboys (12–4) and Los Angeles Rams (9–7) and to the AFC's Seattle Seahawks (9–7) and Denver Broncos (9–7). The Rams and the Seahawks emerged victorious in the wild-card playoff round; Washington, San Francisco, Seattle, and the Raiders advanced to the conference championships, in which the Redskins beat the 49ers, 24–21, and the Raiders clobbered the Sea-

Heisman Trophy winner Mike Rozier of Nebraska (in red jersey) drives through the Miami Hurricane defensive line in the first quarter of the Orange Bowl, on January 2, 1984. The underdog Hurricanes nevertheless went on to win the game, 31–30, and the unofficial national collegiate championship.

hawks, 30–14. In Super Bowl XVIII, played on January 22, 1984, in Tampa, Fla., the Raiders triumphed by a score of 38–9, a record margin for a Super Bowl.

Postseason honors went to Redskins' quarterback Joe Theismann, voted the NFL's Most Valuable Player, and Eric Dickerson of the Los Angeles Rams, voted the league's rookie of the year. Dickerson led the league in rushing with 1,808 yards.

Canadian football. The Edmonton Eskimos, who had won the Canadian Football League title five consecutive years, were eliminated in their first playoff game, paving the way for the Toronto Argonauts to win the clubs first Grey Cup championship game in 31 years. The Argonauts defeated the British Columbia Lions, 18–17, on November 27 in Vancouver.

College football. Nebraska (12–0) and Texas (11–0) were the only National Collegiate Athletic Association Division I colleges to finish

Severiano Ballesteros blasts out of a trap on his way to winning the 1983 Masters. His eight-under-par game outdistanced his closest rivals, Ben Crenshaw and Tom Kite, by four strokes.

the regular season undefeated and untied. Near-perfect records were achieved by Auburn (10–1), Miami of Florida (10–1), Southern Methodist (10–1), Illinois (10–1), Brigham Young (10–1), Georgia (9–1–1), and Clemson (9–1–1). The Nebraska Cornhuskers' mighty offense led the nation in rushing (401.7 yards a game) and scoring (52 points a game); it also provided the Heisman Trophy winner in running back Mike Rozier and the winner of the Lombardi and Outland trophies as the nation's best linemen in guard Dean Steinkuhler.

Nebraska knew that if it defeated the Miami Hurricanes in the Orange Bowl, played on January 2, 1984, in Miami, it would retain its number-one ranking. If Nebraska lost and Texas defeated Georgia in the Cotton Bowl in Dallas on the same day, Texas seemed likely to be named national champion. If Nebraska and Texas lost and if Auburn defeated Michigan in the Sugar Bowl in New Orleans, also on January

2, either Auburn or Miami would take the crown. As it turned out, Georgia upset Texas, 10–9, Auburn beat Michigan, 9–7, and Miami upset Nebraska, 31–30. The next day, Miami was voted national champion in separate polls by the Associated Press, United Press International, the Football Writers Association of America, and the National Football Foundation and Hall of Fame.

In the Orange Bowl, described by many observers as one of the most exciting college games ever played, Miami jumped out to a 17–0 lead before Nebraska roared back to tie the game at 17–17 early in the third period. The underdog Hurricanes then scored two straight touchdowns, but the Cornhuskers replied with two of their own, the last one coming with only 48 seconds left in the game and cutting the Miami lead to 31–30 before the conversion attempt. Unwilling to back into the national championship by settling for a tie on a one-point kick, Nebraska coach Tom Osborne courageously ordered his team to attempt a two-point conversion on a pass by quarterback Turner Gill. The pass failed, and Miami ran out the clock to win the game and the national crown—the first in the school's history.   F.L.

GOLF

During 1983, several bright new stars, such as Hal Sutton, Larry Nelson, Rex Caldwell, and Calvin Peete, became increasingly prominent on the Professional Golfers' Association Tour. Old standbys Jack Nicklaus and Tom Watson, meanwhile, failed to win a single tournament on the tour, which was played for a record purse of $22.6 million. Highlights of the regular tour season included four second-place finishes by Rex Caldwell before he finally won the LaJet Coors Classic, in Abilene, Texas, in September, and two dramatic victories by Calvin Peete—in Atlanta in May, when he came from seven strokes back in the final round, and at the Anheuser-Busch in July, when he made up six shots on the final day.

In the major championships, the Masters was won for the second time by Severiano Ballesteros of Spain, who in 1980 was the youngest golfer ever to win the tournament. Ballesteros won by four over Ben Crenshaw in the first-ever final round played on a Monday

(Friday's round was rained out). Atlanta's Larry Nelson won the U.S. Open at Oakmont, Pa., in June, shooting 65–67 (a record for the course) in the final two rounds to best Tom Watson. In July, Watson came back to win the British Open—his fifth—over Hale Irwin, whose miss-hit of a two-inch putt in the third round cost him a tie for first. Finally, in the PGA at Pacific Palisades, Calif., Hal Sutton won his third tournament of the tour, holding off Nicklaus in the final round. With a total of 274, he became the first player to post a 10-under-par total since the championship switched to medal play in 1958.

On the Ladies Professional Golf Association Tour, Patty Sheehan won the LPGA Championship at King's Island, Ohio, in June, shooting a 66 in the final round to beat Sandra Haynie by two. In the U.S. Women's Open, at Tulsa in late July, Jan Stephenson put together rounds of 72–73–71–74 to beat JoAnne Carner and Patty Sheehan by one. The LPGA's other major, the Peter Jackson Classic, in Quebec in July, went to Hollis Stacy.   T.McC.

GYMNASTICS

The Soviet Union won most of the honors in the 1983 gymnastics world championships, held October 23–29 in Budapest, Hungary. Sixteen-year-old Dmitri Belozerchev and 18-year-old Natalia Yurchenko won the all-around titles. In women's competition, the Soviet team finished first again, with Romania second and the United States seventh. In the men's team competition, China edged the Soviet Union, 591.45 points to 591.30, for its first team title. Belozerchev won gold medals in the pommel horse, high bar, and rings (tying in rings with Koji Gushiken of Japan). Overall, the Soviet Union took nine gold medals. The United States failed to win any medals, although it took three of the first 11 places in the men's all-around.
F.L.

HARNESS RACING

The three-year-old colt Ralph Hanover, who earned a record $1.6 million for the year, set a Messenger Stakes record of 1:57 at Roosevelt Raceway, scored a record 1:57 victory at the Cane Pace at Yonkers Raceway, and won pacing's final Triple Crown race—the Little Brown Jug at Delaware, Ohio—in 1:55 ⅗. In the $1.7 million Woodrow Wilson Pace in East

Rutherford, N.J., a 34–1 shot, Carls Bird, paid $69.40 to his $2 backers.

Duenna defeated Joie de Vie—winner of trotting's first Triple Crown race, the Yonkers Trot—in the Hambletonian at the New Jersey Meadowlands, in 1:57 ⅖. The third trotting Triple Crown event, the Kentucky Futurity, was won by Power Seat, who captured two out of three heats, the last in 1:58. Power Seat also won the World Trotting Derby in Du Quoin, Ill., and the Colonial Trot in Philadelphia. Ideal du Gazeau of France won the Silver Anniversary Roosevelt Raceway International Trot in 2:35 ⅖.   W.L.

HORSE RACING

The 1983 thoroughbred season was dominated by several fine three-year-old colts, a precocious two-year-old colt, and a sensational four-year-old French filly.

For the second year in a row, three different horses won the Triple Crown races for three-year-olds: Canadian-bred Sunny's Halo, after

The sun didn't shine but Sunny's Halo did, as jockey Eddie Delahoussaye rode him to victory in the 109th Kentucky Derby during a light rain.

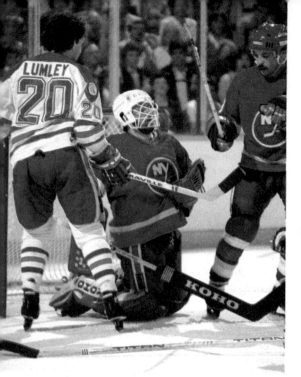

A fourth straight Stanley Cup went to the New York Islanders after they trounced Edmonton in four games. Goaltender Billy Smith (center) was named tournament MVP.

Prix de l'Arc de Triomphe in Paris, the Rothman's International in Toronto, the Aqueduct Turf Classic in New York, and the Washington, D.C., International at Laurel. Her unprecedented sweep of the last three races earned her owners a $1 million bonus.   W.L.

ICE HOCKEY

The New York Islanders rebounded from a disappointing 1982–1983 regular season to capture their fourth successive Stanley Cup. In beating the explosive Edmonton Oilers, four games to none, in the best-of-seven playoff

winning the Rebel Handicap and the Arkansas Derby, triumphed in the Kentucky Derby; Deputed Testamony upset the field in the Preakness; and Caveat, who had run third in Kentucky, took the Belmont Stakes. By the end of the year, however, the finest three-year-old may have been Slew o' Gold, a son of former Triple Crown winner Seattle Slew. Fourth in the Derby, Slew o' Gold finished second in the midsummer Travers Stakes at Saratoga (N.Y.) racetrack and then went on to win two legs of Belmont's prestigious fall championship series (the Woodward Stakes and the Jockey Club Gold Cup) and finish second in the other (the Marlboro Cup). Meanwhile, Devil's Bag emerged as a horse to watch. The two-year-old colt won the Champagne Stakes at Belmont in October, covering the mile in 1:34 ⅕, the fastest mile ever run in New York by a two-year-old. Devil's Bag retired for the season with a perfect five-for-five record and a reputation as one of the fastest horses ever.

The final star to emerge late in the year was the French filly All Along, the winner of the

NATIONAL HOCKEY LEAGUE
1982–1983 Regular Season

PRINCE OF WALES CONFERENCE

Patrick Division	W	L	T	Pts.
Philadelphia Flyers	49	23	8	106
New York Islanders	42	26	12	96
Washington Capitals	39	25	16	94
New York Rangers	35	35	10	80
New Jersey Devils	17	49	14	48
Pittsburgh Penguins	18	53	9	45

Adams Division	W	L	T	Pts.
Boston Bruins	50	20	10	110
Montreal Canadiens	42	24	14	98
Buffalo Sabres	38	29	13	89
Quebec Nordiques	34	34	12	80
Hartford Whalers	19	54	7	45

CAMPBELL CONFERENCE

Norris Division	W	L	T	Pts.
Chicago Black Hawks	47	23	10	104
Minnesota North Stars	40	24	16	96
Toronto Maple Leafs	28	40	12	68
St. Louis Blues	25	40	15	65
Detroit Red Wings	21	44	15	57

Smythe Division	W	L	T	Pts.
Edmonton Oilers	47	21	12	106
Calgary Flames	32	34	14	78
Vancouver Canucks	30	35	15	75
Winnipeg Jets	33	39	8	74
Los Angeles Kings	27	41	12	66

STANLEY CUP PLAYOFFS

Division Semifinals
New York Islanders defeated Washington, 3 games to 1
New York Rangers defeated Philadelphia, 3 games to 0
Boston defeated Quebec, 3 games to 1
Buffalo defeated Montreal, 3 games to 0
Minnesota defeated Toronto, 3 games to 1
Chicago defeated St. Louis, 3 games to 1
Calgary defeated Vancouver, 3 games to 1
Edmonton defeated Calgary, 4 games to 1

Division Finals
New York Islanders defeated New York Rangers, 4 games to 2
Boston defeated Buffalo, 4 games to 3
Chicago defeated Minnesota, 4 games to 1
Edmonton defeated Calgary, 4 games to 1

Conference Finals
New York Islanders defeated Boston, 4 games to 2
Edmonton defeated Chicago, 4 games to 0

Championship Finals
New York Islanders defeated Edmonton, 4 games to 0

finals, the Islanders became only the second team in National Hockey League annals to win four straight Stanley Cups. (The Montreal Canadiens garnered five in a row from 1956 to 1960 and four in a row from 1976 to 1979.) Islander goalie Billy Smith was voted Most Valuable Player of the postseason.

During the regular season, the Islanders finished only sixth in the overall points standings. Boston captured first place, with 110 points, followed by Philadelphia, Edmonton, Chicago, and Montreal. Philadelphia and Montreal were eliminated from the playoffs in the first round, however, and while the Islanders defeated Boston, the Oilers beat Chicago to set up the final confrontation.

Despite a poor showing in the final series, Oiler Wayne Gretzky again was the league's top scorer, with 196 points, and won the Hart Trophy as the NHL's Most Valuable Player—both for a record fourth consecutive year. Steve Larmer of Chicago was selected the Calder Trophy winner as best rookie. Washington's Rod Langway received the Norris Trophy as best defenseman, Islander right wing Mike Bossy the Lady Byng Trophy for sportmanship combined with a high caliber of play, and Boston's Pete Peeters the Vezina Trophy as outstanding goalie.

Prior to the beginning of the 1983–1984 campaign, the NHL instituted a five-minute sudden-death overtime period to resolve ties in regular-season games. If no goal is scored in the overtime period, the game ends in a tie.   B.V.

ICE SKATING

The World Figure Skating Championships were held March 7–13 in Helsinki. In the men's competition, Scott Hamilton of Denver captured his third consecutive world title; Hamilton had also won the national title for the third time at the U.S. championships, in Pittsburgh. The women's event went to Rosalynn Sumners of Edmonds, Wash., also the U.S. champion. Sumners, appearing in only her second Worlds, put on a scintillating free-skating performance to take the crown. Other championships went to the Soviet team of Elena Valova and Oleg Vasiliev in the pairs competition and the dynamic British team of Jayne Torvill and Christopher Dean in ice dancing.

At the World Speed Skating Championships, in February, Rolf Falk-Larssen of Norway won the men's title and Andrea Schoene of East Germany took the women's crown.   I.A.A.

SKIING

In Alpine skiing, Phil Mahre and Tamara McKinney of the U.S. ski team both raced to overall World Cup titles in 1983. They were only the third male-female duo from the same country to win the prestigious crystal World Cup. Mahre, besides winning his third consecutive overall World Cup title, took the giant slalom and combined titles as well. McKinney defeated the 1982 champion, Switzerland's Erica Hess, at Furano, Japan, becoming the first American woman to win the World Cup crown. McKinney also won the World Cup giant slalom title.

Most of the Nordic World Cup season was a dogfight between 1981 champion Alexander Zavjalov of the Soviet Union and 1982 champion Bill Koch of the United States. Toward

Figure skater Scott Hamilton took his third consecutive world title at World Figure Skating Championships in Helsinki.

In 1983 skier Tamara McKinney, who had sat out most of the previous season with a broken wrist, became the first American woman ever to win the overall crown in World Cup competition.

Marja-Liisa Hamalainen of Finland won the women's final 10-kilometer event to take the World Cup cross-country title from Norway's Brit Pettersen, who had led for most of the season.

Another world record was set in speed skiing when Austrian world champion Franz Weber exploded down the speed track at Velocity Peak in Silverton, Colo., at 129.303 miles per hour. R.N.

SOCCER

The late withdrawal of Colombia as host nation for the 1986 World Cup provoked a frenzy of activity as the Fédération Internationale de Football Association (FIFA) sought a replacement. Brazil, Canada, the United States, and late-entry Mexico were the candidates. After Brazil withdrew, FIFA at first announced that Mexico was the only viable candidate, but, following heated protests from Canada and the United States, the association said those countries could make presentations at a May 1983 executive committee meeting in Stockholm. After the presentations were made at the meeting, without a roll-call vote of the committee, it was announced that Mexico had been unanimously selected.

the end of the season, with one event to go, Koch was in first place. However, in the last event, in Labrador City, Newfoundland, Zavjalov reclaimed his crown, winning the championship in the final race.

The unofficial title of world club champion for 1983 went to Gremio of Brazil, the South American club champion, who beat European champion SV Hamburg of West Germany, 2–

Tulsa's Ron Futcher (number 8) led the Roughnecks to a 2–0 win over the Toronto Blizzard in the NASL Soccer Bowl. Suspended for various infractions, Futcher was given a controversial reprieve that enabled him to play in the championship game.

1, in Tokyo in December. By beating Juventus of Italy, 1–0, Hamburg had broken the six-year stranglehold of English clubs on the European Cup. In other European club championships, the Cup Winners' Cup went to Aberdeen of Scotland, who upset Real Madrid, 2–1, in the final, and Anderlecht of Belgium won the UEFA Cup, beating Portugal's Benfica by an aggregate score of 2–1 in the home-and-home series.

In the North American Soccer League (NASL), the Tulsa Roughnecks overcame a disastrous 2–8 start and went on to win the championship in Vancouver by beating the Toronto Blizzard, 2–0. By the end of the season, however, the league was facing its most serious crisis in years. In September, the Seattle Sounders, once a showcase franchise, folded, and in November, Molson Breweries, the owner of Le Manic de Montreal, announced the folding of that team. In addition, rumors circulated about the future prospects of the Roughnecks, the San Diego Sockers, and even the New York Cosmos.

The Major Indoor Soccer League title was won by the San Diego Sockers. In U.S. college soccer, Indiana in 1983 won its second straight National Collegiate Athletic Association Division I title by beating Columbia University, 1–0, in double overtime.   P.G.

SWIMMING

The U.S. Nationals in August produced five world records. Rick Carey set three (55.44 seconds in his heat and 55.38 in the final of the 100-m backstroke, and 1:58.93 in his heat of the 200-m backstroke). One each was set by Steve Lundquist (1:02.34 in the 100-m breaststroke) and Matt Gribble (53.44 seconds in the 100-m butterfly).

At the Pan American Games, the United States won 25 of the 29 swimming finals. Carey, Lundquist, and Bruce Hayes won two individual titles each, as did Brazil's Ricardo Prado and two American women—Tiffany Cohen and Tracy Caulkins. Carey lowered his 100-m backstroke record to 55.19 seconds, and Lundquist his 100-m breaststroke record to 1:02.28. For the 400-m medley relay, the U.S. all-star team of Carey, Lundquist, Gribble, and Ambrose ("Rowdy") Gaines IV set a world record of 3:40.42.

Vladimir Salnikov of the Soviet Union broke

Diver Greg Louganis shows the form that won him two titles at The Woodlands, Texas, and also two gold medals in the Pan American Games.

world records for the 400-m freestyle (3:48.32) and the 1,500-m (14:54.76) at the Soviet winter championships in February and later for the 800-m freestyle (7:52.33). At the European championships in August, Michael Gross of West Germany set world records of 1:47.87 for the 200-m freestyle and 1:57.05 for the 200-m butterfly.

World championships in diving at The Woodlands, Texas, were won by American Greg Louganis (3-m springboard and 10-m platform), and China's Peng Yuanchun (women's springboard) and Chen Xiao Xia (women's platform).   F.L.

TENNIS

In a year devoid of epic on-court confrontations, the top male tennis pros seemed to flounder in a near-constant reshuffling of the upper ranks. Among the women, Martina Navratilova dominated the game.

Navratilova enjoyed an awesome year. The former Czech star (now a U.S. citizen) racked up six wins over Chris Evert Lloyd, her closest competition, en route to compiling an 86–1

Martina Navratilova shows her form in the U.S. Open. By defeating Chris Evert Lloyd, Navratilova won her first U.S. Open championship, during a year in which she dominated women's tennis.

the U.S. Open, McEnroe was upset in the fourth round by Bill Scanlon. Defending champion Jimmy Connors met Lendl in the finals and in a lackluster match, collected his fifth U.S. Open title, 6–3, 6–7, 7–5, 6–0. Wilander staged a major surprise in the Australian Open, beating McEnroe in the semifinals and then defeating Lendl, 6–1, 6–4, 6–4.

In Davis Cup play, the United States was defeated by Argentina in early round action in March, 3–2. In December, Australia captured its 25th cup with a 3–2 win over Sweden.

R.J.L.

TRACK AND FIELD

In 1983, for the first time in history, there was a world championship competition in track and field. Held August 7–14 in Helsinki, Finland, it attracted 1,572 athletes from 157 nations. The medal race was dominated by the United States (24), the Soviet Union (23), and East Germany (22). Carl Lewis of Willingboro, N.J., won three gold medals, taking the 100-meter dash in 10.07 seconds, the long jump with a distance of 28' 3/4'', and the 400-m relay in a world-record 37.86 seconds. Mary Decker, of Eugene, Ore., beat two of the best Soviet runners in close finishes, winning the 3,000 m in 8:34.62 and the 1,500 m in 4:00.90. Jarmila Kratochvilova, of Czechoslovakia, won the 800 m in 1:54.68 and the 400 in a world-record 47.99 seconds. Eamonn Coghlan of Ireland, who ran a world record indoor mile of 3:49.78 on February 27 in East Rutherford, N.J., won the world championship 5,000 m with a strong finishing kick in 13:28.53. A similar finishing sprint allowed Steve Cram of Great Britain to edge out the American Steve Scott in the men's 1,500-m final with a time of 3:41.59.

Lewis was also outstanding in the United States outdoor championships June 17–19 in Indianapolis, becoming the first athlete in 97 years to gain three titles in one national outdoor championship. At the National Sports Festival in July in Colorado Springs, Colo., Evelyn Ashford of Venice, Calif., and Calvin Smith of Bolton, Miss., set world records for 100 m.

Greg Meyer and Joan Benoit, both Massachusetts natives, won the Boston Marathon on April 18. In the October 23 New York Marathon, New Zealand's Rod Dixon passed Geoff

won-lost record. Her only loss came in the French Open, where she was defeated in the fourth round by 17-year-old Kathy Horvath; Evert Lloyd went on to win her fifth French Open crown with a 6–1, 6–2 victory over Mima Jausovec in the final. Navratilova rebounded to win the final at Wimbledon (over Andrea Jaeger, 6–0, 6–3) and capture her first U.S. Open title (defeating Evert Lloyd, 6–1, 6–3). She continued her string of victories in the Australian Open with a 6–2, 7–6 win over Kathy Jordan in the finals.

Among the men, there was no dominant player. After Björn Borg announced his retirement on January 23, Ivan Lendl of Czechoslovakia and Americans John McEnroe and Jimmy Connors took turns beating each other on the men's tour. The best matchups pitted McEnroe against Lendl—touch versus power. The French Open was a surprise, as Yannick Noah defeated defending champion Mats Wilander, 6–2, 7–5, 7–6; Noah was the first French citizen to win the title since 1946.

At Wimbledon, McEnroe beat Lendl in the semifinals, 7–6, 6–4, 6–4, and New Zealander Chris Lewis in the finals, 6–2, 6–2, 6–2. In

Smith of Britain in the last mile to win, while Grete Waitz of Norway took her fifth New York women's title.   F.L.

YACHTING

A non-American boat finally captured the America's Cup in 1983, when the yacht *Australia II*, representing Western Australia, defeated *Liberty*, representing the New York Yacht Club, in an exciting seven-race series in September off Newport, R.I. Prior to the final series, *Australia II* easily disposed of seven other non-U.S. yachts.

In addition to excellent sails and a highly experienced skipper and crew, *Australia II* had a design advantage over her opponents—an unusually short keel with huge wings on either side. The shorter keel allowed the boat to turn more quickly and to sail faster upwind and downwind, while the wings provided stability. The New York Yacht Club in July sought a ruling on the keel's legality from the International Yacht Racing Union, which affirmed that *Australia II* was a legal boat.

In the final series between *Liberty* and *Australia II*, it was apparent that the Australians had the faster boat, but equipment problems

After Australia II's *history-making victory in the America's Cup races, the boat's controversial "mystery keel," which had been kept under cover even when the boat was hoisted out of the water, was finally put on view. The invention of Ben Lexcen, the keel was a major factor in the upset victory.*

and poor tactics cost them three out of the first four races. The challengers then roared back to win the next three races, taking the Cup with a 41-second win in the seventh race.

D.M.P.

SRI LANKA. In 1983, Sri Lankan President J. R. Jayewardene faced riots and security problems, but his United National Party remained in firm control.

Sri Lanka was torn by racial violence that began in late July between the minority Tamil population and the majority Sinhalese. The rioting was touched off when Tamil guerrillas fighting to establish a separate Tamil state ambushed and killed 13 Sinhalese soldiers. The attack led to a spate of selective violence apparently designed to destroy the operations of Tamil traders in the Sinhalese areas of the south. Although security forces initially appeared slow to react to the violence, by early August order was being restored. The rioting took a heavy toll. The number of people killed was officially set at 363, but unofficial estimates ran much higher.

The governing United National Party won a series of parliamentary by-elections and local government elections in May, but as violent incidents became increasingly common, a state of emergency was declared. With security deteriorating, Jayewardene attempted to launch an all-party conference in July to decide on

Sailing to one of three gold medals, Carl Lewis, of Willingboro, N.J., outdistanced other long jumpers on his first try, an impressive 28'3/4", at the World Track and Field Championships in Helsinki.

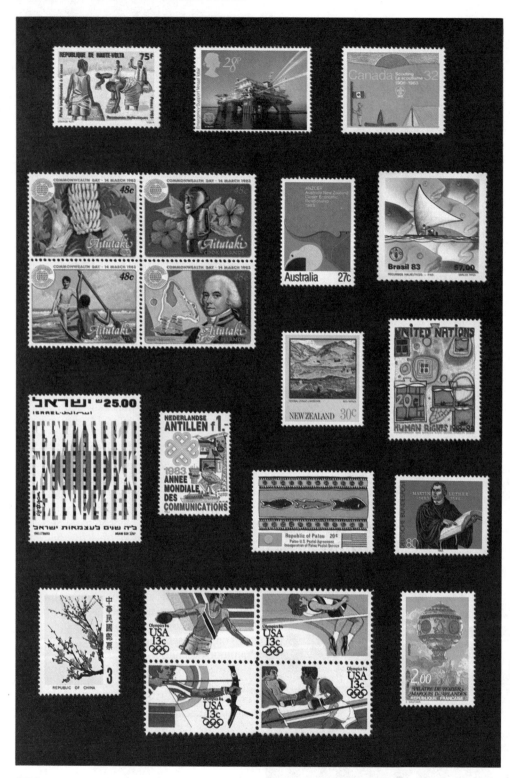

ways to end guerrilla violence. The opposition parties boycotted the opening session on July 20 because they wanted the conference to address Tamil grievances. The government then broadened the conference's scope to include Tamil concerns. In October the government lifted a ban imposed in July on three Marxist parties and tried to resume the talks without the Tamil United Liberation Front, the official opposition party, with little success. It then began informal talks aimed at solving the country's ethnic problems.

The island has attained virtual self-sufficiency in rice production. Sugar is the next crop due for a production boost: the government approved construction of three processing factories. Tea production remained poor.

See STATISTICS OF THE WORLD. C.B.R.

STAMPS AND STAMP COLLECTING. A "space stamp," a Brooklyn Bridge stamp, and three joint U.S.-European issues were among the outstanding new postage stamps of 1983.

American philately soared into space on August 30 as the space shuttle *Challenger* carried into orbit 260,000 covers bearing the new $9.35 express mail stamp. After returning to earth, the covers were sold in souvenir folders by the U.S. Postal Service for $15.35 each. The stamp, which shows the head of a

Opposite page: Some outstanding stamps of 1983. Top row (left to right): Upper Volta, fishing scene marking the 20th anniversary of the World Food Program; Great Britain, Europa stamp showing the emergency support vessel Iolair; Canada, commemorating 76 years of scouting, 1908–1983. Second row: Aitutaki (Cook Islands), block of four in observance of Commonwealth Day (March 14, 1983); Australia, "Australia New Zealand Closer Economic Relationship 1983"; Brazil, marking the 20th anniversary of the World Food Program. Third row: New Zealand, highlighting a 1983 museum exhibit of New Zealand landscapes; United Nations, commemorating the 35th anniversary of the Universal Declaration of Human Rights. Fourth row: Israel, oversized stamp celebrating 35 years of independence; Netherlands Antilles, marking 1983 as World Communications Year; Republic of Palau, commemorating the inauguration of postal service; West Germany, marking the 500th anniversary of Martin Luther's birth. Fifth row: Republic of China (Taiwan), from a series depicting floral blossoms; United States, set of four, publicizing the 1984 Olympic Games; France, celebrating the bicentennial of manned flight.

bald eagle against a NASA photo of the moon, is the largest U.S. stamp ever issued in both denomination and size (3.28 square inches).

For the first time the Postal Service added maximum cards to its philatelic stock. These pictorial postcards, long popular in Europe, feature art related to or reproducing the original design used for a stamp. The new U.S. cards related to the four se tenant (mixed design and/or denomination) sets that publicized the 1984 Olympic Games.

Other se tenant groups featured inventors Philo Farnsworth, Edwin Armstrong, Nikola Tesla, and Charles Steinmetz in one unit and hot-air ballooning in another, which consisted of oversized horizontal and vertical designs. The centennials of the federal Civil Service, the Brooklyn Bridge, and the Metropolitan Opera also rated singles. Joint U.S.-European issues of common design commemorated the tricentennial of German migration to the United States, the bicentennial of a commercial treaty with Sweden, and the 1783 signing of the Treaty of Paris, which ended the Revolutionary War (issued jointly with France).

Personalities honored in the Great American series were Thomas Gallaudet, educator of the deaf; Pearl Buck, novelist; Henry Clay and Carl Schurz, statesmen; and Dorothea Dix, social worker. Scott Joplin appeared in the Black Heritage, Nathaniel Hawthorne in the Literary Arts, and Babe Ruth in the American Sports series. The 500th anniversary of Martin Luther's birth was also commemorated despite a revival of the controversy stirred by 1982 religious-subject stamps.

Commercial philately suffered heavy losses of investment values, resulting from the general economic recession as well as from the shock generated by the sale on December 13, 1982, of the "Princeton" block of four U.S. 24-cent airmail inverts. The block sold for $175,000 (plus a 10 percent buyer's premium), $325,000 less than its investor-owner paid in 1979.

Palau, the westernmost part of the U.S. Trust Territory of the Pacific, became the first of four such political entities to be granted postal independence. In anticipation of achieving a "Compact of Free Association" status with the United States, it issued its own stamps under the name of Republic of Palau on March 10.

Omnibus commemorations, in which many nations use similar designs or symbols, marked World Communications Year and the bicentennial of manned flight. Within the Commonwealth of Nations, Commonwealth Day was noted by all the members with a series of four stamps each. Of these, 20,000 sets were donated to the Commonwealth Secretariat for sale in a fund-raising plan.   B.R.M.

STATE GOVERNMENT REVIEW. Tax increases, budget cutbacks, jobs, and the economy were foremost on the agendas of U.S. governors and state legislators early in 1983. Faced with deficits due to recession, slow revenue growth, and high unemployment, many states took drastic action to avoid deficits and ensure the continuation of vital services. By late summer some 36 states had passed more than $7 billion in tax increases. By year's end, however, many states, feeling the impact of economic recovery, found themselves faced with revenue surpluses. Drunken driving, overcrowded prisons, and fears of declining educational standards were other state concerns.

Fiscal trends. While states continued to increase taxes on such items as gasoline and cigarettes, many turned increasingly toward broad-based taxes that affect the bulk of the population. Sales taxes were increased in 11 states, and income taxes in 17. Most states also made some reduction in services.

The taxes stirred strong protests in some instances. A tax revolt in Ohio was defused in November, when voters turned down initiatives that would have rolled back heavy new taxes and made enactment of future tax increases more difficult. Tax increases in Michigan led to efforts to recall close to 20 members of the legislature and even the new governor, James J. Blanchard. By December, two legislators had been recalled; petitions to unseat others were pending, but the effort to recall the governor failed.

Late in the year, it became evident that many states were reaping higher than anticipated revenues, as the economy improved. California, which had faced an anticipated $1.5 billion deficit early in the year, was now expecting a surplus of more than $400 million by June 1984; other states such as Washington,

Wisconsin, and Minnesota also reported dramatic turnarounds. The trend, however, was by no means universal.

Crime. Drunken driving continued to concern state legislators, and 35 states toughened their penalties for this offense. The legal drinking age was raised in Alaska, Delaware, Oklahoma, Connecticut, North Carolina, Virginia, and West Virginia, but proposals for a higher drinking age were vetoed by Vermont's governor and defeated by Ohio's voters. A number of states continued to try to close loopholes in the "insanity defense." The burden of proving mental illness was placed on the defendant in Arizona, Vermont, and Wyoming. South Dakota legalized a "guilty but mentally ill" verdict.

Because tough new laws and an expanding youthful population resulted in increasingly overcrowded prisons, many states stepped up their efforts to control the size of prison populations or expand prison facilities. New laws in Georgia, South Carolina, Tennessee, and Texas provided for early release of certain offenders in the event of a "prison emergency," a release system already used by Michigan. Construction of new prisons was scheduled in California, Hawaii, Minnesota, Mississippi, and New York. Following a prison riot, Oklahoma funded extensive renovations in its penal institutions. Such alternatives to prison terms as restitution, community service, probation, parole, and halfway houses were receiving increased attention.

More states passed legislation defining victim's rights, which included notification of the release or escape of offenders. The crackdown against child pornography also continued, as several states passed laws aimed at its elimination.

Employment and labor. A report released by the U.S. Labor Department in August noted that West Virginia continued to have the highest civilian unemployment rate in the country (17.5 percent as of June), followed by Michigan (14.6 percent). The unemployment rate was lowest (4.7 percent) in New Hampshire and North Dakota. As of June, unemployment was lower than it had been a year earlier in 28 states, higher in 21 states, and unchanged in one state. This was the first time since 1981 that the majority of states had reported year-to-year drops in unemployment rates.

The recession and unemployment, however, continued to strain state unemployment funds; 27 states owed nearly $13 billion to the federal fund as of August 31. A number of states reduced or froze jobless benefits, raised taxes, or instituted other economy moves in order to keep unemployment compensation funds solvent. To provide at least temporary work for youth or the unemployed, jobs programs were started in Michigan, Minnesota, New York, Vermont, and West Virginia. Other states planned to launch jobs training programs, especially for workers whose jobs had been permanently eliminated; among them were Hawaii, Iowa, New Mexico, and New York. Minnesota, New Mexico, and Pennsylvania passed legislation that provided health insurance for the unemployed.

Although 17 states had worker "right-to-know" laws about toxic substances in the work place, a rule proposed by the Reagan administration in late 1983 was aimed at preempting such laws. The rule was expected to be made binding in 1984. Comparable worth, a policy designed to equalize pay between the sexes, won a victory when a federal court ruled Washington state had illegally paid women less than men for comparable jobs. Attracting high-technology industry and jobs was the goal of many state economic development efforts, which included the establishment of high-technology councils, research centers, and loan funds.

Education. The release of a flurry of national studies indicting American schools for inferior mathematics and science programs, poor teaching, and relaxed graduation requirements engendered widespread concern among state education authorities. California and Florida passed new taxes to fund school improvements and took major steps to upgrade education, which included provision of merit pay for teachers and development of a "master teacher" concept. Mississippi implemented a $500 million package of educational improvements its legislature had passed the previous December. Math and science education were augmented in California, Florida, Indiana, Iowa, and Minnesota. Wyoming took action to equalize school funds for rich and poor districts.

Consumer protection. New car "lemon laws," first passed by Connecticut and California in 1982, were adopted by more states, including Florida, Minnesota, Montana, New Hampshire, New York, and Wyoming. The laws required automobile manufacturers to repair or replace defective new vehicles.

High utility rates resulted in legislative reforms in many states. Arizona established a utility consumers' office; Arkansas, Indiana, and Iowa opened consumer advocates' offices; and Mississippi, South Carolina, Texas, and

This group of Connecticut 19-year-olds toasted farewell to their favorite beverage just before the state law raising the legal drinking age to 20 went into effect. Connecticut was only one of several states taking steps to curb drunk driving among young people.

West Virginia instituted one-year freezes on utility rates. The breakup of the Bell Telephone System caused concern among state regulatory agencies about future price increases for telephone customers. An effort made by 13 states to invalidate the breakup agreement between the federal government and the Bell System was rebuffed in February by the U.S. Supreme Court.

Banking laws were updated by many states, including Maryland, New York, Oklahoma, Rhode Island, Tennessee, Utah, and Virginia. The collapse of the Butcher banking empire in Tennessee and Kentucky was blamed in part on inadequate state auditing procedures.

Elections. Kentucky elected its first woman governor, Martha Layne Collins (D); she had served as the state's lieutenant governor. New governors were also elected in Louisiana (Republican David C. Treen) and Mississippi (Democrat Bill Allain).

In California, Republicans designed an initiative that would have increased their chances of gaining control of at least one of the houses of the legislature by redrawing a Democrat-sponsored reapportionment plan that had been approved by the legislature the previous December. However, a referendum on the initiative, called by Republican Governor George Deukmejian, was barred in September by the state Supreme Court, which cited a provision in the state constitution permitting only one redistricting per decade. (See also ELECTIONS IN THE UNITED STATES.)

Environment. To meet a federal mandate, many states continued to organize regional compacts for disposal of low-level radioactive wastes. Compact states were to be permitted to close their borders to wastes imported from other regions on January 1, 1986. At least a dozen states took legislative action to clean up hazardous waste sites, pursue illegal dumpers, or regulate transport of toxic wastes. Florida appropriated millions of dollars for projects aimed at ensuring clean groundwater, and Louisiana took major steps to clean up its environment.

Governors' conference. When the National Governors Association held its annual convention in August in Portland, Me., the nation's economy was the dominant issue. The 34 Democratic governors attending the meeting reiterated their support for an earlier resolution that called for a reduction of the national deficit, tax increases, decreased military spending, and limitation of some government benefits. Republican governors, however, objected to any official condemnation of the Reagan administration's policies, and the three-day meeting ended without a policy statement. Aside from the partisanship raised by the debate over the economy, the governors left Portland in general agreement on a number of other issues, including the need for augmented spending on health care and education.

Other developments. Missouri became the 32nd state to call for a constitutional convention on a balanced federal budget, but approval of the move remained two states short of the required 34. The deadline for passage of the proposed equal rights amendment to the U.S. Constitution passed without sufficient state ratification.

In a California case decided April 20, the U.S. Supreme Court gave states the power to regulate nuclear power development through local waste disposal regulations.

Pari-mutuel betting on horse racing was approved in Oklahoma and Iowa, and implemented in Minnesota as the result of a November 1982 referendum. In January, Colorado became the 17th state to operate a lottery.

See also STATISTICS OF THE WORLD.   E.S.K.

SUDAN. Sudan faced a series of threats to its security in 1983 that impelled President Jaafar al-Nimeiry to seek external aid. Unrest in the southern part of the country was attributed to Libyan instigation, and in late February, Nimeiry cracked down on a group of armed Libyan "volunteers" alleged to be helping dissident Sudanese troops to plan a coup. In quelling the revolt, Nimeiry drew upon the support of Egyptian President Hosni Mubarak, who visited Khartoum in February to demonstrate support of his Sudanese ally.

Libya's backing of a rebel offensive in Chad beginning in June resulted in great concern in Khartoum. Nimeiry welcomed the American Awacs surveillance aircraft sent to Sudanese air bases for two weeks in August in support of the Chad government, and he offered logistical support to the outlying Chadian government outposts near Sudanese territory.

In Sudan's southern region, Nimeiry's fragile regional autonomy agreements began to disintegrate. Increasing lawlessness became evident in late January, when bandits attacked a railway station in Bahr el-Ghazal province, leaving 13 persons dead.

In spite of the overwhelming turnout to reelect the president in April, when he received a reported 99.6 percent of the vote, the ruling Sudanese Socialist Union (SSU) faced organizational problems. Nimeiry took the major step of dissolving the Khartoum area conference of the party.

Sudan's economic difficulties were exacerbated by the ailing global economy. Extensive foreign-debt negotiations staved off bankruptcy, but the government was forced to adopt austerity measures.

In late September, Nimeiry ordered the release of all prison inmates, including political prisoners. In announcing the pardon of the 13,000 convicts, Nimeiry said that any who returned to crime would be tried under a new Islamic penal code.

See STATISTICS OF THE WORLD.   R.B.

SUPREME COURT OF THE UNITED STATES.

The U.S. Supreme Court was very active in 1983, handing down many full opinions.

Legislative veto. Of all the opinions issued by the Court, none had greater impact than the one in the so-called ''one-house veto'' case. In *Immigration and Naturalization Service* v. *Chadha*, the Court ruled unconstitutional, by a 7–2 vote, a provision of the Immigration and Nationality Act that, in effect, authorized one house of Congress to veto a decision of the executive branch. Five justices joined Chief Justice Warren E. Burger's majority opinion, which said that, given the bicameral structure of the legislative branch, the only permissible way for Congress to override an executive decision was by introduction of legislation to be passed by a majority of both houses and eventually signed by the president. The *Chadha* decision was deemed likely to trigger a flood of federal court decisions striking down other legislative veto provisions. The Supreme Court itself invalidated two more legislative vetos, involving federal regulatory agencies.

Rights of individuals. A close second in significance to the *Chadha* case was *Arizona*

Nathalie Norris (right) with her lawyer Amy Gittler after a Supreme Court appearance on March 28. Norris won her case when the Court ruled that employer-sponsored retirement plans may not provide smaller benefits for women than for men even though women live longer and therefore collect benefits longer.

Governing Committee for Tax Deferred Annuity and Deferred Compensation Plans v. *Norris*. In that case, the Court ruled that the long-established policy whereby employers pay retired women smaller monthly benefits than retired men was a violation of the 1964 Civil Rights Act. Five members of the Court agreed that the practice, even though based upon statistics which accurately show that women as a class live longer than men as a class, constituted sex discrimination because the Civil Rights Act requires employers to treat their employees as individuals, not as members of a group. One of the five, Justice Sandra Day O'Connor, switched to the dissenters' view of the appropriate remedy, however, thus making the majority's holding applicable to future retirees only, not retroactive. Justice O'Connor was concerned that if employers were required by the Court to disburse greater annuity benefits than collected contributions from past years could support, entire pension funds would be jeopardized.

Related to the *Norris* case was *Equal Employment Opportunity Commission* v. *Wyoming*. There, a 5–4 majority held that the federal age discrimination act (which generally prohibits involuntary retirement before age 70)

389

could be applied to state and local governments as employers without violating the Tenth Amendment's reservation of states' rights.

Abortion. In a major abortion decision, the Court, in *Akron* v. *Akron Center for Reproductive Health*, struck down as unconstitutional, by a 6–3 vote, a 1978 Akron, Ohio, ordinance placing restrictions on a woman's right to have an abortion. Reaffirming its landmark 1973 decision in *Roe* v. *Wade*, the Court, in an opinion written by Justice Lewis Powell, found that a woman's constitutional right to an abortion was impeded by a variety of regulatory measures in the Akron ordinance, including a 24-hour waiting period after signing a consent form, hospitalization for abortions performed after the second trimester, and a detailed consent provision that required a doctor to make certain specified statements (for example, "a fetus is a human life from the moment of conception") to a patient to ensure informed consent.

Criminal law and procedure. In *Illinois* v. *Gates*, the Court ruled, 6–3, that a search warrant based in part on a tip from an anonymous informant is constitutionally valid. In another search and seizure decision, *Illinois* v. *Lafayette*, the Court, in a unanimous opinion written by Chief Justice Burger, held that police do not need a warrant to conduct a stationhouse search of an arrested individual's personal effects; the Court said that such a search is proper for inventory purposes and does not offend Fourth Amendment principles. In *United States* v. *Place*, a 6–3 majority, speaking through Justice O'Connor, held that police may use a trained dog to sniff a passenger's luggage on suspicion that it contains proscribed drugs but that the removal of the luggage from its owner constitutes investigatory detention and would become impermissible seizure if the investigation continued for an "unreasonable" time. Again speaking through Justice O'Connor, the Court held, in *Michigan* v. *Long*, that police officers can search an automobile's passenger area without a warrant provided the officers reasonably believe a suspect in the car is dangerous and could reach a weapon.

Besides search and seizure questions, other criminal law concerns were addressed by the Court. In *Barefoot* v. *Estelle*, the Court, through Justice Byron White and over the dissents of Justices William J. Brennan, Jr., Thurgood Marshall, and Harry A. Blackmun, prescribed guidelines intended to shorten the processing of habeas corpus petitions, and the resulting stays of execution, for inmates under sentence of death. In two contrasting 5–4 decisions, *Solem* v. *Helm* and *Jones* v. *United States*, Justice Powell was the swing vote and wrote both majority opinions. In *Solem*, the Court held that a sentence of life imprisonment without parole based upon seven non-violent felony convictions constituted cruel and unusual punishment under the Eighth Amendment. In *Jones*, however, the Court held that a criminal defendant acquitted by reason of insanity could, without any violation of due process, be held in a mental hospital even if the hospital stay exceeded the maximum prison sentence for the crime charged; Justice Powell wrote, "There simply is no necessary correlation between severity of the offense and length of time necessary for recovery."

Religion. In *Marsh* v. *Chambers*, the Court ruled, 6–3, that the First Amendment's prohibition of governmental establishment of religion was not offended by Nebraska's historic tradition of opening its legislative session with a prayer offered by a chaplain, despite the fact that the cleric is paid a salary from public funds.

Religion also figured in several important tax law interpretations rendered by the Court. In *Bob Jones University* v. *United States*, the Court over Justice William Rehnquist's sole dissent, supported the decision of the Internal Revenue Service to deny tax-exempt status to schools practicing racial discrimination in admissions and student activities policies. In *Mueller* v. *Allen*, a 5–4 majority upheld a Minnesota state income tax deduction for expenses for tuition, textbooks, and transportation to send children to private or public schools, even though the actual benefit of the deduction heavily favored families with children in parochial schools.

J.F.H., III

SURINAME. See STATISTICS OF THE WORLD. See also CARIBBEAN COUNTRIES.

SWAZILAND. See STATISTICS OF THE WORLD.

SWEDEN. Prime Minister Olof Palme's Social Democratic government submitted a bill in

November 1983 to the Riksdag (parliament) authorizing five so-called wage-earner funds. The funds were intended to enhance the influence of organized labor in economic decisions and to generate much-needed additional sources of investment capital. They were to be financed through a combination of additional taxes on company profits and a small increase in payroll taxes. Money deposited in the funds would be used to purchase shares in Swedish companies on the domestic stock market. To allay public fears that the funds, which were to be controlled by labor unions, could gain controlling interests in major businesses, the proposal restricted the wage-earner funds and existing pension funds combined to no more than 50 percent of the outstanding stock of any company.

The wage-earner funds concept was bitterly opposed by most nonsocialist groups, and on October 4, in one of the largest demonstrations in Swedish history, 75,000–100,000 people marched on the Riksdag in protest. However, because the Social Democrats held 166 of the Riksdag's 349 seats, and could generally count on the support of the 20 Communist legislators, eventual enactment of the measure seemed certain.

In an effort to siphon off sharply increasing corporate profits, the Riksdag in spring approved two temporary taxes—one a 20 percent tax on dividends, the other a 20 percent surcharge on corporate profits taxes. The government later submitted an austerity budget for the fiscal year beginning July 1, 1983. The deficit for the fiscal year was still expected to amount to 12.5 percent of the nation's gross national product. To restore social service cuts instituted by the previous, nonsocialist government, the Social Democrats raised the value-added tax by two percentage points, to nearly 23.5 percent.

Food-subsidy cuts, further tax increases, and a foreign-aid freeze were announced in October. Unemployment increased slightly to almost 3.5 percent during 1983. The inflation rate remained relatively constant at about 9 percent, and exports rose sharply during the first half of the year, producing a surplus three times the level of January–June 1982.

A commission that had been established to investigate the incursion of a foreign submarine in Swedish waters the previous October reported on April 26 that the intrusion had been one of at least six, including three incursions by "midget" submarines capable of crawling along the sea floor. The government delivered a strong protest note to the Soviets and temporarily recalled the Swedish ambassador from Moscow. By that time, new submarine sightings had been reported along Sweden's east coast north of Stockholm, but a search lasting several days failed to find any intruders.

See STATISTICS OF THE WORLD.   M.D.H.

SWITZERLAND. Swiss-Soviet relations in 1983 were strained by a series of expulsions of Soviet citizens accused of espionage. Early in the year, three Soviet diplomats were forced to leave the country, and in April the Swiss government closed the Bern offices of Novosti, the Soviet news agency, and ordered its chief correspondent out of the country. The government said the news agency had used its Swiss employees to infiltrate dissident groups.

The federal railroad continued to have grave financial problems and accounted for almost half of the nation's 1982 $200 million budget deficit. With an unemployment rate of about 1 percent and an annual inflation rate of around 5 percent, the economy appeared quite stable in 1983. Early in the year, Switzerland was admitted as a full member of the so-called Group of Ten, the inner circle of the largest contributors to the International Monetary Fund.

In October parliamentary elections, the conservative Radical Democrats registered slight gains, taking 54 seats in the lower house, up from 51 in 1979. The Social Democrats won 47 seats, down from 51, and the Christian Democrats took 42 seats, down from 44. The Swiss People's Party retained its 23 seats. The four-party coalition that has governed Switzerland since 1959 thus held 166 of the house's 200 seats.

The Swiss business community witnessed a historic event with the merger of the country's two largest watch manufacturers, Allgemeine Schweizerische Uhrenindustrie AG (Asuag) and Société Suisse pour l'Industrie Horlogère S.A. (SSIH). The action was prompted by declining sales. (In the early 1970's, the Swiss share of the world market in watch sales was 40 per-

Swiss traffic police operate a radar trap to enforce traffic regulations on the Linth Canal. When fishermen complained that motorboat-created waves were killing fish, the Swiss moved quickly to restore law and order on the waterways.

cent; by 1983, it was about 9 percent.) The new corporation, Industrie Horlogère Suisse S.A., will maintain separate marketing operations.

In September, a U.S. federal grand jury indicted Marc Rich and Pincus Green, owners of the Swiss-based Marc Rich & Co. AG, one of the largest commodity trading firms in the world, on 51 counts of tax evasion, racketeering, and fraud. The Swiss company and its former U.S. subsidiary, Marc Rich International, which had been renamed Clarendon Ltd. in July, were also named in the indictment, the biggest tax fraud indictment in U.S. history. Rich and Green did not appear in the United States to answer the charges. Federal prosecutors did not expect they would do so voluntarily, and tax evasion is not an extraditable offense in Switzerland. The IRS calculated that Clarendon owed $90.4 million in back taxes, and it had seized $22 million in cash from the company by the end of October.

See STATISTICS OF THE WORLD.   J.F.S.

SYRIA. Syria played a major role in the Middle East in 1983, especially in the conflicts in Lebanon. Syrian forces continued to occupy large sections of Lebanon and supported Druze, Shiite Muslim, and Palestinian factions that fought the Lebanese government in a renewal of Lebanon's civil war.

A long-standing antagonism between Syria President Hafez al-Assad and Yasir Arafat, chairman of the Palestine Liberation Organization, intensified, largely because Assad feared Arafat was moving the PLO toward accommodation with Israel. After a rebellion by PLO radicals broke out in May in Lebanon's Syrian-controlled Bekaa Valley, Syrian forces backed the rebels with troop and tank support. On June 23, Arafat, during a visit to Damascus, accused Syria of having incited the rebellion; the following day he was abruptly expelled from the country. The PLO rebels ultimately overwhelmed pro-Arafat forces, and in December, Arafat and several thousand followers were evacuated from Lebanon by sea, leaving Syria apparently in control of the remaining PLO forces in the country.

The Soviet Union moved quickly to replace the missile batteries, aircraft, and other equipment that Syria lost in fighting with Israel after the 1982 Israeli invasion of Lebanon. Batteries for the first SAM-5 long-range antiaircraft missiles ever to be deployed outside the Soviet Union were in place in Syria by midyear, reportedly manned by 1,000 Soviet technicians. Syria, meanwhile, showed strong reluctance to withdraw any troops from Lebanon and bitterly objected to the Israeli-Lebanese troop withdrawal agreement signed on May

17. That accord included provision for a "security zone" in southern Lebanon that would be patrolled by Israeli-Lebanese teams and made an Israeli troop withdrawal from Lebanon contingent on the simultaneous pullout of Syrian and Palestinian troops. Syria's opposition in effect nullified the agreement.

The Syrian involvement in Lebanon was aimed at ensuring that any settlement in the region would take Syrian interests into account. As a condition for agreeing to a cease-fire in the civil war in late September (which ultimately broke down), Syria was accorded observer status at Lebanese national reconciliation talks, which began on October 31 but were recessed indefinitely on November 4.

After the October 23 bombing of a U.S. Marine headquarters at the Beirut airport, the U.S. government charged the attack had been carried out with the "sponsorship and knowledge and authority of the Syrian government." Syria sharply denied the charge. Syria was also accused of complicity in the November 4 bombing of an Israeli military compound in Tyre, Lebanon. Tension between Syria and the United States increased further when U.S. fighter-bombers based on offshore aircraft carriers attacked Syrian antiaircraft batteries east of Beirut on December 4, in retaliation for their firing on unarmed U.S. reconnaissance planes. Two U.S. planes were shot down during the raid; one American was killed, and a U.S. Navy flier, Lieutenant Robert O. Goodman, Jr., was captured and held by Syria. After similar attacks on reconnaissance planes later in December, U.S. warships shelled Syrian positions in Lebanon. Lieutenant Goodman was freed by the Syrians on January 3, 1984, after the Reverend Jesse Jackson, a candidate for the Democratic presidential nomination, urged his release in private meetings in Damascus.

Despite its support of Shiite Muslims in Lebanon, the Syrian government itself remained clearly secular in orientation; late in the year, the government reportedly outlawed six religious groups, including the Humane Committee of the Imam Mortada.

See STATISTICS OF THE WORLD. *See also* LEBANON; MIDDLE EAST; PALESTINE LIBERATION ORGANIZATION.   A.D.

T

TAIWAN. Among the issues that dominated Taiwan's politics in 1983 was the eventual choice of a successor to Chiang Ching-kuo, who turned 73 in March and was concurrently president of Taiwan and chairman of the Nationalist Party of Kuomintang (KMT). Chiang has been ailing and had to undergo surgery twice in two years.

Another troubling issue for KMT chieftains was how to democratize the political system and expand participation in response to popular demands, without giving up substantial real power. The advanced age and incapacity of many members of the 371-seat legislative yuan (parliament), elected on the mainland in 1947, has already forced the KMT authorities to "reinterpret" parliamentary rules so as to lower the number of legislators required for a quorum. Nevertheless, the KMT was in no danger of losing its firm grip over the legislature. In elections held on December 3, the ruling party won 62 of the 71 contested seats. Factional fighting among the opposition and an upswing in the economy were believed to have contributed to the KMT's resounding victory.

Taiwan's once booming economy seemed to be rebounding after four years of declining growth and discouraging economic statistics. According to the Board of Foreign Trade, Taiwan's exports in the first eight months of 1983 showed an increase of 9 percent over the same period the previous year. The government predicted that real gross national product would grow more than 6 percent for 1983 as a whole. Taiwan-U.S. trade was expected to reach $15 billion, setting a new record.

In the past several years, Peking has sought to isolate Taiwan from ties with other countries, and many people in Taiwan were alarmed by what they perceived as a progressive weakening in U.S. support—particularly after a U.S. pledge in August 1982 to reduce arms sales to Taiwan from the $600 million level of 1979 and eventually cut them off. In July 1983, however, the U.S. Defense Department announced plans to sell Taiwan a substantial arms package and total U.S. sales for 1983 came to $700 million. The United States claimed that its pledge required reductions only in the inflation-adjusted value of arms.

See STATISTICS OF THE WORLD. P.H.C.

TANZANIA. In early 1983, for the first time in 20 years, an army mutiny broke out in Tanzania, involving soldiers in a northern garrison near Lake Victoria. On January 28 the government of President Julius K. Nyerere indirectly acknowledged that a coup had been averted when some 30 soldiers and civilians were arraigned in a closed session before a security court. (Charges were subsequently dropped against the defendants, but they were held in jail under a preventive detention law.) Possibly in response to this alert, the cabinet was thoroughly reshuffled. Edward M. Sokoine was reappointed to the post of prime minister, which he had resigned for reasons of health in November 1980. The outgoing prime minister, Cleopa Msuya, was shifted to the Finance Ministry, where he was expected to carry on delicate and often acrimonious negotiations with the International Monetary Fund and the World Bank, from which Tanzania has been seeking credit facilities.

In a popular nationwide campaign against corruption, 1,500 people, including a regional governor, were rounded up by authorities during April. On April 22 the National Assembly passed an Economic Sabotage Act establishing a special tribunal and instituting penalties of up to 15 years in jail for specified violations.

Among Tanzania's "serious economic problems," as outlined in a report by Nyerere, was its disappointing performance in agriculture. A consequent shift in priorities was reflected in the 1983–1984 budget, published in June, which allocated 24 percent of expenditures to agriculture—an increase of over 100 percent.

Customs duties and sales taxes were also raised. The currency was devalued by 20 percent in June. The following month, producer prices were increased on five export crops to stimulate production.

See STATISTICS OF THE WORLD. E.B.

TECHNOLOGY. In 1983 a Japanese project to develop a breakthrough artificial-intelligence computer made worldwide headlines. Lasers were put to work in the United States making holograms for ordinary credit cards as well as drilling teeth and etching patterns in materials without producing heat. Also, an innovative technology for mass-producing cars was introduced, the first generation of personal robots went on the market, and a computerized radio-telephone system went into service.

Advanced computers. Developmental work on a new class of artificial-intelligence (AI) computers was pursued intensively in Japan throughout 1983. Scientists and engineers working for the government-sponsored Fifth Generation Computer Project were attempting to build a machine that "thinks" by the early 1990's. Ultimately, they hoped to design a sequential inference machine (SIM) that would make up to 1 million logical inferences per second (LIPS); in contrast, the most powerful computers currently in use can handle only 10,000 LIPS. To achieve the speed aimed at, computer designers must develop a parallel-interface machine (PIM) that can perform many such computations simultaneously. Current plans call for this inference hardware to be combined with complex banks of information (so-called knowledge bases) and intelligent person-machine interfaces—computer circuits that will be able to understand human speech, to read, or to scan and understand pictures or photographs. The resulting machine would mimic many human thought processes. According to Japanese sources, it will initially be used for language translation and as a computer-design tool. In a related project, the Japanese were also developing advanced supercomputers designed for high-speed processing of scientific data. Such advanced "number crunchers" would be of inestimable value in solving the extremely complex problems encountered in weather forecasting, aerodynamic design, and other high-technology areas.

Hologram credit cards. A surge in credit card forgeries in recent years prompted MasterCard International Inc. to begin producing credit cards bearing holograms—three-dimensional images made with lasers. MasterCard planned to distribute 80 million cards carrying a holographic image of the firm's initials within a small globe. When such a card is tilted, the 3-D initials and globe will pass through a series of colors—an effect impossible to achieve without holography. The holograms will add only an estimated 2.5 cents to the cost of each card, but reproducing such an image would pose immense difficulties to forgers.

Heatless laser etching. A new technique for etching patterns in microcircuits, drilling teeth, or cutting bones or tissue with a laser was announced by IBM. IBM researchers discovered that lasers using far-ultraviolet wavelengths can etch plastics or tissue without the charring typical of the infrared lasers currently in use. When applied to such materials, laser light produces what is called ablative photodecomposition—the disruption of the chemical bonds that hold the molecules of the material together. It is believed that as the substance vaporizes, the material that flies away removes the heat energy that would normally cause charring. Far-ultraviolet lasers would be of particular benefit in microcircuit technology. Currently, circuit patterns must be transferred onto a radiation-sensitive surface with the aid of wet chemicals, which can remove more of a circuit pattern than is desirable. With heatless laser etching, however, wet-chemical development would not be required.

Plastic-panel cars. General Motors unveiled a major technological innovation in car making: a manufacturing technique based on plastic panels bolted onto a precision-machined frame. The new technique, which was first used for 1984 model year Pontiac P-cars, starts with a space-frame chassis, onto which 39 body mounts for plastic panels are simultaneously drilled and precision-milled by a mammoth machine tool. Later, plastic panels are bolted to the frame to form the body of the car. If a panel is damaged, either during assembly or later on by the owner, it can easily be replaced. Bolt-on plastic panels may even become available for do-it-yourself replacement. In conventional car manufacturing, a steel body is welded to the chassis at thousands of points; as a result, small errors in the tolerances of parts can accumulate into major errors that result in poor fitting of hoods, doors, trunk lids, and other parts. With the new GM technique, in contrast, body panels are put on as the last step and are fit precisely. The use of bolt-on plastic panels will also make it easier to change car styling, since differently styled panels can be bolted on the same frame.

A new computerized technology will soon allow large numbers of people to use take-along telephones. The so-called cellular mobile telephone is expected to be available in the 30 largest U.S. metropolitan areas by the end of 1984.

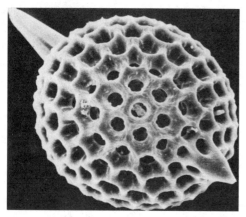

This photograph of the ancient skeleton of a radiolarian, a single-celled marine animal, was taken with a scanning electron microscope by the Monsanto Company and uses an image-processing technique. The same technology is employed in product research to identify defects undetectable with an ordinary microscope.

Personal robots. Most robots in existence today are very expensive industrial robots that can carry out only limited tasks on factory production lines. For several years, however, advanced hobbyists have been building home robots and linking them to personal computers for experiments. In 1983, the first generation of personal robots designed for consumers was introduced. The new machines are not ready to brew coffee or vacuum the rugs by themselves; the robot owner must program the robot to perform each movement required to perform a task. Some home robots, such as BOB ("brains on board"), from Androbot Inc., have one or more built-in microcomputers. Others, such as the same firm's Topo, receive commands beamed by radio or infrared light from a personal computer. Most have built-in speech synthesizers and can be programmed to talk. Some have sensor attachments that enable them to sense when they have bumped into something and to avoid that obstacle in the future. Genus, by Robotico International, has an optional vacuuming attachment and could be programmed to clean the floors of a home. Finally, Heath Company's HERO 1 is one of several home robots with small arms that can lift or manipulate light objects in accordance with meticulously programmed instructions.

Take-along telephones. After more than ten years of delays because of legal battles involving the Federal Communications Commission (FCC), major telephone companies, and radio-common-carrier (RCC) firms, the first stage in what may become a nationwide system of cellular-radio telephones was launched. In cellular radio systems, urban areas are divided into geographic cells, each of which contains a small, low-power radio transmitter linked to a central computer. When a subscriber, using a radio car telephone or a small, walkie-talkie type portable unit, dials a number, the call is received by the nearest cell and then automatically patched into the local telephone network by the central computer. As the caller drives from one cell to another, the computer senses this movement and switches the telephone call among cells without interruption.

The key to setting up a cellular radio system is access to open radio channels, and from the early 1970's telephone companies and RCC's waged a bitter battle over access rights. To settle the issue, the FCC in 1982 authorized 666 new radio channels for cellular systems and allotted each type of carrier half of the new channels. Because of the cellular setup and because the size of each cell can be reduced by adding more low-power transmitters, many callers can use the same channel simultaneously in several parts of a region. In other types of radio-telephone systems, in contrast, a single high-power central transmitter beams a call made on one of the limited number of mobile-telephone frequencies over the entire area—a setup that rules out the simultaneous use of a frequency by more than one caller. Chicago, which has been testing a cellular system for several years, began full cellular service in October. Other cities were expected to follow suit in 1984.

See also COMPUTERS AND ELECTRONICS.

J.F., Jr.

TELEVISION AND RADIO BROADCASTING. Faced with increasing competition, the three major U.S. commercial television networks—CBS, ABC, and NBC—found themselves in increasingly perilous straits. For more than three decades they had thrived, taking a mass viewership largely for granted. As recently as 1977, they could count on regularly capturing

Carol Burnett and Elizabeth Taylor in a scene from Between Friends, *a film made specially for HBO, Time Inc.'s pay-cable subsidiary. By July two out of five U.S. households subscribed to cable, and continued rapid growth was anticipated.*

more than 90 percent of the peak-hour viewing audience. But all that was changing rapidly, in large part because of cable television's inroads into the networks' audience. In Columbus, Ohio, to take one example, the prime-time network share in homes equipped with Warner Amex's Qube cable service was recently reduced to 70 percent. As of July 1983, a little over 39 percent of all U.S. television households were receiving cable, and it seemed likely that the figure could increase dramatically in coming years.

The big three networks also had to contend with the growth of "ad hoc" networks—companies that, on a one-time basis, distribute their own programs, and even, in a new twist, pick up shows canceled by the networks. Ad hoc networks, which had their earliest beginnings in the 1950's, have put on a number of major television programs. The series of interviews with former President Richard Nixon, conducted in 1975 by David Frost, went out over an ad hoc network created expressly for that purpose. The Mobil Showcase Network has presented such acclaimed programs as *Edward and Mrs. Simpson, Ten Who Dared,* and, in 1983, the Royal Shakespeare Company's innovative dramatization of Charles Dickens's *Nicholas Nickleby.* The highly successful *Entertainment Tonight,* a program that provides light, upbeat coverage of the entertainment industry, is produced by Paramount Pictures. The major networks became seriously concerned when their own affiliate stations began preempting network programs for those supplied by ad hoc distributors. NBC, for example, found that the proportion of U.S. television households receiving its full package of programming had fallen to 97 percent, one percentage point behind ABC and CBS. Each percentage point translates into millions of dollars annually in lost advertising revenues.

The ad hoc networks also breathed new life into shows given up by the major networks. *Fame,* an hour-long comedy-drama series about talented youngsters at a special public high school representing New York City's School of Performing Arts, was canceled by NBC after two seasons during which it won critical praise but mediocre ratings. It was popular in Western Europe and Australia, however, which boded well for foreign sales. The program was happily picked up by an ad hoc network that lined up its own stations and advertisers. *Too Close for Comfort,* a comedy series starring Ted Knight as a harried cartoonist with family troubles, also won a new lease on life, after being canceled by ABC.

Syndication rights. The networks could claim one possible victory of great importance. The U.S. Federal Communications Commission, in a tentative decision that could mean substantial revenues for networks, ruled in August that they could buy syndication rights to prime-time entertainment shows. The move, modifying a 1970 regulation, would allow networks to profit from the sale of programs such as *M*A*S*H* and *Dallas* to independent and cable stations after they had been presented in prime time. However, networks would not be allowed to sell directly to stations any prime-time pro-gram they had aired for five years or more; they would be required to contract with a separate company to distribute such programs. Networks claimed that the ruling change would benefit the public, since the extra income from the syndicated programs could help the networks develop high-quality prime-time shows. Hollywood producers and others opposed the change, arguing that network interests in specific programs would lead to a decline in program creativity and quality. Both houses of Congress, however, voted to block the new rules for six months, and President Ronald Reagan endorsed a two-year moratorium. In mid-November the chairman of the FCC said the commission would postpone a final vote on the new rules until spring 1984.

New anchormen. Frank Reynolds, respected co-anchorman for ABC's *World News Tonight* since 1978, died on July 20 at 59, after suffering from viral hepatitis and bone cancer. Before his latest anchor assignment, Reynolds had covered every major U.S. political convention and presidential campaign since 1965, as well as the U.S. manned spaceflight program. Because of his illness, he had been absent from the anchor desk since April, and the program ratings had declined over that period. In early August, Peter Jennings, a Canadian-born newsman who was a co-anchor with Reynolds and had previously served as a London-based

Television's Reigning Substitute

Joan Rivers, who has attracted millions of fans with her raucous brand of comedy ("Can we talk? . . . Marry rich! Buy him a pacemaker, then stand behind him and say boo!"), made news in 1983 by signing an exclusive contract with NBC's *Tonight Show* to serve as acting host during regular host Johnny Carson's annual nine weeks of vacation. The 50-year-old Brooklyn-born comic began as a television comedy writer. She had difficulty catching on as a comedian until Carson invited her on his show one night in 1965, pronounced her "funny," and, exults Rivers, set her upon her subsequent path to stardom. Since then she has frequently served brief stints as a substitute host on the *Tonight Show* when not convulsing audiences on the nightclub circuit.

Joan Rivers

correspondent for ABC, was named sole anchor; Max Robinson, also previously a coanchor on the program, was reassigned to the daily *News Brief* and the Saturday edition of *World News Tonight.* Meanwhile, as of September, Tom Brokaw became sole anchor of NBC's *Nightly News.* Brokaw, who had moved to the evening anchor spot after cohosting the morning news and entertainment program *Today,* had been teamed with Roger Mudd since April 1982. But when NBC's newscasts continued to trail the opposition, the network decided to demote Mudd, who was designated senior political correspondent.

Ratings game. For the fourth straight year, CBS won the network ratings race, with an A. C. Nielsen Company rating of 18.2 for the 1982–1983 season, a half point ahead of second-place ABC. NBC was third, with a rating of 15.1. (A rating denotes the percentage of television households tuned in to a given network.) CBS led the competition by capturing 19 of 29 weeks, on the strength of its regular series and its movies. Of the seven weeks won by ABC, four were attributable to the success of its miniseries *The Winds of War* and *The Thorn Birds,* one to the Oscar telecast, and the rest to regular programming. NBC took three weeks, two because of its telecast of baseball's World Series and one because of the pro football Super Bowl. For the season, the top ten shows, in order, were: *60 Minutes* (CBS), *Dallas* (CBS), *M*A*S*H* (CBS), *Magnum, P.I.* (CBS), *Dynasty* (ABC), *Three's Company* (ABC), *Simon & Simon* (CBS), *Falcon Crest* (CBS), *The Love Boat* (ABC), and *The A Team* (NBC). Besides *The A Team,* only two of the season's 31 new programs made it into the top 20: *Newhart,* a comedy series starring Bob Newhart as the owner of a New England guesthouse, and *Gloria,* another situation comedy, starring Sally Struthers.

Awards. At the 35th annual Emmy awards ceremonies, held on September 25 by the Academy of Television Arts and Sciences, ratings loser NBC came out ahead with 33 awards, followed by ABC with 14 and CBS with 11. For the third year in a row, the award for best dramatic series went to NBC's *Hill Street Blues,* which portrays police officers in a tough inner-city precinct. The show, which

received more nominations than any other program, also won awards for directing and writing. *Cheers,* a new NBC comedy set in a Boston bar, was named outstanding comedy series; *Cheers* star Shelley Long took top honors for outstanding lead actress in a comedy series, and the show's writers and director also received awards. *Taxi,* which was canceled by NBC, won awards for lead actor in a comedy series (Judd Hirsch) and best supporting actor (Christopher Lloyd) and actress (Carol Kane) in a comedy, variety, or music series. *St. Elsewhere,* a new series set in a Boston hospital, also made a strong showing, receiving awards for best lead actor (Ed Flanders), supporting actor (James Coco), and supporting actress (Doris Roberts) in a drama. Best lead actress in a dramatic series was *Cagney and Lacey's* Tyne Daly.

The awards ceremony was hosted by comedians Joan Rivers and Eddie Murphy. Rivers herself had scored a first by signing a contract to become the guest host for the *Tonight Show* for the entire nine weeks of host Johnny Carson's vacation.

CBS News came out on top when Emmys for news and documentaries were awarded in mid-October. The network's *60 Minutes,* a weekly "news magazine," won seven Emmys, including one for reporter Ed Bradley's story "In the Belly of the Beast" on convicted murderer and author Jack Abbott. All told, CBS walked away with 17 awards, followed by ABC News, with 13, the Public Broadcasting Service with 12, and NBC News with three.

The George Foster Peabody Awards, the most esteemed awards in broadcasting, were presented in May by the University of Georgia's Henry W. Grady School of Journalism and Mass Communication. A total of 29 awards were made, selected from 730 entries. Among the winners, NBC News was cited for *The Man Who Shot the Pope: A Study in Terrorism,* which examined alleged links between Mehmet Ali Agca, who attempted to assassinate Pope John Paul II in 1981, and the Bulgarian secret police. NBC News also won an award for *Banks on the Brink,* a program on the NBC radio series *Second Sunday,* and the NBC network shared with producers the awards for *Skeezer* and a *Project Peacock* special called

The Electric Grandmother. CBS shared with the producers an award for *The Wall,* and CBS News won for *Juilliard and Beyond: A Life in Music.* ABC News received an award for its documentary *Vietnam Requiem.* The Canadian Broadcasting Corporation won a Peabody award for *Morningside,* its popular morning radio program featuring interviews, reviews, satire, music, readings, and debate.

Specials. ABC's *The Thorn Birds* emerged as the year's most popular miniseries, deposing the network's own *The Winds of War* as the second most popular program of its kind ever shown on network television. (*Roots,* which was shown on ABC in 1977, remained the all-time ratings winner.) *The Thorn Birds,* a four-part, ten-hour adaptation of Colleen McCullough's novel of love, money, and religion in three generations of an Australian family, was watched in 41.9 percent of all U.S. television households and on 59 percent of all

Robert Mitchum made his TV debut at age 65 in The Winds of War, *ABC's 18-hour miniseries. The adaptation of Herman Wouk's novel drew 140 million viewers—the largest total audience in television history.*

sets that were turned on. ABC estimated that 110 million persons saw some part of *The Thorn Birds* and that, on average, 34.9 million viewers were tuned in for each minute of the show. The miniseries earned generally positive reviews, primarily for its strong performances. Barbara Stanwyck won an Emmy for her role as the mistress of a large sheep station and antagonist to Richard Chamberlain's Father Ralph de Bricassart. Christopher Plummer clearly enjoyed himself as Vittorio Contini-Verchese, the sophisticated churchman who is mentor to Father Ralph. Other stars were Rachel Ward, who falls in love with Father Ralph, and Australian newcomer Bryan Brown.

The Winds of War, shown a month earlier, was a dramatization by Herman Wouk of his own prizewinning novel, built around the events leading to World War II. The sprawling 18-hour drama starred Robert Mitchum, Ali MacGraw, Polly Bergen, Victoria Tennant, David Dukes, and John Houseman. Produced at a cost of $40 million, it was the costliest single dramatic undertaking in television history. Its seven installments also attracted the largest total TV audience ever—140 million.

A number of programs were broadcast in November to mark the 20th anniversary of the assassination of President John F. Kennedy. In addition to such documentaries as ABC's two-hour *JFK* and the two-hour syndicated *Being With John F. Kennedy,* which contained previously unseen footage, they included the seven-hour, three-part NBC miniseries *Kennedy,* which was branded by some critics as a vulgarization, despite strong performances by Martin Sheen as the president and John Shea as Robert Kennedy.

On November 20, ABC aired the controversial made-for-television movie *The Day After,* focusing on life in the Lawrence, Kan., area before and after the holocaust of a U.S.-Soviet nuclear exchange. At least 100 million people were estimated to have watched the $7 million production, whose powerful and graphic depiction of the effects of nuclear war was actually characterized by some experts as understated. After the showing, ABC aired a discussion of the film on *Viewpoint;* participants included Secretary of State George Shultz and former Secretary of State Henry Kissinger.

End of the line. The year marked the finale, after ten and a half years and 250 episodes, of *M*A*S*H*, CBS's enormously popular and highly honored comedy-drama series about U.S. Army surgeons in the Korean War. A concluding show of two and a half hours, which some critics found overlong and sentimental, was aired on February 28. It broke all viewing records for a nonsports, one-evening program by gaining a 60.3 rating and an audience of 125 million. The series, which lasted three times as long as the war that provided its setting, was proof that a commercial venture in a medium dominated by ratings can still achieve high quality—for example, the series won a total of 14 Emmys. At the heart of the show was the writing, which was unvaryingly intelligent, often witty, and laced with irony. Another hallmark of *M*A*S*H* was its high level of ensemble acting, by a cast headed by Alan Alda as the sardonic yet dedicated surgeon Captain Benjamin Franklin ("Hawkeye") Pierce. Explaining the decision to close up shop, the executive producer of *M*A*S*H*, Burt Metcalfe, remarked, "We wanted to stop while we were still doing well, commercially and aesthetically—while we still had pride and a sense of accomplishment in what we were doing." Successful shows never die, however; they breed sequels. In this case the follow-up was *AfterMASH*, starring *M*A*S*H* regulars Jamie Farr, Harry Morgan, and William Christopher and set in a stateside Veterans Administration hospital. The show's premiere episode was seen by 100 million viewers, making it the most popular opener since *Laverne and Shirley* in 1976.

Archie bows out. With the cancellation of *Archie's Place*, a spinoff of the popular and critical success *All in the Family*, television lost one of its most colorful, full-bodied characters: Archie Bunker. Played since 1970 with great zest by Carroll O'Connor, Archie Bunker, the irrepressible blue-collar bigot, became an archetype, the name itself a part of the American lexicon. Although Archie was at first most conspicuous for his use of racial epithets, O'Connor's rich characterization developed other dimensions and wide appeal.

Cable shakeout. In October, cable entrepreneur Ted Turner bought out his sole rival in

Survivors move painfully through the remains of a Kansas town after a nuclear attack, in a scene from the made-for-TV film The Day After. *The controversial drama was shown on ABC November 20.*

the cable news business, the Satellite News Channels, for $25 million. After little more than a year in operation, the 24-hour headline service had proved unable to attract the necessary advertising and faced losses of $40 million. The buyout left Turner's Cable News Network as the only source of general news programming for cable operators.

The Turner deal was just one more development in a general shakeout of the cable television industry. CBS Cable, a cultural service run by CBS Inc., had shut down in November 1982. And in March 1983, after nine months in operation, the Entertainment Channel, a 24-hour pay-cable network devoted to quality programming, ended operations after losing substantial sums for its owners. Showtime and Movie Channel, the second and third largest pay television services, merged. Also merging were the Cable Health Network, a 24-hour health and science channel, and Daytime, a four-hour-a-day channel offering shows devoted to self-help and family topics.

Cable sex. Subscription services—which are not subject to FCC regulations governing obscenity and indecency on public airwaves—were the prime target for viewers worried about what their children might see on the television screen. Pay television offered sexually explicit material not only in such films as *Young Lady Chatterly* and *Carry on Emmannuelle,* but in original shows such as *A New Day in Eden,* a soap opera featuring nudity. Certain subscription services, notably the successful Playboy Network, were devoted entirely to sexually oriented programming. Cable industry groups argued that films rated R ("Restricted") are more popular than films for a general audience and less explicit than X-rated films, shown by only a handful of cable systems.

Radio. National Public Radio, for nearly 15 years virtually ignored as a force in broadcasting, became headline news in 1983. It was revealed that the federally funded network, which produces programs and distributes them to nearly 300 public radio stations, had sustained a $9.1 million deficit. NPR president Frank Mankiewicz and other executives were compelled to resign, and at one point NPR was on the verge of being eliminated by Congress. However, with a new management team at NPR, the budget was slashed, nearly 200 persons were dropped from the payroll, and expenses were cut by 80 percent. Ironically, it was in 1983 that NPR achieved the greatest national listenership in its history. Among its 55 hours of weekly programming were two programs widely considered as among the best news outlets in the nation—*All Things Considered,* hosted by Susan Stamberg and Noah Adams, and *Morning Edition,* with Bob Edwards. Given its newly trimmed budget and tarnished image, NPR faced a struggle to regain its standing.

In late May the FCC approved an expansion of FM radio in the United States that would add 1,000 new stations over the next five years. The new assignments would increase by about 30 percent the total number of FM stations.

D.F.

TENNESSEE. *See* Statistics of the World.

TEXAS. *See* Statistics of the World.

THAILAND. With national elections scheduled for June 1983, the military sought early in the year to amend provisions in the constitution that were to go into effect shortly; the provisions they opposed would have abolished the special powers of the Senate, where appointed military officers constituted a majority, and taken away the right of civil servants and military officers to hold cabinet posts without having to run for election. The military also sought to prevent changes in the electoral system that could make the election of larger opposition parties easier.

In March, after much partisan maneuvering and some violence, Parliament defeated the military's proposed changes by a close vote, 264–254. However, the country's prime minister, General Prem Tinsulanond, responded by dissolving the legislature and scheduling elections for April 18, only three days before the new electoral rules were to go into effect. Prem's sudden move heavily favored the continuation of a strong military role in Thai political affairs.

In the elections a total of 1,862 candidates, representing 14 political parties, ran for 324 seats in the House of Representatives. As expected, no party secured a clear majority of seats. The nation's largest political grouping, the Social Action Party, which had campaigned against military rule, gained 11 new seats, for a total of 93.

When the parties proved unable to form a new coalition government, Prem, who had announced his retirement, said he would accept the office of prime minister for another four years. On May 8, Prem announced a new government, composed of ten military officers with no political affiliation and 30 other ministers selected from the four major parties. The new government, responding to increased popular pressure, declared that its first order of business would be to wage a concerted campaign against poverty.

The Thai government continued to meet with significant successes in its war against Communist insurgents. Communist leaders and thousands of their followers surrendered to government authorities. The Thai army held elaborate ceremonies to welcome the insurgents, who formally surrendered their weapons as they vowed allegiance to king and nation.

During the early months of 1983, the Vietnamese launched severe military attacks against anti-Communist guerrilla forces and Thai military units along the Thai-Cambodian border. The Thai government responded with a large counterattack, using both ground and air forces. The border clash caused Peking to issue a stern warning to the Hanoi government against such military adventurism in the region; it also induced the Reagan administration to offer additional aid to Bangkok.

Late in the year unusually heavy rains caused the worst flooding in Bangkok in four decades. Water-borne diseases spread rapidly, schools and businesses were disrupted, and damages were put at $400 million. In general, however, the year brought good economic news, with a growth rate of 6.5 percent projected by the end of 1983. The economy also received a boost with the first shipment of crude oil from domestic fields in the north.

See STATISTICS OF THE WORLD.   F.C.D.

THEATER. For the American commercial theater, 1983 was a poor year. Broadway was hurt by a lack of popular plays, and only a handful of big-money musicals kept it from disaster. As of June 1, there were 26 shows in Broadway's 37 theaters; by late August, there were only 15. Of these 15, six were sell-out musicals, including the first major hit of the 1983–1984 season, La Cage aux Folles. Most of the others had seats available for same-day half-price tickets.

The statistics show that both Broadway and the commercial road companies took a battering in the 1982–1983 season ending May 31. According to figures published by Variety, the weekly trade paper, Broadway attendance had declined 24 percent from the preceding year. Broadway receipts had declined 8 percent in the same period, and road company receipts had dropped for the first time in ten years, by 26 percent.

Awards. Cats won seven Antoinette Perry (Tony) awards for the 1982–1983 season, including best musical. Harvey Fierstein received Tonys for best performance in a play and best play for Torch Song Trilogy. Tommy Tune was named best actor in a musical and shared the Tony for choreography with Thommie Walsh, for My One and Only. Jessica Tandy was named best actress in a play for her performance in Foxfire, and ballet star Natalia Makarova won as best actress in a musical (On Your Toes), her first acting role ever. Awards for featured performances went to Judith Ivey for Steaming, Matthew Broderick for Brighton Beach Memoirs, Charles (Honi) Coles for My One and Only, and Betty Buckley for Cats. Marsha Norman's 'night, Mother won the Pulitzer Prize for drama, while the New York Drama Critics Circle gave its palm to Neil Simon's Brighton Beach Memoirs.

Broadway productions. Early in 1983, Tony LoBianco was praised for his impassioned portrayal of a Brooklyn longshoreman in a revival of Arthur Miller's A View From the Bridge. The revival of Richard Rodgers and Lorenz Hart's On Your Toes (1936), featuring Natalia Makarova, was directed by the venerable producer-director George Abbott, who also contributed to the book of the original production.

The autobiographical Brighton Beach Memoirs, a comic story of Neil Simon's alter ego stumbling through puberty in a poor Jewish home in Brooklyn, was made particularly memorable by the performance of 21-year-old Matthew Broderick as the 15-year-old boy.

Norman's 'night, Mother, which originated at Robert Brustein's American Repertory Theater in Cambridge, Mass., was about a divorced woman living with her widowed mother in a sterile environment. With nothing to look back on and nothing to look forward to, she tries to explain to her mother why she plans to kill herself, and her mother frantically tries to dissuade her. The acting by Kathy Bates as the woman and Anne Pitoniak as the mother was widely praised.

Edward Albee put all his personal bitterness and frustrations about his recent lack of success and harsh treatment by the critics into The Man Who Had Three Arms. The critics were unrepentant and the public uninterested, and the play ran only 16 performances.

In the spring, there was a string of revivals: Jason Robards and Colleen Dewhurst starred in the 1936 George S. Kaufman and Moss Hart

Tennessee Williams (below), dead at 71, ignited Broadway with such plays as his 1947 A Streetcar Named Desire; in the original cast (above) were Marlon Brando, Kim Hunter, and Jessica Tandy.

comedy *You Can't Take It With You,* directed by Ellis Rabb. Jack O'Brien directed a fine production of the original version of George Gershwin's *Porgy and Bess* (1935). The Royal Shakespeare Company presented its excellent Edwardian production of Shakespeare's *All's Well That Ends Well,* directed by Trevor Nunn, which didn't get the audiences it deserved. Herman Wouk's *Caine Mutiny Court-Martial* featured some first-rate work by Michael Moriarty as Captain Queeg and John Rubinstein as the defense lawyer who destroys him.

A revival of Noel Coward's 1930 comedy *Private Lives* starred Elizabeth Taylor as Amanda and her former husband Richard Burton as Elyot. The evening was less a play than an event, to which the curious thronged to see Taylor's jewels and cleavage and to giggle whenever the dialogue reminded listeners of the two Taylor-Burton marriages. The two stars reportedly got $70,000 a week each.

Cicely Tyson starred as the inspiring teacher in another revival, of Emlyn Williams's *The Corn Is Green,* but it was successful with neither critics nor public and it folded quickly.

Tommy Tune and Twiggy caught the public's fancy in *My One and Only,* a grab bag of songs by George Gershwin (music) and Ira Gershwin (lyrics) put to a suitably daft new book about an aviator and an English Channel swimmer. Frank Langella returned to Broadway in a new play by Peter Nichols. Entitled *Passion,* it was about a middle-aged husband who has an affair with a younger woman; the play featured on-stage doubles to represent the characters' inner selves.

Apart from a brief appearance by Angela Lansbury as *Mame,* Broadway was quiet throughout the summer until *La Cage aux Folles* burst onto the scene in late August. Though some viewers had reservations about the show, it was an undoubted hit—selling $4 million worth of tickets before it opened—and there was nothing but praise for its stars, George Hearn and Gene Barry. With a score by Jerry Herman and book by Harvey (*Torch Song Trilogy*) Fierstein, *La Cage aux Folles* told the story of Georges, the owner and emcee of a transvestite nightclub in St. Tropez, and his male lover of 20 years, Albin, who doubles as the star of the stage show. Soon afterward, Ben

La Cage aux Folles, *starring Gene Barry (left) and George Hearn, was Broadway's first big hit of the 1983/1984 season. An old-fashioned musical with a new-fashioned theme—homosexual love—the show offered lavish costumes and dancing.*

Kingsley, who won a best-actor Oscar for *Gandhi,* starred in Raymund FitzSimmons's one-man show *Edmund Kean,* about the legendary 19th-century actor.

Al Pacino scored the first triumph of the fall season in *American Buffalo,* a revival of David Mamet's 1975 play. The show's success was marred by a tragic note on November 8, when acclaimed cast member James Hayden, who portrayed a drug addict, died at the age of 29, apparently of a heroin overdose. *La Tragédie de Carmen,* Peter Brook's adaptation of Bizet's opera, was widely praised when it opened in the fall at the long-dark Vivian Beaumont Theater at New York's Lincoln Center. Other fall entries included a British comedy, *Noises Off,* starring Dorothy Loudon, and revivals of *Zorba,* with Anthony Quinn; George Bernard Shaw's *Heartbreak House,* with Rex Harrison; and *The Glass Menagerie,* with Jessica Tandy.

Arthur Bicknell's *Moose Murders,* a mystery set in an Adirondacks lodge that housed the oddest assortment of characters ever assembled on a stage, lasted only one night, but that was long enough for *Moose Murders* to become known as the theatrical disaster of the year.

Renaming theaters. Before the telecast of the Tony awards, Alexander M. Cohen, executive producer of the telecast, announced that the Alvin Theater would be renamed the Neil Simon Theater. The move was part of a campaign to name theaters after theater personalities rather than builders and businessmen. The Uris was renamed the Gershwin, and the Little was renamed the Helen Hayes, keeping the actress's name on a marquee following the razing of the original Helen Hayes Theater to make room for a hotel complex.

Chorus Line celebration. On September 29, with its 3,389th performance, *A Chorus Line* became the longest-running show in Broadway history. The musical about Broadway chorus "gypsies," which officially opened at the Shubert Theater on October 25, 1975, knocked *Grease* into second place (3,388 performances), followed by *Fiddler on the Roof* (3,242), *Life With Father* (3,224), and *Tobacco Road* (3,182). Still playing, in sixth place but closing in on *Tobacco Road,* was *Oh! Calcutta!*

Regional theater. Sam Shepard's *Fool for Love,* first staged by the author at San Francisco's Magic Theater, was transferred successfully to

New York by the Circle Repertory Company for an extended run. Less successful was an attempt by the Trinity Square Repertory Company in Providence, R.I., to make a play out of Jack Henry Abbott's book, *In the Belly of the Beast: Letters from Prison*. The Milwaukee Repertory Theater presented the contemporary Mexican play *The Government Man* by Filipe Santander (in a translation by Joe Rosenberg).

Off Broadway. Off Broadway successes included Tina Howe's *Painting Churches*, about the indignities of aging and the alienation of the generations, and *Taking My Turn*, a musical about growing old and enjoying it by composer Gary William Friedman and lyricist Will Holt, starring Margaret Whiting, Marni Nixon, and others. Also notable were Remak Ramsey's performance in Simon Gray's *Quartermaine's Terms*, a British drama about an ineffectual schoolteacher, and the revival of Marc Blitzstein's *The Cradle Will Rock* by John Houseman's Acting Company, a musical about an evil industrialist and a heroic labor organizer. Among Off Broadway's fall 1983 offerings, Christopher Durang's *Baby With the Bathwater* and *The Last of the Knucklemen,* by John Powers, drew special praise.

Final curtain. On March 4, the marquee lights on all operating Broadway theaters were dimmed in a one-minute tribute to Tennessee Williams, who died on February 25. Williams, 71, was the author of *The Glass Menagerie, A Streetcar Named Desire,* and *Cat on a Hot Tin Roof,* among other plays.   G.C.

TOGO. See STATISTICS OF THE WORLD.

TONGA. See STATISTICS OF THE WORLD.

TRANSPORTATION. Many U.S. transportation companies showed improvement in their financial performance in 1983, but the industry's overall growth was not vigorous.

AVIATION

According to the Air Transport Association, U.S. airlines were expected to earn a small profit, in the neighborhood of $200–400 mil-

Passengers board People Express's maiden flight from Newark, N.J., to London. The airline's economy prices—$149 for a one-way transatlantic ticket, for example—were maintained by charging passengers for food and baggage service and employing about half the usual ratio of workers per plane.

A flash fire aboard an Air Canada jet in June forced the plane to make an emergency landing and resulted in 23 deaths.

lion, on $40 billion in revenues, despite a record first-quarter loss of $650 million. In 1982 the industry suffered $733 million in operating losses on revenues of $36.4 billion, its worst performance ever. Air passenger traffic rose a scant 2.9 percent that year, and air freight traffic dropped 4.4 percent.

The 1983 recovery, however, was uneven. For example, formerly troubled Pan Am reported a second-quarter operating profit of $50 million, while traditionally strong Delta lost $51 million in the same quarter. (Delta did report net income of $10.4 million in the third quarter.) Fare discounting continued, although several airlines incorporated higher prices in fare restructurings. Perhaps the most spectacularly low fare was offered by People Express for its new transatlantic service, begun in May; it charged $149 for a one-way, no-frills flight from Newark, N.J., to London. The success of People Express, which had started operations in 1981 as a three-plane fleet serving only four cities (Newark, Buffalo, N.Y., Columbus, Ohio, and Norfolk, Va.), was shared by several smaller airlines spawned after the 1978 air deregulation law. The authority of the Civil Aeronautics Board (CAB) to regulate domestic passenger fares had expired on December 31, 1982, as part of the law.

Bankruptcies. Braniff International, which in 1982 had become the first major U.S. airline to go bankrupt, was expected to be flying again by early 1984. In September 1983, after several earlier reorganization attempts had failed, Braniff's creditors approved a plan by the Hyatt Corporation to acquire control of 80 percent of the carrier. Late in the same month, Continental Air Lines, experiencing continued losses and a reluctance by employees to grant wage concessions, filed for reorganization under the bankruptcy law.

Labor. Industry difficulties prompted many airline labor groups to make concessions. Pay cuts were accepted by 10,000 nonunion TWA workers and by Delta executives and workers. Machinists at Continental, however, went on strike in August after the company refused the wage hike they had requested. Pilots and flight attendants subsequently rejected a Continental request for wage concessions. When it filed for reorganization in September, the airline cut its staff by nearly two-thirds; many of its pilots subsequently went on strike, but Continental continued to operate. In an agreement with three major unions in December, Eastern Airlines won major wage and work rule concessions in exchange for management participation by workers and common stock in the company.

Disasters and skyjackings. On September 1 a Korean Air Lines jumbo jet was shot down over the Sea of Japan by a Soviet interceptor plane, after the Boeing 747 had strayed off course and entered restricted Soviet airspace. All 269 people on board the airliner perished, and the incident precipitated an international crisis. Several countries declared two-week bans on flights to and from the Soviet Union, and Canada announced a 60-day ban on flights by Aeroflot, the Soviet airline. An inquiry team sponsored by the International Civil Aviation Organization, a United Nations affiliate, rejected Soviet assertions that the aircraft had been on a spying mission and also discounted earlier theories that the plane's crew was taking a short cut to save fuel or that its navigation systems had failed. The plane's going off course was blamed on human error.

On June 2 an Air Canada DC-9 was forced by a lavatory fire to make an emergency landing at Greater Cincinnati International Airport; 23 people were killed.

Almost 300 people died in two air crashes in Spain. In one of the ten worst accidents in aviation history, a Colombian Boeing 747 crashed shortly before landing at Madrid's Barajas airport on November 27; only 11 of the 193 people aboard, most of whom were French nationals, survived. Ten days later, 93 people, many of them Japanese tourists, were killed when two Spanish jetliners collided on a runway at the same airport. Pilots blamed the crash on lack of ground radar and multicolored signal lights.

A rash of skyjackings of U.S. airliners distressed air travelers in the spring and summer. Between May 1 and September 22, 12 planes were hijacked. Most skyjackers were Cuban refugees seeking to return to their country.

MOTOR TRANSPORT

The intercity bus industry achieved only a weak recovery. According to Interstate Commerce

As striking Greyhound workers picket the bus station in Baltimore in November, job seekers line up a city block long to apply for possible openings. Workers ended up accepting a 7.8 percent pay cut to reach a settlement.

Commission statistics, the nation's ten largest passenger carriers in 1982 suffered a 3.4 percent decline in revenues, and their net operating income dropped by $41.4 million. The carriers' income decreased slightly through the third quarter of 1983, and ridership levels dropped by 7.9 percent. Bus companies began taking advantage of the new freedoms provided by the Bus Regulatory Reform Act of 1982. Greyhound Lines, the country's biggest bus company, was the most aggressive in this regard. In several cases, Greyhound successfully petitioned the ICC to preempt adverse decisions by state regulatory agencies so that it could abandon unprofitable routes within individual states. Other carriers won ICC permission to implement intrastate fare increases that had been rejected by state commissions.

On November 3, Greyhound bus service was halted as drivers and other employees, balking at a management request for such concessions as a 9.5 percent pay cut, went on strike. After hiring new employees, Greyhound resumed partial service on November 17 despite violence by strikers at some terminals. A union-management compromise, involving a 7.8 percent pay cut, ended the strike in time for the height of the holiday travel season.

The nation's trucking companies experienced an upturn in business, and some of the largest carriers registered substantial gains. The preceding year had turned out to be the industry's worst financially since the introduction of regulation in 1935. According to ICC figures for the nation's 100 largest companies, operating income stood at $200 million in 1982, down from $531 million in 1981; net was $65 million, down from $293 million the year before.

On January 6, President Ronald Reagan signed into law the Surface Transportation Assistance Act (STAA). The law, which increased the federal gasoline tax from 4 to 9 cents a gallon, effective April 1, was aimed largely at providing more funds for highway construction and repair. It benefited the trucking industry by permitting the nationwide use of longer and wider trailers, as well as double trailers on the Interstate Highway System and some federally aided primary roads. Some

Protesting increased federal taxes, independent truckers went on strike early in the year. When some strikers turned to violence—including sniper attacks—many drivers who wanted to stay on the road took to toting guns.

states, however, vigorously opposed allowing big trucks on their highways, and the Federal Highway Administration sought to quiet the controversy by revising the interstate route structure over which the bigger trucks were to be permitted to operate.

STAA provisions raising special truck user taxes from an average of $240 per vehicle this year to $1,900 in 1989 provoked a brief but violent shutdown by independent owner-operators, and howls of protest from the regulated carriers. Between January 31 and February 10, a loose coalition of owner-operators led by the Independent Truckers Association parked their rigs. Hundreds of shooting incidents around the nation were reported against independent and carrier drivers who continued to operate. At least one driver was killed, and more than 1,700 trucks were damaged, over 500 by gunfire.

On the 100th anniversary of the completion of the Northern Pacific Railroad, the hammering of the last spike was reenacted in Deer Lodge, Mont., complete with a genuine 1861 locomotive.

RAILROADS

Railroad freight volumes rose by about 3 percent in the year's first three quarters, but slight declines were reported in the industry's net operation income. Truck-rail traffic, however, showed a 20 percent gain, measured in the number of cars loaded. The ICC's year-end statistics for 1982 revealed that rail freight traffic had dropped 12.3 percent from 1981 levels, and the industry's net operating income had declined 44.6 percent, to $767 million.

Guilford Transportation Industries. Industrialist Timothy Mellon's Guilford Transportation Industries received clearance in June from a federal appeals court for the purchase of the bankrupt Boston & Maine Corporation and the Delaware & Hudson Railway. GTI expected to complete its planned 3,000-mile rail network in the northeastern United States in early 1984, and, as the year drew to a close, was negoti-

ating agreements with two connecting railroads aimed at satisfying competitive concerns raised by the ICC and the court.

Government-owned railroads. Conrail continued to bolster its financial position. The government-owned railroad, created in 1976 from a group of bankrupt carriers, announced 1982 net income of $174 million, which included $44 million for the settlement of various accounts with commuter authorities and Amtrak, the federally subsidized passenger railroad. The net income figure represented a $135 million improvement over 1981. Conrail earned $195.5 million in the first nine months of 1983. In May the U.S. Railway Association made an official determination that the railroad would remain profitable for the foreseeable future, a determination legally required to clear the way for Conrail's sale as a single entity to the private sector.

Amtrak was able to maintain its service level with a $700 million budget for the fiscal year ending September 30. The carrier raised its fares an average of 3 percent in June, and it resurrected late in the year the Virginia-to-Florida passenger-automobile service once provided by the defunct Auto Train Corporation. In February, Amtrak began offering a rail-truck package delivery service to 54 cities.

Under a law effective in January, the federal government began the process of transferring the Alaska Railroad, owned by the U.S. Department of Transportation, to the state of Alaska. The transfer was expected to be completed in 1984.

Deregulation. The ICC took several major actions aimed at helping the railroad industry. The most significant was the agency's proposal to establish new guidelines that effectively eliminate rate ceilings on coal, which is the carriers' most important traffic. Under the ICC's plan, railroads would be authorized to raise their coal rates up to 15 percent annually, plus inflation adjustments, until they reach so-called revenue adequacy, under the agency's generous definition of the term. The ICC also implemented earlier proposals to exempt from economic regulation railroad shipments of export coal, to exempt most agricultural products, except grain and soybeans, to exempt shipments moving in boxcars, and to allow railroad transportation contracts to become effective on short notice.

Labor. President Reagan acted to ensure the long-term viability of the railroad retirement system, which was experiencing a solvency crisis similar to that facing the social security system, by signing the Railroad Retirement Solvency and Railroad Retirement Revenue Acts of 1983 into law in August. The legislation increased railroad retirement and unemployment insurance taxes, deferred cost-of-living benefit increases, modified early retirement programs, and subjected rail retirement annuities to federal income taxes.

SHIPPING

Maritime business was projected to pick up somewhat as the United States led the other industrialized nations out of the trough of the world recession. Optimistic predictions of trade growth for fleets serving the developed nations and the oil market, however, were balanced by the fact that there were too many vessels of all types in the world fleet.

Liner code. The most important event in maritime shipping took place on October 6, when the Code of Conduct for Liner Conferences of the United Nations Conference on Trade and Development entered into force. The code, aimed at encouraging developing nations to build up their shipping fleets, applied only to liner vessels, which haul general or containerized cargo on regular schedules. The code treaty was adopted by UNCTAD in 1974 and had to be ratified by at least 24 countries controlling a minimum of one-fourth of world liner tonnage before it could take effect. As of October it had been signed by 59 nations representing more than 28 percent of world liner tonnage.

Although many signatory nations placed reservations and restrictions on their participation, the code essentially called for cargo-sharing arrangements under which most trade between trading partners would be set aside for national-flag carriers. Countries sending cargoes and countries receiving them would each be entitled to handle 40 percent of the shipping. Third-flag carriers would be allowed 20 percent. This could hurt several U.S.-flag lines operating on routes that do not involve U.S. ports. The Reagan administration refused to ratify the code on grounds that it was anticompetitive. U.S. shippers feared that the code would force them to pay higher freight rates in certain trades.

U.S. maritime policy. Maritime reform legislation that would ease antitrust restrictions on U.S.-flag carriers, a move the carriers believed was critical to their survival in international trade, was passed by the Senate in March. Similar legislation was approved by the House in October, and the measure was referred to a conference committee, which was scheduled to take up the two bills early in 1984.

Company restructuring. Several U.S.-flag shipping companies made significant changes in their corporate structures. United States Lines bought Moore-McCormack Lines for $60 million. USL's parent company, McLean Industries, made a public stock offering of 5 million shares. The stock sale left the company's president, Malcolm P. McLean, in control of 87 percent of the company. Meanwhile, Sea-Land Service Inc., which reported record 1982 earnings of $157 million and held its place as the world's largest private shipping firm, was being positioned for divestiture from its parent corporation, the R. J. Reynolds conglomerate. Additionally, American President Lines Ltd. was spun off from its parent company, the Natomas Company, when Natomas merged with Diamond Shamrock Corporation.

Barge industry. The barge and towing industry continued to slump, although there was a modest upturn in grain volumes during the summer. The industry's 15 largest companies were said to have lost $30 million in 1982.

In a significant compromise, the Reagan administration backed off its earlier insistence that barge and towing companies should be required to pay nearly 100 percent of the costs of building, operating, and maintaining inland waterway projects. Instead, the administration sponsored legislation that would require the private sector to pay 70 percent, with the government picking up 30 percent.

MASS TRANSIT

In August, Dallas-area voters approved a sales tax increase of one percentage point to finance an $8.75 billion mass-transit program, including a 160-mile rail network and increased bus service. Elsewhere in Texas, the Texas Rail Transportation Company purchased the right-of-way for a planned high-speed rail service that could shuttle passengers between Dallas and Houston in two hours. A similar project was under consideration in Pennsylvania, where the Pennsylvania High Speed Rail Passenger Commission was studying the feasibility of a line between Philadelphia and Pittsburgh. Meanwhile, New York City's aging subway system continued to have its troubles. There were 16 derailments by mid-November, due at least in part to the fact that the system had for a few years, when the city was suffering a financial crunch, deferred needed maintenance.

See also AUTOMOBILE INDUSTRY. R.J.K.

TRINIDAD AND TOBAGO. See STATISTICS OF THE WORLD.

TUNISIA. Tunisian foreign-policy makers pursued diplomatic activity early in 1983 designed to improve relations with the country's North African neighbors. On March 19, Tunisia and Algeria signed a 20-year treaty of peace and friendship. Among other things, the accord called for a mutual commitment to maintaining peace and security in the region, rejection of the use of force to resolve differences, and the refusal by each country to tolerate the activities in its territory of any group seeking to change another country's regime. Reaction to the treaty was generally positive. Neighboring Libya dispatched a top official to Tunisia in mid-May to meet with Premier Muhammad M'zali, and M'zali, in turn, traveled to Libya for talks on July 19–20.

The primary cause of Tunisia's diplomatic initiatives was the need to find new sources of support within the region for its sagging economy. The trade deficit, $1.23 billion for 1982, continued to deepen in the first few months of 1983, and by March, Tunisia's foreign debt had surpassed 40 percent of its GNP. Government officials responded with an austerity plan. On June 30 it was announced that imports of a wide range of goods were to be limited to 80 percent of their 1982 levels. By the summer of 1983, petroleum and phosphate exports had surpassed levels for the corresponding period of 1982. Tourism, however, was down 20 percent, and serious economic problems persisted.

In mid-June, Premier M'zali dismissed Mansour Moalla, the architect of the government's austerity policies. Information Minister Tahar Belkhodja was also removed, and both were replaced by longtime Destour Socialist Party members. The shakeup was interpreted as a show of strength by M'zali, who in November seemingly felt confident enough in his political position to agree to the legalization of two opposition political parties.

In an effort to reduce its budget deficit, the government reduced food imports and increased the price of bread by 125 percent in late December, a move that sparked widespread riots as the year drew to a close.

See STATISTICS OF THE WORLD. K.J.B.

TURKEY. After three years of military rule, Turkey in late 1983 returned to democratic rule with the election of a new Parliament and the installation of a civilian prime minister.

National elections. Parliamentary elections on November 6 saw a surprise victory by the Motherland Party of conservative economist Turgut Özal, a former deputy prime minister in the military regime who is generally credited with planning Turkey's economic recovery program. The Motherland Party took 45 percent of the vote, winning 211 seats in the 400-member Parliament. The moderate Populist Party of Necdet Calp, a former provincial governor, received 30 percent of the vote and 117 seats. The law-and-order Nationalist Democracy Party of Turgut Sunalp, a retired general, trailed in third place despite having been endorsed by the military government.

The military's governing National Security Council had authorized only three parties to take part and barred more than 240 former politicians from any political activity for ten years. On December 6 the NSC handed over authority to the new Parliament. Shortly thereafter, on December 13, Özal took office,

heading the country's first civilian government since 1980.

Domestic crackdown. In February a martial law court in Ankara sentenced Necmettin Erbakan, the former chairman of the now defunct National Salvation Party, and 23 other former party members to prison terms for attempting to establish an Islamic state in Turkey. In the southeastern city of Diyarbakir in May, a large number of Kurds were convicted of crimes ranging from murder to attempting to establish a separate Kurdish state; 35 were sentenced to death and 339 to prison terms.

The NSC announced new laws in May, prohibiting unions from engaging in political activity and limiting strikes to 60 days. A press law announced in November provided stiff penalties to editors who publish articles deemed a threat to national security or an offense to public morality.

Economic problems. After two years of impressive gains, Turkey's economy showed signs

Residents of Ankara vote in Turkey's first general election in three years; only three parties were given permission to participate by the military government. The independent conservative Motherland Party led by Turgut Özal scored a surprise victory.

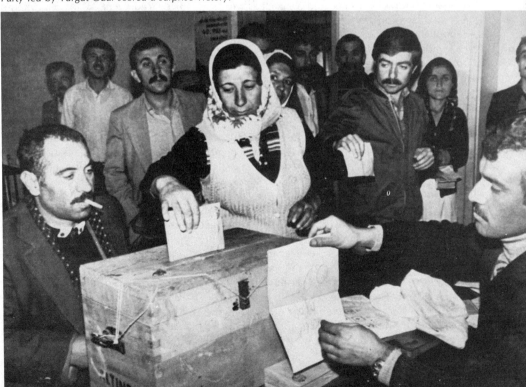

of a downturn in 1983. Inflation, which had been reduced from 120 percent to 30 percent, crept back up to the 50 percent mark. Unemployment was expected to rise above 20 percent. The trade deficit was rising, and remittances from Turkish workers abroad, especially in West Germany and Saudi Arabia, were decreasing sharply.

Foreign affairs. Relations between Turkey and Greece were seriously strained when Ankara extended recognition to a newly proclaimed independent republic in Turkish-held northern Cyprus in November. Turkey's move also drew strong criticism from the United States and other members of the North Atlantic Treaty Organization, which feared renewed tension in the eastern Mediterranean.

Earthquake. A major earthquake struck eastern Turkey on October 30, reportedly killing at least 2,000 people and leaving thousands homeless. Various countries donated relief supplies and emergency aid.

Armenian terrorism. Attacks by Armenian nationalists against Turkish diplomats and agencies continued in 1983. On March 9 the Turkish ambassador to Yugoslavia was fatally shot in Belgrade; on July 15 a bomb explosion at the Turkish Airlines counter at Paris's Orly Airport killed eight and wounded 54; and on July 27 gunmen attacked the Turkish ambassador's residence in Lisbon, Portugal, killing the ambassador's wife.

See STATISTICS OF THE WORLD.   P.J.M.

TUVALU. See STATISTICS OF THE WORLD.

U

UGANDA. In 1983 the prospects for civil peace and national reconciliation in Uganda remained uncertain. Although forces opposed to President Milton Obote appeared weakened by internal dissensions, they nevertheless managed through sporadic attacks to prevent a return to normalcy. Heavy-handed retaliatory action by government troops, in turn, continued to fuel popular resentment in Buganda and other southern districts where opposition to Obote has traditionally been strongest.

Uganda was still unable to solve the problem of the 100,000 Rwandan refugees in the southwest, thousands of whom were being forced over the border into Rwanda, apparently by local pressure rather than as a result of a deliberate governmental policy. The refugees were herded into makeshift, overcrowded, unsanitary camps on both sides of the border, and some have died of malnutrition.

Armed dissidents continued to keep government forces at bay during most of the year. Originally the strongest of the anti-Obote movements, the Uganda National Rescue Front, led by Moses Ali (a former cabinet minister under the regime of Idi Amin), was driven out of its stronghold near the Sudan border by government troops, and the area regained some degree of peace during 1983.

In the south, the National Resistance Army, led by Yoweri Museveni, a former defense minister in the post-Amin provisional government, was active. On December 3 the rebel group took credit for the downing of an army helicopter carrying the chief of staff, Major General David Oyite Ojok, regarded as the second most powerful man in Uganda. Ojok and eight other passengers were killed.

A third opposition group, the Uganda Freedom Movement, was less effective. Government retaliation and reported dissension within its ranks caused its leader, Andrew Lukatome Kayiira, to leave for Kenya early in the year. On June 3, President Obote and Kenyan President Daniel arap Moi met and agreed to curb the activities of dissidents from each other's country. Plans were then announced for the deportation from Kenya of 48 Ugandans; Kayiira subsequently fled to Europe.

At the end of June, the governmment released its 1983–1984 budget and announced economic policy guidelines for the coming year. They included a 50 percent raise in civil service salaries. This measure was expected to undermine the government's commitment to cut inflation to 25 percent, from its reported 1982 level of 50 percent. Public spending was projected to increase 67 percent.

Under the Expropriated Properties Act, signed by President Obote on January 31, Asians and other foreign owners dispossessed by the Amin regime in 1972 were given the option of reclaiming their confiscated properties if they returned to the country or of securing compensation.

See STATISTICS OF THE WORLD.   E.B.

UNION OF SOVIET SOCIALIST REPUBLICS.
The general secretary of the Soviet Communist Party, Yuri Andropov (see biography in PEOPLE IN THE NEWS), appeared to be effectively consolidating support within the Soviet leadership during 1983. He himself was named chairman of the Presidium of the Supreme Soviet in June, thus becoming chief of state. However, he dropped from public view in late August, leaving observers to conclude that he was suffering from a serious illness. Relations with the United States declined, especially after the Soviet downing of a South Korean commercial airliner on September 1. The Soviet economy appeared to be improving after a generally weak year in 1982.

Political leadership. Shortly after becoming general secretary in November 1982, Andropov had shifted key responsibilities away from Konstantin Chernenko, his chief rival, and had a former KGB subordinate, Geidar Aliyev, named a first deputy premier; Aliyev also was made a full, or voting, member of the party's ruling Politburo. Andropov's position was apparently strengthened further at a party Central Committee meeting in December 1983, with the appointment of Mikhail S. Solomentsev and Vitaly I. Vorotnikov as full Politburo members; of Viktor M. Chebrikov, head of the KGB, as a nonvoting Politburo member; and of Yegor K. Ligachev as a secretary of the Central Committee secretariat. Earlier in the year, Foreign Affairs Minister Andrei Gromyko was named a first deputy premier; Mikhail Gorbachev, the Central Committee secretary for agriculture, was given overall responsibility for personnel selection; and Grigori Romanov, the Leningrad party leader, was elected a secretary of the Central Committee and apparently assigned responsibilities in the defense industry.

Personnel changes, in many cases involving relatively young men, were of particular interest as Andropov's health apparently deteriorated. After an appearance in public on August 18, he disappeared from view for the rest of the year, missing such key events as the annual Revolution Day parade in November and the party's Central Committee meeting the following month. However, Andropov's speech, strongly assailing inefficiency in the economic system, was read at that meeting, and the government seemed to be taking pains to stress his continuance in authority.

Foreign policy. There was no apparent major change in foreign policy in 1983. Soviet occupation forces continued their operations against Afghan guerrillas. Relations with China showed some slight improvement, largely on the symbolic and economic levels. Cultural, sports, and tourist ties were strengthened, and Soviet-Chinese foreign trade rose.

The Soviets did increase their involvement in the non-Communist Middle East, installing longer-range SAM-5 antiaircraft missiles in Syria near the Lebanese border, to replace shorter-range SAM's destroyed by Israeli aircraft. The new missiles, moreover, were manned by Soviet specialists.

During the summer there were some signs of a possible improvement in U.S. relations. In July, the Soviet Union permitted a group of Soviet Pentecostal believers who had taken refuge in 1978 in the U.S. embassy in Moscow to emigrate. Both the U.S. and Soviet sides made compromises to permit an agreement to be reached in July at the long-running Conference on European Security and Cooperation in Madrid, called to review the operation of the 1975 Helsinki accords on European security and human rights. In August the United States and the Soviet Union signed a five-year grain agreement that increased guaranteed minimum annual sales to 9 million metric tons and prohibited cancellation for any political reason.

The primary short-term foreign policy goal of the Soviet leaders in 1983 was to prevent the deployment of U.S. Pershing II and cruise missiles in Western Europe beginning at the end of the year. Moscow conducted a vigorous peace campaign, including propaganda efforts (unsuccessful) to influence the West German elections in March and the British elections in June. At U.S.-Soviet talks in Geneva, both sides proposed compromises, with the Soviets offering to reduce the number of SS-20's aimed at Western Europe in return for abandonment of NATO deployment plans. The talks deadlocked, and, after missiles began arriving in Great Britain and West Germany, the Soviet Union on November 23 suspended the talks. The next day, Andropov announced plans to beef up the Soviet nuclear arsenal on land and sea.

On December 8, the separate U.S.-Soviet strategic arms limitation talks in Geneva were suspended indefinitely, and on December 15, East-West talks in Vienna on conventional armed forces in Central Europe also were recessed, with no date set for their resumption. **Korean Air Lines flight 007.** U.S.-Soviet tensions heightened after a Soviet interceptor on September 1 shot down a Korean Air Lines jumbo jet, flight 007, with the loss of all 269 people aboard.

Some of the facts about the incident were quickly established. The airliner, bound for Seoul, South Korea, on a route from Anchorage, Alaska, had left its assigned flight path. It passed first over the Soviet peninsula of Kamchatka, where sensitive Soviet military installations are located. While the airliner was near Kamchatka, at least one U.S. RC-135 spy plane was in the same general area; however, the Soviet Union and the United States later disagreed on the distance between the planes and on the number of spy planes. The Soviet Union sent up fighters to intercept the intruding plane, but flight 007 was over international waters before they found it. The airliner subsequently reentered Soviet airspace over the island of Sakhalin, by now hundreds of miles off course. It was then picked up by fighter planes from Sakhalin, and, just as it was about to pass into

Nine days after Korean Air Lines flight 007 was shot down over the Sea of Japan by a Soviet interceptor, killing all 269 persons aboard, Marshal Nikolai Ogarkov, chief of the Soviet general staff, gave Moscow's official version of the incident. He said that the downing had been a deliberate decision, made after military officers concluded that the plane was on a spy mission.

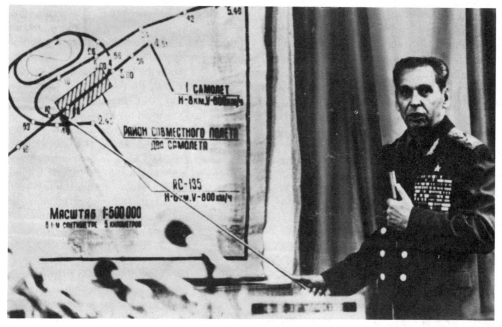

Soviet ships were trapped by ice floes in the Arctic Ocean north of Siberia in October; an unusually abrupt change of season and administrative inefficiency were blamed. Ice breakers finally succeeded in freeing the approximately 40 ships, but not before one freighter was sunk and others extensively damaged.

international airspace once more, it was shot down.

Other details were more difficult to establish. It was unclear why flight 007 was off course, whether its pilot was aware of warning signals given by the Soviet planes, where in the Soviet chain of command the decision to fire was made, or what information it was based upon. On September 9, in an unusual press conference Marshal Nikolai Ogarkov, chief of the Soviet general staff, presented official Soviet answers to some questions. Ogarkov confirmed that the downing of the airliner had been deliberate; the decision, he said, was made by the district commander of the Air Defense Forces, after staff officers decided the plane was on a spy mission. Ogarkov claimed the South Korean pilot had refused to let Soviet pilots escort his plane to a landing.

For several days, the Soviet Union did not even acknowledge that it had shot down the airliner, asserting only that the plane had "left Soviet airspace." The Soviet leadership charged that the airliner was on a spy mission for the Reagan administration—a conclusion later rejected in a report by the International Civil Aviation Agency. Although it eventually expressed regret for the loss of life, the Soviet Union made no apology, and Foreign Minister Gromyko said that the same action would be taken again should similar circumstances arise. Relatives of the victims were not permitted to go to the crash scene for a memorial ceremony.

Immediate reactions from various parts of the world included condemnation of the downing; a widespread boycott of Aeroflot, the Soviet airline; and a vote by international airline pilots to temporarily suspend flights into the Soviet Union. In the weeks following the incident, U.S., Japanese, and Soviet ships searched for wreckage of the jetliner, hoping in particular to recover the plane's flight recorder, which might contain information that could shed light on mysteries surrounding the downing. The U.S. and Japanese ships were repeatedly harassed by Soviet vessels; in early November they abandoned the search.

Economy. Andropov focused attention on the need for economic reform, for tighter discipline and harder work, for an end to corruption, and for more citizen participation in management. The steps actually taken in these areas, however, were not far-reaching. The only reform appearing to have the potential to develop into a major innovation was an experimental system in agriculture in which small production units, or "brigades," on the collective farms enter into contract with the government to deliver a certain amount of output; they may keep and sell for their own account any surplus above the contracted amount.

In 1982, the Soviet economy was generally weak. The energy sector continued to grow rapidly; but agricultural performance was less satisfactory, with grain harvest a disappointing 175 million metric tons, far below the official target of 238 million metric tons. The 1982 industrial growth of 2.8 percent was lower than the average of 7.4 percent a year in 1970–1975 and the 3.4 percent registered in 1981. On the basis of projections, 1983 appeared to be a better year. Growth of the gross national product was expected to exceed 4 percent, and grain production was expected to pass the 200-million-ton mark. Better weather was not the only reason for the economic improvement. Andropov's labor discipline campaign apparently also had at least some short-term effect in industry. A slowdown in the growth of military spending may also have helped.

Ice crisis. In early October about 40 Soviet freighters and tankers were trapped by arctic ice in the Chukchi Sea. One ship sank, but the rest were freed by the end of the month; at least 30, however, were extensively damaged. The disaster was attributed partly to unusually harsh weather and shifts of ice fields and winds, but the bureaucrats in charge of moving cargo in the region also came under attack for inefficiency.

See STATISTICS OF THE WORLD. *See also* AFGHANISTAN; COMMUNISM; MILITARY AND NAVAL AFFAIRS; SPACE SCIENCE AND EXPLORATION.

J.F.H.

UNITED ARAB EMIRATES. *See* STATISTICS OF THE WORLD. *See also* PERSIAN GULF STATES.

UNITED NATIONS, THE, abbreviated UN. The harsh rhetoric and tensions that in 1983 characterized relations between the United States and the Soviet Union, the two most powerful members of the United Nations, virtually paralyzed the Security Council despite ongoing conflicts in the Middle East, Asia, Africa, and Central America.

Korean Air Lines flight 007. Antagonism between the United States and the Soviet Union reached an emotional pitch unmatched since the Cuban missile crisis of 1962 when on September 2 the United States took the lead in the Security Council in condemning the Soviet Union for shooting down a South Korean airliner. (South Korea is not a UN member.) A Soviet jet fighter had shot down the plane on September 1, killing all 269 persons aboard, after it entered Soviet airspace over the Kamchatka Peninsula and Sakhalin Island. The initial Soviet denials were exposed as untruthful when the United States let the Council hear tapes of the Soviet pilot's radio transmissions to ground control confirming that he had destroyed the plane. Insisting that the plane was on a U.S. intelligence mission and that the Soviet pilot had taken appropriate warning measures without response from the airliner, the Soviet government expressed regret for the loss of life but admitted no guilt and made no apology.

However, as further information was released, the expectation that all the Council members except the Soviet Union itself and Poland would vote to condemn the Soviet Union for its action receded. It became known, for example, that a U.S. intelligence-gathering plane had also been in the area, and a revised translation of the Soviet pilot's transmissions suggested that he had made some attempt to attract the Korean pilot's attention.

The resolution that was put to a vote on September 12 merely deplored the plane's destruction and the tragic loss of life. In addition, it urged all states to cooperate fully with the International Civil Aviation Organization in efforts to strengthen the safety of civil aviation and invited the secretary-general to conduct a full investigation into the circumstances of the tragedy. The vote was 9 in favor and 2 opposed (the Soviet Union and Poland), with 4 abstentions. The resolution failed because of the Soviet veto.

Arab-Israeli conflict. On January 18 the Security Council extended the mandate of the UN Interim Force in Lebanon (Unifil), despite the fact that its credibility was diminished by the continuing presence of an Israeli occupation force. The attempt to negotiate the withdrawal of foreign forces from Lebanon was left to the United States. The task of helping the Lebanese government consolidate control over Beirut and its environs was left to the non-UN multinational force. Some 50 UN observers remained in Beirut, however, and the UN

During the UN debate over the Korean jet shot down by the Soviet Union, members of the Security Council watched subtitles on a television screen while listening to the tape-recorded voice of a Soviet pilot during the attack. The words on the screen read, "The target is destroyed."

peacekeeping force on the Golan Heights remained in place.

On August 2 a resolution condemning Israel's settlement policies in the West Bank was approved by 13 Council members and vetoed by the United States. A controversial ten-day conference on the "question of Palestine" began in Geneva later in August, with neither the United States nor Israel participating. While it called for the establishment of a Palestinian state, which was unacceptable to Israel, the final resolution also included implicit recognition of Israel's right to exist.

Other Asian issues. On October 31 the Security Council adopted its fourth resolution calling for a cease-fire in the ongoing Iran-Iraq war since hostilities began in September 1980. The General Assembly, again for the fourth time, passed a resolution calling for the withdrawal of "foreign" troops from Afghanistan. Also passed was a resolution condemning Vietnamese occupation of Cambodia.

Central America. The Security Council met five times in March to debate Nicaraguan charges that the United States was backing antigovernment guerrillas infiltrating from Honduras, but the debates ended without a resolution being presented. The Council met again in May, after Nicaragua had asked the Council to consider measures to halt what it described as a "new stage" in the U.S.-backed invasion from Honduras. The request followed a statement by President Ronald Reagan supporting

the "freedom fighters" who were opposing the Sandinista government. Nicaragua asked the Security Council to approve bilateral talks with the United States and with Honduras under UN auspices; the United States, with Honduran support, proposed instead negotiations encompassing all five Central American states involved in the Nicaraguan dispute, preferably mediated by the Organization of American States. Four Latin American nations (Colombia, Venezuela, Mexico, and Panama), termed the Contadora group after their initial meeting place, Panama's Contadora Island, attempted to reconcile these positions.

On May 19 the Security Council unanimously approved a resolution expressing concern over possible war between Nicaragua and Honduras and supporting the Contadora peace initiative. Nicaragua called the Council into session again on September 13 to accuse the United States of initiating bombing strikes from Honduras against Nicaragua. The United States did not respond, and there was no debate. On November 11 the General Assembly adopted, without a vote, a compromise resolution condemning "acts of aggression" against Nicaragua while at the same time encouraging "democratic, representative, and pluralistic systems" in the area.

Grenada. On October 28, three days after the United States and several Caribbean nations invaded Grenada, the Security Council voted on a resolution deploring the invasion as a

419

"flagrant violation of international law" and calling for the immediate withdrawal of all foreign troops from the country. The tally was 11 to 1 in favor, the one negative vote, a veto, being cast by the United States; Britain, Togo, and Zaire abstained. A virtually identical resolution was adopted by the General Assembly on November 2, by a large margin.

Cyprus. A General Assembly resolution adopted on May 13 called for the withdrawal of occupation troops from Cyprus, which since 1974 had been split into self-governing Turkish and Greek sectors, with a large number of Turkish troops stationed in the northern, Turkish Cypriot zone. Intermittent UN-sponsored talks had been held between the Turkish and Greek communities for years, with the aim of resolving their differences. But on November 15 the Turkish Cypriots proclaimed the establishment of an independent Turkish Republic of Northern Cyprus. The Security Council voted, 13–1, to reject the declaration as "legally invalid."

South West Africa (Namibia). The familiar pattern of raised hopes followed by stalemate continued to characterize the UN-sponsored negotiations for Namibian independence. There was little progress toward fulfillment of the 1978 plan for a cease-fire, elections, and independence monitored by the UN. In late January, South Africa dissolved the territory's National Assembly, resumed direct rule, and began again the task of creating an indigenous interim government.

South Africa also endorsed the U.S. proposal that Cuban troops in neighboring Angola be withdrawn as a precondition for the implementation of the UN plan. Angola and other neighboring African states strongly protested the linkage of the two issues, although Angola predicted that Cuban troops would no longer be needed once its territory ceased to be a target for South African attacks against bases of the South West Africa People's Organization, fighting for the independence of Namibia.

On May 31 the Council resolved unanimously to call on the secretary-general to confer with South Africa and Swapo on implementing the UN plan and to report back by August 31. At that time, Secretary-General Javier Pérez de Cuéllar announced progress on procedural issues, such as the composition of the proposed UN force and the selection of a voting system for the proposed constituent assembly, leaving only the date of a cease-fire to be agreed. This final step, he said, had been impeded by South African insistence that Cuban troops pull out of Angola.

Chad. In March the Security Council considered Chad's charge of Libyan aggression and occupation of the Aozou sector of northern Chad. Libya, with Soviet backing, had been actively assisting rebel leader Goukouni Oueddei, while itself claiming Aozou as a part of Libya. The Council asked Chad and Libya to settle their dispute through the Organization of African Unity, but no progress was reported in that effort. Despite a renewal of the fighting in August, when France sent troops and the United States sent matériel in support of the Hissène Habré government, the Council was not able to reach any agreement on a resolution.

Unctad and Unesco. At a meeting of the UN Conference on Trade and Development (Unctad), held in Belgrade in June and July, the Group of 77 (actually a group of more than 120 states seeking reforms to aid the Third World) proposed a commodity price support program, easier debt repayment terms, reduced trade barriers, and more development aid. These measures were rejected by the major industrialized countries as being costly and unnecessary.

In November, a 161-nation Unesco conference, meeting in Paris, authorized a two-year study to analyze news organizations' impact on developing countries. The compromise move sidestepped Third World demands for a world journalism policy that Western nations said could lead to a restrictive international code for journalists. In late December, nevertheless, the United States formally announced its intention to withdraw from Unesco, effective January 1, 1985. The decision was based on what the U.S. government perceived as a hostile attitude toward the West, wasteful spending habits, and a desire to restrict press freedom. The United States said it might reconsider if Unesco modified its policies.

New member. On September 23, the newly independent nation of St. Christopher and Nevis (St. Kitts–Nevis) became the UN's 158th member.   I.C.B.

United States of America

In 1983, the United States appeared to be making a solid recovery from the economic recession that began in 1981. The administration of President Ronald Reagan faced a deteriorating situation in the Middle East and worsening relations with the Soviet Union but won favor at home for the U.S.-led invasion of Grenada.

The signs of economic recovery in the United States included declining unemployment, solid increases in gross national product, and an apparent growth in consumer confidence. Despite conflicts in Congress over the budget and other matters, the Reagan administration was able to work out compromises on some key issues and appeared to be benefiting politically from the nation's ongoing economic revival.

In a surprise development on October 25, the United States led an invasion of the Caribbean island of Grenada that quickly toppled the nation's Marxist government—and won approval from many Americans. In other areas of the world, the United States faced challenges and crises that were more difficult to deal with. The deteriorating situation in Lebanon was symbolized dramatically in the bombing of a U.S. Marine facility in Beirut on October 23. Relations with the Soviet Union worsened after the Soviet downing of a South Korean commercial airliner in September. U.S.-Soviet negotiations on limitation of medium-range missiles made no progress, and late in the year, the United States began deploying such missiles in Western Europe.

DOMESTIC AFFAIRS

The Reagan administration generally steered clear of the great debates on economic and social policy that characterized its first two years in power. Widespread recovery from the recession was under way, although the federal budget deficit escalated to the $200 billion range. After scandals erupted over environmental policy and the officials that had been chosen to carry it out, new administrators were appointed. Tops on Congress's limited list of accomplishments was a bipartisan measure aimed at shoring up the social security system. In the business world, perhaps the event that promised most to affect the public at large was the breakup of the American Telephone & Telegraph Company (AT&T).

The economy. The economic signs were good during 1983. By November the civilian unemployment rate had dropped to 8.4 percent, its lowest level in two years. During the first ten months of the year the government's index of leading economic indicators rose uninterruptedly (a slight decline was reported for November). Consumer prices moved upward by a modest 3.8 percent for the year. On the New York Stock Exchange, the Dow Jones Industrial Average crashed through the 1200 mark and reached a record high of 1287.20 on November 29. Consumer confidence grew, and by midyear consumer debt was expanding rapidly. Automobile sales surged in the latter part of the year, and despite adverse weather conditions throughout the country, the major chain stores reported that the traditional holiday buying spree was among the most robust of recent years.

The recovery was not universal, however. Layoffs in the mining industry drove West Virginia's jobless rate in February to 21 percent—the highest for any state since the federal government began collecting such totals in the late 1960's. Also slow to rebound was the steel industry, which by the end of the year was operating at only about 60 percent of capacity. Farmers suffered from a blistering summer drought that cut the corn crop in half and sharply reduced yields of many other crops.

Noting that he didn't expect other people to do anything he wouldn't do himself, Agriculture Secretary John R. Block, with his wife, daughter, and the daughter's friend, spent a week this summer living within his department's $58 maximum food stamp allowance for a family of four. Here, the Blocks, who are millionaires, make some basic purchases at a supermarket.

Budget. President Reagan's budget proposal for the 1984 fiscal year (beginning October 1, 1983), submitted to Congress in January, called for spending of $848.5 billion, with a projected deficit of $188.8 billion. After much wrangling, Congress on June 23 set a spending ceiling somewhat higher than the president's with a slower rise in military outlays but more generous funding for social programs.

Fearful of astronomical deficits, Congress in its budget resolution called for $73 billion in additional taxes over the fiscal years 1984–1986. This move was opposed by the Reagan administration, which in the end got most of what it wanted. The third phase of the administration-sponsored 1981 tax cut went into effect on July 1, as scheduled, and no tax increases were enacted.

The administration blamed excessive social spending for the deficits, while its critics pointed to rising military costs. The military spending bill approved by Congress in November amounted to $249.6 billion, not quite 30 percent of the budget total. Also in November,

Congress raised the federal debt ceiling to $1,490 billion, enough to keep the Treasury solvent through April 1984. The new ceiling was triple that of a decade ago. *See also* CONGRESS OF THE UNITED STATES.

Breakups and shakeups. The face of American business changed significantly in 1983. As the air transportation industry continued to reel under the impact of deregulation, Continental Air Lines filed for reorganization under the bankruptcy laws in September, and Eastern Airlines also claimed to be close to insolvency. In the brutally competitive small-computer field, the Osborne Computer Corporation went under, Texas Instruments abandoned its low-priced line, and several other manufacturers swallowed big losses. Meanwhile, the giant of the computer industry, IBM, made an increasing dent in the small-computer market with its Personal Computer (or PC), primarily for business use, and late in the year unveiled its lowest-priced model, the PCjr, intended largely for home use. Another corporate success story was Chrysler, which during the summer repaid the last of $1.2 billion in loans guaranteed by the federal government in 1980.

The year's major corporate transformation involved the American Telephone and Telegraph Company. The $155 billion company, whose 70 million subscribers accounted for about 80 percent of the U.S. telephone service, was to dissolve on January 1, 1984. In its stead there was to be a leaner AT&T, specializing in long-distance telephone service and high technology, plus seven regional telephone holding companies, entrusted with local telephone service. The effect of the breakup on the quality and cost of telephone service remained to be seen. See also ECONOMY AND BUSINESS.

Environment. The U.S. Environmental Protection Agency was a trouble spot for the administration throughout 1983. The investigations of the EPA by Congress and the press revealed a pattern of mismanagement, political favoritism, and demoralization at the agency. The administrator of the toxic waste cleanup program, Rita M. Lavelle, was dismissed, and on December 1 she was found guilty in federal court of perjury and impeding a congressional investigation. Ultimately, more than 20 high officials of the EPA resigned, including chief administrator Anne Burford, who was replaced by William D. Ruckelshaus, a veteran public servant with a reputation for integrity. Meanwhile, Times Beach, Mo. a suburb of St. Louis, was in the news early in the year because of high levels of dioxin contamination there. In February the federal government offered to buy out all homes and businesses in the town.

Environmentalists had continually criticized Secretary of the Interior James G. Watt, but it was his loose talk about affirmative action that finally brought about his downfall in October. After Watt jocularly described an Interior Department advisory panel as ideally balanced because it included "a black, a woman, two Jews, and a cripple," bipartisan outrage in Congress led to his resignation. In a move that surprised many observers, President Reagan named National Security Adviser William P. Clark, a personal friend, to replace Watt. See also ENVIRONMENT.

Women and minorities. The same year that brought The Right Stuff, an epic film about the first American astronauts—all male, all white—

also saw the nation's first female and black astronauts launched into space. In June, Sally K. Ride, a physicist, flew as mission specialist on board the space shuttle Challenger, and in late August and early September, Challenger carried Air Force Lieutenant Colonel Guion S. Bluford, Jr., a black aerospace engineer, into space.

Chicago and Philadelphia elected their first black mayors—Harold Washington and W. Wilson Goode, respectively—and Martha Layne Collins won the Kentucky gubernatorial race, to become the nation's only woman governor. In January, President Reagan named two women to his cabinet: presidential assistant Elizabeth Dole, as secretary of transportation, and former Representative Margaret M. Heckler (R, Mass.) as head of the Department of Health and Human Services.

On August 27, a crowd of some 300,000 gathered in Washington, D.C., to commemorate the 20th anniversary of the 1963 march on Washington led by the late Reverend Martin Luther King, Jr. The civil rights leader, who was slain in Memphis in 1968, was also honored by the establishment of his birthday as a federal holiday, to be celebrated on the third Monday in January, beginning in 1986. See also CIVIL LIBERTIES AND CIVIL RIGHTS; NEGROES IN THE UNITED STATES; WOMEN.

Social security. The bipartisan National Commission on Social Security recommended, Congress enacted, and President Reagan signed into law a complex financial package designed to rescue the system from the threat of bankruptcy. The reforms, which were expected to yield nearly $170 billion in revenues and savings between 1983 and 1989, involved increases in social security taxes, postponement of cost-of-living adjustments, inclusion in the system of new federal employees, and taxing of benefits to higher-income recipients. Next on the reform agenda was the medicare system, whose Hospital Insurance Trust Fund was believed headed for bankruptcy. See also SOCIAL SECURITY. G.M.H.

FOREIGN AFFAIRS

The two most dramatic developments in U.S. foreign affairs came only two days apart in October: a devastating terrorist bombing in Lebanon and a U.S.-led invasion of the tiny island of Grenada. In Washington, for much of the year William P. Clark, the president's national security adviser, exercised a strong influence over administration policy decisions, in some respects eclipsing the influence of Secretary of State George P. Shultz (see biographies in PEOPLE IN THE NEWS). In October, however, President Reagan named Clark to succeed James Watt as secretary of the interior. Robert C. McFarlane, the former U.S. special envoy in the Middle East, was named national security adviser.

Beirut bombing. Shortly after dawn on October 23, a truck full of explosives was driven through barricades at the headquarters of the U.S. Marine peacekeeping force at the Beirut airport and detonated, destroying the building and killing over 240 U.S. troops. For the American military, it was the single bloodiest day since the Vietnam war. The White House suspected a pro-Iranian Shiite Muslim group of the attack, and Defense Secretary Caspar W. Weinberger later said it had been carried out with the "sponsorship and knowledge and authority of the Syrian government." A Pentagon report released in December criticized U.S. security measures and also questioned the wisdom of stationing U.S. Marines in Lebanon as a means of achieving U.S. policy goals.

Grenada invasion. On October 25, a strike force of 1,900 U.S. Marines and Army Rangers spearheaded an invasion of the Caribbean island of Grenada. The invasion came shortly after the overthrow and killing of Prime Minister Maurice Bishop, following a power struggle in the Marxist ruling party. U.S. forces, ultimately including several thousand troops, were accompanied by some 300 troops from seven Caribbean nations.

Initially the administration stressed that the major goal of the operation was to rescue the approximately 1,000 U.S. citizens on Grenada in order to prevent "another hostage crisis." Within a few days, however, administration spokesmen were stressing a restoration of democratic government on Grenada and presenting evidence that they said demonstrated that the island was being developed as a base for Cuba and the Soviet Union. Except for its Caribbean allies, the United States found itself virtually isolated in world opinion after the invasion.

Only a U.S. veto prevented the UN Security Council from condemning the invasion. At home, however, public opinion, at least in the short run, was generally favorable, as was the reported reaction of the islanders.

Central America. The invasion of Grenada was the culmination of deepening U.S. involvement in the politics of the Caribbean Basin. On April 27, President Reagan addressed a joint session of Congress and urged legislators to support his earlier requests for $110 million in supplemental military aid for El Salvador in 1983 as part of an overall $298 million aid package for the Central American region. On May 25, one of the U.S. advisers in El Salvador, Lieutenant Commander Albert A. Schaufelberger III, who was deputy commander of the U.S. Military Group in that country, became the first U.S. military casualty there when he was shot and killed on a San Salvador street. Two days later the administration announced that it was replacing Thomas O. Enders, the assistant secretary of state for inter-American affairs, and Deane Hinton, the U.S. ambassador to El Salvador. The administration apparently felt it needed more forceful defenders of its policies. On June 14, 100 members of the U.S. Special Forces (the Green Berets) arrived in Honduras to train Salvadoran troops. In Nicaragua, the United States insisted that its support for opponents of the leftist Sandinista regime, the "contras," was based on their ability to block the alleged supply of arms from Nicaragua to the insurgents in El Salvador. The contras declared openly, however, that their aim was to overthrow the Sandinistas.

As opposition to the president's Central American policies mounted, Congress approved only $55 million in supplementary military aid to El Salvador, half of what the administration had requested. To conciliate his opponents, the president announced in July that he would establish a bipartisan commission to make long-term recommendations for U.S. policy in Central America. Former Secretary of State Henry A. Kissinger was named to head the group, which toured the region in October. In November, Reagan won congressional approval for part of requested funding for the new fiscal year for military aid to El Salvador and covert aid to Nicaraguan rebels.

Members of the president's bipartisan commission on Central America, headed by former Secretary of State Henry Kissinger, listen to President Ricardo de la Espriella of Panama, in Panama City during a six-nation fact-finding tour in October.

Lebanon. U.S. diplomacy concentrated on securing the removal of all foreign forces from Lebanon (those of Israel, Syria, and the Palestine Liberation Organization) and on aiding the Lebanese government in reconstructing and reunifying the war-shattered country. To help achieve the latter goals, the United States contributed over 1,000 U.S. Marines to a multinational peacekeeping force in Beirut. Even before the October 23 bombing, however, U.S. efforts had suffered repeated setbacks, including an April 18 car bomb explosion that destroyed the U.S. embassy in Beirut, killing 63 people, including 17 Americans. Although an Israeli-Lebanese agreement on troop withdrawals was negotiated, with the help of U.S. mediation, the withdrawal of Israeli troops under its terms was contingent on pullouts by

the PLO and Syria, neither of which was willing to leave.

As fighting intensified in late summer, four U.S. Marines were killed, and President Reagan ordered more U.S. forces to the area. Senate Democrats, meeting in a party caucus in mid-September, voted unanimously to introduce a resolution stating that the Marines in Lebanon were involved in "hostilities," thus making it necessary under the War Powers Act for the president to seek congressional approval to keep them there. Under a compromise plan, which Congress passed in late September, the War Powers Act was declared to be in effect in Lebanon and Marines were authorized to remain there for another 18 months.

In part as a result of U.S. mediation, a cease-fire in the factional fighting went into effect on

September 26. It later broke down, however, and even before that, sniping attacks on the Marines in Beirut continued. In early December, U.S. reconnaissance jets flying over Syrian positions were fired upon; in retaliation, 28 U.S. carrier-based planes bombed Syrian antiaircraft positions. Two of the planes were shot down; one U.S. airman was killed and another captured (he was released in early 1984, after the Reverend Jesse Jackson visited Syria and met with President Hafez al-Assad). On the same day as the U.S. raid, eight Marines were killed in an artillery attack, and later in December, U.S. warships shelled Syrian positions in Lebanon in response to further Syrian attacks on U.S. reconnaissance planes.

Israel. Through most of 1983, U.S.-Israeli relations seemed much improved, although the government of Prime Minister Menachem Begin continued to reject key aspects of Reagan's overall plan for peace in the Mideast. On September 15, Begin resigned from office. His successor, Foreign Minister Yitzhak Shamir, traveled to Washington in late November for a three-day visit that produced a wide-ranging agreement to strengthen U.S.-Israeli strategic cooperation in the face of the Lebanon crisis.

Arms control. The central issue in U.S.-Soviet arms control negotiations was NATO's planned deployment of 108 U.S. Pershing II missiles and 464 U.S. Tomahawk cruise missiles in Western Europe to counter hundreds of Soviet medium-range missiles already in Europe. The Reagan administration had originally proposed abandoning these deployment plans in return for a Soviet decision to dismantle all its me-

In the course of a three-day visit to Japan, President Ronald Reagan and his wife Nancy shared a traditional tea ceremony with Prime Minister Yasuhiro Nakasone and his wife at their country home.

dium-range missiles in Europe—the "zero option." The Soviets were willing to reduce their missiles to 162—the same number already deployed by France and Britain (although the Soviet weapons would have more warheads). During 1983, both sides modified their positions. In mid-November, the United States, elaborating on an interim reduction plan proposed early in the year, offered to deploy only 420 missile warheads in Europe if the Soviet Union cut its arsenal in Europe and Asia to the same number of warheads. The Soviet Union was willing to reduce its three-warhead missiles aimed at Western Europe to about 140, if the United States agreed to drop its deployment plans. No agreement was reached on any of these proposals, and on November 23 the Soviet Union withdrew from talks on limiting medium-range missiles just as the first Pershing missiles arrived in West Germany in preparation for deployment. The first cruise missiles had arrived in Britain earlier in the month.

In separate talks on strategic arms limitation, the Reagan administration softened its earlier positions and proposed that the Soviets keep more of their large, accurate land-based intercontinental ballistic missiles than originally discussed. Despite some concessions on both sides, however, no agreements were reached, and the talks recessed on December 8 with no date set for resumption.

Soviet Union. In March the president caused a flap both at home and abroad by his description of the Soviet Union as "an evil empire." U.S.-Soviet relations seemed to take a modest upturn for a time in the summer. The two countries agreed in July on a final text to conclude the Madrid review conference of the 1975 Helsinki accord on European security and human rights. In August the United States and the Soviet Union also signed a five-year grain agreement. However, relations worsened drastically on September 1 with the news that a Soviet jet fighter had shot down a Korean Air Lines 747 that had strayed over Soviet airspace on a flight from New York to Seoul. All 269 passengers and crew were killed. After denying it at first, Moscow eventually admitted shooting down the plane, but it refused to offer any apology or compensation, claiming that the airliner was on an intelligence-gathering mission. The Reagan administration responded by closing the American offices of Aeroflot, the Soviet airline, and suspending negotiations on scientific, cultural, and consular agreements with Moscow. The United States also sponsored a UN Security Council resolution—which was vetoed by the Soviets—deploring the incident and inviting the UN secretary-general to conduct a full investigation.

Asia. Japanese Prime Minister Yasuhiro Nakasone pleased Washington by increasing defense spending by 6.5 percent in 1983 and, on a trip to the United States in January, remarking that Japan "should be like an unsinkable aircraft carrier." In November, Reagan made a trip to Japan and South Korea, seeking to cement ties with both countries.

U.S. relations with China began on a strained basis. On January 13 the United States unilaterally limited the import of Chinese textiles, and China retaliated by banning the purchase of U.S. soybeans, cotton, and synthetic fibers. The dispute was settled on August 19 when the two sides agreed on a new five-year pact that allowed for 3.5 percent annual growth in Chinese textile exports to the United States. The level of U.S. arms sales to Taiwan remained a major irritant in U.S.-Chinese relations.

On June 1 the United States signed an agreement allowing it to continue to use air and naval bases in the Philippines and agreeing to give Manila $900 million in aid over the next five years. The future of U.S.-Philippine relations was thrown into question, however, when Filipino opposition leader Benigno Aquino, Jr., was shot to death on August 21 at Manila International Airport as he returned from three years of self-imposed exile in the United States. The incident occurred while Aquino was in the custody of security guards, who immediately gunned down the man they claimed had shot Aquino.   C.A.K.

UPPER VOLTA. See STATISTICS OF THE WORLD. See also AFRICA.

URUGUAY. The timetable according to which Uruguay's armed forces are to leave government by March 1985 was seriously endangered in 1983 by a breakdown of negotiations on a new constitution between civilian political leaders and representatives of the military, which has ruled Uruguay since 1973. The talks were interrupted July 5 after seven meetings, with neither side willing to yield on basic—and emotional—issues. Throughout the talks, arrests of student and labor activists, as well as harassment of politicians and newspapers unfriendly to the government, continued.

In the aftermath of the breakdown, the political parties sought to apply pressure on the authorities by organizing a series of peaceful protests. In late October, the government announced it was prepared to hold elections and stage a plebiscite on a draft constitution even if no agreement was reached with the political leaders. Meanwhile, there were a series of large protest demonstrations against military rule.

The economy continued to decline during 1983, after a 10 percent drop in the real gross domestic product in 1982. However, the recession—the most severe in decades—appeared to have bottomed out in March. The further reduction in economic activity in 1983 was the result of a stabilization program required by the International Monetary Fund. Financial assistance from the IMF had been sought in 1982 but was not granted until April 1983, after Uruguay had devalued the peso. The cost of living, which had practically stabilized by November 1982, went up sharply in 1983, with inflation nearly 50 percent by August.

See STATISTICS OF THE WORLD.   A.P.

UTAH. *See* STATISTICS OF THE WORLD.

VANUATU. *See* STATISTICS OF THE WORLD.

VENEZUELA. Venezuelans elected a new president on December 4, 1983, after a year of economic hardship caused by declining oil revenues.

Jaime Lusinchi of the opposition Democratic Action Party won an easy victory over his main competitor, ex-President Rafael Caldera of the ruling COPEI, a Christian democratic party. The campaign had focused more on personalities than on issues, with both candidates pledging to rejuvenate the ailing economy. However, Caldera was hampered by the unpopularity of the COPEI government of incumbent President Luis Herrera Campíns, who was not eligible for reelection. Lusinchi's party also won a majority of the 300 legislative seats at stake.

Lusinchi faced severe debt repayment problems and promised an austerity program. Lower oil prices reduced petroleum revenue in 1983, and Venezuela had difficulty making payments on its nearly $35 billion in foreign debt. It had unilaterally suspended payments on principal and fallen badly behind on interest payments. Foreign banks refused to reschedule the debt until the country agreed to harsh International Monetary Fund conditions, which neither major party would agree to in an election year.

As a member of the Organization of Petroleum Exporting Countries, Venezuela in March accepted an OPEC-mandated petroleum production cut from 1.8 million to 1.7 million barrels per day. Accompanying price cuts reduced the average price per barrel of Venezuelan petroleum to $24.74, but the government raised the price of heavy and extra heavy crudes by $1.00 and $1.25 respectively, effective October 2.

Venezuela joined with Mexico, Colombia, and Panama to form the Contadora group, aimed at furthering peace efforts in Central America. The group is named for the island off Panama where the foreign ministers of the four countries held their first meeting in January. After a series of meetings at the ministerial level, the four presidents gathered in July at Cancún, Mexico, where they reiterated earlier calls for, among other things, the removal of foreign military bases and advisers from Central America and a halt to arms shipments to the region.

See STATISTICS OF THE WORLD.   L.L.P.

VERMONT. *See* STATISTICS OF THE WORLD.

VIETNAM. The Vietnamese government went ahead in 1983 with its economic liberalization program, which had continued to bring modest improvements since its formal inauguration the year before. Because of fears that the reforms might cause a resurgence of capitalistic activity in the southern half of the country (what had been South Vietnam), however, the government took pains to balance its relaxation of business and social rules in the north with tighter controls in the south. Meanwhile, the government began to resettle Vietnamese citizens—reportedly some 100,000 by October—from the cities to the countryside, in so-called new economic zones.

Vietnam's debts remained high—about $2.3 billion to the Soviet bloc and $1.2 billion to non-Communist countries—while its hard currency reserves totaled barely $15 million. The economic reforms have eased life for the peasants, but civil servants in the cities have suffered from the effect of continued high inflation on fixed salaries.

In February the Vietnamese convened an Indochina summit in Vientiane, Laos, that formalized the relations of Vietnam, Laos, and Cambodia (all firmly under Hanoi's domination) with several agreements for cooperation in economic development, trade, and communications. The meeting capped Vietnam's three-year effort to forge an Indochina grouping to ensure that Cambodia would remain part of a bloc under Hanoi's control. To that end, Vietnam maintained an estimated 50,000 troops in Laos and 150,000 troops in Cambodia. In addition, it reportedly launched a program to settle between 100,000 and 400,000 Vietnamese in the eastern regions of Cambodia, bordering Vietnam.

The Vietnamese army early in the year launched its biggest attacks against Cambodian resistance groups since 1979. During intense fighting in March, Vietnamese troops pursued Cambodians into Thai territory and engaged in sustained combat with Thai forces. Thailand protested to the United Nations and asked the United States to speed up a promised shipment of arms and ammunition (a request with which the Reagan administration quickly complied). When the fighting between the Vietnamese and the Cambodian rebels ended in April, the Vietnamese had sustained thousands of casualties but had prevented the Cambodians from making real progress.

Vietnam's relations with the Soviet Union remained close. The annual economic protocol between the two nations was signed before the deadline, and the Soviet aid level to Vietnam appeared to keep pace with Vietnamese inflation. Generous Soviet military assistance allowed Vietnam to continue its occupation of Cambodia. Relations remained poor, however, between Vietnam and the United States, which maintained its embargo against Vietnam in protest against the Vietnamese occupation of Cambodia.

The Vietnamese served as hosts for a scientific conference held early in the year, on the effects of the herbicide Agent Orange, which the U.S. military used in Vietnam during the 1960's and 1970's as a defoliant. European, American, and Japanese experts joined Vietnamese in Ho Chi Minh City (formerly Saigon) to compare their research. The conference ended without arriving at any clear conclusions on the chemical and its effects. Vietnam veterans in the United States have contended that Agent Orange caused severe physical problems among those who had been exposed to it.

See STATISTICS OF THE WORLD.   E.H.B.

VIRGINIA. *See* STATISTICS OF THE WORLD.

VIRGIN ISLANDS. *See* STATISTICS OF THE WORLD.

WARSAW TREATY ORGANIZATION. *See* COMMUNISM.

WASHINGTON. *See* STATISTICS OF THE WORLD.

WESTERN SAHARA. *See* AFRICA; MOROCCO.

WESTERN SAMOA. *See* STATISTICS OF THE WORLD.

WEST VIRGINIA. *See* STATISTICS OF THE WORLD.

WISCONSIN. *See* STATISTICS OF THE WORLD.

WOMEN. In 1983, proponents of women's rights won important victories in U.S. Supreme Court cases. At the same time, women's groups

Television reporter Christine Craft and her attorney smile after a jury in August awarded her $500,000 in a suit against Metromedia, Inc., her former employer, involving sex discrimination and related charges. Although that award was overturned, she eventually won $325,000 in damages.

remained highly dissatisfied with Reagan administration positions on key issues.

"Gender gap." The year was marked by a growing rift between the Reagan administration and women's organizations, which criticized the administration's positions on abortion and the equal rights amendment, its economic and military policies, and its allegedly poor record on the appointment of women to major posts. Polls continued to show that women were considerably less likely than men to favor President Ronald Reagan and his policies. The so-called gender gap was exacerbated August 8 when the Justice Department, in a brief to the Supreme Court on a case to be considered in the 1983–1984 term, favored limiting federal authority to cut off funds to educational institutions that discriminate against women. A few days earlier, Reagan was criticized for insensitivity, after he told a meeting of the International Federation of Business and Professional Women that "I happen to be one who believes that if it wasn't for women, us men would still be walking around in skin suits carrying clubs."

Later in August, the administration was em-barrassed when Barbara Honegger, a political appointee in the Justice Department, resigned after publication of a newspaper article in which she charged Reagan with deliberate failure to fulfill his promises on women's rights. Administration spokesmen minimized the importance of the resignation, dismissing Honegger as a "low-level Munchkin." The incident ended amid newspaper accounts that had Honnegger saying that she received inspiration from occult powers, but its net effect seemed to be a new setback for Reagan.

Job benefits. In two rulings, the Supreme Court held that company medical plans must cover the pregnancies of employees' wives to the same extent as all other dependents' medical expenses and that employer-sponsored pension plans must give men and women equal benefits. The first ruling helped clarify a 1978 federal law that prohibits sex discrimination in employment "on the basis of pregnancy." The pension decision, which will affect millions of public employees and employees of nonprofit organizations, required that benefits under sex-differentiated annuity plans be equalized for all contributions made after August 1. Previously, nearly all annuities paid out lower monthly benefits to women, on the basis that women tend to live longer than men.

Abortion. On June 15 the Supreme Court reaffirmed, by a 6–3 majority, the constitutional right to obtain an abortion and struck down certain local restrictions on access to abortion. The Court declared unconstitutional an Akron, Ohio, ordinance requiring, among other things, that a 24-hour waiting period be observed before obtaining an abortion and that the doctor tell the patient that the fetus "is a human life from the moment of conception" and warn of possible serious physical and emotional consequences.

Legal equality. The proposed equal rights amendment to the Constitution, which failed to gain ratification by two-thirds of the states by the June 30, 1982, deadline, was reintroduced in Congress in 1983. The new ERA measure, however, failed to gain the two-thirds majority needed for passage in the House in a vote taken on November 15.

Foat and Craft cases. In a case that received wide attention, Ginny Foat, former president of the California branch of the National Organization for Women, was indicted for the 1965 robbery-murder of an Argentine businessman in Louisiana. Foat was accused of the crime by former husband John Sidote, who said he had taken part in the murder. After a brief trial in Gretna, La., Foat was acquitted by a jury in November.

A sex discrimination and fraud suit filed by former KMBC (Kansas City) news anchorwoman Christine Craft against Metromedia, Inc., the station's former owner, also attracted wide attention. Craft charged that Metromedia, despite having hired her as a journalist, had demoted her from her coanchor spot because she was not attractive enough and not sufficiently deferential toward men. In August, a federal jury awarded her $500,000 in damages on the fraud charge and recommended that the U.S. district court rule in her favor on the charge of discrimination. The judge rejected the discrimination charge against Metromedia and ordered a new trial on the issue of fraud. In January 1984, a new jury ruled in her favor, awarding her $325,000 in damages.

Achievements. On June 18, physicist Sally K. Ride became the first American woman to go into space; she and four men formed the crew on a six-day mission by the space shuttle *Challenger.* In the political arena, two women joined the Reagan cabinet: Elizabeth Dole, wife of Senator Robert Dole (R, Kan.), became secretary of transportation in February, and Margaret M. Heckler was sworn in as secretary of health and human services in March. In November, Martha Layne Collins was elected the first woman governor of Kentucky, and two prominent women mayors, Dianne Feinstein of San Francisco and Kathryn Whitmire of Houston, retained their posts.   M.Gr. & D.F.

WYOMING. *See* STATISTICS OF THE WORLD.

Ginny Foat, a former official of the National Organization for Women, arrives at court during her trial for the murder of an Argentine businessman. A jury quickly acquitted her.

Y

YEMEN, PEOPLE'S DEMOCRATIC REPUBLIC OF. The People's Democratic Republic of Yemen (South Yemen) continued diplomatic efforts to end its isolation from its Arab neighbors in 1983. The move was believed to be motivated by a desire to obtain financial assistance from Gulf oil-producing states, especially Saudi Arabia, at a time when Soviet aid was declining and efforts to attract foreign investment were largely unsuccessful. In July, South Yemen exchanged ambassadors with Saudi Arabia for the first time since 1977. South Yemen and Oman held several meetings during the year to discuss border questions, but South Yemeni President Ali Nasser Muhammad was still sharply critical of Omani military cooperation with the United States.

There were also efforts to overcome the continuing friction between South Yemen and the Yemen Arab Republic (North Yemen). Federation of the two Yemens has been a stated goal of the two governments. In May, plans to unify the interior ministries of the two countries were approved, but talks in June on economic affairs and a joint constitution demonstrated the wide ideological gap between them. Marxist South Yemen raised questions about the role of Islam in a unified state and opposed large-scale private ownership of property. President Nasser and North Yemeni President Ali Abdullah Saleh met in August in Sana to discuss coordinated foreign policies, but since South Yemen supported the Soviet bloc and Iran, while North Yemen was nonaligned and backed Iraq in the Gulf war, little immediate progress toward unification was expected.

See STATISTICS OF THE WORLD.   C.H.A.

YEMEN ARAB REPUBLIC. The major concern of the Yemen Arab Republic (North Yemen) in 1983 was rebuilding after the devastating December 1982 earthquake. Reconstruction costs were estimated at more than $2 billion. Aid came from Saudi Arabia, a number of European countries, the United States, and international agencies. By midyear, construction of houses, schools, and clinics in the affected region had begun.

Although President Ali Abdullah Saleh had initially stated that he would not stand for reelection, he was nominated and elected without opposition by the People's Constituent Assembly in late May. Saleh began serving his second five-year term on July 17.

In spite of continuing tension with South Yemen, talks aimed at eventual unification of the two countries were conducted at various levels, including a summit meeting between President Saleh and South Yemeni President Ali Nasser Muhammad in August. No immediate results were expected.

Yemen's economy, battered by the 1982 earthquake, continued to decline. The situation was exacerbated by economic slowdown in the Persian Gulf states. Many of the 1.4 million Yemenis who worked in neighboring oil-producing states returned home, causing a decline in the earnings formerly remitted by Yemeni workers.

The government adopted a number of measures to deal with economic problems, including higher tariffs and currency restrictions. These policies will probably be undermined, however, by smuggling, especially by the well-armed northern tribes, who would resist any government attempt to enforce customs regulations. The only good economic news was a survey by the American Hunt Oil Company indicating commercial quantities of oil in the Marib area.

See STATISTICS OF THE WORLD.   C.H.A.

YUGOSLAVIA. Yugoslavia began the year 1983 on the brink of bankruptcy, with a foreign debt of $20 billion, almost half of which was scheduled to be repaid during the year, and with limited foreign currency reserves. After prolonged negotiations, lenders and the Yugoslav authorities were able to agree on an overall financial aid package, including deferment of debts and extension of new credits and loans, worth about $5 billion.

At home, the government's economic policy decisions were announced at a marathon session of the Federal Assembly, held in Belgrade in early July. Prime Minister Milka Planinc presented a bleak picture of the overall economic situation and called for radical measures. In order to reschedule the foreign debt, she said, the government would have to accept "harsh and difficult" conditions laid down by Western governments and banks. Sacrifices would have to be made by every citizen.

In politics, the name of former President (Josip Broz) Tito, who died in 1980, remained well remembered in Yugoslavian daily life, but without his personal presence and unifying influence the country faced strong difficulty in charting a clear course and dealing with its regional antagonisms.

The situation in the autonomous province of Kosovo appeared outwardly quiet in 1983, despite fears by authorities that ethnic Albanian nationalists were regrouping underground, after a series of arrests in 1982, to prepare for renewed hostile activities. Another center of nationalist discontent was the republic of Bosnia-Hercegovina, inhabited largely by Muslims of Slavic blood. In April security agents in Sarajevo, the republic's capital, arrested 11 people, including two Muslim clergymen, on charges of preaching "Muslim nationalism" and spreading "hostile propaganda."

Such charges, combined with the outbreak of nationalism by ethnic Albanians in Kosovo, caused a reaction among Serbians. Serbian nationalism, first revived mainly in cultural circles, has begun affecting an increasingly large segment of the population.

In foreign policy, Yugoslavia's financial links with the West have apparently not affected its relations with the Soviet Union and China. In late March, Soviet Premier Nikolai Tikhonov visited Belgrade, where he met with Prime Minister Planinc and other Yugoslav leaders. During Tikhonov's visit, Yugoslavia and the Soviet Union signed a trade agreement.

See STATISTICS OF THE WORLD. R.A.P.

YUKON TERRITORY. See STATISTICS OF THE WORLD.

Z

ZAIRE. With its reserves of foreign currency nearly depleted in 1983, Zaire agreed in the fall to meet rigorous International Monetary Fund conditions in order to obtain credits through 1984 to keep the economy afloat. Zaire had in the past chronically failed to make all but token payments on its frequently rescheduled debt—believed to be approaching $6 billion. The government introduced fiscal controls, accepted a devaluation of its currency to only 20 percent of its previous level, and liberalized certain business and banking restrictions in order to bypass the bureaucracy and, in this way, attempt to curb rampant corruption. As a result of austerity measures, food and fuel prices rose.

In May, President Mobuto Sese Seko proclaimed a general amnesty for political dissidents and invited all exiles to return to Zaire before the June 30 anniversary of the country's independence. Only a few exiles availed themselves of this much publicized act of clemency; the amnesty did, however, lead to the release of 13 dissidents and former members of Parliament, who had been sentenced to jail in mid-1982 for attempting to organize the Union for Democracy and Social Progress, an opposition group.

Having restored relations with Israel in 1982, Zaire agreed in January to have some of its key army and navy units "restructured" and retrained by Israeli military personnel. Some units completed their training in time to be dispatched to fight in the civil war in Chad, in response to appeals for help by beleaguered President Hissène Habré. When Mobutu visited the United States in August, President Ronald Reagan praised him for rendering this service in Chad. Relations with Zambia continued to be marred by a succession of border incidents and by rumors that guerrillas hostile to the left-wing government in Angola were being secretly

Skulls of rhinos killed by poachers in Zambia's Luangwa Valley Game Reserve were gathered by Phillip Berry, patrol leader of the game scouts charged with protecting the reserve's 1,000 to 1,500 rhinos. Poachers kill the animals for the foot-long horns that command fabulous prices in the Middle and Far East.

and a new two-year agreement restoring the CSO's exclusive rights to market the diamonds was signed in March. Miba diamonds account for approximately one half of Zaire's output.

See STATISTICS OF THE WORLD.   E.B.

ZAMBIA. In 1983, Zambia faced serious economic problems. Kenneth D. Kaunda, the country's first and only president since its independence in 1964, continued to hold power.

In January seven defendants were convicted of treason growing out of an October 1980 coup attempt. The seven, including a former governor of the Bank of Zambia and a former general manager of the National Building Society, were sentenced to death after a lengthy trial; an eighth received a ten-year prison sentence. The death sentences were appealed to the Supreme Court.

President Kenneth Kaunda announced a cabinet reshuffle in January. He coupled his decision with a request to Zambians to accept drastic reductions in living standards. On October 27, Kaunda was elected to a fifth five-year term as president, winning 93 percent of the vote. (Kaunda's United National Independence Party is the country's only legal political organization.)

In January the Bank of Zambia announced interim proposals for the management of its foreign debt obligations. These were confirmed in a deal with the Club of Paris (composed of major Western governments and institutions, such as the IMF). In return for the spreading of 1983 interest payments over ten years and the suspension of principal payments in early 1983, Zambia agreed to scrap most price controls, devalue the kwacha by 20 percent, and impose on commercial banks credit ceilings which they had to pass along to individual loans and overdrafts. By early May the price of mealie meal (a staple) was up by 30 percent and fertilizer by 60 percent.

By February, copper prices had jumped to their highest level in three years on the London Metal Exchange. The price increase, plus increased production of copper, from 614,000 tons in 1982 to about 627,000 in 1983, was expected to ease Zambia's foreign exchange pinch.

See STATISTICS OF THE WORLD.   K.W.G.

reorganized on Zairean soil. Zaire's continuing economic ties with South Africa were also criticized by other African nations.

With declining copper prices, resources for investment and maintenance were scarce; as a result, it was expected that copper production might show significant declines from 1982's 500,000 tons. Cobalt prices remained deeply depressed and production was down. As a result of the continuing closure of the Benguela railroad, manganese ores accumulated at the Kisenge mine, where production was reduced to an absolute minimum. Zaire's attempt to dispense with the services of De Beers' Central Selling Organization (CSO) for the marketing of its Miba diamonds proved unsatisfactory,

ZIMBABWE. Prime Minister Robert Mugabe's government was troubled by continuing civil unrest in 1983. The principal dissidents were identified with opposition leader Joshua Nkomo's Zimbabwe African People's Union (Patriotic Front) and with the Ndebele population of the western province of Matabeleland. Bands of former Zapu-PF fighters engaged in a wave of robberies, assaults, and abductions.

The government accused South Africa of having trained and aided the Ndebele dissidents and, in January, dispatched the North Korea-trained Fifth Brigade to Matabeleland, where it remained until July. According to some press reports, as many as 500 people may have been killed in the course of the disturbances, but the government repudiated any such figure.

In March, Nkomo, claiming that the government was seeking to destroy Zapu-PF by killing its leaders and supporters, fled Zimbabwe illegally for Great Britain. He returned to Zimbabwe in August and, amid speculation about possible prosecution for his flight, reclaimed his seat in Parliament. Treason charges against six leading Zapu-PF officials were dropped in March, and the next month the officials were acquitted of charges of possessing and caching arms for purposes of a coup. Within minutes of their acquittal, however, they were redetained under the Emergency Powers Act. Among the leaders involved were Dumiso Dabengwa and Lieutenant General Lookout Masuku, the former deputy commander of Nkomo's army. In October and November, Zimbabwe's High Court ordered the release of Dabengwa and one of the detained Zapu-PF members of Parliament.

Six white air force officers were brought to trial in May for allegedly helping three unnamed South Africans blow up 13 Zimbabwean warplanes in July 1982. The officers were acquitted in August, but three were deported and three others held in jail until late December. The government's denial of access to defendants by their lawyers and its detention of acquitted prisoners brought criticism from human rights activists.

On October 31, former Prime Minister Bishop Abel Muzorewa, head of the opposition United African National Council Party, was arrested on suspicion of "clandestine activities." He reportedly went on a week-long hunger strike upon being jailed.

Serious drought caused crop losses estimated as high as $500 million in 1983. The Zimbabwe Development Bank was established in January, and in May, the government took over the business of fuel procurement and storage from a private consortium. Zimbabwe's balance-of-payments deficit, increasing steadily, reached between 10 percent and 12 percent of the GNP, but the government was largely effective in curbing foreign borrowing.

In a drive that began in late October, soldiers and police officers arrested hundreds of women as part of what the government called an antiprostitution campaign. Many observers claimed that the arrests were made at random with no clear criterion for detaining suspects. Those found to be prostitutes were being sent to job training centers for rehabilitation, according to government sources.

See STATISTICS OF THE WORLD.   K.W.G.

Early in the year, opposition leader Joshua Nkomo had his bags packed to leave Zimbabwe for a conference abroad, but the government confiscated his passport. Alleging attempts to kill him, he fled the country secretly, but later returned to reclaim his seat in Parliament.

THE COUNTRIES OF THE WORLD

Nation Capital	Population	Area of Country (sq mi/ sq km)	Type of Government	Heads of State and Government	Currency: Value in U.S. Dollars	GNP (000,000): GNP Per Capita
AFGHANISTAN Kabul	14,200,000 913,164	250,000 647,497	People's republic	President, Revolutionary Council: Babrak Karmal Prime Minister: Soltan Ali Keshtmand	Afghani 0.02	$ NA NA
ALBANIA Tiranë	2,900,000 250,000	11,100 28,748	People's socialist republic	Chairman, Presidium of the People's Assembly: Ramiz Alia Chairman, Council of Ministers (Premier): Adil Çarçani	Lek 0.15	NA NA
ALGERIA Algiers	20,700,000 2,000,000	919,595 2,381,741	Republic	President: Col. Chadli Benjedid Premier: Col. Mohamed Benahmed Abdelghani	Dinar 0.21	42,010 2,140
ANGOLA Luanda	7,600,000 800,000	481,353 1,246,700	People's republic	President: José Eduardo dos Santos	Kwanza 0.03	NA NA
ANTIGUA AND BARBUDA St. John's	74,000 24,000	171 442	Parliamentary state (C)	Governor-General: Sir Wilfred E. Jacobs Prime Minister: Vere C. Bird, Sr.	East Caribbean dollar 0.37	120 1,550
ARGENTINA Buenos Aires	29,100,000 2,908,000	1,068,301 2,766,889	Federal republic	President: Raúl Alfonsín	New peso 0.12	72,120 2,560
AUSTRALIA Canberra	15,276,000 230,800	2,967,907 7,686,848	Federal parliamentary state (C)	Governor-General: Sir Ninian M. Stephen Prime Minister: Robert Hawke	Dollar 0.88	165,460 11,080
AUSTRIA Vienna	7,600,000 1,531,346	32,374 83,849	Federal republic	President: Rudolf Kirchschläger Chancellor: Fred Sinowatz	Schilling 0.06	77,120 10,210
BAHAMAS Nassau	200,000 138,500	5,380 13,935	Parliamentary state (C)	Governor-General: Sir Gerald C. Cash Prime Minister: Lynden O. Pindling	Dollar 1.01	780 3,620
BAHRAIN Manama	400,000 121,986	240 622	Emirate	Emir: Isa bin Sulman al-Khalifah Prime Minister: Khalifah bin Sulman al-Khalifah	Dinar 2.65	3,240 8,960
BANGLADESH Dhaka	96,500,000 3,605,000	55,598 143,998	Republic (C)	President: A. F. M. Ahsanuddin Choudhury Chief Martial Law Administrator: Gen. H. M. Ershad	Taka 0.04	12,840 140
BARBADOS Bridgetown	250,500 7,552	166 431	Parliamentary state (C)	Governor-General: Sir Deighton H. L. Ward Prime Minister: Tom Adams	Dollar 0.50	880 3,500
BELGIUM Brussels	9,900,000 1,000,221	11,781 30,513	Constitutional monarchy	King: Baudouin Prime Minister: Wilfried Martens	Franc 0.02	117,510 11,920

The section on countries presents the latest information available. All monetary figures are expressed in United States dollars. The symbol (C) signifies that the country belongs to the Commonwealth of Nations. NA means that the data were not available. * indicates that the category does not apply to the country under discussion. Footnotes at the end of the section contain more specialized information.

Imports Exports	Revenue Expenditure	Elementary Schools: Teachers Students	Secondary Schools: Teachers Students	Colleges and Universities: Teachers Students
$ 776,000,000 .... $ 373,000,000	667,078,000 667,078,000	32,937 1,006,094	6,114 133,498	818 13,204
246,000,000[1] .... 267,000,000[1]	1,268,000,000 1,260,000,000	25,900 555,910	NA 156,984	907 12,500
10,937,000,000 12,533,000,000	12,557,000,000 9,144,000,000	88,481 3,118,827	37,269 933,335	7,903 68,416
1,001,000,000 1,730,000,000	3,593,000,000 3,593,000,000	25,000 1,388,110	4,393 153,000	333 4,746
NA .... NA	21,154,240 21,154,240	414 10,159	358 6,927	* *
5,396,000,000 7,407,000,000	26,600,000,000 29,400,000,000	200,388 4,035,404	178,681 1,296,839	29,661 413,542
26,576,000,000 22,077,000,000	46,623,000,000 48,343,000,000	91,280 1,688,121	85,340 1,095,610	20,822 323,716
19,495,000,000 15,642,000,000	43,000,000,000 44,500,000,000	27,525 400,397	63,678 739,702	11,792 118,186
4,050,000,000 1,530,000,000	273,600,000 288,200,000	NA 32,854	1,018 .... NA	NA 4,396
4,035,000,000 3,518,000,000	1,270,000,000 1,010,000,000	2,479 48,672	844 21,485	125 1,314
2,334,000,000 768,000,000	1,381,000,000 996,776,000	188,234 8,236,526	111,927 2,362,906	2,364 30,699
515,700,000 251,600,000	239,700,000 263,700,000	1,172 31,147	1,231 28,818	NA 1,140
57,976,000,000[2] .... 52,363,000,000[2]	26,100,000,000 38,000,000,000	46,430 842,117	71,170 811,608	NA 95,246

Nation Capital	Population	Area of Country (sq mi/ sq km)	Type of Government	Heads of State and Government	Currency: Value in U.S. Dollars	GNP (000,000): GNP Per Capita
BELIZE Belmopan	200,000 2,932	8,867 22,965	Parliamentary state (C)	Governor-General: Minita Gordon Prime Minister: George C. Price	Dollar 0.50	$ 160 1,080
BENIN Porto-Novo	3,800,000 104,000	43,484 112,622	People's republic	President: Lt. Col. Ahmed Kérékou	CFA franc[3] 0.0026	1,140 320
BHUTAN Thimphu	1,400,000 16,500	18,147 47,000	Monarchy	King: Jigme Singye Wangchuk	Ngultrum 0.10	110 80
BOLIVIA Sucre La Paz	5,900,000 80,000 881,400	424,164 1,098,581	Republic	President: Hernán Siles Zuazo	Peso 0.02	3,440 600
BOTSWANA Gaborone	900,000 59,700	231,805 600,372	Republic (C)	President: Quett K. J. Masire	Pula 0.94	940 1,010
BRAZIL Brasilia	131,300,000 411,305	3,286,487 8,511,965	Federal republic	President: Gen. João Baptista de Oliveira Figueiredo	Cruzeiro 0.0021	267,730 2,220
BULGARIA Sofia	8,900,000 1,139,000	42,823 110,912	People's republic	Chairman, Council of State: Todor Zhivkov Chairman, Council of Ministers (Premier): Grisha Filipov	Lev 1.034	NA NA
BURMA Rangoon	37,900,000 3,186,886	261,218 676,552	Socialist republic	President: U San Yu Prime Minister: U Maung Maung Kha	Kyat 0.13	6,540 190
BURUNDI Bujumbura	4,500,000 146,000	10,747 27,834	Republic	President: Col. Jean-Baptiste Bagaza	Franc 0.011	990 230
CAMBODIA (PEOPLE'S REPUBLIC OF KAMPUCHEA) Phnom Penh	6,000,000 400,000	69,898 181,035	People's republic	President, Council of State: Heng Samrin Chairman, Council of Ministers (Premier): Chan Sy	New riel NA	NA NA
CAMEROON Yaoundé	9,100,000 430,000	183,569 475,442	Republic	President and Prime Minister: Paul Biya	CFA franc[3] 0.0026	7,630 880
CANADA Ottawa	24,900,000 295,163	3,851,809 9,976,139	Federal parliamentary state (C)	Governor-General: Edward R. Schreyer Prime Minister: Pierre Elliott Trudeau	Dollar 0.815	276,220 11,400
CAPE VERDE Praia	400,000 21,494	1,557 4,033	Republic	President: Aristides M. Pereira Premier: Cmdt. Pedro Rodrigues Pires	Escudo 0.014	100 340
CENTRAL AFRICAN REPUBLIC Bangui	2,500,000 200,000	240,535 622,984	Republic	Head of State and Chairman, Military Committee for National Recovery (President): Gen. André Kolingba	CFA franc[3] 0.0026	770 320
CHAD N'Djamena	4,700,000 303,000	495,755 1,284,000	Republic	President: Hissène Habré	CFA franc[3] 0.0026	490 110
CHILE Santiago	11,500,000 3,905,000	292,258 756,945	Republic	President: Gen. Augusto Pinochet Ugarte	Peso 0.013	28,890 2,560
CHINA, PEOPLE'S REPUBLIC OF Peking (Beijing)	1,023,300,000 5,600,000	3,705,406 9,596,961	People's republic	Chairman, Standing Committee of the National People's Congress: Marshal Ye Jianying (Yeh Chian-ying) Premier: Zhao Ziyang (Chao Chi-yang)	Yuan 0.50	299,770 300
COLOMBIA Bogotá	27,700,000 4,300,000	439,737 1,138,914	Republic	President: Belisario Betancur Cuartas	Peso 0.013	36,390 1,380
COMOROS Moroni	400,000 19,800	838 2,171	Federal islamic republic	President: Ahmed Abdallah Abderemane Premier: Ali Mroudjae	CFA franc[3] 0.0026	110 320

Imports Exports	Revenue Expenditure	Elementary Schools: Teachers Students	Secondary Schools: Teachers Students	Colleges and Universities: Teachers Students
$ 134,000,000.............$ 85,000,000	40,300,000............. 44,500,000	1,310............. 35,628	470............. 6,131	20 580
889,000,000............. 34,000,000	125,690,000............. 125,690,000	7,994............. 379,926	1,215............. 64,275	234 2,704
NA............. NA	13,473,000............. 22,355,000	897............. 22,648	NA............. 1,733	15 180
598,000,000............. 732,000,000	281,480,000............. 612,900,000	48,894............. 978,250	7,143............. 130,029	NA 41,408
NA............. NA	387,600,000............. 384,700,000	5,316............. 171,914	1,137............. 20,969	90 1,052
21,069,000,000............. 20,168,000,000	25,700,000,000............. 25,700,000,000	863,335............. 22,025,449	180,782............. 2,537,949	104,231 1,225,557
2,281,000,000[1]............. 1,969,000,000[1]	15,000,000,000............. 14,980,000,000	51,581............. 994,018	25,666............. 314,753	12,503 89,083
863,000,000............. 390,000,000	3,144,000,000............. 3,412,000,000	68,251............. 3,711,464	23,853............. 885,621	2,260 27,830
214,000,000............. 88,000,000	167,400,000............. 234,000,000	4,623............. 159,729	919............. 14,891	231 1,784
62,000,000............. 40,000,000	NA............. NA	12,000............. 1,328,033	NA............. NA	NA NA
1,846,000,000............. 1,721,000,000	1,090,000,000............. 1,050,000,000	25,289............. 1,302,974	8,374............. 212,860	439 11,901
58,164,000,000............. 71,130,000,000	44,950,000,000............. 64,796,000,000	119,200............. 2,205,865	139,100............. NA	32,953 601,225
70,000,000............. 3,000,000	28,097,900............. 24,203,800	1,436............. 50,661	293............. 8,716	* *
91,000,000............. 106,000,000	101,980,000............. 129,890,000	3,690............. 238,605	462............. 46,084	405 7,547
132,000,000............. 101,000,000	44,828,000............. 44,828,000	2,610............. 210,882	NA............. 19,580	62 758
3,536,000,000............. 3,836,000,000	9,040,000,000............. 7,670,000,000	66,354............. 2,235,861	27,207............. 536,428	11,419 149,647
18,694,000,000............. 21,632,000,000	59,500,000,000............. 61,100,000,000	5,499,400............. 146,270,000	3,171,500............. 56,777,800	236,637 1,019,950
5,350,000,000............. 2,992,000,000	4,240,000,000............. 4,510,000,000	136,381............. 4,168,200	88,905............. 1,811,003	26,600 269,183
NA............. NA	6,270,000............. 10,590,000	1,292............. 59,709	449............. 13,798	* *

Nation Capital	Population	Area of Country (sq mi/ sq km)	Type of Government	Heads of State and Government	Currency: Value in U.S. Dollars	GNP (000,000): GNP Per Capita
CONGO .... Brazzaville	1,700,000.... 400,000	132,047.... 342,000	People's republic	President: .... Col. Denis Sassou-Nguesso Premier: Col. Louis Sylvain Goma	CFA franc[3] 0.0026	$ 7,840 1,110
COSTA RICA .... San José	2,400,000.... 265,445	19,575.... 50,700	Republic	President .... Luis Alberto Monge Alvarez	Colón 0.03	3,340 1,430
CUBA .... Havana	9,800,000.... 2,003,587	44,218.... 114,524	Socialist republic	President of the .... Councils of State and Ministers: Fidel Castro Ruz	Peso 1.17	NA NA
CYPRUS .... Nicosia	700,000.... 161,000[5]	3,572.... 9,251	Republic (C)	President: .... Spyros Kyprianou	Pound 1.96	2,330 3,740
CZECHOSLOVAKIA ... Prague	15,400,000.... 1,185,958	49,370.... 127,869	Federal socialist republic	President: .... Gustáv Husák Premier: Lubomir Štrougal	Koruna 0.16	NA NA
DENMARK[8] Copenhagen	5,200,000.... 645,198	16,629.... 43,069	Constitutional monarchy	Queen: .... Margrethe II Prime Minister: Poul Schlüter	Krone 0.11	67,190 13,120
DJIBOUTI .... Djibouti	300,000.... 175,000	8,494.... 22,000	Republic	President: .... Hassan Gouled Aptidon Premier: Barkad Gourad Hamadou	Djibouti .... franc 0.0056	180 480
DOMINICA .... Roseau	74,089.... 16,800	290.... 751	Republic (C)	President: .... Aurelius Marie Prime Minister: (Mary) Eugenia Charles	East ..... Caribbean dollar 0.37	60 750
DOMINICAN REPUBLIC Santo Domingo	6,200,000.... 1,300,000	18,816.... 48,734	Republic	President: .... Salvador Jorge Blanco	Peso 1.00	7,070 1,260
ECUADOR .... Quito	8,800,000.... 700,000	109,483.... 283,561	Republic	President: .... Osvaldo Hurtado Larrea	Suore 0.0124	10,120 1,180
EGYPT .... Cairo	45,900,000.... 5,084,463	386,661.... 1,001,449	Republic	President: .... Hosni Mubarak Prime Minister: Ahmed Fuad Mohieddin	Pound 1.209	28,160 650
EL SALVADOR .... San Salvador	4,700,000.... 800,000	8,124.... 21,041	Republic	President: .... Alvaro Alfredo Magaña	Colón 0.40	3,040 650
EQUATORIAL GUINEA Malabo	300,000.... 23,000	10,831.... 28,051	Republic	President, Supreme Military ...... Council: Lt. Col. Teodoro Obiang Nguema Mbasogo	Ekuele 0.004	60 180
ETHIOPIA .... Addis Ababa	31,300,000.... 1,125,340	471,778.... 1,221,900	Socialist state	Head of State, Chairman .... of the Provisional Military Administrative Council, and Chairman of the Council of Ministers: Lt. Col. Mengistu Haile Mariam	Birr 0.49	4,530 140
FIJI .... Suva	700,000.... 68,178	7,056.... 18,274	Parliamentary state (C)	Governor-General: .... Ratu Sir George K. Cakobau Prime Minister: Ratu Sir Kamisese Mara	Dollar 0.97	1,290 2,000
FINLAND .... Helsinki	4,800,000.... 483,051	130,129.... 337,032	Republic	President: .... Mauno Koivisto Prime Minister: Kalevi Sorsa	Markka 0.18	51,270 10,680
FRANCE .... Paris	54,600,000.... 2,317,227	211,208.... 547,026	Republic	President: .... François Mitterrand Premier: Pierre Mauroy	Franc 0.13	657,560 12,190
GABON .... Libreville	700,000.... 250,000	103,347.... 267,667	Republic	President: .... Omar Bongo Premier: Léon Mébiame	CFA franc[3] 0.0026	2,550 3,810

Imports Exports	Revenue Expenditure	Elementary Schools: Teachers Students	Secondary Schools: Teachers Students	Colleges and Universities: Teachers Students
$ 970,000,000	$ 734,536,000	7,186	5,117	681
923,000,000	734,536,000	390,676	187,585	6,848
870,000,000	858,700,000	12,596	7,157	4,382
898,000,000	1,210,000,000	348,674	135,830	50,812
1,415,000,000[1]	13,128,000,000	86,519	42,306	10,736
1,328,000,000[1]	13,124,000,000	1,550,323	554,365	146,240
NA	455,700,000[6]	2,193[7]	2,953[7]	205
NA	616,200,000[6]	48,701[7]	47,599[7]	1,522
3,794,000,000[1]	47,490,000,000	90,380	33,227	22,595
5,176,000,000[1]	47,135,000,000	1,904,476	388,561	179,780
17,304,000,000	24,378,000,000	64,118	NA	6,702
15,638,000,000	34,744,000,000	448,370	365,561	84,895
240,000,000	107,500,000	375	174	NA
25,000,000	161,500,000	16,841	3,812	150
53,146,800	12,010,200	423	299	8
10,089,900	19,758,000	15,220	9,814	514
1,438,000,000	1,233,000,000	17,932	6,702	1,435
809,000,000	1,233,000,000	911,142	178,249	42,412
2,360,000,000	1,420,000,000	39,825	31,489	10,335
2,671,000,000	2,030,000,000	1,427,627	535,445	230,637
9,077,000,000	13,531,000,000	167,821	121,999	21,680
3,120,000,000	19,560,000,000	4,662,816	2,929,168	486,067
929,000,000	436,200,000	17,364	3,080	2,427
879,000,000	677,800,000	834,101	73,030	32,189
42,000,000	26,600,000	630	165	*
26,000,000	148,900,000	35,977	4,523	*
686,000,000	797,100,000	33,329	8,992	662
400,000,000	1,400,000,000	2,130,716	371,301	10,392
509,200,000	301,300,000	4,058	2,053	105
283,600,000	343,200,000	129,298	37,036	1,386
13,388,000,000	12,000,000,000	25,949	33,958	6,041
13,074,000,000	11,900,000,000	373,347	444,165	83,461
115,705,000,000	125,800,000,000	232,405	364,758	40,512
96,688,000,000	131,800,000,000	4,650,954	5,007,508	811,258
934,000,000	1,190,000,000	3,441	1,510	231
1,946,000,000	1,190,000,000	155,081	26,750	3,878

Nation Capital	Population	Area of Country (sq mi/ sq km)	Type of Government	Heads of State and Government	Currency: Value in U.S. Dollars	GNP (000,000): GNP Per Capita
GAMBIA, THE .... Banjul	600,000.... 45,600	4,361.... 11,295	Republic...... (C)	President: .... Sir Dawda K. Jawara	Dalasi ....$ 0.39	220 370
GERMAN............ DEMOCRATIC REPUBLIC East Berlin	16,700,000.... 1,165,677	41,768.... 108,178	Socialist ...... republic	Chairman, Council of State: ...... Erich Honecker Chairman, Council of Ministers (Premier): Willi Stoph	Mark 0.37	NA NA
GERMANY, FEDERAL REPUBLIC OF Bonn	61,500,000.... 289,400	95,976.... 248,577	Federal...... republic	President: .... Karl Carstens Chancellor: Helmut Kohl	Deutsche ..... mark 0.39	829,600 13,450
GHANA .... Accra	13,900,000.... 840,000	92,100.... 238,537	Republic...... (C)	Chairman, Provisional............ National Defense Council: Flight Lt. Jerry J. Rawlings	Cedi 0.36	4,770 400
GREAT BRITAIN[9] ..... London	56,000,000.... 6,690,000	94,227.... 244,046	Limited ...... monarchy (C)	Queen:......................... Elizabeth II Prime Minister: Margaret Thatcher	Pound 1.53	510,310 8,950
GREECE .... Athens	9,900,000.... 885,136	50,944.... 131,944	Republic...... 	President:.................... Constantine Caramanlis Prime Minister: Andreas Papandreou	Drachma 0.01	42,890 4,420
GRENADA .... St. George's	110,394.... 30,813	133.... 344	Parliamentary state (C)	Governor-General:.............. Sir Paul Scoon	East. Caribbean dollar 0.37	100 850
GUATEMALA .... Guatemala City	7,900,000.... 1,000,000	42,042.... 108,889	Republic...... 	President:.................... Oscar Mejía Victores	Quetzal...... 1.00	8,510 1,140
GUINEA............. Conakry	5,400,000.... 763,000	94,926.... 245,857	Republic...... 	President:.................... Sékou Touré Premier: Louis Lansana Béavogui	Syli 0.04	1,660 300
GUINEA-BISSAU...... Bissau	800,000.... 109,486	13,948.... 36,125	Republic...... 	President, Council of............ the Revolution: Cmdr. João Bernardo Vieira Premier: Vítor Saúde Maria	Escudo 0.024	150 190
GUYANA .... Georgetown	800,000.... 187,600	83,000.... 214,969	Republic...... (C)	President:.................... Forbes Burnham Prime Minister: Ptolemy A. Reid	Dollar 0.33	580 720
HAITI .... Port-au-Prince	5,700,000.... 719,671	10,714.... 27,750	Republic...... 	President:.................... Jean-Claude Duvalier	Gourde 0.20	1,510 300
HONDURAS .... Tegucigalpa	4,100,000.... 472,700	43,277.... 112,088	Republic...... 	President:.................... Roberto Suazo Córdova	Lempira 0.50	2,270 600
HUNGARY .... Budapest	10,700,000.... 2,060,644	35,919.... 93,030	People's ...... republic	Chairman, Presidential Council: ... Pál Losonczi Chairman, Council of Ministers (Premier): György Lázár	Forint 0.02	22,550 2,100
ICELAND............. Reykjavik	200,000.... 85,782	39,769.... 103,000	Republic...... 	President:.................... Vigdís Finnbogadóttir Prime Minister: Steingrímur Hermannsson	New króna 0.04	2,970 12,860
INDIA .... New Delhi	730,000,000.... 1,500,000	1,269,345.... 3,287,590	Federal...... republic (C)	President:.................... Zail Singh Prime Minister: Indira Gandhi	Rupee......... 0.10	176,660 260
INDONESIA .... Djakarta	155,600,000.... 6,503,449	782,662.... 2,027,087	Republic...... 	President:.................... Suharto	Rupiah 0.001	78,750 530
IRAN................ Tehran	42,500,000.... 7,000,000	636,296.... 1,648,000	Islamic .... republic	President:.................... Hojatoleslam Sayed Ali Khamenei Prime Minister: Mir Hussein Moussavi	Rial 0.01	NA NA

Imports Exports	Revenue Expenditure	Elementary Schools: Teachers Students	Secondary Schools: Teachers Students	Colleges and Universities: Teachers Students
$ 120,000,000 ....$ 33,000,000	56,340,000 59,930,000	1,808 43,432	620 9,657	* *
3,609,000,000[1] .... 4,630,000,000[1]	78,330,000,000 78,300,000,000	168,849 2,203,991	NA 506,412	28,275 135,666
155,372,000,000 176,432,000,000	91,700,000,000 106,700,000,000	273,556 5,044,424	298,277 4,300,740	113,975 970,284
703,000,000 929,000,000	2,078,000,000 3,610,000,000	48,397 1,294,872	31,812 613,710	963 7,179
99,567,000,000 96,948,000,000	183,733,110,000 185,120,820,000	270,346 5,133,710	274,100 4,574,000	43,017 330,619
10,025,000,000 4,294,000,000	8,500,000,000 11,000,000,000	35,750 922,698	NA 710,169	6,129 83,485
37,900,000 16,700,000	62,530,000 62,530,000	704 23,065	284 6,120	77 614
1,340,000,000 1,245,000,000	749,100,000 1,110,000,000	23,770 803,404	8,604 132,258	2,845 34,301
296,000,000 411,000,000	493,875,000 493,875,000	7,165 257,547	3,700 106,000	650 24,000
60,000,000 10,000,000	21,129,000 34,993,000	3,102 76,709	213 2,153	* *
290,000,000 388,000,000	336,431,000 393,058,000	5,831 159,749	2,513 46,595	332 1,527
525,000,000 380,000,000	176,300,000 366,500,000	13,472 580,127	4,018 91,247	451 3,801
711,000,000 745,000,000	385,100,000 574,800,000	13,305 543,021	4,417 125,018	1,278 21,454
8,333,000,000 8,078,000,000	13,200,000,000 13,600,000,000	75,422 1,162,203	24,235 198,225	10,319 63,732
944,000,000 685,000,000	536,000,000 516,700,000	1,732 25,924	2,387 25,853	527 2,789
16,131,000,000 8,559,000,000	27,854,000,000 29,219,000,000	1,599,182 68,602,224	1,694,651 28,372,339	244,448 5,038,369
15,647,000,000 20,004,000,000	16,600,000,000 18,400,000,000	787,400 25,537,053	261,864 4,364,598	29,128 173,537
11,231,000,000 16,379,000,000	23,895,000,000 38,940,000,000	154,577 5,020,686	96,395 2,356,878	8,184 72,929

Nation Capital	Population	Area of Country (sq mi/ sq km)	Type of Government	Heads of State and Government	Currency: Value in U.S. Dollars	GNP (000,000): GNP Per Capita
IRAQ.............. Baghdad	14,500,000.... 3,300,000	167,925.... 434,924	Republic......	President and Chairman, Revolutionary Command Council: Saddam Hussein al-Takriti	Dinar........ 3.24	$ NA NA
IRELAND,........... **REPUBLIC OF** Dublin	3,500,000.... 543,563	27,136.... 70,283	Republic......	President: .... Patrick J. Hillery Prime Minister: Garret FitzGerald	Pound....... 1.23	17,990 5,230
ISRAEL............. Jerusalem	4,100,000.... 410,000	8,019.... 20,770	Republic......	President: .... Chaim Herzog Prime Minister: Yitzhak Shamir	Shekel....... 0.01	20,420 5,160
ITALY.............. Rome	56,300,000.... 2,828,067	116,304.... 301,225	Republic......	President: .... Alessandro Pertini Prime Minister: Bettino Craxi	Lira....... 0.00067	391,440 6,960
IVORY COAST....... Abidjan	8,900,000.... 1,800,000	124,504.... 322,463	Republic......	President: .... Félix Houphouët-Boigny	CFA franc[3].... 0.0026	10,190 1,200
JAMAICA........... Kingston	2,300,000.... 600,000	4,244.... 10,991	Parliamentary state (C)	Governor-General:.............. Florizel A. Glasspole Prime Minister: Edward P. G. Seaga	Dollar 0.56	2,600 1,180
JAPAN.............. Tokyo	119,200,000.... 8,152,336	143,751.... 372,313	Constitutional monarchy	Emperor:.................. Hirohito Prime Minister: Yasuhiro Nakasone	Yen.......... 0.004	1,186,430 10,080
JORDAN............. Amman	3,600,000.... 1,300,000	37,738.... 97,740	Constitutional monarchy	King:.................. Hussein I Prime Minister: Mudar Badran	Dinar......... 2.77	3,880 1,620
KENYA.............. Nairobi	18,600,000.... 1,100,000	224,961.... 582,646	Republic...... (C)	President: .... Daniel arap Moi	Shilling....... 0.078	7,280 420
KIRIBATI (GILBERT... **ISLANDS)** Tarawa	58,518.... 1,800	332.... 861	Republic...... (C)	President: .... Ieremia T. Tabai	Dollar........ 0.91	30 420
KOREA,............. **DEMOCRATIC PEOPLE'S REPUBLIC OF** P'yŏngyang	19,200,000.... 1,800,000	46,540.... 120,538	People's republic	President:....... Marshal Kim Il Sung Premier: Li Chlong Ok	Won....... 1.06	NA NA
KOREA,............. **REPUBLIC OF** Seoul	41,300,000.... 8,366,756	38,025.... 98,484	Republic......	President: .... Chun Doo Hwan Prime Minister: Chin Iee Jong	Won....... 0.0013	66,090 1,700
KUWAIT............. Al Kuwait	1,600,000.... 78,116	6,880.... 17,818	Constitutional emirate	Emir:........................ Sheikh Jabir al-Ahmad al-Sabah Prime Minister: Sheikh Saad al-Abdullah al-Salem al-Sabah	Dinar........ 3.44	30,600 20,900
LAOS.............. Vientiane	3,600,000.... 90,000	91,429.... 236,800	People's republic	President:................... Prince Souphanouvong Premier: Kaysone Phomvihan	New kip...... 0.10	290 80
LEBANON........... Beirut	2,600,000.... 702,000	4,015.... 10,400	Republic......	President:................... Amin Gemayel Prime Minister: Shafik al-Wazzan	Pound........ 0.24	NA NA
LESOTHO........... Maseru	1,400,000.... 45,000	11,720.... 30,355	Constitutional monarchy (C)	King:.................. Moshoeshoe II Prime Minister: Chief Leabua Jonathan	Loti 0.93	740 540
LIBERIA............ Monrovia	2,100,000.... 208,600	43,000.... 111,369	Republic......	Head of State and............ Chairman, People's Redemption Council: Gen. Samuel K. Doe	Dollar........ 1.00	1,010 520

Imports Exports	Revenue Expenditure	Elementary Schools: Teachers Students	Secondary Schools: Teachers Students	Colleges and Universities: Teachers Students
$ 21,182,000,000 11,210,000,000	$ 62,297,000,000 62,297,000,000	94,000 2,615,910	33,514 1,033,418	4,627 81,782
9,782,000,000 8,083,000,000	7,340,000,000 10,200,000,000	14,636 419,998	20,965 300,601	2,242 27,859
15,200,000,000 10,700,000,000	27,000,000,000 29,690,000,000	39,401 605,933	14,434 181,094	8,850 44,022
86,213,000,000 73,374,000,000	116,400,000,000 159,400,000,000	269,279 4,562,441	493,513 5,270,298	43,220 1,090,644
2,094,000,000 2,441,000,000	1,730,528,000 1,730,528,000	24,441 954,190	NA 119,482	NA 9,831
1,397,000,000 858,000,000	1,234,000,000 1,354,000,000	8,783 363,420	6,473 216,248	367 13,556
131,566,000,000 138,443,000,000	209,400,000,000 165,820,000,000	470,991 11,826,573	554,078 9,745,517	167,757 1,947,351
4,897,000,000 563,000,000	1,020,000,000 2,000,000,000	14,303 454,391	12,153 248,643	1,023 10,063
1,650,000,000 1,125,000,000	1,860,000,000 2,410,000,000	92,762 3,698,246	15,726 388,216	NA 7,251
13,610,000 21,200,000	13,050,000 10,780,000	447 13,383	108 1,766	NA 741
899,000,000[1] 843,000,000[1]	23,985,000,000 23,985,000,000	100,000[4] 2,561,674	[4] 2,000,000	NA 100,000
25,466,000,000 22,251,000,000	12,600,000,000 11,800,000,000	122,727 5,586,494	113,185 4,396,984	14,969 436,918
8,863,000,000 9,797,000,000	22,800,000 9,250,000	8,035 148,983	15,342 181,882	584 8,974
83,000,000 24,000,000	119,000,000 215,200,000	14,983 463,098	3,705 82,618	118 1,157
3,567,000,000 923,000,000	NA NA	22,646 405,402	NA 287,310	NA 85,087
NA NA	200,597,000 250,590,000	4,782 235,604	885 18,677	115 727
2,463,000,000 1,200,000,000	399,600,000 420,100,000	9,099 227,431	2,974 51,231	190 3,702

Nation Capital	Population	Area of Country (sq mi/ sq km)	Type of Government	Heads of State and Government	Currency: Value in U.S. Dollars	GNP (000,000): GNP Per Capita
LIBYA............... Tripoli	3,300,000.... 1,000,000	679,362.... 1,759,540	Socialist republic	Revolutionary Leader (Head of State): Col. Muammar al-Qaddafi Secretary-General, General People's Congress: Muhammad az-Zarrouk Ragab	Dinar......... 3.38	$ 26,080 8,450
LIECHTENSTEIN...... Vaduz	26,130.... 4,980	61.... 157	Constitutional monarchy	Sovereign:..................... Prince Francis Joseph II Chief of Government: Hans Brunhart	Swiss franc ... 0.48	NA NA
LUXEMBOURG .... Luxembourg	400,000.... 78,900	998.... 2,586	Constitutional monarchy	Grand Duke:.................... Jean Prime Minister: Pierre Werner	Franc 0.02	5,790 15,910
MADAGASCAR .... Antananarivo	9,500,000.... 525,000	226,658.... 587,041	Socialist republic	President: Cmdr. Didier Ratsiraka Prime Minister: Lt. Col. Désiré Rakotoarijaona	Franc 0.002	2,970 330
MALAWI .... Lilongwe	6,800,000.... 98,718	45,747.... 118,484	Republic (C)	President:...... Hastings Kamuzu Banda	Kwacha 0.89	1,250 200
MALAYSIA .... Kuala Lumpur	15,000,000.... 937,875	127,317.... 329,749	Federal constitutional monarchy (C)	Supreme Head of State: .... Sultan Haji Ahmad Shah al Musta'in Bilah ibni al-Marhum Prime Minister: Datuk Seri Mahathir bin Mohamad	Ringgit 0.43	26,110 1,840
MALDIVES .... Male	200,000.... 29,555	115.... 298	Republic	President: Maumoon Abdul Gayoom	Rupee...... 0.25	NA NA
MALI................. Bamako	7,300,000.... 404,000	478,766.... 1,240,000	Republic	President: Brig. Gen. Moussa Traoré	Franc 0.0014	1,340 190
MALTA .... Valletta	400,000.... 14,249	122.... 316	Republic (C)	President: .... Agatha Barbara Prime Minister: Dom Mintoff	Pound 2.36	1,310 3,600
MAURITANIA .... Nouakchott	1,800,000.... 135,000	397,955.... 1,030,700	Islamic republic	President and Chairman, Military Committee for National Salvation: Lt. Col. Mohamed Khouna Ould Haidalla Prime Minister: Lt. Col. Maaouya Ould Sidi Ahmed Taya	Ouguiya 0.019	710 460
MAURITIUS .... Port Louis	1,000,000.... 148,389	790.... 2,045	Parliamentary state (C)	Governor-General:............... Sir Dayendranath Burrenchobay Prime Minister: Aneerood Jugnauth	Rupee...... 0.09	1,230 1,270
MEXICO.............. Mexico City	75,700,000.... 9,991,000	761,604.... 1,972,547	Federal republic	President: Miguel de la Madrid Hurtado	Peso 0.0067	160,230 2,250
MONACO .... Monaco-Ville	28,000.... 1,700	0.58.... 1.49	Constitutional monarchy	Prince:...................... Rainier III Minister of State: Jean Herly	French franc .. 0.13	NA NA
MONGOLIAN PEOPLE'S REPUBLIC Ulan Bator	1,800,000.... 435,400	604,250.... 1,565,000	People's republic	Presidium Chairman: Yumzhagiyen Tsedenbal Chairman, Council of Ministers (Premier): Zhambyn Batmunkh	Tugrik 0.30	NA NA
MOROCCO .... Rabat	22,900,000.... 1,000,000	172,414.... 446,550	Constitutional monarchy	King:....................... Hassan II Prime Minister: Maati Bouabid	Dirham 0.15	17,960 860
MOZAMBIQUE....... Maputo	13,100,000.... 755,000	309,496.... 801,590	People's republic	President: .... Samora M. Machel	Metical 0.03	NA NA
NAURU .... Yaren	7,254.... NA	8.... 21	Republic (C)	President: .... Hammer DeRoburt	Australian..... dollar 0.91	155 21,400

Imports Exports	Revenue Expenditure	Elementary Schools: Teachers Students	Secondary Schools: Teachers Students	Colleges and Universities: Teachers Students
$ 8,177,000,000	$ NA	28,229	21,026	1,340
12,892,000,000	13,018,000,000	600,747	280,215	15,036
[10]	123,960,000	95	92	NA
[10]	123,780,000	1,899	1,831	NA
[11]	1,370,000,000	1,449	1,801	168
[11]	1,410,000,000	27,510	24,984	404
522,000,000	685,400,000	23,937	5,709	557
433,000,000	685,400,000	1,311,000	113,270	16,226
291,000,000	218,600,000	12,540	931	190
232,000,000	306,800,000	809,862	16,797	2,000
12,543,000,000	7,070,000,000	63,479[12]	43,797[12]	3,100
11,789,000,000	9,510,000,000	1,675,340[12]	987,624[12]	23,625
113,300,000	4,170,000	49	94	*
12,300,000	10,500,000	2,662	1,760	*
318,000,000	115,020,000	7,214	NA	489
93,000,000	115,020,000	298,831	55,465	5,281
783,000,000	408,200,000	1,567	2,229	174
411,000,000	380,300,000	32,448	27,673	868
445,000,000	200,576,000	2,183	511	110
256,000,000	200,576,000	90,530	11,957	477
463,000,000	228,000,000	6,177	3,101	137
365,000,000	324,900,000	123,666	82,748	646
15,372,000,000	29,400,000,000	375,220	250,890	68,617
21,163,000,000	32,700,000,000	14,666,257	4,285,016	811,281
NA	128,330,540	400[4]	[4]	*
NA	81,828,370	1,017	2,065	*
29,000,000[1]	1,537,000,000	4,482	10,215	834
37,000,000[1]	1,534,000,000	141,306	237,190	9,970
4,351,000,000	5,378,000,000	63,157	37,323	2,561
2,130,000,000	7,899,000,000	2,411,000	805,016	74,465
792,000,000	634,550,000	17,030	2,831	244
303,000,000	732,991,000	1,387,192	102,745	804
11,830,000	116,050,000	129[4]	[4]	*
75,340,000	90,720,000	1,500	600	*

447

Nation Capital	Population	Area of Country (sq mi/ sq km)	Type of Government	Heads of State and Government	Currency: Value in U.S. Dollars	GNP (000,000): GNP Per Capita
NEPAL .... Katmandu	15,800,000.... 195,300	54,362.... 140,797	Constitutional monarchy	King: .... Birendra Bir Bikram Shah Deva Prime Minister: Lokendra Bahadur Chand	Rupee 0.07	$ 2,300 150
NETHERLANDS, THE Amsterdam	14,400,000.... 700,759	15,770.... 40,844	Constitutional monarchy	Queen: .... Beatrix Prime Minister: Ruud Lubbers	Guilder 0.35	167,980 11,790
NEW ZEALAND ...... Wellington	3,200,000...... 349,000	103,736.... 368,676	Parliamentary state (C)	Governor-General: .... Sir David S. Beattie Prime Minister: Robert D. Muldoon	Dollar 0.66	25,460 7,700
NICARAGUA .... Managua	2,800,000.... 660,846	50,193.... 130,000	Republic	Coordinator, Junta of .... the Government of National Reconstruction: Cmdr. Daniel Ortega Saavedra	Córdoba 0.10	2,400 860
NIGER .... Niamey	6,100,000.... 200,000	489,191.... 1,267,000	Republic	President, Supreme .... Military Council: Col. Seyni Kountché Premier: Dumarov Mamane	CFA franc[3] 0.0026	1,890 330
NIGERIA .... Lagos	84,200,000.... 4,200,000	356,669.... 923,768	Federal republic (C)	President: .... Gen. Muhammad Buhari	Naira 1.4751	76,170 870
NORWAY .... Oslo	4,100,000.... 452,023	125,182.... 324,219	Constitutional monarchy	King: .... Olav V Prime Minister: Kaare Willoch	Krone 0.14	57,640 14,060
OMAN .... Muscat	1,000,000.... 6,000	82,030.... 212,457	Sultanate	Sultan and Prime Minister: .... Qabus bin Sa'id	Rial 2.89	5,440 5,920
PAKISTAN .... Islamabad	95,700,000.... 350,000	310,404.... 803,943	Federal republic	President and Chief .... Martial Law Administrator: Gen. Muahmmad Zia ul-Haq	Rupee 0.08	29,800 350
PANAMA .... Panamá	2,100,000.... 467,000	29,762.... 77,082	Republic	President: .... Ricardo de la Espriella	Balboa 1.00	3,580 1,910
PAPUA NEW GUINEA Port Moresby	3,100,000.... 122,761	178,260.... 461,691	Parliamentary state (C)	Governor-General: .... Kingsford Dibela Prime Minister: Michael Somare	Kina 1.19	2,570 840
PARAGUAY .... Asunción	3,500,000.... 474,122	157,048.... 406,752	Republic	President: .... Gen. Alfredo Stroessner	Guarani 0.008	4,970 1,630
PERU .... Lima	19,200,000.... 4,900,000	496,224.... 1,285,216	Republic	President: .... Fernando Belaúnde Terry Prime Minister: Fernando Schwalb	Sol 0.00064	19,980 1,170
PHILIPPINES .... Manila	52,800,000.... 1,630,485	115,831.... 300,000	Republic	President: .... Ferdinand E. Marcos Prime Minister: César Virata	Peso 0.09	39,010 790
POLAND .... Warsaw	36,600,000.... 1,572,000	120,725.... 312,677	People's republic	Chairman, Council of State: ...... Henryk Jabloński Chairman, Military Council of National Salvation, and Chairman, Council of Ministers (Premier): Gen. Wojciech W. Jaruzelski	Zloty 0.01	NA NA
PORTUGAL .... Lisbon	9,900,000.... 850,500	35,553.... 92,082	Republic	President: .... Gen. António Ramalho Eanes Prime Minister: Mário Soares	Escudo 0.009	24,750 2,520
QATAR .... Doha	300,000.... 190,000	4,247.... 11,000	Constitutional emirate	Emir and Prime Minister: .... Sheikh Khalifa bin Hamad al-Thani	Riyal 0.27	6,540 27,720
ROMANIA .... Bucharest	22,700,000.... 1,861,007	91,699.... 237,500	Socialist republic	Head of State and .... President, State Council: Nicolae Ceaușescu Chairman, Council of Ministers (Premier): Constantin Dăscălescu	Leu 0.22	57,030 2,540

Imports Exports	Revenue Expenditure	Elementary Schools: Teachers Students	Secondary Schools: Teachers Students	Colleges and Universities: Teachers Students
$ 252,000,000.............$ 46,000,000	202,000,000.............. 404,800,000	27,805.............. 1,067,912	16,376.............. 512,434	2,311 31,942
64,221,000,000.............. 66,362,000,000	47,200,000,000.............. 55,300,000,000	57,536.............. 1,333,342	103,369.............. 1,394,939	28,500 280,948
5,913,000,000.............. 5,512,000,000	8,160,000,000.............. 9,390,000,000	22,658.............. 381,262	15,743.............. 370,001	4,780 43,933
686,000,000.............. 366,000,000	460,910,000.............. 609,210,000	13,318.............. 472,167	2,720.............. 98,874	1,266 26,734
480,000,000.............. 307,000,000	320,758,000.............. 320,758,000	4,298.............. 176,397	961.............. 27,196	224 1,435
13,902,000,000.............. 14,901,000,000	8,327,000,000.............. 6,088,000,000	NA.............. 12,556,881	NA.............. 1,826,629	5,748 57,592
15,466,000,000.............. 17,538,000,000	23,600,000,000.............. 21,900,000,000	46,604.............. 394,510	14,939.............. 183,664	3,879 40,643
2,683,000,000.............. 4,115,000,000	2,300,000,000.............. 2,300,000,000	3,959.............. 91,895	934.............. 8,534	* *
5,231,000,000.............. 2,374,000,000	3,850,000,000.............. 4,150,000,000	147,000.............. 6,601,227	129,035.............. 2,244,500	6,074 148,451
2,901,000,000.............. 309,000,000	1,060,000,000.............. 1,400,000,000	12,361.............. 337,522	8,138.............. 171,273	1,948 40,369
1,171,000,000.............. 727,000,000	506,100,000.............. 873,000,000	9,935.............. 300,536	2,289.............. 49,334	578 2,887
672,000,000.............. 330,000,000	492,000,000.............. 67,000,000	17,525...\.............. 493,231	9,830.............. 110,095	1,945 20,496
4,006,000,000.............. 3,196,000,000	3,510,000,000.............. 3,200,000,000	80,331.............. 3,117,055	37,383.............. 1,095,085	11,324 192,686
8,229,000,000.............. 5,010,000,000	6,520,000,000.............. 7,740,000,000	264,241.............. 8,033,642	85,779.............. 2,928,525	40,022 1,182,103
4,645,000,000[1].............. 5,012,000,000[1]	41,540,000,000.............. 48,928,000,000	212,050.............. 4,167,313	139,412.............. 1,673,869	55,941 469,368
9,385,000,000.............. 4,029,000,000	4,214,000,000.............. 4,214,000,000	65,124.............. 1,220,527	21,847.............. 499,557	6,330 65,701
2,075,000,000.............. 449,000,000	3,690,000,000.............. 3,470,000,000	2,037.............. 28,472	1,369.............. 14,360	261 2,025
8,074,000,000.............. 8,493,000,000	18,500,000,000.............. 17,200,000,000	156,817.............. 3,236,808	48,082.............. 871,257	14,592 192,769

Nation Capital	Population	Area of Country (sq mi/ sq km)	Type of Government	Heads of State and Government	Currency: Value in U.S. Dollars	GNP (000,000): GNP Per Capita
RWANDA	5,600,000....	10,169....	Republic	President:	Franc	$ 1,340
Kigali	143,000	26,338		Maj. Gen. Juvénal Habyarimana	0.01	250
ST. CHRISTOPHER AND NEVIS	44,404....	104.... 269	Parliamentary state (C)	Governor-General: Sir Clement Arrindell	East Caribbean	41 920
Basseterre	14,725			Prime Minister: Kennedy Simmonds	dollar 0.37	
ST. LUCIA	115,783....	238....	Parliamentary	Governor-General:	East	120
Castries	45,000	616	state (C)	Boswell Williams Prime Minister: John G. M. Compton	Caribbean dollar 0.37	970
ST. VINCENT AND THE GRENADINES	119,942....	150.... 388	Parliamentary state (C)	Governor-General: Sir Sydney Douglas Gun-Munro Prime Minister:	East Caribbean dollar	70 630
Kingstown	22,782			R. Milton Cato	0.37	
SAN MARINO	21,622....	24....	Republic	Co-Regents:	Italian lira	NA
San Marino	8,600	61		Renzo Renzi Germano De Biagi	0.00067	NA
SÃO TOMÉ AND PRÍNCIPE	100,000....	372.... 964	Republic	President and Prime Minister:	Dobra 0.025	40 370
São Tomé	20,000			Manuel Pinto da Costa		
SAUDI ARABIA	10,400,000....	830,000....	Monarchy	King and Prime Minister:	Riyal	117,240
Riyadh	680,000	2,149,690		Fahd ibn Abdul-Aziz	0.29	12,600
SENEGAL	6,100,000....	75,750....	Republic	President:	CFA franc[3]	2,530
Dakar	978,553	196,192		Abdou Diouf Premier: Habib Thiam	0.0026	430
SEYCHELLES	100,000....	108....	Republic	President:	Rupee	110
Victoria	23,000	280	(C)	France Albert René	0.14	1,800
SIERRA LEONE	3,800,000....	27,699....	Republic	President:	Leone	1,140
Freetown	274,000	71,740	(C)	Siaka P. Stevens	0.40	320
SINGAPORE	2,500,000....	224....	Republic	President:	Dollar	12,800
Singapore	2,322,000	581	(C)	C. V. Devan Nair Prime Minister: Lee Kuan Yew	0.47	5,240
SOLOMON ISLANDS	300,000....	10,983....	Parliamentary	Governor-General:	Dollar	150
Honiara	18,346	28,446	state (C)	Sir Baddeley Devesi Prime Minister: Solomon Mamaloni	0.83	640
SOMALIA	5,300,000....	246,201....	Republic	President and Chairman,	Shilling	1,240
Mogadishu	400,00	637,657		Council of Ministers: Maj. Gen. Muhammad Siad Barre	0.066	280
SOUTH AFRICA,[14] REPUBLIC OF	24,885,000....	471,445.... 1,221,037	Republic	President: Marais Viljoen	Rand 0.92	81,840 2,770
Cape Town	790,880			Prime Minister:		
Prètoria	528,407			P. W. Botha		
SPAIN	38,400,000....	194,897....	Constitutional	King:	Peseta	214,300
Madrid	3,300,000	504,782	monarchy	Juan Carlos I Prime Minister: Felipe González Márquez	0.007	5,640
SRI LANKA (CEYLON)	15,600,000....	25,332.... 65,610	Republic (C)	President: Junius R. Jayewardene	Rupee 0.04	4,460 300
Colombo	585,776			Prime Minister: Ranasinghe Premadasa		
SUDAN	20,600,000....	967,499....	Republic	President and Prime Minister:	Pound	7,390
Khartoum	1,000,000	2,505,813		Maj. Gen. Jaafar al-Nimeiry	0.76	380
SURINAME	400,000....	63,037....	Republic	President:	Guilder	1,070
Paramaribo	200,000	163,265		Desi Bouterse Prime Minister: Errol Alibux	0.56	3,030
SWAZILAND	600,000....	6,704....	Monarchy	Queen:	Lilangeni	480
Mbabane	22,262	17,363	(C)	Ntombi Prime Minister: Prince Bhekimpi Dlamini	0.92	760

Imports Exports	Revenue Expenditure	Elementary Schools: Teachers Students	Secondary Schools: Teachers Students	Colleges and Universities: Teachers Students
$ 206,000,000..........$ 82,000,000	134,300,000.............. 148,500,000	11,912.............. 704,924	887.............. 10,667	111 809
47,656,000.............. 22,385,000	38,887,000.............. 38,702,000	295.............. 7,074	271.............. 4,334	NA 197[13]
127,169,000.............. 82,103,000	NA.............. 34,743,000	942.............. 30,610	297.............. 4,552	51 437
NA.............. NA	29,535,868.............. 26,986,046	1,210.............. 21,854	243.............. 5,084	41 259
NA.............. NA	96,549,010.............. 96,549,010	132.............. 1,535	112.............. 1,228	* *
25,000,000.............. 9,000,000	6,740,000.............. 17,700,000	527.............. 14,162	111.............. 3,300	* *
40,979,000,000.............. 77,370,000,000	98,600,000,000.............. 86,420,000,000	50,511.............. 926,531	26,788.............. 348,996	6,598 56,252
1,108,000,000.............. 482,000,000	759,600,000.............. 759,600,000	9,178.............. 392,541	2,934.............. 87,755	638 12,373
60,000,000.............. 34,000,000	65,800,000.............. 65,800,000	405.............. 9,978	288.............. 5,143	28 144
199,000,000.............. 169,000,000	201,800,000.............. 398,200,000	7,943.............. 250,480	2,596.............. 50,478	289 1,642
28,176,000,000.............. 20,787,000,000	4,630,000,000.............. 3,140,000,000	9,463.............. 291,649	9,298.............. 169,538	1,178 7,137
53,600,000.............. 59,400,000	39,000,000.............. 69,000,000	1,148.............. 28,870	257.............. 4,030	* *
468,000,000.............. 143,000,000	219,100,000.............. 219,100,000	8,693.............. 271,139	1,405.............. 22,691	286 1,936
18,956,000,000[15].............. 17,597,000,000[15]	15,200,000,000.............. 17,400,000,000	164,149[4].............. 4,480,493	[4].............. 1,225,153	16,708 218,275
31,465,000,000.............. 20,498,000,000	27,100,000,000.............. 37,400,000,000	228,307.............. 6,778,877	92,716.............. 1,650,005	40,321 649,098
1,813,000,000.............. 1,033,000,000	855,700,000.............. 1,710,000,000	138,488[4].............. 1,975,749	[4].............. 1,159,967	1,623 26,791
1,914,000,000.............. 583,000,000	2,510,000,000.............. 3,570,000,000	43,451.............. 1,464,227	18,831.............. 384,194	6,081 25,151
486,000,000.............. 370,000,000	289,400,000.............. 441,500,000	3,068.............. 85,060	1,867.............. 34,372	118 900
NA.............. NA	162,600,000.............. 147,300,000	3,278.............. 112,019	1,073.............. 20,084	91 885

451

Nation Capital	Population	Area of Country (sq mi/ sq km)	Type of Government	Heads of State and Government	Currency: Value in U.S. Dollars	GNP (000,000): GNP Per Capita
SWEDEN	8,300,000	173,732 . . .	Constitutional	King:	Krona	$ 123,770
Stockholm	1,535,539	449,964	monarchy	Carl XVI Gustaf	0.13	14,870
				Prime Minister:		
				Olof Palme		
SWITZERLAND	6,500,000	15,941 . . .	Federal	President:	Franc	112,850
Bern	145,300	41,288	republic	Pierre Aubert	0.48	17,430
SYRIA	9,700,000	71,498 . . .	Socialist	President:	Pound	14,660
Damascus	1,097,205	185,180	republic	Lt. Gen. Hafez al-Assad	0.26	1,570
				Prime Minister:		
				Abdel al-Raouf al-Kassem		
TAIWAN or	18,900,000	13,892 . . .	Republic	President:	New Taiwan . .	NA
FORMOSA		35,981		Chiang Ching-kuo	dollar	NA
(REPUBLIC OF				Premier:	0.03	
CHINA)				Sun Yun-suan		
Taipei	2,270,000					
TANZANIA	20,500,000	364,900 . . .	Republic	President:	Shilling	5,260
Dar es Salaam	900,000	945,087	(C)	Julius K. Nyerere	0.08	280
				Prime Minister:		
				Edward Sokoine		
THAILAND	50,800,000	198,456 . . .	Constitutional	King:	Baht	36,900
Bangkok	5,500,000	514,000	monarchy	Bhumibol Adulyadej	0.04	770
				Prime Minister:		
				Gen. Prem Tinsulanonda		
TOGO	2,800,000	21,925 . . .	Republic	President:	CFA franc3	1,010
Lomé	250,000	56,785		Gen. Gnassingbe Eyadéma	0.0026	380
TONGA . . . . , ...	100,143	270 . . .	Constitutional	King:	Pa'anga	50
Nuku'alofa	18,312	699	monarchy	Taufa'ahau Tupou IV	0.92	530
				Prime Minister:		
				Prince Fatafehi Tu'ipelehake		
TRINIDAD AND	1,200,000	1,981 . . .	Republic	President:	Dollar	6,720
TOBAGO		5,130	(C)	Sir Elllis E. I. Clarke	0.42	5,670
Port-of-Spain	250,000			Prime Minister:		
				George M. Chambers		
TUNISIA	6,800,000	63,170 . . .	Republic	President:	Dinar	9,300
Tunis	550,400	163,610		Habib Bourguiba	1.49	1,420
				Prime Minister:		
				Muhammad M'zali		
TURKEY	49,200,000	301,382 . . .	Republic	President and Chief	Lira	70,210
Ankara	1,877,755	780,576		of the General Staff:	0.005	1,540
				Gen. Kenan Evren		
TUVALU	7,349	10 . . .	Parliamentary	Governor-General:	Dollar	5
(ELLICE ISLANDS)		26	state (C)	Sir Penitala Fiatau Teo	0.91	680
Funafuti	2,200			Prime Minister:		
				Tomasi Puapua		
UGANDA	13,800,000	91,134 . . .	Republic	President:	Shilling	2,890
Kampala	458,000	236,036	(C)	Milton Obote	0.007	220
				Prime Minister:		
				Erifasi Otema Alimadi		
UNION OF SOVIET	272,000,000	8,649,534	Federal	Chairman, Presidium	Ruble	NA
SOCIALIST		22,402,200	socialist	of the Supreme Soviet:	1.37	NA
REPUBLICS			state	Yuri Andropov		
Moscow	8,396,000			Chairman, Council of Ministers		
				(Premier):		
				Nikolai A. Tikhonov		
UNITED ARAB	1,400,000	32,278 . . .	Federal	President:	Dirham	26,910
EMIRATES		83,600	state	Sheikh Zayed bin	0.27	24,660
Abu Dhabi	449,000			Sultan al-Nahayan		
				Prime Minister:		
				Sheikh Rashid bin Saeed		
				al-Maktloum		
UNITED STATES	234,200,000	3,618,770 . . .	Federal	President:	Dollar	3,270,000
OF AMERICA		9,372,569	republic	Ronald W. Reagan	*	13,962
Washington, D.C.	631,000					

Imports Exports	Revenue Expenditure	Elementary Schools: Teachers Students	Secondary Schools: Teachers Students	Colleges and Universities: Teachers Students
$ 27,619,000,000	$ 33,800,000,000	40,204	61,759	NA
26,733,000,000	50,200,000,000	677,349	536,287	198,798
28,675,000,000[16]	9,290,000,000	NA	NA	5,872
26,014,000,000[16]	8,870,000,000	450,942	459,590	58,953
3,567,000,000	3,510,000,000	49,431	31,916	1,332
1,524,000,000	4,720,000,000	1,450,045	588,865	65,348
193,231,000,000	13,406,000,000	69,143	70,688	17,452
103,051,000,000	13,380,000,000	2,202,904	1,620,165	358,437
1,046,000,000	1,070,000,000	81,153	3,218	847
480,000,000	1,410,000,000	3,359,966	62,998	3,240
8,940,000,000	5,050,000,000	304,400	59,161	10,851
7,040,000,000	6,820,000,000	7,370,846	1,386,136	335,997
526,000,000	344,700,000	9,193	2,377	269
213,000,000	349,900,000	506,356	96,065	3,430
29,000,000	14,350,000	818	685	*
8,000,000	14,330,000	19,744	12,843	*
3,529,000,000	1,578,000,000	6,363	1,745	500
3,008,000,000	1,648,000,000	181,863	91,501	4,940
3,367,000,000	2,790,000,000	27,375	14,328	3,647
1,974,000,000	2,790,000,000	1,054,027	293,351	30,150
8,533,000,000	11,400,000,000	212,456	95,827	12,919
5,565,000,000	14,700,000,000	5,656,494	2,225,533	116,986
1,440,000	NA	44	10	*
67,000	3,185,000	1,226	250	*
339,000,000	507,300,000	36,442	3,775	304
371,000,000	537,300,000	1,223,850	77,929	3,932
35,885,000,000[1]	461,804,000,000	2,638,000[4]	[4]	317,152
36,232,000,000[1]	461,255,000,000	34,400,000	9,900,000	4,853,958
9,830,000,000	6,120,000,000	5,424	2,819	76
18,540,000,000	5,080,000,000	88,617	31,560	1,015
254,881,000,000	600,563,000,000	1,351,000	1,100,000	822,000
212,274,000,000	795,917,000,000	28,559,209	15,204,233	11,569,899

453

Nation Capital	Population	Area of Country (sq mi/ sq km)	Type of Government	Heads of State and Government	Currency: Value in U.S. Dollars	GNP (000,000): GNP Per Capita
UPPER VOLTA Ouagadougou	6,800,000 172,661	105,869 274,200	Republic	Head of Government: Thomas Sankara	CFA franc[3] 0.0026	$ 1,490 240
URUGUAY Montevideo	3,000,000 1,400,000	68,037 176,215	Republic	President: Gen. Gregorio Conrado Alvarez Armelino	New peso 0.03	8,260 2,820
VANUATU (NEW HEBRIDES) Vila	125,600 14,600	5,700 14,763	Republic (C)	President: Ati George Sokomanu Prime Minister: Rev. Walter H. Lini	Vatu 0.01	40 350
VENEZUELA Caracas	18,000,000 2,950,000	352,144 912,050	Federal republic	President: Luis Herrera Campins	Bolivar 0.09	65,080 4,220
VIETNAM Hanoi	57,000,000 2,800,000	127,242 329,556	Socialist republic	Chairman, Council of State (President): Truong Chinh Chairman, Council of Ministers (Premier): Pham Van Dong	Dong 0.46	NA NA
WESTERN SAMOA Apia	200,000 32,099	1,097 2,842	Constitutional monarchy (C)	Head of State: Malietoa Tanumafili II Prime Minister: Tupuola Efi	Tala 0.62	NA NA
YEMEN, PEOPLE'S DEMOCRATIC REPUBLIC OF Aden	2,100,000 271,953	128,560 332,968	People's republic	President: Chairman of the Presidium of the Supreme People's Council, and Prime Minister: Ali Nasser Muhammad al-Hasani	Dinar 2.90	910 460
YEMEN ARAB REPUBLIC San'a	5,700,000 277,817	75,290 195,000	Republic	President: Col. Ali Abdullah Saleh Prime Minister: Abdul Karim al-Iryani	Rial 0.22	3,310 460
YUGOSLAVIA Belgrade	22,800,000 1,455,046	98,766 255,804	Federal socialist republic	President: Mika Spiljak President, Federal Executive Council (Prime Minister): Milka Planinć	Dinar 0.01	62,930 2,790
ZAIRE Kinshasa	31,300,000 3,500,000	905,567 2,345,409	Republic	President: Mobutu Sese Seko First State Commissioner (Prime Minister): Kengo wa Dondo	Zaire 0.17	6,280 210
ZAMBIA Lusaka	6,200,000 641,000	290,586 752,614	Republic (C)	President: Kenneth D. Kaunda Prime Minister: Nalumino Mundia	Kwacha 0.50	3,490 600
ZIMBABWE (RHODESIA) Harare	8,400,000 654,000	150,804 390,580	Republic (C)	President: Rev. Canaan S. Banana Prime Minister: Robert G. Mugabe	Dollar 1.01	6,260 870

1. Trade figures for these countries, chiefly members of the Soviet bloc, exclude trade among themselves.
2. Figure includes data for Luxembourg.
3. "CFA" stands for Communauté Financière Africaine.
4. Combined figure for elementary and secondary education.
5. Excluding Turkish part of Nicosia.
6. Excluding budget of Turkish Federated State of Cyprus, which was balanced at $51,785,900 in 1982–1983.
7. Figure for Greek schools only.
8. Figures generally include data for Greenland and Faeroe Islands.

Imports Exports	Revenue Expenditure	Elementary Schools: Teachers Students	Secondary Schools: Teachers Students	Colleges and Universities: Teachers Students
$ 267,000,000..............$ 80,000,000	142,200,000.............. 151,900,000	3,700.............. 201,595	818.............. 16,227	116 1,281
1,058,000,000.............. 1,032,000,000	2,670,000,000.............. 8,870,000,000	14,768.............. 331,247	18,180.............. 218,632	3,847 36,298
37,600,000.............. 15,500,000	3,724,000,000.............. 3,724,000,000	986.............. 23,264	157.............. 2,360	* *
12,982,000,000.............. 17,047,000,000	22,700,000,000.............. 19,300,000,000	88,493.............. 2,456,815	45,888.............. 820,660	20,744 239,233
637,000,000.............. 188,000,000	4,817,000,000.............. 4,817,000,000	217,493.............. 7,923,495	115,348.............. 2,987,997	15,082 132,380
48,500,000.............. 12,700,000	20,570,000.............. 39,350,000	1,913[4].............. 33,012	[4].............. 19,299	54 388
1,193,000,000.............. 580,000,000	278,000,000.............. 278,000,000	10,078.............. 212,795	2,194.............. 46,341	246 2,517
1,987,000,000.............. 44,000,000	719,500,000.............. 1,360,000,000	10,576.............. 460,630	1,345.............. 24,822	NA 4,058
12,783,000,000.............. 10,049,000,000	9,510,000,000.............. 9,730,000,000	59,391.............. 1,431,582	131,348.............. 2,426,164	19,757 336,472
963,000,000.............. 1,713,000,000	1,450,000,000.............. 1,640,000,000	NA.............. 3,919,395	NA.............. 704,332	2,782 28,430
885,000,000.............. 880,000,000	724,200,000.............. 1,200,000,000	19,868.............. 964,475	4,236.............. 94,930	412 9,192
1,635,000,000.............. 1,057,000,000	1,600,000,000.............. 2,940,000,000	36,734.............. 1,714,266	6,148.............. 149,018	483 2,525

9. Figures include data for Northern Ireland.
10. Included in figure for Switzerland.
11. Included in figure for Belgium.
12. Figure is for peninsular Malaysia.
13. Enrollment figure includes nondegree programs.
14. Data generally exclude the homelands that have been granted independence. Population of the homelands (including homeland citizens residing in South Africa) is: Bophuthatswana, 2,300,000; Ciskei, 2,060,000; Transkei, 4,200,000; Venda, 473,000.
15. Figures include data for Botswana, Lesotho, South West Africa, and Swaziland.
16. Figure includes data for Liechtenstein.

THE STATES AND OUTLYING AREAS OF THE UNITED STATES

State Capital	Population	Area (sq mi/ sq km)	Per Capita Personal Income	Governor Lieutenant-Governor	Revenue Expenditure	Roads (Miles)
ALABAMA Montgomery	3,943,000 177,857	51,705 133,915	$ 8,649	George Wallace (D) William Baxley (D)	$ 5,105,000,000 4,374,000,000	87,240
ALASKA Juneau	438,000 19,528	591,004 1,530,693	16,257	William J. Sheffield (D) Stephen McAlpine (D)	5,134,000,000 2,543,000,000	9,085
ARIZONA Phoenix	2,860,000 789,704	114,000 295,259	10,173	Bruce E. Babbitt (D) *	3,405,000,000 3,076,000,000	78,286
ARKANSAS Little Rock	2,291,000 158,461	53,187 137,753	8,479	Bill Clinton (D) Winston Bryant (D)	2,529,000,000 2,356,000,000	76,764
CALIFORNIA Sacramento	24,724,000 292,600	158,706 411,047	12,567	George Deukmejian (R) Leo McCarthy (D)	39,552,000,000 38,846,000,000	176,665
COLORADO Denver	3,045,000 490,000	104,091 269,594	12,302	Richard D. Lamm (D) Nancy Dick (D)	3,501,000,000 3,311,000,000	75,708
CONNECTICUT Hartford	3,153,000 135,350	5,018 12,997	13,748	William A. O'Neill (D) Joseph J. Fauliso (D)	3,873,000,000 3,740,000,000	19,442
DELAWARE Dover	602,000 23,512	2,044 5,295	11,731	Pierre S. du Pont 4th (R) Michael N. Castle (R)	1,123,000,000 1,029,000,000	5,249
DISTRICT OF COLUMBIA *	631,000	69 178	14,550	Mayor: Marion S. Barry, Jr. (D)	1,596,000,000 1,537,000,000	1,102
FLORIDA Tallahassee	10,416,000 81,548	58,664 151,938	10,978	D. Robert Graham (D) Wayne Mixson (D)	9,029,000,000 8,274,000,000	97,186
GEORGIA Atlanta	5,639,000 425,022	58,910 152,575	9,583	Joe Frank Harris (D) Zell B. Miller (D)	5,848,000,000 5,401,000,000	104,253
HAWAII Honolulu	994,000 365,048	6,471 16,759	11,652	George R. Ariyoshi (D) John Waihee (D)	2,085,000,000 1,838,000,000	4,107
IDAHO Boise	965,000 102,451	83,564 216,431	9,029	John V. Evans (D) David Leroy (R)	1,224,000,000 1,139,000,000	67,442
ILLINOIS Springfield	11,448,000 99,637	56,345 145,933	12,100	James R. Thompson, Jr. (R) George H. Ryan (R)	14,250,000,000 13,934,000,000	133,672
INDIANA Indianapolis	5,471,000 700,807	36,185 93,720	10,021	Robert D. Orr (R) John M. Mutz (R)	5,488,000,000 5,664,000,000	91,676
IOWA Des Moines	2,905,000 191,003	56,275 145,752	10,791	Terry E. Branstad (R) Robert Anderson (D)	3,670,000,000 3,617,000,000	112,487
KANSAS Topeka	2,408,000 115,266	82,277 213,097	11,765	John W. Carlin (D) Tom Docking (D)	2,715,000,000 2,618,000,000	132,209
KENTUCKY Frankfort	3,667,000 25,973	40,409 104,660	8,934	Martha Layne Collins (D) Steven Beshear (D)	4,618,000,000 4,821,000,000	68,429

The material in the following tables is the latest available. As before, it should be noted that the symbol * indicates that the category is not applicable to the area mentioned, and that NA means that the data were not available. The Office of Territorial Affairs was helpful in supplying some data for the table on Outlying Areas.

Railways (Miles)	Commercial Radio and Television Stations	English-language Daily Newspapers	Public Elementary Schools (K–8): Teachers / Students	Public Secondary Schools (9–12): Teachers / Students	Colleges and Universities: Institutions / Students
4,455	220 / 17	28	20,100 / 536,000	16,100 / 221,000	59 / 164,306
582	34 / 7	6	2,800 / 59,000	2,400 / 26,000	15 / 21,296
1,865	94 / 13	19	17,900 / 360,000	7,800 / 155,000	28 / 202,716
5,308	147 / 9	28	11,800 / 310,000	12,300 / 135,000	35 / 77,607
7,600	443 / 55	136	115,200 / 2,750,000	78,600 / 1,318,000	272 / 1,790,993
3,322	125 / 12	29	14,800 / 377,000	15,000 / 164,000	45 / 162,916
950	64 / 5	25	12,800 / 349,000	21,800 / 156,000	47 / 159,632
290	17 / *	3	3,000 / 53,000	2,600 / 41,000	8 / 32,939
55	17 / 5	2	3,100 / 67,000	2,100 / 27,000	19 / 86,675
3,698	318 / 32	51	39,900 / 1,051,000	34,100 / 450,000	81 / 411,891
5,417	280 / 19	33	34,500 / 738,000	22,000 / 320,000	78 / 184,159
0	34 / 10	5	4,000 / 108,000	3,200 / 55,000	12 / 47,181
2,504	67 / 8	11	5,300 / 147,000	4,600 / 57,000	9 / 43,018
10,672	260 / 24	86	54,600 / 1,307,000	53,500 / 617,000	158 / 644,245
5,948	181 / 20	70	26,500 / 695,000	26,600 / 333,000	74 / 247,253
6,900	152 / 13	40	15,500 / 343,000	17,200 / 174,000	60 / 140,449
7,621	107 / 12	47	14,200 / 280,000	12,200 / 126,000	52 / 136,605
3,300	211 / 11	26	21,100 / 461,000	11,800 / 200,000	57 / 143,066

State Capital	Population	Area (sq mi/ sq km)	Per Capita Personal Income	Governor Lieutenant-Governor	Revenue Expenditure	Roads (Miles)
LOUISIANA	4,362,000	47,752	10,231	Edwin W. Edwards (D)	$ 5,895,000,000	56,676
Baton Rouge	219,419	123,676		Robert L. Freeman (D)	5,825,000,000	
MAINE	1,133,000	33,265	9,042	Joseph E. Brennan (D)	1,504,000,000	21,902
Augusta	21,819	86,156		*	1,420,000,000	
MARYLAND	4,265,000	10,460	12,238	Harry R. Hughes (D)	5,891,000,000	27,005
Annapolis	31,740	27,092		Joseph Curran (D)	5,788,000,000	
MASSACHUSETTS	5,781,000	8,284	12,088	Michael Dukakis (D)	7,676,000,000	33,772
Boston	562,994	21,456		John Kerry (D)	7,986,000,000	
MICHIGAN	9,109,000	58,527	10,956	James J. Blanchard (D)	15,035,000,000	117,396
Lansing	130,414	151,585		Martha W. Griffiths (D)	13,295,000,000	
MINNESOTA	4,133,000	84,402	11,175	Rudy Perpich (DFL)	6,729,000,000	130,834
St. Paul	267,290	218,600		Marlene Johnson (DFL)	6,050,000,000	
MISSISSIPPI	2,551,000	47,689	7,778	Bill Allain (D)	3,053,000,000	70,442
Jackson	202,895	123,515		Brad Dye (D)	2,985,000,000	
MISSOURI	4,951,000	69,697	10,170	Christopher S. Bond (R)	4,435,000,000	118,403
Jefferson City	33,619	180,515		Kenneth J. Rothman (D)	4,422,000,000	
MONTANA	801,000	147,046	9,580	Ted Schwinden (D)	1,269,000,000	71,703
Helena	23,938	380,846		George Turman (D)	1,096,000,000	
NEBRASKA	1,586,000	77,355	10,683	Robert Kerrey (D)	1,583,000,000	91,828
Lincoln	171,932	200,349		Don McGinley (D)	1,558,000,000	
NEVADA	881,000	110,561	11,981	Richard Bryan (D)	1,324,000,000	43,442
Carson City	32,022	286,351		Robert Cashell (R)	1,230,000,000	
NEW HAMPSHIRE	951,000	9,279	10,729	John Sununu (R)	944,000,000	14,412
Concord	32,460	24,031		*	952,000,000	
NEW JERSEY	7,438,000	7,787	13,089	Thomas H. Kean (R)	10,269,000,000	33,490
Trenton	91,903	20,169		*	10,280,000,000	
NEW MEXICO	1,359,000	121,593	9,190	Toney Anaya (D)	2,687,000,000	53,715
Santa Fe	48,953	314,923		Mike Runnels (D)	2,039,000,000	
NEW YORK	17,659,000	49,108	12,314	Mario M. Cuomo (D)	30,003,000,000	109,639
Albany	101,727	127,189		Alfred B. DeBello (D)	27,780,000,000	
NORTH CAROLINA	6,019,000	52,669	9,044	James B. Hunt, Jr. (D)	6,721,000,000	92,587
Raleigh	150,255	136,412		James C. Green (D)	6,571,000,000	
NORTH DAKOTA	670,000	70,702	10,876	Allen I. Olson (R)	1,204,000,000	85,904
Bismarck	44,485	183,118		Ernest M. Sands (R)	1,013,000,000	
OHIO	10,791,000	41,330	10,677	Richard F. Celeste (D)	14,241,000,000	110,845
Columbus	564,871	107,043		Myrl H. Shoemaker (D)	13,269,000,000	
OKLAHOMA	3,177,000	69,956	11,370	George Nigh (D)	4,094,000,000	109,946
Oklahoma City	403,136	181,185		Spencer Bernard (D)	3,791,000,000	
OREGON	2,649,000	97,073	10,335	Victor G. Atiyeh (R)	4,423,000,000	121,408
Salem	91,400	251,417		*	3,817,000,000	
PENNSYLVANIA	11,865,000	45,308	10,955	Richard L. Thornburgh (R)	15,348,000,000	117,103
Harrisburg	53,264	117,347		William W. Scranton 3rd (R)	14,094,000,000	
RHODE ISLAND	958,000	1,212	10,723	J. Joseph Garrahy (D)	1,535,000,000	6,275
Providence	156,804	3,140		Thomas R. DiLuglio (D)	1,461,000,000	
SOUTH CAROLINA	3,203,000	31,113	8,502	Richard W. Riley (D)	3,948,000,000	62,731
Columbia	100,385	80,582		Michael Daniel (D)	3,952,000,000	
SOUTH DAKOTA	691,000	77,116	9,666	William J. Janklow (R)	805,000,000	73,018
Pierre	11,973	199,729		Lowell C. Hansen 2nd (R)	836,000,000	

Railways (Miles)	Commercial Radio and Television Stations	English-language Daily Newspapers	Public Elementary Schools (K–8): Teachers Students	Public Secondary Schools (9–12): Teachers Students	Colleges and Universities: Institutions Students
3,700	160 16	24	24,000 536,000	19,900 222,000	32 160,058
2,000	71 7	8	7,800 148,000	4,000 67,000	29 43,264
1,192	88 6	14	19,300 475,000	21,600 249,000	56 225,526
1,310	106 12	52	28,700 657,000	36,300 336,000	118 418,415
6,153	253 24	47	48,000 1,210,000	36,400 621,000	91 520,131
7,510	167 12	28	21,000 468,000	23,100 263,000	70 206,691
3,107	182 11	23	14,300 326,000	11,600 142,000	41 102,364
6,109	192 24	48	24,700 556,000	24,200 261,000	89 234,421
3,802	71 12	11	5,200 104,000	4,200 47,000	16 35,177
7,342	86 14	19	8,500 186,000	8,300 86,000	31 89,488
1,553	35 8	8	3,500 102,000	3,600 49,000	7 40,455
826	43 2	8	5,600 110,000	2,800 55,000	26 46,794
1,576	75 5	27	45,400 795,000	31,200 414,000	61 321,610
1,964	86 9	18	6,900 184,000	7,200 82,000	19 58,283
3,891	281 31	80	80,100 1,771,000	75,200 991,000	294 992,237
4,000	304 19	55	33,000 780,000	23,200 331,000	127 287,537
5,262	38 13	10	4,600 76,000	2,800 38,000	17 34,069
7,400	254 25	94	56,000 1,276,000	44,500 611,000	136 489,145
5,005	120 14	49	18,500 400,000	15,400 173,000	44 160,295
4,428	117 12	17	12,300 322,000	10,300 140,000	45 157,458
7,788	304 28	102	53,200 1,194,000	56,700 648,000	202 507,716
135	22 2	7	5,100 90,000	4,100 52,000	13 66,869
2,939	164 12	19	19,900 430,000	12,300 189,000	60 132,476
2,024	52 11	12	5,200 82,000	2,800 42,000	20 32,761

State Capital	Population	Area (sq mi/ sq km)	Per Capita Personal Income	Governor Lieutenant-Governor	Revenue Expenditure	Roads (Miles)
TENNESSEE .... Nashville	4,651,000...... 455,651	42,144...... 109,151	8,906....	Lamar Alexander (R) ....$ John S. Wilder (D)	4,271,000,000.... 4,231,000,000	83,497
TEXAS .... Austin	15,280,000..... 375,000	266,807...... 691,026	11,419....	Mark White (D)................ William P. Hobby (D)	15,252,000,000.... 12,910,000,000	268,253
UTAH .... Salt Lake City	1,554,000...... 163,697	84,899...... 219,888	8,875....	Scott M. Matheson (D) .... David S. Monson (R)	2,053,000,000.... 1,896,000,000	43,735
VERMONT........... Montpelier	516,000...... 8,241	9,614...... 24,900	9,507....	Richard A. Snelling (R)......... Peter Smith (R)	795,000,000.... 724,000,000	13,942
VIRGINIA .... Richmond	5,491,000..... 218,000	40,767...... 105,585	11,095....	Charles S. Robb (D) .... Richard J. Davis (D)	6,484,000,000.... 6,092,000,000	64,683
WASHINGTON........ Olympia	4,245,000...... 27,447	68,139...... 176,478	11,560....	John Spellman (R) .... John A. Cherberg (D)	6,916,000,000.... 6,911,000,000	83,291
WEST VIRGINIA ...... Charleston	1,948,000...... 63,968	24,231...... 62,759	8,769....	John D. Rockefeller 4th (D)...... *	2,931,000,000.... 2,863,000,000	34,999
WISCONSIN .... Madison	4,765,000...... 173,003	56,153...... 145,435	10,774....	Anthony S. Earl (D)............. James Flynn (D)	7,201,000,000.... 6,838,000,000	108,110
WYOMING........... Cheyenne	502,000...... 47,283	97,809...... 253,325	12,372....	Ed Herschler (D) .... *	1,158,000,000.... 968,000,000	36,709

OUTLYING AREAS OF THE U.S.

Area Capital	Population	Area (sq mi/ sq km)	Status	Governor Lieutenant-Governor	Revenue Expenditure	Roads (Miles)
AMERICAN SAMOA..... Pago Pago	32,000.... 2,732	77.... 199	Unorganized,........ unincorporated territory	Peter T. Coleman.............$ Tufele Li'a	49,800,000.... NA	94
GUAM .... Agaña	105,800.... 881	209.... 541	Unincorporated ...... territory	Ricardo J. Bordallo .... Edward D. Reyes	185,800,000.... NA	419
PUERTO RICO.......... San Juan	3,196,520.... 433,901	3,515.... 9,103	Commonwealth...... 	Carlos Romero Barceló........ 	4,420,000,000.... 3,919,000,000	10,456
TRUST TERRITORY..... **OF THE PACIFIC** **ISLANDS**[1] Capitol Hill, on Saipan Island	116,974.... NA	533.... 1,380	UN Trust .... Territory	High Commissioner: .... Janet J. McCoy	114,100,000.... NA	64
VIRGIN ISLANDS .... Charlotte Amalie	95,591.... 11,756	133.... 344	Unincorporated ...... territory	Juan Luis .... Julio Brady	225,600,000.... 225,300,000	532

1. The Northern Mariana Islands in 1983 were an internally self-governing part of the Trust Territory of the Pacific Islands. The government of the Northern Marianas was headed by Gov. Pedro P. Tenorio and Lt.-Gov. Pedro A. Tenorio. The capital was Susupe, on Saipan Island.

Railways (Miles)	Commercial Radio and Television Stations	English-language Daily Newspapers	Public Elementary Schools (K–8): Teachers Students	Public Secondary Schools (9–12): Teachers Students	Colleges and Universities: Institutions Students
3,500	245 / 19	29	25,300 / 602,000	15,900 / 243,000	79 / 204,581
19,134	489 / 59	107	86,300 / 2,087,000	73,200 / 836,000	156 / 701,391
1,734	57 / 4	5	7,600 / 263,000	6,100 / 91,000	14 / 93,987
724	31 / 2	9	3,400 / 65,000	3,100 / 29,000	21 / 30,628
3,705	212 / 16	39	32,100 / 697,000	24,900 / 290,000	69 / 280,504
6,057	145 / 15	25	20,100 / 517,000	15,400 / 234,000	50 / 303,603
3,941	97 / 9	25	13,400 / 268,000	8,300 / 110,000	28 / 81,973
5,160	196 / 20	35	26,700 / 515,000	21,800 / 288,000	64 / 269,086
2,528	41 / 6	10	3,200 / 73,000	3,200 / 28,000	9 / 21,147

Railways (Miles)	Radio and Television Stations	Daily Newspapers	Public Elementary and Secondary School Teachers	Public School Students: Elementary Secondary	Higher Education: Institutions Students
0	1 / 1	1	559	7,174 / 2,473	1 / 1,007
0	5 / 3	2	1,466	19,603 / 6,817	2 / 5,041
60	93 / 11	5	31,964	521,865 / 191,015	39 / 153,350
0	6 / 3	0	NA	18,117 / 3,997	2 / 598
0	7 / 3	2	1,567	19,716 / 5,485	1 / 2,744

THE PROVINCES AND TERRITORIES OF CANADA

Province Capital	Population	Area (sq mi/ sq km)	Per Capita Personal Income	Premier Lieutenant-Governor
ALBERTA	2,237,724	255,285	$12,779	Peter Lougheed
Edmonton	532,246	661,185		Frank Lynch-Staunton
BRITISH COLUMBIA	2,744,467	366,255	12,538	William Bennett
Victoria	64,379	948,596		Robert Gordon Rogers
MANITOBA	1,026,241	251,000	10,806	Howard R. Pawley
Winnipeg	562,059	650,087		Pearl McGonigal
NEW BRUNSWICK	696,403	28,354	8,272	Richard B. Hatfield
Fredericton	43,723	73,436		George F. G. Stanley
NEWFOUNDLAND	567,681	156,185	7,528	Brian Peckford
St. John's	83,770	404,517		William A. Paddon
NORTHWEST TERRITORIES	45,471	1,304,903	11,797[1]	Commissioner:
Yellowknife	9,483	3,379,684		John H. Parker
NOVA SCOTIA	847,442	21,425	9,041	John Buchanan
Halifax	114,594	55,491		John Elvin Shaffner
ONTARIO	8,625,107	412,582	12,386	William G. Davis
Toronto	599,217	1,068,582		John Black Aird
PRINCE EDWARD ISLAND	122,506	2,184	7,829	James M. Lee
Charlottetown	15,282	5,657		Joseph Aubin Doiron
QUÉBEC	6,438,403	594,860	10,661	René Lévesque
Québec	166,474	1,540,680		Jean-Pierre Côté
SASKATCHEWAN	968,313	251,700	11,583	Grant Devine
Regina	162,613	651,900		Frederick Johnston
YUKON TERRITORY	23,153	186,300	11,797[1]	Commissioner:
Whitehorse	14,814	482,515		Douglas Bell

1. Figure is the combined average for the Northwest Territories and Yukon Territory.

462

The material in this table has been prepared with the assistance of Statistics Canada, Ottawa. It should be noted that all dollar figures are in Canadian dollars.

Revenue Expenditure	Motor Vehicle Registrations	Railways (Miles)	Radio and Television Stations	Daily Newspapers	Elementary and Secondary Schools: Teachers Enrollment	Postsecondary Education: Institutions Enrollment
$ 8,800,000,000 9,700,000,000	1,598,912	5,760	69 19	10	24,690 464,580	23 59,570
6,840,000,000 8,450,000,000	1,630,357	4,531	86 5	19	28,840 530,030	27 56,590
2,748,000,000 3,327,000,000	638,604	3,996	32 17	6	12,280 217,410	15 24,660
2,199,000,000 2,389,000,000	342,779	1,633	28 2	6	7,720 147,390	13 16,180
2,059,000,000 2,100,000,000	207,342	906	33 10	3	8,055 146,880	7 10,150
314,700,000 316,600,000	15,161	130	9 1	0	700 12,910	0 0
2,142,000,000 2,587,000,000	508,892	1,223	34 9	6	10,585 177,620	23 25,130
22,150,000,000 24,710,000,000	4,521,584	9,549	201 27	48	94,320 1,856,100	53 275,870
394,600,000 415,400,000	66,600	253	6 3	3	1,355 25,440	3 2,560
21,110,000,000 24,295,000,000	2,943,906	5,171	166 14	12	70,800 1,149,920	91 244,290
2,808,000,000 3,125,000,000	666,351	7,696	39 10	5	11,210 211,000	7 21,020
143,200,000 135,700,000	17,753	58	3 2	1	250 4,430	0 0

KEY TO
SIGNED ARTICLES

Here is a list of contributors to this Yearbook. The initials at the end of an article are those of the author, or authors, of that article.

A.C.-C., ANGEL CALDERÓN-CRUZ, A.B., M.S.
Director, Office of Planning & Development, Center for Energy & Environment Research, University of Puerto Rico. Coauthor, *Contemporary Caribbean Issues.*

A.D., ALASDAIR DRYSDALE, PH.D.
Assistant Professor, University of New Hampshire.

A.E.J., ANTONIO E. JIMENEZ, A.B.
Latin American correspondent at the United Nations for *Voice of America.*

A.E.N., ANNE E. NOLAN, A.B.
Yearbook Staff Editor.

A.L.R., ARTHUR L. ROBINSON, PH.D.
Senior Writer, Research News section, *Science* magazine.

A.P., ARTURO PORZECANSKI, PH.D.
International Economist, Morgan Guaranty Trust Company. Author, *Uruguay's Tupamaros: The Urban Guerrilla.*

A.T.S., ANN T. SCHULZ, PH.D.
Research Associate Professor, Clark University. United Nations Consultant. Author, *Local Politics and Nation States: Case Studies in Politics and Policy.*

B.B.S., BONNIE BARRETT STRETCH, A.B., M.S.
Art Market Columnist, *Portfolio.* Contributing Editor, *Art & Antiques.*

B.G.V., BRUCE G. VANDEN BERGH, A.B., M.S., PH.D.
Associate Professor of Advertising, Michigan State University.

B.J., BRUCE JUDDERY, A.B.
Canberra Branch Secretary, Australian Journalists Association.

B.R., BEA RIEMSCHNEIDER, A.B., M.A.
Editor in Chief, *Archaeology.* Associate Trustee, American Schools of Oriental Research.

B.R.M., BARBARA R. MUELLER
Editor, *The Essay-Proof Journal.* Special Publications Editor, *Bureau Issues Association.* Author, *Common Sense Philately.*

B.V., BOB VERDI, A.B.
Columnist, *Chicago Tribune.*

C.A.K., CHRISTOPHER A. KOJM, A.B., M.P.A.
Senior Editor, Foreign Policy Association. Editor, *U.S. Defense Policy.*

C.B.R., CHRISTOPHER B. REYNOLDS, M.A.
Lecturer in Sinhalese, University of London.

C.D.N., CLARK D. NEHER, PH.D.
Professor of Political Science, Northern Illinois University. President, Council on Thai Studies. Author, *Politics in Southeast Asia.*

C.H.A., CALVIN H. ALLEN, JR., A.B., M.A., PH.D.
Associate Professor of History, School of the Ozarks, Mo.

C.L.K., CHARLES L. KIMBELL, B.S.
Physical Scientist, U.S. Bureau of Mines.

D.F., DON FREEMAN
Television editor and Columnist, San Diego *Union* and Copley News Service.

D.F.A., DONALD F. ANTHROP, PH.D.
Professor of Environmental Studies, San Jose State University. Author, *Noise Pollution.*

D.G., DAWN GORDON, B.S.
Freelance Writer. Contributor, *Rolling Stone, Popular Mechanics, Home Electronics and Entertainment, Electronic Games, Easy Home Computers.*

D.G.S., DAVID G. SAVAGE, A.B., M.S.
Education Writer, Los Angeles *Times.*

D.J.C., DONALD J. CANTY, A.B., M.A.
Editor in Chief, *AIA Journal.* Former Editor, *City* magazine.

D.J.F., DANIEL J. FLANAGAN, A.B.
Yearbook Staff Editor.

D.L.L., DAVID L. LEWIS, B.S., M.S., M.A., PH.D.
Professor of Business History, Graduate School of Business Administration, University of Michigan.

D.M.P., DAVID M. PHILIPS, A.B.
Boating and Yachting Writer, Providence *Journal.*

D.P., DON PERETZ, A.B., M.A., PH.D.
Professor of Political Science at State University of New York at Binghamton. Author, *Middle East Today.*

D.R., DIANE ROBACK, A.B.
Freelance Writer and Reviewer; Contributor, *Publishers Weekly.*

D.R.F., DAVID R. FRANCIS, B.J., A.B.
Business Editor, *The Christian Science Monitor.*

D.R.W., DONALD R. WHITAKER, A.B.
Economist, Office of Policy and Planning, National Marine Fisheries Service. Contributor, *Fishing Gazette, Commercial Fisheries Review.*

D.S.M., DONALD S. MACDONALD, PH.D.
Research Professor of Korean Studies, School of Foreign Service, Georgetown University. Former State Department Intelligence Officer.

E.B., EDOUARD BUSTIN, PH.D.
Professor of Political Science, Boston University. Author, *Lunda Under Belgian Rule.*

E.C.R., EDWARD C. ROCHETTE, B.S.
Executive Director, American Numismatic Association.

E.H.B., ELIZABETH H. BECKER, A.B.
Freelance Writer. Former Indochina Correspondent, Washington *Post.*

E.J.F., ERIK J. FRIIS, B.S., M.A.
Editor and Publisher, *The Scandinavian-American Bulletin.*

E.J.G., ELLEN J. GREENFIELD, A.B., M.A.
Freelance Writer. Former Textiles Editor, *Women's Wear Daily.*

E.S.K., ELAINE S. KNAPP, A.B.
Editor, *Council of State Governments.*

E.S.R., EUGENIA S. ROBBINS, A.B.
Freelance Writer and Editor. News Editor, *Art Express.* Coauthor, *Henri de Toulouse-Lautrec.*

E.W., ED WARD
Music Critic, Austin *American-Statesman.*

F.C.D., FRANK C. DARLING, A.B., M.A., PH.D.
Professor of Political Science, Department Chairman, Principia College, Ill. Author, *Thailand: The Modern Kingdom, The Westernization of Asia.*

F.D.S., FREDERICK D. SCHNEIDER, PH.D.
Professor of History, Vanderbilt University.

F.L., FRANK LITSKY, B.S.
Assistant Sports Editor, New York *Times.*

Author, *Superstars, Winners in Gymnastics, Winners on the Ice, The Winter Olympics.*

F.M.N., FREDERICK M. NUNN, A.B., M.A., PH.D.
Professor of History, Portland State University. Author, *Chilean Politics, 1920–1931: The Honorable: Mission of the Armed Forces; Yesterday's Soldiers: European Military Professionalism in South America, 1890–1940.*

G.B., GEORGE BLOOSTON, A.B., M.A.
Freelance Writer. Regular Contributor, *Publishers Weekly.*

G.C., GLENNE CURRIE
Lively Arts Editor, United Press International.

G.L., GEORGE LAMSON, PH.D.
Professor of Economics, Carleton College, Northfield, Minn.

G.M.H., GEOFFREY M. HORN, A.B., M.A.
Freelance Writer. Coauthor, *Bible Stories for Children.*

G.W., GAYE WARD, A.B.
Freelance Writer and Editor, based in Ontario.

H.C.H., HAROLD C. HINTON, PH.D.
Professor of Political Science and International Affairs, George Washington University. Editor, *The People's Republic of China, 1949–1979: A Documentary Survey.*

H.W.H., HARRY W. HENDERSON, A.B.
Freelance Writer. Former Writer–Economist, U.S. Department of Agriculture.

I.A.A., IAN A. ANDERSON, A.B.
Publications Director, U.S. Figure Skating Association.

I.C.B., IRIRANGI COATES BLOOMFIELD, A.B., M.A., PH.D.
Lecturer, Boston University. Researcher and Writer.

I.K., INDULIS KEPARS, A.B., A.L.A.A.
Chief Reference Librarian, Australian Reference, National Library of Australia.

J.A.P., JOHN A. PETROPULOS, PH.D.
Professor of History, Amherst College. Author, *Politics and Statecraft in the Kingdom of Greece.*

J.A.R., JAMES A. ROTHERHAM, A.B., M.A., M.A.L.D., PH.D.
Deputy Associate Director, Committee on the Budget, U.S. House of Representatives.

J.C., JAMES CARPER, B.S.
Associate Editor, *Professional Builder/Apartment Business.*

J.C.L., JEAN CAFFEY LYLES, A.B.
Associate Editor, *The Christian Century.* Editorial Consultant, *The Christian Ministry.*

J.D., JOHN DAMIS, PH.D.
Professor of Political Science, Portland State University. Consultant, U.S. Department of State.

J.F., JULIE FREDERIKSE, A.B.
Southern Africa Correspondent, National Public Radio.

J.F., JR. JOHN FORAN, JR., A.B., M.A.
Graduate Fellow in Sociology, University of California, Berkeley.

J.F.H., JERRY F. HOUGH, PH.D.
Professor of Political Science, Duke University. Staff Member, Brookings Institution. Author, *Soviet Leadership in Transition.*

J.F.H., III, JEREMIAH F. HEALY, III, A.B., J.D.
Associate Professor, New England School of Law, Boston. Freelance Writer.

J.F.J., JAMES F. JEKEL, M.D., M.P.H.
Professor of Epidemiology and Public Health, Yale Medical School. Former Epidemiologist, Centers for Disease Control.

J.F.S., JOANNE F. SCHNEIDER, A.B., M.A., PH.D.
Visiting Assistant Professor of History, Wheaton College.

J.G.D., JOHN G. DEEDY, A.B., M.A.
Former Managing Editor, *Commonweal.* Contributor, New York *Times, U.S. Catholic, Informations Catholiques Internationales.*

J.H.B., JAMES H. BUDD
Freelance Writer based in Mexico. Correspondent, Ziff–Davis magazines and Gemini News Service.

J.J., JULIAN JOSEPHSON, A.B., M.S.E.E.
Associate Editor, *Environmental Science and Technology.*

J.J.Z., JOSEPH J. ZASLOFF, A.B., M.A., PH.D.
Professor of Political Science, University of Pittsburgh. Specialist in Southeast Asian Affairs.

J.K., JON KRAUS, PH.D.
Professor of Political Science, State University of New York, Fredonia.

J.L., JOHN LUTER, A.B.
Professor and Chairman, Journalism Department, University of Hawaii. Former Coordinator, Advanced International Reporting Program, Columbia University Graduate School of Journalism.

J.N.C., JAMES N. CRUTCHFIELD
Assistant City Editor, Detroit *Free Press.*

J.O.S., JAMES O. SAFFORD III, A.S., M.A., PH.D.
Instructor of History, The Shipley School, Bryn Mawr, Pa.

J.R.C., JOHN ROSS CARTER, A.B., B.D., M.TH., PH.D.
Professor of Philosophy and Religion, Colgate University. Director, Fund for the Study of the Great Religions of the World. Author, *Dhamma: Western Academic and Sinhalese Buddist Interpretations—a Study of a Religious Concept.*

J.R.F., JOHN R. FREE, A.B.
Senior Editor, *Technology, Popular Science.* Former Associate Editor, *Radio Electronics.*

J.R.O., JAMES R. OESTREICH, A.B. Former Classical Music Editor, *High Fidelity*.

K.F.R., KARL F. REULING Managing Editor, *Ballet News*.

K.J.B., KIRK J. BEATTIE, A.B., M.A. Researcher in Egyptian Politics.

K.M., KENT MULLINER, B.S., M.A. Executive Committee, Malaysia/Singapore/Brunei Studies Group. Assistant to the Director, Ohio University Libraries.

K.W.G., KENNETH W. GRUNDY, A.B., M.A., PH.D. Professor of Political Science, Case Western Reserve University.

L.A.K., LAWRENCE A. KLETTER, A.B., M.A., J.D. Certificate in Middle Eastern Studies, Columbia University. Associate, Testa Hurwitz and Thibeault, Boston.

L.D., LARRY DIAMOND, A.B., M.A., PH.D. Assistant Professor of Sociology, Vanderbilt University. Fulbright Visiting Lecturer, Bayero University, Nigeria.

L.G., LOIS GOTTESMAN, A.B., M.A. Research Analyst, American Jewish Committee.

L.J.R., LEIF J. ROBINSON Editor, *Sky & Telescope*.

L.L.P., LARRY L. PIPPIN, A.B., M.A., PH.D. Professor of Political Science, Elbert Covell College, University of the Pacific.

L.R.H., LINDLEY R. HIGGINS, P.E., A.B., M.S. Consulting Engineer. President, Piedmont Publications. Author, *Handbook of Construction Equipment Maintenance* and *Maintenance Engineering Handbook*.

L.Z., LAWRENCE ZIRING, B.S., M.I.A., PH.D. Director, Institute of Government and Politics, Professor of Political Science, Western Michigan University. Author, *Pakistan: The Enigma of Political Development*.

M.D., MICHAEL DIRDA, A.B., M.A., PH.D. Daily Book Review Editor, *The Washington Post Book World*.

M.D.H., M. DONALD HANCOCK, PH.D. Professor of Political Science, Vanderbilt University.

M.D.W., MICHAEL D. WORMSER, A.B., M.A. Freelance Writer on Government and Politics.

M.E.A., MICHAEL E. AGNES, A.B. Yearbook Staff Editor.

M.G., MURIEL GRINDROD, A.B. Author, *Italy, Rebuilding of Italy*.

M.Gr. MILTON GREENBERG, A.B., M.A., PH.D. Provost, The American University. Coauthor, *The American Political Dictionary*, *Political Science Dictionary*.

M.G.G., M. GRANT GROSS, A.B., M.S., PH.D. Director, Division of Ocean Sciences, National Science Foundation. Author, *Oceanography: A View of the Earth*.

M.H., MARJORIE HOLT, A.B. Yearbook Staff Editor.

M.K., MARC KUSINITZ, M.S., PH.D. News Correspondent, *New York State Medical Journal*.

M.L., MIKE LITTWIN Sports Writer, *Los Angeles Times*.

M.S.B., MICHAEL S. BAKER, A.B., M.A. Japan Foundation Research Fellow and Ph.D. Candidate, Columbia University.

M.W., MARGARET WILLY, F.R.S.L. Lecturer, City Literary Institute, London. Lecturer, Morley College, London. Poetry collected in *The Invisible Sun, Every Star a Tongue*.

N.M.R., NATHAN M. REISS, PH.D. Associate Professor of Meteorology, Cook College, Rutgers University.

N.P., NEAL PRONEK, B.B.A. Managing Editor, *Tropical Fish Hobbyist*. Former editor, *Pet Industry*.

N.P.N., NANCY PEABODY NEWELL, A.B. Coauthor, *The Struggle for Afghanistan*.

P.G., PAUL GARDNER Freelance Writer. Author, *The Simplest Game, Nice Guys Finish Last*. Commentator, ABC national soccer telecasts.

P.H.C., PARRIS H. CHANG, PH.D. Professor of Political Science, Chairman of Asian Area Studies, Pennsylvania State University. Author, *Power and Policy in China*.

P.J.M., PAUL J. MAGNARELLA, A.M., PH.D. Professor of Anthropology, University of Florida. Author, *Tradition and Change in a Turkish Town, The Peasant Venture*.

P.L.W., PENELOPE L. WANG, A.B., M.A. Editorial Assistant, *Newsweek*.

P.W., PETER WINN, A.B., PH.D. Associate Professor of History, Tufts University. Senior Research Fellow, Research Institute on International Change, Columbia University.

R.A., RICHARD ALLINSON, A.B., M.A. Editor and Publisher, *Criminal Justice Abstracts*.

R.A.M., ROBERT A. MORTIMER, A.B., M.A., PH.D. Professor of Political Science, Haverford College. Author, *The Third World Coalition in International Politics*.

R.A.P., RICHARD A. PIERCE, PH.D. Professor of History, Queen's University, Ontario. Author, *Eastward to Empire: Exploration and Conquest on the Russian Open Frontier to 1750*.

R.B., RICHARD E. BISSELL, A.B., M.A., PH.D. Professorial Lecturer, Johns Hopkins School of Advanced International Studies. Author, *South Africa and the United States: Erosion of an Influence Relationship*.

R.D., ROGER DeGARIS, A.B., M.A. Yearbook Staff Editor.

R.E.B., ROGER E. BILSTEIN, PH.D. Professor of History, University of Houston at Clear Lake City. Author, *Stages to Saturn: A Technological History of the Apollo/Saturn Launch Vehicles*.

R.E.K., ROGER E. KANET, A.B., M.A., PH.D. Professor of Political Science, University of Illinois at Urbana–Champaign. Editor, *Background to Crisis: Policies and Politics in Gierek's Poland*.

R.J.K., ROBERT J. KURSAR, A.B. Assistant Editor, *Traffic World* magazine.

R.J.L., ROBERT J. LaMARCHE, A.B. Associate Editor, *TENNIS* magazine.

R.J.S., ROGER J. SOUTHERN Geography Teacher, Scotch College, Melbourne, Australia.

R.J.Sh., ROBERT J. SHAW, B.S., A.B., M.A. Freelance Writer. Author, *Libraries: Building for the Future*.

R.J.W., RICHARD J. WILLEY, A.B., M.A., PH.D. Professor of Political Science, Vassar College. Author, *Democracy in the West German Trade Unions*. Contributor, New York Times.

R.L.B., RICHARD L. BUTWELL, A.B., M.A., D.Phil. Vice–president for Academic Affairs and Professor of Political Science, University of South Dakota. Author, *Southeast Asia, A Political Introduction; U Nu of Burma*.

R.L.K., ROBERT L. KOVACH, M.A., PH.D. Associate Dean for Research and Professor of Geophysics, School of Earth Sciences, Stanford University.

R.L.M., RICHARD L. MILLETT, A.B., M.A., PH.D. Professor of History, Southern Illinois University. Coeditor, *The Restless Caribbean*.

R.M.L., ROBERT M. LEVINE, A.B., M.A., PH.D. Professor of History, University of Miami. Author, *Brazil Since 1930, The Vargas Regime, A Historical Dictionary of Brazil*.

R.N., RICHARD NEEDHAM, A.B., M.A. Editor, *Ski* magazine, *The Encyclopedia of Skiing*.

R.O.F., ROBERT O, FREEDMAN, PH.D. Dean and Professor of Political Science, School of Graduate Studies, Baltimore Hebrew College. Author, *Soviet Policy Toward the Middle East Since 1970*.

R.S., ROBERT SCHWARZ, A.B., M.A., PH.D. Professor of Philosophy, Florida Atlantic University. Author, *Sozialismus der Propaganda*.

R.Y.D., RICHARD Y. DOW, B.S., M.S. Staff Officer, Geophysics Research Board and Space Science Board.

S.-A.R., SALLY-ANN RAY, PH.D.
Lecturer in Politics, Canberra College for Advanced Education, Australia.

S.A.W., STANLEY A. WOLPERT, A.B., A.M., PH.D.
Professor of History, University of California, Los Angeles. Author, *A New History of India*.

S.E., SANFORD ELWITT, PH.D.
Professor of History, University of Rochester. Author, *The Making of the Third Republic*. Contributor, *Journal of Modern History, French Historical Studies*.

S.F., SHIRLEY FLEMING, A.B., M.A.
Editor, *Musical America*.

S.G., SAM GOLDAPER
Sports Reporter, New York *Times*. New York Area Chairman, Pro Basketball Writers' Association.

S.L.D., SPENCER L. DAVIDSON
Associate editor, *Time*.

S.L.W., SEYMOUR L. WOLFBEIN, A.B., M.A., PH.D.
J.E. Boettner Professor of Business Administration, Professor of Economics, Temple University, Philadelphia.

S.M., SIEGFRIED MANDEL, A.B., M.A., PH.D.
Professor of English and Comparative Literature, University of Colorado. Author, *Contemporary European Novelists*.

S.M.H., STEPHEN M. HEAD, M.A., PH.D.
Lecturer in Zoology, University of the West Indies, Jamaica.

S.W., SUSAN WALTON, A.B., M.A.
Assistant Editor, *Education Week*. Former News and Features Editor, *BioScience* magazine.

T.C., TERESA CARSON, A.B.
Former Staff Writer, *The American Banker*.

T.G.S., T. G. STAVROU, A.B.
Yearbook Staff Editor.

T.H.M., THOMAS H. MAUGH, II, PH.D.
Senior Science Writer, *Science* magazine. Coauthor, *Energy and the Future, Seeds of Destruction: The Science Report on Cancer Research*.

T.J.O.H., T.J.O. HICKEY
Member, Editorial Staff, *The Times* of London.

T.McC., TOM McCOLLISTER, A.B.
Sports Writer, Atlanta *Constitution*.

V.L., VINCE LOVETT
Public Information Specialist, Bureau of Indian Affairs, U.S. Department of the Interior. Writer, *Indian News Notes*, for Indian tribal and organizational publications.

W.C.C., WILLIAM C. CROMWELL, A.B., M.A., PH.D.
Professor of International Relations, American University. Author, *The Eurogroup and NATO*.

W.E., WILLIAM EATON, B.S., M.S.
New Delhi Bureau Chief and former Washington Correspondent, Los Angeles

Times. Coauthor, *Reuther*. Winner of the 1970 Pulitzer Prize for National Reporting.

W.H.G., WILLIAM H. GRIMES, A.B., M.A., PH.D.
Yearbook Staff Editor.

W.H.N., WILLIAM H. NEW, PH.D.
Professor of English, University of British Columbia. Editor, *Canadian Literature*.

W.L., WILLIAM LEGGETT, A.B.
Senior Writer, *Sports Illustrated*.

W.M., WILLIAM MINTER, PH.D.
Staff Writer, Africa News Service. Author, *Portuguese Africa and the West*.

W.M.W., W. MARVIN WILL, PH.D.
Associate Professor of Political Science, University of Tulsa, Okla. Coeditor, *The Restless Caribbean*. Former Editor, *Caribbean Studies Newsletter*.

W.N., WILLIAM NEIKIRK, A.B.
Economics Correspondent, Washington Bureau, Chicago *Tribune*.

W.W., WILLIAM WOLF, A.B.
Contributing Editor, *New York* magazine. Lecturer, New York University and St. John's University. Author, *Landmark Films, The Marx Brothers*.

W.W.H., WILLIAM W. HADDAD, A.B., M.A., PH.D.
Professor of History, Illinois State University at Normal. Coauthor, *Nationalism in a Non–National State: The Dissolution of the Ottoman Empire*.

PICTURE CREDITS

2 Vic DeLucia/The New York *Times*   **8** Mike Keza/Liaison   **10** Dennis Fisher/International Stock Photo   **11** *Left:* Jim Balog/Black Star; *Right:* Mark Tuschman/Phototake   **12** *Top:* Bill Pierce/*Time Magazine*; *Bottom:* D. Goldberg/Sygma   **13** Wide World   **14** Sidney Harris   **15** Jon Reis/ The Stock Market   **16** Mike Keza/Liaison   **17** Xerox Corp.   **18** Tom Kelly/PAR-NYC   **19** Tom Zimberoff/Sygma   **20** *Top, Left and Right:* Milton Bradley Company; *Bottom:* Michael Philip Manheim/The Stock Shop   **21** D. Goldberg/Sygma   **22** Scala, Istituto Editoriale, Florence   **23** Enrico Ferorelli/Wheeler Pictures   **24–25** *All:* Scala, Istituto Editoriale, Florence   **26** *Above:* Scala, Istituto Editoriale, Florence; *Below:* Biblioteca Apostolica Vaticana, Museo Sacra   **27–29** *All:* Scala, Istituto Editoriale, Florence   **30** *Above:* Biblioteca Apostolica Vaticana, Archivo Fotografico; *Below:* Scala, Istituto Editoriale, Florence   **31–35** *All:* Scala, Istituto Editoriale, Florence   **36** Patricia Caulfield   **37** Patricia Caulfield   **38** Martin Eichterscheimer   **39** Michal Heron   **40** *Top:* UPI; *Bottom:* Wide World   **41** Andrew Rakoczy   **42** Andrew Rakoczy   **43** *Top:* Florida State News Bureau; *Bottom:* Patricia Caulfield   **44** Suzanne J. Engelmann   **45** Patricia Caulfield   **46** Richard Frear/National Park Service   **47** George Grant/National Park Service   **48** Michal Heron   **50** Richard S. Nichols/Gamma-Liaison   **51** Fouad/Sygma   **52** Peter Jordan/*Time* Magazine   **53–55** UPI   **56** *Both: Time* Magazine   **61** Pierre Perrin/Gamma   **62** Mark Peters/Black Star   **63** Daniel Bissonet/The New York *Times*   **64** Danek/Liaison   **68** Ken Heyman   **70** Bill Deane/National Geographic Society   **71** Steve Rosenthal   **72** I. M. Pei and Partners   **73** Barbara Karant/Kohn Pedersen Fox Assoc.   **75** UPI   **76** Wide World   **77** Wolfgang Volz/Outline   **78** The Metropolitan Museum of Art/Courtauld Institute Galleries   **79** Christie's, New York   **81** UPI   **82** UPI   **83** Peter Kelly/Australian Information Service   **84** Wide World   **87** Wide World   **89** Cartoon, MacNelly/Chicago *Tribune*; Chart, Martin Eichtersheimer   **91** UPI   **92** Meyer/San Francisco *Chronicle*   **94** Schiffman/Gamma-Liaison   **96** UPI   **97** UPI   **99** Wide World   **101** Canapress Photo Service   **102** Michael T. Kaufman/The New York *Times*   **104** Canapress Photo Service   **107** J. Bryan Stiles   **109** C. Spengler/Sygma   **110** Eastfoto   **111** UPI   **113** UPI   **115** UPI   **118** *Time* Magazine   **121** *Left:* Vic DeLucia/The New York *Times*; *Right:* UPI   **123** Wide World   **124** Atlan/Sygma   **129** Yvonne Hemsey/Liaison   **131** UPI   **132** © 1983 Washington Post Co. Reprinted with permission.   **134** UPI   **135** UPI   **138** Martha Swope   **139** Martha Swope   **140** *Left:* Wide World; *Right:* Alex Webb/Magnum   **142–144** UPI   **146** Dan Miller/The New York *Times*   **147** © 1983 Osrin/The *Plain Dealer*   **148** Chris Harris/Gamma-Liaison   **149** UPI   **151** Timothy A. Murphy/U.S. News & World Report, Inc.   **152** George Brich/The New York *Times*   **155** UPI   **156** Jim Richardson/The Denver *Post*   **157** UPI   **160** Terrence McCarthy/The New York *Times*   **162** UPI   **163** John Barr/Liaison   **164** Wide World   **167** UPI   **168** UPI   **169** Daniel Simon/Gamma   **170** Erica Lennard/Courtesy of Perry Ellis   **173** *Bottom:* Sygma; *Right:* UPI   **174** Alain Guillou/Visions   **175** Jürgens/Katherine Young   **177** UPI   **178** Jean Claude Francolon/Gamma   **180** Stuart Franklin/Sygma   **181** Stuart Franklin/Sygma   **183** UPI   **185** Wide World   **187** UPI   **188** UPI   **189** Wide World   **191** Bob Sacha/*Time* Magazine   **192** Timothy A. Murphy/U.S. News & World Report, Inc.   **193** Claude Urraca/Sygma   **195** David Strick/The New York *Times*   **197** Baldev/Sygma   **200** Alain Nogues/Sygma   **203** M. Kalari/Sygma   **204** Alfred/Gamma   **206** UPI   **207** Moshe Milner/Sygma   **208–213** *All:* UPI   **216** Matsumoto/Sygma   **218** Wide World   **220** Dan Brinzac/New York *Post*   **222** Yan Morvan/Sipa/Black Star   **223** Wide World   **226** Ed Fisher © 1975, The New Yorker Magazine, Inc.   **229** Jerome Wexler   **230** Eastfoto   **231** Zoological Society of San Diego   **233** UPI   **235** Australian Information Service   **236** *Both:* Canapress   **237** D. McCullin/Magnum   **238** UPI   **239** UPI   **241** Courtesy of Charles Scribner's Sons, N.Y.   **245** UPI   **247** UPI   **249** Laurent Maous/Gamma-Liaison   **250** Wide World   **251** Wide World   **252** UPI   **254** UPI   **255** Don Jones/Liaison   **256** Randy Taylor/Sygma   **257** UPI   **258** Wide World   **260** Don Connolly/Gamma-Liaison   **261** The New York *Times*   **263** Lucasfilm   **264** Lynn Goldsmith/LGI © 1983   **265** John Bryson/Sygma   **266** Kerry Hayes   **267** Photo Trends SN   **268** G. Mathieson/Liaison   **269** Jim Wilson/The New York *Times*   **270** Louise Gubb/Gamma-Liaison   **271** Nova Press/Sygma   **272** Wide World   **273** J. Hefferman   **277** George Tames/The New York *Times*   **278** Photo Trends   **280** Claude Urraca/Sygma   **283** Wide World   **285** Doug Wilson/Black Star   **286–288** UPI   **289** George Cohen/Liaison   **290** Katherine Young   **291** *Top:* UPI; *Bottom:* Theo Westenberger/Liaison   **292** UPI   **293** *Both:* UPI   **294** UPI   **295** Wide World   **296–301** *All:* UPI   **303** Steve McCurry/Liaison   **304** UPI   **305** UPI   **306** Mario Suriani/Uniphoto   **307–309** UPI   **310** Martha Swope   **311** *Both:* UPI   **312** Raeanne Rubenstein/People Weekly/© 1983 Time Inc.   **313** Wide World   **314** Sven Simon Bonn/Katherine Young   **315** Wide World   **316** *Top:* Australian Information Service; *Bottom:* Kathy Arkell/Spooner/Gamma   **317** Czarnecki/Gamma-Liaison   **318** Gamma   **319** *Left:* Goldberg/Sygma; *Right:* C. Simonpietri/Gamma   **320** Clark/UPC   **321** Moshe Milner/Sygma   **322** UPI   **325** Chart by Martin Eichtersheimer   **327** UPI   **328** UPI   **329** *Both:* © Karsh, Ottawa/Woodfin Camp   **331** Fermilab   **333** UPI   **334** Gamma/Liaison   **337–339** UPI   **340** Bill Adler/The New York *Times*   **341** UPI   **343** *Both:* Reprinted with permission from *Vanity Fair*; Copyright: © 1983, The Conde Nast Publications, Inc.   **344** Linda Bartlett   **348** UPI   **349** Wide World   **350** UPI   **353** Wally McNamme/Newsweek   **354** Dean Conger © 1983 National Geographic Society   **358** Francois Lochon/Gamma   **360** Dirck Halstead/*Time* Magazine   **362** Mark Peters/The New York *Times*   **363** NASA   **364** NASA   **365** UPI   **366** UPI   **368** UPI   **370** Richard Pilling/Focus on Sports   **371** Focus on Sports   **373** UPI   **374** Wide World   **375–377** UPI   **378–379** Focus on Sports   **380** *Top:* UPI; *Bottom:* Focus on Sports   **381** Focus on Sports   **382** UPI   **383** *Top:* UPI; *Bottom:* Paul J. Sutton/Duomo   **387** Rollin A. Riggs/The New York *Times*   **389** Wide World   **392** UPI   **395** Ameritech Mobile Communications, Inc.   **396** UPI   **397** HBO Premiere Films   **398** UPI   **400** Wide World   **401** Wide World   **404** *Top:* Culver Pictures; *Bottom:* © 1983 Martha Swope   **405** © 1983 Martha Swope   **406** Richard Marin/*Time* Magazine   **407** UPI   **408** UPI   **409** Wide World   **410** Terrence Moore/The New York *Times*   **413** UPI   **416** Wide World   **417** UPI   **419** UPI   **422** Wide World   **425–431** *All:* UPI   **434** Alan Cowell/The New York *Times*   **435** William Campbell/*Time* Magazine

INDEX TO THE
1984 YEARBOOK
EVENTS OF 1983

INTRODUCTION

This index is a comprehensive listing of persons, organizations, and events that are discussed in the 1984 yearbook. Entries in **boldface** letters indicate subjects on which the Yearbook has an individual article. Entries in lightface type indicate individual references within articles. In either type of entry, the letters a and b refer, respectively, to the left and right column of the page cited. If no letter follows a page number, the reference is to text that is printed across the full width of a page. Only the first significant mention of a subject in a given article has been included in the Index.

In a main entry such as **Australia:** 82b, the first number refers to the page on which the article begins. The succeeding lightface page numbers refer to other text discussions in the volume. The first number in lightface entries, when not in numerical order, will similarly provide the most extensive information on the subject. Subtitles following major entries refer to further references on the main subject, as in **Congress of the United States:** 122a; Elections, 154a. In the case of comprehensive articles such as the **United States of America,** reference is made to the page location of the beginning of the article. The discussion of foreign relations of the United States in that article may be augmented by reference to separate articles on the countries and international organizations concerned.

When an entry is followed by the abbreviation **illus.,** the reference is to a caption and picture on the page mentioned. When a text mention and an illustration of the same subject fall within the same article, only the text location is included in the index.

LIST OF ABBREVIATIONS USED IN THE INDEX

NATO   North Atlantic Treaty Organization
OPEC   Organization of Petroleum Exporting Countries
PLO   Palestine Liberation Organization
U.N.   United Nations
U.S.   United States
U.S.S.R.   Union of Soviet Socialist Republics

Papandreou, Andreas: 182b; **illus.** 167
paper industry: 245b
Papau New Guinea: 448
Paraguay: 305a, 448
paraquat: 108a
Parker, Robert A.: 364b
particle physics: 330b
Payne, Robert: 295b
peace movement: 347b; Canada, 103a; Europe, 282a, 136b, 176a, 180b, 196b; nuclear freeze resolution, 124b
Peace Prize, Nobel: 339a
Peacock, Andrew: 84a
Peete, Calvin: 376b
Pei, I. M.: 72b
Pelkey, Edward: 296a
Pelshe, Arvid Yanovich: 296a
Peña, Federico: 156a
Penn, Sean: 265a
Pennsylvania: 387a, 412a, 458
pension plans: 114a, 389b, 430b
People in the News: 306a
Pepper, Claude: 360
Percy, Charles: **illus.** 123
Pérez de Cuéllar, Javier: 420a
periodicals: 58a, 343a
Perón, Isabel: 75a
Persian Gulf States: 324a
Peru: 324a, 56a, 64b, 448
pesticides: 163a
Peterson, Donald H.: 364a
Petroleum and Natural Gas: 324b; Africa, 66b, 67a, 281a; Canada, 103b; Europe, 206b, 284a; Latin America, 150b, 246b, 428b; Middle East, 203b, 205a, 217b, 324a, 358a; OPEC, 300b
Pets: 326b
Pevsner, Nikolaus Bernhard Leon: 296a
Philadelphia: 155b, 276a
Philadelphia Phillies: 369a
Philadelphia 76ers: 371b
Philadelphia Stars: 375a
philately. See STAMPS AND STAMP COLLECTING
Philip, Prince: 182a, 308a
Philippines: 328a, 57a, 448; religion, 350a; U.S., 427b
Phoenix, Ariz.: 156b
Photography: 329a, 341a
Physics: 330b, 339b
physiology or medicine, Nobel Prize in: 340a
Picasso, Pablo: 78b
Pickens, Slim: 296a
Pike, Anne Marie: 373a
Piltdown hoax: 67b
Pinheiro de Azevedo, José Baptista: 296a
Pinochet Ugarte, Augusto: 108b
Piquet, Nelson: 368a
plague: 191a
Planinc, Milka: 432b
plants. See BOTANY
PLO. See PALESTINE LIBERATION ORGANIZATION
pneumonia: 186a

Podgorny, Nikolai: 296a
Poland: 332b, 116a, 118a, 347a, 352b, 448
Polisario Front: 60b, 66a, 225a, 262a
popular music: 268a
Portland Building: 73a
Portland Museum of Art: 71b
Portugal: 335a, 240a, 448; Communism, 120a
Powell, Anthony: 237a
Prem Tinsulanond: 402b
President of the United States: 335b. See also REAGAN, RONALD W.
Presser, Jackie: 220b
Prince Edward Island: 462
prisons: 134b, 386b
prison sentences: 115a, 390b
Prizes and Awards: 338a, 74a, 234b, 266b, 274a, 349b, 399a, 403a
Protestant churches: 350b
Pryor, Aaron: 373b
psychology. See BEHAVIORAL SCIENCES
Public Broadcasting Service: 58a
Publishing: 342b, 352a
Puerto Rico: 346a, 460
Pulitzer Prizes: 340b
pulsars: 82a

Q

Qaddafi, Muammar al-: 224b, 106b, 262b
Qatar: 448
Qiao Guanhua: 296a
Quebec: 462
Queensland: 85a
Quisenberry, Dan: 370b

R

rabies: 191a
radio. See TELEVISION AND RADIO BROADCASTING
radioactive wastes: 164a, 285b
railroads: 55b, 103b, 410a
Ralph Hanover (horse): 377a
Raphaelson, Samson: 296a
rats: 108a
Rawlings, Jerry: 178b
Reagan, Maureen: 307a
Reagan, Michael: 306b
Reagan, Nancy: 306b; **illus.** 426
Reagan, Ron: 306b
Reagan, Ronald W.: 335b, 306b, 421a; **illus.** 124; arms control, 282a; Cabinet, 99a; Civil Rights, 113a; Congress, 122a; El Salvador, 158a; Environment, 161a; Grenada, 184a, 255a; Indian policy, 199a; Japan, 214a; Korea, 217a; Middle East peace plan, 250b, 303b; Military Affairs, 253b; Negroes, 276b; Republican Party, 356b; Social Security, 360a; Women, 430a

recording equipment: 121b
recordings: 274b
referendums: 156b, 388a
refugees: 414a; **illus.** 303
Religion: 347a, 342b, 390b
REM sleep: 93b
Renault, Mary: 296a
Republican Party: 356b, 122a, 154b, 388a
restaurants: 58b
retirement age: 360b, 389b
Return of the Jedi: 262b
Rey, Jean: 167b
Reynolds, Frank: 296a, 398b
Rhode Island: 458
Rhodesia. See ZIMBABWE
Rice, Jim: 370b
Richards, Keith: 310b
Richardson, Sir Ralph: 296b
Ride, Sally K.: 364, 431b
Ridge, Julie: 312b
Right Stuff, The: 264a, 423a
right-to-work laws: 387a
Ríos Montt, Efraín: 184b
Ripken, Cal, Jr.: 370b
Rivers, Joan: 398
Robberies: 133a, 182a
Robbins, Jerome: 137a
Robinson, Joan Violet: 296b
Robinson, John Arthur Thomas: 296b
robots: 396a; **illus.** 121
rodenticides: 108a
Roman Catholicism: 347a, 136b, 243b, 333b
Romania: 357a, 119a, 361b, 448
Romero Barceló, Carlos: 346b
Rosenberg, Anna Marie: 296b
Rosenberg, Julius and Ethel: 234a, 263b
Rosenthal, Benjamin Stanley: 297a
Ross, Diana: 269b
Rostow, Eugene: 337a
Roth, Philip: 233a
Rothko, Mark: 80a
Roy, Gabrielle: 297a, 236b
Rozier, Mike: 376a
Ruckelshaus, William D.: 161b, 337b, 423a
Russia. See UNION OF SOVIET SOCIALIST REPUBLICS
Rwanda: 414a, 450

S

safety: automobiles, 86b
Sagan, Françoise: 239a
Sahara, Western. See WESTERN SAHARA
St. Christopher and Nevis (St. Kitts-Nevis): 106a, 117b, 420b, 450
St. Louis Globe-Democrat: 345b
St. Lucia: 450
St. Vincent and the Grenadines: 450
Saleh, Ali Abdullah: 432a, 432b
Salnikov, Vladimir: 381a
salt, dietary: 189b
Samoa, American. See AMERICAN SAMOA